Business Law & the Legal Environment

Standard Edition

Selected Chapters

Sixth Edition

Jeffrey F. Beatty | Susan S. Samuelson | Dean Bredeson

Australia • Brazil • Japan • Korea • Mexico • Singapore • Spain • United Kingdom • United States

Business Law & the Legal Environment: Standard Edition, Selected Chapters, Sixth Edition

Jeffrey F. Beatty | Susan S. Samuelson
Dean Bredeson

Executive Editors:
Maureen Staudt
Michael Stranz

Senior Project Development Manager:
Linda deStefano

Marketing Specialist:
Courtney Sheldon

Senior Production/Manufacturing Manager:
Donna M. Brown

Production Editorial Manager:
Kim Fry

Sr. Rights Acquisition Account Manager:
Todd Osborne

Business Law and the Legal Environment, Standard Edition, 6th Edition
Jeffrey F. Beatty | Susan S. Samuelson | Dean Bredeson

ISBN-13: 978-1-285-02595-7

ISBN-10: 1-285-02595-4

Cengage Learning
5191 Natorp Boulevard
Mason, Ohio 45040
USA

Cengage Learning is a leading provider of customized learning solutions with office locations around the globe, including Singapore, the United Kingdom, Australia, Mexico, Brazil, and Japan. Locate your local office at:
international.cengage.com/region.
Cengage Learning products are represented in Canada by Nelson Education, Ltd.
For your lifelong learning solutions, visit **www.cengage.com/custom.**
Visit our corporate website at **www.cengage.com.**

Printed in the United States of America

Brief Contents

Chapter 1 ***Introduction To Law*** 1

Chapter 3 ***Dispute Resolution*** 42

Chapter 4 ***Common Law, Statutory Law, and Administrative Law*** 75

Chapter 5 ***Constitutional Law*** 102

Chapter 6 ***Intentional Torts and Business Torts*** 130

Chapter 7 ***Negligence and Strict Liability*** 156

Chapter 8 ***Crime*** 178

Chapter 10 ***Introduction to Contracts*** 230

Chapter 11 ***The Agreement: Offers and Acceptances*** 251

Chapter 12 ***Consideration*** 275

Chapter 13 ***Legality*** 295

Chapter 14 ***Voidable Contracts: Capacity and Consent*** 316

Chapter 15 ***Written Contracts*** 339

Chapter 17 ***Performance and Discharge*** 381

Chapter 18 ***Remedies*** 403

Chapter 28 ***Agency Law*** 670

Chapter 31 ***Starting a Business: LLCs and Other Options*** 762

Chapter 32 ***Partnerships*** 787

Chapter 33 ***Life and Death of a Corporation*** 815

Chapter 34 ***Corporate Management*** 839

Chapter 35 ***Shareholders*** 862

UNIT 1

The Legal Environment

CHAPTER 1

INTRODUCTION TO LAW

© r.nagy/Shutterstock.com

Near Campus

Alan Dawson dumped his Calculus II textbook into his backpack. Outside, a light snow began to fall. With a sigh, he left his apartment and headed out into the early December evening.

Halfway to the library, he encountered a group of his friends "Hey, Alan, we're done with finals," said Gary with a flourish. "You should come to Thirsty's with us."

"I can't. I have my Calculus final tomorrow."

"Carrie's going to be there." Gary raised his eyebrows.

"Come on, Dawson! Be a man! Come on!" said the others. Without a word, Alan reversed direction and headed away from the library. His friends cheered loudly.

> When he opened the door, he saw Alan rolling around on the floor, groaning.

At Thirsty's Bar

Anna stood behind the bar and watched four bikers enter. They wore jackets with gang insignia, and purple headscarves. One of them approached the bar. "Four Budweisers," he said to Anna.

After gathering her courage, Anna said, "Look, you guys know you can't wear your colors in here."

"What are you gonna do about it, missy?" the biker asked. When she didn't reply, he leaned closer to her. "Four beers."

Anna thought about it for a moment, then gathered four Budweiser longnecks and placed them on the bar. The biker tossed down a $10 bill, took the beers, and joined his three associates at a table.

Anna eyed the telephone on the counter behind her. The owner of Thirsty's had told her to call the cops immediately if she saw any gang colors in there. But the bikers were watching her, and she decided not to make a call right away.

At a back table

"I'm not going home for a few more days," Alan said to Carrie.

"I'm not either. We should do something," Carrie said.

"Yeah," Alan said, trying hard to not seem too excited. "Have you, ah, seen the new DiCaprio movie? We could go see that."

"That would be great."

Alan blissfully made small talk with Carrie, unaware of the bikers or anyone else in the bar.

Eventually, he excused himself and made his way to the restroom.

As he washed his hands, he saw two bikers in the mirror. "Howdy, college boy," one of them said. It was the last thing Alan remembered for awhile.

Twenty minutes later

"Hey, where's Alan?" Gary asked

Carrie said, "I think he went to the restroom."

Frowning, Gary headed back to the men's room. When he opened the door, he saw Alan rolling around on the floor, groaning. His shirt was torn, his face bloody.

"Oh, man, what happened? Are you OK?" Gary asked.

"No," Alan replied.

Gary thumbed 911 on his cell phone.

"Wait a moment," you may be thinking. "Are we reading a chapter on business law or one about biker crimes in a roadside tavern?" Both. Later in the chapter we examine a real case that mirrors the opening scenario. The crime committed against Alan will enable us to explore one of the law's basic principles, negligence. Should a pub owner pay money damages to the victim of gang violence? The owner herself did nothing aggressive. Should she have prevented the harm? Does her failure to stop the assault make her responsible? What begins as a gang incident ends up an issue of commercial liability.

Law is powerful, essential, and fascinating. We hope this book will persuade you of all three ideas. We place great demands on our courts, asking them to make our large, complex, and sometimes violent society into a safer, fairer, more orderly place. Judges must reason their way through countless complex issues.

Three Important Ideas about Law

Power

The strong reach of the law touches nearly everything we do, especially at work. Consider a mid-level manager at Sublime Corp., which manufactures and distributes video games.

During the course of a day's work, she might negotiate a deal with a game developer (contract law). Before signing any deals, she might research whether similar games already exist which might diminish her ability to market the proposed new game (intellectual property law). One of her subordinates might complain about being harassed by a coworker (employment law). Another worker may complain about being required to work long hours (administrative law). And she may consider investing her own money in her company's stock, but she may wonder whether she will get into trouble if she invests based on inside information (securities law).

It is not only as a corporate manager that you will confront the law. As a voter, investor, juror, entrepreneur, and community member, you will influence and be affected by the law. Whenever you take a stance about a legal issue, whether in the corporate office, in the voting booth, or as part of local community groups, you help to create the fabric of our nation. Your views are vital. This book will offer you knowledge and ideas from which to form and continually reassess your legal opinions and values.

Importance

Law is also essential. *Every* society of which we have any historical record has had some system of laws. For example, consider the Visigoths, a nomadic European people who overran much of present-day France and Spain during the fifth and sixth centuries A.D. Their code admirably required judges to be "quick of perception, clear in judgment, and lenient in the infliction of penalties." It detailed dozens of crimes.

Our legal system is largely based upon the English model, but many societies contributed ideas. The Iroquois Native Americans, for example, played a role in the creation of our own government. Five major nations made up the Iroquois group: the Mohawk, Cayuga, Oneida, Onondaga, and Seneca. Each nation governed its own domestic issues. But each nation also elected "sachems" to a League of the Iroquois. The league had authority over any matters that were common to all, such as relations with outsiders. Thus, by the fifteenth century, the Iroquois had solved the problem of *federalism:* how to have two levels of government, each with specified powers. Their system impressed Benjamin Franklin and others and influenced the drafting of our Constitution, with its powers divided between state and federal governments.[1]

Fascination

In 1835, the young French aristocrat Alexis de Tocqueville traveled through the United States, observing the newly democratic people and the qualities that made them unique. One of the things that struck de Tocqueville most forcefully was the American tendency to file suit: "Scarcely any political question arises in the United States that is not resolved, sooner or later, into a judicial question."[2] De Tocqueville got it right: For better or worse, we do expect courts to solve many problems.

Not only do Americans litigate—they watch each other do it. Every television season offers at least one new courtroom drama to a national audience breathless for more cross-examination. Almost all of the states permit live television coverage of real trials. The most heavily viewed event in the history of the medium was the O.J. Simpson murder trial. In most nations, coverage of judicial proceedings is not allowed.[3]

The law is a big part of our lives, and it is wise to know something about it. Within a few weeks, you will probably find yourself following legal events in the news with keener

---

[1]JackWeatherford, *Indian Givers* (New York: Fawcett Columbine, 1988), pp. 133–150.

[2]Alexis deTocqueville, *Democracy in America* (1835), Vol. 1, Ch. 16.

[3]Regardless of whether we allow cameras, it is an undeniable benefit of the electronic age that we can obtain information quickly. From time to time, we will mention websites of interest. Some of these are for nonprofit groups, while others are commercial sites. We do not endorse or advocate on behalf of any group or company; we simply wish to alert you to what is available.

interest and deeper understanding. In this chapter, we develop the background for our study. We look at where law comes from: its history and its present-day institutions. In the section on jurisprudence, we examine different theories about what "law" really means. And finally we see how courts—and students—analyze a case.

Origins of Our Law

It would be nice if we could look up "the law" in one book, memorize it, and then apply it. But the law is not that simple, and *cannot* be that simple, because it reflects the complexity of contemporary life. In truth, there is no such thing as "the law." Principles and rules of law actually come from *many different* sources. Why is this so? In part because we inherited a complex structure of laws from England.

Additionally, ours is a nation born in revolution and created, in large part, to protect the rights of its people from the government. The Founding Fathers created a national government but insisted that the individual states maintain control in many areas. As a result, each state has its own government with exclusive power over many important areas of our lives. To top it off, the Founders guaranteed many rights to the people alone, ordering national *and* state governments to keep clear. This has worked, but it has caused a multilayered system, with 50 state governments and one federal government all creating and enforcing law.

English Roots

England in the tenth century was a rustic agricultural community with a tiny population and very little law or order. Vikings invaded repeatedly, terrorizing the Anglo-Saxon peoples. Criminals were hard to catch in the heavily forested, sparsely settled nation. The king used a primitive legal system to maintain a tenuous control over his people.

England was divided into shires, and daily administration was carried out by a "shire reeve," later called a sheriff. The shire reeve collected taxes and did what he could to keep peace, apprehending criminals and acting as mediator between feuding families. Two or three times a year, a shire court met; lower courts met more frequently. Today, this method of resolving disputes lives on as mediation, which we will discuss in Chapter 3.

Because there were so few officers to keep the peace, Anglo-Saxon society created an interesting method of ensuring public order. Every freeman belonged to a group of 10 freemen known as a "tithing," headed by a "tithingman." If anyone injured a person outside his tithing or interfered with the king's property, all 10 men of the tithing could be forced to pay. Today, we still use this idea of collective responsibility in business partnerships. All partners are personally responsible for the debts of the partnership. They could potentially lose their homes and all assets because of the irresponsible conduct of one partner. That liability has helped create new forms of business organization, including limited liability companies.

When cases did come before an Anglo-Saxon court, the parties would often be represented either by a clergyman, by a nobleman, or by themselves. There were few professional lawyers. Each party produced "oath helpers," usually 12, who would swear that one version of events was correct. The Anglo-Saxon oath helpers are forerunners of our modern jury of 12 persons.

Medieval tenants in demesne *harrowing, plowing, and seeding a field.*

In 1066, the Normans conquered England. William the Conqueror made a claim never before made in England: that he owned all of the land. The king then granted sections of his lands to his favorite noblemen, as his tenants in chief, creating the system of feudalism. These tenants in chief then granted parts of their land to *tenants in demesne,* who actually occupied a particular estate. Each tenant in demesne owed fidelity to his lord (hence, "landlord"). So what? Just this: land became the most valuable commodity in all of England, and our law still reflects that. One thousand years later, American law still regards land as special. The statute of frauds, which we study in the section on contracts, demands that contracts for the sale or lease of property be in writing. And landlord-tenant law, vital to students and many others, still reflects its ancient roots. Some of a landlord's rights are based on the 1,000-year-old tradition that land is uniquely valuable.

In 1250, Henry de Bracton (d. 1268) wrote a legal treatise that still influences us. *De Legibus et Consuetudinibus Angliae* (*On the Laws and Customs of England*), written in Latin, summarized many of the legal rulings in cases since the Norman Conquest. De Bracton was teaching judges to rule based on previous cases. He was helping to establish the idea of **precedent**. The doctrine of precedent, which developed gradually over centuries, requires that judges decide current cases based on previous rulings. This vital principle is the heart of American common law. Precedent ensures predictability. Suppose a 17-year-old student promises to lease an apartment from a landlord, but then changes her mind. The landlord sues to enforce the lease. The student claims that she cannot be held to the agreement because she is a minor. The judge will look for precedent, that is, older cases dealing with the same issue, and he will find many holding that a contract generally may not be enforced against a minor. That precedent is binding on this case, and the student wins. The accumulation of precedent, based on case after case, makes up the **common law**.

Precedent
The tendency to decide current cases based on previous rulings.

Common law
Judge-made law.

In the end, today's society is dramatically different from that of medieval English society. But interestingly, legal disputes from hundreds of years ago are often quite recognizable today. Some things have changed but others never do.

Here is an actual case from more than six centuries ago, in the court's own language. The plaintiff claims that he asked the defendant to heal his eye with "herbs and other medicines." He says the defendant did it so badly that he blinded the plaintiff in that eye.

The Oculist's Case (1329)

LI MS. Hale 137 (1), fo. 150, Nottingham[4]

Attorney Launde [for defendant]: Sir, you plainly see how [the plaintiff claims] that he had submitted himself to [the defendant's] medicines and his care; and after that he can assign no trespass in his person, inasmuch as he submitted himself to his care: but this action, if he has any, sounds naturally in breach of covenant. We demand [that the case be dismissed].

Excerpts from Judge Denum's Decision: I saw a Newcastle man arraigned before my fellow justice and me for the death of a man. I asked the reason for the indictment, and it was said that he had slain a man under his care, who died within four days afterwards. And because I saw that he was a [doctor] and that he had not done the thing feloniously but [accidentally] I ordered him to be discharged. And suppose a blacksmith, who is a man of skill, injures your horse with a nail, whereby you lose your horse: you shall never have recovery against him. No more shall you here.

Afterwards the plaintiff did not wish to pursue his case any more.

[4]J.Baker and S.Milsom, Sources of English Legal History (London: Butterworth & Co., 1986).

This case from 1329 is an ancient medical malpractice action. Attorney Launde does not deny that his client blinded the plaintiff. He claims that the plaintiff has brought the wrong kind of lawsuit. Launde argues that the plaintiff should have brought a case of "covenant," that is, a lawsuit about a contract.

Judge Denum decides the case on a different principle. He gives judgment to the defendant because the plaintiff voluntarily sought medical care. He implies that the defendant would lose only if he had attacked the plaintiff. As we will see when we study negligence law, this case might have a different outcome today. Note also the informality of the judge's ruling. He rather casually mentions that he came across a related case once before and that he would stand by that outcome. The idea of precedent is just beginning to take hold.

Law in the United States

The colonists brought with them a basic knowledge of English law, some of which they were content to adopt as their own. Other parts, such as religious restrictions, were abhorrent to them. Many had made the dangerous trip to America precisely to escape persecution, and they were not interested in recreating their difficulties in a new land. Finally, some laws were simply irrelevant or unworkable in a world that was socially and geographically so different. American law ever since has been a blend of the ancient principles of English common law and a zeal and determination for change.

During the nineteenth century, the United States changed from a weak, rural nation into one of vast size and potential power. Cities grew, factories appeared, and sweeping movements of social migration changed the population. Changing conditions raised new legal questions. Did workers have a right to form industrial unions? To what extent should a manufacturer be liable if its product injured someone? Could a state government invalidate an employment contract that required 16-hour workdays? Should one company be permitted to dominate an entire industry?

In the twentieth century, the rate of social and technological change increased, creating new legal puzzles. Were some products, such as automobiles, so inherently dangerous that the seller should be responsible for injuries even if no mistakes were made in manufacturing? Who should clean up toxic waste if the company that had caused the pollution no longer existed? If a consumer signed a contract with a billion-dollar corporation, should the agreement be enforced even if the consumer never understood it? New and startling questions arise with great regularity. Before we can begin to examine the answers, we need to understand the sources of contemporary law.

Sources of Contemporary Law

Throughout the text, we will examine countless legal ideas. But binding rules come from many different places. This section describes the significant *categories* of laws in the United States.

United States Constitution

America's greatest legal achievement was the writing of the United States Constitution in 1787. It is the supreme law of the land.[5] Any law that conflicts with it is void. This federal Constitution does three basic things. First, it establishes the national government of the

[5]The Constitution took effect in 1788, when 9 of 13 colonies ratified it. Two more colonies ratified it that year, and the last of the 13 did so in 1789, after the government was already in operation. The complete text of the Constitution appears in Appendix A.

United States, with its three branches. Second, it creates a system of checks and balances among the branches. And third, the Constitution guarantees many basic rights to the American people.

Branches of Government

The Founding Fathers sought a division of government power. They did not want all power centralized in a king or in anyone else. And so, the Constitution divides legal authority into three pieces: legislative, executive, and judicial power.

Legislative power gives the ability to create new laws. In Article I, the Constitution gives this power to the Congress which is comprised of two chambers—a Senate and a House of Representatives. Voters in all 50 states elect representatives who go to Washington, D.C., to serve in the Congress and debate new legal ideas.

The House of Representatives has 435 voting members. A state's voting power is based on its population. Large states (Texas, California, and Florida) send dozens of representatives to the House. Some small states (Wyoming, North Dakota, and Delaware) send only one. The Senate has 100 voting members—two from each state.

Executive power is the authority to enforce laws. Article II of the Constitution establishes the president as commander-in-chief of the armed forces and the head of the executive branch of the federal government.

Judicial power gives the right to interpret laws and determine their validity. Article III places the Supreme Court at the head of the judicial branch of the federal government. Interpretive power is often underrated, but it is often every bit as important at the ability to create laws in the first place. For instance, the Supreme Court ruled that privacy provisions of the Constitution protect a woman's right to abortion, although neither the word "privacy" nor "abortion" appears in the text of the Constitution.[6]

At times, courts void laws altogether. For example, in 1995, the Supreme Court ruled that the *Gun-Free School Zones Act of 1990* was unconstitutional because Congress did not have the authority to pass such a law.[7]

Checks and Balances

Sidney Crosby would score 300 goals per season if checking were not allowed in the National Hockey League. But because opponents are allowed to hit Crosby and the rest of his teammates on the Penguins, he is held to a much more reasonable 50 goals per year.

Political checks work in much the same way. They allow one branch of the government to trip up another.

The authors of the Constitution were not content merely to divide government power three ways. They also wanted to give each part of the government some power over the other two branches. Many people complain about "gridlock" in Washington, but the government is slow and sluggish by design. The Founding Fathers wanted to create a system that, without broad agreement, would tend towards inaction.

The president can veto Congressional legislation. Congress can impeach the president. The Supreme Court can void laws passed by Congress. The president appoints judges to the federal courts, including the Supreme Court, but these nominees do not serve unless approved by the Senate. Congress (with help from the 50 states) can override the Supreme Court by amending the Constitution. The president and the Congress influence the Supreme Court by controlling who is placed on the court in the first place.

Many of these checks and balances will be examined in more detail in Chapter 4.

---

[6]*Roe v. Wade*, 410 U.S. 113 (1973).

[7]*United States v. Alfonso Lopez, Jr.*, 514 U.S. 549 (1995).

Fundamental Rights

The Constitution also grants many of our most basic liberties. For the most part, they are found in the amendments to the Constitution. The First Amendment guarantees the rights of free speech, free press, and the free exercise of religion. The Fourth, Fifth, and Sixth Amendments protect the rights of any person accused of a crime. Other amendments ensure that the government treats all people equally and that it pays for any property it takes from a citizen.

By creating a limited government of three branches and guaranteeing basic liberties to all citizens, the Constitution became one of the most important documents ever written.

Statutes

The second important source of law is statutory law. The Constitution gave to the United States Congress the power to pass laws on various subjects. These laws are called **statutes,** and they can cover absolutely any topic, so long as they do not violate the Constitution.

Statute
A law created by a legislative body.

Almost all statutes are created by the same method. An idea for a new law—on taxes, health care, texting while driving, or any other topic, big or small—is first proposed in the Congress. This idea is called a *bill.* The House and Senate then independently vote on the bill. To pass Congress, the bill must win a simple majority vote in each of these chambers.

If Congress passes a bill, it goes to the White House for the president's approval. If the president signs it, a new statute is created. It is no longer a mere idea; it is the law of the land. If the president refuses to approve, or *vetoes* a bill, it does not become a statute unless Congress overrides the veto. To do that, both the House and the Senate must approve the bill by a two-thirds majority. If this happens, it becomes a statute without the president's signature.

Common Law

Binding legal ideas often come from the courts. Judges generally follow *precedent.* When courts decide a case, they tend to apply the legal rules that other courts have used in similar cases.

The principle that precedent is binding on later cases is called *stare decisis,* which means "let the decision stand." *Stare decisis* makes the law predictable, and this in turn enables businesses and private citizens to plan intelligently.

It is important to note that precedent is binding only on *lower* courts. For example, if the Supreme Court decided a case in one way in 1965, it is under no obligation to follow precedent if the same issue arises in 2015.

Sometimes, this is quite beneficial. In 1896, the Supreme Court decided (unbelievably) that segregation—separating people by race in schools, hotels, public transportation, and other public services—was legal under certain conditions.[8] In 1954, on the exact same issue, the court changed its mind.[9]

In other circumstances, it is more difficult to see the value in breaking with an established rule.

Court Orders

Judges have the authority to issue court orders that place binding obligations on specific people or companies. An injunction, for example, is a court order to stop doing something. A judge might order a stalker to stay more than 500 yards away from an ex-boyfriend or -girlfriend. Lindsey Lohan might be ordered to stop drinking and enter rehab. Courts have the authority to imprison or fine those who violate their orders.

---

[8] *Plessy v. Ferguson*, 163 U.S.537 (1896).

[9] *Brown v. Board of Education of Topeka*, 347 U.S. 483 (1954) .

Administrative Law

In a society as large and diverse as ours, the executive and legislative branches of government cannot oversee all aspects of commerce. Congress passes statutes about air safety, but United States senators do not stand around air traffic towers, serving coffee to keep everyone awake. The executive branch establishes rules concerning how foreign nationals enter the United States, but presidents are reluctant to sit on the dock of the bay, watching the ships come in. Administrative agencies do this day-to-day work.

Most government agencies are created by Congress. Familiar examples are the Environmental Protection Agency (EPA), the Securities and Exchange Commission (SEC), and the Internal Revenue Service (IRS), whose feelings are hurt if it does not hear from you every April 15. Agencies have the power to create laws called *regulations.*

Treaties

The Constitution authorizes the president to make treaties with foreign nations. These must then be ratified by the United States Senate by a two-thirds vote. When they are ratified, they are as binding upon all citizens as any federal statute. In 1994 the Senate ratified the North American Free Trade Agreement (NAFTA) with Mexico and Canada. NAFTA was controversial then and remains so today—but it is the law of the land.

CLASSIFICATIONS

We have seen where law comes from. Now we need to classify the various types of laws. First, we will distinguish between criminal and civil law. Then, we will take a look at the intersection between law and morality.

Criminal and Civil Law

Criminal law
Criminal law prohibits certain behavior.

It is a crime to embezzle money from a bank, to steal a car, to sell cocaine. **Criminal law** concerns behavior so threatening that society outlaws it altogether. Most criminal laws are statutes, passed by Congress or a state legislature. The government itself prosecutes the wrongdoer, regardless of what the bank president or car owner wants. A district attorney, paid by the government, brings the case to court. The injured party, for example the owner of the stolen car, is not in charge of the case, although she may appear as a witness. The government will seek to punish the defendant with a prison sentence, a fine, or both. If there is a fine, the money goes to the state, not to the injured party.

Civil law
Civil law regulates the rights and duties between parties.

Civil law is different, and most of this book is about civil law. **The civil law regulates the rights and duties between parties.** Tracy agrees in writing to lease you a 30,000-square-foot store in her shopping mall. She now has a *legal duty* to make the space available. But then another tenant offers her more money, and she refuses to let you move in. Tracy has violated her duty, but she has not committed a crime. The government will not prosecute the case. It is up to you to file a civil lawsuit. Your case will be based on the common law of contract. You will also seek equitable relief, namely, an injunction ordering Tracy not to lease to anyone else. You should win the suit, and you will get your injunction and some money damages. But Tracy will not go to jail.

Some conduct involves both civil and criminal law. Suppose Tracy is so upset over losing the court case that she becomes drunk and causes a serious car accident. She has committed the crime of driving while intoxicated, and the state will prosecute. Tracy may be fined or imprisoned. She has also committed negligence, and the injured party will file a lawsuit against her, seeking money. We will again see civil and criminal law joined together in the *Pub Zone* case, later in the chapter.

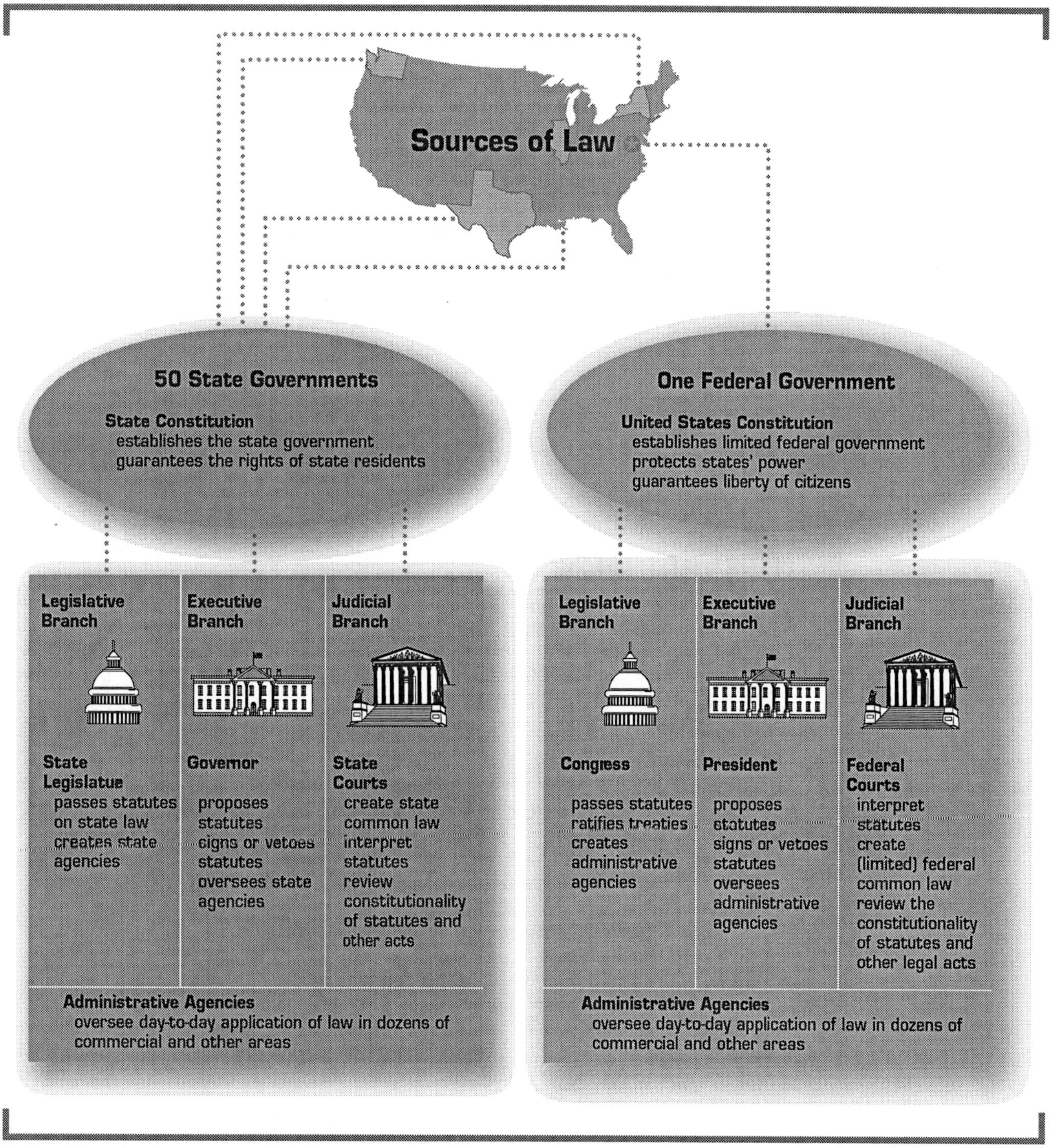

Sources of Law

50 State Governments

State Constitution
establishes the state government
guarantees the rights of state residents

Legislative Branch	Executive Branch	Judicial Branch
State Legislatue passes statutes on state law creates state agencies	**Governor** proposes statutes signs or vetoes statutes oversees state agencies	**State Courts** create state common law interpret statutes review constitutionality of statutes and other acts

Administrative Agencies
oversee day-to-day application of law in dozens of commercial and other areas

One Federal Government

United States Constitution
establishes limited federal government
protects states' power
guarantees liberty of citizens

Legislative Branch	Executive Branch	Judicial Branch
Congress passes statutes ratifies treaties creates administrative agencies	**President** proposes statutes signs or vetoes statutes oversees administrative agencies	**Federal Courts** interpret statutes create (limited) federal common law review the constitutionality of statutes and other legal acts

Administrative Agencies
oversee day-to-day application of law in dozens of commercial and other areas

Federal Form of Government. Principles and rules of law come from many sources. The government in Washington creates and enforces law throughout the nation. But 50 state governments exercise great power in local affairs. And citizens enjoy constitutional protection from both state and federal government. The Founding Fathers wanted this balance of power and rights, but the overlapping authority creates legal complexity.

Law and Morality

Law is different from morality, yet the two are obviously linked. There are many instances when the law duplicates what all of us would regard as a moral position. It is negligent to drive too fast in a school district, and few would dispute the moral value of seeking to limit harm to students. And the same holds with contract law: If the owner of land agrees in writing to sell property to a buyer at a stated price, both the buyer and the seller must go through with the deal, and the legal outcome matches our moral expectations.

On the other hand, we have had laws that we now clearly regard as immoral. At the turn of the century, a factory owner could typically fire a worker for any reason at all—including, for example, his religious or political views. It is immoral to fire a worker because she is Jewish—and today the law prohibits it.

Finally, there are legal issues where the morality is less clear. You are walking down a country lane and notice a three-year-old child playing with matches near a barn filled with hay. Are you obligated to intervene? No, says the law, though many think that is preposterous. (See Chapter 4, on common law, for more about this topic.) A company buys property and then discovers, buried under the ground, toxic waste that will cost $300,000 to clean up. The original owner has gone bankrupt. Should the new owner be forced to pay for the cleanup? If the new owner fails to pay for the job, who will? (See Chapter 40, on environmental law, for more discussion on this issue.)

Chapter 2 will further examine the bond between law and morality.

JURISPRUDENCE

Jurisprudence
The philosophy of law.

We have had a glimpse of legal history and a summary of the present-day sources of American law. But what *is* law? That question is the basis of a field known as **jurisprudence**. What is the real nature of law? Can there be such a thing as an "illegal" law?

Legal Positivism

Sovereign
The recognized political power, whom citizens obey.

This philosophy can be simply stated: Law is what the sovereign says it is. The **sovereign** is the recognized political power whom citizens obey, so in the United States, both state and federal governments are sovereign. A legal positivist holds that whatever the sovereign declares to be the law *is* the law, whether it is right or wrong.

The primary criticism of legal positivism is that it seems to leave no room for questions of morality. A law permitting a factory owner to fire a worker because she is Catholic is surely different from a law prohibiting arson. Do citizens in a democracy have a duty to consider such differences? Consider the following example.

Most states allow citizens to pass laws directly at the ballot box, a process called voter referendum. California voters often do this, and during the 1990s, they passed one of the state's most controversial laws. Proposition 187 was designed to curb illegal immigration into the state by eliminating social spending for undocumented aliens. Citizens debated the measure fiercely but passed it by a large margin. One section of the new law forbade public schools from educating illegal immigrants. The law obligated a principal to inquire into the immigration status of all children enrolled in the school and to report undocumented students to immigration authorities. Several San Diego school principals rejected the new rules, stating that they would neither inquire into immigration status nor report undocumented aliens. Their statements produced a heated response. Some San Diego residents castigated the school officials as lawbreakers, claiming that

- A school officer who knowingly disobeyed a law was setting a terrible example for students, who would assume they were free to do the same;
- The principals were advocating permanent residence and a free education for anyone able to evade our immigration laws; and

- The officials were scorning grass-roots democracy by disregarding a law passed by popular referendum.

Others applauded the principals' position, asserting that

- The referendum's rules would transform school officials from educators into border police, forcing them to cross-examine young children and their parents;
- The new law was foolish because it punished innocent children for violations committed by their parents; and
- Our nation has long respected civil disobedience based on humanitarian ideals, and these officials were providing moral leadership to the whole community.

Ultimately, no one had to decide whether to obey Proposition 187. A federal court ruled that only Congress had the power to regulate immigration and that California's attempt was unconstitutional and void. The debate over immigration reform—and ethics—did not end, however. It continues to be a thorny issue.

Natural Law

St. Thomas Aquinas (1225–1274) answered the legal positivists even before they had spoken. In his *Summa Theologica,* he argued that an unjust law is no law at all and need not be obeyed. It is not enough that a sovereign makes a command. The law must have a moral basis.

> St. Thomas Aquinas argued that an unjust law is no law at all ...

Where do we find the moral basis that would justify a law? Aquinas says that "good is that which all things seek after." Therefore, the fundamental rule of all laws is that "good is to be done and promoted, and evil is to be avoided." This sounds appealing, but also vague. Exactly which laws promote good and which do not? Is it better to have a huge corporation dominate a market or many smaller companies competing? Did the huge company get that way by being better than its competitors? If Wal-Mart moves into a rural area, establishes a mammoth store, and sells inexpensive products, is that "good"? Yes, if you are a consumer who cares only about prices. No, if you are the owner of a Main Street store driven into bankruptcy. Maybe, if you are a resident who values small-town life but wants lower prices.

Legal Realism

Legal realists take a very different tack. They claim it does not matter what is written as law. What counts is who enforces that law and by what process. All of us are biased by issues such as income, education, family background, race, religion, and many other factors. These personal characteristics, they say, determine which contracts will be enforced and which ignored, why some criminals receive harsh sentences while others get off lightly, and so on.

Judge Jones hears a multimillion dollar lawsuit involving an airplane crash. Was the airline negligent? The law is the same everywhere, but legal realists say that Jones's background will determine the outcome. If she spent 20 years representing insurance companies, she will tend to favor the airline. If her law practice consisted of helping the "little guy," she will favor the plaintiff.

Other legal realists argue, more aggressively, that those in power use the machinery of the law to perpetuate their control. The outcome of a given case will be determined by the needs of those with money and political clout. A court puts "window dressing" on a decision, they say, so that society thinks there are principles behind the law. A problem with legal realism, however, is its denial that any lawmaker can overcome personal bias. Yet clearly some do act unselfishly.

SUMMARY OF JURISPRUDENCE	
Legal Positivism	Law is what the sovereign says.
Natural Law	An unjust law is no law at all.
Legal Realism	Who enforces the law counts more than what is in writing.

No one school of jurisprudence is likely to seem perfect. We urge you to keep the different theories in mind as you read cases in the book. Ask yourself which school of thought is the best fit for you.

Working with the Book's Features

In this section, we introduce a few of the book's features and discuss how you can use them effectively. We will start with *cases.*

Analyzing a Case

A law case is the decision a court has made in a civil lawsuit or criminal prosecution. Cases are the heart of the law and an important part of this book. Reading them effectively takes practice. This chapter's opening scenario is fictional, but the following real case involves a similar situation. Who can be held liable for the assault? Let's see.

Kuehn v. Pub Zone

364 N.J. Super. 301, 835 A.2d 692
Superior Court of New Jersey, Appellate Division, 2003

Facts: Maria Kerkoulas owned the Pub Zone bar. She knew that several motorcycle gangs frequented the tavern. From her own experience tending bar, and conversations with city police, she knew that some of the gangs, including the Pagans, were dangerous and prone to attack customers for no reason. Kerkoulas posted a sign prohibiting any motorcycle gangs from entering the bar while wearing "colors," that is, insignia of their gangs. She believed that gangs without their colors were less prone to violence, and experience proved her right.

Rhino, Backdraft, and several other Pagans, all wearing colors, pushed their way past the tavern's bouncer and approached the bar. Although Kerkoulas saw their colors, she allowed them to stay for one drink. They later moved towards the back of the pub, and Kerkoulas believed they were departing. In fact, they followed a customer named Karl Kuehn to the men's room, where without any provocation they savagely beat him. Kuehn was knocked unconscious and suffered brain hemorrhaging, disc herniation, and numerous fractures of facial bones. He was forced to undergo various surgeries, including eye reconstruction.

Although the government prosecuted Rhino and Backdraft for their vicious assault, our case does not concern that prosecution. Kuehn sued the Pub Zone, and that is the case we will read. The jury awarded him $300,000 in damages. However, the trial court judge overruled the jury's verdict. He granted a judgment for the Pub Zone, meaning that the tavern owed nothing. The judge ruled that the pub's owner could not have foreseen the attack on Kuehn, and had no duty to protect him from an outlaw motorcycle gang. Kuehn appealed, and the appeals court's decision follows:

Issue: ***Did the Pub Zone have a duty to protect Kuehn from the Pagans' attack?***

Excerpts from Judge Payne's Decision: Whether a duty exists depends upon an evaluation of a number of factors including the nature of the underlying risk of harm, that is, its foreseeability and severity, the opportunity and ability to exercise care to prevent the harm, the comparative interests of and the relationships between or among the parties, and, ultimately, based on considerations of public policy and fairness, the societal interest in the proposed solution.

Since the possessor [of a business] is not an insurer of the visitor's safety, he is ordinarily under no duty to exercise any care until he knows or has reason to know that the acts of the third person are occurring, or are about to occur. He may, however, know or have reason to know, from past experience, that there is a likelihood of conduct on the part of third persons in general which is likely to endanger the safety of the visitor, even though he has no reason to expect it on the part of any particular individual.

We find the totality of the circumstances presented in this case give rise to a duty on the part of the Pub Zone to have taken reasonable precautions against the danger posed by the Pagans as a group. In this case, there was no reason to suspect any particular Pagan of violent conduct. However, the gang was collectively known to Kerkoulas to engage in random violence. Thus, Kerkoulas had knowledge as the result of past experience and from other sources that there was a likelihood of conduct on the part of third persons in general that was likely to endanger the safety of a patron at some unspecified future time. A duty to take precautions against the endangering conduct thus arose.

We do not regard our recognition of a duty in this case to give rise to either strict or absolute liability on the part of the Pub Zone. To fulfill its duty in this context, the Pub Zone was merely required to employ "reasonable" safety precautions. It already had in place a prohibition against bikers who were wearing their colors, and that prohibition, together with the practice of calling the police when a breach occurred, had been effective in greatly diminishing the occurrence of biker incidents on the premises. The evidence establishes that the prohibition was not enforced on the night at issue, that three Pagans were permitted entry while wearing their colors, and the police were not called. Once entry was achieved, the Pub Zone remained under a duty to exercise reasonable precautions against an attack.

The jury's verdict must therefore be reinstated.

Analysis

Let's take it from the top. The case is called *Kuehn v. Pub Zone.* Karl Kuehn is the **plaintiff**, the person who is suing. The Pub Zone is being sued, and is called the **defendant**. In this example, the plaintiff's name happens to appear first but that is not always true. When a defendant loses a trial and files an appeal, *some* courts reverse the names of the parties.

Plaintiff
The party who is suing.

Defendant
The party being sued.

The next line gives the legal citation, which indicates where to find the case in a law library. We explain in the footnote how to locate a book if you plan to do research.[10]

The *Facts* section provides a background to the lawsuit, written by the authors of this text. The court's own explanation of the facts is often many pages long, and may involve complex matters irrelevant to the subject covered in this book, so we relate only what is necessary. This section will usually include some mention of what happened at the trial

[10]If you want to do legal research, you need to know where to find particular legal decisions. A case citation guides you to the correct volume(s). The full citation of our case is *Kuehn v. Pub Zone,* 364 N.J. Super. 301, 835 A.2d 692. The string of numbers identifies two different books in which you can find the full text of this decision. The first citation is to "N.J. Super," which means the official court reporter of the state of New Jersey. New Jersey, like most states, reports its law cases in a series of numbered volumes. This case appears in volume 364 of the New Jersey Superior Court reporters. If you go to a law library and find that book, you can then turn to page 301 and—*voila!*—you have the case. The decision is also reported in another set of volumes, called the regional reporters. This series of law reports is grouped by geographic region. New Jersey is included in the Atlantic region, so our case appears in reporters dedicated to that region. The "A" stands for Atlantic. After a series of reporters reaches volume 999, a second set begins. Our case appears in volume 835 of the second set of the Atlantic reporters ("A.2d"), at page 692. In addition, most cases are now available online, and your professor or librarian can show you how to find them electronically.

court. Lawsuits always begin in a trial court. The losing party often appeals to a court of appeals, and it is usually an appeals court decision that we are reading. The trial judge ruled in favor of Pub Zone, but later, in the decision we are reading, Kuehn wins.

The *Issue* section is very important. It tells you what the court had to decide—and also why you are reading the case. In giving its decision, a court may digress. If you keep in mind the issue and relate the court's discussion to it, you will not get lost.

Excerpts from Judge Payne's Decision begins the court's discussion. This is called the *holding,* meaning a statement of who wins and who loses. The holding also includes the court's *rationale,* which is the reasoning behind the decision.

The holding that we provide is an edited version of the court's own language. Some judges write clear, forceful prose, others do not. Either way, their words give you an authentic feel for how judges think and rule, so we bring it to you in the original. Occasionally we use brackets [ ] to substitute our language for that of the court, either to condense or to clarify. Notice the brackets in the second paragraph of the Pub Zone decision. Judge Payne explains the point at much greater length, so we have condensed some of his writing into the phrase "of a business."

We omit a great deal. A court's opinion may be 3 pages or it may be 75. We do not use ellipses (…) to indicate these deletions, because there is more taken out than kept in, and we want the text to be clean. When a court quotes an earlier decision verbatim but clearly adopts those words as its own, we generally delete the quotation marks, as well as the citation to the earlier case. If you are curious about the full holding, you can always look it up.

Let us look at a few of Judge Payne's points. The holding begins with a discussion of *duty*. The court explains that whether one person (or bar) owes a duty to protect another depends upon several factors, including whether the harm could be foreseen, how serious the injury could be, and whether there was an opportunity to prevent it.

Judge Payne then points out that the owner of a business is not an insurer of a visitor's safety. Typically, the owner has a duty to a visitor *only* if he has a reason to know that some harm is likely to occur. How would a merchant know that? Based on the character of the business, suggests the judge, or the owner's experience with particular people.

The judge then applies this general rule to the facts of this case. He concludes that the Pub Zone did in fact have a duty to protect Kuehn from the Pagans' attack. Based on Kerkoulas's experience, and warnings received from the police, she knew that the gang was dangerous and should have foreseen that admitting them in their "colors" greatly increased the chance of an attack.

Next, the court points out that it is not requiring the Pub Zone to *guarantee* everyone's safety. The bar was merely obligated to do a *reasonable* job. The prohibition on colors was a good idea, and calling the police had also proven effective. The problem of course was that in this case, Kerkoulas ignored her own rule about gang insignia and failed to call the police.

Based on all the evidence, the jury's finding of liability was reasonable, and its verdict must be reinstated. In other words, Kuehn, who lost at the trial, wins on appeal. What the court has done is to *reverse* the lower court's decision, meaning to turn the loser into the winner. In other cases, we will see an appellate court *remand* the case, meaning to send it back down to the lower court for additional steps. Or the appellate judges could *affirm* the lower court's decision, meaning to leave it unchanged.

Devil's Advocate

Each chapter has several cases. After some of them, a "Devil's Advocate" feature offers you a contrasting view of the legal issue. This is not part of the case, but is instead a suggestion of another perspective on the problem discussed. The authors take no position for or against the court's decision, but merely want you to consider an alternate view, and decide which analysis of the law makes more sense to you—that of the court or the Devil's Advocate. Is the following view persuasive?

Devil's Advocate A court should not force small businesses to guarantee their customers' safety. Two or three violent men, whether motorcycle gang members or frustrated professors, could enter a grocery store or clothing retailer at any time and mindlessly attack innocent visitors. Random attacks are just that—random, unforeseeable. No merchant should be required to anticipate them. Send the criminals to jail, but do not place the burden on honest business people.

Exam Strategy

This feature gives you practice analyzing cases the way lawyers do—and the way *you* must on tests. Law exams are different from most others because you must determine the issue from the facts provided. Too frequently, students faced with a law exam forget that the questions relate to the issues in the text and those discussed in class. Understandably, students new to law may focus on the wrong information in the problem or rely on material learned elsewhere. Exam Strategy teaches you to figure out exactly what issue is at stake, and then analyze it in a logical, consistent manner. Here is an example, relating to the element of "duty," which the court discussed in the Pub Zone case.

EXAM Strategy

Question: The Big Red Traveling (BRT) Carnival is in town. Tony arrives at 8:00 p.m., parks in the lot—and is robbed at gunpoint by a man who beats him and escapes with his money. There are several police officers on the carnival grounds, but no officer is in the parking lot at the time of the robbery. Tony sues, claiming that brighter lighting and more police in the lot would have prevented the robbery. There has never before been any violent crime—robbery, beating, or otherwise—at any BRT carnival. BRT claims it had no duty to protect Tony from this harm. Who is likely to win?

Strategy: Begin by isolating the legal issue. What are the parties disputing? They are debating whether BRT had a duty to protect Tony from an armed robbery, committed by a stranger. Now ask yourself: How do courts decide whether a business has a duty to prevent this kind of harm? The Pub Zone case provides our answer. A business owner is not an ensurer of the visitor's safety. The owner generally has no duty to protect a customer from the criminal act of a third party, unless the owner knows the harm is occurring or could foresee it is about to happen. (In the Pub Zone case, the business owner *knew* of the gang's violent history, and could have foreseen the assault.) Now apply that rule to the facts of this case.

Result: There has never been a violent attack of any kind at a BRT carnival. BRT cannot foresee this robbery, and has no duty to protect against it. The carnival wins.

You Be the Judge

Many cases involve difficult decisions for juries and judges. Often both parties have legitimate, opposing arguments. Most chapters in this book will have a feature called "You Be the Judge," in which we present the facts of a case but not the court's holding.

We offer you two opposing arguments based on the kinds of claims the lawyers made in court. We leave it up to you to debate and decide which position is stronger or to add your own arguments to those given.

The following case is another negligence lawsuit, with issues that overlap those of the Pub Zone case. This time the court confronts a fight that resulted in a death. The victim's distraught family sued the owner of a bar, claiming that one of his employees was partly responsible for the death. Once again, the defendant asked the court to dismiss the case, claiming that he owed no duty to protect the victim—the same argument made by the Pub Zone.

But there is a difference here—this time the defendant owned the bar across the street, not the one where the fight took place. Could he be held legally responsible for the death? You be the judge.

You be the Judge

Soldano v. O'Daniels

141 Cal. App. 3d 443
Court of Appeal of California, 5th Appellate District, 1983

Facts: In the days before cell phones, a fight broke out at Happy Jack's Saloon. A good Samaritan ran across the street to the Circle Inn. He asked the bartender at the Circle Inn to let him use the telephone to call the police, but he refused.

Back at Happy Jack's Saloon, the fight escalated, and a man shot and killed Soldano's father. Soldano sued the owner of the Circle Inn for negligence. He argued that the bartender violated a legal duty when he refused to hand over the inn's telephone and that, as the employer of the bartender, O'Daniels was partially liable for Soldano's father's death.

The lower court dismissed the case, citing the principle that generally, a person does not have a legal responsibility to help another unless he created the dangerous situation in the first place. Soldano appealed.

You Be The Judge: ***Did the bartender have a duty to allow the use of the Circle Inn's telephone?***

Argument for the Defendant: Your honors, my client did not act wrongfully. He did nothing to create the danger. The fight was not even on his property. We sympathize with the plaintiff, but it is the shooter, and perhaps the bar where the fight took place, who are responsible for his father's death. Our client was not involved. Liability can be stretched only so far.

The court would place a great burden on the citizens of California by going against precedent. The Circle Inn is Mr. O'Daniel's private property. If the court imposes potential liability on him in this case, would citizens be forced to open the doors of their homes whenever a stranger claims that there is an emergency? Criminals would delight in their newfound ability to gain access to businesses and residences by simply demanding to use a phone to "call the police."

The law has developed sensibly. People are left to decide for themselves whether to help in a dangerous situation. They are not legally required to place themselves in harm's way.

Argument for the Plaintiff: Your honors, the Circle Inn's bartender had both a moral and a legal duty to allow the use of his establishment's telephone. The Circle Inn may be privately owned, but it is a business and is open to the public. Anyone in the world is invited to stop by and order a drink or a meal. The good Samaritan had every right to be there.

We do not argue that the bartender had an obligation to break up the fight or endanger himself in any way. We simply argue he had a responsibility to stand aside and allow a free call on his restaurant's telephone. Any "burden" on him or on the Circle Inn was incredibly slight. The potential benefits were enormous. The trial court made a mistake in concluding that a person *never* has a duty to help another. Such an interpretation makes for poor public policy.

There is no need to radically change the common law. Residences can be excluded from this ruling. People need not be required to allow telephone-seeking strangers into their homes. This court can simply determine that businesses have a legal duty to allow the placement of emergency calls during normal business hours.

Chapter Conclusion

We depend upon the law to give us a stable nation and economy, a fair society, a safe place to live and work. These worthy goals have occupied ancient kings and twenty-first-century lawmakers alike. But while law is a vital tool for crafting the society we want, there are no easy answers about how to create it. In a democracy, we all participate in the crafting. Legal rules control us, yet *we* create *them.* A working knowledge of the law can help build a successful career—and a solid democracy.

EXAM REVIEW

1. **THE FEDERAL SYSTEM** Our federal system of government means that law comes from a national government in Washington, D.C., and from 50 state governments. (p. 7)

2. **LEGAL HISTORY** The history of law foreshadows many current legal issues, including mediation, partnership liability, the jury system, the role of witnesses, the special value placed on land, and the idea of precedent. (pp. 5–6)

3. **PRIMARY SOURCES OF LAW** The primary sources of contemporary law are

   - United States Constitution and state constitutions;
   - Statutes, which are drafted by legislatures;
   - Common law, which is the body of cases decided by judges, as they follow earlier cases, known as precedent;
   - Court orders, which place obligations on specific people or companies;
   - Administrative law, the rules and decisions made by federal and state administrative agencies; and
   - Treaties, agreements between the United States and foreign nations. (p. 7)

EXAM Strategy

Question: The stock market crash of 1929 and the Great Depression that followed were caused in part because so many investors blindly put their money into stocks they knew nothing about. During the 1920s, it was often impossible for an investor to find out what a corporation was planning to do with its money, who was running the corporation, and many other vital things. Congress responded by passing the Securities Act of 1933, which required a corporation to divulge more information about itself before it could seek money for a new stock issue. What kind of law did Congress create?

Strategy: What is the question seeking? The question asks you which *type* of law Congress created when it passed the 1933 Securities Act. What are the primary kinds of law? Administrative law consists of rules passed by agencies. Congress is not a federal agency. Common law is the body of cases decided by judges. Congress is not a judge. Statutes are laws passed by legislatures. Congress is a legislature. (See the "Result" at the end of this section.)

4. **CRIMINAL LAW** Criminal law concerns behavior so threatening to society that it is outlawed altogether. Civil law deals with duties and disputes between parties, not with outlawed behavior. (p. 10)

EXAM Strategy

Question: Bill and Diane are hiking in the woods. Diane walks down a hill to fetch fresh water. Bill meets a stranger, who introduces herself as Katrina. Bill sells a kilo of cocaine to Katrina, who then flashes a badge and mentions how much she enjoys her job at the Drug Enforcement Agency. Diane, heading back to camp with the water, meets Freddy, a motorist whose car has overheated. Freddy is late for a meeting where he expects to make a $30 million profit; he's desperate for water for his car. He promises to pay Diane $500 tomorrow if she will give him the pail of water, which she does. The next day, Bill is in jail and Freddy refuses to pay for Diane's water. Explain the criminal law/civil law distinction and what it means to Bill and Diane. Who will do what to whom, with what results?

Strategy: You are asked to distinguish between criminal and civil law. What is the difference? The criminal law concerns behavior that threatens society and is therefore outlawed. The government prosecutes the defendant. Civil law deals with the rights and duties between parties. One party files a suit against the other. Apply those different standards to these facts. (See the "Result" at the end of this section.)

5. **JURISPRUDENCE** Jurisprudence is concerned with the basic nature of law. Three theories of jurisprudence are

- Legal positivism: The law is what the sovereign says it is.
- Natural law: An unjust law is no law at all.
- Legal realism: Who enforces the law is more important than what the law says. (pp. 12–15)

3. Result: The Securities Act of 1933 is a statute.

4. Result: The government will prosecute Bill for dealing in drugs. If convicted, he will go to prison. The government will take no interest in Diane's dispute. However, if she chooses, she may sue Freddy for $500, the amount he promised her for the water. In that civil lawsuit, a court will decide whether Freddy must pay what he promised; however, even if Freddy loses, he will not go to jail.

Multiple-Choice Questions

1. The United States Constitution is among the finest legal accomplishments in the history of the world. Which of the following influenced Ben Franklin, Thomas Jefferson, and the rest of the Founding Fathers?
   (a) English common-law principles
   (b) The Iroquois's system of federalism
   (c) Both A and B
   (d) None of the above

2. Which of the following parts of the modern legal system are "borrowed" from medieval England?
   (a) Jury trials
   (b) Special rules for selling land
   (c) Following precedent
   (d) All of the above

3. Union organizers at a hospital wanted to distribute leaflets to potential union members, but hospital rules prohibited leafleting in areas of patient care, hallways, cafeterias, and any areas open to the public. The National Labor Relations Board, a government agency, ruled that these restrictions violated the law and ordered the hospital to permit the activities in the cafeteria and coffee shop. What kind of law was it creating?
   (a) A statute
   (b) Common law
   (c) A constitutional amendment
   (d) Administrative regulation

4. If the Congress creates a new statute with the president's support, it must pass the idea by a ____________ majority vote in the House and the Senate. If the president vetoes a proposed statute and the Congress wishes to pass it without his support, the idea must pass by a ____________ majority vote in the House and Senate.
   (a) simple; simple
   (b) simple; two-thirds
   (c) simple; three-fourths
   (d) two-thirds; three-fourths

5. What part of the Constitution addresses the most basic liberties?
   (a) Article I
   (b) Article II
   (c) Article III
   (d) Amendments

Essay Questions

1. Burglar Bob breaks into Vince Victim's house. Bob steals a flat-screen TV and laptop and does a significant amount of damage to the property before he leaves. Fortunately, Vince has a state-of-the-art security system. It captures excellent images of Bob, who is soon caught by police.

   Assume that two legal actions follow, one civil and one criminal. Who will be responsible for bringing the civil case? What will be the outcome if the jury believes that Bob burgled Vince's house? Who will be responsible for bringing the criminal case? What will be the outcome if the jury believes that Bob burgled Vince's house?

2. As "The Oculist's Case" indicates, the medical profession has faced a large number of lawsuits for centuries. In Texas, a law provides that, so long as a doctor was not reckless and did not intentionally harm a patient, recovery for "pain and suffering" is limited to $750,000. In many other states, no such limit exists. If a patient will suffer a lifetime of pain after a botched operation, for example, he might recover millions in compensation.

   Which rule seems more sensible to you – the "Texas" rule, or the alternative?

3. **YOU BE THE JUDGE WRITING PROBLEM** Should trials be televised? Here are a few arguments to add to those in the chapter. You be the judge. **Arguments against live television coverage:** We have tried this experiment and it has failed. Trials fall into two categories: Those that create great public interest and those that do not. No one watches dull trials, so we do not need to broadcast them. The few that are interesting have all become circuses. Judges and lawyers have shown that they cannot resist the temptation to play to the camera. Trials are supposed to be about justice, not entertainment. If a citizen seriously wants to follow a case, she can do it by reading the daily newspaper. **Arguments for live television coverage:** It is true that some televised trials have been unseemly affairs, but that is the fault of the presiding judges, not the media. Indeed, one of the virtues of television coverage is that millions of people now understand that we have a lot of incompetent people running our courtrooms. The proper response is to train judges to run a tight trial by prohibiting grandstanding by lawyers. Access to accurate information is the foundation on which a democracy is built, and we must not eliminate a source of valuable data just because some judges are ill-trained or otherwise incompetent.

4. Leslie Bergh and his two brothers, Milton and Raymond, formed a partnership to help build a fancy saloon and dance hall in Evanston, Wyoming. Later, Leslie met with his friend and drinking buddy, John Mills, and tricked Mills into investing in the saloon. Leslie did not tell Mills that no one else was investing cash or that the entire enterprise was already bankrupt. Mills mortgaged his home, invested $150,000 in the saloon—and lost every penny of it. Mills sued all three partners for fraud. Milton and Raymond defended on the grounds that they did not commit the fraud; only Leslie did. The defendants lost. Was that fair? By holding them liable, what general idea did the court rely on? What Anglo-Saxon legal custom did the ruling resemble?

5. *Kuehn v. Pub Zone* and *Soldano v. O'Daniels* both involve attacks in a bar. Should they have the same result? If so, in which way—in favor of the injured plaintiffs or owner-defendants? If not, why should they have different outcomes? What are the key facts that lead you to believe as you do?

Discussion Questions

1. Do you believe that there are too many lawsuits in the United States? If so, do you place more blame for the problem on lawyers or on individuals who go to court? Is there anything that would help the problem, or will we always have large numbers of lawsuits?

2. In the 1980s, the Supreme Court ruled that it is legal for protesters to burn the American flag. This activity counts as free speech under the Constitution. If the Court hears a new flag-burning case in this decade, should it consider changing its ruling, or should it follow precedent? Is following past precedent something that seems sensible to you: always, usually, sometimes, rarely, or never?

3. When should a business be held legally responsible for customer safety? Consider the following statements, and circle the appropriate answer:
   a. A business should keep customers safe from its own employees.
      strongly agree agree neutral disagree strongly disagree
   b. A business should keep customers safe from other customers.
      strongly agree agree neutral disagree strongly disagree
   c. A business should keep customers safe from themselves. (Example: an intoxicated customer who can no longer walk straight.)
      strongly agree agree neutral disagree strongly disagree
   d. A business should keep people outside its own establishment safe if it is reasonable to do so.
      strongly agree agree neutral disagree strongly disagree

4. In his most famous novel, *The Red and the Black*, the French author Stendhal (1783–1842) wrote: "There is no such thing as 'natural law': this expression is nothing but old nonsense. Prior to laws, what is natural is only the strength of the lion, or the need of the creature suffering from hunger or cold, in short, need." What do you think? Does legal positivism or legal realism seem more sensible to you?

5. At the time of this writing, voters are particularly disgruntled. A good many people seem to be disgusted with government. For this question, we intentionally avoid distinguishing between Democrats and Republicans, and we intentionally do not name any particular president. Consider the following statements, and circle the appropriate answer:
   a. I believe that members of Congress usually try to do the right thing for America.
      strongly agree agree neutral disagree strongly disagree
   b. I believe that presidents usually try to do the right thing for America.
      strongly agree agree neutral disagree strongly disagree
   c. I believe that Supreme Court justices usually try to do the right thing for America.
      strongly agree agree neutral disagree strongly disagree

CHAPTER 3

DISPUTE RESOLUTION

© r.nagy/Shutterstock.com

Tony Caruso had not returned for dinner, and his wife, Karen, was nervous. She put on some sandals and hurried across the dunes, a half mile to the ocean shore. She soon came upon Tony's dog, Blue, tied to an old picket fence. Tony's shoes and clothing were piled neatly nearby. Karen and friends searched frantically throughout the evening.

A little past midnight, Tony's body washed ashore, his lungs filled with water. A local doctor concluded he had accidentally drowned.

A little past midnight, Tony's body washed ashore, his lungs filled with water.

Karen and her friends were not the only ones who were distraught. Tony had been partners with Beth Smiles in an environmental consulting business, Enviro-Vision. They were good friends, and Beth was emotionally devastated. When she was able to focus on business issues, Beth filed an insurance claim with the Coastal Insurance Group. Beth hated to think about Tony's death in financial terms, but she was relieved that the struggling business would receive $2 million on the life insurance policy.

Several months after filing the claim, Beth received this reply from Coastal: "Under the policy issued to Enviro-Vision, we are conditionally liable in the amount of $1 million in the event of Mr. Caruso's death. If his death is accidental, we are conditionally liable to pay double indemnity of $2 million. But pursuant to section H(5), death by suicide is not covered.

"After a thorough investigation, we have concluded that Anthony Caruso's death was an act of suicide, as defined in section B(11) of the policy. Your claim is denied in its entirety." Beth was furious. She was convinced Tony was incapable of suicide. And her company could not afford the $2 million loss. She decided to consult her lawyer, Chris Pruitt.

Three Fundamental Areas of Law

This case is a fictionalized version of several real cases based on double indemnity insurance policies. In this chapter, we follow Beth's dispute with Coastal from initial interview through appeal, using it to examine three fundamental areas of law: the structure of our court systems, civil lawsuits, and alternative dispute resolution.

When Beth Smiles meets with her lawyer, Chris Pruitt brings a second attorney from his firm, Janet Booker, who is an experienced **litigator**, that is, a lawyer who handles court cases. If they file a lawsuit, Janet will be in charge, so Chris wants her there for the first meeting. Janet probes about Tony's home life, the status of the business, his personal finances, everything. Beth becomes upset that Janet doesn't seem sympathetic, but Chris explains that Janet is doing her job: she needs all the information, good and bad.

Litigation versus Alternative Dispute Resolution

Janet starts thinking about the two methods of dispute resolution: litigation and alternative dispute resolution. **Litigation** refers to lawsuits, the process of filing claims in court, and ultimately going to trial. **Alternative dispute resolution** is any other formal or informal process used to settle disputes without resorting to a trial. It is increasingly popular with corporations and individuals alike because it is generally cheaper and faster than litigation, and we will focus on this topic in the last part of this chapter.

Litigation
The process of filing claims in court and ultimately going to trial.

Alternative dispute resolution
Any other formal or informal process used to settle disputes without resorting to a trial.

Court Systems

The United States has over 50 *systems* of courts. One nationwide system of *federal* courts serves the entire country. In addition, each individual *state*—such as Texas, California, and Florida—has its court system. The state and federal courts are in different buildings, have different judges, and hear different kinds of cases. Each has special powers and certain limitations.

State Courts

The typical state court system forms a pyramid, as Exhibit 3.1 shows. Some states have minor variations on the exhibit. For example, Texas has two top courts: A Supreme Court for civil cases and a Court of Criminal Appeals for criminal cases.

Trial Courts

Almost all cases start in trial courts, which are endlessly portrayed on television and in film. There is one judge, and there will often (but not always) be a jury. This is the only court to hear testimony from witnesses and receive evidence. **Trial courts** determine the facts of a particular dispute and apply to those facts the law given by earlier appellate court decisions.

Trial courts
Determine the facts of a particular dispute and apply to those facts the law given by earlier appellate court decisions.

In the Enviro-Vision dispute, the trial court will decide all important facts that are in dispute. Did Tony Caruso die? Did he drown? Assuming he drowned, was his death accidental or suicide? Once the jury has decided the facts, it will apply the law to those facts. If Tony Caruso died accidentally, contract law provides that Beth Smiles is entitled to double indemnity benefits. If the jury decides he killed himself, Beth gets nothing.

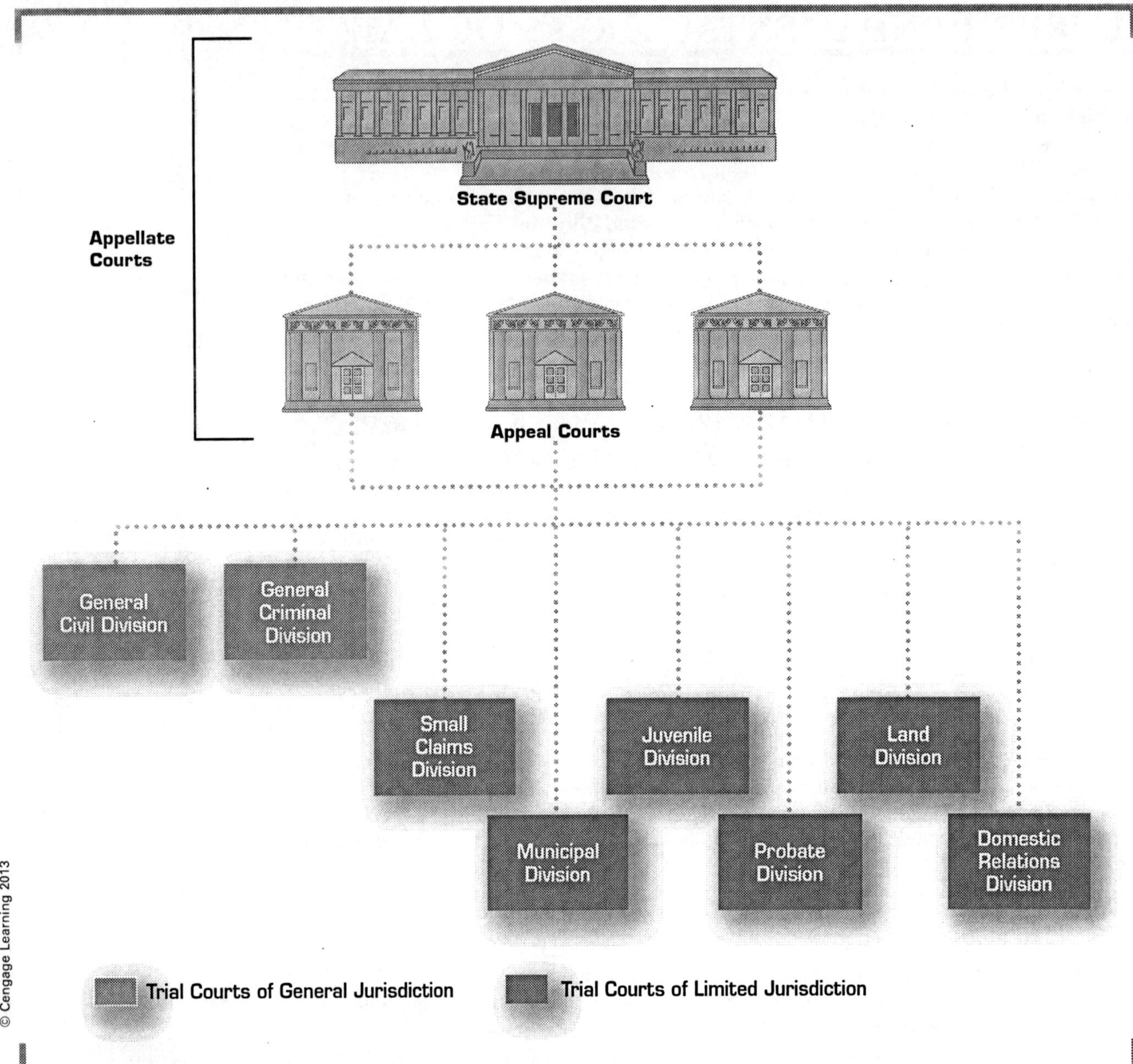

EXHIBIT 3.1 A trial court determines facts, while an appellate court ensures that the lower court correctly applied the law to those facts.

Facts are critical. That may sound obvious, but in a course devoted to legal principles, it is easy to lose track of the key role that factual determinations play in the resolution of any dispute. In the Enviro-Vision case, we will see that one bit of factual evidence goes undetected, with costly consequences.

Jurisdiction
A court's power to hear a case.

Jurisdiction refers to a court's power to hear a case. In state or federal court, a plaintiff may start a lawsuit only in a court that has jurisdiction over that kind of case. Some courts have very limited jurisdiction, while others have the power to hear almost any case.

Subject Matter Jurisdiction

Subject matter jurisdiction means that a court has the authority to hear a particular type of case.

Trial Courts of Limited Jurisdiction. These courts may hear only certain types of cases. Small claims court has jurisdiction only over civil lawsuits involving a maximum of, say, $5,000 (the amount varies from state to state). A juvenile court hears only cases involving minors. Probate court is devoted to settling the estates of deceased persons, though in some states it will hear certain other cases as well.

Trial Courts of General Jurisdiction. Trial courts of general jurisdiction, however, can hear a very broad range of cases. The most important court, for our purposes, is the general civil division. This court may hear virtually any civil lawsuit. In one day it might hear a $450 million shareholders' derivative lawsuit, an employment issue involving freedom of religion, and a foreclosure on a mortgage. Most of the cases we study start in this court.[1] If Enviro-Vision's case against Coastal goes to trial in a state court, it will begin in the trial court of general jurisdiction.

Personal Jurisdiction

In addition to subject matter jurisdiction, courts must also have **personal jurisdiction** over the defendant. Personal jurisdiction is the legal authority to require the defendant to stand trial, pay judgments, and the like. When plaintiffs file lawsuits, defendants sometimes make a *special appearance* to challenge a court's personal jurisdiction. If the court agrees with the defendant's argument, the lawsuit will be dismissed.

Personal jurisdiction generally exists, if:

1. For individuals, the defendant is a resident of the state in which a lawsuit is filed. For companies, the defendant is doing business in that state.
2. The defendant takes a formal step to defend a lawsuit. Most papers filed with a court count as formal steps, but special appearances do not.
3. A **summons** is *served* on a defendant. A summons is the court's written notice that a lawsuit has been filed against the defendant, The summons must be delivered to the defendant when she is physically within the state in which the lawsuit is filed.

For example, Texarkana straddles the Texas/Arkansas border. If a lawsuit is filed in a Texas court, a defendant who lives in Arkansas can be served if, when walking down the street in Texarkana, she steps across the state line into Texas. Corporations are required to hire a registered agent in any state in which they do business. If a registered agent receives a summons, then the corporation is served.

[1]Note that the actual name of the court will vary from state to state. In many states it is called *superior court* because it has power superior to the courts of limited jurisdiction. In New York it is called *supreme court* (anything to confuse the layperson); in some states it is called *court of common pleas;* in Oregon and other states it is a *circuit court.* They are all civil trial courts of general jurisdiction. Within this branch, some states are beginning to establish specialized business courts to hear complex commercial disputes. At least one state has created a cybercourt for high-tech cases. Lawyers will argue their cases by teleconference and present evidence via streaming video.

4. A **long-arm statute** applies. If all else fails—the defendant does not reside in the state, does not defend the lawsuit, and has not been served with a summons while in the state—a court still can obtain jurisdiction under long-arm statutes. These statutes typically claim jurisdiction over someone who commits a tort, signs a contract, or conducts "regular business activities" in the state.

As a general rule, courts tend to apply long-arm statutes aggressively, hauling defendants into their courtrooms. However, the due process guarantees in the United States Constitution require fundamental fairness in the application of long-arm statutes. Therefore, courts can claim personal jurisdiction only if a defendant has had *minimum contacts* with a state. In other words, it is unfair to require a defendant to stand trial in another state if he has had no meaningful interaction with that state.

In the following Landmark Case, the Supreme Court explains its views on this important constitutional issue.

Landmark Case

International Shoe Co. v. State of Washington

326 U.S. 310
Supreme Court of the United States, 1945

Facts: Although International Shoe manufactured footwear only in St. Louis, Missouri, it sold its products nationwide. It did not have offices or warehouses in Washington State, but it did send about a dozen salespeople there. The salespeople rented space in hotels and businesses, displayed sample products, and took orders. They were not authorized to collect payments from customers.

When Washington State sought contributions to the state's unemployment fund, International Shoe refused to pay. Washington sued. The company argued that it was not engaged in business in the state, and, therefore, that Washington courts had no jurisdiction over it.

The Supreme Court of Washington ruled that International Shoe did have sufficient contacts with the state to justify a lawsuit there. International Shoe appealed to the United States Supreme Court.

Issue: ***Did International Shoe have sufficient minimum contacts in Washington State to permit jurisdiction there?***

Excerpts from Chief Justice Stone's Decision: Appellant insists that its activities within the state were not sufficient to manifest its "presence" there and that in its absence, the state courts were without jurisdiction, that consequently, it was a denial of due process for the state to subject appellant to suit. Appellant [International Shoe] refers to those cases in which it was said that the mere solicitation of orders for the purchase of goods within a state, to be accepted without the state and filled by shipment of the purchased goods interstate, does not render the corporation seller amenable to suit within the state.

Historically the jurisdiction of courts to render judgment is grounded on their power over the defendant's person. Hence his presence within the territorial jurisdiction of a court was prerequisite to a judgment personally binding him. But now due process requires that [a defendant] have certain minimum contacts with it such that the maintenance of the suit does not offend "traditional notions of fair play and substantial justice."

Since the corporate personality is a fiction, its "presence" without can be manifested only by those activities of the corporation's agent within the state which courts will deem to be sufficient to satisfy the demands of due process.

"Presence" in the state in this sense has never been doubted when the activities of the corporation there have not only been continuous and systematic, but also give rise to the liabilities sued on, even though no consent to be sued or authorization to an agent to accept service of process has been given. Conversely, it has been generally recognized that the casual presence of the corporate agent or even his conduct of single or isolated items of activities in a state in the corporation's behalf are not enough to subject it to suit on causes of action unconnected with the activities there. To require the corporation in such circumstances to defend the suit away from its home or other jurisdiction where it carries on more substantial activities has been thought to lay too great and unreasonable a burden on the corporation to comport with due process.

But to the extent that a corporation exercises the privilege of conducting activities within a state, it enjoys the benefits and protection of the laws of that state. The exercise of that privilege may give rise to obligations.

Applying these standards, the activities carried on in behalf of appellant in the State of Washington were neither irregular nor casual. They were systematic and continuous throughout the years in question. They resulted in a large volume of interstate business, in the course of which appellant received the benefits and protection of the laws of the state, including the right to resort to the courts for the enforcement of its rights. The obligation which is here sued upon arose out of those very activities. It is evident that these operations establish sufficient contacts or ties with the state of the forum to make it reasonable and just, according to our traditional conception of fair play and substantial justice, to permit the state to enforce the obligations which appellant has incurred there.

The state may maintain the present suit to collect the tax.

Affirmed.

Appellate Courts

Appellate courts are entirely different from trial courts. Three or more judges hear the case. There are no juries, ever. These courts do not hear witnesses or take new evidence. They hear appeals of cases already tried below. **Appeals courts** generally accept the facts given to them by trial courts and review the trial record to see if the court made errors of law.

Appeals courts
Have the right to review decisions of trial courts.

Higher courts generally defer to lower courts on factual findings. Juries and trial court judges see all evidence as it is presented, and they are in the best position to evaluate it. An appeals court will accept a factual finding unless there was *no evidence at all* to support it. If the jury decides that Tony Caruso committed suicide, the appeals court will normally accept that fact, even if the appeals judges consider the jury's conclusion dubious. On the other hand, if a jury concluded that Tony had been murdered, an appeals court would overturn that finding if neither side had introduced any evidence of murder during the trial.

An appeals court reviews the trial record to make sure that the lower court correctly applied the law to the facts. If the trial court made an **error of law**, the appeals court may require a new trial. Suppose the jury concludes that Tony Caruso committed suicide but votes to award Enviro-Vision $1 million because it feels sorry for Beth Smiles. That is an error of law: if Tony committed suicide, Beth is entitled to nothing. An appellate court will reverse the decision. Or suppose that the trial judge permitted a friend of Tony's to state that he was certain Tony would never commit suicide. Normally, such opinions are not permissible in trial, and it was a legal error for the judge to allow the jury to hear it.

Court of Appeals. The party that loses at the trial court may appeal to the intermediate court of appeals. The party filing the appeal is the **appellant**. The party opposing the appeal (because it won at trial) is the **appellee**.

Appellant
The party filing the appeal.

Appellee
The party opposing the appeal.

This court allows both sides to submit written arguments on the case, called **briefs**. Each side then appears for oral argument, usually before a panel of three judges. The appellant's lawyer has about 15 minutes to convince the judges that the trial court made serious errors of law, and that the decision should be **reversed**, that is, nullified. The appellee's lawyer has the same time to persuade the court that the trial court acted correctly, and that the result should be **affirmed**, that is, permitted to stand.

Briefs
Written arguments on the case.

Reversed
Nullified.

Affirmed
Permitted to stand.

State Supreme Court. This is the highest court in the state, and it accepts some appeals from the court of appeals. In most states, there is no absolute right to appeal to the Supreme Court. If the high court regards a legal issue as important, it accepts the case. It then takes briefs and hears oral argument just as the appeals court did. If it considers the matter unimportant, it refuses to hear the case, meaning that the court of appeals' ruling is the final word on the case.[2]

In most states, seven judges, often called *justices*, sit on the Supreme Court. They have the final word on state law.

Federal Courts

As discussed in Chapter 1, federal courts are established by the United States Constitution, which limits what kinds of cases can be brought in any federal court. See Exhibit 3.2. For our purposes, two kinds of civil lawsuits are permitted in federal court: federal question cases and diversity cases.

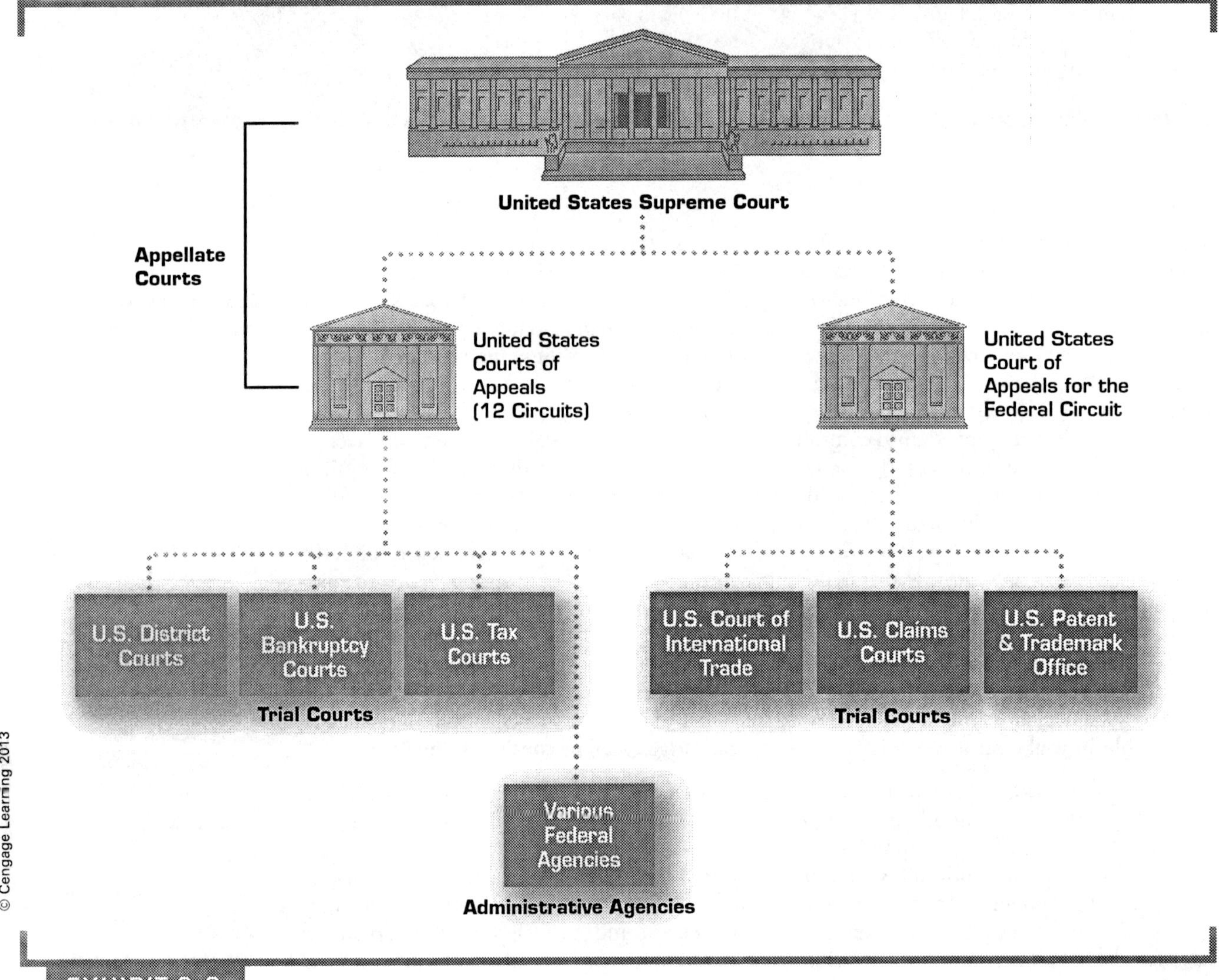

EXHIBIT 3.2

[2]In some states with smaller populations, there is no intermediate appeals court. All appeals from trial courts go directly to the state supreme court.

Federal Question Cases

A claim based on the United States Constitution, a federal statute, or a federal treaty is called a **federal question** case.[3] Federal courts have jurisdiction over these cases. If the Environmental Protection Agency (a part of the federal government) orders Logging Company not to cut in a particular forest, and Logging Company claims that the agency has wrongly deprived it of its property, that suit is based on a federal statute and is thus a federal question. If Little Retailer sues Mega Retailer, claiming that Mega has established a monopoly, that claim is also based on a statute—the Sherman Antitrust Act—and creates federal question jurisdiction. Enviro-Vision's potential suit merely concerns an insurance contract. The federal district court has no federal question jurisdiction over the case.

Federal question
A case in which the claim is based on the United States Constitution, a federal statute, or a federal treaty.

Diversity Cases

Even if no federal law is at issue, federal courts have **diversity jurisdiction** when (1) the plaintiff and defendant are citizens of different states *and* (2) the amount in dispute exceeds $75,000. The theory behind diversity jurisdiction is that courts of one state might be biased against citizens of another state. To ensure fairness, the parties have the option to use a federal court as a neutral playing field.

Diversity jurisdiction
(1) The plaintiff and defendant are citizens of different states *and* (2) the amount in dispute exceeds $75,000.

Enviro-Vision is located in Oregon and Coastal Insurance is incorporated in Georgia.[4] They are citizens of different states and the amount in dispute far exceeds $75,000. Janet could file this case in United States District Court based on diversity jurisdiction.

Trial Courts

United States District Court. This is the primary trial court in the federal system. The nation is divided into about 94 districts, and each has a district court. States with smaller populations have one district. States with larger populations have several; Texas is divided geographically into four districts.

Other Trial Courts. There are other, specialized trial courts in the federal system. Bankruptcy Court, Tax Court, and the United States Court of International Trade all handle name-appropriate cases. The United States Claims Court hears cases brought against the United States, typically on contract disputes. The Foreign Intelligence Surveillance Court is a very specialized, secret court, which oversees requests for surveillance warrants against suspected foreign agents.

Judges. The president of the United States nominates all federal court judges, from district court to Supreme Court. The nominees must be confirmed by the Senate. Once confirmed, federal judges serve for "life in good behavior." Many federal judges literally stay on the job for life. Recently, still-active Judge Wesley Brown of Kansas tied a record as the oldest federal judge in history when he turned 103.

Appellate Courts

United States Courts of Appeals. These are the intermediate courts of appeals. As the map below shows, they are divided into "circuits," which are geographical areas. There are 11 numbered circuits, hearing appeals from district courts. For example, an appeal from the Northern District of Illinois would go to the Court of Appeals for the Seventh Circuit.

A 12th court, the Court of Appeals for the District of Columbia, hears appeals only from the district court of Washington, D.C. This is a particularly powerful court because so many

[3] 28 U.S.C. §1331 governs federal question jurisdiction and 28 U.S.C. §1332 covers diversity jurisdiction.

[4] For diversity purposes, a corporation is a citizen of the state in which it is incorporated and the state in which it has its principal place of business.

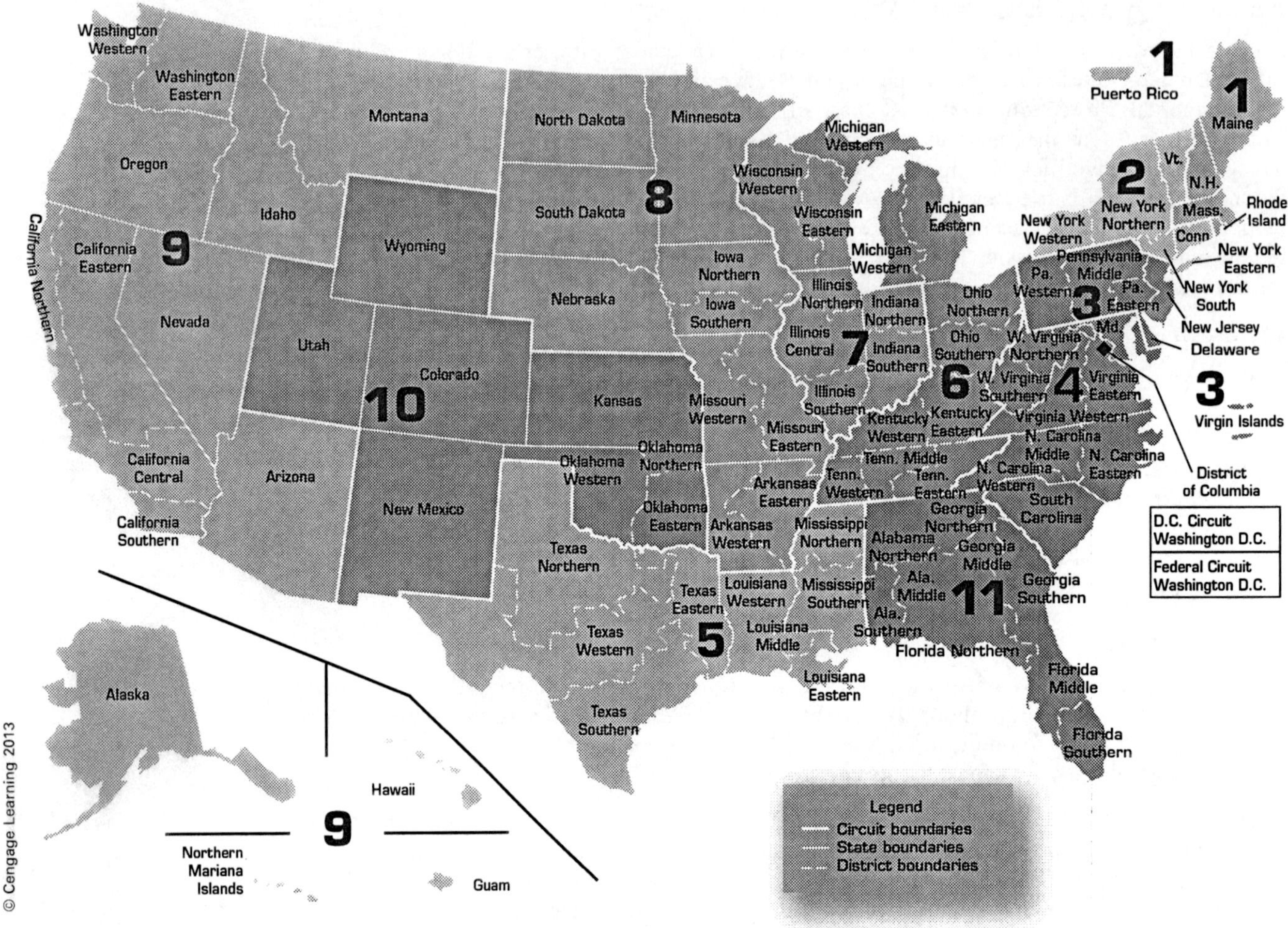

suits about federal statutes begin in the district court for the District of Columbia. Also in Washington is the 13th Court of Appeals, known as the Federal Circuit. It hears appeals from specialized trial courts, as shown in Exhibit 3.2.

Within one circuit there are many circuit judges, up to about 50 judges in the largest circuit, the Ninth. When a case is appealed, three judges hear the appeal, taking briefs and hearing oral arguments.

United States Supreme Court. This is the highest court in the country. There are nine justices on the Court. One justice is the chief justice and the other eight are associate justices. When they decide a case, each justice casts an equal vote. The chief justice's special power comes from his authority to assign opinions to a given justice. The justice assigned to write an opinion has an opportunity to control the precise language and thus to influence the voting by other justices.

The Supreme Court has the power to hear appeals in any federal case and in certain cases that began in state courts. Generally, it is up to the Court whether or not it will accept a case. A party that wants the Supreme Court to review a lower court ruling must file a petition for a **writ of *certiorari***, asking the Court to hear the case. Four of the nine justices must vote in favor of hearing a case before a writ will be granted. The Court receives several thousand requests every year but usually accepts fewer than 100. Most

Writ of certiorari
A petition asking the Supreme Court to hear a case.

cases accepted involve either an important issue of constitutional law or an interpretation of a major federal statute.

EXAM Strategy

Question: Mark has sued Janelle, based on the state common law of negligence. He is testifying in court, explaining how Janelle backed a rented truck out of her driveway and slammed into his Lamborghini, causing $82,000 in damages. Where would this take place?

(a) State appeals court

(b) United States Court of Appeals

(c) State trial court

(d) Federal District Court

(e) Either state trial court or Federal District Court

Strategy: The question asks about trial and appellate courts, and also about state versus federal courts. One issue at a time, please. What are the different functions of trial and appellate courts? *Trial* courts use witnesses, and often juries, to resolve factual disputes. *Appellate* courts never hear witnesses and never have juries. Applying that distinction to these facts tells us whether we are in a trial or appeals court.

Next Issue: *State* trial courts may hear lawsuits on virtually any issue. *Federal District Courts* may only hear two kinds of cases: Federal question (those involving a statute or constitutional provision); or diversity (where the parties are from different states *and* the amount at issue is $75,000 or higher). Apply what we know to the facts here.

Result: We are in a trial court because Mark is testifying. Could we be in Federal District Court? No. The suit is based on state common law. This is not a diversity case because the parties live in the same state. We are in a state trial court.

LITIGATION

Janet Booker decides to file the Enviro-Vision suit in the Oregon trial court. She thinks that a state court judge may take the issue more seriously than a federal district court judge.

Pleadings

The documents that begin a lawsuit are called the **pleadings.**These consist of the complaint, the answer, and sometimes a reply.

Pleadings
The documents that begin a lawsuit, consisting of the complaint, the answer, and sometimes a reply.

Complaint

The plaintiff files in court a **complaint**, which is a short, plain statement of the facts she is alleging and the legal claims she is making. The purpose of the complaint is to inform the defendant of the general nature of the claims and the need to come into court and protect his interests.

Complaint
A short, plain statement of the facts alleged and the legal claims made.

Janet Booker files the complaint, as shown below. Since Enviro-Vision is a partnership, she files the suit on behalf of Beth personally.

STATE OF OREGON
CIRCUIT COURT

Multnomah County — Civil Action No. ________

Elizabeth Smiles,
Plaintiff

JURY TRIAL DEMANDED

v.
Coastal Insurance Company, Inc.,
Defendant

COMPLAINT

Plaintiff Elizabeth Smiles states that:

1. She is a citizen of Multnomah County, Oregon.
2. Defendant Coastal Insurance Company, Inc., is incorporated under the laws of Georgia and has as its usual place of business 148 Thrift Street, Savannah, Georgia.
3. On or about July 5, 2012, plaintiff Smiles ("Smiles"), Defendant Coastal Insurance Co, Inc. ("Coastal") and Anthony Caruso entered into an insurance contract ("the contract"), a copy of which is annexed hereto as Exhibit "A." This contract was signed by all parties or their authorized agents, in Multnomah County, Oregon.
4. The contract obligates Coastal to pay to Smiles the sum of two million dollars ($2 million) if Anthony Caruso should die accidentally.
5. On or about September 20, 2012, Anthony Caruso accidentally drowned and died while swimming.
6. Coastal has refused to pay any sum pursuant to the contract.
7. Coastal has knowingly, willingly and unreasonably refused to honor its obligations under the contract.

WHEREFORE, plaintiff Elizabeth Smiles demands judgment against defendant Coastal for all monies due under the contract; demands triple damages for Coastal's knowing, willing, and unreasonable refusal to honor its obligations; and demands all costs and attorney's fees, with interest.
ELIZABETH SMILES,
By her attorney,
[Signed]
Janet Booker
Pruitt, Booker & Bother
983 Joy Avenue
Portland, OR
October 18, 2012

Service

When she files the complaint in court, Janet gets a summons, which is a paper ordering the defendant to answer the complaint within 20 days. A sheriff or constable then *serves* the two papers by delivering them to the defendant. Coastal's headquarters are in Georgia, so the state of Oregon has required Coastal to specify someone as its agent for receipt of service in Oregon.

Answer

Once the complaint and summons are served, Coastal has 20 days in which to file an answer. Coastal's answer, shown below, is a brief reply to each of the allegations in the complaint. The answer tells the court and the plaintiff exactly what issues are in dispute. Since Coastal admits that the parties entered into the contract that Beth claims they did, there is no need for her to prove that in court. The court can focus its attention on the disputed issue: whether Tony Caruso died accidentally.

STATE OF OREGON
CIRCUIT COURT

Multnomah County

Civil Action No. 09-5626

Elizabeth Smiles,
Plaintiff
v.
Coastal Insurance Company, Inc.,
Defendant

ANSWER

Defendant Coastal Insurance Company, Inc., answers the complaint as follows:

1. Admit.
2. Admit.
3. Admit.
4. Admit.
5. Deny.
6. Admit.
7. Deny.

COASTAL INSURANCE COMPANY, INC.,
By its attorney,
[Signed]
Richard B. Stewart
Kiley, Robbins, Stewart & Glote
333 Victory Boulevard
Portland, OR
October 30, 2012

If the defendant fails to answer in time, the plaintiff will ask for a **default judgment**. In granting a default judgment, the judge accepts every allegation in the complaint as true and renders a decision that the plaintiff wins without a trial.

Default judgment
A decision that the plaintiff wins without a trial because the defendant failed to answer in time.

Recently, two men sued PepsiCo, claiming that the company stole the idea for Aquafina water from them. They argued that they should receive a portion of the profits for every bottle of Aquafina ever sold.

PepsiCo failed to file a timely answer, and the judge entered a default judgment in the amount of $1.26 billion. On appeal, the default judgment was overturned and PepsiCo was able to escape paying the massive sum, but other defendants are sometimes not so lucky.

It is important to respond to courts on time.

Counter-Claim

Sometimes a defendant does more than merely answer a complaint and files a **counter-claim**, meaning a second lawsuit by the defendant against the plaintiff. Suppose that after her complaint was filed in court, Beth had written a letter to the newspaper, calling Coastal a bunch of "thieves and scoundrels who spend their days mired in fraud and larceny." Coastal would not have found that amusing. The company's answer would have included a counter-claim against Beth for libel, claiming that she falsely accused the insurer of serious criminal acts. Coastal would have demanded money damages.

Counter-claim
A second lawsuit by the defendant against the plaintiff.

If Coastal counter-claimed, Beth would have to file a **reply**, which is simply an answer to a counter-claim. Beth's reply would be similar to Coastal's answer, admitting or denying the various allegations.

Reply
An answer to a counter-claim.

Class Actions

Suppose Janet uncovers evidence that Coastal denies 80 percent of all life insurance claims, calling them suicide. She could ask the court to permit a **class action**. If the court granted her request, she would represent the entire group of plaintiffs, including those

Class action
One plaintiff represents the entire group of plaintiffs, including those who are unaware of the lawsuit or even unaware they were harmed.

who are unaware of the lawsuit or even unaware they were harmed. Class actions can give the plaintiffs much greater leverage, since the defendant's potential liability is vastly increased. In the back of her mind, Janet has thoughts of a class action, *if* she can uncover evidence that Coastal has used a claim of suicide to deny coverage to a large number of claimants.

Notice how potent a class action can be. From his small town in Maine, Ernie decides to get rich quickly. On the Internet, he advertises "Energy Breakthrough! Cut your heating costs 15 percent for only $25." In response, 100,000 people send him their money, and they receive a photocopied graph, illustrating that if you wear two sweaters instead of one, you will feel 15 percent warmer. Ernie has deceitfully earned $2,500,000 in pure profit. What can the angry homeowners do? Under the laws of fraud and consumer protection, they have a legitimate claim to their $25, and perhaps even to treble damages ($75). But few will sue, because the time and effort required would be greater than the money recovered.

Economists analyze such legal issues in terms of *efficiency*. The laws against Ernie's fraud are clear and well intended, but they will not help in this case because it is too expensive for 100,000 people to litigate such a small claim. The effort would be hugely *inefficient,* both for the homeowners and for society generally. The economic reality may permit Ernie to evade the law's grasp.

That is one reason we have class actions. A dozen or so "heating plan" buyers can all hire the same lawyer. This attorney will file court papers in Maine on behalf of *everyone,* nationwide, who has been swindled by Ernie—including the 99,988 people who have yet to be notified that they are part of the case. Now the con artist, instead of facing a few harmless suits for $25, must respond to a multimillion-dollar claim being handled by an experienced lawyer. Treble damages become menacing: three times $25 times 100,000 is no joke, even to a cynic like Ernie. He may also be forced to pay for the plaintiffs' attorney, as well as all costs of notifying class members and disbursing money to them. With one lawyer representing an entire class, the legal system has become fiercely efficient.

Congress recently passed a statute designed to force large, multi-state class actions out of state courts, into federal. Proponents of the new law complained that state courts often gave excessive verdicts, even for frivolous lawsuits. They said the cases hurt businesses while enriching lawyers. Opponents argued that the new law was designed to shield large corporations from paying for the harm they caused by sending the cases into a federal system that is often hostile to such suits.

Judgment on the Pleadings

Motion
A formal request to the court to take some step or issue an order.

A party can ask the court for a judgment based simply on the pleadings themselves, by filing a motion to dismiss. A **motion** is a formal request to the court that the court take some step or issue some order. During a lawsuit, the parties file many motions. A **motion to dismiss** is a request that the court terminate a case without permitting it to go further. Suppose that a state law requires claims on life insurance contracts to be filed within three years, and Beth files her claim four years after Tony's death. Coastal would move to dismiss based on this late filing. The court might well agree, and Beth would never get into court.

Discovery

Discovery
The pre-trial opportunity for both parties to learn the strengths and weaknesses of the opponent's case.

Few cases are dismissed on the pleadings. Most proceed quickly to the next step. **Discovery** is the critical, pre-trial opportunity for both parties to learn the strengths and weaknesses of the opponent's case.

The theory behind civil litigation is that the best outcome is a negotiated settlement and that parties will move toward agreement if they understand the opponent's case. That is likeliest to occur if both sides have an opportunity to examine most of the evidence the other side will bring to trial. Further, if a case does go all the way to trial, efficient and fair litigation cannot take place in a courtroom filled with surprises. On television dramas, witnesses say astonishing things that amaze the courtroom (and keep viewers hooked through the next commercial). In real trials, the lawyers know in advance the answers to practically all questions asked because discovery has allowed them to see the opponent's documents and question its witnesses. The following are the most important forms of discovery.

© Digital Vision/Getty Images

Depositions provide a chance for one party's lawyer to question the other party, or a potential witness, under oath.

Interrogatories. These are written questions that the opposing party must answer, in writing, under oath.

Depositions. These provide a chance for one party's lawyer to question the other party, or a potential witness, under oath. The person being questioned is the **deponent**. Lawyers for both parties are present. During depositions, and in trial, good lawyers choose words carefully and ask questions calculated to advance their cause. A fine line separates ethical, probing questions from those that are tricky, and a similar line divides answers that are merely unhelpful from perjury.

Deponent
The person being questioned.

Production of Documents and Things. Each side may ask the other side to produce relevant documents for inspection and copying; to produce physical objects, such as part of a car alleged to be defective; and for permission to enter on land to make an inspection, for example, at the scene of an accident.

Physical and Mental Examination. A party may ask the court to order an examination of the other party, if his physical or mental condition is relevant, for example, in a case of medical malpractice.

Janet Booker begins her discovery with interrogatories. Her goal is to learn Coastal's basic position and factual evidence and then follow up with more detailed questioning during depositions. Her interrogatories ask for every fact Coastal relied on in denying the claim. She asks for the names of all witnesses, the identity of all documents, including electronic records, the description of all things or objects that they considered. She requests the names of all corporate officers who played any role in the decision and of any expert witnesses Coastal plans to call. Interrogatory No. 18 demands extensive information on all *other* claims in the past three years that Coastal has denied based on alleged suicide. Janet is looking for evidence that would support a class action.

Beth remarks on how thorough the interrogatories are. "This will tell us what their case is." Janet frowns and looks less optimistic: she's done this before.

Coastal has 30 days to answer Janet's interrogatories. Before it responds, Coastal mails to Janet a notice of deposition, stating its intention to depose Beth Smiles. Beth and Janet will go to the office of Coastal's lawyer, and Beth will answer questions under oath. But at the same time Coastal sends this notice, it sends *25 other notices of deposition.* The company will depose Karen Caruso as soon as Beth's deposition is over. Coastal also plans to depose all seven employees of Enviro-Vision; three neighbors who lived near Tony and Karen's beach house; two policemen who participated in the search; the doctor and two nurses involved in the case; Tony's physician; Jerry Johnson, Tony's tennis partner; Craig Bergson, a college roommate; a couple who had dinner with Tony and Karen a week before his death; and several other people.

Beth is appalled. Janet explains that some of these people might have relevant information. But there may be another reason that Coastal is doing this: the company wants to make this litigation hurt. Janet will have to attend every one of these depositions. Costs will skyrocket.

Motion for a protective order
A request that the court limit discovery.

Janet files a **motion for a protective order.** This is a request that the court limit Coastal's discovery by decreasing the number of depositions. Janet also calls Rich Stewart and suggests that they discuss what depositions are really necessary. Rich insists that all of the depositions are important. This is a $2 million case and Coastal is entitled to protect itself. As both lawyers know, **the parties are entitled to discover anything that could reasonably lead to valid evidence**.

But there may be another reason that Coastal is doing this: the company wants to make this litigation hurt.

Before Beth's deposition date arrives, Rich sends Coastal's answers to Enviro-Vision's interrogatories. The answers contain no useful information whatsoever. For example, Interrogatory No. 10 asked, "If you claim that Anthony Caruso committed suicide, describe every fact upon which you rely in reaching that conclusion." Coastal's answer simply says, "His state of mind, his poor business affairs, and the circumstances of his death all indicate suicide."

Janet calls Rich and complains that the interrogatory answers are a bad joke. Rich disagrees, saying that it is the best information they have so early in the case. After they debate it for 20 minutes, Rich offers to settle the case for $100,000. Janet refuses and makes no counteroffer.

Janet files a **motion to compel answers to interrogatories**, in other words, a formal request that the court order Coastal to supply more complete answers. Janet submits a **memorandum** with the motion, which is a supporting argument. Although it is only a few pages long, the memorandum takes several hours of online research and writing to prepare—more costs. Janet also informs Rich Stewart that Beth will not appear for the deposition, since Coastal's interrogatory answers are inadequate.

Rich now files *his* motion to compel, asking the court to order Beth Smiles to appear for her deposition. The court hears all of the motions together. Janet argues that Coastal's interrogatory answers are hopelessly uninformative and defeat the whole purpose of discovery. She claims that Coastal's large number of depositions creates a huge and unfair expense for a small firm.

Rich claims that the interrogatory answers are the best that Coastal can do thus far and that Coastal will supplement the answers when more information becomes available. He argues against Interrogatory No. 18, the one in which Janet asked for the names of other policyholders whom Coastal considered suicides. He claims that Janet is engaging in a fishing expedition that would violate the privacy of Coastal's insurance customers and provide no information relevant to this case. He demands that Janet make Beth available for a deposition.

These discovery rulings are critical because they will color the entire lawsuit. A trial judge has to make many discovery decisions before a case reaches trial. At times, the judge must weigh the need of one party to see documents against the other side's need for privacy. One device a judge can use in reaching a discovery ruling is an **in camera inspection**, meaning that the judge views the requested documents alone, with no lawyers present, and decides whether the other side is entitled to view them.

E-Discovery. The biggest change in litigation in the last decade is the explosive rise of electronic discovery. Companies send hundreds, or thousands, or millions of e-mails—every day. Many have attachments, sometimes hundreds of pages long. In addition, businesses large and small have vast amounts of data stored electronically. All of this information is potentially subject to discovery.

It is enormously time-consuming and expensive for companies to locate all of the relevant material, separate it from irrelevant or confidential matter, and furnish it. A firm may be obligated to furnish *millions* of e-mails to the opposing party. In one recent case, a defendant had to pay 31 lawyers full time, for six months, just to wade through the e-ocean of documents and figure out which had to be supplied and how to produce it. Not surprisingly, this data eruption has created a new industry: high-tech companies that assist law firms in finding, sorting, and delivering electronic data.

Who is to say what must be supplied? What if an e-mail string contains individual e-mails that are clearly privileged (meaning a party need not divulge them), but others that are not privileged? May a company refuse to furnish the entire string? Many will try. However, some courts have ruled that companies seeking to protect e-mail strings must create a log describing every individual e-mail and allow the court to determine which are privileged.[5]

When the cost of furnishing the data becomes burdensome, who should pay, the party seeking the information or the one supplying it? In a recent $4 million corporate lawsuit, the defendant turned over 3,000 e-mails and 211,000 other documents. But the trial judge noted that many of the e-mail attachments—sometimes 12 to an e-mail—had gone missing, and required the company to produce them. The defendant protested that finding the attachments would cost an additional $206,000. The judge ordered the company to do it, and bear the full cost.

Both sides in litigation sometimes use gamesmanship during discovery. Thus, if an individual sues a large corporation, for example, the company may deliberately make discovery so expensive that the plaintiff cannot afford the legal fees. And if a plaintiff has a poor case, he might intentionally try to make the discovery process more expensive for the defendant than his settlement offer. Even if a defendant expects to win at trial, an offer to settle a case for $50,000 can look like a bargain if discovery alone will cost $100,000. Some defendants refuse, but others are more pragmatic.

The following case illustrates another common discovery problem: refusal by one side to appear for deposition. Did the defendant cynically believe that long delay would win the day, given that the plaintiff was 78 years old? What can a court do in such a case?

Stinton v. Robin's Wood, Inc.

45 A.D. 3d 203, 842 NYS2d 477
New York App. Div., 2007

Facts: Ethel Flanzraich, 78 years old, slipped and fell on the steps of property owned by Robin's Wood. She broke her left leg and left arm. Flanzraich sued, claiming that Robin's Wood caused her fall because its employee, Anthony Monforte, had negligently painted the stairs. In its answer to the complaint, Robin's Wood denied all of the significant allegations.

During a preliminary conference with the trial judge, the parties agreed to hold depositions of both parties on August 4. Flanzraich appeared for deposition but Robin's Wood did not furnish its employee, Monforte, nor did it offer any other company representative. The court then ordered the deposition of the defendant to take place the following April 2. Again, Robin's Wood produced neither Monforte nor anyone else. On July 16, the court ordered the defendant to produce its representative within 30 days. Once more, no one showed up for deposition.

[5] *Universal Service Fund Telephone Billing Practices Litigation*, 232 F.R.D. 669 (D. Kan. 2005).

On August 18—over *one year* after the original deposition date—Flanzraich moved to strike the defendant's answer, meaning that the plaintiff would win by default. The company argued that it had made diligent efforts to locate Monforte and force him to appear. However, all of the letters sent to Monforte were addressed care of Robin's Wood. Finally, the company stated that it no longer employed Monforte.

The trial judge granted the motion to strike the answer. That meant that Robin's Wood was liable for Flanraich's fall. The only remaining issue was damages. The court determined that Robin's Wood owed $22,631 for medical expenses, $150,000 for past pain and suffering, and $300,000 for future pain and suffering. One day later, Flanraich died, of other causes. Robin's Wood appealed.

Issue: ***Did the trial court abuse its discretion by striking the defendant's answer?***

Excerpts from Judge McCarthy's Decision: We find no merit to the defendant's claim that the [trial court] improvidently exercised its discretion in striking its answer. An action should be determined on the merits whenever possible. However, a court, in its discretion, may invoke the drastic remedy of striking an answer if it determines that the defendant's failure to comply with discovery demands is willful and contumacious.

The willful and contumacious character of [defendant's] conduct may be inferred from the defendant's noncompliance with [three] court orders directing such a deposition. Although the defendant may not have been able to produce Monforte after he left its employ, the defendant failed to explain why it produced neither another representative for the deposition nor timely disclosed to the decedent that it no longer employed Monforte. Either of these actions would have afforded the decedent the opportunity to subpoena Monforte for a nonparty deposition, had she so desired. For instance, by producing its representative for a deposition, the decedent would have had the ability to explore the whereabouts of Monforte and, in all likelihood, would have obtained information regarding how to contact him since the record indicates that the defendant had such information. This is especially important here where the decedent was elderly at the time of the accident and delays in discovery could only serve to prejudice her and unjustly benefit the defendant. Moreover, the defendant failed to explain why it did not produce Monforte for a deposition during the time he was under its employ.

Affirmed.

In the Enviro-Vision case, the judge rules that Coastal must furnish more complete answers to the interrogatories, especially as to why the company denied the claim. However, he rules against Interrogatory No. 18, the one concerning other claims Coastal has denied. This simple ruling kills Janet's hope of making a class action of the case. He orders Beth to appear for the deposition. As to future depositions, Coastal may take any 10 but then may take additional depositions only by demonstrating to the court that the deponents have useful information.

Rich proceeds to take Beth's deposition. It takes two full days. He asks about Enviro-Vision's past and present. He learns that Tony appeared to have won their biggest contract ever from Rapid City, Oregon, but that he then lost it when he had a fight with Rapid City's mayor. He inquires into Tony's mood, learns that he was depressed, and probes in every direction he can to find evidence of suicidal motivation. Janet and Rich argue frequently over questions and whether Beth should have to answer them. At times, Janet is persuaded and permits Beth to answer; other times, she instructs Beth not to answer. For example, toward the end of the second day, Rich asks Beth whether she and Tony had been sexually involved. Janet instructs Beth not to answer. This fight necessitates another trip into court to determine whether Beth must answer. The judge rules that Beth must discuss Tony's romantic life only if Coastal has some evidence that he was involved with someone outside his marriage. The company lacks any such evidence.

Now limited to 10 depositions, Rich selects his nine other deponents carefully. For example, he decides to depose only one of the two nurses; he chooses to question Jerry Johnson, the tennis partner, but not Craig Bergson, the former roommate; and so forth. When we look at the many legal issues this case raises, his choices seem minor. In fact, unbeknownst to Rich or anyone else, his choices may determine the outcome of the case.

As we will see later, Craig Bergson has evidence that is possibly crucial to the lawsuit. If Rich decides not to depose him, neither side will ever learn the evidence and the jury will never hear it. A jury can decide a case only based on the evidence presented to it. *Facts are elusive—and often controlling.*

In each deposition, Rich carefully probes with his questions, sometimes trying to learn what he actually does not know, sometimes trying to pin down the witness to a specific version of facts so that Rich knows how the witness will testify at trial. Neighbors at the beach testify that Tony seemed tense; one testifies about seeing Tony, unhappy, on the beach with his dog. Another testifies he had never before seen Blue tied up on the beach. Karen Caruso admits that Tony had been somewhat tense and unhappy the last couple of months. She reluctantly discusses their marriage, admitting there were problems.

Other Discovery. Rich sends Requests to Produce Documents, seeking medical records about Tony. Once again, the parties fight over which records are relevant, but Rich gets most of what he wants. Janet does less discovery than Rich because most of the witnesses she will call are friendly witnesses. She can interview them privately without giving any information to Coastal. With the help of Beth and Karen, Janet builds her case just as carefully as Rich, choosing the witnesses who will bolster the view that Tony was in good spirits and died accidentally.

She deposes all the officers of Coastal who participated in the decision to deny insurance coverage. She is particularly aggressive in pinning them down as to the limited information they had when they denied Beth's claim.

Summary Judgment

When discovery is completed, both sides may consider seeking summary judgment. **Summary judgment** is a ruling by the court that no trial is necessary because some essential facts are not in dispute. The purpose of a trial is to determine the facts of the case, that is, to decide who did what to whom, why, when, and with what consequences. If there are no relevant facts in dispute, then there is no need for a trial.

Summary judgment
A ruling by the court that no trial is necessary because some essential facts are not in dispute.

In the following case, the defendant won summary judgment, meaning that the case never went to trial. And yet, this was only the beginning of trouble for that defendant, Bill Clinton.

Jones v. Clinton

990 F. Supp. 657, 1998 U.S. Dist. LEXIS 3902
United States District Court for the Eastern District of Arkansas, 1998

Facts: In 1991, Bill Clinton was governor of Arkansas. Paula Jones worked for a state agency, the Arkansas Industrial Development Commission (AIDC). When Clinton became president, Jones sued him, claiming that he had sexually harassed her. She alleged that, in May 1991, the governor arranged for her to meet him in a hotel room in Little Rock, Arkansas. When they were alone, he put his hand on her leg and slid it toward her pelvis. She escaped from his grasp, exclaimed, "What are you doing?" and said she was "not that kind of girl." She was upset and confused, and sat on a sofa near the door. She claimed that Clinton approached her, "lowered his trousers and underwear, exposed his penis and told her to kiss it." Jones was horrified, jumped up and said she had to leave. Clinton responded by saying, "Well, I don't want to make you do anything you don't want to do," and pulled his pants up. He added that if she got in trouble for leaving work, Jones should "have Dave call me immediately and I'll take care of it." He also said, "You are smart. Let's keep this between ourselves." Jones remained at AIDC until February 1993, when she moved to California because of her husband's job transfer.

President Clinton denied all of the allegations. He also filed for summary judgment, claiming that Jones had not alleged facts that justified a trial. Jones opposed the motion for summary judgment.

Issue: ***Was Clinton entitled to summary judgment or was Jones entitled to a trial?***

Excerpts from Judge Wright's Decision: [To establish this type of a sexual harassment case, a plaintiff must show that her refusal to submit to unwelcome sexual advances resulted in a tangible job detriment, meaning that she suffered a specific loss. Jones claims that she was denied promotions, given a job with fewer responsibilities, isolated physically, required to sit at a workstation with no work to do, and singled out as the only female employee not to be given flowers on Secretary's Day.]

There is no record of plaintiff ever applying for another job within AIDC, however, and the record shows that not only was plaintiff never downgraded, her position was reclassified upward from a Grade 9 classification to a Grade 11 classification, thereby increasing her annual salary. Indeed, it is undisputed that plaintiff received every merit increase and cost-of-living allowance for which she was eligible during her nearly two-year tenure with the AIDC and consistently received satisfactory job evaluations.

Although plaintiff states that her job title upon returning from maternity leave was no longer that of purchasing assistant, her job duties prior to taking maternity leave and her job duties upon returning to work both involved data input. That being so, plaintiff cannot establish a tangible job detriment. A transfer that does not involve a demotion in form or substance and involves only minor changes in working conditions, with no reduction in pay or benefits, will not constitute an adverse employment action, otherwise every trivial personnel action that an irritable employee did not like would form the basis of a discrimination suit.

Finally, the Court rejects plaintiff's claim that she was subjected to hostile treatment having tangible effects when she was isolated physically, made to sit in a location from which she was constantly watched, made to sit at her workstation with no work to do, and singled out as the only female employee not to be given flowers on Secretary's Day. Plaintiff may well have perceived hostility and animus on the part of her supervisors, but these perceptions are merely conclusory in nature and do not, without more, constitute a tangible job detriment. Although it is not clear why plaintiff failed to receive flowers on Secretary's Day in 1992, such an omission does not give rise to a federal cause of action.

In sum, the Court finds that a showing of a tangible job detriment or adverse employment action is an essential element of plaintiff's sexual harassment claim and that plaintiff has not demonstrated any tangible job detriment or adverse employment action for her refusal to submit to the Governor's alleged advances. The President is therefore entitled to summary judgment [on this claim].

In other words, the court acknowledged that there were factual disputes, but concluded that even if Jones proved each of her allegations, she would *still* lose the case, because her allegations fell short of a legitimate case of sexual harassment. Jones appealed the case. Later the same year, as the appeal was pending and the House of Representatives was considering whether to impeach President Clinton, the parties settled the dispute. Clinton, without acknowledging any of the allegations, agreed to pay Jones $850,000 to drop the suit.

Janet and Rich each consider moving for summary judgment, but both correctly decide that they would lose. There is one major fact in dispute: Did Tony Caruso commit suicide? Only a jury may decide that issue. As long as there is *some evidence* supporting each side of a key factual dispute, the court may not grant summary judgment.

EXAM strategy

Question: You are a judge. Mel has sued Kevin, claiming that while Kevin was drunk, he negligently drove his car down Mel's street, and destroyed rare trees on a lot that Mel owns, next to his house. Mel's complaint stated that three witnesses at a bar saw Kevin take at least eight drinks less than an hour before the damage was done. In Kevin's answer, he denied causing the damage and denied being in the bar that night.

Kevin's lawyer has moved for summary judgment. He proves that three weeks before the alleged accident, Mel sold the lot to Tatiana.

Mel's lawyer opposes summary judgment. He produces a security camera tape proving that Kevin was in the bar, drinking beer, 34 minutes before the damage was done. He produces a signed statement from Sandy, a landscape gardener who lives across the street from the scene. Sandy states that she heard a crash, hurried to the windows, and saw

Kevin's car weaving away from the damaged trees. She is a landscape gardener and estimates the tree damage at $30,000 to $40,000. How should you rule on the motion?

Strategy: Do not be fooled by red herrings about Kevin's drinking or the value of the trees. Stick to the question: Should you grant summary judgment? Trials are necessary to resolve disputes about essential factual issues. Summary judgment is appropriate when there are no essential facts in dispute. Is there an essential fact not in dispute? Find it. Apply the rule. Being a judge is easy!

Result: It makes no difference whether Kevin was drunk or sober, whether he caused the harm or was at home in bed. Because Mel does not own the property, he cannot recover for the damage to it. He cannot win. You should grant Kevin's summary judgment motion.

Final Preparation

Well over 90 percent of all lawsuits are settled before trial. But the parties in the Enviro-Vision dispute are unable to compromise, so each side gears up for trial. The attorneys make lists of all witnesses they will call. They then prepare each witness very carefully, rehearsing the questions they will ask. It is considered ethical and proper to rehearse the questions, provided the answers are honest and come from the witness. It is unethical and illegal for a lawyer to tell a witness what to say. It also makes for a weaker presentation of evidence—witnesses giving scripted answers are often easy to spot. The lawyers also have colleagues cross-examine each witness, so that the witnesses are ready for the questions the other side's lawyer will ask.

This preparation takes hours and hours, for many days. Beth is frustrated that she cannot do the work she needs to for Enviro-Vision because she is spending so much time preparing the case. Other employees have to prepare as well, especially for cross-examination by Rich Stewart, and it is a terrible drain on the small firm. More than a year after Janet filed her complaint, they are ready to begin trial.

Trial

Adversary System

Our system of justice assumes that the best way to bring out the truth is for the two contesting sides to present the strongest case possible to a neutral factfinder. Each side presents its witnesses and then the opponent has a chance to cross-examine. The adversary system presumes that by putting a witness on the stand and letting both lawyers question her, the truth will emerge.

The judge runs the trial. Each lawyer sits at a large table near the front. Beth, looking tense and unhappy, sits with Janet. Rich Stewart sits with a Coastal executive. In the back of the courtroom are benches for the public. On one bench sits Craig Bergson. He will watch the entire proceeding with intense interest and a strange feeling of unease. He is convinced he knows what really happened.

Janet has demanded a jury trial for Beth's case, and Judge Rowland announces that they will now impanel the jury.

Right to Jury Trial

Not all cases are tried to a jury. As a general rule, both plaintiff and defendant have a right to demand a jury trial when the lawsuit is one for money damages. For example, in a typical contract lawsuit, such as Beth's insurance claim, both plaintiff and defendant have a jury trial right whether they are in state or federal court. Even in such a case, though, the parties may *waive* the jury right, meaning they agree to try the case to a judge. Also, if the plaintiff is seeking an equitable remedy such as an injunction, there is no jury right for either party.

Voir Dire

Voir dire
The process of selecting a jury.

The process of selecting a jury is called **voir dire**, which means "to speak the truth."[6] The court's goal is to select an impartial jury; the lawyers will each try to get a jury as favorable to their side as possible. A court sends letters to potential jurors who live in its county. Those who do not report for jury duty face significant consequences.

Challenges for cause
A claim that a juror has demonstrated probable bias.

Peremptory challenges
The right to excuse a juror for virtually any reason.

When voir dire begins, potential jurors are questioned individually, sometimes by the judge and sometimes by the two lawyers, as each side tries to ferret out potential bias. Each lawyer may make any number of **challenges for cause**, claiming that a juror has demonstrated probable bias. For example, if a prospective juror in the Enviro-Vision case works for an insurance company, the judge will excuse her on the assumption that she would be biased in favor of Coastal. If the judge perceives no bias, the lawyer may still make a limited number of **peremptory challenges**, entitling him to excuse that juror for virtually any reason, which need not be stated in court. For example, if Rich Stewart believes that a juror seems hostile to him personally, he will use a peremptory challenge to excuse that juror, even if the judge sensed no animosity. The process continues until 14 jurors are seated. Twelve will comprise the jury; the other two are alternates who hear the case and remain available in the event one of the impaneled jurors becomes ill or otherwise cannot continue.

Although jury selection for a case can sometimes take many days, in the Enviro-Vision case, the first day of the hearing ends with the jury selected. In the hallway outside the court, Rich offers Janet $200,000 to settle. Janet reports the offer to Beth and they agree to reject it. Craig Bergson drives home, emotionally confused. Only three weeks before his death, Tony had accidentally met his old roommate and they had had several drinks. Craig believes that what Tony told him answers the riddle of this case.

Pereda v. Parajon

957 So.2d 1194
Florida Court of Appeals, 2007

Facts: Maria Parajon sued Diana Pereda for injuring her in a car accident. During voir dire, Parajon's lawyer asked the panel of prospective jurors these questions: "Is there anybody sitting on this panel now that has ever been under the care of a physician for personal injuries, whether you had a lawsuit or not? In other words, you may not have had any sort of lawsuit, but you slipped and fell—you had any accidents?"

Several of the prospective jurors raised their hands, allowing the lawyers to question more deeply into possible bias. However, Lisa Berg, a prospective juror who happened to be a lawyer, did not respond. Berg and others were seated as jurors, and ultimately awarded Parajon $450,000 for medical damages and pain and suffering.

After the trial, questioned in court by the judge, Berg admitted that three years earlier she had been injured in a

[6]Students of French note that *voir* means "to see" and assume that *voir dire* should translate as "to see, to speak." However, the legal term is centuries old and derives not from modern French but from Old French, in which *voir* meant "truth."

car accident, hired a lawyer to sue, and settled out of court for $4,000. Asked about the settlement, Berg replied, "I think everyone always wants more money."

Parajon moved for a new trial but the judge denied the motion. Parajon appealed.

Issue: ***Is Parajon entitled to a new trial based on Berg's failure to disclose her own personal injury lawsuit?***

Excerpts from Judge Rothenberg's Decision: To determine whether a juror's nondisclosure warrants a new trial, the complaining party must show that: (1) the information is relevant and material to jury service in the case; (2) the juror concealed the information during questioning; and (3) the failure to disclose the information was not attributable to the complaining party's lack of diligence.

Both Parajon's and Pereda's respective counsels may indeed have been influenced to challenge Berg peremptorily had the facts of her personal injury litigation history been known. Berg's personal injury claim was not remote in time. Berg settled out of court at the urging of her parents in order to put the matter behind her. Her involvement in this matter may have affected her point of view in [this case]. Her nondisclosure, which precluded counsel's ability to question Berg about the experience and to fairly evaluate her as a prospective juror, was material.

It is clear from the record that Berg concealed her personal injury litigation history. She is a lawyer and an officer of the court. It is, therefore, difficult to imagine that she did not think the questions posed by Parajon's counsel applied to her.

The record evidence demonstrates that other prospective jurors, none of whom were lawyers, clearly understood what type of information Parajon's counsel was asking them to disclose. We find that Parajon's counsel made a diligent inquiry.

Reversed and remanded for a new trial.

Opening Statements

The next day, each attorney makes an opening statement to the jury, summarizing the proof he or she expects to offer, with the plaintiff going first. Janet focuses on Tony's successful life, his business and strong marriage, and the tragedy of his accidental death.[7]

Rich works hard to establish a friendly rapport with the jury. If members of the jury like him, they will tend to pay more attention to his presentation of evidence. He expresses regret about the death. Nonetheless, suicide is a clear exclusion from the policy. If insurance companies are forced to pay claims never bargained for, everyone's insurance rates will go up.

Burden of Proof

In civil cases, the plaintiff has the burden of proof. That means that the plaintiff must convince the jury that its version of the case is correct; the defendant is not obligated to disprove the allegations.

The plaintiff's burden in a civil lawsuit is to prove its case by a **preponderance of the evidence**. It must convince the jury that its version of the facts is at least *slightly more likely* than the defendant's version. Some courts describe this as a "51–49" persuasion, that is, that plaintiff's proof must "just tip" credibility in its favor. By contrast, in a criminal case, the prosecution must demonstrate **beyond a reasonable doubt** that the defendant is guilty. The burden of proof in a criminal case is much tougher because the likely consequences are, too. See Exhibit 3.3.

Preponderance of the evidence
The plaintiff's burden in a civil lawsuit.

Beyond a reasonable doubt
The government's burden in a criminal prosecution.

[7]Janet Booker has dropped her claim for triple damages against Coastal. To have any hope of such a verdict, she would have to show that Coastal had no legitimate reason at all for denying the claim. Discovery has convinced her that Coastal will demonstrate some rational reasons for what it did.

EXHIBIT 3.3 *Burden of Proof.* In a civil lawsuit, a plaintiff wins with a mere preponderance of the evidence. But the prosecution must persuade a jury beyond a reasonable doubt in order to win a criminal conviction.

Plaintiff's Case

Because the plaintiff has the burden of proof, Janet puts in her case first. She wants to prove two things. First, that Tony died. That is easy because the death certificate clearly demonstrates it and Coastal does not seriously contest it. Second, in order to win double indemnity damages, she must show that the death was accidental. She will do this with the testimony of the witnesses she calls, one after the other. Her first witness is Beth. When a lawyer asks questions of her own witness, it is **direct examination.** Janet brings out all the evidence she wants the jury to hear: that the business was basically sound, though temporarily troubled, that Tony was a hard worker, why the company took out life insurance policies, and so forth.

Direct examination
When a lawyer asks questions of her own witness.

Cross-examine
To ask questions of an opposing witness.

Then Rich has a chance to **cross-examine** Beth, which means to ask questions of an opposing witness. He will try to create doubt in the jury's mind. He asks Beth only questions for which he is certain of the answers, based on discovery. Rich gets Beth to admit that the firm was not doing well the year of Tony's death; that Tony had lost the best client the firm ever had; that Beth had reduced salaries; and that Tony had been depressed about business.

Rules of Evidence

The lawyers are not free simply to ask any question they want. The **law of evidence** determines what questions a lawyer may ask and how the questions are to be phrased, what answers a witness may give, and what documents may be introduced. The goal is to get the best evidence possible before the jurors so they can decide what really happened. In general, witnesses may only testify about things they saw or heard.

These rules are complex, and a thorough look at them is beyond the scope of this chapter. However, they can be just as important in resolving a dispute as the underlying substantive law. Suppose that a plaintiff's case depends upon the jury hearing about a certain conversation, but the rules of evidence prevent the lawyer from asking about it. That conversation might just as well never have occurred.

Janet calls an expert witness, a marine geologist, who testifies about the tides and currents in the area where Tony's body was found. The expert testifies that even experienced swimmers can be overwhelmed by a sudden shift in currents. Rich objects strenuously that this is irrelevant, because there is no testimony that there *was* such a current at the time of Tony's death. The judge permits the testimony.

Karen Caruso testifies that Tony was in "reasonably good" spirits the day of his death, and that he often took Blue for walks along the beach. Karen testifies that Blue was part Newfoundland. Rich objects that testimony about Blue's pedigree is irrelevant, but Janet insists it will show why Blue was tied up. The judge allows the testimony. Karen says that whenever Blue saw them swim, he would instinctively go into the water and pull them to shore. Does that explain why Blue was tied up? Only the jury can answer.

Cross-examination is grim for Karen. Rich slowly but methodically questions her about Tony's state of mind and brings out the problems with the company, his depression, and tension within the marriage. Janet's other witnesses testify essentially as they did during their depositions.

Is the breed relevant?

Motion for Directed Verdict

At the close of the plaintiff's case, Rich moves for a directed verdict, that is, a ruling that the plaintiff has entirely failed to prove some aspect of her case. Rich is seeking to win without even putting in his own case. He argues that it was Beth's burden to prove that Tony died accidentally and that she has entirely failed to do that.

Directed verdict
A ruling that the plaintiff has entirely failed to prove some aspect of her case.

A directed verdict is permissible only if the evidence so clearly favors the defendant that reasonable minds could not disagree on it. If reasonable minds could disagree, the motion must be denied. Here, Judge Rowland rules that the plaintiff has put in enough evidence of accidental death that a reasonable person could find in Beth's favor. The motion is denied.

There is no downside for Rich to ask for a directed verdict. The trial continues as if he had never made such a motion.

Defendant's Case

Rich now puts in his case, exactly as Janet did, except that he happens to have fewer witnesses. He calls the examining doctor, who admits that Tony could have committed suicide by swimming out too far. On cross-examination, Janet gets the doctor to acknowledge that he has no idea whether Tony intentionally drowned. Rich also questions several neighbors as to how depressed Tony had seemed and how unusual it was that Blue was tied up. Some of the witnesses Rich deposed, such as the tennis partner Jerry Johnson, have nothing that will help Coastal's case, so he does not call them.

Craig Bergson, sitting in the back of the courtroom, thinks how different the trial would have been had he been called as a witness. When he and Tony had the fateful drink, Tony had been distraught: business was terrible, he was involved in an extramarital affair that he could not end, and he saw no way out of his problems. He had no one to talk to and had been hugely relieved to speak with Craig. Several times Tony had said, "I just can't go on like this. I don't want to, anymore." Craig thought Tony seemed suicidal and urged him to see a therapist Craig knew and trusted. Tony had said that it was good advice, but Craig is unsure whether Tony sought any help.

This evidence would have affected the case. Had Rich Stewart known of the conversation, he would have deposed Craig and the therapist. Coastal's case would have been far stronger, perhaps overwhelming. But Craig's evidence will never be heard. Facts are critical. Rich's decision to depose other witnesses and omit Craig may influence the verdict more than any rule of law.

Closing Arguments

Both lawyers sum up their case to the jury, explaining how they hope the jury will interpret what they have heard. Janet summarizes the plaintiff's version of the facts, claiming that Blue was tied up so that Tony could swim without worrying about him. Rich claims that business and personal pressures had overwhelmed Tony. He tied up his dog, neatly folded his clothes, and took his own life.

Jury Instructions

Judge Rowland instructs the jury as to its duty. He tells them that they are to evaluate the case based only on the evidence they heard at trial, relying on their own experience and common sense.

He explains the law and the burden of proof, telling the jury that it is Beth's obligation to prove that Tony died. If Beth has proven that Tony died, she is entitled to $1 million; if she has proven that his death was accidental, she is entitled to $2 million. However, if Coastal has proven suicide, Beth receives nothing. Finally, he states that if they are unable to decide between accidental death and suicide, there is a legal presumption that it was accidental. Rich asks Judge Rowland to rephrase the "legal presumption" part but the judge declines.

Verdict

The jury deliberates informally, with all jurors entitled to voice their opinion. Some deliberations take two hours; some take two weeks. Many states require a unanimous verdict; others require only, for example, a 10–2 vote in civil cases.

This case presents a close call. No one saw Tony die. Yet even though they cannot know with certainty, the jury's decision will probably be the final word on whether he took his own life. After a day and a half of deliberating, the jury notifies the judge that it has reached a verdict. Rich Stewart quickly makes a new offer: $350,000. (The two sides have the right to settle a case until the moment when the last appeal is decided.) Beth hesitates but turns it down.

The judge summons the lawyers to court, and Beth goes as well. The judge asks the foreman if the jury has reached a decision. He states that it has: the jury finds that Tony Caruso drowned accidentally, and awards Beth Smiles $2 million.

Motions after the Verdict

Judgment *non obstante veredicto*
A judgment notwithstanding the jury's verdict.

Rich immediately moves for a **judgment *non obstante veredicto*** (JNOV), meaning a judgment notwithstanding the jury's verdict. He is asking the judge to overturn the jury's verdict. Rich argues that the jury's decision went against all of the evidence. He also claims that the judge's instructions were wrong and misled the jury.

Judge Rowland denies the JNOV. Rich immediately moves for a new trial, making the same claim, and the judge denies the motion. Beth is elated that the case is finally over—until Janet says she expects an appeal. Craig Bergson, leaving the courtroom, wonders if he did the right thing. He felt sympathy for Beth and none for Coastal. Yet now he is neither happy nor proud.

APPEALS

Two days later, Rich files an appeal to the court of appeals. The same day, he phones Janet and increases his settlement offer to $425,000. Beth is tempted but wants Janet's advice. Janet says the risks of an appeal are that the court will order a new trial, and they would start all over. But to accept this offer is to forfeit over $1.5 million. Beth is unsure what to do. The firm desperately needs cash now, and appeals may take years. Janet suggests they wait until oral argument, another eight months.

Rich files a brief arguing that there were two basic errors at the trial: first, that the jury's verdict is clearly contrary to the evidence; and second, that the judge gave the wrong instructions to the jury. Janet files a reply brief, opposing Rich on both issues. In her brief, Janet cites many cases that she claims are **precedent**: earlier decisions by the state appellate courts on similar or identical issues.

Precedent
Earlier decisions by the state appellate courts on similar issues.

Eight months later, the lawyers representing Coastal and Enviro-Vision appear in the court of appeals to argue their case. Rich, the appellant, goes first. The judges frequently interrupt his argument with questions. They show little sympathy for his claim that the verdict was against the facts. They seem more sympathetic with his second point, that the instructions were wrong.

When Janet argues, all of their questions concern the judge's instructions. It appears they believe the instructions were in error. The judges take the case under advisement, meaning they will decide some time in the future—maybe in two weeks, maybe in five months.

Appeals Court Options

The court of appeals can **affirm** the trial court, allowing the decision to stand. The court may **modify** the decision, for example, by affirming that the plaintiff wins but decreasing the size of the award. (That is unlikely here; Beth is entitled to $2 million or nothing.) The court might **reverse and remand**, nullifying the lower court's decision and returning the case to the lower court for a new trial. Or it could simply **reverse**, turning the loser (Coastal) into the winner, with no new trial.

Affirm
To allow the decision to stand.

Modify
To affirm the outcome but with changes.

Reverse and remand
To nullify the lower decision and return the case for reconsideration or retrial.

Reverse
To turn the loser into the winner.

What will it do here? On the factual issue it will probably rule in Beth's favor. There *was* evidence from which a jury could conclude that Tony died accidentally. It is true that there was also considerable evidence to support Coastal's position, but that is probably not enough to overturn the verdict. If reasonable people could disagree on what the evidence proves, an appellate court generally refuses to change the jury's factual findings. The court of appeals is likely to rule that a reasonable jury *could* have found accidental death, even if the appellate judges personally suspect that Tony may have killed himself.

The judge's instructions raise a more difficult problem. Some states would require a more complex statement about "presumptions."[8]

What does a court of appeals do if it decides the trial court's instructions were wrong? If it believes the error rendered the trial and verdict unfair, it will remand the case, that is, send it back to the lower court for a new trial. However, the court may conclude that the mistake was **harmless error**. A trial judge cannot do a perfect job, and not every error is fatal. The court may decide the verdict was fair in spite of the mistake.

Harmless error
A mistake by the trial judge that was too minor to affect the outcome.

Janet and Beth talk. Beth is very anxious and wants to settle. She does not want to wait four or five months, only to learn that they must start all over. Janet urges that they wait a few weeks to hear from Rich: they don't want to seem too eager.

A week later, Rich telephones and offers $500,000. Janet turns it down, but says she will ask Beth if she wants to make a counter-offer. She and Beth talk. They agree that they will settle for $1 million. Janet then calls Rich and offers to settle for $1.7 million. Rich and Janet

[8]Judge Rowland probably should have said, "The law presumes that death is accidental, not suicide. So if there were no evidence either way, the plaintiff would win because we presume accident. But if there is competing evidence, the presumption becomes irrelevant. If you think that Coastal Insurance has introduced some evidence of suicide, then forget the legal presumption. You must then decide what happened based on what you have seen and heard in court, and on any inferences you choose to draw." Note that the judge's instructions were different, though similar.

debate the merits of the case. Rich later calls back and offers $750,000, saying he doubts that he can go any higher. Janet counters with $1.4 million, saying she doubts she can go any lower. They argue, both predicting that they will win on appeal.

Rich calls, offers $900,000 and says, "That's it. No more." Janet argues for $1.2 million, expecting to nudge Rich up to $1 million. He doesn't nudge, instead saying, "Take it or leave it." Janet and Beth talk it over. Janet telephones Rich and accepts $900,000 to settle the case.

If they had waited for the court of appeals decision, would Beth have won? It is impossible to know. It is certain, though, that whoever lost would have appealed. Months would have passed waiting to learn if the state supreme court would accept the case. If that court had agreed to hear the appeal, Beth would have endured another year of waiting, brief writing, oral argument, and tense hoping. The high court has all of the options discussed: to affirm, modify, reverse and remand, or simply reverse.

Alternative Dispute Resolution

As we have seen in the previous section, trials can be trying. Lawsuits can cause prolonged periods of stress, significant legal bills, and general unpleasantness. Many people and companies prefer to settle cases out of court. Alternative dispute resolution (ADR) provides several semi-formal methods of resolving conflicts. We will look at different types of ADR and analyze their strengths and weaknesses.

Negotiation

In most cases, the parties negotiate, whether personally or through lawyers. Fortunately, the great majority of disputes are resolved this way. Negotiation often begins as soon as a dispute arises and may last a few days or several years.

Mediation

Mediation is the fastest growing method of dispute resolution in the United States. Here, a neutral person, called a *mediator*, attempts to guide the two disputing parties toward a voluntary settlement. (In some cases, there may be two or more mediators, but we will use the singular.) Generally, the two disputants voluntarily enter mediation, although some judges order the parties to try this form of ADR before allowing a case to go to trial.

A mediator does not render a decision in the dispute, but uses a variety of skills to move the parties toward agreement. Often a mediator will shuttle between the antagonists, hearing their arguments, sorting out the serious issues from the less important, prompting the parties and lawyers alike to consider new perspectives, and looking for areas of agreement. Mediators must earn the trust of both parties, listen closely, try to diffuse anger and fear, and build the will to settle. Good mediators do not need a law degree, but they must have a sense of humor and low blood pressure.

Mediation has several major advantages. Because the parties maintain control of the process, the two antagonists can speak freely. They need not fear conceding too much, because no settlement takes effect until both parties sign. All discussions are confidential, further encouraging candid talk. This is particularly helpful in cases involving proprietary information that might be revealed during a trial.

Of all forms of dispute resolution, mediation probably offers the strongest "win–win" potential. Since the goal is voluntary settlement, neither party needs to fear that it will end up the loser. This is in sharp contrast to litigation, where one party is very likely to lose.

Removing the fear of defeat often encourages thinking and talking that are more open and realistic than negotiations held in the midst of a lawsuit. Studies show that over 75 percent of mediated cases do reach a voluntary settlement. Such an agreement is particularly valuable to parties that wish to preserve a long-term relationship. Consider two companies that have done business successfully for 10 years but now are in the midst of a million-dollar trade dispute. A lawsuit could last three or more years and destroy any chance of future trade. However, if the parties mediate the disagreement, they might reach an amicable settlement within a month or two and could quickly resume their mutually profitable business.

This form of ADR works for disputes both big and small. Two college roommates who cannot get along may find that a three-hour mediation session restores tranquility in the apartment. On a larger scale, consider the work of former U.S. Senator George Mitchell, who mediated the Anglo-Irish peace agreement, setting Northern Ireland on the path to peace for the first time in three centuries. Like most good mediators, Mitchell was remarkably patient. In an early session, Mitchell permitted the head of one militant party to speak without interruption—for seven straight hours. The diatribe yielded no quick results, but Mitchell believed that after Northern Ireland's tortured history, any nonviolent discussions represented progress.

Arbitration

In this form of ADR, the parties agree to bring in a neutral third party, but with a major difference: the arbitrator has the power to impose an award. The arbitrator allows each side equal time to present its case and, after deliberation, issues a binding decision, generally without giving reasons. Unlike mediation, arbitration ensures that there will be a final result, although the parties lose control of the outcome.

Judge Judy and similar TV court shows are examples of arbitration. Before the shows are taped, people involved in a real dispute sign a contract in which they give up the right to go to court over the incident and agree to be bound by the judge's decision.

Parties in arbitration give up many additional rights that litigants retain, including discovery and class action. In arbitration, as already discussed as applied to trials, *discovery* allows the two sides in a lawsuit to obtain documentary and other evidence from the opponent before the dispute is decided. Arbitration permits both sides to keep secret many files that would have to be divulged in a court case, potentially depriving the opposing side of valuable evidence. A party may have a stronger case than it realizes, and the absence of discovery may permanently deny it that knowledge. As discussed earlier in this chapter, a *class action* is a suit in which one injured party represents a large group of people who have suffered similar harm. Arbitration eliminates this possibility, since injured employees face the employer one at a time. Finally, the fact that an arbitrator may not provide a written, public decision bars other plaintiffs, and society generally, from learning what happened.

Traditionally, parties sign arbitration agreements *after* some incident took place. A car accident would happen first, and the drivers would agree to arbitration second. But today, many parties agree *in advance* to arbitrate any disputes that may arise in the future. For example, a new employee may sign an agreement requiring arbitration of any future disputes with his employer; a customer opening an account with a stock-broker or bank—or health plan—may sign a similar form, often without realizing it. The good news is fewer lawsuits; the bad news is you might be the person kept out of court.

Assume that you live in Miami. Using the Internet, you order a $1,000 ThinkLite laptop computer, which arrives in a carton loaded with six fat instructional manuals and many small leaflets. You read some of the documents and ignore others. For four weeks, you struggle to make your computer work, to no avail. Finally, you call ThinkLite and demand a refund, but the company refuses. You file suit in your local court, at which time the company points out that buried among the hundreds of pages it mailed you was a *mandatory arbitration form*. This document prohibits you from filing suit against the company and states that if you have any complaint with the company, you must fly to Chicago, pay a $2,000 arbitrator's fee, plead your case before an arbitrator selected by the Laptop Trade Association of America, and, should you lose, pay ThinkLite's attorneys' fees, which could be several thousand dollars. Is that mandatory arbitration provision valid? It is too early to say with finality, but thus far, the courts that have faced such clauses have enforced them.[9]

Chapter Conclusion

No one will ever know for sure whether Tony Caruso took his own life. Craig Bergson's evidence might have tipped the scales in favor of Coastal. But even that is uncertain, since the jury could have found him unpersuasive. After two years, the case ends with a settlement and uncertainty—both typical lawsuit results. The missing witness is less common but not extraordinary. The vaguely unsatisfying feeling about it all is only too common and indicates why most parties settle out of court.

EXAM REVIEW

1. **COURT SYSTEMS** There are many *systems* of courts, one federal and one in each state. A federal court will hear a case only if it involves a federal question or diversity jurisdiction. (pp. 43–49)

2. **TRIAL AND APPELLATE COURTS** Trial courts determine facts and apply the law to the facts; appeals courts generally accept the facts found by the trial court and review the trial record for errors of law. (pp. 49–51)

EXAM Strategy

Question: Jade sued Kim, claiming that Kim promised to hire her as an in-store model for $1,000 per week for 8 weeks. Kim denied making the promise, and the jury was persuaded: Kim won. Jade has appealed, and now offers Steve as a witness. Steve will testify to the Appeals Court that he saw Kim hire Jade as a model, exactly as Jade claimed. Will Jade win on appeal?

Strategy: Before you answer, make sure you know the difference between trial and appellate courts. What is the difference? Apply that distinction here. (See the "Result" at the end of this section.)

---

[9]See, e.g., *Hill v. Gateway* 2000, 105 F.3d 1147, 1997 U.S. App. LEXIS 1877 (7th Cir. 1997), upholding a similar clause.

3. **PLEADINGS** A complaint and an answer are the two most important pleadings, that is, documents that start a lawsuit. (pp. 51–54)

4. **DISCOVERY** Discovery is the critical pre-trial opportunity for both parties to learn the strengths and weaknesses of the opponent's case. Important forms of discovery include interrogatories, depositions, production of documents and objects, physical and mental examinations, and requests for admission. (pp. 54–59)

5. **MOTIONS** A motion is a formal request to the court. (pp. 54, 66)

6. **SUMMARY JUDGMENT** Summary judgment is a ruling by the court that no trial is necessary because there are no essential facts in dispute. (pp. 59–61)

7. **JURY TRIALS** Generally, both plaintiff and defendant may demand a jury in any lawsuit for money damages. (pp. 61–66)

8. **VOIR DIRE** Voir dire is the process of selecting jurors in order to obtain an impartial panel. (p. 62)

EXAM Strategy

Question: You are a lawyer, representing the plaintiff in a case of alleged employment discrimination. The court is selecting a jury. Based on questions you have asked, you believe that juror number 3 is biased against your client. You explain this to the judge, but she disagrees. Is there anything you can do?

Strategy: The question focuses on your rights during voir dire. If you believe that a juror will not be fair, you may make two different types of challenge. What are they? (See the "Result" at the end of this section.)

9. **BURDEN OF PROOF** The plaintiff's burden of proof in a civil lawsuit is preponderance of the evidence, meaning that its version of the facts must be at least slightly more persuasive than the defendant's. In a criminal prosecution, the government must offer proof beyond a reasonable doubt in order to win a conviction. (pp. 63–64)

10. **RULES OF EVIDENCE** The rules of evidence determine what questions may be asked during trial, what testimony may be given, and what documents may be introduced. (pp. 65–65)

11. **VERDICTS** The verdict is the jury's decision in a case. The losing party may ask the trial judge to overturn the verdict, seeking a JNOV or a new trial. Judges seldom grant either. (pp. 65–66)

12. **APPEALS** An appeals court has many options. The court may affirm, upholding the lower court's decision; modify, changing the verdict but leaving the same party victorious; reverse, transforming the loser into the winner; and/or remand, sending the case back to the lower court. (pp. 47–50, 66–68)

13. **ADR** Alternative dispute resolution is any formal or informal process to settle disputes without a trial. Mediation, arbitration, and other forms of ADR are growing in popularity. (pp. 68–70)

2. Result: Trial courts use witnesses to help resolve fact disputes. Appellate courts review the record to see if there have been errors of law. Appellate courts never hear witnesses, and they will not hear Steve. Jade will lose her appeal.

8. Result: You have already made a *challenge for cause*, claiming bias, but the judge has rejected your challenge. If you have not used up all of your *peremptory challenges*, you may use one to excuse this juror, without giving any reason.

MULTIPLE-CHOICE QUESTIONS

1. The burden of proof in a civil trial is to prove a case ________________. The burden of proof rests with the ________________.
   (a) beyond a reasonable doubt; plaintiff
   (b) by a preponderance of the evidence; plaintiff
   (c) beyond a reasonable doubt; defendant
   (d) by a preponderance of the evidence; defendant

2. Alice is suing Betty. After the discovery process, Alice believes that no relevant facts are in dispute, and that there is no need for a trial. She should move for...
   (a) a judgment on the pleadings
   (b) a directed verdict
   (c) a summary judgment
   (d) a JNOV

3. Glen lives in Illinois. He applies for a job with an Missouri company, and he is told, amazingly, that the job is open only to white applicants. He will now sue the Missouri company under the Civil Rights Act, a federal statute. Can Glen sue in federal court?
   (a) Yes, absolutely.
   (b) Yes, but only if he seeks damages of at least $75,000. Otherwise, he must sue in a state court.
   (c) Yes, but only if the Missouri company agrees. Otherwise, he must sue in a state court.
   (d) No, absolutely not. He must sue in a state court.

4. A default judgment can be entered if which of the following is true?
   (a) A plaintiff presents her evidence at trial and clearly fails to meet her burden of proof.
   (b) A defendant loses a lawsuit and does not pay a judgment within 180 days.
   (c) A defendant fails to file an answer to a plaintiff's complaint on time.
   (d) A citizen fails to obey an order to appear for jury duty.

5. Barry and Carl are next-door neighbors. Barry's dog digs under Carl's fence and does $500 worth of damage to Carl's garden. Barry refuses to pay for the damage, claiming that Carl's cats "have been digging up my yard for years."

The two argue repeatedly, and the relationship turns frosty. Of the following choices, which has no outside decision maker and is most likely to allow the neighbors to peacefully coexist after working out the dispute?

(a) Trial
(b) Arbitration
(c) Mediation

Essay Questions

1. You plan to open a store in Chicago, specializing in rugs imported from Turkey. You will work with a native Turk who will purchase and ship the rugs to your store. You are wise enough to insist on a contract establishing the rights and obligations of both parties and would prefer an ADR clause. But you do not want a clause that will alienate your overseas partner. What kind of ADR clause should you include, and why?

2. Which court(s) have jurisdiction over each of these lawsuits—state or federal? Explain your reasoning for each answer.

   - Pat wants to sue his next-door neighbor, Dorothy, claiming that Dorothy promised to sell him the house next door.
   - Paula, who lives in New York City, wants to sue Dizzy Movie Theatres, whose principal place of business is Dallas. She claims that while she was in Texas on holiday, she was injured by their negligent maintenance of a stairway. She claims damages of $30,000.
   - Phil lives in Tennessee. He wants to sue Dick, who lives in Ohio. Phil claims that Dick agreed to sell him 3,000 acres of farmland in Ohio, worth over $2 million.
   - Pete, incarcerated in a federal prison in Kansas, wants to sue the United States government. He claims that his treatment by prison authorities violates three federal statutes.

3. British discovery practice differs from that in the United States. Most discovery in Britain concerns documents. The lawyers for the two sides, called *solicitors,* must deliver to the opposing side a list of all relevant documents in their possession. Each side may then request to look at and copy those it wishes. Depositions are rare. What advantages and disadvantages are there to the British practice?

4. Trial practice also is dramatically different in Britain. The parties' solicitors do not go into court. Courtroom work is done by different lawyers, called barristers. The barristers have very limited rights to interview witnesses before trial. They know the substance of what each witness intends to say but do not rehearse questions and answers, as in the United States. Which approach do you consider more effective? More ethical? What is the purpose of a trial? Of pre-trial preparation?

5. Claus Scherer worked for Rockwell International and was paid over $300,000 per year. Rockwell fired Scherer for alleged sexual harassment of several workers, including his secretary, Terry Pendy. Scherer sued in United States District Court, alleging that Rockwell's real motive in firing him was his high salary.

Rockwell moved for summary judgment, offering deposition transcripts of various employees. Pendy's deposition detailed instances of harassment, including comments about her body, instances of unwelcome touching, and discussions of extramarital affairs. Another deposition, from a Rockwell employee who investigated the allegations, included complaints by other employees as to Scherer's harassment. In his own deposition, which he offered to oppose summary judgment, Scherer testified that he could not recall the incidents alleged by Pendy and others. He denied generally that he had sexually harassed anyone. The district court granted summary judgment for Rockwell. Was its ruling correct?

Discussion Questions

1. In the Tony Caruso case described throughout this chapter, the defendant offers to settle the case at several stages. Knowing what you do now about litigation, would you have accepted any of the offers? If so, which one(s)? If not, why not?

2. The burden of proof in civil cases is fairly low. A plaintiff wins a lawsuit if he is 51 percent convincing, and then he collects 100 percent of his damages. Is this result reasonable? Should a plaintiff in a civil case be required to prove his case beyond a reasonable doubt? Or, if a plaintiff is only 51 percent convincing, should he get only 51 percent of his damages?

3. Large numbers of employees have signed mandatory arbitration agreements in employment contracts. Courts usually uphold these clauses. Imagine that you signed a contract with an arbitration agreement, that the company later mistreated you, and that you could not sue in court. Would you be upset? Or would you be relieved to go through the faster and cheaper process of arbitration?

4. Imagine a state law that allows for residents to sue "spammers"—those who send uninvited commercial messages through e-mail—for $30. One particularly prolific spammer sends messages to hundreds of thousands of people.

   John Smith, a lawyer, signs up 100,000 people to participate in a class-action lawsuit. According to the agreements with his many clients, Smith will keep one-third of any winnings. In the end, Smith wins a $3 million verdict and pockets $1 million. Each individual plaintiff receives a check for $20.

   Is this lawsuit a reasonable use of the court's resources? Why or why not?

5. Higher courts are reluctant to review a lower court's *factual* findings. Should this be so? Would appeals be fairer if appellate courts reviewed *everything*?

CHAPTER 4

Common Law, Statutory Law, and Administrative Law

© r.nagy/Shutterstock.com

Harry Homicide captures Gary and hauls him to the Old Abandoned Mill. Inside the mill, Harry sets a plank of wood atop a conveyor belt and ties Gary securely to the board.

"And now, Gary … my arch-enemy … I will have my REVENGE," Harry shouts. With a flourish, he presses a large green button marked START. The conveyor belt starts to move. A very large circular blade at the end of the belt begins to turn and cut into the plank. "Bwah hah hah hah!" Harry laughs in triumph.

Gary moves slowly toward the blade. Very, very slowly. Harry Homicide taps his foot. He sighs, frowns, and checks his watch. "Well," he says, "I think it is safe to assume that it's all over for you, Gary. You should never have crossed me. And so, farewell!" Harry makes a dramatic exit.

Gary works at his bonds frantically. He begins to weep. But then—a hiker appears in the doorway! "Hey! Help! Untie me!" Gary shouts. He can't believe his good fortune.

The hiker mumbles something. "What's that?" Gary shouts. "I can't hear you. Help me—hurry!"

The hiker speaks up. "I said I'm not any good untying knots. Never have been."

Gary's mouth drops open. "Fine, that's fine," he says. "Just hit the big red STOP button on the wall next to you, and I'll untie myself."

> "Just hit the big red STOP button on the wall next to you, and I'll untie myself."
> The hiker looks at the button, then back at Gary.
> "I really need to go," he says.
> "WHAT?!"
> "If I don't get home soon, I'm going to miss *Oprah.*"

The hiker looks at the button, then back at Gary. "I really need to go," he says.

"WHAT?!"

"If I don't get home soon, I'm going to miss *Oprah.*"

"You can't be serious!"

"I am serious. I find her empathy and common sense refreshing."

"Oh, boy," Gary mutters to himself. Then, louder, "That's fine, just fine. Just punch the button and you can be on your way in two seconds. Please!"

The hiker takes one last look at the STOP button. "I have to go," he says. Without another word, he leaves.

In his last moments, Gary cannot decide whether he is more irritated with the hiker or Harry Homicide.

Common Law

Gary and the hiker present a classic legal puzzle: what, if anything, must a bystander do when he sees someone in danger? We will examine this issue to see how the common law works.

Common law
Judge-made law.

The **common law** is judge-made law. It is the sum total of all the cases decided by appellate courts. The common law of Pennsylvania consists of all cases decided by appellate courts in that state. The Illinois common law is made up of all of the cases decided by Illinois appellate courts. Two hundred years ago, almost all of the law was common law. Today, common law still predominates in tort, contract, and agency law, and it is very important in property, employment, and some other areas.

Stare Decisis

Stare decisis
"Let the decision stand," that is, the ruling from a previous case.

Precedent
An earlier case that decided the issue.

Nothing perks up a course like Latin. ***Stare decisis*** means "let the decision stand." It is the essence of the common law. Once a court has decided a particular issue, it will generally apply the same rule in similar cases in the future . Suppose the highest court of Arizona must decide whether a contract signed by a 16-year-old can be enforced against him. The court will look to see if there is **precedent**, that is, whether the high court of Arizona has already decided a similar case. The Arizona court looks and finds several earlier cases, all holding that such contracts may not be enforced against a minor. The court will probably apply that precedent and refuse to enforce the contract in this case. Courts do not always follow precedent, but they generally do: *stare decisis.*

A desire for predictability created the doctrine of *stare decisis.* The value of predictability is apparent: people must know what the law is. If contract law changed daily, an entrepreneur who leased factory space and then started buying machinery would be uncertain if the factory would actually be available when she was ready to move in. Will the landlord slip out of the lease? Will the machinery be ready on time? The law must be knowable. Yet there must also be flexibility in the law, some means to respond to new problems and a changing social climate. Sometimes, we are better off if we are not encumbered by ironclad rules established before electricity was discovered. These two ideas are in conflict: the more flexibility we permit, the less predictability we enjoy. We will watch the conflict play out in the bystander cases.

Bystander Cases

This country inherited from England a simple rule about a **bystander's obligations: you have no duty to assist someone in peril unless you created the danger.** In *Union Pacific Railway Co. v. Cappier,*[1] through no fault of the railroad, a train struck a man. Railroad employees saw the incident happen but did nothing to assist him. By the time help arrived, the victim had died. The court held that the railroad had no duty to help the injured man:

> With the humane side of the question courts are not concerned. It is the omission or negligent discharge of legal duties only which come within the sphere of judicial cognizance. For withholding relief from the suffering, for failure to respond to the calls of worthy charity, or for faltering in the bestowment of brotherly love on the unfortunate, penalties are found not in the laws of men but in [the laws of God].

As harsh as this judgment might seem, it was an accurate statement of the law at that time in both England and the United States: bystanders need do nothing. Contemporary writers found the rule inhumane and cruel, and even judges criticized it. But—*stare decisis*—they followed it. With a rule this old and well established, no court was willing to scuttle it. What courts did do was seek openings for small changes.

Eighteen years after the Kansas case of *Cappier,* a court in nearby Iowa found the basis for one exception. Ed Carey was a farm laborer, working for Frank Davis. While in the fields, Carey fainted from sunstroke and remained unconscious. Davis simply hauled him to a nearby wagon and left him in the sun for an additional four hours, causing serious permanent injury. The court's response:

> It is unquestionably the well-settled rule that the master is under no legal duty to care for a sick or injured servant for whose illness or injury he is not at fault. Though not unjust in principle, this rule, if carried unflinchingly and without exception to its logical extreme, is sometimes productive of shocking results. To avoid this criticism [we hold that where] a servant suffers serious injury, or is suddenly stricken down in a manner indicating the immediate and emergent need of aid to save him from death or serious harm, the master, if present is in duty bound to take such reasonable measures as may be practicable to relieve him, even though such master be not chargeable with fault in bringing about the emergency.[2]

And this is how the common law often changes: bit by tiny bit. In Iowa, a bystander could now be liable *if* he was the employer and *if* the worker was suddenly stricken and *if* it was an emergency and *if* the employer was present. That is a small change but an important one.

For the next 50 years, changes in bystander law came very slowly. Consider *Osterlind v. Hill,* a case from 1928.[3] Osterlind rented a canoe from Hill's boatyard, paddled into the lake, and promptly fell into the water. For *30 minutes,* he clung to the side of the canoe and shouted for help. Hill heard the cries but did nothing; Osterlind drowned. Was Hill liable? No, said the court: a bystander has no liability. Not until half a century later did the same court reverse its position and begin to require assistance in extreme cases. Fifty years is a long time for the unfortunate Osterlind to hold on.[4]

In the 1970s, changes came more quickly.

---

[1]66 Kan. 649, 72 P. 281 (1903).

[2]*Carey v. Davis,* 190 Iowa 720, 180 N.W. 889 (1921).

[3]263 Mass. 73, 160 N.E. 301 (1928).

[4]*Pridgen v. Boston Housing Authority,* 364 Mass. 696, 308 N.E.2d 467 (Mass. 1974).

Tarasoff v. Regents of the University of California

17 Cal. 3d 425, 551 P.2d 334, 131 Cal. Rptr. 14
Supreme Court of California, 1976

Facts: On October 27, 1969, Prosenjit Poddar killed Tatiana Tarasoff. Tatiana's parents claimed that two months earlier, Poddar had confided his intention to kill Tatiana to Dr. Lawrence Moore, a psychologist employed by the University of California at Berkeley. They sued the university, claiming that Dr. Moore should have warned Tatiana and/or should have arranged for Poddar's confinement.

Issue: ***Did Dr. Moore have a duty to Tatiana Tarasoff, and did he breach that duty?***

Excerpts from Justice Tobriner's Decision: Although under the common law, as a general rule, one person owed no duty to control the conduct of another, nor to warn those endangered by such conduct, the courts have carved out an exception to this rule in cases in which the defendant stands in some special relationship to either the person whose conduct needs to be controlled or in a relationship to the foreseeable victim of that conduct. Applying this exception to the present case, we note that a relationship of defendant therapists to either Tatiana or Poddar will suffice to establish a duty of care.

We recognize the difficulty that a therapist encounters in attempting to forecast whether a patient presents a serious danger of violence. Obviously we do not require that the therapist, in making that determination, render a perfect performance; the therapist need only exercise that reasonable degree of skill, knowledge, and care ordinarily possessed and exercised by members of [the field] under similar circumstances.

In the instant case, however, the pleadings do not raise any question as to failure of defendant therapists to predict that Poddar presented a serious danger of violence. On the contrary, the present complaints allege that defendant therapists did in fact predict that Poddar would kill, but were negligent in failing to warn.

In our view, once a therapist does in fact determine, or under applicable professional standards reasonably should have determined, that a patient poses a serious danger of violence to others, he bears a duty to exercise reasonable care to protect the foreseeable victim of that danger.

[The Tarasoffs have stated a legitimate claim against Dr. Moore.]

The *Tarasoff* exception applies when there is some special relationship, such as therapist–patient. What if there is no such relationship? Remember the *Soldano v. O'Daniels* case from Chapter 1, in which the bartender refused to call the police.

As in the earlier cases we have seen, this lawsuit presented an emergency. But the exception created in *Carey v. Davis* applied only if the bystander was an employer, and that in *Tarasoff* only for a doctor. In *Soldano*, the bystander was neither. Should the law require him to act, that is, should it carve a new exception? Here is what the California court decided:

> Many citizens simply "don't want to get involved." No rule should be adopted [requiring] a citizen to open up his or her house to a stranger so that the latter may use the telephone to call for emergency assistance. As Mrs. Alexander in Anthony Burgess' *A Clockwork Orange* learned to her horror, such an action may be fraught with danger. It does not follow, however, that use of a telephone in a public portion of a business should be refused for a legitimate emergency call.
>
> We conclude that the bartender owed a duty to [Soldano] to permit the patron from Happy Jack's to place a call to the police or to place the call himself. It bears emphasizing that the duty in this case does not require that one must go to the aid of another. That is not the issue here. The employee was not the good samaritan intent on aiding another. The patron was.

And so, courts have made several subtle changes to the common law rule. Let's apply them to the opening scenario. If Gary's family sues the hiker, will they be successful? Probably not.

The hiker did not employ Gary, nor did the two men have any special relationship. The hiker did not stand in the way of someone else trying to call the police. He may be morally culpable for refusing to press a button and save a life, but he will not be legally liable unless an entirely new change to the common law occurs.

The bystander rule, that hardy oak, is alive and well. Various initials have been carved into its bark—the exceptions we have seen and a variety of others—but the trunk is strong and the leaves green. Perhaps someday the proliferating exceptions will topple it, but the process of the common law is slow and that day is nowhere in sight.

EXAM Strategy

Question: When Rachel is walking her dog, Bozo, she watches a skydiver float to earth. He lands in an enormous tree, suspended 45 feet above ground. "Help!" the man shouts. Rachel hurries to the tree and sees the skydiver bleeding profusely. She takes out her cell phone to call 911 for help, but just then Bozo runs away. Rachel darts after the dog, afraid that he will jump in a nearby pond and emerge smelling of mud. She forgets about the skydiver and takes Bozo home. Three hours later, the skydiver expires.

The victim's family sues Rachel. She defends by saying she feared that Bozo would have an allergic reaction to mud, and that in any case she could not have climbed 45 feet up a tree to save the man. The family argues that the dog is not allergic to mud, that even if he is, a pet's inconvenience pales compared to human life, and that Rachel could have phoned for emergency help without climbing an inch. Please rule.

Strategy: The family's arguments might seem compelling, but are they relevant? Rachel is a bystander, someone who perceives another in danger. What is the rule concerning a bystander's obligation to act? Apply the rule to the facts of this case.

Result: A bystander has no duty to assist someone in peril unless she created the danger. Rachel did not create the skydiver's predicament. She had no obligation to do anything. Rachel wins.

STATUTORY LAW

More law is created by statute than by the courts. Statutes affect each of us every day, in our business, professional, and personal lives. When the system works correctly, this is the one part of the law over which "we the people" have control. We elect the legislators who pass state statutes; we vote for the senators and representatives who create federal statutes.

Every other November, voters in all 50 states cast ballots for members of Congress. The winners of congressional elections convene in Washington, D.C. and create statutes. In this section, we look at how Congress does its work creating statutes.[5] Using the Civil Rights Act as a backdrop, we will follow a bill as it makes its way through Congress and beyond.

[5]State legislatures operate similarly in creating state laws.

Bills

Bill
A proposed statute.

Veto
The power of the president to reject bills passed by Congress.

Congress is organized into two houses, the House of Representatives and the Senate. Either house may originate a proposed statute, which is called a **bill**. To become law, the bill must be voted on and approved by both houses. Once both houses pass it, they will send it to the president. If the president signs the bill, it becomes law and is then a statute. If the president opposes the bill, he will **veto** it, in which case it is not law.[6]

If you visit either house of Congress, you will probably find half a dozen legislators on the floor, with one person talking and no one listening. This is because most of the work is done in committees. Both houses are organized into dozens of committees, each with special functions. The House currently has about 25 committees (further divided into about 150 subcommittees) and the Senate has approximately 20 committees (with about 86 subcommittees). For example, the armed services committee of each house oversees the huge defense budget and the workings of the armed forces. Labor committees handle legislation concerning organized labor and working conditions. Banking committees develop expertise on financial institutions. Judiciary committees review nominees to the federal courts. There are dozens of other committees, some very powerful, because they control vast amounts of money, and some relatively weak. Few of us ever think about the House Agricultural Subcommittee on Specialty Crops. But if we owned a family peanut farm, we would pay close attention to the subcommittee's agenda, because those members of Congress would pay close attention to us.

When a bill is proposed in either house, it is referred to the committee that specializes in that subject. Why are bills proposed in the first place? For any of several reasons:

- ***New Issue, New Worry.*** If society begins to focus on a new issue, Congress may respond with legislation. We consider below, for example, the congressional response in the 1960s to employment discrimination.
- ***Unpopular Judicial Ruling.*** If Congress disagrees with a judicial interpretation of a statute, the legislators may pass a new statute to modify or "undo" the court decision. For example, if the Supreme Court misinterprets a statute about musical copyrights, Congress may pass a new law correcting the Court's error. However, the legislators have no such power to modify a court decision based on the Constitution. When the Supreme Court ruled that lawyers had a right *under the First Amendment* to advertise their services, Congress lacked the power to change the decision.
- ***Criminal Law.*** Statutory law, unlike common law, is prospective. Legislators are hoping to control the future. And that is why almost all criminal law is statutory. A court cannot retroactively announce that it *has been* a crime for a retailer to accept kickbacks from a wholesaler. Everyone must know the rules in advance because the consequences—prison, a felony record—are so harsh.

Discrimination: Congress and the Courts

The civil rights movement of the 1950s and 1960s convinced most citizens that African Americans suffered significant and unacceptable discrimination in jobs, housing, voting, schools, and other basic areas of life. Demonstrations and boycotts, marches and counter-marches, church bombings and killings persuaded the nation that the problem was vast and urgent.

In 1963 President Kennedy proposed legislation to guarantee equal rights in these areas. The bill went to the House Judiciary Committee, which heard testimony for

[6]Congress may, however, attempt to override the veto. See the discussion following.

weeks. Witnesses testified that blacks were often unable to vote because of their race, that landlords and home sellers adamantly refused to sell or rent to African Americans, that education was grossly unequal, and that blacks were routinely denied good jobs in many industries. Eventually, the Judiciary Committee approved the bill and sent it to the full House.

The bill was dozens of pages long and divided into "titles," with each title covering a major issue. Title VII concerned employment. We will consider the progress of Title VII in Congress and in the courts. Here is one section of Title VII, as reported to the House floor:[7]

> Sec. 703(a). It shall be an unlawful employment practice for an employer—
>
> (1) to fail or refuse to hire or to discharge any individual, or otherwise to discriminate against any individual with respect to his compensation, terms, conditions, or privileges of employment, because of such individual's race, color, religion, or national origin; or
>
> (2) to limit, segregate, or classify his employees in any way which would deprive or tend to deprive any individual of employment opportunities or otherwise adversely affect his status as an employee, because of such individual's race, color, religion, or national origin.

A civil rights demonstrator being arrested by the police.

Debate

The proposed bill was intensely controversial and sparked argument throughout Congress. Here are some excerpts from one day's debate on the House floor, on February 8, 1964:[8]

> MR. WAGGONNER. I speak to you in all sincerity and ask for the right to discriminate if I so choose because I think it is my right. I think it is my right to choose my social companions. I think it is my right if I am a businessman to run it as I please, to do with my own as I will. I think that is a right the Constitution gives to every man. I want the continued right to discriminate and I want the other man to have the right to continue to discriminate against me, because I am discriminated against every day. I do not feel inferior about it.
>
> I ask you to forget about politics, forget about everything except the integrity of the individual, leaving to the people of this country the right to live their lives in the manner they choose to live. Do not destroy this democracy for a Socialist government. A vote for this bill is no less.
>
> MR. CONTE. If the serious cleavage which pitted brother against brother and citizen against citizen during the tragedy of the Civil War is ever to be justified, it can be justified in this House and then in the other body with the passage of this legislation which can and must reaffirm the rights to all individuals which are inherent in our Constitution.
>
> The distinguished poet Mark Van Doren has said that "equality is absolute or no, nothing between can stand," and nothing should now stand between us and the passage of strong and effective civil rights legislation. It is to this that we are united in a strong bipartisan coalition today, and when the laws of the land proclaim that the 88th Congress acted effectively, judiciously, and wisely, we can take pride in our accomplishments as free men.

[7]The section number in the House bill was actually 704(a); we use 703 here because that is the number of the section when the bill became law and the number to which the Supreme Court refers in later litigation.
[8]The order of speakers is rearranged, and the remarks are edited.

Other debate was less rhetorical and aimed more at getting information. The following exchange anticipates a 30-year controversy on quotas:

> MR. JOHANSEN. I have asked for this time to raise a question and I would ask particularly for the attention of the gentleman from New York [MR. GOODELL] because of a remark he made—and I am not quarreling with it. I understood him to say there is no plan for balanced employment or for quotas in this legislation.... I am raising a question as to whether in the effort to eliminate discrimination—and incidentally that is an undefined term in the bill—we may get to a situation in which employers and conceivably union leaders, will insist on legislation providing for a quota system as a matter of self-protection.
>
> Now let us suppose this hypothetical situation exists with 100 jobs to be filled. Let us say 150 persons apply and suppose 75 of them are Negro and 75 of them are white. Supposing the employer... hires 75 white men. [Does anyone] have a right to claim they have been discriminated against on the basis of color?
>
> MR. GOODELL. It is the intention of the legislation that if applicants are equal in all other respects there will be no restriction. One may choose from among equals. So long as there is no distinction on the basis of race, creed, or color it will not violate the act.

The debate on racial issues carried on. Later in the day, Congressman Smith of Virginia offered an amendment that could scarcely have been smaller—or more important:

> Amendment offered by MR. SMITH of Virginia: On page 68, line 23, after the word "religion," insert the word "sex."

In other words, Smith was asking that discrimination on the basis of sex also be outlawed, along with the existing grounds of race, color, national origin, and religion. Congressman Smith's proposal produced the following comments:

> MR. CELLER. You know, the French have a phrase for it when they speak of women and men. They say "vive la difference." I think the French are right. Imagine the upheaval that would result from adoption of blanket language requiring total equality. Would male citizens be justified in insisting that women share with them the burdens of compulsory military service? What would become of traditional family relationships? What about alimony? What would become of the crimes of rape and statutory rape? I think the amendment seems illogical, ill timed, ill placed, and improper.
>
> MRS. ST. GEORGE. Mr. Chairman, I was somewhat amazed when I came on the floor this afternoon to hear the very distinguished chairman of the Committee on the Judiciary [MR. CELLER] make the remark that he considered the amendment at this point illogical. I can think of nothing more logical than this amendment at this point.
>
> There are still many States where women cannot serve on juries. There are still many States where women do not have equal educational opportunities. In most States and, in fact, I figure it would be safe to say, in all States—women do not get equal pay for equal work. That is a very well known fact. And to say that this is illogical. What is illogical about it? All you are doing is simply correcting something that goes back, frankly to the Dark Ages.

The debate continued. Some supported the "sex" amendment because they were determined to end sexual bias. But politics are complex. Some *opponents* of civil rights supported the amendment because they believed that it would make the legislation less popular and cause Congress to defeat the entire Civil Rights bill.

That strategy did not work. The amendment passed, and sex was added as a protected trait. And, after more debate and several votes, the entire bill passed the House. It went to the Senate, where it followed a similar route from Judiciary Committee to full Senate. Much of the Senate debate was similar to what we have seen. But some senators raised a new issue, concerning §703(2), which prohibited *segregating or classifying* employees based on any of the protected categories (race, color, national origin, religion, or sex). Senator Tower was concerned that §703(2) meant that an employee in a protected category could never be given any sort of job test. So the Senate amended §703 to include a new subsection:

> Sec. 703(h). Notwithstanding any other provision of this title, it shall not be an unlawful employment practice for an employer ... to give and to act upon the results of any professionally developed ability test provided that such test ... is not designed, intended or used to discriminate because of race, color, religion, sex or national origin.

With that amendment, and many others, the bill passed the Senate.

Conference Committee

Civil rights legislation had now passed both houses, but the bills were no longer the same due to the many amendments. This is true with most legislation. The next step is for the two houses to send representatives to a House–Senate Conference Committee. This committee examines all of the differences between the two bills and tries to reach a compromise. With the Civil Rights bill, Senator Tower's amendment was left in; other Senate amendments were taken out. When the Conference Committee had settled every difference between the two versions, the new, modified bill was sent back to each house for a new vote.

The House of Representatives and the Senate again angrily debated the compromise language reported from the Conference Committee. Finally, after years of violent public demonstrations and months of debate, each house passed the same bill. President Johnson promptly signed it. The Civil Rights Act of 1964 was law. See Exhibit 4.1.

But the passing of a statute is not always the end of the story. Sometimes courts must interpret congressional language and intent.

Statutory Interpretation

Title VII of the Civil Rights Act obviously prohibited an employer from saying to a job applicant, "We don't hire minorities." In some parts of the country, that had been common practice; after the Civil Rights Act passed, it became rare. Employers who routinely hired whites only, or promoted only whites, found themselves losing lawsuits. A new group of cases arose, those in which some job standard was set that appeared to be racially neutral, yet had a discriminatory effect. In North Carolina, the Duke Power Co. required that applicants for higher paying, promotional positions meet two requirements: they must have a high school diploma, and they must pass a standardized written test. There was no evidence that either requirement related to successful job performance. Blacks met the requirements in lower percentages than whites, and consequently whites obtained a disproportionate share of the good jobs.

Title VII did not precisely address this kind of case. It clearly outlawed overt discrimination. Was Duke Power's policy overt discrimination, or was it protected by Senator Tower's amendment, §703(h)? The case went all the way to the Supreme Court, where the Court had to interpret the new law.

Courts are often called upon to interpret a statute, that is, to explain precisely what the language means and how it applies in a given case. There are three primary steps in a court's statutory interpretation:

- ***Plain Meaning Rule.*** When a statute's words have ordinary, everyday significance, the court will simply apply those words. Section 703(a)(1) of the Civil Rights Act prohibits firing someone because of her religion. Could an employer who had fired a Catholic because of her religion argue that Catholicism is not really a religion, but more of a social group? No. The word "religion" has a plain meaning and courts apply its commonsense definition.

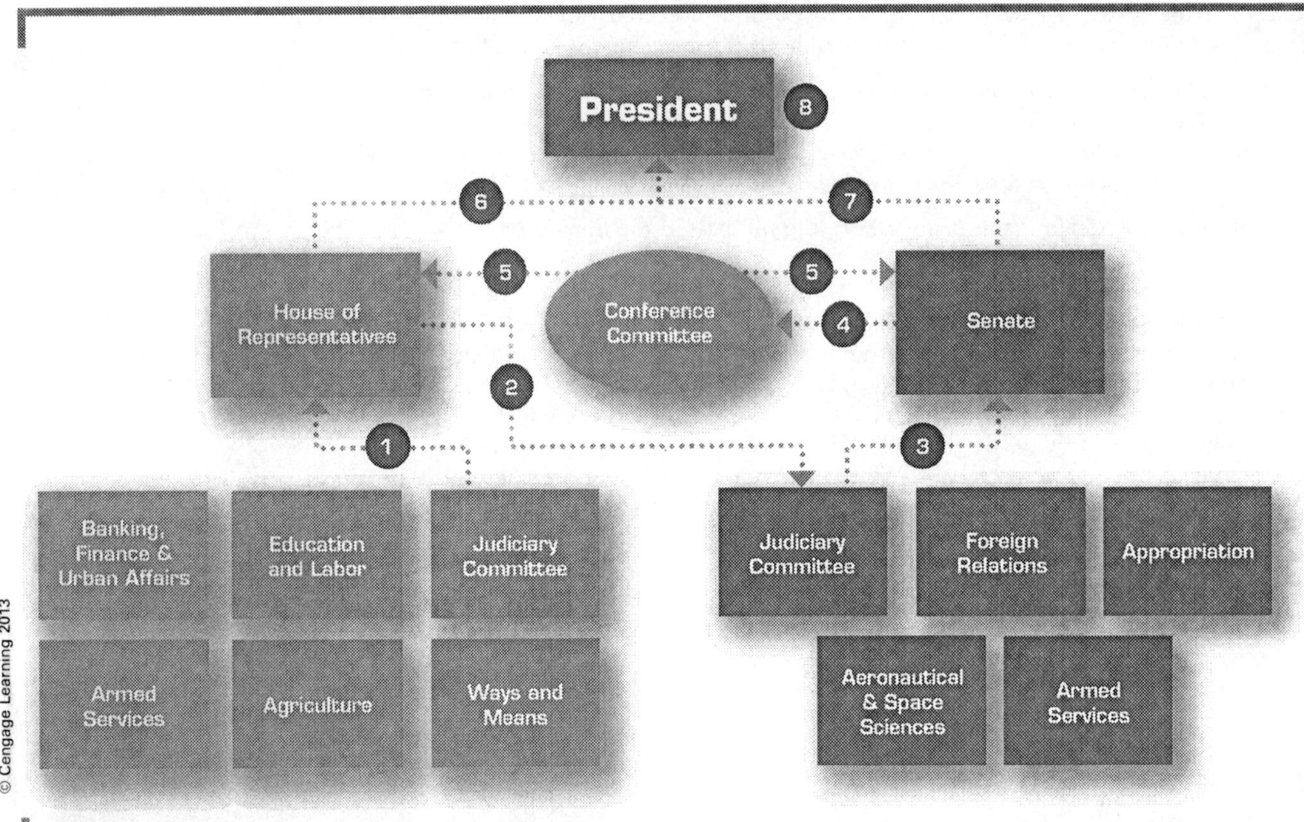

EXHIBIT 4.1 The two houses of Congress are organized into dozens of committees, a few of which are shown here. The path of the 1964 Civil Rights Act (somewhat simplified) was as follows: (1) The House Judiciary Committee approved the bill and sent it to the full House; (2) the full House passed the bill and sent it to the Senate, where it was assigned to the Senate Judiciary Committee; (3) the Senate Judiciary Committee passed an amended version of the bill and sent it to the full Senate; (4) the full Senate passed the bill with additional amendments. Since the Senate version was now different from the bill the House passed, the bill went to a Conference Committee. The Conference Committee (5) reached a compromise and sent the new version of the bill back to both houses. Each house passed the compromise bill (6 and 7) and sent it to the president, who signed it into law (8).

- ***Legislative History and Intent.*** If the language is unclear, the court must look deeper. Section 703(a)(2) prohibits classifying employees in ways that are discriminatory. Does that section prevent an employer from requiring high school diplomas, as Duke Power did? The explicit language of the statute does not answer the question. The court will look at the law's history to determine the intent of the legislature. The court will examine committee hearings, reports, and the floor debates that we have seen.
- ***Public Policy.*** If the legislative history is unclear, courts will rely on general public policies, such as reducing crime, creating equal opportunity, and so forth. They may include in this examination some of their own prior decisions. Courts assume that the legislature is aware of prior judicial decisions, and if the legislature did not change those decisions, the statute will be interpreted to incorporate them.

Here is how the Supreme Court interpreted the 1964 Civil Rights Act.

Landmark Case

GRIGGS V. DUKE POWER CO.

401 U.S. 424, 91 S. Ct. 849, 1971 U.S. LEXIS 134
United States Supreme Court, 1971

Facts: See the discussion of the Duke Power Company's job requirements in the "Conference Committee" section above.

Issue: ***Did Title VII of the 1964 Civil Rights Act require that employment tests be job-related?***

Excerpts from Chief Justice Burger's Decision: The objective of Congress in the enactment of Title VII is plain from the language of the statute. It was to achieve equality of employment opportunities and remove barriers that have operated in the past to favor an identifiable group of white employees over other employees. Under the Act, practices, procedures, or tests neutral on their face, and even neutral in terms of intent, cannot be maintained if they operate to "freeze" the status quo of prior discriminatory employment practices.

The Act proscribes not only overt discrimination but also practices that are fair in form, but discriminatory in operation. The touchstone is business necessity. If an employment practice which operates to exclude Negroes cannot be shown to be related to job performance, the practice is prohibited.

On the record before us, neither the high school completion requirement nor the general intelligence test is shown to bear a demonstrable relationship to successful performance of the jobs for which it was used.

Senator Tower offered an amendment which was adopted verbatim and is now the testing provision of section 703(h). Speaking for the supporters of Title VII, Senator Humphrey endorsed the amendment, stating: "Senators on both sides of the aisle who were deeply interested in Title VII have examined the text of this amendment and have found it to be in accord with the intent and purpose of that title." The amendment was then adopted. From the sum of the legislative history relevant in this case, the conclusion is inescapable that the ... requirement that employment tests be job related comports with congressional intent.

And so the highest Court ruled that if a job requirement had a discriminatory impact, the employer could use that requirement only if it was related to job performance. Many more cases arose. For almost two decades courts held that, once workers showed that a job requirement had a discriminatory effect, the employer had the burden to prove that the requirement was necessary for the business. The requirement had to be essential to achieve an important goal. If there was any way to achieve that goal without discriminatory impact, the employer had to use it.

Changing Times

But things changed. In 1989, a more conservative Supreme Court decided *Wards Cove Packing Co. v. Atonio.*[9] The plaintiffs were nonwhite workers in salmon canneries in Alaska. The canneries had two types of jobs, skilled and unskilled. Nonwhites (Filipinos and native Alaskans) invariably worked as low-paid, unskilled workers, canning the fish. The higher paid, skilled positions were filled almost entirely with white workers, who were hired during the off-season in Washington and Oregon.

There was no overt discrimination. But plaintiffs claimed that various practices led to the racial imbalances. The practices included failing to promote from within the company, hiring through separate channels (cannery jobs were done through a union hall, skilled positions were

[9]490 U.S. 642, 109 S. Ct. 2115, 1989 U.S. LEXIS 2794 (1989).

filled out of state), nepotism, and an English language requirement. Once again the case reached the Supreme Court, where Justice White wrote the Court's opinion.

If the plaintiffs succeeded in showing that the job requirements led to racial imbalance, said the Court, the employer now only had to demonstrate that the requirement or practice "serves, in a significant way, the legitimate employment goals of the employer.... [T]here is no requirement that the challenged practice be 'essential' or 'indispensable' to the employer's business." In other words, the Court removed the "business necessity" requirement of *Griggs* and replaced it with "legitimate employment goals."

Voters' Role

The response to *Wards Cove* was quick. Liberals decried it; conservatives hailed it. Everyone agreed that it was a major change that would make it substantially harder for plaintiffs to bring successful discrimination cases. Democrats introduced bills to reverse the interpretation of *Wards Cove.* President George H.W. Bush strongly opposed any new bill. He said it would lead to "quotas," that is, that employers would feel obligated to hire a certain percentage of workers from all racial categories to protect themselves from suits. This was the issue that Congressman Johansen had raised in the original House debate in 1964.

Both houses passed bills restoring the "business necessity" holding of *Griggs.* Again there were differences, and a Conference Committee resolved them. After acrimonious debate, both houses passed the compromise bill in October 1990. Was it therefore law? No. President Bush immediately vetoed the bill. He said it would compel employers to adopt quotas.

Congressional Override

When the president vetoes a bill, Congress has one last chance to make it law: an override. If both houses repass the bill, each by a two-thirds margin, it becomes law over the president's veto. Congress attempted to pass the 1990 Civil Rights bill over the Bush veto, but it fell short in the Senate by one vote.

Civil rights advocates tried again, in January 1991, introducing a new bill to reverse the *Wards Cove* rule. Again both houses debated and bargained. The new bill stated that, once an employee proves that a particular employment practice causes a discriminatory impact, the employer must "demonstrate that the challenged practice is job related for the position in question and consistent with business necessity."

Now the two sides fought over the exact meanings of two terms: "job related" and "business necessity." Each side offered definitions, but they could not reach agreement. It appeared that the entire bill would founder over those terms. So Congress did what it often does when faced with a problem of definition: it dropped the issue. Liberals and conservatives agreed not to define the troublesome terms. They would leave that task to courts to perform through statutory interpretation.

With the definitions left out, the new bill passed both houses. In November 1991, President Bush signed the bill into law. The president stated that the new bill had been improved and no longer threatened to create racial quotas. His opponents charged he had reversed course for political reasons, anticipating the 1992 presidential election.

And so, the Congress restored the "business necessity" interpretation to its own 1964 Civil Rights Act. No one would say, however, that it had been a simple process.

EXAM Strategy

Question: Kelly Hackworth took a leave of absence from her job at Progressive Insurance to care for her ailing mother. When she offered to return, Progressive refused to give her the same job or one like it. She sued based on the Family Medical Leave Act, a federal statute that requires firms to give workers returning from family leave their original job or an equivalent one. However, the statute excludes from its coverage workers whose company employs "fewer than 50 people within 75 miles" of the worker's jobsite. Between Ms. Hackworth's job site in Norman, Oklahoma, and the company's Oklahoma City workplace (less than 75 miles away), Progressive employed 47 people. At its Lawton, Oklahoma facility, Progressive employed three more people – but Lawton was 75.6 miles (wouldn't you know it) away from Norman. Progressive argued that the job was not covered by the statute. Hackworth claimed that this distance should be considered "within 75 miles," thereby rendering her eligible for FMLA leave. Even if it were not, she urged, it would be absurd to disqualify her from important rights based on a disparity of six-tenths of a mile. Please rule.

Strategy: The question asks you to interpret a statute. How do courts do that? There are three steps: the plain meaning rule; legislative history; and public policy. Apply those steps to these facts.

Result: In this real case, the court ruled that the plain meaning of "within 75 miles" was *75 miles or less.* Lawton was not 75 miles or less from Norman. The statute did not apply and Ms. Hackworth lost.[10]

Administrative Law

Before beginning this section, please return your seat to its upright position. Stow the tray firmly in the seatback in front of you. Turn off any laptops, cell phones, or other electronic devices. Sound familiar? Administrative agencies affect each of us every day in hundreds of ways. They have become the fourth branch of government. Supporters believe that they provide unique expertise in complex areas; detractors regard them as unelected government run amok.

Before beginning this section, please return your seat to its upright position. Stow the tray firmly in the seatback in front of you.

Many administrative agencies are familiar. The Federal Aviation Administration, which requires all airlines to ensure that your seats are upright before takeoff and landing, is an administrative agency. The Internal Revenue Service expects to hear from us every April 15. The Environmental Protection Agency regulates the water quality of the river in your town. The Federal Trade Commission oversees the commercials that shout at you from your television set.

Other agencies are less familiar. You may never have heard of the Bureau of Land Management, but if you go into the oil and gas industry, you will learn that this powerful agency has more control over your land than you do. If you develop real estate in Palos Hills, Illinois, you will tremble every time the Appearance Commission of the City of Palos Hills speaks, since you cannot construct a new building without its approval. If your software corporation wants to hire an Argentine expert on databases, you will get to know the complex workings of Immigration and Customs Enforcement: no one lawfully enters this country without its nod of approval.

[10] *Hackworth v. Progressive Casualty Ins. Co.*, 468 F.3d 722, 10th Cir. 2006 (10th Cir. 2006).

Background

By the 1880s, trains crisscrossed America. But this technological miracle became an economic headache. Congress worried that the railroads' economic muscle enabled a few powerful corporations to reap unfair profits. The railroad industry needed closer regulation. Who would do it? Courts decide individual cases, they do not regulate industries. Congress itself passes statutes, but it has no personnel to oversee the day-to-day working of a huge industry. For example, Congress lacks the expertise to establish rates for freight passing from Kansas City to Chicago, and it has no personnel to enforce rates once they are set.

A new entity was needed. Congress passed the Interstate Commerce Act, creating the Interstate Commerce Commission (ICC), the first administrative agency. The ICC began regulating freight and passenger transportation over the growing rail system and continued to do so for over 100 years. Congress gave the ICC power to regulate rates and investigate harmful practices, to hold hearings, issue orders, and punish railroads that did not comply.

The ICC was able to hire and develop a staff that was expert in the issues that Congress wanted controlled. The agency had enough flexibility to deal with the problems in a variety of ways: by regulating, investigating, and punishing. And that is what has made administrative agencies an attractive solution for Congress: one entity, focusing on one industry, can combine expertise and flexibility. However, the ICC also developed great power, which voters could not reach, and thereby started the great and lasting conflict over the role of agencies.

During the Great Depression of the 1930s, the Roosevelt administration and Congress created dozens of new agencies. Many were based on social demands, such as the need of the elderly population for a secure income. Political and social conditions dominated again in the 1960s, as Congress created agencies, such as the Equal Employment Opportunity Commission, to combat discrimination.

Then during the 1980s the Reagan administration made an effort to decrease the number and strength of the agencies. For several years some agencies declined in influence, though others did not. Today, there is still controversy about how much power agencies should have.

Classification of Agencies

Agencies exist at the federal, state, and local level. We will focus on federal agencies because they have national impact and great power. Most of the principles discussed apply to state and local agencies as well. Virtually any business or profession you choose to work in will be regulated by at least one administrative agency, and it may be regulated by several.

Executive-Independent

Some federal agencies are part of the executive branch while others are independent agencies. This is a major distinction. The president has much greater control of executive agencies for the simple reason that he can fire the agency head at any time. An executive agency will seldom diverge far from the president's preferred policies. Some familiar executive agencies are the Internal Revenue Service (part of the Treasury Department); the Federal Bureau of Investigation (Department of Justice); the Food and Drug Administration (Department of Health and Human Services); and the Nuclear Regulatory Commission (Department of Energy).

The president has no such removal power over independent agencies. The Federal Communications Commission (FCC) is an independent agency. For many corporations involved in broadcasting, the FCC has more day-to-day influence on their business than

Congress, the courts, and the president combined. Other powerful independent agencies are the Federal Trade Commission, the Securities and Exchange Commission, the National Labor Relations Board, and the Environmental Protection Agency.

Enabling Legislation

Congress creates a federal agency by passing **enabling legislation**. The Interstate Commerce Act was the enabling legislation that established the ICC. Typically, the enabling legislation describes the problems that Congress believes need regulation, establishes an agency to do it, and defines the agency's powers.

Critics argue that Congress is delegating to another body powers that only the legislature or courts are supposed to exercise. This puts administrative agencies above the voters. But legal attacks on administrative agencies have consistently failed for several decades. Courts acknowledge that agencies have become an integral part of a complex economy, and so long as there are some limits on an agency's discretion, courts will generally uphold its powers

POWER OF AGENCIES

Administrative agencies use three kinds of power to do the work assigned to them: they make rules, they investigate, and they adjudicate.

Rulemaking

One of the most important functions of an administrative agency is to make rules. In doing this, the agency attempts, prospectively, to establish fair and uniform behavior for all businesses in the affected area. **To create a new rule is to promulgate it**. Agencies promulgate two types of rules: legislative and interpretive.

Types of Rules: Legislative and Interpretive

Legislative rules are the most important agency rules, and they are much like statutes. Here, an agency creates law by requiring businesses or private citizens to act in a certain way. Suppose you operate a website for young shoppers, aged 10 to 18. Like most online merchants, you consider yourself free to collect as much data as possible about consumers. Wrong. The Federal Trade Commission, a federal agency, has promulgated detailed rules governing any site directed to young children. Before obtaining private data from these immature consumers, you must let them know exactly who you are, how to contact site operators, precisely what you are seeking, and how it will be used. You must also obtain verifiable parental consent before collecting, using, or disclosing any personal information. Failure to follow the rules can result in a substantial civil penalty. This modest legislative rule, in short, will be more important to your business than most statutes passed by Congress.

Interpretive rules do not change the law. They are the agency's interpretation of what the law already requires. But they can still affect all of us. For example, in 1977 Congress amended the Clean Air Act in an attempt to reduce pollution from factories. The act required the Environmental Protection Agency (EPA) to impose emission standards on "stationary sources" of pollution. But what did "stationary source" mean? It was the EPA's job to define that term. Obscure work, to be sure, yet the results could be seen and even smelled, because the EPA's definition would determine the quality of air entering our lungs every time we breathe. Environmentalists wanted the term defined to include every smokestack in a factory so that the EPA could regulate each one. The EPA, however, developed the "bubble concept," ruling that "stationary

© Photodisc/Getty Images

An agency's interpretation of an environmental statue may be obscure, but the consequences affect us all.

source" meant an entire factory, but not the individual smokestacks. As a result, polluters could shift emission among smokestacks in a single factory to avoid EPA regulation. Environmentalists howled that this gutted the purpose of the statute, but to no avail. The agency had spoken, merely by interpreting a statute.[11]

How Rules Are Made

Corporations fight many a court battle over whether an agency has the right to issue a particular rule and whether it was promulgated properly. The critical issue is this: how much participation is the public entitled to before an agency issues a rule? There are two basic methods of rulemaking.[12]

Informal Rulemaking. On many issues, agencies may use a simple "notice and comment" method of rulemaking. The agency must publish a proposed rule in advance and permit the public a comment period. During this period, the public may submit any objections and arguments, with supporting data. The agency will make its decision and publish the final rule.

For example, the Department of Transportation may use the informal rulemaking procedure to require safety features for all new automobiles. The agency must listen to objections from interested parties, notably car manufacturers, and it must give a written response to the objections. The agency is required to have rational reasons for the final choices it makes. However, it is not obligated to satisfy all parties or do their bidding.

Formal Rulemaking. In the enabling legislation, Congress may require that an agency hold a hearing before promulgating rules. Congress does this to make the agency more accountable to the public. After the agency publishes its proposed rule, it must hold a public hearing. Opponents of the rule, typically affected businesses, may cross-examine the agency experts about the need for the rule and may testify against it. When the agency makes its final decision about the rule, it must prepare a formal, written response to everything that occurred at the hearing.

When used responsibly, these hearings give the public access to the agency and can help formulate sound policy. When used irresponsibly, hearings can be manipulated to stymie needed regulation. The most famous example concerns peanut butter. The Food and Drug Administration (FDA) began investigating peanut butter content in 1958. It found, for example, that Jif peanut butter, made by Procter & Gamble, had only 75 percent peanuts and 20 percent of a Crisco-type base. P&G fought the investigation, and any changes, for years. Finally, in 1965, the FDA proposed a minimum of 90 percent peanuts in peanut butter; P&G wanted 87 percent. The FDA wanted no more than 3 percent hydrogenated vegetable oil; P&G wanted no limit.

The hearings dragged on for months. One day, the P&G lawyer objected to the hearing going forward because he needed to vote that day. Another time, when an FDA official testified that consumer letters indicated the public wanted to know what was really in peanut butter, the P&G attorney demanded that the official bring in and identify the

---

[11]An agency's interpretation can be challenged in court, and this one was.

[12]Certain rules may be made with no public participation at all. For example, an agency's internal business affairs and procedures can be regulated without public comment, as can its general policy statements. None of these directly affect the public, and the public has no right to participate.

letters—all 20,000 of them. Finally, in 1968, a decade after beginning its investigation, the FDA promulgated final rules requiring 90 percent peanuts but eliminating the 3 percent cap on vegetable oil.[13]

Investigation

Agencies do an wide variety of work, but they all need broad factual knowledge of the field they govern. Some companies cooperate with an agency, furnishing information and even voluntarily accepting agency recommendations. For example, the U.S. Consumer Product Safety Commission investigates hundreds of consumer products every year and frequently urges companies to recall goods that the agency considers defective. Many firms comply.

Other companies, however, jealously guard information, often because corporate officers believe that disclosure would lead to adverse rules. To force disclosure, agencies use *subpoenas* and *searches.*

Subpoenas

A **subpoena** is an order to appear at a particular time and place to provide evidence. A **subpoena *duces tecum*** requires the person to appear and bring specified documents. Businesses and other organizations intensely dislike subpoenas and resent government agents plowing through records and questioning employees. What are the limits on an agency's investigation? The information sought:

Subpoena
An order to appear at a particular place and time. A subpoena *duces tecum* requires the person to produce certain documents or things.

- Must be *relevant* to a lawful agency investigation. The FCC is clearly empowered to investigate the safety of broadcasting towers, and any documents about tower construction are obviously relevant. Documents about employee racial statistics might indicate discrimination, but the FCC lacks jurisdiction on that issue and thus may not demand such documents.
- Must not be *unreasonably burdensome.* A court will compare the agency's need for the information with the intrusion on the corporation.
- Must not be *privileged.* The Fifth Amendment privilege against self-incrimination means that a corporate officer accused of criminal securities violations may not be compelled to testify about his behavior.

Search and Seizure. At times an agency will want to conduct a surprise **search** of an enterprise and **seize** any evidence of wrongdoing. May an agency do that? Yes, although there are limitations. When a particular industry is *comprehensively regulated,* courts will assume that companies know they are subject to periodic, unannounced inspections. In those industries, an administrative agency may conduct a search without a warrant and seize evidence of violations. For example, the mining industry is minutely regulated, with strict rules covering equipment, mining depths, and air quality. Mining executives understand that they are closely watched. Accordingly, the Bureau of Mines may make unannounced, warrantless searches to ensure safety.[14]

The following case established many of the principles just described.

[13]For an excellent account of this high-fat hearing, see Mark J. Green, *The Other Government* (New York: W. W. Norton & Co., 1978), pp. 136–150.

[14]*Donovan v. Dewey*, 452 U.S. 594, 101 S. Ct. 2534, 1980 U.S. LEXIS 58 (1981).

Landmark Case

UNITED STATES v. BISWELL

406 U.S. 311
Supreme Court Of The United States (1972)

Facts: Biswell operated a pawnshop and had a license to sell "sporting weapons." Treasury agents demanded to inspect Biswell's locked storeroom. The officials claimed that the Gun Control Act of 1968 gave them the right to search without a warrant.

That law says, in part, "the Secretary [of the Treasury] may enter during business hours the premises of any firearms dealer for the purpose of inspecting or examining (1) any records or documents required to be kept by such dealer, and (2) any firearms or ammunition kept or stored by such dealer."

Biswell voluntarily opened the storeroom, and the agent found two sawed-off rifles inside. The guns did not remotely meet the definition of "sporting weapons," and Biswell was convicted on firearms charges.

The appellate court found that because the search violated the Fourth Amendment, the rifles could not be admitted as evidence. It reversed the conviction, and the government appealed to the Supreme Court.

Issue: ***Did the agent's warrantless search violate the Constitution?***

Excerpts from Justice White's Decision: When the officers asked to inspect respondent's locked storeroom, they were merely asserting their statutory right, and respondent was on notice as to their identity and the legal basis for their action. Respondent's submission to lawful authority and his decision to step aside and permit the inspection rather than face a criminal prosecution is analogous to a householder's acquiescence in a search pursuant to a warrant when the alternative is a possible criminal prosecution for refusing entry or a forcible entry. In neither case does the lawfulness of the search depend on consent; in both, there is lawful authority independent of the will of the householder who might, other things being equal, prefer no search at all.

In the context of a regulatory inspection system of business premises that is carefully limited in time, place, and scope, the legality of the search depends not on consent but on the authority of a valid statute.

Federal regulation of the interstate traffic in firearms is undeniably of central importance to federal efforts to prevent violent crime. Large interests are at stake, and inspection is a crucial part of the regulatory scheme.

Here, if inspection is to be effective and serve as a credible deterrent, unannounced, even frequent, inspections are essential. In this context, the prerequisite of a warrant could easily frustrate inspection; and if the necessary flexibility as to time, scope, and frequency is to be preserved, the protections afforded by a warrant would be negligible.

It is also plain that inspections for compliance with the Gun Control Act pose only limited threats to the dealer's justifiable expectations of privacy. When a dealer chooses to engage in this pervasively regulated business and to accept a federal license, he does so with the knowledge that his business records, firearms, and ammunition will be subject to effective inspection. Each licensee is annually furnished with a revised compilation of ordinances that describe his obligations. The dealer is not left to wonder about the purposes of the inspector or the limits of his task.

We have little difficulty in concluding that where, as here, regulatory inspections further urgent federal interest, and the possibilities of abuse and the threat to privacy are not of impressive dimensions, the inspection may proceed without a warrant where specifically authorized by statute. The seizure of respondent's sawed-off rifles was not unreasonable under the *Fourth Amendment*, the judgment of the Court of Appeals is reversed, and the case is remanded to that court.

Adjudication

To **adjudicate** a case is to hold a hearing about an issue and then decide it. Agencies adjudicate countless cases. The FCC adjudicates which applicant for a new television license is best qualified. The Occupational Safety and Health Administration (OSHA) holds adversarial hearings to determine whether a manufacturing plant is dangerous.

Adjudicate
To hold a formal hearing about an issue and then decide it.

Most adjudications begin with a hearing before an **administrative law judge** (ALJ). There is no jury. An ALJ is an employee of the agency but is expected to be impartial in her rulings. All parties are represented by counsel. The rules of evidence are informal, and an ALJ may receive any testimony or documents that will help resolve the dispute.

Administrative law judge
An agency employee who acts as an impartial decision maker.

After all evidence is taken, the ALJ makes a decision. The losing party has a right to appeal to an appellate board within the agency. The appellate board may ignore the ALJ's decision. If it does not, an unhappy party may appeal to federal court.

Limits on Agency Power

There are four primary methods of reining in these powerful creatures: statutory, political, judicial, and informational.

Statutory Control

As discussed, the enabling legislation of an agency provides some limits. It may require that the agency use formal rulemaking or investigate only certain issues. The Administrative Procedure Act imposes additional controls by requiring basic fairness in areas not regulated by the enabling legislation.

Political Control

The president's influence is greatest with executive agencies. Congress, though, "controls the purse." No agency, executive or independent, can spend money it does not have. An agency that angers Congress risks having a particular program defunded or its entire budget cut. Further, Congress may decide to defund an agency as a cost-cutting measure. In its effort to balance the budget, Congress abolished the Interstate Commerce Commission, transferring its functions to the Transportation Department.

Congress has additional control because it must approve presidential nominees to head agencies. Before approving a nominee, Congress will attempt to determine her intentions. And, finally, Congress may amend an agency's enabling legislation, limiting its power.

Judicial Review

An individual or corporation directly harmed by an administrative rule, investigation, or adjudication may generally have that action reviewed in federal court.[15] The party seeking review, for example, a corporation, must have suffered direct harm; the courts will not listen

[15] In two narrow groups of cases, a court may not review an agency action. In a few cases, courts hold that a decision is "committed to agency discretion," a formal way of saying that courts will keep hands off. This happens only with politically sensitive issues, such as international air routes. In some cases, the enabling legislation makes it absolutely clear that Congress wanted no court to review certain decisions. Courts will honor that.

to theoretical complaints about an agency action.[16] And that party must first have taken all possible appeals within the agency itself.[17]

Standard on Review

Suppose OSHA promulgates a new rule limiting the noise level within steel mills. Certain mill operators are furious because they will have to retool their mills in order to comply. After exhausting their administrative appeals, they file suit seeking to force OSHA to withdraw the new rule. How does a court decide the case? Or, in legal terms, what standard does a court use in reviewing the case? Does it simply substitute its own opinion for that of the agency? No, it does not. The standard a court uses must take into account:

Facts. Courts generally defer to an agency's fact finding. If OSHA finds that human hearing starts to suffer when decibels reach a particular level, a court will probably accept that as final. The agency is presumed to have expertise on such subjects. As long as there is *substantial evidence* to support the fact decision, it will be respected.

Law. Courts often—but not always—defer to an agency's interpretation of the law. This is due in part to the enormous range of subjects that administrative agencies monitor. Consider the following example. "Chicken catchers" work in large poultry operations, entering coops, manually capturing broilers, loading them into cages, and driving them to a processing plant where they... well, never mind. On one farm, the catchers wanted to organize a union, but the company objected, pointing out that *agricultural* workers had no right to do so. Were chicken catchers agricultural workers? The National Labor Relations Board, an administrative agency, declared that chicken catchers were in fact *ordinary* workers, entitled to organize. The Supreme Court ruled that courts were obligated to give deference to the agency's decision about chicken catchers. If the agency's interpretation was *reasonable* it was binding, even if the court itself might not have made the same analysis. The workers were permitted to form a union—though the chickens were not.

The following case contains vulgar language, so *please do not read it.*

Fox Television Stations, Inc. v. Federal Communications Commission

613 F.3d 317
Second Circuit Court of Appeals, 2010

Facts: "People have been telling me I'm on the way out every year, right? So f*** 'em," said Cher, on a televised Billboard Music Awards ceremony. A year later, on the same program, Nicole Richie asked, "Have you ever tried to get cow s*** out of a Prada purse? It's not so f****** simple." The FCC, which regulates the broadcast industry, received complaints about this and other profanity on the airwaves.

[16]The law describes this requirement by saying that a party must have standing to bring a case. A college student who has a theoretical belief that the EPA should not interfere with the timber industry has no standing to challenge an EPA rule that prohibits logging in a national forest. A lumber company that was ready to log that area has suffered a direct economic injury: it has standing to sue.

[17]This is the doctrine of exhaustion of remedies. A lumber company may not go into court the day after the EPA publishes a proposed ban on logging. It must first exhaust its administrative remedies by participating in the administrative hearing and then pursuing appeals within the agency before venturing into court.

The FCC declared that these words were *invariably* indecent, explicit, and shocking. Their utterance violated the Commission's decency standards, and the Commission had the right to fine the networks for broadcasting them. The networks protested, arguing that the utterances were fleeting and isolated. They claimed that the Commission had traditionally permitted such sporadic usage, that this new ruling was an arbitrary change of policy, and that it violated the networks' First Amendment free speech rights. The Commission disagreed, declaring that it had the right to prohibit even the *occasional* use of the words. The networks appealed to federal court.

Issue: ***Did the FCC abuse its discretion and violate the First Amendment by prohibiting even the occasional use of profanity?***

Excerpts from Judge Pooler's Decision: In 2001, in an attempt to provide guidance to the broadcast industry regarding enforcement policies, the FCC issued a statement in which it explained that an indecency finding involved the following two determinations: (1) whether the material describe[s] or depict[s] sexual or excretory organs or activities; and (2) whether the broadcast is patently offensive as measured by contemporary community standards for the broadcast medium. The Industry Guidance reiterated that fleeting and isolated expletives were not actionably indecent.

In 2004, however, the FCC's policy on indecency changed. During the 2003 Golden Globe Awards, U2 band member Bono exclaimed, upon receiving an award, "this is really, really, f****** brilliant." In response to complaints filed after the incident, the FCC declared, for the first time, that a single, nonliteral use of an expletive (a so-called "fleeting expletive") could be actionably indecent.

A law or regulation is impermissibly vague if it does not "give the person of ordinary intelligence a reasonable opportunity to know what is prohibited." The First Amendment places a special burden on the government to ensure that restrictions on speech are not impermissibly vague.

The Networks argue that the FCC's indecency test is unconstitutionally vague because it provides no clear guidelines as to what is covered and thus forces broadcasters to steer far wider of the unlawful zone, rather than risk massive fines. The FCC argues that the indecency policy in its Industry Guidance, together with its subsequent decisions, give the broadcasters sufficient notice as to what will be considered indecent.

We agree with the Networks that the indecency policy is impermissibly vague. As we stated in a previous opinion:

> Although the Commission has declared that all variants of "f***" and "s***" are presumptively indecent and profane, repeated use of those words in "Saving Private Ryan," for example, was neither indecent nor profane. And while multiple occurrences of expletives in "Saving Private Ryan" was not gratuitous, a single occurrence in the Golden Globe Awards was shocking and gratuitous.

There is little rhyme or reason to these decisions and broadcasters are left to guess.

The FCC's application of its policy to live broadcasts creates an even more profound chilling effect. In the case of the 2003 Billboard Music Awards broadcasts, Fox had an audio delay system in place to bleep fleeting expletives. It also pre-cleared the scripts of the presenters. Ritchie, however, departed from her script and used three expletives in rapid sequence. While the person employed to monitor and bleep expletives was bleeping the first, the following two slipped through. Even elaborate precautions will not protect a broadcaster against such occurrences. In fact, the only way that Fox can be sure that it won't be sanctioned by the FCC is by refusing to air the broadcast live. The absence of reliable guidance in the FCC's standards chills a vast amount of protected speech.

For the foregoing reasons, we strike down the FCC's indecency policy.

Informational Control and the Public

We started this section describing the pervasiveness of administrative agencies. We should end it by noting one way in which all of us have some direct control over these ubiquitous authorities: information.

> A popular government, without popular information, or the means of acquiring it, is but a Prologue to a Farce or a Tragedy—or perhaps both. Knowledge will forever govern ignorance, and a people who mean to be their own Governors must arm themselves with the power which knowledge gives.
>
> *James Madison, President, 1809–17*

Two federal statutes arm us with the power of knowledge.

Freedom of Information Act

Congress passed the landmark Freedom of Information Act (known as "FOIA") in 1966. It is designed to give all of us, citizens, businesses, and organizations alike, access to the information that federal agencies are using. The idea is to avoid government by secrecy.

Any citizen or executive may make a "FOIA request" to any federal government agency. It is simply a written request that the agency furnish whatever information it has on the subject specified. Two types of data are available under FOIA. Anyone is entitled to information about how the agency operates, how it spends its money, and what statistics and other information it has collected on a given subject. People routinely obtain records about agency policies, environmental hazards, consumer product safety, taxes and spending, purchasing decisions, and agency forays into foreign affairs. A corporation that believes that OSHA is making more inspections of its textile mills than it makes of the competition could demand all relevant information, including OSHA's documents on the mill itself, comparative statistics on different inspections, OSHA's policies on choosing inspection sites, and so forth.

Second, all citizens are entitled to any records the government has *about them*. You are entitled to information that the Internal Revenue Service, or the Federal Bureau of Investigation, has collected about you.

FOIA does not apply to Congress, the federal courts, or the executive staff at the White House. Note also that, since FOIA applies to federal government agencies, you may not use it to obtain information from state or local governments or private businesses.

Exemptions. An agency officially has 10 days to respond to the request. In reality, most agencies are unable to meet the deadline but are obligated to make good faith efforts. FOIA exempts altogether nine categories from disclosure. The most important exemptions permit an agency to keep confidential information that relates to national security, criminal investigations, internal agency matters such as personnel or policy discussions, trade secrets or financial institutions, or an individual's private life.

Privacy Act

This 1974 statute prohibits federal agencies from giving information about an individual to other agencies or organizations without written consent. There are exceptions, but overall this act has reduced the government's exchange of information about us "behind our back."

EXAM Strategy

Question: Builder wants to develop 1,000 acres in rural Montana, land that is home to the Kite Owl. The EPA rules that the Kite Owl is an endangered species, and prohibits development of the property. The developer appeals to court. The EPA based its decision on five statistical studies, and the opinions of three out of seven experts. The court looks at the same evidence and acknowledges that the EPA decision is carefully reasoned and fair. However, the judges believe that the other four experts were right: the owl is *not* endangered. Should the court permit development?

Strategy: What is the legal standard for deciding whether a court should affirm or reverse an agency decision? As long as there is *substantial evidence* to support the factual conclusions, and a *reasonable basis* for the legal conclusion, the court should not impose its judgment. Agencies are presumed to have special expertise in their areas. As the *Fox Television* case tells us, an agency ruling should generally be affirmed unless it is arbitrary and capricious. Apply that standard here.

Result: The EPA made a careful, reasoned decision. The court may disagree, but it should not impose its views. The court must affirm the agency's ruling and prohibit development.

Chapter Conclusion

"Why can't they just fix the law?" They can, and sometimes they do—but it is a difficult and complex task. "They" includes a great many people and forces, from common law courts to members of Congress to campaign donors to administrative agencies. The courts have made the bystander rule slightly more humane, but it has been a long and bumpy road. Congress managed to restore the legal interpretation of its own 1964 Civil Rights Act, but it took months of debate and compromising. The FDA squeezed more peanuts into a jar of Jif, but it took nearly a decade to get the lid on.

A study of law is certain to create some frustrations. This chapter cannot prevent them all. However, an understanding of how law is made is the first step toward controlling that law.

Exam Review

1. **COMMON LAW** The common law evolves in awkward fits and starts because courts attempt to achieve two contradictory purposes: predictability and flexibility. (pp. 77–79)

2. **STARE DECISIS** *Stare decisis* means "let the decision stand," and indicates that once a court has decided a particular issue, it will generally apply the same rule in future cases. (p. 77)

3. **BYSTANDER RULE** The common law bystander rule holds that, generally, no one has a duty to assist someone in peril unless the bystander himself created the danger. Courts have carved some exceptions during the last 100 years, but the basic rule still stands. (pp. 77–79)

4. **LEGISLATION** Bills originate in congressional committees and go from there to the full House of Representatives or Senate. If both houses pass the bill, the legislation normally must go to a Conference Committee to resolve differences between the two versions. The compromise version then goes from the Conference Committee back to both houses, and if passed by both, to the president. If the president signs the bill, it becomes a statute; if he vetoes it, Congress can pass it over his veto with a two-thirds majority in each house. (pp. 80–83)

5. **STATUTORY INTERPRETATION** Courts interpret a statute by using the plain meaning rule; then, if necessary, legislative history and intent; and finally, if necessary, public policy. (p. 83)

EXAM Strategy

Question: Whitfield, who was black, worked for Ohio Edison. Edison fired him, but then later offered to rehire him. Another employee argued that Edison's original termination of Whitfield had been race discrimination. Edison rescinded its offer to rehire Whitfield. Whitfield sued Edison, claiming that the company was retaliating for the other employee's opposition to discrimination. Edison pointed out that Title VII of the 1964 Civil Rights Act did not explicitly apply in such cases. Among other things, Title VII prohibits an employer from retaliating against *an employee* who has opposed illegal discrimination. But it does not say anything about retaliation based on *another employee's* opposition to discrimination. Edison argued that the statute did not protect Whitfield.

Strategy: What three steps does a court use to interpret a statute? First, the plain meaning rule. Does that rule help us here? The statute neither allows nor prohibits Edison's conduct. The law does not mention this situation, and the plain meaning rule is of no help. Second step: Legislative history and intent. What did Congress intend with Title VII generally? With the provision that bars retaliation against a protesting employee? Resolving those issues should give you the answer to this question. (See the "Result" at the end of this section.)

6. **ADMINISTRATIVE AGENCIES** Congress creates federal administrative agencies with enabling legislation. The Administrative Procedure Act controls how agencies do their work. (pp. 87–89)

7. **RULEMAKING** Agencies may promulgate legislative rules, which generally have the effect of statutes, or interpretive rules, which merely interpret existing statutes. (pp. 89–91)

8. **INVESTIGATION** Agencies have broad investigatory powers and may use subpoenas and, in some cases, warrantless searches to obtain information. (pp. 91–93)

EXAM Strategy

Question: When Hiller Systems, Inc., was performing a safety inspection on board the M/V *Cape Diamond,* an ocean-going vessel, an accident killed two men. The Occupational Safety and Health Administration (OSHA), a federal agency, attempted to investigate, but Hiller refused to permit any of its employees to speak to OSHA investigators. What could OSHA do to pursue the investigation? What limits would there have been on OSHA's actions?

Strategy: Agencies make rules, investigate, and adjudicate. Which is involved here? Investigation. During an investigation, what power has an agency to force a company to produce data? What are the limits on that power? (See the "Result" at the end of this section.)

9. **ADJUDICATION** Agencies adjudicate cases, meaning that they hold hearings and decide issues. Adjudication generally begins with a hearing before an administrative law judge and may involve an appeal to the full agency or ultimately to federal court. (p. 93)

10. **AGENCY LIMITATIONS** The four most important limitations on the power of federal agencies are statutory control in the enabling legislation and the APA; political control by Congress and the president; judicial review; and the informational control created by the FOIA and the Privacy Act. (pp. 93–95)

5. Result: Congress passed Title VII as a bold, aggressive move to end race discrimination in employment. Further, by specifically prohibiting retaliation against an employee, Congress indicated it was aware that companies might punish those who spoke in favor of the very goals of Title VII. Protecting an employee from anti-discrimination statements made by a *co-worker* is a very slight step beyond that, and appears consistent with the goals of Title VII and the anti-retaliation provision. Whitfield should win, and in the real case, he did.[18]

9. Result: OSHA can issue a subpoena *duces tecum*, demanding that those on board the ship, and their supervisors, appear for questioning, and bring with them all relevant documents. OSHA may ask for anything that is (1) relevant to the investigation, (2) not unduly burdensome, and (3) not privileged. Conversations between one of the ship inspectors and his supervisor is clearly relevant; a discussion between the supervisor and the company's lawyer is privileged.

Multiple-Choice Questions

1. A bill is vetoed by ___________.
   (a) the Speaker of the House
   (b) a majority of the voting members of the Senate
   (c) the president
   (d) the Supreme Court

2. If a bill is vetoed, it may still become law if it is approved by ___________.
   (a) two-thirds of the Supreme Court
   (b) two-thirds of registered voters
   (c) two-thirds of the Congress
   (d) the president
   (e) an independent government agency

3. Which of the following presidents was most influential in the passing of the Civil Rights Act?
   (a) Franklin D. Roosevelt
   (b) Ronald Reagan
   (c) Abraham Lincoln
   (d) John F. Kennedy
   (e) George W. Bush

[18] *EEOC v. Ohio Edison*, 7 F.3d 541 (6th Cir. 1993).

4. Under FOIA, any citizen may demand information about ____________.
   (a) how an agency operates
   (b) how an agency spends its money
   (c) files that an agency has collected on the citizen herself
   (d) all of the above

5. If information requested under FOIA is not exempt, an agency has ____________ to comply with the request.
   (a) 10 days
   (b) 30 days
   (c) 3 months
   (d) 6 months

Essay Questions

1. Until recently, every state had a statute outlawing the burning of American flags. But in *Texas v. Johnson*,[19] the Supreme Court declared such statutes unconstitutional, saying that flag burning is symbolic speech protected by the First Amendment. Does Congress have the power to overrule the Court's decision?

2. In 1988, terrorists bombed Pan Am Flight 103 over Lockerbie, Scotland, killing all passengers on board. Congress sought to remedy security shortcomings by passing the Aviation Security Improvement Act of 1990, which, among other things, ordered the Federal Aviation Authority (FAA) to prescribe minimum training requirements and staffing levels for airport security. The FAA promulgated rules according to the informal rulemaking process. However, the FAA refused to disclose certain rules concerning training at specific airports. A public interest group called Public Citizen, Inc., along with family members of those who had died at Lockerbie, wanted to know the details of airport security. What steps should they take to obtain the information? Are they entitled to obtain it?

3. The Aviation Security Improvement Act (ASIA) states that the FAA can refuse to divulge information about airport security. The FAA interprets this to mean that it can withhold data in spite of the FOIA. Public Citizen and the Lockerbie family members interpret FOIA as being the controlling statute, requiring disclosure. Is the FAA interpretation binding?

4. An off-duty, out-of-uniform police officer and his son purchased some food from a 7-Eleven store and were still in the parking lot when a carload of teenagers became rowdy. The officer went to speak to them, and the teenagers assaulted him. The officer shouted to his son to get the 7-Eleven clerk to call for help. The son entered the store, told the clerk that a police officer needed help, and instructed the clerk to call the police. He returned 30 seconds later and repeated the request, urging the clerk to say it was a Code 13. The son claimed that the clerk laughed at him and refused to do it. The policeman sued the store. **Argument for the Store:** We sympathize with the policeman and his family, but the store has no liability.

[19] 491 U.S. 397, 109 S. Ct. 2533, 1989 U.S. LEXIS 3115 (1989).

A bystander is not obligated to come to the aid of anyone in distress unless the bystander created the peril, and obviously the store did not do so. The policeman should sue those who attacked him. **Argument for the Police Officer:** We agree that in general a bystander has no obligation to come to the aid of one in distress. However, when a business that is open to the public receives an urgent request to call the police, the business should either make the call or permit someone else to do it

5. Federal antitrust statutes are complex, but the basic goal is straightforward: to prevent a major industry from being so dominated by a small group of corporations that they destroy competition and injure consumers. Does Major League Baseball violate the antitrust laws? Many observers say that it does. A small group of owners not only dominate the industry, but actually *own* it, controlling the entry of new owners into the game. This issue went to the United States Supreme Court in 1922. Justice Holmes ruled, perhaps surprisingly, that baseball is exempt from the antitrust laws, holding that baseball is not "trade or commerce." Suppose that members of Congress dislike this ruling and the current condition of baseball. What can they do?

Discussion Questions

1. Courts generally follow precedent, but in the *Tarasoff* and *Soldano* cases discussed earlier in this chapter, they did not. Consider the opening scenario at the Old Abandoned Mill. *Should* the hiker bear any *legal* responsibility for Gary's untimely end; or should a court follow precedent and hold the lazy hiker blameless?

2. Revisit the *Fox Television Stations* case. Do you agree with the opinion? What would a sensible broadcast obscenity policy contain? When (if ever) should a network face fines for airing bad language?

3. In 2010, President Barack Obama signed a major health care reform bill into law. Seventeen state attorneys general filed a lawsuit challenging the constitutionality of the new statute. A key argument in the case will revolve around "interstate commerce." The states will argue that a provision in the law that requires Americans to purchase health insurance or face fines should be struck down because the Constitution allows for the *regulation* of commerce but does not allow the federal government to require people to *participate in* commerce; that is, to buy something.

   Does this argument seem sensible to you? Should the government be able to require those who can afford to purchase health insurance to purchase it?

4. FOIA applies to government agencies, but it exempts Congress. Should top lawmakers be obligated to comply with FOIA requests, or would that create more problems than it would solve?

5. Suppose you were on a state supreme court and faced with a restaurant-choking case. Should you require restaurant employees to know and employ the Heimlich maneuver to assist a choking victim? If they do a bad job, they could cause additional injury. Should you permit them to do nothing at all? Is there a compromise position? What social policies are most important?

CHAPTER 5

CONSTITUTIONAL LAW

© r.nagy/Shutterstock.com

The consultant started his presentation to the energy company's board of directors. "So I don't have to tell you that if the Smith-Jones bill ever passes Congress, it will be an utter disaster for your company. The House has already passed it. The president wants it. The only thing that kept it from becoming law this summer is that the Senate was too chicken to bring it up for a vote in an election year.

"Here's the bottom line: to be comfortable, you need three candidates who see things your way to beat current senators who support the bill."

The next slide showed a large map of the United States with three states highlighted in red. "These are your best bets. Attempting wins here would cost $60 million total—not so much for a billion-dollar-a-year operation like yours.

> "In state #3, we go negative. Really negative."

"The money would go to saturation advertising from Labor Day to Election Day. I want to buy TV ads during local news programs all day, and during most prime time shows. I want the viewers to see your ads at least a dozen times before they go to the polls.

"In state #1, the challenger—your candidate—is a squeaky-clean state representative, but no one knows much about her outside her own district. She carries herself well, has a nice family. People will like her if they see her. Your money makes sure people will see her.

"In state #2, your guy hasn't really done much. But his grandfather was a hero at Normandy, and his dad was a coal miner. Great-grandparents were immigrants who came through New York with nothing in their pockets—I can see the ad with the Statue of Liberty already. A lot of voters will appreciate his family's story. This strategy will work if we have the funds to tell the story often enough.

"In state #3, we go negative. Really negative. Our opponent has been in the Senate a long time, and he's taken maybe 100,000 photos. We have three of them showing him with world leaders who have become unpopular of late. We're going to use them to tell a story about the senator putting foreign interests above American jobs and national security. People are angry—they think America is losing its place in the world. Our polling shows that this kind of campaign will be highly effective.

"You need to get into this election. All of your stakeholders benefit if the Smith-Jones bill dies—your workers stay on the job, your shareholders make more money, and your customers pay lower prices. Corporations are nothing more or less than the people who work for them, and they have the right to express their political opinions. These ads would simply give your workers the chance to exercise their right to free speech."

The CFO interrupted, "Look, we're all against the Smith-Jones bill. But is this plan *legal*?"

Government Power

One in a Million

The Constitution of the United States is the greatest legal document ever written. No other written constitution has lasted so long, governed so many, or withstood such challenge. This amazing work was drafted in 1787, when two weeks were needed to make the horseback ride from Boston to Philadelphia, a pair of young cities in a weak and disorganized nation. Yet today, when that trip requires less than two hours by jet, the same Constitution successfully governs the most powerful country on earth. This longevity is a tribute to the wisdom and idealism of the Founding Fathers.The Constitution is not perfect, but overall, it has worked astonishingly well and has become the model for many constitutions around the world.

The Constitution sits above everything else in our legal system. No law can conflict with it. The chapter opener raises a constitutional issue: does Congress have the right to prohibit corporations from spending money to affect elections, or are these actions protected as free speech under the First Amendment? We will explore this later in the chapter when we discuss the *Citizens United* case.

The Constitution is short and relatively easy to read. This brevity is potent. The Founding Fathers, or **Framers**, wanted it to last for centuries, and they understood that would happen only if the document permitted interpretation and "fleshing out" by later generations. The Constitution's versatility is striking. In this chapter, the first part provides an overview of the Constitution, discussing how it came to be and how it is organized. The second part describes the power given to the three branches of government. The third part explains the individual rights the Constitution guarantees to citizens.

Overview

Thirteen American colonies declared independence from Great Britain in 1776, and gained it in 1783. The new status was exhilarating. Ours was the first nation in modern history founded on the idea that the people could govern themselves, democratically. The idea was daring, brilliant, and fraught with difficulties. The states were governing themselves under the Articles of Confederation, but these articles gave the central government no real power. The government could not tax any state or its citizens and had no way to raise money. The national government also lacked the power to regulate commerce between the states or between foreign nations and any state. This was disastrous. States began to impose taxes on goods entering from other states. The young "nation" was a collection of poor relations, threatening to squabble themselves to death.

In 1787, the states sent a group of 55 delegates to Philadelphia. Rather than amend the old articles, the Framers set out to draft a new document and to create a government that had never existed before. It was hard going. What structure should the government have? How much power? Representatives like Alexander Hamilton, a *federalist*, urged a strong central government. The new government must be able to tax and spend, regulate commerce, control the borders, and do all things that national governments routinely do. But Patrick Henry and other *antifederalists* feared a powerful central government. They had fought a bitter war precisely to get rid of autocratic rulers; they had seen the evil that a distant government could inflict. The antifederalists insisted that the states retain maximum authority, keeping political control closer to home.

The debate continues to this day, and periodically it plays a key role in elections. The "tea party" movement, for example, is a modern group of antifederalists with a growing political influence.

Another critical question was how much power the *people* should have. Many of the delegates had little love for the common people and feared that extending this idea of democracy too far would lead to mob rule. Antifederalists again disagreed. The British had been thrown out, they insisted, to guarantee individual liberty and a chance to participate in the government. Power corrupted. It must be dispersed amongst the people to avoid its abuse.

How to settle these basic differences? By compromise, of course. **The Constitution is a series of compromises about power.** We will see many provisions granting power to one branch of the government while at the same time restraining the authority given.

Separation of Powers

The Framers did not want to place too much power in any single place. One method of limiting power was to create a national government divided into three branches, each independent and equal. Each branch would act as a check on the power of the other two. Article I of the Constitution created a Congress, which was to have legislative, or lawmaking, power. Article II created the office of president, defining the scope of executive, or enforcement, power. Article III established judicial, or interpretive, power by creating the Supreme Court and permitting additional federal courts.

Consider how the three separate powers balance one another: Congress was given the power to pass statutes, a major grant of power. But the president was permitted to veto, or block, proposed statutes, a nearly equal grant. Congress, in turn, had the right to override the veto, ensuring that the president would not become a dictator. The president was allowed to appoint federal judges and members of his cabinet, but only with a consenting vote from the Senate.

Individual Rights

The original Constitution was silent about the rights of citizens. This alarmed many who feared that the new federal government would have unlimited power over their lives. So in 1791 the first 10 amendments, known as the **Bill of Rights,** were added to the Constitution, guaranteeing many liberties directly to individual citizens.

In the next two sections, we look in more detail at the two sides of the great series of compromises: power granted and rights protected.

POWER GRANTED

Congressional Power

To recap two key ideas from Chapter 1:

1. Voters in all 50 states elect representatives who go to Washington, D.C., to serve in Congress.
2. The Congress is comprised of the House of Representatives and the Senate. The House has 435 voting members, and states with large populations send more representatives. The Senate has 100 members—two from each state.

Congress wields tremendous power. Its members create statutes that influence our jobs, money, health care, military, communications, and virtually everything else. But can Congress create *any* kind of law that it wishes? No.

Article I, section 8 is a critically important part of the Constitution. It lists the 18 types of statutes that Congress is allowed to pass, such as imposing taxes, declaring war, and coining money. Thus, only the national government may create currency. The state of Texas cannot print $20 bills with George W. Bush's profile.

States like Texas *are* supposed to create all other kinds of laws for themselves because the Tenth Amendment says, "All powers not delegated to the United States by the Constitution ... are reserved to the States."

The **Commerce Clause** is the specific item in Article I, Section 8, most important to your future as a businessperson. It calls upon Congress "to regulate commerce ... among the several States," and its impact is described in the next section.

Commerce Clause
The part of Article I, Section 8, that gives Congress the power to regulate commerce with foreign nations and among states.

Interstate Commerce

With the Commerce Clause, the Framers sought to accomplish several things in response to the commercial chaos that existed under the Articles of Confederation. They wanted the federal government to speak with one voice when regulating commercial relations with foreign governments.[1] The Framers also wanted to give Congress the power to bring coordination and fairness to trade among the states, and to stop the states from imposing the taxes and regulations that were wrecking the nation's domestic trade.

Virtually all of the numerous statutes that affect businesses are passed under the Commerce Clause. But what does it mean to regulate interstate commerce? Are all business transactions "interstate commerce," or are there exceptions? In the end, the courts must interpret what the Constitution means.

Substantial Effect Rule

An important test of the Commerce Clause came in the Depression years of the 1930s, in *Wickard v. Filburn*.[2] The price of wheat and other grains had fluctuated wildly, severely harming farmers and the national food market. Congress sought to stabilize prices by limiting the bushels per acre that a farmer could grow. Filburn grew more wheat than federal law allowed and was fined. In defense, he claimed that Congress had no right to regulate him because none of his wheat went into *interstate* commerce. He sold some locally and used the rest on his own farm as food for livestock and as seed. The Commerce Clause, Filburn claimed, gave Congress no authority to limit what he could do.

[1] *Michelin Tire Corp. v. Wages, Tax Commissioner*, 423 U.S. 276, 96 S. Ct. 535, 1976 U.S. LEXIS 120 (1976).
[2] 317 U.S. 111, 63 S. Ct. 82, 1942 U.S. LEXIS 1046 (1942).

The Supreme Court disagreed and held that **Congress may regulate any activity that has a substantial economic effect on interstate commerce.** Filburn's wheat *affected* interstate commerce because the more he grew for use on his own farm, the less he would need to buy in the open market of interstate commerce. In the end, "interstate commerce" does not require that things travel from one state to another.

In *United States v. Lopez,*[3] however, the Supreme Court ruled that Congress *had* exceeded its power under the Commerce Clause. Congress had passed a criminal statute called the "Gun-Free School Zones Act," which forbade any individual from possessing a firearm in a school zone. The goal of the statute was obvious: to keep schools safe. Lopez was convicted of violating the act and appealed his conviction all the way to the high Court, claiming that Congress had no power to pass such a law. The government argued that the Commerce Clause gave it the power to pass the law, but the Supreme Court was unpersuaded.

> The possession of a gun in a local school zone is in no sense an economic activity that might, through repetition elsewhere, substantially affect any sort of interstate commerce. [Lopez] was a local student at a local school; there is no indication that he had recently moved in interstate commerce, and there is no requirement that his possession of the firearm have any concrete tie to interstate commerce. To uphold the Government's contentions here, we would have to pile inference upon inference in a manner that would bid fair to convert congressional authority under the Commerce Clause to a general police power of the sort retained by the States. [The statute was unconstitutional and void.]
>
> Congress's power is great—but still limited.

Current Application: The Affordable Healthcare Act. In 2010, Congress passed the Affordable Healthcare Act and President Barack Obama signed it into law. The wide-ranging legislation may result in as many as 30 million uninsured Americans gaining health care coverage. Almost immediately after it passed, many states sued and argued that the law violated the Constitution by exceeding Congress's power to regulate interstate commerce.

The challenge centers on a provision (which the press refers to as the "individual mandate") in the Act that requires many people to purchase health insurance or face fines. The states argue that requiring people to buy something is fundamentally different from regulating people who *voluntarily* decided to participate in commerce.

At this writing, the lower courts are divided on whether the healthcare statute is constitutional. The Supreme Court will surely have the final word. In the end, the fate of this law hinges upon how the justices define "commerce."

State Legislative Power

The "dormant" or "negative" aspect of the Commerce Clause governs state efforts to regulate interstate commerce. **The dormant aspect holds that a state statute which discriminates against interstate commerce is almost always unconstitutional.** Here is an example, but please do not read it if you plan to drive later today. Michigan and New York permitted in-state wineries to sell directly to consumers. They both denied this privilege to out-of-state producers, who were forced to sell to wholesalers, who offered the wine to retailers, who sold to consumers. This created an impossible barrier for many small vineyards, which did not produce enough wine to attract wholesalers. Even if they did, the multiple resales drove their prices prohibitively high.

Local residents and out-of-state wineries sued, claiming that the state regulations violated the dormant Commerce Clause. The Supreme Court ruled that these statutes obviously discriminated against out-of-state vineyards; the schemes were illegal unless Michigan and

[3]514 U.S. 549, 115 S. Ct. 1624, 1995 U.S. LEXIS 3039 (1995).

New York could demonstrate an important goal that could not be met any other way. The states' alleged motive was to prevent minors from purchasing wine over the Internet. However, Michigan and New York offered no evidence that such purchases were really a problem. The Court said that minors seldom drink wine, and when they do, they seek instant gratification, not a package in the mail. States that allowed direct shipment to consumers reported no increase in purchases by minors. This discrimination against interstate commerce, like most, was unconstitutional.[4]

Devil's Advocate Underage drinking is a serious problem. The Court should allow states wide leeway in their efforts to limit the harm. Even if the regulations are imperfect, they may help reduce the damage.

Supremacy Clause

What happens when both the federal and state governments pass regulations that are permissible, but conflicting? For example, Congress passed the federal Occupational Safety and Health Act (OSHA) establishing many job safety standards, including those for training workers who handle hazardous waste. Congress had the power to do so under the Commerce Clause. Later, Illinois passed its own hazardous waste statutes, seeking to protect both the general public and workers. The state statute did not violate the Commerce Clause because it imposed no restriction on interstate commerce.

Each statute specified worker training and employer licensing. But the requirements differed. Which statute did Illinois corporations have to obey? Article VI of the Constitution contains the answer. **The Supremacy Clause** states that the Constitution, and federal statutes and treaties, shall be the supreme law of the land.

The Supremacy Clause
Makes the Constitution, and federal statutes and treaties, the supreme law of the land.

- If there is a conflict between federal and state statutes, the federal law **preempts** the field, meaning it controls the issue. The state law is void.
- Even in cases where there is no conflict, if Congress demonstrates that it intends to exercise exclusive control over an issue, federal law preempts.

Thus state law controls only when there is no conflicting federal law *and* Congress has not intended to dominate the issue. In the Illinois case, the Supreme Court concluded that Congress intended to regulate the issue exclusively. Federal law therefore preempted the field, and local employers were obligated to obey only the federal regulations.

EXAM Strategy

Question: Dairy farming was more expensive in Massachusetts than in other states. To help its farmers, Massachusetts taxed all milk sales, regardless of where the milk was produced. The revenues went into a fund that was then distributed to in-state dairy farmers. Discuss.

[4] *Granholm v. Heald,* 544 U.S. 460, 1255 S.Ct. 1885 (2005).

Strategy: By giving a subsidy to local farmers, the state is treating them differently than out-of-state dairies. This raises Commerce Clause issues. The dormant aspect applies. What does it state? Apply that standard to theses facts.

Result: The dormant aspect holds that a state statute which discriminates against interstate commerce is almost always invalid. Massachusetts was subsidizing its farmers at the expense of those from other states. The tax violates the Commerce Clause and is void.

Executive Power

Article II of the Constitution defines executive power. The president's most basic job function is to enforce the nation's laws. Three of his key powers concern appointment, legislation, and foreign policy.

Appointment

Administrative agencies play a powerful role in business regulation, and the president nominates the heads of most of them. These choices dramatically influence what issues the agencies choose to pursue and how aggressively they do it. For example, a president who seeks to expand the scope of regulations on air quality may appoint a forceful environmentalist to run the Environmental Protection Agency (EPA), whereas a president who dislikes federal regulations will choose a more passive agency head.[5]

Legislation

The president and his advisers propose bills to Congress. During the last 50 years, a vast number of newly proposed bills have come from the executive branch. Some argue that *too many* proposals come from the president and that Congress has become overly passive. When a president proposes controversial legislation on a major issue, such as Social Security reform, the bill can dominate the news—and Congress—for months or even years. The president, of course, also has the power to veto bills.[6]

Foreign Policy

The president conducts the nation's foreign affairs, coordinating international efforts, negotiating treaties, and so forth. The president is also the commander in chief of the armed forces, meaning that he heads the military. But Article II does not give him the right to declare war—only the Senate may do that. A continuing tension between the president and Congress has resulted from the president's use of troops overseas *without* a formal declaration of war.

Judicial Power

Article III of the Constitution creates the Supreme Court and permits Congress to establish lower courts within the federal court system.[7] Federal courts have two key functions: adjudication and judicial review.

---

[5]For a discussion of administrative agency power, see Chapter 4, on administrative law.

[6]For a discussion of the president's veto power and Congress's power to override a veto, see Chapter 4, on statutory law.

[7]For a discussion of the federal court system, see Chapter 3, on dispute resolution.

Adjudicating Cases

The federal court system hears criminal and civil cases. Generally, prosecutions of federal crimes begin in United States District Court. That same court has limited jurisdiction to hear civil lawsuits, a subject discussed in Chapter 3, on dispute resolution.

Judicial Review

One of the greatest "constitutional" powers appears nowhere in the Constitution. In 1803, the Supreme Court decided *Marbury v. Madison.*[8] Congress had passed a relatively minor statute that gave certain powers to the Supreme Court, and Marbury wanted the Court to use those powers. The Court refused. In an opinion written by Chief Justice John Marshall, the Court held that the statute violated the Constitution because Article III of the Constitution did not grant the Court those powers. The details of the case were insignificant, but the ruling was profound: because the statute violated the Constitution, said the Court, it was void. **Judicial review refers to the power of federal courts to declare a statute or governmental action unconstitutional and void.**

Chief Justice John Marshall

This formidable grab of power has produced two centuries of controversy. The Court was declaring that it alone had the right to evaluate acts of the other two branches of government—the Congress and the executive—and to decide which were valid and which void. The Constitution nowhere grants this power. Undaunted, Marshall declared that "[I]t is emphatically the province and duty of the judicial department to say what the law is." In later cases, the Supreme Court expanded on the idea, holding that it could also nullify state statutes, rulings by state courts, and actions by federal and state officials. In this chapter we have already encountered an example of judicial review in the *Lopez* case, where the justices declared that Congress lacked the power to pass local gun regulations.

Is judicial review good for the nation? Those who oppose it argue that federal court judges are all appointed, not elected, and that we should not permit judges to nullify a statute passed by elected officials because that diminishes the people's role in their government. Those who favor judicial review insist that there must be one cohesive interpretation of the Constitution and the judicial branch is the logical one to provide it. The following example of judicial review shows how immediate and emotional the issue can be. This is a criminal prosecution for a brutal crime. Cases like this force us to examine two

Kennedy v. Louisiana

128 S.Ct. 2641
United States Supreme Court, 2008

Facts: Patrick Kennedy raped his eight-year-old stepdaughter. Her injuries were the most severe that the forensic expert had ever seen. Kennedy was convicted of aggravated rape because the victim was under 12 years of age.

The jury voted to sentence Kennedy to death, which was permitted by the Louisiana statute. The state supreme court affirmed the death sentence, and Kennedy appealed to the United States Supreme Court. He argued

[8] 5 U.S. 137, 1 Cranch 137 (1803).

that the Louisiana statute was unconstitutional. The Eighth Amendment prohibits cruel and unusual punishment, which includes penalties that are out of proportion to the crime. Kennedy claimed that capital punishment was out of proportion to rape and violated the Eighth Amendment.

Issues: ***Did the Louisiana statute violate the Constitution by permitting the death penalty in a case of child rape? Is it proper for the Supreme Court to decide this issue?***

Excerpts from Justice Kennedy's Decision: The constitutional prohibition against excessive or cruel and unusual punishments mandates that the State's power to punish be exercised within the limits of civilized standards. Evolving standards of decency that mark the progress of a maturing society counsel us to be most hesitant before interpreting the Eighth Amendment to allow the extension of the death penalty, a hesitation that has special force where no life was taken in the commission of the crime.

Consistent with evolving standards of decency and the teachings of our precedents we conclude that, in determining whether the death penalty is excessive, there is a distinction between intentional first-degree murder on the one hand and nonhomicide crimes against individual persons, even including child rape, on the other. The latter crimes may be devastating in their harm, as here, but in terms of moral depravity and of the injury to the person and to the public, they cannot be compared to murder in their severity and irrevocability.

Louisiana reintroduced the death penalty for rape of a child in 1995. Five States have since followed Louisiana's lead: Georgia, Montana, Oklahoma, South Carolina, and Texas. By contrast, 44 States have not made child rape a capital offense. As for federal law, Congress in the Federal Death Penalty Act of 1994 expanded the number of federal crimes for which the death penalty is a permissible sentence, including certain nonhomicide offenses; but it did not do the same for child rape or abuse. [The court concludes that there is a national consensus against imposing the death penalty for rape, and strikes down the Louisiana statute.]

Justice Alito, dissenting: If anything can be inferred from state legislative developments, the message is very different from the one that the Court perceives. In just the past few years, five States have enacted targeted capital child-rape laws. Such a development would not be out of step with changes in our society's thinking. During that time, reported instances of child abuse have increased dramatically; and there are many indications of growing alarm about the sexual abuse of children.

questions about judicial review. What is the proper punishment for such a horrible crime? Just as important, *who should make that decision*—appointed judges, or elected legislators?

Judicial Activism/Judicial Restraint. The power of judicial review is potentially dictatorial. The Supreme Court nullifies statutes passed by Congress (*Marbury v. Madison*, *United States v. Lopez*) and executive actions. May it strike down any law it dislikes? In theory, no—the Court should nullify only laws that violate the Constitution. But in practice, yes—the Constitution means whatever the majority of the current justices says that it means, since it is the Court that tells us which laws are violative.

Judicial activism
A court's willingness to decide issues on constitutional grounds.

Judicial restraint
A court's attitude that it should leave law making to legislators.

Judicial activism refers to a court's willingness, or even eagerness, to become involved in major issues and to decide cases on constitutional grounds. Activists are sometimes willing to "stretch" laws beyond their most obvious meaning. **Judicial restraint** is the opposite, an attitude that courts should leave lawmaking to legislators and nullify a law only when it unquestionably violates the Constitution. Some justices believe that the Founding Fathers never intended the judicial branch to take a prominent role in sculpting the nation's laws and its social vision.

From the 1950s through the 1970s, the Supreme Court took an activist role, deciding many major social issues on constitutional grounds. The landmark 1954 decision in *Brown v. Board of Education* ordered an end to racial segregation in public schools, not only changing the nation's educational systems but altering forever its expectations about race.[9] The Court also struck down many state laws that denied minorities the right to vote. Beginning with *Miranda v. Arizona*, the Court began a sweeping reappraisal of the police power of the state and the rights of criminal suspects during searches, interrogations, trials, and appeals.[10] And in *Roe v. Wade*, the

9 347 U.S. 483, 74 S. Ct. 686, 1954 U.S. LEXIS 2094 (1954).
10 384 U.S. 436, 86 S. Ct. 1602, 1966 U.S. LEXIS 2817 (1966).

Supreme Court established certain rights to abortion, most of which remain after nearly 40 years of continuous litigation.[11]

Beginning in the late 1970s, and lasting to the present, the Court has pulled back from its social activism. Exhibit 5.1 illustrates the balance among Congress, the president, and the Court.

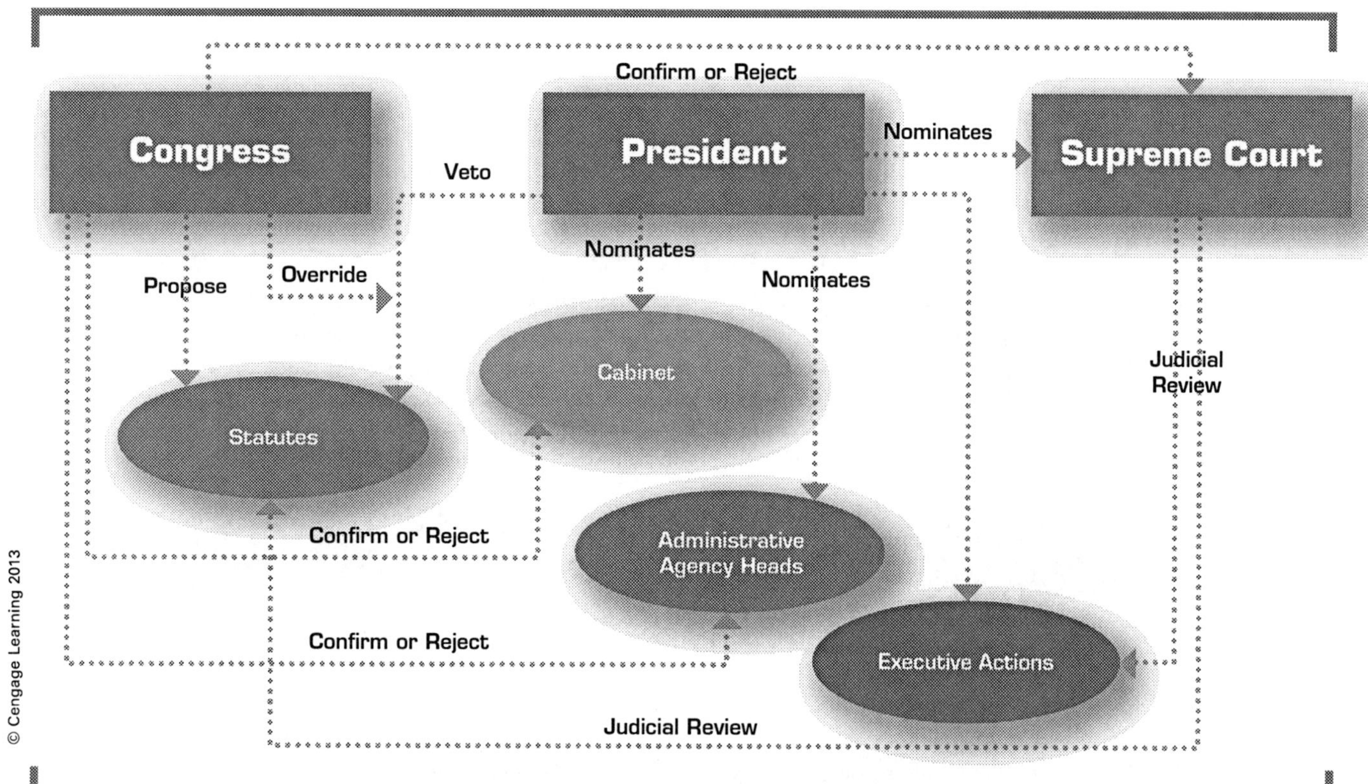

EXHIBIT 5.1 The Constitution established a federal government of checks and balances. Congress may propose statutes; the president may veto them; and Congress may override the veto. The president nominates cabinet officers, administrative heads, and Supreme Court justices, but the Senate must confirm his nominees. Finally, the Supreme Court (and lower federal courts) exercise judicial review over statutes and executive actions. Unlike the other checks and balances, judicial review is not provided for in the Constitution, but is a creation of the Court itself in *Marbury v. Madison.*

PROTECTED RIGHTS

The amendments to the Constitution protect the people of this nation from the power of state and federal government. The First Amendment guarantees rights of free speech, free press, and religion; the Fourth Amendment protects against illegal searches; the Fifth Amendment ensures due process; the Sixth Amendment demands fair treatment for defendants in criminal prosecutions; and the Fourteenth Amendment guarantees equal protection of the law. We consider the First, Fifth, and Fourteenth Amendments in this chapter and the Fourth, Fifth, and Sixth Amendments in Chapter 8, on crime.

[11] 410 U.S. 113, 93 S. Ct. 705, 1973 U.S. LEXIS 159 (1973).

The "people" who are protected include citizens and, for most purposes, corporations. Corporations are considered persons and receive most of the same protections. The great majority of these rights also extend to citizens of other countries who are in the United States.

Constitutional rights generally protect only against governmental acts. The Constitution generally does not protect us from the conduct of private parties, such as corporations or other citizens.

Incorporation

A series of Supreme Court cases has extended virtually all of the important constitutional protections to *all levels* of national, state, and local government. This process is called **incorporation** because rights explicitly guaranteed at one level are incorporated into rights that apply at other levels.

First Amendment: Free Speech

The First Amendment states that "Congress shall make no law ... abridging the freedom of speech...." In general, we expect our government to let people speak and hear whatever they choose. The Founding Fathers believed democracy would work only if the members of the electorate were free to talk, argue, listen, and exchange viewpoints in any way they wanted. The people could only cast informed ballots if they were informed. "Speech" also includes symbolic conduct, as the following case flamingly illustrates.

Texas v. Johnson

491 U.S. 397, 109 S. Ct. 2533, 1989 U.S. LEXIS 3115
United States Supreme Court, 1989

Facts: Outside the Republican National Convention in Dallas, Gregory Johnson participated in a protest against policies of the Reagan administration. Participants gave speeches and handed out leaflets. Johnson burned an American flag. He was arrested and convicted under a Texas statute that prohibited desecrating the flag, but the Texas Court of Criminal Appeals reversed on the grounds that the conviction violated the First Amendment. Texas appealed to the United States Supreme Court.

Issue: ***Does the First Amendment protect flag burning?***

Excerpts from Justice Brennan's Decision: The First Amendment literally forbids the abridgment only of "speech," but we have long recognized that its protection does not end at the spoken or written word. While we have rejected the view that an apparently limitless variety of conduct can be labeled "speech," we have acknowledged that conduct may be sufficiently imbued with elements of communication to fall within the scope of the First and Fourteenth Amendments.

In deciding whether particular conduct possesses sufficient communicative elements to bring the First Amendment into play, we have asked whether an intent to convey a particularized message was present, and [whether] the likelihood was great that the message would be understood by those who viewed it. Hence, we have recognized the expressive nature of students' wearing of black armbands to protest American military involvement in Vietnam; of a sit-in by blacks in a "whites only" area to protest segregation; of the wearing of American military uniforms in a dramatic presentation criticizing American involvement in Vietnam; and of picketing about a wide variety of causes.

[The Court concluded that burning the flag was in fact symbolic speech.]

It remains to consider whether the State's interest in reserving the flag as a symbol of nationhood and national unity justifies Johnson's conviction. Johnson was prosecuted because he knew that his politically charged expression would cause "serious offense."

If there is a bedrock principle underlying the First Amendment, it is that the Government may not prohibit the expression of an idea simply because society finds the idea itself offensive or disagreeable. Nothing in our precedents suggests that a State may foster its own view of the flag by prohibiting expressive conduct relating to it.

Could the Government, on this theory, prohibit the burning of state flags? Of copies of the Presidential seal? Of the Constitution? In evaluating these choices under the First Amendment, how would we decide which symbols were sufficiently special to warrant this unique status? To do so, we would be forced to consult our own political preferences, and impose them on the citizenry, in the very way that the First Amendment forbids us to do.

The way to preserve the flag's special role is not to punish those who feel differently about these matters. It is to persuade them that they are wrong. We can imagine no more appropriate response to burning a flag than waving one's own, no better way to counter a flagburner's message than by saluting the flag that burns, no surer means of preserving the dignity even of the flag that burned than by—as one witness here did—according its remains a respectful burial. We do not consecrate the flag by punishing its desecration, for in doing so we dilute the freedom that this cherished emblem represents.

The judgment of the Texas Court of Criminal Appeals is therefore *affirmed.*

Political Speech

Because the Framers were primarily concerned with enabling democracy to function, political speech has been given an especially high degree of protection. Such speech may not be barred even when it is offensive or outrageous. A speaker, for example, could accuse a U.S. senator of being insane and could use crude, violent language to describe him. The speech is still protected. **Political speech is protected unless it is intended and likely to create imminent lawless action.**[12] For example, suppose the speaker said, "The senator is inside that restaurant. Let's get some matches and burn the place down." Speech of this sort is not protected. The speaker could be arrested for attempted arson or attempted murder.

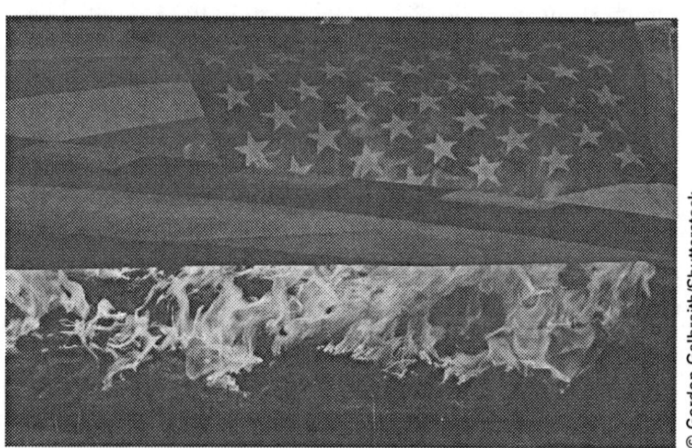

Protected speech?

© Gordon Galbraith/Shutterstock

One of the most important recent developments in constutitional law concerns the ability of *organizations* to engage in political speech. In the case that follows, a sharply divided Supreme Court weighed in on the issue raised in this chapter's opening scenario.

Citizens United v. Federal Election Commission

130 S. Ct. 876
Supreme Court of the United States, 2010

Facts: Citizens United, a nonprofit organization, produced a documentary on presidential candidate Hillary Clinton. The group wanted to run television ads promoting *Hillary: The Movie.* The Bipartisan Campaign Reform Act of 2002 banned "electioneering communication" by corporations and unions for the 30 days before a presidential primary. Citizens United challenged the Act, arguing that it violated the First Amendment.

Issue: ***Did the Bipartisan Campaign Reform Act violate the First Amendment?***

Excerpts from Justice Kennedy's Decision: The First Amendment provides that "Congress shall make no law … abridging the freedom of speech." The law before us makes it a felony for all corporations—including nonprofit advocacy corporations—either to expressly advocate the election

[12]*Brandenburg v. Ohio,* 395 U.S. 444, 89 S. Ct. 1827, 1969 U.S. LEXIS 1367 (1969).

or defeat of candidates or to broadcast electioneering communications within 30 days of a primary election and 60 days of a general election. These prohibitions are classic examples of censorship.

As a restriction on the amount of money a person or group can spend on political communication during a campaign, that statute necessarily reduces the quantity of expression by restricting the number of issues discussed, the depth of their exploration, and the size of the audience reached.

Speech is an essential mechanism of democracy, for it is the means to hold officials accountable to the people. The right of citizens to inquire, to hear, to speak, and to use information to reach consensus is a precondition to enlightened self-government and a necessary means to protect it. For these reasons, political speech must prevail against laws that would suppress it, whether by design or inadvertence.

The Government may not deprive the public of the right and privilege to determine for itself what speech and speakers are worthy of consideration. The First Amendment protects speech and speaker, and the ideas that flow from each.

The Court has recognized that First Amendment protection extends to corporations. This protection has been extended by explicit holdings to the context of political speech. Corporations and other associations, like individuals, contribute to the discussion, debate, and the dissemination of information and ideas that the First Amendment seeks to foster. The Court has thus rejected the argument that political speech of corporations or other associations should be treated differently under the First Amendment simply because such associations are not "natural persons."

The Government falls back on the argument that corporate political speech can be banned in order to prevent corruption or its appearance. We must give weight to attempts by Congress to seek to dispel either the appearance or the reality of these influences. The remedies enacted by law, however, must comply with the First Amendment; and, it is our law and our tradition that more speech, not less, is the governing rule. An outright ban on corporate political speech during the critical preelection period is not a permissible remedy.

Modern-day movies, television comedies, or skits on YouTube might portray public officials or public policies in unflattering ways. Yet if a covered transmission during the blackout period creates the background for candidate endorsement or opposition, a felony occurs solely because a corporation has made the purchase in order to engage in political speech. Speech would be suppressed in the realm where its necessity is most evident: in the public dialogue preceding a real election. Governments are often hostile to speech, but under our law and our tradition it seems stranger than fiction for our Government to make this political speech a crime. Yet this is the statute's purpose and design.

Some members of the public might consider Hillary to be insightful and instructive; some might find it to be neither high art nor a fair discussion on how to set the Nation's course; still others simply might suspend judgment on these points but decide to think more about issues and candidates. Those choices and assessments, however, are not for the Government to make.

The judgment of the District Court is reversed.

It is so ordered.

Time, Place, and Manner

Even when speech is protected, the government may regulate the *time, place,* and *manner* of such speech. A town may require a group to apply for a permit before using a public park for a political demonstration. The town may insist that the demonstration take place during daylight hours and that there be adequate police supervision and sanitation provided. However, the town may not prohibit such demonstrations outright.

Many public universities have designated "free speech zones" located in high-traffic areas of campus which are not immediately adjacent to a large number of classrooms. The zones allow for debates to proceed and reach many students, but they minimize the chances that noisy demonstrations will interfere with lectures.

Morality and Obscenity

The regulation of morality and obscenity presents additional problems. Obscenity has never received constitutional protection. The Supreme Court has consistently held that it does not play a valued role in our society and has refused to give protection to obscene works. That is well and good, but it merely forces the question: what is obscene?

In *Miller v. California*,[13] the Court created a three-part test to determine if a creative work is obscene. The basic guidelines for the factfinder are:

- Whether the average person, applying contemporary community standards, would find that the work, taken as a whole, appeals to the prurient interest;
- Whether the work depicts or describes, in a patently offensive way, sexual conduct specifically defined by the applicable state law; and
- Whether the work, taken as a whole, lacks serious literary, artistic, political, or scientific value.

If the trial court finds that the answer to all three of those questions is "yes," it may judge the material obscene; the state may then prohibit the work. If the state fails to prove any one of the three criteria, though, the work is not obscene.[14] A United States District Court ruled that "As Nasty As They Wanna Be," recorded by 2 Live Crew, was obscene. The appeals court, however, reversed, finding that the state had failed to prove lack of artistic merit.[15]

Commercial Speech

This refers to speech that has a dominant theme to propose a commercial transaction. For example, most advertisements on television and in the newspapers are commercial speech. This sort of speech is protected by the First Amendment, but the government is permitted to regulate it more closely than other forms of speech. Commercial speech that is false or misleading may be outlawed altogether. **The government may regulate other commercial speech, provided that the rules are reasonable, and directed to a legitimate goal.** The following case demonstrates the very different treatment given to this type of speech.

Commercial speech Communication, such as advertisements, that has the dominant theme of proposing a business transaction.

Salib v. City of Mesa

133 P.3d 756, 212 Ariz. 446
Arizona Court of Appeals, 2006

Facts: Edward Salib owned a Winchell's Donut House in Mesa, Arizona. To attract customers, he displayed large signs in his store window. The city ordered him to remove the signs, because they violated its Sign Code, which prohibited covering more than 30% of a store's windows with signs. Salib sued, claiming that the Sign Code violated his First Amendment free speech rights. The trial court gave summary judgment for Mesa, and the store owner appealed.

Issue: ***Did Mesa's Sign Code violate the First Amendment?***

Excerpts from Judge Irvine's Decision: Under [a Supreme Court case called] *Central Hudson*, commercial speech that concerns unlawful activity or is misleading is not protected by the First Amendment. Commercial speech that falls into neither of these categories may be regulated if the government satisfies a three-prong test. First, the government must assert a substantial interest in support of the regulation. Mesa argues, and Salib concedes, that the governmental regulation of aesthetics constitutes a substantial interest, so the first prong of *Central Hudson* is not at issue.

Under the second prong of *Central Hudson*, the government must demonstrate that the challenged regulation advances its interest in a direct and material way. Salib argues that this prong has not been met because no

[13] 413 U.S. 15, 93 S. Ct. 2607, 1973 U.S. LEXIS 149 (1973).
[14] *Penthouse Intern Ltd. v. McAuliffe*, 610 F.2d 1353 (5th Cir. 1980).
[15] *Luke Records, Inc. v. Navarro*, 960 F.2d 134, 1992 U.S. App. LEXIS 9592 (11th Cir. 1992).

studies were conducted to determine what aesthetic or safety problems existed and how the Sign Code could solve such problems.

Mesa responds that the Sign Code was enacted because of legitimate concerns among business owners that many businesses in the area had 100% coverage of their storefront windows and that this total coverage was unattractive and detracted from the aesthetics of the city. The First Amendment does not require a formal study before a regulation may be enacted. The record shows that the city council received considerable input on the subject of window coverage and aesthetics before enacting the Sign Code. Although its final adoption of the Sign Code may have rested on anecdote, history, consensus or simple common sense, rather than a formal study or survey addressed specifically to the window coverage provision, the constitution requires no greater proof.

Salib argues the restriction is not narrow enough and therefore violates the third prong of *Central Hudson*. It is clear from the First Amendment cases that narrowly tailored or narrowly drawn does not mean that the least restrictive means must be used. Rather, a "reasonable fit" between the intent and purpose of the regulation and the means chosen to accomplish those goals is required. The regulation does not have to be perfect, but its scope must be in proportion to the interest served.

Mesa argues that 30% is a reasonable compromise between 100% coverage and a total ban of signage. Further, Mesa argues, the Sign Code is narrow because it only addresses signs that are inside the pane, and the Code allows alternative methods of communication, including signs hanging outside of the window sill area. Additionally, Mesa conducted comparisons with other communities and found that the 30% restriction on window coverage was comparable to other cities' restrictions.

We are not in a position to determine what percentage of window coverage is optimal. Rather, we only decide if the 30% figure that was adopted by the Sign Code is a reasonable fit to further the goal of improving aesthetics. We conclude that it is. Reasonable minds can differ as to whether Mesa's interest would best be served by a 15%, 25%, 30% or 40% limitation on window coverage, but under the facts of this case we cannot conclude that these differences of degree are of a constitutional dimension. The exact balance between the size of the signs and the aesthetic benefits attained is ultimately a subjective decision best left to the city council.

We conclude the Sign Code directly advances a substantial governmental interest and is narrowly tailored to directly advance the goal of improved aesthetics. We therefore affirm the trial court's granting of Mesa's Motion for Summary Judgment.

EXAM Strategy

Question: Maria owns a lot next to a freeway that passes through Tidyville. She has rented a billboard to Huge Mart, a nearby retailer, and a second billboard to Green, a political party. However, Tidyville prohibits off-premises signs (those not on the advertiser's property) that are visible from the freeway. Tidyville's rule is designed to make the city more attractive, to increase property values, and to eliminate distractions that may cause freeway accidents. Huge Mart and Green sue, claiming that Tidyville's law violates their First Amendment rights.

A. Huge Mart is likely to win; Green is likely to lose.

B. Green is likely to win; Huge Mart is likely to lose.

C. Huge Mart and Green are both likely to win.

D. Huge Mart and Green are both likely to lose.

Strategy: What is the difference between the two cases? Huge Mart wants the billboard for commercial speech, Green wants it for a political message. What are the legal standards for commercial and political free speech? Apply those standards.

Result: The government may regulate commercial speech, provided that the rules are reasonable and directed to a legitimate goal. Political speech is given much stronger protection, and can be prohibited only if it is intended and likely to create imminent lawless action. The regulation outlawing *advertising* will be upheld, but Tidyville will not be allowed to block political messages.

Fifth Amendment: Due Process and the Takings Clause

You are a senior at a major state university. You feel great about a difficult exam you took in Professor Watson's class. The Dean's Office sends for you, and you enter curiously, wondering if your exam was so good that the dean is awarding you a prize. Not quite. The exam proctor has accused you of cheating. Based on the accusation, Watson has flunked you. You protest that you are innocent and demand to know what the accusation is. The dean says that you will learn the details at a hearing, if you wish to have one. She reminds you that if you lose the hearing, you will be expelled from the university. Four years of work and your entire career are suddenly on the line.

> Four years of work and your entire career are suddenly on the line.

The hearing is run by Professor Holmes, who will make the final decision. Holmes is a junior faculty member in Watson's department. (Next year, Watson will decide Holmes's tenure application.) At the hearing, the proctor accuses you of copying from a student sitting in front of you. Both Watson and Holmes have already compared the two papers and concluded that they are strongly similar. Holmes tells you that you must convince him the charge is wrong. You examine the papers, acknowledge that there are similarities, but plead as best you can that you never copied. Holmes doesn't buy it. The university expels you, placing on your transcript a notation of cheating.

Have you received fair treatment? To answer that, we must look to the Fifth Amendment, which provides several vital protections. We will consider two related provisions, the Due Process Clause and the Takings Clause. Together, they state: "No person shall be . . . deprived of life, liberty, or property without due process of law; nor shall private property be taken for public use, without just compensation." These clauses prevent the government from arbitrarily taking the most valuable possessions of a citizen or corporation. The government has the right to take a person's liberty or property. But there are three important limitations:

- ***Procedural Due Process.*** Before depriving anyone of liberty or property, the government must go through certain steps, or procedures, to ensure that the result is fair.
- ***The Takings Clause.*** When the government takes property for public use, such as to build a new highway, it has to pay a fair price.
- ***Substantive Due Process.*** Some rights are so fundamental that the government may not take them from us at all. The substance of any law or government action may be challenged on fundamental fairness grounds.

Takings Clause
A clause in the Fifth Amendment which ensures that when any governmental unit takes private property for public use, it must compensate the owner.

Procedural Due Process

The government deprives citizens or corporations of their property in a variety of ways. The Internal Revenue Service may fine a corporation for late payment of taxes. The Customs Service may seize goods at the border. As to liberty, the government may take it by confining someone in a mental institution or by taking a child out of the home because of

ocedural due process The doctrine which ensures that before the government takes liberty or property, the affected person has a fair chance to oppose the action.

parental neglect. The purpose of **procedural due process** is to ensure that before the government takes liberty or property, the affected person has a fair chance to oppose the action.

There are two steps in analyzing a procedural due process case:

- Is the government attempting to take liberty or property?
- If so, how much process is due? (If the government is *not* attempting to take liberty or property, there is no due process issue.)

Is the Government Attempting to Take Liberty or Property? Liberty interests are generally easy to spot: confining someone in a mental institution and taking a child from her home are both deprivations of liberty. A property interest may be obvious. Suppose that, during a civil lawsuit, the court **attaches** a defendant's house, meaning it bars the defendant from selling the property at least until the case is decided. This way, if the plaintiff wins, the defendant will have assets to pay the judgment. The court has clearly deprived the defendant of an important interest in his house, and the defendant is entitled to due process. However, a property interest may be subtler than that. A woman holding a job with a government agency has a "property interest" in that job, because her employer has agreed not to fire her without cause, and she can rely on it for income. If the government does fire her, it is taking away that property interest, and she is entitled to due process. A student attending any public school has a property interest in her education. If a public university suspends a student as described above, it is taking her property, and she, too, should receive due process.

How Much Process Is Due? Assuming that a liberty or property interest is affected, a court must decide how much process is due. Does the person get a formal trial, or an informal hearing, or merely a chance to reply in writing to the charges against her? If she gets a hearing, must it be held before the government deprives her of her property, or is it enough that she can be heard shortly thereafter? **What sort of hearing the government must offer depends upon how important the property or liberty interest is and on whether the government has a competing need for efficiency.** The more important the interest, the more formal the procedures must be.

Neutral Factfinder. Regardless of how formal the hearing, one requirement is constant: the factfinder must be neutral. Whether it is a superior court judge deciding a multimillion dollar contract suit or an employment supervisor deciding the fate of a government employee, the factfinder must have no personal interest in the outcome. In *Ward v. Monroeville*,[16] the plaintiff was a motorist who had been stopped for traffic offenses in a small town. He protested his innocence and received a judicial hearing. But the "judge" at the hearing was the town mayor. Traffic fines were a significant part of the town's budget. The motorist argued that the town was depriving him of procedural due process because the mayor had a financial interest in the outcome of the case. The United States Supreme Court agreed and reversed his conviction.

Attachment of Property. As described earlier, a plaintiff in a civil lawsuit often seeks to *attach* the defendant's property. This protects the plaintiff, but it may also harm the defendant if, for example, he is about to close a profitable real estate deal. Attachments used to be routine. In *Connecticut v. Doehr*, the Supreme Court required more caution.[17] Based on *Doehr*, when a plaintiff seeks to attach at the beginning of the trial, a court must look at the plaintiff's likelihood of winning. Generally, the court must grant the defendant a hearing

---

[16]409 U.S. 57, 93 S. Ct. 80, 1972 U.S. LEXIS 11 (1972).

[17]501 U.S. 1, 111 S. Ct. 2105, 1991 U.S. LEXIS 3317 (1991).

before attaching the property. The defendant, represented by a lawyer, may offer evidence as to how attachment would harm him and why it should be denied.

Government Employment. A government employee must receive due process before being fired. Generally, this means some kind of hearing, but not necessarily a formal court hearing. The employee is entitled to know the charges against him, to hear the employer's evidence, and to have an opportunity to tell his side of the story. He is not entitled to have a lawyer present. The hearing "officer" need only be a neutral employee. Further, in an emergency, where the employee is a danger to the public or the organization, the government may suspend with pay, before holding a hearing. It then must provide a hearing before the decision becomes final.

Academic Suspension. There is still a property interest here, but it is the least important of those discussed. When a public school concludes that a student has failed to meet its normal academic standards, such as by failing too many courses, it may dismiss him without a hearing. Due process is served if the student receives notice of the reason and has some opportunity to respond, such as by writing a letter contradicting the school's claims.

In cases of disciplinary suspension or expulsion, courts generally require schools to provide a higher level of due process. In the hypothetical at the beginning of this section, the university has failed to provide adequate due process.[18] The school has accused the student of a serious infraction. The school must promptly provide details of the charge and cannot wait until the hearing to do so. The student should see the two papers and have a chance to rebut the charge. Moreover, Professor Holmes has demonstrated bias. He appears to have made up his mind in advance. He has placed the burden on the student to disprove the charges. And he probably feels obligated to support Watson's original conclusion, since Watson will be deciding his tenure case next year.

The Takings Clause

Florence Dolan ran a plumbing store in Tigard, Oregon. She and her husband wanted to enlarge it on land they already owned. But the city government said that they could expand only if they dedicated some of their own land for use as a public bicycle path and for other public use. Does the city have the right to make them do that? For an answer we must look to a different part of the Fifth Amendment.

The Takings Clause prohibits a state from taking private property for public use without just compensation. A town wishing to build a new football field may boot you out of your house. But the town must compensate you. The government takes your land through the power of **eminent domain**. Officials must notify you of their intentions and give you an opportunity to oppose the project and to challenge the amount the town offers to pay. But when the hearings are done, the town may write you a check and level your house, whether you like it or not.

Eminent domain
The power of the government to take private property for public use.

More controversial issues arise when a local government does not physically take the property but passes regulations that restrict its use. Tigard is a city of 30,000 in Oregon. The city developed a comprehensive land use plan for its downtown area in order to preserve green space, to encourage transportation other than autos, and to reduce its flooding problems. Under the plan, when a property owner sought permission to build in the downtown section, the city could require some of her land to be used for public purposes. This has become a standard method of land use planning throughout the nation. States have used it to preserve coastline, urban green belts, and many environmental features.

When Florence Dolan applied for permission to expand, the city required that she dedicate a 15-foot strip of her property to the city as a bicycle pathway and that she

[18]See, e.g., *University of Texas Medical School at Houston v. Than*, 901 S.W.2d 926, 1995 Tex. LEXIS 105 (Tex. 1995).

preserve, as greenway, a portion of her land within a floodplain. She sued, and though she lost in the Oregon courts, she won in the United States Supreme Court. The Court held that Tigard City's method of routinely forcing all owners to dedicate land to public use violated the Takings Clause. The city was taking the land, even though title never changed hands.[19]

The Court did not outlaw all such requirements. What it required was that, **before a government may require an owner to dedicate land to a public use, it must show that this owner's proposed building requires this dedication of land.** In other words, it is not enough for Tigard to have a general plan, such as a bicycle pathway, and to make all owners participate in it. Tigard must show that it needs *Dolan's* land *specifically for a bike path and greenway.* This will be much harder for local governments to demonstrate than merely showing a city-wide plan. A related issue arose in the following controversial case. A city used eminent domain to take property on behalf of *private developers.* Was this a valid public use?

The Kelo decision was controversial, and in response some states passed statutes prohibiting eminent domain for private development.

Kelo v. City of New London, Connecticut

545 U.S. 469, 125 S.Ct. 2655
United States Supreme Court, 2005

Facts: New London, Connecticut, was declining economically. The city's unemployment rate was double that of the state generally, and the population at its lowest point in 75 years. In response, state and local officials targeted a section of the city, called Fort Trumbull, for revitalization. Located on the Thames River, Fort Trumbull comprised 115 privately owned properties and 32 additional acres of an abandoned naval facility. The development plan included one section for a waterfront conference hotel and stores; a second one for 80 private residences; and one for research facilities.

The state bought most of the properties from willing sellers. However, nine owners of 15 properties refused to sell, and filed suit. The owners claimed that the city was trying to take land for *private* use, not public, in violation of the Takings Clause. The case reached the United States Supreme Court.

Issue: ***Did the city's plan violate the Takings Clause?***

Excerpts from Justice Stevens' Decision: It has long been accepted that the sovereign may not take the property of *A* for the sole purpose of transferring it to another private party *B*, even though *A* is paid just compensation. On the other hand, it is equally clear that a State may transfer property from one private party to another if future "use by the public" is the purpose of the taking; the condemnation of land for a railroad with common-carrier duties is a familiar example.

This is not a case in which the City is planning to open the condemned land—at least not in its entirety—to use by the general public. Nor will the private lessees of the land in any sense be required to operate like common carriers, making their services available to all comers. But this Court long ago rejected any literal requirement that condemned property be put into use for the general public, [embracing] the broader and more natural interpretation of public use as "public purpose." Thus, in a case upholding a mining company's use of an aerial bucket line to transport ore over property it did not own, Justice Holmes' opinion for the Court stressed "the inadequacy of use by the general public as a universal test."

The City has carefully formulated an economic development plan that it believes will provide appreciable benefits to the community, including—but by no means limited to—new jobs and increased tax revenue. As with other exercises in urban planning and development, the City is endeavoring to coordinate a variety of commercial, residential, and recreational uses of land, with the hope that they will form a whole greater than the sum of its parts. Because that plan unquestionably serves a public purpose, the takings challenged here satisfy the public use requirement of the Fifth Amendment.

[19]*Dolan v. City of Tigard,* 512 U.S. 374, 114 S. Ct. 2309, 1994 U.S. LEXIS 4826 (1994).

To avoid this result, petitioners urge us to adopt a new bright-line rule that economic development does not qualify as a public use. [However, promoting] economic development is a traditional and long accepted function of government. There is, moreover, no principled way of distinguishing economic development from the other public purposes that we have recognized. In our cases upholding takings that facilitated agriculture and mining, for example, we emphasized the importance of those industries to the welfare of the States in question. Clearly, there is no basis for exempting economic development from our traditionally broad understanding of public purpose.

The judgment of the Supreme Court of Connecticut is affirmed.

Justice O'Connor, dissenting: The Court today significantly expands the meaning of public use. It holds that the sovereign may take private property currently put to ordinary private use, and give it over for new, ordinary private use, so long as the new use is predicted to generate some secondary benefit for the public—such as increased tax revenue, more jobs, maybe even esthetic pleasure. But nearly any lawful use of real private property can be said to generate some incidental benefit to the public. Thus, if predicted (or even guaranteed) positive side-effects are enough to render transfer from one private party to another constitutional, then the words "for public use" do not realistically exclude *any* takings, and thus do not exert any constraint on the eminent domain power.

Any property may now be taken for the benefit of another private party, but the fallout from this decision will not be random. The beneficiaries are likely to be those citizens with disproportionate influence and power in the political process, including large corporations and development firms. As for the victims, the government now has license to transfer property from those with fewer resources to those with more.

Substantive Due Process

This doctrine is part of the Due Process Clause, but it is entirely different from procedural due process and from government taking. During the first third of the twentieth century, the Supreme Court frequently nullified state and federal laws, asserting that they interfered with basic rights. For example, in a famous 1905 case, *Lochner v. New York*,[20] the Supreme Court invalidated a New York statute that had limited the number of hours that bakers could work in a week. New York had passed the law to protect employee health. But the Court declared that private parties had a basic constitutional right to contract. In this case, the statute interfered with the rights of the employer and the baker to make any bargain they wished. Over the next three decades, the Court struck down dozens of state and federal laws that were aimed at working conditions, union rights, and social welfare generally. This was called **substantive due process**[21] because the Court was looking at the underlying rights being affected, such as the right to contract, not at any procedures.

Substantive due process
A form of due process that holds that certain rights are so fundamental that the government may not eliminate them.

Critics complained that the Court was interfering with the desires of the voting public by nullifying laws that the justices personally disliked (judicial activism). During the Great Depression, however, things changed. Beginning in 1934, the Court completely reversed itself and began to uphold the types of laws it earlier had struck down.

The Supreme Court made an important substantive due process ruling in the case of *BMW v. Gore*[22]. A BMW dealership sold Gore a car that had sustained water damage. Instead of telling him of the damage, they simply repainted the car and sold it as new.

In Chapter 6, we will examine two different types of cash awards that juries may make in tort cases. For now, let's call them "ordinary" and "punitive" damages. When plaintiffs win tort cases, juries may always award ordinary damages to offset real, measureable losses. In addition, juries are sometimes allowed to add to an award to further punish a defendant for bad behavior.

[20]198 U.S. 45, 25 S. Ct. 539, 1905 U.S. LEXIS 1153 (1905).

[21]Be the first on your block to pronounce this word correctly. The accent goes on the first syllable: *sub*stantive.

[22]517 U.S. 559 (1996).

In the BMW case, the jury awarded Gore $4,000 in ordinary damages as the difference in value between a flawless new car and a water-damaged car. The jury then awarded a delighted Gore $4 *million* in punitive damages. In the end, the Supreme Court decided that the punitive award was so disproportionate to the harm actually caused that it violated substantive due process rights.

Fourteenth Amendment: Equal Protection Clause

Shannon Faulkner wanted to attend The Citadel, a state-supported military college in South Carolina. She was a fine student who met every admission requirement that The Citadel set except one: she was not a man. The Citadel argued that its long and distinguished history demanded that it remain all male. Faulkner responded that she was a citizen of the state and ought to receive the benefits that others got, including the right to a military education. Could the school exclude her on the basis of gender?

Equal Protection Clause
A clause in the Fourteenth Amendment that generally requires the government to treat people equally.

The Fourteenth Amendment provides that "No State shall ... deny to any person within its jurisdiction the equal protection of the laws." This is the **Equal Protection Clause**, and it means that, generally speaking, **governments must treat people equally**. Unfair classifications among people or corporations will not be permitted. A notorious example of unfair classification would be race discrimination: permitting only white children to attend a public school violates the Equal Protection Clause.

Yet clearly, governments do make classifications every day. People with high incomes pay a higher tax rate than those with low incomes; some corporations are permitted to deal in securities, while others are not. To determine which classifications are constitutionally permissible, we need to know what is being classified. There are three major groups of classifications. The outcome of a case can generally be predicted by knowing which group it is in.

- ***Minimal Scrutiny: Economic and Social Relations.*** Government actions that classify people or corporations on these bases are almost always upheld.
- ***Intermediate Scrutiny: Gender.*** Government classifications are sometimes upheld.
- ***Strict Scrutiny: Race, Ethnicity, and Fundamental Rights.*** Classifications based on any of these are almost never upheld.

Minimal Scrutiny: Economic and Social Regulation

Just as with the Due Process Clause, laws that regulate economic or social issues are presumed valid. They will be upheld if they are *rationally related to a legitimate goal.* This means a statute may classify corporations and/or people and the classifications will be upheld if they make any sense at all. The New York City Transit Authority excluded all methadone users from any employment. The United States District Court concluded that this violated the Equal Protection Clause by unfairly excluding all those who were on methadone. The court noted that even those who tested free of any illegal drugs and were seeking non-safety-sensitive jobs, such as clerks, were turned away. That, said the district court, was irrational.

Not so, said the United States Supreme Court. The Court admitted that the policy might not be the wisest. It would probably make more sense to test individually for illegal drugs rather than automatically exclude methadone users. But, said the Court, it was not up to the justices to choose the best policy. They were only to decide if the policy was rational. Excluding methadone users related rationally to the safety of public transport and therefore did not violate the Equal Protection Clause.[23]

Intermediate Scrutiny: Gender

Classifications based on sex must meet a tougher test than those resulting from economic or social regulation. Such laws must *substantially relate to important government objectives.* Courts have increasingly nullified government sex classifications as societal concern with gender equality has grown.

[23] *New York City Transit Authority v. Beazer*, 440 U.S. 568, 99 S. Ct. 1355, 1979 U.S. LEXIS 77 (1979).

At about the same time Shannon Faulkner began her campaign to enter The Citadel, another woman sought admission to the Virginia Military Institute, an all-male state school. The Supreme Court held that Virginia had violated the Equal Protection Clause by excluding women from VMI. The Court ruled that gender-based government discrimination requires an "exceedingly persuasive justification," and that Virginia had failed that standard of proof. The Citadel promptly opened its doors to women as well.[24]

Strict Scrutiny: Race, Ethnicity, and Fundamental Rights

Any government action that intentionally discriminates against racial or ethnic minorities, or interferes with a fundamental right, is presumed invalid. In such cases, courts will look at the statute or policy with *strict scrutiny;* that is, courts will examine it very closely to determine whether there is compelling justification for it. The law will be upheld only if it is *necessary to promote a compelling state interest.* Very few meet that test.

- ***Racial and Ethnic Minorities.*** Any government action that intentionally discriminates on the basis of race, or ethnicity is presumed invalid. For example, in *Palmore v. Sidoti,*[25] the state had refused to give child custody to a mother because her new spouse was racially different from the child. The practice was declared unconstitutional. The state had made a racial classification, it was presumed invalid, and the government had no *compelling need* to make such a ruling.
- ***Fundamental Rights.*** A government action interfering with a fundamental right also receives strict scrutiny and will likely be declared void. For example, New York State gave an employment preference to any veteran who had been a state resident when he entered the military. Newcomers who were veterans were less likely to get jobs, and therefore this statute interfered with the right to travel, a fundamental right. The Supreme Court declared the law invalid.[26]

Fundamental rights
Rights so basic that any governmental interference with them is suspect and likely to be unconstitutional.

EXAM Strategy

Question: Megan is a freshman at her local public high school; her older sister Jenna attends a nearby private high school. Both girls are angry because their schools prohibit them from joining their respective wrestling teams, where only boys are allowed. The two girls sue based on the U.S. Constitution. Discuss the relevant law and predict the outcomes.

Strategy: One girl goes to private and one to public school. Why does that matter? Now ask what provision of the Constitution is involved, and what legal standard it establishes.

Result: The Constitution offers protection from the *government.* A private high school is not part of the government, and Jenna has no constitutional case. Megan's suit is based on the Equal Protection Clause. This is gender discrimination, meaning that Megan's school must convince the court that keeping girls off the team *substantially relates to an important government objective.* The school will probably argue that wrestling with stronger boys will be dangerous for girls. However, courts are increasingly suspicious of any gender discrimination and are unlikely to find the school's argument persuasive.

---

[24] *United States v. Virginia,* 518 U.S. 515, 116 S. Ct. 2264, 1996 U.S. LEXIS 4259 (1996).
[25] 466 U.S. 429, 104 S. Ct. 1879, 1984 U.S. LEXIS 69 (1984).
[26] *Attorney General of New York v. Soto-Lopez,* 476 U.S. 898, 106 S. Ct. 2317, 1986 U.S. LEXIS 59 (1986).

Chapter Conclusion

The legal battle over power never stops. The obligation of a state to provide equal educational opportunity for both genders relates to whether Tigard, Oregon, may demand some of Ms. Dolan's store lot for public use. Both issues are governed by one amazing document. That same Constitution determines what tax preferences are permissible, and even whether a state may require you to wear clothing. As social mores change in step with broad cultural developments, as the membership of the Supreme Court changes, the balance of power between federal government, state government, and citizens will continue to evolve. There are no easy answers to these constitutional questions because there has never been a democracy so large, so diverse, or so powerful.

Exam Review

1. **CONSTITUTION** The Constitution is a series of compromises about power. (pp. 103–105)

2. **ARTICLES I, II AND III** Article I of the Constitution creates the Congress and grants all legislative power to it. Article II establishes the office of president and defines executive powers. Article III creates the Supreme Court and permits lower federal courts; the article also outlines the powers of the federal judiciary. (pp. 105–111)

3. **COMMERCE CLAUSE** Under the Commerce Clause, Congress may regulate any activity that has a substantial effect on interstate commerce. (pp. 105–107)

4. **INTERSTATE COMMERCE** A state may not regulate commerce in any way that will interfere with interstate commerce. (p. 105)

EXAM Strategy

Question: Maine exempted many charitable institutions from real estate taxes but denied this benefit to a charity that primarily benefited out-of-state residents. Camp Newfound was a Christian Science organization, and 95 percent of its summer campers came from other states. Camp Newfound sued Maine. Discuss.

Strategy: The state was treating organizations differently depending on what states their campers come from. This raised *Commerce Clause* issues. Did the positive aspect or dormant aspect of that clause apply? The dormant aspect applied. What does it state? Apply that standard to theses facts. (See the "Result" at the end of this section.)

5. **SUPREMACY CLAUSE** Under the Supremacy Clause, if there is a conflict between federal and state statutes, the federal law preempts the field. Even without a conflict, federal law preempts if Congress intended to exercise exclusive control. (p. 107)

6. **PRESIDENTIAL POWERS** The president's key powers include making agency appointments, proposing legislation, conducting foreign policy, and acting as commander in chief of the armed forces. (p. 108)

7. **FEDERAL COURTS** The federal courts adjudicate cases and also exercise judicial review, which is the right to declare a statute or governmental action unconstitutional and void. (pp. 108–111)

8. **FREEDOM OF SPEECH** Freedom of speech includes symbolic acts. Political speech by both people and organizations is protected unless it is intended and likely to create imminent lawless action. (pp. 112–117)

9. **REGULATION OF SPEECH** The government may regulate the time, place, and manner of speech. (p. 114)

10. **COMMERCIAL SPEECH** Commercial speech that is false or misleading may be outlawed; otherwise, regulations on this speech must be reasonable and directed to a legitimate goal. (pp. 115–117)

EXAM Strategy

Question: A federal statute prohibits the broadcasting of lottery advertisements, except by stations that broadcast in states permitting lotteries. The purpose of the statute is to support efforts of states that outlaw lotteries. Truth Broadcasting operates a radio station in State A (a nonlottery state) but broadcasts primarily in State B (a lottery state). Truth wants to advertise State A's lottery but is barred by the statute. Does the federal statute violate Truth's constitutional rights?

Strategy: This case involves a particular kind of speech. What kind? What is the rule about that kind of speech? (See the "Result" at the end of this section.)

11. **PROCEDURAL DUE PROCESS** Procedural due process is required whenever the government attempts to take liberty or property. The amount of process that is due depends upon the importance of the liberty or property threatened. (pp. 117–119)

EXAM Strategy

Question: Fox's Fine Furs claims that Ermine owes $68,000 for a mink coat on which she has stopped making payments. Fox files a complaint and also asks the court clerk to *garnish* Ermine's wages. A garnishment is a court order to an employer to withhold an employee's wages, or a portion of them, and pay the money into court so that there will be money for the plaintiff, if it wins. What constitutional issue does Fox's request for garnishment raise?

Strategy: Ermine is in danger of losing part of her income, which is property. The Due Process Clause prohibits the government (the court) from taking life, liberty or property without due process. What process is Ermine entitled to? (See the "Result" at the end of this section.)

12. **TAKINGS CLAUSE** The Takings Clause prohibits a state from taking private property for public use without just compensation. (pp. 119–121)

13. **SUBSTANTIVE DUE PROCESS** A substantive due process analysis presumes that any economic or social regulation is valid, and presumes invalid any law that infringes upon a fundamental right. (pp. 121–122)

14. **EQUAL PROTECTION CLAUSE** The Equal Protection Clause generally requires the government to treat people equally. Courts apply strict scrutiny in any equal protection case involving race, ethnicity, or fundamental rights; intermediate scrutiny to any case involving gender; and minimal scrutiny to an economic or social regulation. (pp. 122–123)

4. Result: The dormant aspect holds that a state statute which discriminates against interstate commerce is almost always invalid. Maine was subsidizing charities that served in-state residents, and penalizing those that attracted campers from elsewhere. The tax rules violated the Commerce Clause and was void.[27]

10. Result: An advertisement is *commercial* speech. The government may regulate this speech as long as the rules are reasonable and directed to a legitimate goal. The goal of supporting nonlottery states is reasonable, and there is no violation of Truth's free speech rights.[28]

11. Result: Ermine is entitled to notice of Fox's claim and to a hearing *before* the court garnishes her wages.[29]

MULTIPLE-CHOICE QUESTIONS

1. Greenville College, a public community college, has a policy of admitting only male students. If the policy is challenged under the Fourteenth Amendment, ______________ scrutiny will be applied.
   (a) strict
   (b) intermediate
   (c) rational
   (d) none of the above

2. You begin work at Everhappy Corp. at the beginning of November. On your second day at work, you wear a political button on your overcoat, supporting your choice for governor in the upcoming election. Your boss glances at it and says, "Get that stupid thing out of this office or you're history, chump." Your boss ______________ violated your First Amendment rights. After work, you put the button back on and start walking home. You pass a police officer who blocks your path and says, "Take off that stupid button or you're going to jail, chump." The officer ____________ violated your First Amendment rights.

[27] *Camps Newfound/Owatonna, Inc. v. Town of Harrison, Maine,* 520 U.S. 564, 117 S.Ct. 1590 (1997).
[28] *United States v. Edge Broadcasting,* 509 U.S. 418, 113 S.Ct. 2696 (1993).
[29] *Sniadach v. Family Finance Corp.,* 395 U.S. 337 (1969).

(a) has; has
(b) has; has not
(c) has not; has
(d) has not; has not

3. Which of the following statements accurately describes statutes that Congress and the president may create?
   (a) Statutes must be related to a power listed in Article I, section 8 of the Constitution.
   (b) Statutes must not infringe on the liberties in the Bill of Rights.
   (c) Both A and B
   (d) None of the above

4. Which of the following is true of the origin of judicial review?
   (a) It was created by Article II of the Constitution.
   (b) It was created by Article III of the Constitution.
   (c) It was created in the *Marbury v. Madison* case.
   (d) It was created by the Fifth Amendment.
   (e) It was created by the Fourteenth Amendment.

5. Consider *Kelo v. City of New London,* in which a city with a revitalization plan squared off against property owners who did not wish to sell their property. The key constitutional provision was the Takings Clause in the ______________ Amendment. The Supreme Court decided the city ______________ use eminent domain and take the property from the landowners.
   (a) Fifth; could
   (b) Fifth; could not
   (c) Fourteenth; could
   (d) Fourteenth; could not

Essay Questions

1. **YOU BE THE JUDGE WRITING PROBLEM** Scott Fane was a CPA licensed to practice in New Jersey and Florida. He built his New Jersey practice by making unsolicited phone calls to executives. When he moved to Florida, the Board of Accountancy there prohibited him (and all CPAs) from personally soliciting new business. Fane sued. Does the First Amendment force Florida to forgo foreclosing Fane's phoning? **Argument for Fane:** The Florida regulation violates the First Amendment, which protects commercial speech. Fane was not saying anything false or misleading, but was just trying to secure business. This is an unreasonable regulation, designed to keep newcomers out of the marketplace and maintain steady business and high prices for established CPAs. **Argument for the Florida Board of Accountancy:** Commercial speech deserves—and gets—a lower level of protection than other speech. This regulation is a reasonable method of ensuring that the level of CPA work in our state remains high. CPAs who personally solicit

clients are obviously in need of business. They are more likely to bend legal and ethical rules to obtain clients and keep them happy, and will lower the standards throughout the state.

2. President George H.W. Bush insisted that he had the power to send American troops into combat in the Middle East, without congressional assent. Yet before authorizing force in Operation Desert Storm, he secured congressional authorization. President Bill Clinton stated that he was prepared to invade Haiti without a congressional vote. Yet he bargained hard to avoid an invasion, and ultimately American troops entered without the use of force. Why the seeming doubletalk by both presidents?

3. In the landmark 1965 case of *Griswold v. Connecticut,* the Supreme Court examined a Connecticut statute that made it a crime for any person to use contraception. The majority declared the law an unconstitutional violation of the right of privacy. Justice Black dissented, saying, "I do not to any extent whatever base my view that this Connecticut law is constitutional on a belief that the law is wise or that its policy is a good one. [It] is every bit as offensive to me as it is to the majority. [There is no criticism by the majority of this law] to which I cannot subscribe—except their conclusion that the evil qualities they see in the law make it unconstitutional." What legal doctrines are involved here? Why did Justice Black distinguish between his personal views on the statute and the power of the Court to overturn it?

4. Gilleo opposed American participation in the war in the Persian Gulf. She displayed a large sign on her front lawn that read, "Say No to War in the Persian Gulf, Call Congress Now." The city of Ladue prohibited signs on front lawns and Gilleo sued. The city claimed that it was regulating "time, place, and manner." Explain that statement, and decide who should win.

5. David Lucas paid $975,000 for two residential lots on the Isle of Palms near Charleston, South Carolina. He intended to build houses on them. Two years later, the South Carolina legislature passed a statute that prohibited building seaward of a certain line, and Lucas's property fell in the prohibited zone. Lucas claimed that his land was now useless and that South Carolina owed him its value. Explain his claim. Should he win?

Discussion Questions

1. Return to the opening scenario and the *Citizens United* case. Is political advertising purchased by corporations appropriate? Do you agree with the five members of the Supreme Court who voted to allow it, or with the four who dissented and would have drawn distinctions between free speech by individuals and organizations? Why?

2. **Ethics** Is political advertising by a nonprofit political organization like Citizens United any more or less appropriate than advertising by for-profit corporations like the one described in the opening scenario? If you were a board member in the opening scenario, which (if any) of the three ads would you vote to authorize?

3. Consider the "tea party" movement. Do you believe that the federal government should be able to create whatever laws it deems to be in the country's best interests, or do you believe that individual states, like Florida and California, should have more control over the laws within their own borders?

4. This chapter is filled with examples of statutes that have been struck down by the courts. A Texas law banning flag burning was rejected by the Supreme Court, as was a Louisiana death penalty statute. The Affordable Healthcare Act has been voided by two lower court judges, and the Supreme Court may or may not agree with the action.

   Do you like the fact that courts can void laws that they determine to be in violation of the Constitution? Or is it wrong for appointed judges to overrule "the will of the majority," as expressed by elected members of Congress and state legislatures?

5. Gender discrimination currently receives "intermediate" Fourteenth Amendment scrutiny. Is this right? Should gender receive "strict" scrutiny as does race? Why or why not?

CHAPTER 6

Intentional Torts and Business Torts

© r.nagy/Shutterstock.com

In a small Louisiana town, Don Mashburn ran a restaurant called Maison de Mashburn. The *New Orleans States-Item* newspaper reviewed his eatery, and here is what the article said:

> "'Tain't Creole, 'tain't Cajun, 'tain't French, 'tain't country American, 'tain't good. I don't know how much real talent in cooking is hidden under the mélange of hideous sauces which make this food and the menu a travesty of pretentious amateurism, but I find it all quite depressing. Put a yellow flour sauce on top of the duck, flame it for drama, and serve it with some horrible multiflavored rice in hollowed-out fruit and what have you got? A well-cooked duck with an ugly sauce that tastes too sweet and thick and makes you want to scrape off the glop to eat the plain duck. [The stuffed eggplant was prepared by emptying] a shaker full (more or less) of paprika on top of it. [One sauce created] trout à la green plague [while another should have been called] yellow death on duck."

'Tain't Creole, 'tain't Cajun, 'tain't French, 'tain't country American, 'tain't good.

Mashburn sued, claiming that the newspaper had committed libel, damaging his reputation and hurting his business.[1] Trout à la green plague will be the first course on our menu of tort law. Mashburn learned, as you will, why filing such a lawsuit is easier than winning it.

[1] *Mashburn v. Collin*, 355 So.2d 879 (La. 1977).

The odd word "tort" is borrowed from the French, meaning "wrong." And that is what it means in law: a wrong. More precisely, a **tort** is a violation of a duty imposed by the civil law. When a person breaks one of those duties and injures another, it is a tort. The injury could be to a person or her property. Libel, which the restaurant owner in the opening scenario alleged, is one example of a tort. A surgeon who removes the wrong kidney from a patient commits a different kind of tort, called negligence. A business executive who deliberately steals a client away from a competitor, interfering with a valid contract, commits a tort called interference with a contract. A con artist who tricks you out of your money with a phony offer to sell you a boat commits fraud, yet another tort.

Tort
A violation of a duty imposed by the civil law.

Because tort law is so broad, it takes a while—and two chapters—to understand its boundaries. To start with, we must distinguish torts from two other areas of law: criminal law and contract law.

It is a *crime* to steal a car, to embezzle money from a bank, to sell cocaine. As discussed in Chapter 1, society considers such behavior so threatening that the government itself will prosecute the wrongdoer, whether or not the car owner or bank president wants the case to go forward. A district attorney, who is paid by the government, will bring the case to court, seeking to send the defendant to prison, fine him, or both. If there is a fine, the money goes to the state, not to the victim.

In a tort case, it is up to the injured party to seek compensation. She must hire her own lawyer, who will file a lawsuit. Her lawyer must convince the court that the defendant breached some legal duty and ought to pay money damages to the plaintiff. The plaintiff has no power to send the defendant to jail. Bear in mind that a defendant's action might be both a crime and a tort. A man who punches you in the face for no reason commits the tort of battery. You may file a civil suit against him and will collect money damages if you can prove your case. He has also committed a crime, and the state may prosecute, seeking to imprison and fine him.

Differences between Contract, Tort, and Criminal Law

Type of Obligation	Contract	Tort	Criminal Law
How the obligation is created	The parties agree on a contract, which creates duties for both.	The civil law imposes duties of conduct on all persons.	The criminal law prohibits certain conduct.
How the obligation is enforced	Suit by plaintiff.	Suit by plaintiff.	Prosecution by government.
Possible result	Money damages for plaintiff.	Money damages for plaintiff.	Punishment for defendant, including prison and/or fine.
Example	Raul contracts to sell Deirdre 5,000 pairs of sneakers at $50 per pair, but fails to deliver them. Deirdre buys the sneakers elsewhere for $60 per pair and receives $50,000, her extra expense.	A newspaper falsely accuses a private citizen of being an alcoholic. The plaintiff sues and wins money damages to compensate for her injured reputation.	Leo steals Kelly's car. The government prosecutes Leo for grand theft, and the judge sentences him to two years in prison. Kelly gets nothing.

A tort is also different from a contract dispute. A contract case is based on an agreement two people have already made. For example, Deirdre claims that Raul promised to sell her 10,000 pairs of sneakers at a good price but has failed to deliver them. She files a contract lawsuit. In a tort case, there is usually no "deal" between the parties. Don Mashburn had never met the restaurant critic who attacked his restaurant and obviously had never made any kind of contract. The plaintiff in a tort case claims that the law itself creates a duty that the defendant has breached.

Intentional torts
Harm caused by a deliberate action.

Tort law is divided into categories. In this chapter, we consider **intentional torts**, that is, harm caused by a deliberate action. The newspaper columnist who wrongly accuses someone of being a drunk has committed the intentional tort of libel. In the next chapter, we examine negligence and strict liability, which involve injuries and losses caused by neglect and oversight rather than by deliberate conduct.

A final introductory point: when we speak of intentional torts, we do not necessarily mean that the defendant intended to harm the plaintiff. If the defendant does something deliberately and it ends up injuring somebody, she is probably liable even if she meant no harm. For example, intentionally throwing a snowball at a friend is a deliberate act. If the snowball permanently damages his eye, the *harm* is unintended, but the defendant is liable for the intentional tort of battery because the *act* was intentional.

We look first at the most common intentional torts and then at the most important intentional torts that are related to business.

INTENTIONAL TORTS

Defamation

The First Amendment guarantees the right to free speech, a vital freedom that enables us to protect other rights. But that freedom is not absolute.

The law of defamation concerns false statements that harm someone's reputation. Defamatory statements can be written or spoken. Written defamation is called **libel**. Suppose a newspaper accuses a local retail store of programming its cash registers to overcharge customers when the store has never done so. That is libel. Oral defamation is **slander**. If Professor Wisdom, in class, refers to Sally Student as a drug dealer when she has never sold drugs, he has slandered her.

There are four elements to a defamation case. An element is something that a plaintiff must prove to win a lawsuit. The plaintiff in any kind of lawsuit must prove *all* of the elements to prevail. The elements in a defamation case are

- **Defamatory statement.** This is a statement likely to harm another person's reputation. Professor Wisdom's accusation will clearly harm Sally's reputation.
- **Falseness.** The statement must be false. If Sally Student actually sold marijuana to a classmate, then Professor Wisdom has a defense to slander.
- **Communicated.** The statement must be communicated to at least one person *other than the plaintiff*. If Wisdom speaks privately to Sally and accuses her of dealing drugs, there is no slander.
- **Injury.** In many slander cases, the plaintiff generally must show some injury. Sally's injury would be lower reputation in the school, embarrassment, and humiliation. But in slander cases that involve false statements about sexual behavior, crimes, contagious diseases, and professional abilities, the law is willing to assume injury without requiring the plaintiff to prove it. Lies in these four categories amount to **slander per se**.

Libel cases are treated like cases of slander per se, and courts award damages without proof of injury.[2]

Opinion

Thus far, what we have seen is uncontroversial. If a television commentator refers to Frank Landlord as a "vicious slumlord who rents uninhabitable units," and Frank actually maintains his buildings perfectly, Frank will be compensated for the harm. But what if the television commentator states a harsh *opinion* about Frank? Remember that the plaintiff must demonstrate a "false" statement. Opinions generally cannot be proven true or false, and so they do not usually amount to defamation.

Suppose that the television commentator says, "Frank Landlord certainly does less than many rich people do for our community." Is that defamation? Probably not. Who are the "rich people"? How much do they do? How do we define "does less"? These vague assertions indicate the statement is one of opinion. Even if Frank works hard feeding homeless families, he will probably lose a defamation case.

A related defense involves cases where a supposed statement of fact clearly should not be taken literally. Mr. Mashburn, who opened the chapter suing over his restaurant review, lost his case. The court held that a reasonable reader would have understood the statements to be opinion only. "A shaker full of paprika" and "yellow death on duck" were not to be taken literally but were merely the author's expression of his personal dislike.

Public Personalities

The rules of the game change for those who play in the open. Government officials and other types of public figures such as actors and athletes receive less protection from defamation. In the landmark case *New York Times Co. v. Sullivan*,[3] the Supreme Court ruled that the free exchange of information is vital in a democracy and is protected by the First Amendment to the Constitution.

The rule from the *New York Times* case is that a public official or public figure can win a defamation case only by proving **actual malice** by the defendant. Actual malice means that the defendant knew the statement was false or acted with reckless disregard of the truth. If the plaintiff merely shows that the defendant newspaper printed incorrect statements, even

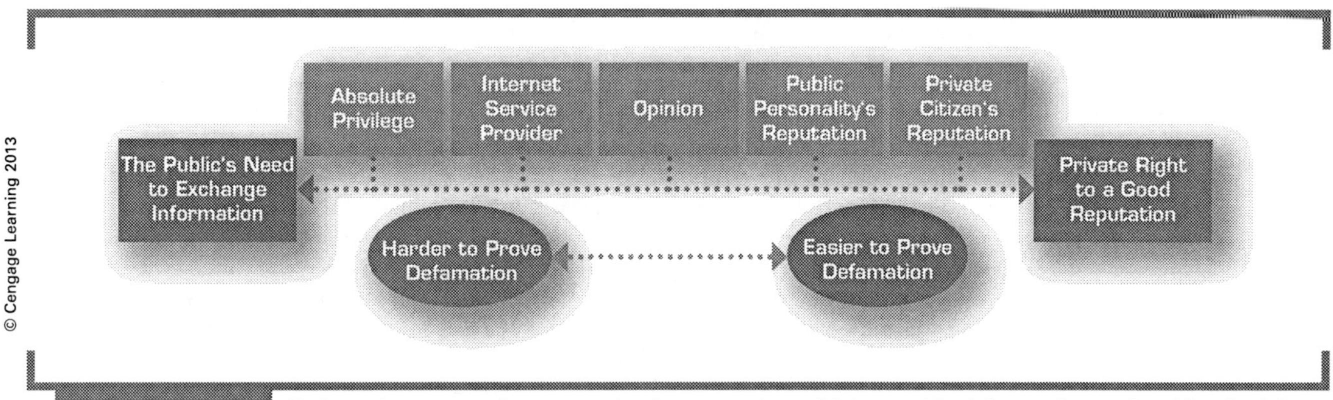

EXHIBIT 6.1 Defamation cases show a tension between the public's need for information and a citizen's right to protect his reputation.

[2]When defamation by radio and television became possible, the courts chose to consider it libel, analogizing it to newspapers because of the vast audience. This means that in broadcasting cases, a plaintiff generally does not have to prove damages.

[3]376 U.S. 254, 84 S.Ct. 710, 1964 U.S. LEXIS 1655 (1964).

very damaging ones, that will not suffice to win the suit. In the *New York Times* case, the police chief of Birmingham, Alabama, claimed that the *Times* falsely accused him of racial violence in his job. He lost because he could not prove that the *Times* had acted with actual malice. If he had shown that the *Times* knew the accusation was false, he would have won.

Online Defamation

Kenneth Zeran awoke one day to learn he had become notorious. An unidentified person had posted a message on an AOL bulletin board advertising "Naughty Oklahoma T-Shirts." The shirts featured deeply offensive slogans relating to the 1995 bombing of a federal building in Oklahoma City, in which hundreds of innocent people died. Those interested in purchasing such a t-shirt were instructed to call "Ken" at Zeran's home telephone number. In fact, Zeran had nothing to do with the posting or the t-shirts. He was quickly inundated with phone messages from furious callers, some of whom made death threats.

Zeran could not conveniently change his number because he ran his business from his home. A radio talk show host in Oklahoma City angrily urged its listeners to call Zeran, which they did. Before long, Zeran was receiving an abusive call every two minutes. He sued AOL for defamation—and lost.

The court held that AOL was immune from a defamation suit based on a third-party posting, based on the Communications Decency Act (CDA). Section 230 of the CDA creates this immunity for any Internet service provider, the court declared, adding:

> It would be impossible for service providers to screen each of their millions of postings for possible problems. Faced with potential liability for each message republished by their services, interactive computer service providers might choose to severely restrict the number and type of messages posted. Congress considered the weight of the speech interests implicated and chose to immunize service providers to avoid any such restrictive effect.[4]

Privilege

Absolute privilege
A witness testifying in a court or legislature may never be sued for defamation.

Defendants receive additional protection from defamation cases when it is important for them to speak freely. **Absolute privilege** exists in courtrooms and legislative hearings. Anyone speaking there, such as a witness in court, can say anything at all and never be sued for defamation. (Deliberately false testimony would be *perjury*, but still not *slander*.)

False Imprisonment

False imprisonment
Is the intentional restraint of another person without reasonable cause and without consent.

False imprisonment is the intentional restraint of another person without reasonable cause and without consent. Suppose that a bank teller becomes seriously ill and wants to go to the doctor, but the bank will not permit her to leave until she makes a final tally of her accounts. Against her wishes, company officials physically bar her from leaving the bank. That is false imprisonment. The restraint was unreasonable because her accounts could have been verified later.[5]

False imprisonment cases most commonly arise in retail stores, which sometimes detain employees or customers for suspected theft. Most states now have statutes governing the detention of suspected shoplifters. **Generally, a store may detain a customer or worker for alleged shoplifting provided there is a reasonable basis for the suspicion and the detention is done reasonably**. To detain a customer in the manager's office for 20 minutes and question him about where he got an item is lawful. To chain that customer to a display counter for three hours and humiliate him in front of other customers is unreasonable and constitutes false imprisonment.

---

[4] *Zeran v. America Online, Inc.*, 129 F.3d 327, 1997 U.S. App. LEXIS 31791 (4th Cir. 1997).

[5] *Kanner v. First National Bank of South Miami*, 287 So.2d 715, 1974 Fla. App. LEXIS 8989 (Fla. Dist. Ct. App. 1974).

Intentional Infliction of Emotional Distress

What should happen when a defendant's conduct hurts a plaintiff emotionally but not physically? Historically, not much did happen. Courts once refused to allow recovery, assuming that if they awarded damages for mere emotional injury, they would be inviting a floodgate of dubious claims. But gradually judges reexamined their thinking and reversed this tendency. Today, most courts allow a plaintiff to recover for emotional injury that a defendant intentionally caused. As we see in the next chapter, some courts will also permit recovery when a defendant's negligent conduct caused the emotional injury.

The **intentional infliction of emotional distress** results from extreme and outrageous conduct that causes serious emotional harm. A credit officer was struggling vainly to locate Sheehan, who owed money on his car. The officer phoned Sheehan's mother, falsely identified herself as a hospital employee, and said she needed to find Sheehan because his children had been in a serious auto accident. The mother provided Sheehan's whereabouts, which enabled the company to seize his car. But Sheehan spent seven hours frantically trying to locate his supposedly injured children, who in fact were fine. The credit company was liable for the intentional infliction of emotional distress.[6]

Intentional infliction of emotional distress
An intentional tort in which the harm results from extreme and outrageous conduct that causes serious emotional harm.

By contrast, a muffler shop, trying to collect a debt from a customer, made six phone calls over three months, using abusive language. The customer testified that this caused her to be upset, to cry, and to have difficulty sleeping. The court ruled that the muffler shop's conduct was neither extreme nor outrageous.[7]

The following case arose in a setting that guarantees controversy—an abortion clinic.

Jane Doe and Nancy Roe v. Lynn Mills

212 Mich. App. 73, 536 N.W.2d 824, 1995 Mich. App. LEXIS 313
Michigan Court of Appeals, 1995

Facts: Late one night, an anti-abortion protestor named Robert Thomas climbed into a dumpster located behind the Women's Advisory Center, an abortion clinic. He found documents indicating that the plaintiffs were soon to have abortions at the clinic. Thomas gave the information to Lynn Mills. The next day, Mills and Sister Lois Mitoraj created signs, using the women's names, indicating that they were about to undergo abortions, and urging them not to "kill their babies."

Doe and Roe (not their real names) sued, claiming intentional infliction of emotional distress (as well as breach of privacy, discussed later in this chapter). The trial court dismissed the lawsuit, ruling that the defendants' conduct was not extreme and outrageous. The plaintiffs appealed.

Issue: ***Have the plaintiffs made a valid claim of intentional infliction of emotional distress?***

Excerpts from the Court's *Per Curiam* Decision: Liability for the intentional infliction of emotional distress has been found only where the conduct complained of has been so outrageous in character, and so extreme in degree, as to go beyond all possible bounds of decency, and to be regarded as atrocious and utterly intolerable in a civilized community. Liability does not extend to mere insults, indignities, threats, annoyances, petty oppressions, or other trivialities. It has been said that the case is generally one in which the recitation of the facts to an average member of the community would arouse his resentment against the actor, and lead him to exclaim, "Outrageous!"

The conduct in this case involved defendants identifying plaintiffs by name and publicizing the fact of their abortions by displaying such information on large signs that were held up for public view. In ruling that defendants'

[6] *Ford Motor Credit Co. v. Sheehan*, 373 So.2d 956, 1979 Fla. App. LEXIS 15416 (Fla. Dist. Ct. App. 1979).
[7] *Midas Muffler Shop v. Ellison*, 133 Ariz. 194, 650 P.2d 496, 1982 Ariz. App LEXIS 488 (Ariz. Ct. App. 1982).

conduct was not sufficiently extreme and outrageous so as to permit recovery, the trial court was influenced in part by its conclusion that the information disclosed did not concern a private matter, inasmuch as it was obtained from a document that had been discarded into the trash. [But the plaintiffs themselves never placed their names on the discarded papers, and even if they had, such an act would not have indicated consent to such publicity.] The trial court also observed that defendants have a constitutional right to "protest peaceably against abortion." However, the objectionable aspect of defendants' conduct does not relate to their views on abortion or their right to express those views, but, rather, to the fact that defendants gave unreasonable or unnecessary publicity to purely private matters involving plaintiffs. Finally, the trial court observed that there is no statute prohibiting the kind of activity engaged in by defendants. It is not necessary, however, that a defendant's conduct constitute a statutory violation in order for it to be found extreme and outrageous.

We are of the opinion that the trial court erred in granting the defendants' motion for summary disposition of plaintiffs' claim of intentional infliction of emotional distress. Defendants' conduct involved more than mere insults, indignities, threats, annoyances, or petty oppressions. We believe this is the type of case that might cause an average member of the community, upon learning of defendants' conduct, to exclaim, "Outrageous!" Because reasonable men may differ with regard to whether defendants' conduct may be considered sufficiently outrageous and extreme so as to subject them to liability for intentional infliction of emotional distress, this matter should be determined by the trier of fact.

[Summary judgment for the defendants is reversed, and the case is remanded for trial.]

Battery and Assault

Battery
An intentional touching of another person in a way that is harmful or offensive.

Assault and battery are related, but not identical. **Battery** is an intentional touching of another person in a way that is harmful or offensive.

If an irate parent throws a chair at a referee during his daughter's basketball game, breaking the man's jaw, he has committed battery. But a parent who cheerfully slaps the winning coach on the back has not committed battery because a reasonable coach would not be offended.

As mentioned earlier, there need be no intention to hurt the plaintiff. If the defendant intended to do the physical act, and a reasonable plaintiff would be offended by it, battery has occurred. An executive who gives an unwanted sexual caress to a secretary also commits this tort, even if he assumed that any normal female would be ecstatic over his attentions. (This is also sexual harassment, discussed in Chapter 29, on employment law.)

Assault
An act that makes a person reasonably fear an imminent battery.

Assault occurs when a defendant does some act that makes a plaintiff *fear* an imminent battery. This tort is based on apprehension—it does not matter whether a battery ever occurs. Suppose Ms. Wilson shouts "Think fast!" at her husband and hurls a toaster at him. He turns and sees it flying at him. His fear of being struck is enough to win a case of assault, even if the toaster misses. If the toaster happens to strike him, Ms. Wilson has also committed battery.

Recall the shoplifting problem. Assume that a store guard pulls an unloaded pistol on Sandra Shopper, suspecting her of theft. Sandra faints and strikes her head on a counter. When sued for assault, the store defends by claiming the guard never touched her and the gun was unloaded. Obviously, the store did not have the benefit of this law course. A reasonable shopper would have feared imminent battery, and the store is liable for assault.

EXAM Strategy

Question: Mark is furious because his girlfriend, Denise, just told him she is leaving him. He never saw it coming. On the sidewalk, he picks up a rock and hurls it at Denise's head. She *does* see it coming, and she ducks. The rock misses Denise but hits Terrance (who never saw it coming) in the back of his head. Denise and Terrance both sue Mark for assault and for battery. Outcomes?

Strategy: Separate the two plaintiffs. What injury did Denise suffer? She saw a rock flying at her and thought she would be struck. Now recall the elements of the two torts. Battery is an intentional touching that is offensive. Assault is an act that makes another person *fear* an imminent battery.

Result: Was Denise touched? No. Did she fear an imminent battery? Yes. Denise wins a suit for assault but loses one for battery. Now Terrance: Was he touched? Yes. Did he fear an imminent battery? No. Terrance wins a suit for battery but loses one for assault.

Trespass, Conversion, and Fraud

Trespass

Trespass is intentionally entering land that belongs to someone else or remaining on the land after being asked to leave. It is also trespass if you have some object, let's say a car, on someone else's property and refuse to remove it. "Intentionally" means that you deliberately walk onto the land. If you walk through a meadow, believing it to be a public park, and it belongs to a private owner, you have trespassed.

Trespass
Intentionally entering land that belongs to someone else or remaining on the land after being asked to leave.

Conversion

Conversion is taking or using someone's personal property without consent. Personal property is any possession other than land or structures permanently attached to land, such as houses. Priceless jewels, ratty sneakers, and sailboats are all personal property. If Stormy sails away in Jib's sailboat and keeps it all summer, that is conversion. Stormy owes Jib the full value of the boat. This, of course, is similar to the crime of theft. The tort of conversion enables a plaintiff to pursue the case herself, without awaiting a criminal prosecution, and to obtain compensation.

© GSPhotography /Shutterstock.com

When does a trespasser intentionally enter onto another's property?

Fraud

Fraud is injuring another person by deliberate deception. Later in this chapter, a plaintiff claims that for many years a cigarette manufacturer fraudulently suggested its product was safe, knowing its assurances were deadly lies. Fraud is a tort, but it typically occurs during the negotiation or performance of a contract, and it is discussed in detail in Unit 2, on contracts.

Conversion
Taking or using someone's personal property without consent.

Fraud
Injuring another person by deliberate deception.

EXAM Strategy

Question: Raymond, a billionaire businessman widely known in the state, is running for the U.S. Senate. A newspaper reports that Raymond received $150,000 from an organization with "proven links to terrorist groups." The story came from a woman working in Raymond's own campaign, and two other witnesses, all three of whom had proven reliable in the past. Raymond, leading in the polls by 18%, plummets in popularity and loses the election. Raymond sues the paper. Outcome?

Strategy: First, determine the injury that Raymond has suffered. His reputation has been damaged. Second, ask what tort protects reputation. Defamation. Third, apply the elements to these facts.

Result: The newspaper's story, very likely to harm reputation, was widely communicated and did injure Raymond. But we don't know whether the article was true or false. Do we need to know? Usually we do, because a defendant is only liable for false statements. However, notice that a public personality must also prove *actual malice.* Was Raymond a public figure? Yes, he was a prominent billionaire and Senate candidate. There was no actual malice. The paper acted in good faith, using three credible sources. Raymond loses his lawsuit.

DAMAGES

Compensatory Damages

> Bien becomes frantic, writing a dozen notes, begging to leave, threatening to call the police.

Mitchel Bien, who is deaf and mute, enters the George Grubbs Nissan dealership, where folks sell cars aggressively. Very aggressively. Maturelli, a salesman, and Bien communicate by writing messages back and forth. Maturelli takes Bien's own car keys, and the two then test drive a 300ZX. Bien says he does not want the car, but Maturelli escorts him back inside and fills out a sales sheet. Bien repeatedly asks for his keys, but Maturelli only laughs, pressuring him to buy the new car. Minutes pass. Hours pass. Bien becomes frantic, writing a dozen notes, begging to leave, threatening to call the police. Maturelli mocks Bien and his physical disabilities. Finally, after four hours, the customer escapes.

Bien sues for the intentional infliction of emotional distress. Two former salesmen from Grubbs testify they have witnessed customers cry, yell, and curse as a result of the aggressive tactics. Doctors state that the incident has traumatized Bien, dramatically reducing his confidence and self-esteem and preventing his return to work even three years later.

The jury awards Bien damages. But how does a jury calculate the money? For that matter, why should a jury even try? Money can never erase pain or undo a permanent injury. The answer is simple: money, however inexact, is often the only thing a court has to give.

Compensatory damages
Money intended to restore a plaintiff to the position he was in before the injury.

Single recovery principle
Requires a court to settle the matter once and for all, by awarding a lump sum for past and future expenses.

A successful plaintiff generally receives **compensatory damages**, meaning an amount of money that the court believes will restore him to the position he was in before the defendant's conduct caused injury. Here is how damages are calculated.

First, a plaintiff receives money for medical expenses that he has proven by producing bills from doctors, hospitals, physical therapists, and psychotherapists. Bien receives all the money he has paid. If a doctor testifies that he needs future treatment, Bien will offer evidence of how much that will cost. The **single recovery principle** requires a court to settle the matter once and for all, by awarding a lump sum for past *and future* expenses, if there will be any. A plaintiff may not return in a year and say, "Oh, by the way, there are some new bills."

Second, the defendants are liable for lost wages. The court takes the number of days or months that Bien missed work and multiplies that times his salary. If Bien is currently unable to work, a doctor estimates how many more months he will miss work, and the court adds that to his damages.

Third, a plaintiff is paid for pain and suffering. Bien testifies about how traumatic the four hours were and how the experience has affected his life. He may state that he now fears shopping, suffers nightmares, and seldom socializes. To bolster the case, a plaintiff uses expert testimony, such as the psychiatrists who testified for Bien. Awards for pain and suffering vary enormously, from a few dollars to many millions, depending on the injury and depending on the jury. In some lawsuits, physical and psychological pain are momentary and insignificant; in other cases, the pain is the biggest part of the verdict. In this case, the jury awarded Bien $573,815, calculated as in the following table.[8]

Past medical	$ 70.00
Future medical	6,000.00
Past rehabilitation	3,205.00
Past lost earning capacity	112,910.00
Future lost earning capacity	34,650.00
Past physical symptoms and discomfort	50,000.00
Future physical symptoms and discomfort	50,000.00
Past emotional injury and mental anguish	101,980.00
Future emotional injury and mental anguish	200,000.00
Past loss of society and reduced ability to socially interact with family, former fiancée, and friends, and hearing (i.e., nondeaf) people in general	10,000.00
Future loss of society and reduced ability to socially interact with family, former fiancee, and friends, and hearing people	5,000.00
TOTAL	**$573,815.00**

[8]The compensatory damages are described in *George Grubbs Enterprises v. Bien*, 881 S.W.2d 843, 1994 Tex. App. LEXIS 1870 (Tex. Ct. App. 1994). In addition to the compensatory damages described, the jury awarded $5 million in punitive damages. The Texas Supreme Court reversed the award of punitive damages, but not the compensatory. *Id.*, 900 S.W.2d 337, 1995 Tex. LEXIS 91 (Tex. 1995). The high court did not dispute the appropriateness of punitive damages, but reversed because the trial court failed to instruct the jury properly as to how it should determine the assets actually under the defendants' control, an issue essential to punitive damages but not compensatory.

Awards for future harm (such as future pain and suffering) involve the court making its best estimate of the plaintiff's hardship in the years to come. This is not an exact science. If the judgment is reasonable, it will rarely be overturned. Ethel Flanzraich, aged 78, fell on stairs that had been badly maintained. In addition to her medical expense, the court awarded her $150,000 for future pain and suffering. The day after the court gave its award, Ms. Flanzraich died of other causes. Did that mean her family must forfeit that money? No. The award was reasonable when made and had to be paid.[9]

Punitive Damages

Punitive damages
Damages that are intended to punish the defendant for conduct that is extreme and outrageous.

Here we look at a different kind of award, one that is more controversial and potentially more powerful: punitive damages. The purpose is not to compensate the plaintiff for harm, because compensatory damages will have done that. **Punitive damages** are intended to punish the defendant for conduct that is extreme and outrageous. Courts award these damages in relatively few cases. The idea behind punitive damages is that certain behavior is so unacceptable that society must make an example of it. A large award of money should deter the defendant from repeating the mistake and others from ever making it. Some believe punitive damages represent the law at its most avaricious, while others attribute to them great social benefit.

Although a jury has wide discretion in awarding punitive damages, the Supreme Court has ruled that a verdict must be reasonable. Ira Gore purchased a new BMW automobile from an Alabama dealer and then discovered that the car had been repainted. He sued. At trial, BMW acknowledged a nationwide policy of not informing customers of predelivery repairs when the cost was less than 3% of the retail price. The company had sold about 1,000 repainted cars nationwide. The jury concluded that BMW had engaged in gross, malicious fraud and awarded Gore $4,000 in compensatory damages and $4 million in punitive damages. The Alabama Supreme Court reduced the award to $2 million, but the United States Supreme Court ruled that even that amount was grossly excessive. The Court held that in awarding punitive damages, a court must consider three "guideposts":

- The reprehensibility of the defendant's conduct;
- The ratio between the harm suffered and the award; and
- The difference between the punitive award and any civil penalties used in similar cases.

The Court concluded that BMW had shown no evil intent and that Gore's harm had been purely economic (as opposed to physical). Further, the Court found the ratio of 500 to 1, between punitive and compensatory damages, to be excessive, although it offered no definitive rule about a proper ratio. On remand, the Alabama Supreme Court reduced the punitive damages award to $50,000.[10]

The U.S. Supreme Court gave additional guidance on punitive damages in the following landmark case.

---

[9]We looked at discovery issues from this case in Chapter 3. *Stinton v. Robin's Wood,* 45 A.D.3d 203, 842 N.Y.S.2d 477 (N.Y.App.Div., 2007).

[10]*BMW of North America, Inc. v. Gore,* 517 U.S. 559, 116 S.Ct. 1589, 1996 U.S. LEXIS 3390 (1996).

Landmark Case

STATE FARM V. CAMPBELL

538 U.S. 408
Supreme Court of the United States (2003)

Facts: While attempting to pass several cars on a two-lane road, Campbell drove into oncoming traffic. An innocent driver swerved to avoid Campbell and died in a collision with a third driver. The family of the deceased driver and the surviving third driver both sued Campbell.

As Campbell's insurer, State Farm represented him in the lawsuit. It turned down an offer to settle the case for $50,000, the limit of Campbell's policy. The company had nothing to gain by settling because even if Campbell lost big at trial, State Farm's liability was capped at $50,000.

A jury returned a judgment against Campbell for $185,000. He was responsible for the $135,000 that exceeded his policy limit. He argued with State Farm, claiming that it should have settled the case. Eventually, State Farm paid the entire $185,000, but Campbell still sued the company, alleging fraud and intentional infliction of emotional distress.

His lawyers presented evidence that State Farm had deliberately acted in its own best interests rather than his. The jury was convinced, and in the end, Campbell won an award of $1 million in compensatory damages and $145 million in punitive damages. State Farm appealed.

Issue: ***What is the limit on punitive damages?***

Excerpts from Justice Kennedy's Opinion: We address whether an award of $145 million in punitive damages, where full compensatory damages are $1 million, is excessive and in violation of the Due Process Clause. The Utah Supreme Court relied upon testimony indicating that State Farm's actions, because of their clandestine nature, will be punished at most in 1 out of every 50,000 cases as a matter of statistical probability, and concluded that the ratio between punitive and compensatory damages was not unwarranted.

Compensatory damages are intended to redress the concrete loss that the plaintiff has suffered by reason of the defendant's wrongful conduct. By contrast, punitive damages serve a broader function; they are aimed at deterrence and retribution.

The Due Process Clause prohibits the imposition of grossly excessive or arbitrary punishments. The reason is that elementary notions of fairness dictate that a person receive fair notice not only of the conduct that will subject him to punishment, but also of the severity of the penalty that a State may impose. To the extent an award is grossly excessive, it furthers no legitimate purpose and constitutes an arbitrary deprivation of property. A defendant should be punished for the conduct that harmed the plaintiff, not for being an unsavory.

We decline to impose a bright-line ratio which a punitive damages award cannot exceed. Our jurisprudence and the principles it has now established demonstrate, however, that, in practice, few awards exceeding a single-digit ratio between punitive and compensatory damages, to a significant degree, will satisfy due process. Single-digit multipliers are more likely to comport with due process, while still achieving the State's goals of deterrence and retribution, than awards with ratios in the range of 145 to 1.

Nonetheless, because there are no rigid benchmarks that a punitive damages award may not surpass, ratios greater than those we have previously upheld may comport with due process where a particularly egregious act has resulted in only a small amount of economic damages. The precise award in any case must be based upon the facts and circumstances of the defendant's conduct and the harm to the plaintiff.

In sum, courts must ensure that the measure of punishment is both reasonable and proportionate to the amount of harm to the plaintiff and to the general damages recovered. In the context of this case, we have no doubt that there is a presumption against an award that has a 145-to-1 ratio. The compensatory award in this case was substantial; the Campbells were awarded $ 1 million for a year and a half of emotional distress. This was complete compensation. The harm arose from a transaction in the economic realm, not from some physical assault or trauma; there were no physical injuries; and State Farm paid the excess verdict before the complaint was filed, so the Campbells suffered only minor economic injuries.

The judgment of the Utah Supreme Court is reversed, and the case is remanded for proceedings not inconsistent with this opinion.

Dramatic cases may *still* lead to very large awards.

And so, the Supreme Court seeks to limit, but not completely prohibit, enormous punitive damages. A California Court of Appeals decided the following case two years after *State Farm v. Campbell*. How should it implement the Supreme Court's guidelines? You be the judge.

You be the Judge

Boeken v. Philip Morris, Incorporated

127 Cal. App.4th 1640, 26 CalRptr.3d 638
California Court of Appeals, 2005

Facts: In the mid-1950s, Richard Boeken began smoking Marlboro cigarettes at the age of 10. Countless advertisements, targeted at boys aged 10 to 18, convinced him and his friends that the "Marlboro man" was powerful, healthy, and manly. Eventually Richard changed to "Marlboro Lite" cigarettes but continued smoking into the 1990s, when he was diagnosed with lung cancer. He filed suit against Philip Morris, the cigarette manufacturer, for fraud and other torts. He died of cancer before the case was concluded.

Evidence at trial demonstrated that by the mid-1950s, scientists uniformly accepted that cigarette smoking caused lung cancer. However, at about the same time, Philip Morris and other tobacco companies began a decades-long campaign to convince the public that there was substantial doubt about any link between smoking and illness. The plaintiffs also demonstrated that tobacco was physically addictive, and that Philip Morris added ingredients such as urea to its cigarettes to increase their addictive power. Boeken testified that in the late 1960s he saw the Surgeon General warnings about the risk of smoking but trusted the cigarette company's statements that smoking was safe. By the 1970s he tried many times, and many cures, to stop smoking but always failed. He finally quit just before surgery to remove part of his lung but resumed after the operation.

The jury found Philip Morris liable for fraudulently concealing that cigarettes were addictive and carcinogenic. It awarded Boeken $5.5 million in compensatory damages, and also assessed punitive damages—of $3 *billion*. The trial judge reduced the punitive award to $100 million. Philip Morris appealed.

You Be the Judge: ***Was the punitive damage award too high, too low, or just right?***

Argument for Philip Morris: The court should substantially reduce the $100 million punitive award because it constitutes an "arbitrary deprivation of property." The Supreme Court has indicated that punitive awards should not exceed compensatory damages by more than a factor of nine. The jury awarded Mr. Boeken $5.5 million in compensatory damages, which means that punitive damages should absolutely not exceed $49.5 million. We argue that they should be even lower.

Cigarettes are a legal product, and our packages have displayed the Surgeon General's health warnings for decades. Mr. Boeken's death is tragic, but his cancer was not necessarily caused by Marlboro cigarettes. And even if cigarettes did contribute to his failing health, Mr. Boeken chose to smoke throughout his life, even after major surgery on one of his lungs.

Argument for Boeken: The Supreme Court says that "few" cases may exceed the 9-to-1 ratio, but that "the precise award in any case must be based upon the facts and circumstances of the defendant's conduct and the harm to the plaintiff." Phillip Morris created ads that targeted children, challenged clear scientific data that its products caused cancer, and added substances to its cigarettes to make them more addictive. Does it get worse than that?

As for harm to the plaintiff, he died a terrible death from cancer. Philip Morris cigarettes kill 200,000 American customers each year. The defendant's conduct could not be more reprehensible. Philip Morris's weekly profit is roughly $100 million. At a minimum, the court should keep the punitive award at that figure. But we ask that the court reinstate the jury's original $3 billion award.

Tort Reform and The Exxon Valdez

Some people believe that jury awards are excessive and need statutory reform, while others argue that the evidence demonstrates excessive awards are rare and modest in size. About one-half of the states have passed limits. The laws vary, but many distinguish between **economic damage** and **non-economic damages**. In such a state, a jury is permitted to award any amount for economic damages, meaning lost wages, medical expenses, and other measureable losses. However, noneconomic damages—pain and suffering and other losses that are difficult to measure—are capped at some level, such as $500,000. In some states, punitive awards have similar caps. These restrictions can drastically lower the total verdict.

In the famous *Exxon Valdez* case, the Supreme Court placed a severe limit on a certain type of punitive award. It is unclear how influential the decision will be because the case arises in the isolated area of maritime law, which governs ships at sea. Nonetheless, the justices wrote at length about punitive awards, and the decision may reverberate in future holdings. This is what happened.

Captain Joseph Hazelwood's negligence caused the *Exxon Valdez* to run aground off the coast of Alaska. The ship dumped 11 million gallons of oil into the sea, damaging 3,000 square miles of vulnerable ecosystem. The oil spill forced fishermen into bankruptcy, disrupted entire communities, and killed hundreds of thousands of birds and marine animals. A decade later, many of the damaged species had not recovered. The jury decided that Exxon had been reckless by allowing Hazelwood to pilot the ship when the company knew he was an alcoholic. The jury awarded compensatory damages to the plaintiffs, and punitive damages of $5 *billion*. Exxon appealed.

Almost two decades after the accident, the Supreme Court ruled. The justices discussed punitive damages in general, noting that much of the criticism of punitive awards appeared overstated. The court declared there had been no major increase in how frequently juries gave punitive damages. In the unusual cases where jurors made such awards, the sums were modest. The problem, declared the justices, was the unpredictability of punitive damages.

The court ruled that *in maritime cases*, the ratio should be no higher than 1:1. The court approved the jury's compensatory award of $507 million, and then reduced the punitive award from $5 billion to $507 million. Supporters of the court's decision stated that it would allow businesses to make plans based on predictable outcomes. Opponents said that the justices ignored the jury's finding of reckless behavior and calamitous environmental harm.[11]

EXAM Strategy

Question: Patrick owns a fast food restaurant which is repeatedly painted with graffiti. He is convinced that 15-year-old John, a frequent customer, is the culprit. The next time John comes to the restaurant, Patrick locks the men's room door while John is inside. Patrick calls the police, but because of a misunderstanding, the police are very slow to arrive. John shouts and cries for help, banging on the door, but Patrick does not release him for two hours. John sues. He claims that he has suffered great psychological harm because of the incident; his psychiatrist asserts that John may have unpredictable suffering in the future. John sues for assault, battery, and false imprisonment. Will he win? May John return to court in the future to seek further damages?

[11]*Exxon Shipping Co. v. Baker*, 128 S.Ct. 2605 (2008).

Strategy: The question focuses on two issues: First, the distinction between several intentional torts; second, damages. Analyze one issue at a time. As to the intentional torts, what injury has John suffered? He was locked in the men's room and suffered psychological harm. Recall the elements of the three possible torts. Battery concerns an offensive touching. A defendant commits assault by causing an imminent fear of battery. False imprisonment: a store may detain someone if it does so reasonably.

As to damages, review the *single recovery principle.*

© Sean Gladwell/Shutterstock

Is it reasonable for the owner of this property to detain the suspected vandal?

Result: Locking John up for two hours, based on an unproven suspicion, was clearly unreasonable. Patrick has committed false imprisonment. The single recovery principle forces John to recover now for all past and future harm. He may not return to court later and seek additional damages.

BUSINESS TORTS

In this section, we look at several intentional torts that occur almost exclusively in a commercial setting: interference with a contract, interference with a prospective advantage, the rights to privacy and publicity, and Lanham Act violations. Note that several business torts are discussed elsewhere in the book:

- Patents, copyrights, and trademarks are discussed in Chapter 42, on intellectual property.
- False advertising, discussed in part under the Lanham Act section (later in this chapter), is considered more broadly in Chapter 39, on consumer law.
- Consumer issues are also covered in Chapter 39. The material in the present chapter focuses not on consumer claims but on disputes between businesses.

Tortious Interference with Business Relations

Competition is the essence of business. Successful corporations compete aggressively, and the law permits and expects them to. But there are times when healthy competition becomes illegal interference. This is called tortious interference with business relations. It can take one of two closely related forms—interference with a contract or interference with a prospective advantage.

Tortious Interference with a Contract

Tortious interference with a contract exists if the plaintiff can establish the following four elements:

Tortious interference with a contract
An intentional tort in which the defendant improperly induced a third party to breach a contract with the plaintiff.

- There was a contract between the plaintiff and a third party;
- The defendant knew of the contract;
- The defendant improperly *induced* the third party to breach the contract or made performance of the contract impossible; and
- There was injury to the plaintiff.

Because businesses routinely compete for customers, employees, and market share, it is not always easy to identify tortious interference. There is nothing wrong with two companies bidding against each other to buy a parcel of land, and nothing wrong with one corporation doing everything possible to convince the seller to ignore all competitors. But once a company has signed a contract to buy the land, it is improper to induce the seller to break the deal. The most commonly disputed issues in these cases concern elements one and three: was there a contract between the plaintiff and another party? Did the defendant improperly induce a party to breach it? Defendants will try to show that the plaintiff had no contract.

A defendant may also rely on the defense of **justification**, that is, a claim that special circumstances made its conduct fair. To establish justification, a defendant must show that:

- It was acting to protect an existing economic interest, such as its own contract with the third party;
- It was acting in the public interest, for example, by reporting to a government agency that a corporation was overbilling for government services; or
- The existing contract could be terminated at will by either party, meaning that although the plaintiff had a contract, the plaintiff had no long-term assurances because the other side could end it at any time.

Texaco v. Pennzoil

The jury returned an enormous verdict in a famous case of contract interference. *Texaco, Inc. v. Pennzoil Co.* illustrates the two key issues: did a contract exist, and was the defendant's behavior improper? Pennzoil made an unsolicited bid to buy 20 percent of Getty Oil at \$100 per share. This offer was too low to satisfy the Getty board of directors, but it got the parties talking. The price increased to \$110 per share, and the two sides began to put together pieces of a complicated deal: Gordon Getty would control four-sevenths of the Getty Oil stock, and Pennzoil would control three-sevenths. The J. Paul Getty Museum, which owned 11.8 percent of Getty stock, agreed to sell its shares provided it was paid immediately. Talks continued, the price moved up to \$112.50 a share, and finally

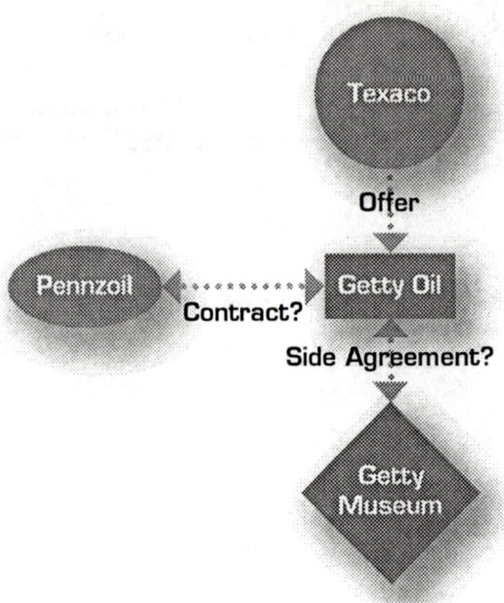

EXHIBIT 6.2 The $10 *billion* question. Texaco offered to pay $125 per share for Getty stock. The key issue was this: when Texaco made the offer, did a contract exist between Pennzoil and Getty? If, as the jury decided, there was a binding agreement, then Texaco committed tortious interference with a contract. If, however, Getty Corp. had a side agreement with the Getty Museum (one of its owners), then arguably there could be no contract between Getty and Pennzoil, and Texaco would have committed no tort at all.

the Getty board voted to approve the deal. A press release announced an agreement in principle between Pennzoil and Getty.

Before the lawyers for both sides could complete the paperwork for the deal, Texaco appeared and offered Getty stockholders $125 per share for the entire company and later upped that offer to $128. Getty turned its attention to Texaco, leaving Pennzoil the jilted lover. This lover, though, decided to sue. In Texas state court, Pennzoil claimed that Texaco had maliciously interfered with a Pennzoil–Getty contract, costing Pennzoil vast amounts of money.

Texaco argued that it had acted in good faith, asserting that there was no binding contract between the other two. But the jury bought Pennzoil's argument, and they bought it big: $7.53 billion in actual damages, plus $3 billion more in punitive damages. Texaco did not happen to have $10 billion it could spare, and the verdict threatened to destroy the oil company. Texaco appealed, but Texas appeals courts require a bond, in this case a $10 billion bond, meaning that the money must be paid into court while the appeal goes forward. Texaco filed for bankruptcy.

At the state supreme court, Texaco based its argument on an obscure rule of the Securities and Exchange Commission (SEC), Rule 10B-13. This rule prevents the parties in a takeover negotiation from arranging a "side deal" while an offer is pending. Texaco's argument thus became: Pennzoil's original $100 per share offer was still pending when the two sides came up with their $112.50 per share, "three-sevenths/four-sevenths" deal. That deal involved a side arrangement with the Getty Museum, which would get its money faster than any other shareholders would. Because it would get about $1 billion, early receipt was a major financial advantage. The deal violated Rule 10B-13 and was therefore invalid. There was no contract, and Texaco could not legally have interfered.

A $10 billion case would be decided on the classic "interference" issue of whether a contract existed. Then the SEC entered the case, filing a brief that appeared strongly to support Texaco's interpretation of the law. Pennzoil could sense that the tide was turning, and the companies settled: Texaco agreed to pay Pennzoil $3 billion as settlement for having wrongfully interfered with Pennzoil's agreement to buy Getty.

Tortious Interference with a Prospective Advantage

Interference with a prospective advantage is an awkward name for a tort that is simply a variation on interference with a contract. The difference is that, for this tort, there need be no contract; the plaintiff is claiming outside interference with an expected economic relationship. Obviously, the plaintiff must show more than just the hope of a profit. **A plaintiff who has a definite and reasonable expectation of obtaining an economic advantage may sue a corporation that maliciously interferes and prevents the relationship from developing.**

Tortious interference with a prospective advantage Malicious interference with a developing economic relationship.

The defense of justification, discussed above, applies here as well. A typical example of justification is that the defendant is simply competing for the same business that the plaintiff seeks. There is nothing wrong with that.

To demonstrate interference with a prospective advantage, most courts require a plaintiff to show that the defendant's conduct was independently unlawful. Suppose Pink manufactures valves used in heart surgery. Pink is about to sign a deal for Rabbit to distribute the products. Zebra then says to Pink, "I want that deal. If you sign with Rabbit, I'll spread false rumors that the valves are unreliable." Pink gives in and signs a contract with Zebra. Zebra has committed interference with a prospective advantage because slander is independently illegal.[12]

The ice cream fight that follows demonstrates why plaintiffs often file but seldom win these cases.

Carvel v. Noonan

3 N.Y.3d 182, 785 N.Y.S.2d 359, 818 N.E.2d 1100
New York Court of Appeals, 2004

Facts: For decades, Carvel sold its ice cream only through franchised stores. However, a decline in revenues caused the company to begin selling its product in supermarkets. That effort expanded quickly, but many of the franchised stores (franchisees) went out of business. Franchisees filed suit, claiming tortious interference with a prospective advantage. In particular, the plaintiffs argued that Carvel undersold them in supermarkets and issued coupons only redeemable there. The case reached New York's highest court.

Issue: ***Had Carvel committed tortious interference with a prospective advantage?***

Excerpts from Justice Smith's Decision: The franchisees' tort claim is that Carvel unlawfully interfered with the relationships between the franchisees and their customers. The franchisees do not claim that the customers had binding contracts that Carvel induced them to breach; they allege only that, by implementing its supermarket program, Carvel induced the customers not to buy Carvel products from the franchisees. The juries have found that Carvel did so induce customers, and the question for us is whether that inducement was tortious interference under New York law.

We have recognized that inducing breach of a binding agreement and interfering with a nonbinding "economic relation" can both be torts, but that the elements of the two torts are not the same. Where there has been no breach of an existing contract, but only interference with prospective contract rights, however, plaintiff must show

[12] For a more detailed explanation, see *Wal-Mart Stores, Inc. v. Sturges*, 52 S.W.3d 711, 2001 Tex. LEXIS 18 (Tex. 2001).

more culpable conduct on the part of the defendant. The implication is that, as a general rule, the defendant's conduct must amount to a crime or an independent tort.

The franchisees claim that Carvel did use wrongful "economic pressure" but that argument is ill-founded for two independent reasons. First, it is ill-founded because the economic pressure that must be shown is not, as the franchisees assume, pressure on the franchisees, but on the franchisees' customers. Conduct constituting tortious interference with business relations is, by definition, conduct directed not at the plaintiff itself, but at the party with which the plaintiff has or seeks to have a relationship.

Here, all Carvel did to the franchisees' customers was to make Carvel goods available in supermarkets at attractive prices; this was not "pressure" on these third parties but legitimate "persuasion," and thus tortious interference with economic relations was not established.

The franchisees' argument is also ill-founded because the Carvel activities they complain of do not amount to the sort of extreme and unfair "economic pressure" that might be "wrongful." The crux of the franchisees' complaint is that Carvel distributed its products through competitive channels, to an extent and in a way that was inconsistent with the franchisor-franchisee relationship. But the relationship between franchisors and franchisees is a complex one; while cooperative, it does not preclude all competition; and the extent to which competition is allowed should be determined by the contracts between the parties, not by courts or juries seeking after the fact to devise a code of conduct.

Apart from attacking the supermarket program in general as excessively and destructively competitive, the franchisees also attack the coupon-redemption element of that program as excessive "economic pressure." The essence of the coupon program was to give customers who used coupons a better price when they shopped in supermarkets. The mere institution of a coupon program was not "economic pressure" rising to the level of "wrongful" or "culpable" conduct.

[Carvel's conduct was not tortious interference with a prospective advantage.]

Privacy and Publicity

We live in a world of dazzling technology, and it is easier than ever—and more profitable—to spy on someone. Does the law protect us? What power do we have to limit the intrusion of others into our lives and to prohibit them from commercially exploiting information about us?

Intrusion

Intrusion
A tort in which a reasonable person would find the invasion of her private life offensive.

Intrusion into someone's private life is a tort if a reasonable person would find it offensive. Peeping through someone's windows or wiretapping his telephone are obvious examples of intrusion. In a famous case involving a "paparazzo" photographer and Jacqueline Kennedy Onassis, the court found that the photographer had invaded her privacy by making a career out of photographing her. He had bribed doormen to gain access to hotels and restaurants she visited, had jumped out of bushes to photograph her young children, and had driven power boats dangerously close to her. The court ordered him to stop.[13] Nine years later the paparazzo was found in contempt of court for again taking photographs too close to Ms. Onassis. He agreed to stop once and for all—in exchange for a suspended contempt sentence.

Commercial Exploitation

The right to commercial exploitation prohibits the use of someone's likeness or voice for commercial purposes without permission. This business tort is the flip side of privacy and covers the right to make money from publicity. For example, it would be illegal to run a

[13] *Galella v. Onassis*, 487 F.2d 986, 1973 U.S. App. LEXIS 7901 (2d Cir. 1973).

magazine ad showing Keira Knightley holding a can of soda without her permission. The ad would imply that she endorses the product. Someone's identity is her own, and it cannot be used for commercial gain unless she permits it.

Ford Motor Co. hired a singer to imitate Bette Midler's version of a popular song. The imitation was so good that most listeners were fooled into believing that Ms. Midler was endorsing the product. That, ruled a court, violated her right to commercial exploitation.[14]

The Lanham Act

The Lanham Act provides broad protection against false statements intended to hurt another business. In order to win a case, a plaintiff must prove three things:

- That the defendants made false or misleading fact statements about the plaintiff's business. This could be a false comparative ad, showing the plaintiff's product to be worse than it is, or it could be a misleading ad, which, though literally accurate, is misleading about the defendant's own product.
- That the defendants used the statements in commercial advertising or promotion. In order to protect First Amendment rights of free speech, particularly political and social commentary, this act covers only commercial speech. A radio ad for beer could violate the Lanham Act; but a radio ad urging that smoking be abolished in public places is not a commercial statement and cannot violate the act.
- That statements created the likelihood of harm to the plaintiff.[15]

"Knock It Off brand food supplement will help you lose weight and gain muscle faster than any competing supplement," shrieks the television commercial, offering an independent study as proof. However, a competitor sues, and demonstrates that during the study, users of Knock It Off received free health club memberships and low-fat gourmet meals, distorting the results. Knock It Off has violated the Lanham Act. The court will order the company to knock it off and stop showing the commercial, and also to pay damages to the injured competitor.

Chapter Conclusion

This chapter has been a potpourri of misdeeds, a bubbling cauldron of conduct best avoided. Although tortious acts and their consequences are diverse, two generalities apply. First, the boundaries of intentional torts are imprecise, the outcome of a particular case depending to a considerable extent upon the factfinder who analyzes it. Second, the thoughtful executive and the careful citizen, aware of the shifting standards and potentially vast liability, will strive to ensure that his or her conduct never provides that factfinder an opportunity to give judgment.

[14] 18 U.S.C. § 2701.
[15] 18 U.S.C. § 2511.

EXAM REVIEW

1. **TORT** A tort is a violation of a duty imposed by the civil law. (pp. 131–132)

EXAM Strategy

Question: Keith is driving while intoxicated. He swerves into the wrong lane and causes an accident, seriously injuring Caroline. Which statement is true?

a. Caroline could sue Keith, who might be found guilty in her suit.

b. Caroline and the state could start separate criminal cases against Keith.

c. Caroline could sue Keith, and the state could prosecute Keith for drunk driving.

d. The state could sue Keith but only with Caroline's consent.

e. The state could prosecute Keith and sue him at the same time, for drunk driving.

Strategy: What party prosecutes a criminal case? The government does, not the injured party. What is the result in a criminal case? Guilt or innocence. What about a tort lawsuit? The injured party brings a tort suit. The defendant may be found liable but never guilty. (See the "Result" at the end of this section.)

2. **DEFAMATION** Defamation involves a defamatory statement that is false, uttered to a third person, and causes an injury. Opinion and privilege are valid defenses. (pp. 132–134)

EXAM Strategy

Question: Benzaquin had a radio talk show. On the program, he complained about an incident in which state trooper Fleming had stopped his car, apparently for lack of a proper license plate and safety sticker. Benzaquin explained that the license plate had been stolen and the sticker fallen onto the dashboard, but Fleming refused to let him drive away. Benzaquin and two young grandsons had to find other transportation. On the show, Benzaquin angrily recounted the incident, then described Fleming and troopers generally: "we're not paying them to be dictators and Nazis"; "this man is an absolute barbarian, a lunkhead, a meathead." Fleming sued Benzaquin for defamation. Comment.

Strategy: Review the elements of defamation. Can these statements be proven true or false? If not, what is the result? Look at the defenses. Does one apply? (See the "Result" at the end of this section.)

3. **MALICE** Public personalities can win a defamation suit only by proving actual malice. (pp. 133–134)

4. **FALSE IMPRISONMENT** False imprisonment is the intentional restraint of another person without reasonable cause and without consent. (p. 134)

5. **EMOTIONAL DISTRESS** The intentional infliction of emotional distress involves extreme and outrageous conduct that causes serious emotional harm. (pp. 135–136)

6. **BATTERY** Battery is an intentional touching of another person in a way that is unwanted or offensive. Assault involves an act that makes the plaintiff fear an imminent battery. (p. 136)

EXAM Strategy

Question: Caudle worked at Betts Lincoln-Mercury dealer. During an office party, many of the employees, including president Betts, were playing with an electric auto condenser, which gave a slight shock when touched. Some employees played catch with it. Betts shocked Caudle on the back of his neck, and chased him around. The shock later caused Caudle to suffer headaches, pass out, feel numbness, and eventually to require nerve surgery. He sued Betts for battery. Betts defended by saying that it was all horseplay and that he had intended no harm. Please rule.

Strategy: Betts argues he intended no harm. Is intent to harm an element? (See the "Result" at the end of this section.)

7. **DAMAGES** Compensatory damages are the normal remedy in a tort case. In unusual cases, the court may award punitive damages, not to compensate the plaintiff but to punish the defendant. (pp. 138–144)

8. **TORTIOUS INTERFERENCE** Tortious interference with business relations involves the defendant harming an existing contract or a prospective relationship that has a definite expectation of success. (pp. 145–148)

9. **PRIVACY AND PUBLICITY** The related torts of privacy and publicity involve unreasonable intrusion into someone's private life and unfair commercial exploitation by using someone's name, likeness, or voice without permission. (p. 148)

10. **LANHAM ACT** The Lanham Act prohibits false statements in commercial advertising or promotion. (p. 149)

1. Result: (a) is wrong because a defendant cannot be found guilty in a civil suit. (b) is wrong because a private party has no power to prosecute a criminal case. (c) is correct. (d) is wrong because the state will prosecute Keith, not sue him. (e) is wrong for the same reason.

2. Result: The court ruled in favor of Benzaquin because a reasonable person would understand the words to be opinion and ridicule. They are not statements of fact because most of them could not be proven true or false. A statement like "dictators and Nazis" is not taken literally by anyone.[16]

[16] *Fleming v. Benzaquin*, 390 Mass. 175, 454 N.E.2d 95 (1983).

6. Result: The court held that it was irrelevant that Betts had shown no malice toward Caudle nor intended to hurt him. Betts *intended the physical contact* with Caudle, and even though he could not foresee everything that would happen, he is liable for all consequences of his intended physical action.[17]

MULTIPLE-CHOICE QUESTIONS

1. Jane writes an article for a newspaper reporting that Ann was arrested for stealing a car. The story is entirely false. Ann is not a public figure. Which of the following torts has Jane committed?
   (a) Ordinary slander
   (b) Slander per se
   (c) Libel
   (d) None of the above

2. Refer back to Question 1. If Ann decides to sue, she _______________ have to show evidence that she suffered an injury. If she ultimately wins her case. a jury _______________ have the option to award punitive damages.
   (a) will; will
   (b) will; will not
   (c) will not; will
   (d) will not; will not

3. Sam sneaks up on Tom, hits him with a baseball bat, and knocks him unconscious. Tom never saw Sam coming. He wakes up with a horrible headache. Which of the following torts has Sam committed?
   (a) Assault
   (b) Battery
   (c) Both A and B
   (d) None of the above

4. Imagine a case in which a jury awards compensatory damages of $1 million. If this is not a maritime case, a jury would rarely be allowed to award more than _________________ in punitive damages.
   (a) $1 million
   (b) $3 million
   (c) $9 million
   (d) $10 million
   (e) $25 million

[17] *Caudle v. Betts*, 512 So.2d 389 (La.1987).

5. Al runs a red light and hits Carol's car. She later sues, claiming the following losses:

   $10,000—car repairs

   $10,000—medical expenses

   $10,000—lost wages (she could not work for two months after the accident)

   $10,000—pain and suffering

   If the jury believes all of Carol's evidence and she wins her case, how much will she receive in *compensatory* damages?

   (a) $40,000
   (b) $30,000
   (c) $20,000
   (d) $10,000
   (e) $0

ESSAY QUESTIONS

1. You are a vice president in charge of personnel at a large manufacturing company. In-house detectives inform you that Gates, an employee, was seen stealing valuable computer equipment. Gates denies the theft, but you believe the detectives and fire him. The detectives suggest that you post notices around the company, informing all employees what happened to Gates and why, because it will discourage others from stealing. While you are considering that, a phone call from another company's personnel officer asks for a recommendation for Gates. Should you post the notices? What should you say to the other officer?

2. Caldwell was shopping in a K-Mart store, carrying a large purse. A security guard observed her looking at various small items such as stain, hinges, and antenna wire. On occasion, she bent down out of sight of the guard. The guard thought he saw Caldwell put something in her purse. Caldwell removed her glasses from her purse and returned them a few times. After she left, the guard approached her in the parking lot and said that he believed she had store merchandise in her pocketbook, but he could not say what he thought was put there. Caldwell opened the purse, and the guard testified that he saw no K-Mart merchandise in it. The guard then told Caldwell to return to the store with him. They walked around the store for approximately 15 minutes, while the guard said six or seven times that he saw her put something in her purse. Caldwell left the store after another store employee indicated she could go. Caldwell sued. What kind of suit did she file, and what should the outcome be?

3. Tata Consultancy of Bombay, India, is an international computer consulting firm. It spends considerable time and effort recruiting the best personnel from India's leading technical schools. Tata employees sign an initial three-year employment commitment, often work overseas, and agree to work for a specified additional time when they return to India. Desai worked for Tata, but then he quit and formed a competing company, which he called Syntel. His new company contacted Tata employees by phone, offering higher salaries, bonuses, and assistance in obtaining permanent resident visas in the United States if they would come work for Syntel. At least 16 former Tata employees left their jobs without completing their contractual

obligations and went to work for Syntel. Tata sued. What did it claim, and what should be the result?

4. Pacific Express began operating as an airline in 1982. It had routes connecting western cities with Los Angeles and San Francisco, and by the summer of 1983, it was beginning to show a profit. In 1983, United Airlines tried to enter into a cooperative arrangement with Pacific in which United would provide Pacific with passengers for some routes so that United could concentrate on its longer routes. Negotiations failed. Later that year, United expanded its routes to include cities that only Pacific had served. United also increased its service to cities in which the two airlines were already competing. By early 1984, Pacific Express was unable to compete and sought protection under bankruptcy laws. It also sued United, claiming interference with a prospective advantage. United moved for summary judgment. Comment.

5. **YOU BE THE JUDGE WRITING PROBLEM** Johnny Carson was for many years the star of a well-known television show, *The Tonight Show*. For about 20 years, he was introduced nightly on the show with the phrase, "Here's Johnny!" A large segment of the television watching public associated the phrase with Carson. A Michigan corporation was in the business of renting and selling portable toilets. The company chose the name "Here's Johnny Portable Toilets," and coupled the company name with the marketing phrase, "The World's Foremost Commodian." Carson sued, claiming that the company's name and slogan violated his right to commercial exploitation.

   Argument for Carson: The toilet company is deliberately taking advantage of Johnny Carson's good name. He worked hard for decades to build a brilliant career and earn a reputation as a creative, funny, likable performer. No company has the right to use his name, his picture, or anything else closely identified with him, such as the phrase "Here's Johnny." The pun is personally offensive and commercially unfair.

   Argument for Here's Johnny Portable Toilets: Johnny Carson doesn't own his first name. It is available for anyone to use for any purpose. Further, the popular term "john," meaning toilet, has been around much longer than Carson or even television. We are entitled to make any use of it we want. Our corporate name is amusing to customers who have never heard of Carson, and we are entitled to profit from our brand recognition.

Discussion Questions

1. The Supreme Court limits punitive damages in most cases to nine times the compensatory damages awarded in the same case. Is this a sensible guideline? If not, should it be higher or lower?

2. You have most likely heard of the *Liebeck v. McDonalds* case. Liebeck spilled hot McDonald's coffee in her lap and suffered third-degree burns. At trial, evidence showed that her cup of coffee was brewed at 190 degrees, and that, more typically, a restaurant's "hot coffee" is in the range of 140 to 160 degrees.

A jury awarded Liebeck $160,000 in compensatory damages and $2.7 million in punitive damages. The judge reduced the punitive award to $480,000, or three times the compensatory award.

Comment on the case and whether the result was reasonable.

3. Celebrities often have problems with tabloids and the paparazzi. It is difficult for public figures to win libel lawsuits because they must show actual malice. Intrusion lawsuits are also tricky, and flocks of photographers often stalk celebrities at all hours.

   Is this right? Should the law change to offer more privacy to famous people? Or is a loss of privacy just the price of success?

4. With a national debt in the trillions, people are desensitized to "mere" billions. Stop for a moment and consider $1 billion. If you had that sum, invested it conservatively, and got a 5 percent return, you could spend roughly $1 million *a week* for the rest of your life *without reducing your principal.*

   This chapter described three lawsuits with jackpot punitive damage awards. The jury award was $10 billion in *Texaco v. Pennzoil,* $5 billion in the *Exxon Valdez* case, and $3 billion in *Boeken v. Philip Morris.* Is there any point at which the raw number of dollars awarded is just too large? Was the original jury award excessive in any of these cases? If so, which one(s)?

5. Many retailers have policies that instruct employees *not* to attempt to stop shoplifters. Some store owners fear false imprisonment lawsuits and possible injuries to workers more than losses related to stolen merchandise.

   Are these "don't be a hero" policies reasonable? Would you put one in place if you owned a retail store?

CHAPTER 7

NEGLIGENCE AND STRICT LIABILITY

© r.nagy/Shutterstock.com

If you give a party, should *you* be responsible for any damage caused by intoxicated guests?

Submitted for your consideration: a timeline.

3:25 p.m.—Jake, an 18-year-old freshman, sits in his Calculus I class, bored to tears. He receives a text: "Beta Zeta rush party TONIGHT!!!" He perks up.

9:15 p.m.—Jake drives with his roommate over to the Beta Zeta rush party.

9:32 p.m.—Jake and his roommate arrive at the Beta Zeta house. No one checks for ID.

9:36 p.m.—Jake gets a beer from a keg and drinks it.

9:37 p.m.—Jake pours himself another beer and heads outside.

9:58 p.m.—After listening to the band for awhile, Jake returns to the keg and gets a third beer.

10:24 p.m.—Jake faces off with his roommate. He chugs a beer slightly faster than the roommate, and his skills are praised by the Beta Zetas.

10:48 p.m.—Jake bongs a beer.

10:51 p.m.—Jake bongs another beer.

12:26 p.m.—Jake poses slightly off-balance, and his roommate takes an iPhone photo.

12:27 a.m.—Jake's roommate sends the picture to everyone on his contact list.

12:28 a.m.—Jake receives the first of many texts making fun of him.

12:35 a.m.—Jake finds his roommate, shoves him, and threatens to kick his ***.

12:38 a.m.—Jake tells his roommate, "I love you man," and heads off to find another beer.

1:14 a.m.—Jake drinks a seventh and final beer.

1:48 a.m.—Jake and his roommate leave the Beta Zeta house. Jake drives his car.

1:49 a.m.—Jake's roommate suggests getting some tacos.

1:54 a.m.—Jake tries to park his car at Taco Bell, but he misses the brake pedal. He drives his car through a large plate glass window and does $50,000 damage to the restaurant.

Who should pay for this damage? Jake is clearly at fault, but should the Beta Zetas share legal responsibility for the property damage? The question leads to other, similar issues: should a restaurant that serves alcohol to a minor be liable for harm that the youth might cause? Should the restaurant be responsible for serving an intoxicated adult who causes damage? If you give a party, should *you* be responsible for any damage caused by intoxicated guests?

These are all practical questions—worth considering before you entertain—and moral ones as well. They are also typical issues of negligence law. In this contentious area, courts continually face one question: *when someone is injured, how far should responsibility extend?*

NEGLIGENCE

We might call negligence the "unintentional" tort because it concerns harm that arises by accident. Should a court impose liability? The fraternity members who gave the party were not trying to damage the Taco Bell, but the damage occurred all the same. Is it in society's interest to hold the fraternity responsible?

Things go wrong all the time, and people are hurt in large ways and small. Society needs a means of analyzing negligence cases consistently and fairly. We cannot have each court that hears such a lawsuit extend or limit liability based on an emotional response to the facts. One of America's greatest judges, Benjamin Cardozo, offered an analysis more than 80 years ago. In a case called *Palsgraf v. Long Island Railroad,* he made a decision that still influences negligence thinking today.

Landmark Case

PALSGRAF V. LONG ISLAND RAILROAD

248 N.Y. 339; 162 N.E. 99
Court of Appeals of New York, 1928

Facts: Helen Palsgraf was waiting on a railroad platform. As a train began to leave the station, a man carrying a package ran to catch it. He jumped aboard but looked unsteady, so a guard on the car reached out to help him as another guard, on the platform, pushed from behind. The man dropped the package, which struck the tracks and exploded—since it was packed with fireworks. The shock knocked over some heavy scales at the far end of the platform, and one of them struck Palsgraf, who was injured as a result. She sued the railroad.

Issue: ***Was the railroad liable for Palsgraf's injuries?***

Excerpts from Judge Cardozo's Decision: The conduct of the defendant's guard was not a wrong in its relation to the plaintiff, standing far away. Relatively to her it was not negligence at all. Nothing in the situation gave notice that the falling package had in it the potency of peril to persons thus removed. Negligence is not actionable unless it involves the invasion of a legally protected interest, the violation of a right. Negligence is the absence of care, according to the circumstances.

If no hazard was apparent to the eye of ordinary vigilance, an act innocent and harmless, at least to outward seeming, with reference to her, did not take to itself the quality of a tort because it happened to be a wrong with reference to some one else. "In every instance, before negligence can be predicated of a given act, back of the act must be sought and found a duty to the individual complaining.

What the plaintiff must show is "a wrong" to herself and not merely a wrong to someone else. We are told that one who drives at reckless speed through a crowded city street is guilty of a negligent act because the eye of vigilance perceives the risk of damage. The risk reasonably to be perceived defines the duty to be obeyed.

Here, by concession, there was nothing in the situation to suggest to the most cautious mind that the parcel wrapped in newspaper would spread wreckage through the station.

The law of causation, remote or proximate, is thus foreign to the case before us. If there is no tort to be redressed, there is no occasion to consider what damage might be recovered if there were a finding of a tort. The consequences to be followed must first be rooted in a wrong.

Judge Cardozo ruled that the guard's conduct might have been a wrong as to the passenger, but not as to Ms. Palsgraf, standing far away. Her negligence case failed. "Proof of negligence in the air, so to speak, will not do," declared the judge. Courts are still guided by Judge Cardozo's ruling.

To win a negligence case, a plaintiff must prove five elements. Much of the remainder of the chapter will examine them in detail. They are:

- ***Duty of Due Care.*** The defendant had a legal responsibility *to the plaintiff*. This is the point from the *Palsgraf* case.
- ***Breach.*** The defendant breached her duty of care or failed to meet her legal obligations.
- ***Factual Cause.*** The defendant's conduct actually caused the injury.
- ***Proximate Cause.*** It was *foreseeable* that conduct like the defendant's might cause *this type of harm*.
- ***Damages.*** The plaintiff has actually been hurt or has actually suffered a measureable loss.

To win a case, a plaintiff must prove all the elements listed above. If a defendant eliminates only one item on the list, there is no liability.

Duty of Due Care

Each of us has a duty to behave as a reasonable person would under the circumstances. If you are driving a car, you have a duty to all the other people near you to drive like a reasonable person. If you drive while drunk, or send text messages while behind the wheel, then you fail to live up to your duty of care.

But how *far* does your duty extend? Most courts accept Cardozo's viewpoint in the *Palsgraf* case. Judges draw an imaginary line around the defendant and say that she owes a duty to the people within the circle, but not to those outside it. The test is generally "foreseeability." If the defendant could have foreseen injury to a particular person, she has a duty to him. Suppose that one of your friends posts a YouTube video of you texting behind the wheel and her father is so upset from watching it that he falls down the stairs. You would not be liable for the father's downfall because it was not foreseeable that he would be harmed by your texting.

Let us apply these principles to a case that, like the opening scenario, involves a fraternity party.

Hernandez v. Arizona Board of Regents

177 Ariz. 244, 866 P.2d 1330, 1994 Ariz. LEXIS 6
Arizona Supreme Court, 1994

Facts: At the University of Arizona, the Epsilon Epsilon chapter of Delta Tau Delta fraternity gave a welcoming party for new members. The fraternity's officers knew that the majority of its members were under the legal drinking age, but they permitted everyone to consume alcohol. John Rayner, who was under 21 years of age, left the party. He drove negligently and caused a collision with an auto driven by Ruben Hernandez. At the time of the accident, Rayner's blood alcohol level was .15, exceeding the legal limit. The crash left Hernandez blind and paralyzed.

Hernandez sued Rayner, who settled the case based on the amount of his insurance coverage. The victim also sued the fraternity, its officers and national organization, all fraternity members who contributed money to buy alcohol, the university, and others. The trial court granted summary judgment for all defendants and the court of appeals affirmed. Hernandez appealed to the Arizona Supreme Court.

Issue: ***Did the fraternity and the other defendants have a duty of due care to Hernandez?***

Excerpts from Justice Feldman's Decision: Before 1983, this court arguably recognized the common-law rule of non-liability for tavern owners and, presumably, for social hosts. Traditional authority held that when "an able-bodied man" caused harm because of his intoxication, the act from which liability arose was the consuming not the furnishing of alcohol.

However, the common law also provides that:

> One who supplies [a thing] for the use of another whom the supplier knows or has reason to know to be likely because of his youth, inexperience, or otherwise to use it in a manner involving unreasonable risk of physical harm to himself and others is subject to liability for physical harm resulting to them.

We perceive little difference in principle between liability for giving a car to an intoxicated youth and liability for giving drinks to a youth with a car. A growing number of cases have recognized that one of the very hazards that makes it negligent to furnish liquor to a minor is the foreseeable prospect that the [youthful] patron will become drunk and injure himself or others. Accordingly, modern authority has increasingly recognized that one who furnishes liquor to a minor breaches a common-law duty owed to innocent third parties who may be injured.

Furnishing alcohol to underaged drinkers violates numerous statutes. The conduct in question violates well-established common-law principles that recognize a duty to avoid furnishing dangerous items to those known to have diminished capacity to use them safely. We join the majority of other states and conclude that as to Plaintiffs and the public in general, Defendants had a duty of care to avoid furnishing alcohol to underage consumers.

Arizona courts, therefore, will entertain an action for damages against [one] who negligently furnishes alcohol to those under the legal drinking age when that act is a cause of injury to a third person. [Reversed and remanded.]

Ethics As the Arizona court notes, its decision agrees with the majority of courts that have considered the issue. In most (but not all) states, anyone serving alcohol to a minor is liable for injuries that result to a third party. The case raises other important issues.

- Should a social host who serves alcohol to an *adult* be liable for resulting harm? New Jersey has answered "Yes" to this question. In the Garden State, if a social host pours drinks for a friend, aware that he is becoming drunk, and the friend injures a third party, the host is fully liable. The majority of states to consider this issue have reached the opposite conclusion, holding that a social host is not liable for harm caused by an adult drinker. Are the majority of states correct to distinguish between adult and underage guests, holding a social host liable only for serving minors? Or is New Jersey correct to scrap this distinction?
- Many states now have some type of **dram act**, making liquor stores, bars, and restaurants liable for serving drinks to intoxicated customers who later cause harm. Dram shop laws force a financial dilemma on such firms. The more a tavern or café encourages its customers to drink, the greater its revenue—but also the larger its risk of a liability lawsuit. Do dram shop laws work? Yes, answer the authors of one economic study. In states with such statutes, bars monitor underage drinking more aggressively, refuse drinks earlier to an intoxicated customer, check the references of their own employees more carefully, and prohibit their workers from drinking on the job. Dram shop laws may be a promising way to reduce drunk driving accidents.[1] But are these laws reasonable? Is holding a bar responsible more reasonable than holding liable a person hosting a party at his house?
- There are many signs that society is fed up with drunk drivers. Some states have considered reducing blood alcohol limits for drunk driving to .05, which would place a typical person "over the limit" after two drinks. Are such proposals reasonable?

Dram act
A law that makes businesses liable for serving drinks to intoxicated customers who later cause harm.

In several circumstances, people have special duties to others. Three of them are outlined below.

Special Duty: Landowners

The common law applies special rules to a landowner for injuries occurring on her property. In most states, the owner's duty depends on the type of person injured.

Trespasser
A person on another's property without consent.

Lowest Liability: Trespassing Adults. A **trespasser** is anyone on the property without consent. A landowner is liable to a trespasser only for intentionally injuring him or for some other gross misconduct. The landowner has no liability to a trespasser for mere negligence. Jake is not liable if a vagrant wanders onto his land and is burned by defective electrical wires.

Mid-level Liability: Trespassing Children. The law makes exceptions when the trespassers are **children**. If there is some manmade thing on the land *that may be reasonably expected to attract children*, the landowner is probably liable for any harm. Daphne lives next door to a day-care center and builds a treehouse on her property. Unless she has fenced off the dangerous area, she is probably liable if a small child wanders onto her property and injures himself when he falls from the rope ladder to the treehouse.

[1]Sloan, Liang, Stout, and Whetten-Goldstein, "Liability, Risk Perceptions, and Precautions at Bars," *Journal of Law and Economics*, 2000, vol. 43, p. 473.

Higher Liability: Licensee. A **licensee** is anyone on the land for her own purposes but with the owner's permission. A social guest is a typical licensee. A licensee is entitled to a warning of hidden dangers that the owner knows about. If Juliet invites Romeo for a late supper on the balcony and fails to mention that the wooden railing is rotted, she is liable when her hero plunges to the courtyard.

But Juliet is liable only for injuries caused by *hidden* dangers—she has no duty to warn guests of obvious dangers. She need not say, "Romeo, oh Romeo, don't place thy hand in the toaster, Romeo."

© Sonya Etchison/Shutterstock

Can the owner of this trampoline be liable?

Highest Liability: Invitee. An **invitee** is someone who has a right to be on the property because it is a public place or a business open to the public. The owner has a duty of reasonable care to an invitee. Perry is an invitee when he goes to the town beach. If riptides have existed for years and the town fails to post a warning, it is liable if Perry drowns. Perry is also an invitee when he goes to Dana's coffee shop. Dana is liable if she ignores spilled coffee that causes Perry to slip.

Licensee
A person on another's land for her own purposes but with the owner's permission.

Invitee
A person who has a right to enter another's property because it is a public place or a business open to the public.

With social guests, you must have *actual knowledge* of some specific hidden danger to be liable. Not so with invitees. You are liable even if you had *no idea* that something on your property posed a hidden danger. Therefore, if you own a business, you must conduct inspections of your property on a regular basis to make sure that nothing is becoming dangerous.

The courts of some states have modified these distinctions, and a few have eliminated them altogether. California, for example, requires "reasonable care" as to all people on the owner's property, regardless of how or why they got there. But most states still use the classifications outlined above.

Special Duty: Professionals

A person at work has a heightened duty of care. While on the job, she must act as a reasonable person *in her profession*. A taxi driver must drive as a reasonable taxi driver would. A heart surgeon must perform bypass surgery with the care of a trained specialist in that field.

Two medical cases illustrate the reasonable person standard. A doctor prescribes a powerful drug without asking his patient about other medicines she is currently taking. The patient suffers a serious drug reaction from the combined medications. The physician is liable for the harm. A reasonable doctor *always* checks current medicines before prescribing new ones.

On the other hand, assume that a patient dies on the operating table in an emergency room. The physician followed normal medical procedures at every step of the procedure and acted with reasonable speed. In fact, the man had a fatal stroke. The surgeon is not liable. A doctor must do a reasonable professional job, but she cannot guarantee a happy outcome.

Special Duty: Hiring and Retention

Employers also have special responsibilities.

In a recent one-year period, more than 1,000 homicides and 2 million attacks occurred in the workplace. Companies must beware because they can be liable for hiring or retaining violent employees. A mailroom clerk with a previous rape and robbery conviction followed a secretary home after work and killed her. Even though the murder took place off the company premises, the court held that the defendant would be liable if it knew or should have known of the mail clerk's criminal history.[2] In other cases, companies have been found liable for failing to check an applicant's driving record, contact personal references, or search criminal records.

Courts have also found companies negligent for *retaining* dangerous workers. If an employee threatens a coworker, the organization is not free to ignore the menacing conduct. If the employee acts on his threats, the company may be liable.[3]

What can an employer do to diminish the likelihood of workplace violence? Many things

- Install adequate lighting in parking lots and common areas, hire security guards if necessary, and use closed-circuit television and identification cards. The judicial trend is toward greater liability. Two decades ago, the victim of a parking lot assault could rarely recover from the store; today, such lawsuits are common and frequently successful. The financial liability can be enormous.
- Ensure that the company uses thorough pre-hire screening, contacts all former employers, and checks all references and criminal records. Nursing homes have been among the most delinquent at this, too often hiring applicants with a violent past who have later attacked elderly residents.
- Respond quickly to dangerous behavior. In many cases of workplace violence, the perpetrator had demonstrated repeated bizarre, threatening, or obsessive behavior on the job, but his supervisors had not taken it seriously. Offer counseling where appropriate and fire employees when necessary.

Breach of Duty

The second element of a plaintiff's negligence case is **breach of duty**. If a legal duty of care exists, then a plaintiff must show that the defendant did not meet it. Did the defendant act as a reasonable person, or as a reasonable professional? Did he warn social guests of hidden dangers he knew to exist in her apartment?

Normally, a plaintiff proves this part of a negligence case by convincing a jury that they would not have behaved as the defendant did—indeed, that no reasonable person would.

Negligence Per Se

In certain areas of life, courts are not free to decide what a "reasonable" person would have done because the state legislature has made the decision for them. **When a legislature sets a minimum standard of care for a particular activity, in order to protect a certain group of people, and a violation of the statute injures a member of that group, the defendant has committed negligence per se.** A plaintiff who can show negligence per se need not prove breach of duty.

In Minnesota, the state legislature became alarmed about children sniffing glue, which they could easily purchase in stores. The legislature passed a statute prohibiting the sale to a minor of any glue containing toluene or benzene. About one month later, 14-year-old Steven Zerby purchased Weldwood Contact Cement from the Coast-to-Coast Store in his hometown. The glue contained toluene. Steven inhaled the glue and died from injury to his central nervous system.

The store clerk had not realized that the glue was dangerous. Irrelevant: he was negligent per se because he violated the statute. Perhaps a reasonable person would have made the same error. Irrelevant. The legislature had passed the statute to protect children,

---

[2] *Gaines v. Monsanto*, 655 S.W.2d 568, 1983 Mo. App. LEXIS 3439 (Mo. Ct. App. 1983).

[3] *Yunker v. Honeywell*, 496 N.W.2d 419, 1993 Minn. App. LEXIS 230 (Minn. Ct. App. 1993).

the sale of the glue violated the law, and a child was injured. The store was automatically liable.

Causation

We have seen that a plaintiff must show that the defendant owed him a duty of care and that the defendant breached the duty. To win, the plaintiff must also show that the defendant's breach of duty *caused* the plaintiff's harm. Courts look at two separate causation issues: Was the defendant's behavior the *factual cause* of the harm? Was it the *proximate cause?*

Factual Cause

If the defendant's breach led to the ultimate harm, it is the factual cause. Suppose that Dom's Brake Shop tells a customer his brakes are now working fine, even though Dom knows that is false. The customer drives out of the shop, cannot stop at a red light, and hits a bicyclist crossing the intersection. Dom is liable to to the cyclist. Dom's unreasonable behavior was the factual cause of the harm. Think of it as a row of dominoes. The first domino (Dom's behavior) knocked over the next one (failing brakes), which toppled the last one (the cyclist's injury).

Suppose, alternatively, that just as the customer is exiting the repair shop, the cyclist hits a pothole and tumbles off her cycle. Dom has breached his duty to his customer, but he is not liable to the cyclist—she would have been hurt anyway. This is a row of dominoes that veers off to the side, leaving the last domino (the cyclist's injury) untouched. No factual causation.

Proximate Cause

For the defendant to be liable, the *type of harm* must have been reasonably *foreseeable.* In the first example just discussed, Dom could easily foresee that bad brakes would cause an automobile accident. He need not have foreseen *exactly* what happened. He did not know there would be a cyclist nearby. What he could foresee was this *general type* of harm involving defective brakes. Because the accident that occurred was of the type he could foresee, he is liable.

By contrast, assume the collision of car and bicycle produces a loud crash. Two blocks away, a pet pig, asleep on the window ledge of a twelfth-story apartment, is startled by the noise, awakens with a start, and plunges to the sidewalk, killing a veterinarian who was making a house call. If the vet's family sues Dom, should it win? Dom's negligence was the factual cause: it led to the collision, which startled the pig, which flattened the vet. Most courts would rule, though, that Dom is not liable. The type of harm is too bizarre. Dom could not reasonably foresee such an extraordinary chain of events, and it would be unfair to make him pay for it. See Exhibit 7.1. Another way of stating that Dom is not liable to the vet's family is by calling the falling pig a *superseding cause.* When one of the "dominoes" in the row is entirely unforeseeable, courts will call that event a superseding cause, letting the defendant off the hook.

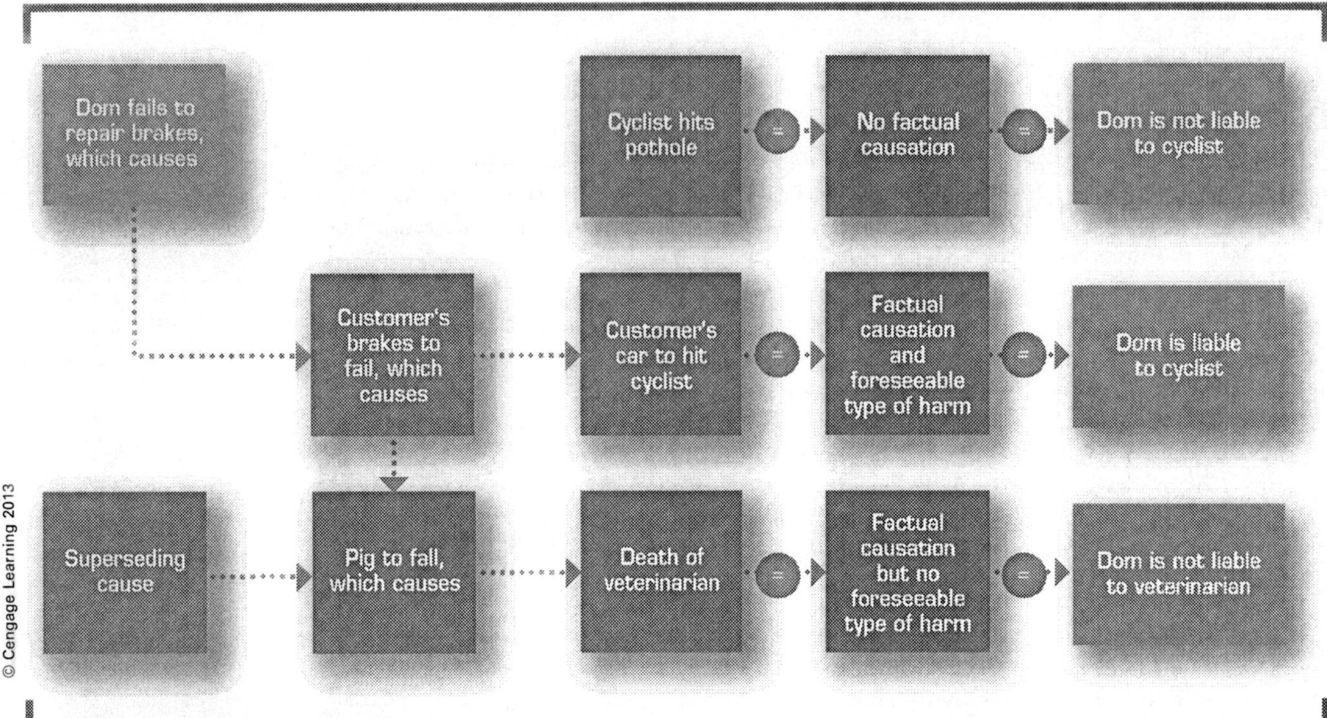

EXHIBIT 7.1

EXAM Strategy

Question: Jenny asked a neighbor, Tom, to water her flowers while she was on vacation. For three days, Tom did this without incident, but on the fourth day, when he touched the outside faucet, he received a violent electric shock that shot him through the air, melted his sneakers and glasses, set his clothes on fire, and seriously burned him. Tom sued, claiming that Jenny had caused his injuries by negligently repairing a second-floor toilet. Water from the steady leak had flooded through the walls, soaking wires and eventually causing the faucet to become electrified. You are Jenny's lawyer. Use one (and only one) element of negligence law to move for summary judgment.

Strategy: The four elements of negligence we have examined thus far are: duty to this plaintiff, breach, factual cause, and proximate cause. Which element seems to be most helpful to Jenny's defense? Why?

Result: Jenny is entitled to summary judgment because this was not a foreseeable type of injury. Even if she did a bad job of fixing the toilet, she could not reasonably have anticipated that her poor workmanship could cause *electrical* injuries to anyone.[4]

[4]Based on *Hebert v. Enos*, 60 Mass. App. Ct. 817, 806 N.E.2d 452 (Mass. Ct. App. 2004).

Res Ipsa Loquitur

Normally, a plaintiff must prove factual cause and foreseeable type of harm in order to establish negligence. But in a few cases, a court may be willing to *infer* that the defendant caused the harm under the doctrine of **res ipsa loquitur** ("the thing speaks for itself"). Suppose a pedestrian is walking along a sidewalk when an air conditioning unit falls on his head from a third-story window. The defendant, who owns the third-story apartment, denies any wrongdoing, and it may be difficult or impossible for the plaintiff to prove why the air conditioner fell. In such cases, many courts will apply *res ipsa loquitur* and declare that **the facts imply that the defendant's negligence caused the accident.** If a court uses this doctrine, then the defendant must come forward with evidence establishing that it did *not* cause the harm.

Res ipsa loquitur
The facts *imply* that the defendant's negligence caused the accident.

Because res ipsa loquitur dramatically shifts the burden of proof from plaintiff to defendant, it applies only when (1) the defendant had exclusive control of the thing that caused the harm, (2) the harm normally would not have occurred without negligence, and (3) the plaintiff had no role in causing the harm. In the air conditioner example, most states would apply the doctrine and force the defendant to prove she did nothing wrong.

The following case illustrates several of the elements of negligence that we have examined so far.

You be the Judge

Griffith v. Valley of Sun Recovery, Inc.

126 Ariz. 227, 613 P.2d 1283
Arizona Court of Appeals, 1980

Facts: Don Gorney was a "repo man"—someone authorized to find and take cars whose owners are behind on payments. A repossessor is allowed to drive away in such a car, provided he can do it peacefully. Gorney worked for Valley of Sun Recovery. He sought a car belonging to Linda Marsalek and Bob Williams. Gorney knew that there had been other, failed efforts to repossess the Marsalek car, including a violent confrontation involving attack dogs. He thought he could do better.

Gorney went to the car at 4:00 in the morning. He unscrewed the bulb in an overhead street lamp. He unlocked the car, setting off its alarm, and quickly hid. The alarm aroused the neighborhood. Williams and a neighbor, Griffith, investigated and concluded it was an attempted theft. They called the police. Gorney watched all of this from his hiding place. When everyone had gone, Gorney entered the car, again setting off the alarm and arousing the neighborhood. Williams and Griffith again emerged, as did another neighbor, dressed in his underwear and carrying a shotgun. They all believed they had caught a thief. Williams shouted for the gun and the neighbor passed it to him, but it went off accidentally and severely injured Griffith.

Griffith sued Valley of Sun. The trial court granted summary judgment for Valley of Sun, and Griffith appealed.

You Be the Judge:

- ***Did Valley of Sun have a duty to Griffith?***
- ***If so, did the company breach its duty?***
- ***If so, was the breach the factual cause of the injury?***
- ***If so, was this type of injury foreseeable?***

Argument for Griffith: Your honors, Mr. Griffith should be allowed to make his case to a jury and let it decide whether Valley of Sun's repossession led to his injury. Mr. Griffith has demonstrated every element of negligence. Valley of Sun had a duty to everyone in the area when it attempted to repossess a car. It could easily have foreseen injury. Car repossessions always involve antagonism between the car owner and the repo company.

Obviously, Gorney breached his duty. He was caught up in some fantasy, dreaming that he was Harrison Ford in an adventure film. He knew from previous repossession attempts that trouble was certain. But rather than minimizing the danger, he exacerbated it. He unscrewed a lightbulb, guaranteeing poor visibility and confusion. He set off the car alarm twice, making the whole neighborhood jittery.

Factual causation is indisputable. Had it not been for his preposterous game playing, no neighbors would have been outside, no guns present—and no accidental shooting. And this type of harm is easily foreseeable. We should have a chance to take our case to a jury.

Argument for Valley of Sun Recovery: Your honors, there are three good reasons to end this case today: no duty, no breach, no causation.

It is preposterous to suggest that Valley of Sun has a legal duty to an entire neighborhood. Car owners who are behind on their payments live in all parts of all communities. Is a repossession company to become an insurer of the entire city?

Yes, some danger is involved because delinquent owners are irresponsible and sometimes dangerous. Should we therefore allow them to keep their cars? Of course not. We must act, and that is what Valley of Sun does.

They do it safely, your honors. Even if there had been a duty, there was no breach. Mr. Gorney attempted to repossess when it was least likely anyone would see him. What should Mr. Gorney have done, asked for permission to take the car? *That* is a recipe for violence. If the owner were reasonable, there would be no repossession in the first place.

Factual causation? Valley of Sun did not create this situation. The car owners did. They bought the car and failed to pay for it. Even if there were factual causation, Valley of Sun is not liable because there is a superseding cause: the negligent use of a firearm by one of Mr. Griffith's neighbors. No jury should hear this case, your honors, because there is no case.

Damages

Finally, a plaintiff must prove that he has been injured, or that he has had some kind of measureable losses. In some cases, injury is obvious. For example, Ruben Hernandez suffered grievous harm when struck by the drunk driver. But in other cases, injury is unclear. **The plaintiff must persuade the court that he has suffered harm that is genuine, not speculative.**

Some cases raise tough questions. Among the most vexing are suits involving *future* harm. Exposure to toxins or trauma may lead to serious medical problems down the road—or it may not. A woman's knee is damaged in an auto accident, causing severe pain for two years. She is clearly entitled to compensation for her suffering. After two years, all pain may cease for a decade—or forever. Yet there is also a chance that in 15 or 20 years, the trauma will lead to painful arthritis. A court must decide today the full extent of present *and future* damages; the single recovery principle, discussed in Chapter 6, prevents a plaintiff from returning to court years later and demanding compensation for newly arisen ailments. The challenge to our courts is to weigh the possibilities and percentages of future suffering and decide whether to compensate a plaintiff for something that might never happen.

The following case examines a different issue: May a plaintiff recover damages because of the emotional injury suffered when a relative is harmed *if she does not see the accident that led to the harm*?

Ra v. Superior Court

154 Cal. App. 4th 142, 64 Ca. Rptr. 3d 539
California Court of Appeals, 2007

Facts: Michelle Ra and her husband, Phil Ra, were shopping in an Armani Exchange in Old Town, Pasadena. Michelle was looking at merchandise in the women's section while Phil examined men's sweaters about 10 or 15 feet away. Michelle was not facing her husband when she heard a loud bang. A large, overhead store sign had fallen, striking Phil and seriously injuring him. Michelle turned, saw her husband bent over in pain, and hurried to him.

The Ras sued Armani for negligence in permitting the sign to fall, and also for the emotional distress suffered by Michelle. This case concerns only Michelle's claim. The trial court granted summary judgment to the store, declaring that Michelle had not made out a valid claim of bystander recovery because she had not seen the accident occur. She appealed.

Issue: ***May a bystander recover for emotional distress caused by an accident that she did not see?***

Excerpts from Judge Perluss's Decision: [In a pretrial deposition, Michelle was asked:] At that moment you heard the sound, did you know your husband had been involved in any kind of accident; this is before you looked anywhere else?" Ra testified, "I was not sure if he was involved, but I knew the sound came from the direction—the part of the store he was in." [Later, she added that] "although I had some doubt, I believed more likely than not when I heard the loud bang in the Armani store that my husband was involved in an accident. I believed this because when I heard the loud bang, I knew the sound came from where I knew my husband was located. I then immediately turned to look at my husband."

[The state Supreme Court has held that] to recover for negligent infliction of emotional distress as a bystander the plaintiff must prove she (1) is closely related to the injury victim; (2) is present at the scene of the injury-producing event at the time it occurs and is then aware that it is causing injury to the victim; and (3) as a result suffers serious emotional distress—a reaction beyond that which would be anticipated in a disinterested witness and which is not an abnormal response to the circumstances. The [Supreme Court] expressly disapproved suggestions that a negligent actor is liable to all those "who may have suffered emotional distress on viewing or learning about the injurious consequences of his conduct," rather than on viewing the injury-producing event itself.

Although a plaintiff may establish presence at the scene through non-visual sensory perception, "someone who hears an accident but does not then know it is causing injury to a relative does not have a viable bystander claim for emotional distress, even if the missing knowledge is acquired moments later."

In restricting bystander claims to "closely related percipient witnesses," the Supreme Court explained [that it] is the traumatic effect of the perception of the infliction of injury on a closely related person that is actionable, not the observation of the consequences. Absent a reasonable certainty her husband was being injured by whatever caused the loud bang she heard, what Ra experienced at that time was simply fear. Although the emotional distress caused by that fear was no doubt real and substantial (as was the distress resulting from the subsequently acquired knowledge her husband had in fact been injured by the falling sign), it is not compensable in a bystander claim.

In sum, Ra's fear for her husband's safety at the time she heard the loud bang emanating from the part of the store where she knew he was shopping and her belief the possibility of his injury was more likely than not are insufficient as a matter of law to establish contemporaneous awareness of her husband's injuries at the time of the injury-producing accident.

[Affirmed.]

DEFENSES

Contributory and Comparative Negligence

Sixteen-year-old Michelle Wightman was out driving at night, with her friend Karrie Wieber in the passenger seat. They came to a railroad crossing, where the mechanical arm had descended and warning bells were sounding. They had been sounding for a long time. A Conrail train had suffered mechanical problems and was stopped 200 feet from the crossing, where it had stalled for roughly an hour. Michelle and Karrie saw several cars ahead of them go around the barrier and cross the tracks. Michelle had to decide whether she would do the same.

... the mechanical arm had descended and warning bells were sounding. They had been sounding for a long time.

Long before Michelle made her decision, the train's engineer had seen the heavy Saturday night traffic crossing the tracks and realized the danger. The conductor and brakeman also understood the peril, but rather than posting a flagman, who could have stopped traffic when a train approached, they walked to the far end of their train to repair the mechanical problem. A police officer had come upon the scene, told his dispatcher to notify the train's parent company Conrail of the danger, and left.

Michelle decided to cross the tracks. She slowly followed the cars ahead of her. Seconds later, both girls were dead. A freight train traveling at 60 miles per hour struck the car broadside, killing both girls instantly.

Michelle's mother sued Conrail for negligence. The company claimed that it was Michelle's foolish risk that led to her death. Who wins when both parties are partly responsible? It depends on whether the state uses a legal theory called contributory negligence. **Under contributory negligence, if the plaintiff is even slightly negligent, she recovers nothing.** If Michelle's death occurred in a contributory negligence state, and the jury considered her even minimally responsible, her estate would receive no money.

Critics attacked this rule as unreasonable. A plaintiff who was 1 percent negligent could not recover from a defendant who was 99 percent responsible. So most states threw out the contributory negligence rule, replacing it with comparative negligence. **In a comparative negligence state, a plaintiff may generally recover even if she is partially responsible.** The jury will be asked to assess the relative negligence of the two parties.

Michelle died in Ohio, which is a comparative negligence state. The jury concluded that reasonable compensatory damages were $1 million. It also concluded that Conrail was 60 percent responsible for the tragedy and Michelle 40 percent. See Exhibit 7.2. The girl's mother received $600,000 in compensatory damages.

Today, most but not all states have adopted some form of comparative negligence. Critics claim that this principle rewards a careless plaintiff. If Michelle had obeyed the law,

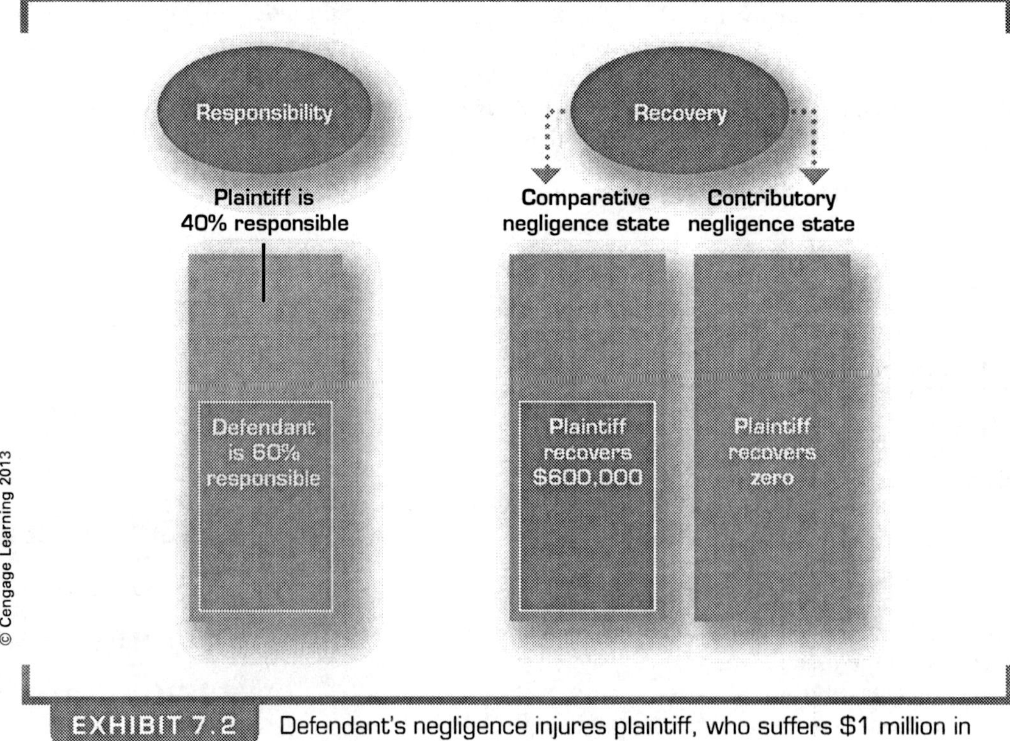

EXHIBIT 7.2 Defendant's negligence injures plaintiff, who suffers $1 million in damages.

she would still be alive. In response to this complaint, many comparative negligence states do *not* permit a plaintiff to recover anything if he was more than 50 percent responsible for his own injury.

In the Conrail case, the jury decided that the rail company was extraordinarily negligent. Expert witnesses testified that similar tragedies occurred every year around the nation and the company knew it. Conrail could easily have prevented the loss of life by posting a flagman on the road. The jury awarded the estate $25 million in punitive damages. The trial judge reduced the verdict by 40 percent to $15 million. The state supreme court affirmed the award.[5]

Assumption of the Risk

Good Guys, a restaurant, holds an ice-fishing contest on a frozen lake to raise money for accident victims. Margie grabs a can full of worms and strolls to the middle of the lake to try her luck, but slips on the ice and suffers a concussion. If she sues Good Guys, how will she fare? She will fall a second time. Wherever there is an obvious hazard, a special rule applies. **Assumption of the risk: a person who voluntarily enters a situation that has an obvious danger cannot complain if she is injured.** Ice is slippery and we all know it. If you venture onto a frozen lake, any falls are your own tough luck.

Do NFL players assume the risk of all on-field injuries?

© REUTERS/Matt Sullivan

However, the doctrine does not apply if someone is injured in a way that is not an inherent part of the dangerous activity. NFL players assume substantial risks each time they take the field, but some injuries fall outside the rule. In a game between the Jets and the Dolphins, Jets assistant coach Sal Alosi, standing on the sideline, tripped Dolphins player Nolan Carroll during a punt return. The trip was not a "normal" part of a football game, and the "assumption of the risk" doctrine would not prevent Carroll from recovering damages.

The following case involves a lake, jet skis—and a great tragedy.

Truong v. Nguyen

67 Cal. Rptr.3d 675, 156 Cal.App.4th 865
California Court of Appeals, 2007

Facts: On a warm California day, there were about 30 personal watercraft (jet skis) operating on Coyote Lake. The weather was fair and visibility good. Anthony Nguyen and Rachael Truong went for a ride on Anthony's Polaris watercraft. Cu Van Nguyen and Chuong Nguyen (neither of whom were related to Anthony) were both riding a Yamaha Waverunner. Both jet skis permitted a driver and passenger, each seated. The two watercraft collided near the middle of the lake. Rachael was killed, and the others all injured.

[5]*Wightman v. Consolidated Rail Corporation*, 86 Ohio St. 3d 431, 715 N.E.2d 546, 1999 Ohio LEXIS 2924 (Ohio 1999).

Rachael's parents sued Anthony, Cu Van, and Chuong, alleging that negligent operation of their watercraft caused their daughter's death. The defendants moved for summary judgment, claiming that assumption of the risk applies to jet skiing. The parents appealed, arguing that jet skiing was not a sport and Rachael never assumed any risk.

Issue: ***Does assumption of the risk apply to jet skiing?***

Excerpts from Judge McAdams's Decision: In a sports context, [assumption of the risk] bars liability because the plaintiff is said to have assumed the particular risks inherent in a sport by choosing to participate. Thus, a court need not ask what risks a particular plaintiff subjectively knew of and chose to encounter, but instead must evaluate the fundamental nature of the sport and the defendant's role in or relationship to that sport.

In baseball, a batter is not supposed to carelessly throw the bat after getting a hit and starting to run to first base. However, assumption of risk recognizes that vigorous bat deployment is an integral part of the sport and a risk players assume when they choose to participate. A batter does not have a duty to another player to avoid carelessly throwing the bat after getting a hit.

Even when a participant's conduct violates a rule of the game and may subject the violator to internal sanctions prescribed by the sport itself, imposition of legal liability for such conduct might well alter fundamentally the nature of the sport by deterring participants from vigorously engaging in activity. Coparticipants' limited duty of care is to refrain from intentionally injuring one another or engaging in conduct that is so reckless as to be totally outside the range of the ordinary activity involved in the sport.

It appears that an activity falls within the meaning of 'sport' if the activity is done for enjoyment or thrill, requires physical exertion as well as elements of skill, and involves a challenge containing a potential risk of injury.

As a matter of common knowledge, jet skiing is an active sport involving physical skill and challenges that pose a significant risk of injury, particularly when it is done—as it often is—together with other jet skiers in order to add to the exhilaration of the sport by racing, jumping the wakes of the other jet skis or nearby boats, or in other respects making the sporting activity more challenging and entertaining. In response to the plaintiff's complaint that the trial court erroneously assumed that the litigants were contestants in some sort of consensual competition event and/or spectator sport, [we conclude] that the doctrine applies equally to competitive and non-competitive but active sports.

Plaintiffs urge [that] Rachael was merely a passenger on the Polaris and was not actively involved in the sport. The record supports the conclusion that riding as a passenger on a personal watercraft [is participating in a sport], because it is done for enjoyment or thrill, requires physical exertion as well as elements of skill, and involves a challenge containing a potential risk of injury. The vessel is open to the elements, with no hull or cabin. It is designed for high performance, speed, and quick turning maneuvers. The thrill of riding the vessel is shared by both the operator and the passenger. Obstacles in the environment such as spraying water, wakes to be crossed, and other watercraft are part of the thrill of the sport, both for the operator and the passenger.

The summary judgment is affirmed.

Strict Liability

Some activities are so naturally dangerous that the law places an especially high burden on anyone who engages in them. A corporation that produces toxic waste can foresee dire consequences from its business that a stationery store cannot. This higher burden is **strict liability**. There are two main areas of business that incur strict liability: *ultrahazardous activity* and *defective products*. Defective products are discussed in Chapter 22, on product liability.

Strict liability
A branch of tort law that imposes a much higher level of liability when harm results from ultrahazardous acts or defective products.

Ultrahazardous Activity

Ultrahazardous activities include using harmful chemicals, operating explosives, keeping wild animals, bringing dangerous substances onto property, and a few similar activities where the danger to the general public is especially great. **A defendant engaging in an ultrahazardous activity is almost always liable for any harm that results.** Plaintiffs do not have to prove duty or breach or foreseeable harm. Recall the deliberately bizarre case we posed earlier of the pig falling from a window ledge and killing a veterinarian. Dom, the mechanic whose negligence caused the car crash, could not be liable for the veterinarian's death because the plunging pig was a superseding cause.

But now imagine that the pig is jolted off the window ledge by a company engaged in an ultrahazardous activity. Sam's Blasting Co. sets off a perfectly lawful blast to clear ground for a new building down the street. When the pig is startled and falls, the blasting company is liable. Even if Sam took extraordinary care, it will do him no good at trial. The "reasonable person" rule is irrelevant in a strict liability case.

Because "strict liability" translates into "defendant is liable," parties in tort cases often fight over whether the defendant was engaged in an ultrahazardous activity. If the court rules that the activity was ultrahazardous, the plaintiff is assured of winning. If the court rules that it was not ultrahazardous, the plaintiff must prove all elements of negligence.

The line is often hazy. A lawful fireworks display does not incur strict liability, but crop dusting does. Cutting timber is generally not abnormally dangerous, but hauling logs might be. The enormous diversity of business activities in our nation ensures continual disputes over this important principle.

New Jersey Department of Environmental Protection v. Alden Leeds, Inc.

153 N.J. 272, 708 A.2d 1161, 1998 N.J. LEXIS 212
Supreme Court of New Jersey, 1998

Facts: The Alden Leeds Company packages, stores, and ships swimming pool chemicals. The firm does most of its work at its facility in Kearns, New Jersey. At any given time, about 21 different hazardous chemicals are present.

The day before Easter, a fire of unknown origin broke out in "Building One" of the company's site, releasing chlorine gas and other potentially dangerous by-products into the air. There were no guards or other personnel on duty. The fire caused $9 million in damage to company property. Because of the potentially dangerous gas, the Department of Environmental Protection (DEP) closed the New Jersey Turnpike along with half a dozen other major highways, halted all commuter rail and train service in the area, and urged residents to stay indoors with windows closed. An unspecified number of residents went to local hospitals with respiratory problems.

Based on New Jersey's Air Pollution Control Act (APCA), the DEP imposed a civil fine on Alden Leeds for releasing the toxic chemicals. The appellate court reversed, finding that there was no evidence the company had caused the fire or the harm, and the case reached the state's high court.

Issue: ***Did the company cause the harm?***

Excerpts from Justice Coleman's Decision: In 1962, this Court adopted the proposition that "an ultrahazardous activity which introduces an unusual danger into the community should pay its own way in the event it actually causes damage to others." In 1983, the Court expressly recognized "that the law of liability has evolved so that a landowner is strictly liable to others for harm caused by toxic wastes that are stored on his property and flow onto the property of others." The Court explained "that those who use, or permit others to use, land for the conduct of abnormally dangerous activities are strictly liable for resultant damages." The same rationale applies to pollution that is released into the air from chemicals stored at a chemical facility.

An actor who chooses to store dangerous chemicals should be responsible for the release of those chemicals into the air. That Alden Leeds lawfully and properly stored chemicals does not alter that conclusion. The risks attendant to the storage of dangerous substances counsel in favor of precautions to prevent their release. Alden Leeds took no such precautions. On the day of the fire, there was no one stationed at the plant to alert the authorities as soon as a fire or other unforeseen calamity erupted. Nor was there any other early warning system in place. A burglar or smoke alarm sounded, but there was no response to that alarm. The law imposes a duty upon those who store hazardous substances to ensure that the substances on their property do not escape in a manner harmful to the public. Alden Leeds failed to meet that burden.

Although Alden Leeds was not found responsible for the fire, the company's facility caused a release of air pollutants. The required nexus is satisfied by the knowing storage of hazardous chemicals. Regardless of what started the fire, it was the knowing storage of chemicals by Alden

Leeds that caused the release of air contaminants once the fire reached the chemicals.

[Affirmed that the APCA is a strict liability statute and that there must be a causal nexus between the defendant and the harm. Reversed that the storing of hazardous chemicals by Alden Leeds does not satisfy that nexus. The DEP does *not* have to prove that the chemical operator started the fire.]

EXAM Strategy

Facts: Ahmed plans to transport a 25-foot boa constrictor from one zoo to another. The snake is locked in a special cage in Ahmed's truck, approved by the American Zoo Society. Experts check the cage to be sure it is locked and entirely secure. Then Ahmed himself checks the cage. During the transport, his engine begins to fail. He pulls into the breakdown lane and sets up four flares, warning motorists of the stalled vehicle. Katy drives off the road and slams into Ahmed's truck. She is badly injured. Somehow the snake escapes and eats a champion show dog, worth $35,000. Katy and the dog's owner both sue Ahmed. What will be the result in each case?

Strategy: Ahmed's behavior seems reasonable throughout this incident. However, the two suits against him are governed by different rules: negligence in one case, strict liability in the other. Apply each rule to the correct case.

Result: The dog was killed by a dangerous snake. Transporting wild animals is an ultrahazardous activity, and Ahmed is strictly liable. His reasonable behavior will not save him. However, when he parked his truck in the breakdown lane, he did a reasonable job. Katy cannot prove that he breached his duty to her, and she loses.

Chapter Conclusion

Tort issues necessarily remain in flux, based on changing social values and concerns. There is no final word on what is an ultrahazardous activity, or how thoroughly an employer must conduct background checks, or whether a social host can be liable for the destruction caused by a guest. What is clear is that a working knowledge of these issues and pitfalls can help everyone—business executive and ordinary citizen alike.

Exam Review

1. **ELEMENTS** The five elements of negligence are duty of due care, breach, factual causation, proximate causation, and damage. (p. 158)

2. **DUTY** If the defendant could foresee that misconduct would injure a particular person, he probably has a duty to her. Special duties exist for people on the job, landowners, and employers. (pp. 158–162)

EXAM Strategy

Question: A supervisor reprimanded an employee for eating in a restaurant when he should have been at work. Later, the employee showed up at the supervisor's office and shot him. Although the employee previously had been violent, management withheld this information from supervisory personnel. Is the company liable for the supervisor's injury?

Strategy: An employer must do a *reasonable* job of hiring and retaining employees. (See the "Result" at the end of this section.)

3. **BREACH OF DUTY** A defendant breaches his duty of due care by failing to meet his duty of care. (p. 162)
4. **NEGLIGENCE PER SE** If a legislature sets a minimum standard of care for a particular activity in order to protect a certain group of people, and a violation of the statute injures a member of that group, the defendant has committed negligence per se. (pp. 162–163)
5. **FACTUAL CAUSE** If one event directly led to the ultimate harm, it is the factual cause. (p. 163)
6. **PROXIMATE CAUSE** For the defendant to be liable, the type of harm must have been reasonably foreseeable. (p. 163)
7. **DAMAGE** The plaintiff must persuade the court that he has suffered a harm that is genuine, not speculative. Damages for emotional distress, without a physical injury, are awarded only in select cases. (pp. 163–164)
8. **CONTRIBUTORY AND COMPARATIVE NEGLIGENCE** In a contributory negligence state, a plaintiff who is even slightly responsible for his own injury recovers nothing; in a comparative negligence state, the jury may apportion liability between plaintiff and defendant. (pp. 167–169)

EXAM Strategy

Question: There is a collision between cars driven by Candy and Zeke. The evidence is that Candy is about 25 percent responsible, for failing to stop quickly enough, and Zeke about 75 percent responsible, for making a dangerous turn. Candy is most likely to win:

(a) A lawsuit for battery

(b) A lawsuit for negligence in a comparative negligence state

(c) A lawsuit for negligence in a contributory negligence state

(d) A lawsuit for strict liability

(e) A lawsuit for assault

Strategy: Battery and assault are intentional torts, irrelevant in a typical car accident. Are such collisions strict liability cases? No; therefore, the answer must be either (b) or (c). Apply the distinction between comparative and contributory negligence to the evidence here. (See the "Result" at the end of this section.)

9. **STRICT LIABILITY** A defendant is strictly liable for harm caused by an ultrahazardous activity or a defective product. Ultrahazardous activities include using harmful chemicals, blasting, and keeping wild animals. Strict liability means that if the defendant's conduct led to the harm, the defendant is liable, even if she exercises extraordinary care. (pp. 170–172)

EXAM Strategy

Question: Marko owned a cat and allowed it to roam freely outside. In the three years he had owned the pet, the animal had never bitten anyone. The cat entered Romi's garage. When Romi attempted to move it outside, the cat bit her. Romi underwent four surgeries, was fitted with a plastic finger joint, and spent more than $39,000 in medical bills. She sued Marko, claiming both strict liability and ordinary negligence. Assume that state law allows a domestic cat to roam freely. Evaluate both of Romi's claims.

Strategy: Negligence requires proof that the defendant breached a duty to the plaintiff by behaving unreasonably, and that the resulting harm was foreseeable. Was it? When would harm by a domestic cat be foreseeable? A defendant can be strictly liable for keeping a wild animal. Apply that rule as well. (See the "Result" at the end of this section.)

2. Result: This employer *may* have been liable for negligently hiring a previously violent employee, and it *certainly* did an unreasonable job in retaining him without advising his supervisor of the earlier violence. The assault was easily foreseeable, and the employer is liable.[6]

8. Result. In a contributory negligence state, a plaintiff even 1 percent responsible for the harm loses. Candy was 25 percent responsible. She can win *only* in a comparative negligence state.

9. Result: If Marko's cat had bitten or attacked people in the past, this harm was foreseeable and Marko is liable. If the cat had never done so, and state law allows domestic animals to roam, Romi probably loses her suit for negligence. Her strict liability case definitely fails: a housecat is not a wild animal.

MULTIPLE-CHOICE QUESTIONS

1. Two cars, driven by Fred and Barney, collide. At trial, the jury determines that the accident was 90 percent Fred's fault and 10 percent Barney's fault. Barney's losses total $100,000. If he lives in a state that uses contributory negligence, Barney will recover ________________.

[6]Based on *Smith v. National R.R. Passenger Corp.*, 856 F.2d 467 (2d Cir. 1988).

(a) $0
(b) $10,000
(c) $50,000
(d) $90,000
(e) $100,000

2. Assume the same facts as in Question 1, except now Barney lives in a state that follows comparative negligence. Now Barney will recover ______________.
(a) $0
(b) $10,000
(c) $50,000
(d) $90,000
(e) $100,000

3. Zack lives in a state that prohibits factory laborers from working more than 12 hours in any 24-hour period. The state legislature passed the law to cut down on accidents caused by fatigued workers.

Ignoring the law, Zack makes his factory employees put in 14-hour days. Eventually, a worker at the end of a long shift makes a mistake and severely injures a coworker. The injured worker sues Zack.

Which of the following terms will be most relevant to the case?
(a) *Res ipsa loquitur*
(b) Assumption of the risk
(c) Negligence per se
(d) Strict liability

4. Randy works for a vending machine company. One morning, he fills up an empty vending machine that is on the third floor of an office building. Later that day, Mark buys a can of PepsiCo from that machine. He takes the full can to a nearby balcony and drops it three floors onto Carl, a coworker who recently started dating Mark's ex-girlfriend. Carl falls unconscious. Which of the following can be considered a factual cause of Carl's injuries?
(a) Randy
(b) Mark
(c) Both Randy and Mark
(d) None of the above

5. For this question, assume the same facts as in Question 4. Now determine which of the following can be considered a proximate cause of Carl's injuries?
(a) Randy
(b) Mark
(c) Both Randy and Mark
(d) None of the above

Essay Questions

1. At approximately 7:50 p.m, bells at the train station rang and red lights flashed, signaling an express train's approach. David Harris walked onto the tracks, ignoring a yellow line painted on the platform instructing people to stand back. Two men shouted to Harris, warning him to get off the tracks. The train's engineer saw him too late to stop the train, which was traveling at approximately 55 mph. The train struck and killed Harris as it passed through the station. Harris's widow sued the railroad, arguing that the railroad's negligence caused her husband's death. Evaluate her argument.

2. Ryder leased a truck to Florida Food Service; Powers, an employee, drove it to make deliveries. He noticed that the strap used to close the rear door was frayed, and he asked Ryder to fix it. Ryder failed to do so in spite of numerous requests. The strap broke, and Powers replaced it with a nylon rope. Later, when Powers was attempting to close the rear door, the nylon rope broke and he fell, sustaining severe injuries to his neck and back. He sued Ryder. The trial court found that Powers's attachment of the replacement rope was a superseding cause, relieving Ryder of any liability, and granted summary judgment for Ryder. Powers appealed. How should the appellate court rule?

3. A new truck, manufactured by General Motors Corp. (GMC), stalled in rush hour traffic on a busy interstate highway because of a defective alternator, which caused a complete failure of the truck's electrical system. The driver stood nearby and waved traffic around his stalled truck. A panel truck approached the GMC truck, and immediately behind the panel truck, Davis was driving a Volkswagen fastback. Because of the panel truck, Davis was unable to see the stalled GMC truck. The panel truck swerved out of the way of the GMC truck, and Davis drove straight into it. The accident killed him. Davis's widow sued GMC. GMC moved for summary judgment, alleging (1) no duty to Davis, (2) no factual causation, and (3) no foreseeable harm. Comment.

4. ***YOU BE THE JUDGE*** **WRITING PROBLEM** When Thomas and Susan Tamplin were shopping at Star Lumber with their six-year-old daughter Ann Marie, a 150-pound roll of vinyl flooring fell on the girl, seriously injuring her head and pituitary gland. Ann was clearly entitled to recover for the physical harm, such as her fractured skull. The plaintiffs also sought recovery for potential future harm. Their medical expert was prepared to testify that although Ann would probably develop normally, he could not rule out the slight possibility that her pituitary injury might prevent her from sexually maturing. Is Ann entitled to damages for future harm? **Argument for Ann:** This was a major trauma, and it is impossible to know the full extent of the future harm. Sexual maturation is a fundamental part of life; if there is a possibility that Ann will not develop normally, she is entitled to present her case to a jury and receive damages. **Argument for Star Lumber:** A plaintiff may not recover for speculative harm. The "slight possibility" that Ann could fail to develop is not enough for her to take her case to the jury.

5. Irving was a lawyer who prepared income tax returns for Maroevich. Irving agreed to draft a will for Maroevich, leaving all of the property to Maroevich's sister, Biakanja. When Maroevich died, the probate court refused to accept the will because Irving had failed to have the signatures properly witnessed. As a result, Biakanja inherited only

one-eighth of the estate. She sued Irving, who defended by saying that he had no duty of due care to Biakanja because all his dealings were with Maroevich and none were with her. Do you agree?

Discussion Questions

1. Imagine an undefeated high school football team on which the average lineman weighs 300 pounds. Also, imagine an 0–10 team on which the average lineman weighs 170 pounds. The undefeated team sets out to hit as hard as they can on every play and to run up the score as much as possible. Before the game is over, 11 players from the lesser team have been carried off the field with significant injuries. All injuries were the result of "clean hits"—none of the plays resulted in a penalty. Even late in the game, when the score is 70–0, the undefeated team continues to deliver devastating hits that are far beyond what would be required to tackle and block. The assumption of the risk doctrine exempts the undefeated team from liability. Is this reasonable?

2. Should the law hold landowners to different standards of care for trespassers, social guests, and invitees? Or do the few states that say, "Just always be reasonable," have a better rule?

3. Are strict liability rules fair? Someone has to dispose of chemicals. Someone has to use dynamite if road projects are to be completed. Is it fair to say to those companies, "You are responsible for all harm caused by your activities, even if you are as careful as you can possibly be?"

4. Steve is making copies. Lonnie, his coworker, politely asks, "When will you be done with the copier?" Steve punches Lonnie in the face. Later, Lonnie learns that Steve's last two employers fired him for punching coworkers. He also finds out that his company did not do a background check of any kind on Steve before hiring him. Would it be fair to hold Lonnie's company liable for the attack, or should Lonnie's only action be against Steve?

5. People who serve alcohol to others take a risk. In some circumstances, they can be held legally responsible for the actions of the people they serve. Is this fair? Should an intoxicated person be the only one liable if harm results? If not, in what specific circumstances is it fair to stretch liablility to other people?

CHAPTER 8

CRIME

© r.nagy/Shutterstock.com

Crime can take us by surprise. Stacey tucks her nine-year-old daughter, Beth, into bed. Promising her husband, Mark, that she will be home by 11:00 PM, she jumps into her car and heads back to Be Patient, Inc. She plugs her iPhone into the player of her $85,000 sedan and tries to relax by listening to music. Be Patient is a health care organization that owns five geriatric hospitals. Most of its patients use Medicare, and Stacey supervises all billing to their largest client, the federal government.

She parks in a well-lighted spot on the street and walks to her building, failing to notice two men, collars turned up, watching from a parked truck. Once in her office, she goes straight to her computer and works on billing issues. Tonight's work goes more quickly than she expected, thanks to new software she helped develop. At 10:30 she emerges from the building with a quick step and a light heart, walks to her car—and finds it missing.

A major crime has occurred during the 90 minutes Stacey was at her desk, but she will never report it to the police. It is a crime that costs Americans countless dollars each year, yet Stacey will not even mention it to friends or family. Stacey is the criminal.

A major crime has occurred during the 90 minutes Stacey was at her desk, but she will never report it to the police.

When we think of crime, we imagine the drug dealers and bank robbers endlessly portrayed on television. We do not picture corporate executives sitting at polished desks. "Street crimes" are indeed serious threats to our security and happiness. They deservedly receive the attention of the public and the law. But when measured only in dollars, street crime takes second place to white-collar crime, which costs society *tens of billions* of dollars annually.

The hypothetical about Stacey is based on many real cases and is used to illustrate that crime does not always dress the way we expect. Her car was never stolen; it was simply towed. Two parking bureau employees, watching from their truck, saw Stacey park illegally and did their job. It is Stacey who committed a crime—Medicare fraud. Every month, she has billed the government about $10 million for work that her company has not performed. Stacey's scheme was quick and profitable—and a distressingly common crime.

Crime, whether violent or white-collar, is detrimental to all society. It imposes a huge cost on everyone. Just the *fear* of crime is expensive—homeowners buy alarm systems and businesses hire security guards. But the anger and fear that crime engenders sometimes tempt us to forget that not all accused people are guilty. Everyone suspected of a crime should have the protections that you yourself would want in that situation. As the English jurist William Blackstone said, "Better that ten guilty persons escape than that one innocent suffer."

Thus, criminal law is a balancing act—between making society safe and protecting us all from false accusations and unfair punishment.

This chapter has four parts:

- The differences between a civil and criminal case;
- **Criminal procedure**—the *process* by which criminals are accused, tried, and sentenced;
- Crimes that *harm* businesses;
- Crimes committed *by* businesses.

Criminal procedure
The process by which criminals are accused, tried, and sentenced.

THE DIFFERENCES BETWEEN A CIVIL AND CRIMINAL CASE

Most of this book focuses on civil law, so we begin with a discussion of the differences between a civil and criminal case.

Civil law involves the rights and liabilities that exist between private parties. As we have seen, if one person claims that another has caused her a civil injury, she must file a lawsuit and convince a court of her damages.

Criminal law is different. Conduct is criminal when society outlaws it. When a state legislature or Congress concludes that certain behavior threatens public safety and welfare, it passes a statute forbidding that behavior; in other words, declaring it criminal. Medicare fraud, which Stacey committed, is a crime because Congress has outlawed it. Money laundering is a crime because Congress concluded that it was a fundamental part of the drug trade and prohibited it.

Criminal law
Prohibits and punishes conduct that threatens public safety and welfare.

Prosecution

Suppose the police arrest Roger and accuse him of breaking into a store and stealing 50 computers. The owner of the store is the one harmed, and he has the right to sue the thief in civil court to recover money damages. But **only the government can prosecute a crime and punish Roger by sending him to prison.** The government may also impose a fine on Roger, but it keeps the fine and does not share it with the victim. (However, the court will sometimes order **restitution**, meaning that the defendant must reimburse the victim for

Restitution
A court order that a guilty defendant reimburse the victim for the harm suffered.

harm suffered.) The local prosecutor has total discretion in deciding whether to bring Roger to trial on criminal charges.

Burden of Proof

Beyond a reasonable doubt
The very high burden of proof in a criminal trial, demanding much more certainty than required in a civil trial.

In a civil case, the plaintiff must prove her case only by a preponderance of the evidence.[1] But because the penalties for conviction in a criminal case are so serious, the government must prove its case **beyond a reasonable doubt**. Also, the stigma of a criminal conviction would stay with Roger forever, making it more difficult to obtain work and housing. Therefore, in all criminal cases, if the jury has any significant doubt at all that Roger stole the computers, it *must* acquit him.

Right to a Jury

The facts of a case are decided by a judge or jury. A criminal defendant has a right to a trial by jury for any charge that could result in a sentence of six months or longer. The defendant may demand a jury trial or may waive that right, in which case the judge will be the factfinder.

Felony/Misdemeanor

Felony
A serious crime, for which a defendant can be sentenced to one year or more in prison.

Misdemeanor
A less serious crime, often punishable by less than a year in a county jail.

A **felony** is a serious crime, for which a defendant can be sentenced to one year or more in prison. Murder, robbery, rape, drug dealing, money laundering, wire fraud, and embezzlement are felonies. A **misdemeanor** is a less serious crime, often punishable by a year or less in a county jail. Public drunkenness, driving without a license, and simple possession of a single marijuana cigarette are considered misdemeanors in most states.

Criminal Procedure

The title of a criminal case is usually the government versus someone: *The United States of America v. Simpson* or *The State of Texas v. Simpson*, for example. This name illustrates a daunting thought—if you are Simpson, the vast power of the government is against you. Because of the government's great power and the severe penalties it can impose, criminal procedure is designed to protect the accused and ensure that the trial is fair. Moreover, a criminal defendant is often engaged in an uphill climb from the beginning because people often assume that anyone accused of a crime must be guilty. Many of the protections for those accused of a crime are found in the first 10 amendments to the United States Constitution, known as the Bill of Rights.

Conduct Outlawed

Crimes are created by statute. The prosecution must demonstrate to the court that the defendant's conduct is indeed outlawed by a statute. Returning to Roger, the alleged computer thief, the state charges that he stole computer equipment from a store, a crime clearly defined by statute as larceny.

The Fifth and Fourteenth Amendments to the Constitution require that the language of criminal statutes be clear and definite enough that (1) ordinary people can understand what conduct is prohibited and (2) the police are discouraged from arbitrary and discriminatory enforcement. Thus, for example, the Supreme Court ruled that a statute that prohibited loitering was unconstitutionally vague because it did not clarify exactly what behavior was prohibited and it tended to be enforced arbitrarily.[2]

---

[1]See the earlier discussion in Chapter 3, on dispute resolution.

[2]*Kolender v. Lawson*, 461 U.S. 352 (S. Ct., 1983).

State of Mind

Voluntary Act

A defendant is not guilty of a crime if she was forced to commit it. In other words, she is not guilty if she acted under duress. However, the defendant bears the burden of proving by a preponderance of the evidence that she did act under duress. In 1974, a terrorist group kidnapped heiress Patricia Hearst from her apartment near the University of California at Berkeley. After being tortured for two months, she participated in a bank robbery with the group. Despite opportunities to escape, she stayed with the criminals until her capture by the police a year later. The State of California put on her on trial for bank robbery. One question for the jury was whether she had voluntarily participated in the crime. This was an issue on which many people had strong opinions. Ultimately Hearst was convicted, sent to prison, and then later pardoned.

Guilty
A judge or jury's finding that a defendant has committed a crime.

© Bettmann/CORBIS

Patty Hearst, before she was kidnapped.

Entrapment

When the government induces the defendant to break the law, the prosecution must prove beyond a reasonable doubt that the defendant was predisposed to commit the crime. The goal is to separate the cases where the defendant was innocent before the government tempted him from those where the defendant was only too eager to break the law.

Kalchinian and Sherman met in the waiting room of a doctor's office where they were both being treated for drug addiction. After several more meetings, Kalchinian told Sherman that the treatment was not working for him and he was desperate to buy drugs. Could Sherman help him? Sherman repeatedly refused, but ultimately agreed to help end Kalchinian's suffering by providing him with drugs. Little did Sherman know that Kalchinian was a police informant. Sherman sold drugs to Kalchinian a number of times. Kalchinian rewarded this act of friendship by getting Sherman hooked again and then turning him in to the police. A jury convicted Sherman of drug dealing, but the Supreme Court overturned the conviction on the grounds that Sherman had been entrapped.[3] The court felt there was no evidence that Sherman was predisposed to commit the crime.

Gathering Evidence: The Fourth Amendment

If the police suspect that a crime has been committed, they will need to obtain evidence. **The Fourth Amendment to the Constitution prohibits the government from making illegal searches and seizures of individuals, corporations, partnerships, and other organizations.** The goal of the Fourth Amendment is to protect the individual from the powerful state.

Warrant

As a general rule, the police must obtain a warrant before conducting a search. A warrant is written permission from a neutral official, such as a judge or magistrate, to conduct a search.[4] **The warrant must specify with reasonable certainty the place to be searched and the items to be seized.** Thus, if the police say they have reason to believe that they will find bloody clothes in the suspect's car in his garage, they cannot also look through his house and confiscate file folders.

---

[3]*Sherman v. United States*, 356 U.S. 369 (S. Ct., 1958).

[4]A magistrate is a judge who tries minor criminal cases or undertakes primarily administrative responsibilities.

If the police search without a warrant, they have violated the Fourth Amendment. **But even a search conducted with a warrant violates the Fourth Amendment if:**

- There was no probable cause to issue the warrant;
- The warrant does not specify the place to be searched and the things sought; or
- The search extends beyond what is specified in the warrant.

Probable Cause

Probable cause
It is likely that evidence of crime will be found in the place to be searched.

The magistrate will issue a warrant only if there is probable cause. **Probable cause** means that based on all the information presented, **it is likely that evidence of a crime will be found in the place to be searched.** Often, the police base their applications for a warrant on data provided by an informant. The magistrate will want evidence to support the informant's reliability. If it turns out that this informant has been wrong the last three times he gave evidence to the police, the magistrate will probably refuse the request for a warrant.

Searches Without a Warrant

There are seven circumstances under which police may **search without a warrant**:

- **Plain View.** Police may search if they see a machine gun, for example, sticking out from under the front seat of a parked car.
- **Stop and Frisk.** None of us wants to live in a world in which police can randomly stop and frisk us on the street anytime they feel like it. The police do have the right to stop and frisk, but *only if* they have a clear and specific reason to suspect that criminal activity may be afoot and that the person may be armed and dangerous.[5]
- **Emergencies.** If, for example, the police believe that evidence is about to be destroyed, they can search.
- **Automobiles.** If police have lawfully stopped a car and observe evidence of other crimes in the car, such as burglary tools, they may search.
- **Lawful Arrest.** Police may always search a suspect they have arrested. The point of this exception is to protect the officers and preserve evidence.
- **Consent.** Anyone lawfully living in a house can allow the police in to search without a warrant. If your roommate gives the police permission to search your house, that search is legal.
- **No Expectation of Privacy.** The police have a right to search any area in which the defendant does not have a reasonable expectation of privacy. For example, Rolando Crowder was staying at his friend Bobo's apartment. Hearing the police in the hallway, he ran down to the basement. The police found Crowder in the basement with drugs nearby. Crowder argued that the police should have obtained a warrant, but the court ruled that Crowder had no expectation of privacy in Bobo's basement.[6]

Apart from these seven exceptions, a warrant is required.

Exclusionary Rule

Under the exclusionary rule, evidence obtained illegally may not be used at trial. The Supreme Court created the exclusionary rule to ensure that police conduct legal searches. The theory is simple: if police know in advance that illegally obtained evidence cannot be

[5]*Terry v. Ohio*, 392 U.S. 1 (S. Ct., 1968).
[6]*Ohio v. Crowder*, 2010 Ohio 3766; 2010 Ohio App. LEXIS 3210 (2010).

used in court, they will not be tempted to make improper searches. Is the exclusionary rule a good idea?

Opponents of the rule argue that a guilty person may go free because one police officer bungled. They are outraged by cases like *Coolidge v. New Hampshire.*[7] Pamela Mason, a 14-year-old babysitter, was brutally murdered. Citizens of New Hampshire were furious, and the state's attorney general personally led the investigation. Police found strong evidence that Edward Coolidge had done it. They took the evidence to the attorney general, who personally issued a search warrant. A search of Coolidge's car uncovered incriminating evidence, and he was found guilty of murder and sentenced to life in prison. But the United States Supreme Court reversed the conviction. The warrant had not been issued by a neutral magistrate. A law officer may not lead an investigation and simultaneously decide what searches are permissible.

After the Supreme Court reversed Coolidge's conviction, New Hampshire scheduled a new trial, attempting to convict him with evidence lawfully obtained. Before the trial began, Coolidge pleaded guilty to second degree murder. He was sentenced and remained in prison until his release years later.

In fact, very few people do go free because of the exclusionary rule. One study showed that evidence is actually excluded in only 1.3 percent of all prosecutions; and in about one-half of *those* cases, the court convicted the defendant on other evidence. Only in 0.7 percent of all prosecutions did the defendant go free after the evidence was suppressed.[8]

There are two exceptions to the exclusionary rule:

- **Inevitable Discovery.** The inevitable discovery exception permits the use of evidence that would inevitably have been discovered even without the illegal search. If an informant was about to tell the police about Coolidge's car, then the evidence found there would have been admissible, so long as the court believed the testimony was true.
- **Good Faith Exception.** Suppose the police use a search warrant believing it to be proper, but it later proves to have been defective. Is the search therefore illegal? No, so long as the police reasonably believed the warrant was valid, the search is legal.[9]

Should the exclusionary rule apply in the following case? You be the judge.

---

[7]403 U.S. 443, 91 S. Ct. 2022, 1971 U.S. LEXIS 25 (S. Ct., 1971).

[8]See the discussion in *United States v. Leon* (Justice Brennan, dissenting), 468 U.S. 897, 1985 U.S. LEXIS 153 (S. Ct., 1984).

[9]Ibid.

You be the **Judge**

OHIO V. SMITH

2009 Ohio 6426; 920 N.E.2d 949; 2009 Ohio Lexis 3496 Supreme Court of Ohio, 2009

Facts: Wendy Northern was hospitalized for a drug overdose. When police questioned her in the hospital, she identified her drug dealer as Antwaun Smith. She then called him to arrange for the purchase of crack cocaine at her house that evening. When Smith arrived at her house, the police arrested him, searched him, and confiscated his cell phone. When the police looked at the phone some time later, they discovered call records and phone numbers confirming that this phone had been used to speak with Northern.

The police had neither a warrant nor Smith's consent to search the phone. Smith filed a motion requesting that the evidence from his cell phone be excluded because it had been obtained without a warrant. After the judge denied this motion, Smith was found guilty and sentenced to 12 years in prison. The appeals court upheld his conviction. He appealed to the Ohio Supreme Court.

You Be the Judge: ***Was the search of Smith's cell phone legal? Should the evidence found on the phone be excluded?***

Argument for the Police: The police have the right to search anyone they arrest. During a perfectly legal search, they discovered Smith's cell phone. Prior courts have ruled that defendants have a low expectation of privacy in address books and that police can search them without a warrant. A cell phone is an electronic address book. Therefore, the search of Smith and the subsequent search of the contents of the phone were both legal. The evidence was properly admitted in court.

Argument for Smith: Police have the right to search someone they have arrested so that they can protect themselves and prevent evidence from being destroyed. A search of the cell phone's contents was not necessary to ensure officer safety, and there was no evidence that the call records and phone numbers were in danger of being destroyed. Once the police had the phone, they had plenty of time to ensure that the data were preserved. In addition, they might have been able to obtain Smith's phone records from his service provider.

The police were entitled to search Smith and discover his cell phone. But they did not have the right to search the phone without a warrant. Modern cell phones are much more similar to a laptop than to an old-fashioned address book—they have the ability to transmit large amounts of personal data in various forms. Courts have ruled that defendants have a high expectation of privacy in laptop computers and that the police must obtain a warrant before searching one. It would be a terrible precedent to declare that the police could search cell phones without a warrant.

The Patriot Act

In response to the devastating attacks of September 11, 2001, Congress passed a sweeping antiterrorist law known as the Patriot Act. The statute was designed to give law enforcement officials greater power to investigate and prevent potential terrorist assaults. The bill raced through Congress nearly unopposed. Proponents hailed it as a vital weapon for use against continuing lethal threats. Opponents argued that the hastily passed law would not provide serious benefits but did threaten the liberties of the very people it purported to shield.

In an early legal test, a federal judge permitted the government to use secret evidence in its effort to freeze the assets of Global Relief Foundation, a religious organization suspected of terrorist activity. The group, which claimed to be purely humanitarian, asserted that it could hardly defend itself against unseen evidence. Finding "acute national security concerns," the judge allowed the government to introduce the evidence in private, without the foundation ever seeing it.[10]

The law also permitted the FBI to issue a **national security letter** (NSL) to communications firms such as Internet service providers (ISPs) and telephone companies. An NSL typically demanded that the recipient furnish to the government its customer records, *without ever divulging* to anyone what it had done. NSLs could be used to obtain access to subscriber billing records, phone, financial, credit, and other information—even records of books taken from libraries. However, an appeals court ruled that a secret NSL could be issued only if the government first demonstrated to a court's satisfaction that disclosure of the NSL would risk serious harm.[11]

[10] *Global Relief Found., Inc. v. O'Neill*, 315 F.3d 748, 2002 U.S. App. LEXIS 27172 (7th Cir., 2002).

[11] *Doe v. Mukasey*, 549 F.3d 861; 2008 U.S. App. LEXIS 25193, (2d Cir., 2008).

EXAM Strategy

Question: Police bang down the door of Mary Beth's apartment, enter without her permission, and search the apartment. They had no warrant. When the officers discover that she is smoking marijuana, they arrest her. What motion will the defense lawyer make before trial? Please rule on the defendant's motion. Are there any facts that would make you change your ruling?

Strategy: The defendant's motion is based on the police conduct. What was wrong with that conduct, and what are the consequences?

Result: The defense lawyer will argue that the police violated the Fourth Amendment because they lacked a warrant for the search. He will ask that the court suppress the drug evidence. Ordinarily, the court would grant that motion unless there was other evidence—for example, the police smelled marijuana from the hallway and Mary Beth would have smoked it all if the police had taken the time to obtain a warrant.

The Case Begins

The trial is now ready to begin. But, the government may not be able to use all the evidence it has gathered.

The Fifth Amendment

The Fifth Amendment to the Constitution protects criminal defendants—both the innocent and the guilty—in several ways.

Due Process **Due process** requires fundamental fairness at all stages of the case. The basic elements of due process are discussed in Chapter 5, on constitutional law. In the context of criminal law, due process sets additional limits. The requirement that the prosecution disclose evidence favorable to the defendant is a due process rule. Similarly, if a witness says that a tall white male robbed the liquor store, it would violate due process for the police to place the male suspect in a lineup with four short women.

Due process
Requires fundamental fairness at all stages of the case.

Self-Incrimination The Fifth Amendment bars the government from forcing any person to provide evidence against himself. In other words, the police may not use mental or physical coercion to force a confession or any other information out of someone. Society does not want a government that engages in torture. Such abuse might occasionally catch a criminal, but it would grievously injure innocent people and make all citizens fearful of the government that is supposed to represent them. Also, coerced confessions are inherently unreliable. The defendant may confess simply to end the torture. (The protection against self-incrimination applies only to people; corporations and other organizations are not protected and may be required to provide incriminating information.)

Exclusionary Rule (Again) If the police do force a confession, the exclusionary rule prohibits the prosecution from using it or any information they obtain as a result of what the defendant has said. (This secondary information is referred to as "the fruit of the poisonous tree.") For example, when the police illegally arrest Alice, she tells them that she has bought drugs from Beau. The police go to Beau's house, where they find drugs. He tells them that Caitlyn is his dealer and, indeed, the police find drugs in Caitlyn's bedroom. None of this evidence—neither the confessions nor the drugs—is admissible in court because it all stemmed from Alice's illegal arrest.

The rationale is the same as for Fourth Amendment searches: suppressing the evidence means that police will not attempt to get it illegally. But remember that the confession is void only if it results from custodial questioning. Suppose a policeman, investigating a bank robbery, asks a pedestrian if he noticed anything peculiar. The pedestrian says, "You mean after I robbed the bank?" Result? There was no custodial questioning, and the confession *may* be used against him.

Miranda Rights The police cannot legally force a suspect to provide evidence against himself. But sometimes, under forceful interrogation, he might forget his constitutional rights. In the following landmark case, the Supreme Court established the requirement that police remind suspects of their rights—with the very same warning that we have all heard so many times on television shows.

Landmark Case

Miranda v. Arizona

384 U.S. 436; 1966 U.S. Lexis 2817
Supreme Court of the United States, 1966

Facts: Ernesto Miranda was a mentally ill, indigent citizen of Mexico. The Phoenix police arrested him at his home and brought him to a police station, where a rape victim identified him as her assailant. Two police officers took him to an interrogation room but did not tell him that he had a right to have a lawyer present during the questioning. Two hours later, the officers emerged with a written confession signed by Miranda. At the top of the statement was a typed paragraph stating that the confession was made voluntarily "with full knowledge of my legal rights, understanding any statement I make may be used against me."

At Miranda's trial, the judge admitted this written confession into evidence over the objection of defense counsel. The officers testified that Miranda had also made an oral confession during the interrogation. The jury found Miranda guilty of kidnapping and rape. He was sentenced to 20 to 30 years imprisonment. On appeal, the Supreme Court of Arizona affirmed the conviction. In reaching its decision, the court relied heavily on the fact that Miranda did not specifically request a lawyer. The Supreme Court of the United States granted *certiorari*.

Issues: ***Was Miranda's confession admissible at trial? Should his conviction be upheld?***

Excerpts from Chief Justice Warren's Decision: Our holding briefly stated is this: the prosecution may not use statements, whether exculpatory or inculpatory, stemming from custodial interrogation of the defendant unless it demonstrates the use of procedural safeguards effective to secure the privilege against self-incrimination. By custodial interrogation, we mean questioning initiated by law enforcement officers after a person has been taken into custody or otherwise deprived of his freedom of action in any significant way. As for the procedural safeguards to be employed, the following measures are required. Prior to any questioning, the person must be warned that he has a right to remain silent, that any statement he does make may be used as evidence against him, and that he has a right to the presence of an attorney, either retained or appointed.

The defendant may waive these rights, provided the waiver is made voluntarily, knowingly, and intelligently. If, however, he indicates in any manner and at any stage of the process that he wishes to consult with an attorney before speaking, there can be no questioning. Likewise, if the individual is alone and indicates in any manner that he does not wish to be interrogated, the police may not question him. The mere fact that he may have answered some questions or volunteered some statements on his own does not deprive him of the right to refrain from answering any further inquiries until he has consulted with an attorney and thereafter consents to be questioned.

In a series of cases decided by this Court, the police resorted to physical brutality—beating, hanging, whipping—and to sustained and protracted questioning incommunicado in order to extort confessions. Only recently in Kings County, New York, the police brutally beat, kicked, and placed lighted cigarette butts on the back of a potential witness under interrogation for the purpose of securing a statement incriminating a third party.

Unless a proper limitation upon custodial interrogation is achieved, there can be no assurance that practices of this nature will be eradicated in the foreseeable future. Not only does the use of the third degree involve a flagrant violation of law by the officers of the law, but it involves also the dangers of false confessions, and it tends to make police and prosecutors less zealous in the search for objective evidence. As [an official] remarked: "If you use your fists, you are not so likely to use your wits."

[C]oercion can be mental as well as physical, and the blood of the accused is not the only hallmark of an unconstitutional inquisition. In a serious case, the interrogation may continue for days, with the required intervals for food and sleep, but with no respite from the atmosphere of domination. It is possible in this way to induce the subject to talk without resorting to duress or coercion.

Even without employing brutality, the very fact of custodial interrogation exacts a heavy toll on individual liberty and trades on the weakness of individuals. In [this case before the Court], the defendant was thrust into an unfamiliar atmosphere and run through menacing police interrogation procedures. It is obvious that such an interrogation environment is created for no purpose other than to subjugate the individual to the will of his examiner. This atmosphere carries its own badge of intimidation. To be sure, this is not physical intimidation, but it is equally destructive of human dignity. The current practice of incommunicado interrogation is at odds with one of our Nation's most cherished principles—that the individual may not be compelled to incriminate himself.

All these policies point to one overriding thought: the constitutional foundation underlying the privilege is the respect a government—state or federal—must accord to the dignity and integrity of its citizens. To maintain a fair state-individual balance, to respect the inviolability of the human personality, our accusatory system of criminal justice demands that the government seeking to punish an individual produce the evidence against him by its own independent labors, rather than by the cruel, simple expedient of compelling it from his own mouth.

From the testimony of the officers and by the admission of [the defendant], it is clear that Miranda was not in any way apprised of his right to consult with an attorney and to have one present during the interrogation, nor was his right not to be compelled to incriminate himself effectively protected in any other manner. Without these warnings, the statements were inadmissible. The mere fact that he signed a statement which contained a typed-in clause stating that he had "full knowledge" of his "legal rights" does not approach the knowing and intelligent waiver required to relinquish constitutional rights.

Right to a Lawyer

As *Miranda* made clear, a criminal defendant has the right to a lawyer before being interrogated by the police. The Sixth Amendment guarantees the **right to a lawyer** at all important stages of the criminal process. Because of this right, the government must **appoint a lawyer** to represent, free of charge, any defendant who cannot afford one.

After Arrest

Indictment

Once the police provide the local prosecutor with evidence, he presents this evidence to a **grand jury** and asks its members to indict the defendant. The grand jury is a group of ordinary citizens, like a trial jury, but the grand jury holds hearings for several weeks at a time, on many different cases. It is the grand jury's job to determine whether there is

Grand jury
A group of ordinary citizens that decides whether there is probable cause the defendant committed the crime with which she is charged.

probable cause that this defendant committed the crime with which she is charged. At the hearing in front of the grand jury, only the prosecutor presents evidence, not the defense attorney because it is better for the defendant to save her evidence for the trial jury. After all, the defense attorney may want to see what evidence the prosecution has before deciding how to present the case.

Indictment
The government's formal charge that the defendant has committed a crime and must stand trial.

If the grand jury determines that there is probably cause, an **indictment** is issued. An indictment is the government's formal charge that the defendant has committed a crime and must stand trial.

Arraignment

At an arraignment, a clerk reads the formal charges of the indictment. The judge asks whether the defendant has a lawyer. If she does not, the judge urges her to get one quickly. If a defendant cannot afford a lawyer, the court will appoint one to represent her free of charge. The judge now asks the lawyer how the defendant pleads to the charges. At this stage, most defendants plead not guilty.

Discovery

During the months before trial, both prosecution and defense will prepare the most effective case possible. There is less formal discovery than in civil trials. The prosecution is obligated to hand over any evidence favorable to the defense that the defense attorney requests. The defense has a more limited obligation to inform the prosecution of its evidence. In most states, for example, if the defense will be based on an alibi, counsel must reveal the alibi to the government before trial.

Plea Bargaining

Plea bargain
An agreement in which the defendant pleads guilty to a reduced charge, and the prosecution recommends to the judge a relatively lenient sentence.

Sometime before trial, the two attorneys will meet to try to negotiate a plea bargain. A **plea bargain** is an agreement between prosecution and defense that the defendant will plead guilty to a reduced charge, and the prosecution will recommend to the judge a relatively lenient sentence. In the federal court system, about 75 percent of all prosecutions end in a plea bargain. In state court systems, the number is often higher. A judge need not accept the bargain but usually does.

For example, astronaut Lisa Nowak drove across country dressed in a wig and trench-coat to attack fellow astronaut Colleen Shipman, whom she viewed as a romantic rival. After Nowak's arrest, police found in her car a BB gun, a knife, and surgical tubing, which was thought to be evidence of her violent intent. Nowak was charged with attempted murder and attempted kidnapping, but much of the evidence was thrown out of court under the exclusionary rule because of police misconduct. Nowak ultimately pleaded guilty to battery and burglary of a car. At that point, she had served two days in jail. She did not receive further jail time, but she was required to complete 50 hours of community service and to attend anger-management classes.

Trial and Appeal

When there is no plea bargain, the case must go to trial. The mechanics of a criminal trial are similar to those for a civil trial, described in Chapter 3, on dispute resolution. It is the prosecution's job to convince the jury beyond a reasonable doubt that the defendant committed every element of the crime charged. The defense counsel will do everything possible to win an acquittal. In federal courts, prosecutors obtain a conviction in about 80 percent of cases; in state courts, the percentage is slightly lower. Convicted defendants have a right to appeal, and again, the appellate process is similar to that described in Chapter 3.

Double Jeopardy

The prohibition against **double jeopardy** means that a defendant may be prosecuted only once for a particular criminal offense. The purpose is to prevent the government from destroying the lives of innocent citizens with repetitive prosecutions. Imagine that Rod and Lucy are accused of murdering a taxi driver. Rod is tried first and wins an acquittal. At Lucy's trial, Rod testifies that he is, indeed, the murderer. The jury acquits Lucy. The Double Jeopardy Clause prohibits the state from retrying Rod again for the same offense, even though he has now confessed to it.

Double jeopardy
A criminal defendant may be prosecuted only once for a particular criminal offense.

Punishment

The Eighth Amendment prohibits cruel and unusual punishment. The most dramatic issue litigated under this clause is the death penalty. The Supreme Court has ruled that capital punishment is not inherently unconstitutional. Most state statutes divide a capital case into two parts, so that the jury first considers only guilt or innocence, and then, if the defendant is found guilty, deliberates on the death penalty. As part of that final decision, the jury must consider aggravating and mitigating circumstances that may make the ultimate penalty more or less appropriate.[12]

As you might expect from the term "cruel and unusual," courts are generally unsympathetic to such claims unless the punishment is truly outrageous. For example, Mickle pleaded guilty to rape. The judge sentenced him to prison for five years and also ordered that he undergo a vasectomy. The appeals court ruled that this sentence was cruel and unusual. Although the operation in itself is not cruel (indeed, many men voluntarily undergo it), when imposed as punishment, it is degrading and in that sense cruel. It is also an unusual punishment.[13]

In the following case, the Supreme Court was not moved to overturn a harsh punishment.

Ewing v. California

538 U.S. 11, 123 S. Ct. 1179, 155 L. Ed. 2d 108
United States Supreme Court, 2003

Facts: California passed a "three strikes" law, dramatically increasing sentences for repeat offenders. A defendant with two or more serious convictions, who was convicted of a third felony, had to receive a sentence of life imprisonment. Such a sentence required the defendant to serve a minimum of 25 years, and in some cases much more.

Gary Ewing, on parole from a nine-year prison term, stole three golf clubs worth $399 each, and was prosecuted. Because he had prior convictions, the crime, normally a misdemeanor, was treated as a felony. Ewing was convicted and sentenced to 25 years to life. He appealed, claiming that the sentence violated the Eighth Amendment.

Issue: ***Did Ewing's sentence violate the Eighth Amendment?***

Excerpts from Justice O'Connor's Decision: When the California Legislature enacted the three strikes law, it made a judgment that protecting the public safety requires incapacitating criminals who have already been convicted of at least one serious or violent crime. Nothing in the Eighth Amendment prohibits California from making that choice. To the contrary, our cases establish that States have a valid interest in deterring and segregating habitual criminals.

California's justification is no pretext. Recidivism is a serious public safety concern in California and throughout the Nation. According to a recent report, approximately 67 percent of former inmates released from state prisons were charged with at least one "serious" new crime within

[12] *Gregg v. Georgia*, 428 U.S. 153, 96 S. Ct. 2909, 1976 U.S. LEXIS 82 (S. Ct., 1976).
[13] *Mickle v. Henrichs*, 262 F. 687 (1918).

three years of their release. In particular, released property offenders like Ewing had higher recidivism rates than those released after committing violent, drug, or public-order offenses.

To be sure, California's three strikes law has sparked controversy. Critics have doubted the law's wisdom, cost-efficiency, and effectiveness in reaching its goals. This criticism is appropriately directed at the legislature, which has primary responsibility for making the difficult policy choices that underlie any criminal sentencing scheme. We do not sit as a "superlegislature" to second-guess these policy choices.

Ewing's sentence is justified by the State's public-safety interest in incapacitating and deterring recidivist felons, and amply supported by his own long, serious criminal record. Ewing has been convicted of numerous misdemeanor and felony offenses, served nine separate terms of incarceration, and committed most of his crimes while on probation or parole. His prior "strikes" were serious felonies, including robbery and three residential burglaries. To be sure, Ewing's sentence is a long one. But it reflects a rational legislative judgment, entitled to deference, that offenders who have committed serious or violent felonies and who continue to commit felonies must be incapacitated. The State of California was entitled to place upon Ewing the onus of one who is simply unable to bring his conduct within the social norms prescribed by the criminal law of the State.

We hold that Ewing's sentence of 25 years to life in prison, imposed for the offense of felony grand theft under the three strikes law, is not grossly disproportionate and therefore does not violate the Eighth Amendment's prohibition on cruel and unusual punishments.

Devil's Advocate Are we really going to send Ewing to prison for a minimum of 25 years—for *shoplifting?* It is true that Ewing is a recidivist, and undoubtedly a state is entitled to punish chronic troublemakers more harshly than first-time offenders. However, this still seems excessive. In California, a first-time offense of "arson causing *great bodily injury*" incurs a maximum nine-year sentence. A first-time offender convicted of voluntary manslaughter receives a sentence of no more than 11 years. Only a first-time murderer receives a penalty equal to Ewing's—25 years to life. It is unfair to Ewing to equate his property crimes with a homicide, and foolish for society to spend this much money locking him up.

The Eighth Amendment also outlaws excessive fines. Forfeiture is the most controversial topic under this clause. **Forfeiture** is a *civil* law proceeding that is permitted by many different *criminal* statutes. Once a court has convicted a defendant under certain criminal statutes—such as a controlled substance law—the government may seek forfeiture of property associated with the criminal act. *How much* property can the government take? To determine if forfeiture is fair, courts generally look at three factors: whether the property was used in committing the crime, whether it was purchased with proceeds from illegal acts, and whether the punishment is disproportionate to the defendant's wrongdoing. Neal Brunk pleaded guilty to selling 2.5 ounces of marijuana, and the government promptly sought forfeiture of his house on 90 acres, worth about $99,000. The court found that forfeiture was legitimate because Brunk had used drug money to buy the land and then sold narcotics from the property.[14] By contrast, Hosep Bajakajian attempted to leave the United States without reporting $375,000 cash to customs officials as the law requires. The government demanded forfeiture of the full sum, but the Supreme Court ruled that seizure of the entire amount was grossly disproportionate to the minor crime of failing to report cash movement.[15]

[14] *U.S. v. Brunk*, 2001 U.S. App. LEXIS 7566 (4th Cir., 2001).

[15] *U.S. v. Bajakajian*, 524 U.S. 321, 118 S. Ct. 2028, 1998 U.S. LEXIS 4172 (S. Ct., 1998).

Crimes that Harm Business

Businesses must deal with four major crimes: larceny, fraud, arson, and embezzlement.

Larceny

It is holiday season at the mall, the period of greatest profits—and the most crime. At the Foot Forum, a teenager limps in wearing ragged sneakers and sneaks out wearing Super Sneakers, valued at $145. Down the aisle at a home furnishing store, a man is so taken by a $375 power saw that he takes it. Sweethearts swipe sweaters, pensioners pocket produce. All are committing larceny.

Economists estimate that *12 cents out of every dollar* spent in retail stores covers the cost of shoplifting.

Larceny is the trespassory taking of personal property with the intent to steal it. "Trespassory taking" means that someone else originally has the property. The Super Sneakers are personal property (not real estate), they were in the possession of the Foot Forum, and the teenager deliberately left without paying, intending never to return the goods. That is larceny. By contrast, suppose Fast Eddie leaves Bloomingdale's in New York, descends to the subway system, and jumps over a turnstile without paying. Larceny? No. He has "taken" a service—the train ride—but not personal property.

Each year, about $10 billion in merchandise is stolen from retail stores in the United States. Economists estimate that *12 cents out of every dollar* spent in retail stores covers the cost of shoplifting. Some criminal experts believe that drug addicts commit over half of all shoplifting to support their habits. Stores have added electronic surveillance, security patrols, and magnetic antitheft devices, but the problem will not disappear.

Fraud

Robert Dorsey owned Bob's Chrysler in Highland, Illinois. When he bought cars, the First National Bank of Highland paid Chrysler, and Dorsey—supposedly—repaid the bank as he sold the autos. Dorsey, though, began to suffer financial problems, and the bank suspected he was selling cars without repaying his loans. A state investigator notified Dorsey that he planned to review all dealership records. One week later, a fire engulfed the dealership. An arson investigator discovered that an electric iron, connected to a timer, had been placed on a pile of financial papers doused with accelerant.

The saddest part of this true story is that it is only too common. Some experts suggest that 1 percent of corporate revenues are wasted on fraud alone. Dorsey was convicted and imprisoned for committing two crimes that cost business billions of dollars annually—fraud (for failing to repay the loans) and arson (for burning down the dealership).[16]

Fraud refers to various crimes, all of which have a common element: **the deception of another person for the purpose of obtaining money or property from him**. Robert Dorsey's precise violation was bank fraud, a federal crime.[17] It is bank fraud to use deceit to obtain money, assets, securities, or other property under the control of any financial institution.

Fraud
Deception for the purpose of obtaining money or property.

[16] *United States v. Dorsey*, 27 F.3d 285, 1994 U.S. App. LEXIS 15010 (7th Cir., 1994).

[17] 18 U.S.C. §1344.

Wire Fraud and Mail Fraud

Wire and mail fraud are additional federal crimes, involving the use of interstate mail, telegram, telephone, radio, or television to obtain property by deceit.[18] For example, if Marsha makes an interstate phone call to sell land that she does not own, that is wire fraud.

Theft of Honest Services

Under traditional standards, a culprit could only be convicted of fraud if he had deceived the victim to get something of value from *her*. But what if a CEO manipulates the financial results of his company and otherwise misleads investors to keep the stock price high? He has not committed fraud under this traditional definition because he did not personally obtain money from the investors—they bought their stock either from other shareholders or from the company.

To find a way to punish these wrongdoers, prosecutors looked to a statute that prohibits the **theft of honest services.**[19] Originally, this law was used to prosecute public officials who took bribes or kickbacks. But then prosecutors began to apply it to employees in the private sector as well. Prosecutors took the view that an employee violated this law if she did not fully perform the job for which she was paid. Thus, the CEO could be charged for not having done his job properly. But under this standard, the scope of the statute became enormous. In theory, an employee who called in sick so that he could watch his son's play has violated this statute. The scope of the statute permitted enormous discretion on the part of prosecutors.

The Supreme Court recently stepped in to limit its scope. As the following case reveals, **the theft of honest services statute prohibits public and private employees from taking bribes or kickbacks**.

SKILLING V. UNITED STATES

130 S. Ct. 2896, 2010 U.S. LEXIS 5259
Supreme Court of the United States, 2010

Facts: The Enron Corporation was founded as an energy company in Houston, Texas, Five years later, it hired Jeffrey Skilling, a young Harvard Business School graduate, to run one of its subsidiaries. He was promoted to president and chief operating officer 11 years later. At that time, only six companies in the United States had higher revenues than Enron. Six months after Skilling's promotion, he resigned. Four months after that, Enron filed for bankruptcy protection.

The company's stock, which had been trading at $90 per share, became virtually worthless. A government investigation uncovered an elaborate conspiracy to prop up Enron's stock prices by overstating the company's financial well-being. The government prosecuted dozens of Enron employees who participated in the scheme. Skilling's indictment charged that he had violated the honest services statute. He was convicted and sentenced to 292 months imprisonment, 3 years supervised release, and $45 million in restitution. Skilling appealed, arguing that he had not violated the honest services statute because it only applied to bribery and kickback schemes. The Fifth Circuit affirmed his conviction. The Supreme Court granted *certiorari*.

Issue: ***Did Skilling violate the honest services statute?***

Excerpts from Justice Ginsburg's Opinion: Unlike fraud, in which the victim's loss of money or property supplied the defendant's gain, with one the mirror image of the other, the honest-services theory targeted corruption that lacked similar symmetry. While the offender profited, the betrayed party suffered no deprivation of money or

[18] 18 U.S.C. §§1341–1346.
[19] 18 U.S.C. § 1346.

property; instead, a third party, who had not been deceived, provided the enrichment. For example, if a city mayor (the offender) accepted a bribe from a third party in exchange for awarding that party a city contract, yet the contract terms were the same as any that could have been negotiated at arm's length, the city (the betrayed party) would suffer no tangible loss. Even if the scheme occasioned a money or property *gain* for the betrayed party, courts reasoned, actionable harm lay in the denial of that party's right to the offender's "honest services." Over time, an increasing number of courts recognized that a recreant employee—public or private—could be prosecuted under this statute if he breached his allegiance to his employer by accepting bribes or kickbacks in the course of his employment.

Skilling asserts that [the honest services statute] is unconstitutionally vague. To satisfy due process, a penal statute must define the criminal offense [1] with sufficient definiteness that ordinary people can understand what conduct is prohibited and [2] in a manner that does not encourage arbitrary and discriminatory enforcement. According to Skilling, [the honest services statute] meets neither of the two due process essentials. First, the phrase "the right of honest services," he contends, does not adequately define what behavior it bars. Second, he alleges, [the honest services statute's] standardless sweep allows policemen, prosecutors, and juries to pursue their personal predilections, thereby facilitating opportunistic and arbitrary prosecutions.

In the main, prosecutions under this statute involved fraudulent schemes to deprive another of honest services through bribes or kickbacks supplied by a third party who had not been deceived. Confined to these paramount applications, [the honest services statute] presents no vagueness problem. Reading the statute to proscribe a wider range of offensive conduct, we acknowledge, would raise the due process concerns underlying the vagueness doctrine. To preserve the statute without transgressing constitutional limitations, we now hold that [the honest services statute] criminalizes only the bribe-and-kickback core.

The Government did not, at any time, allege that Skilling solicited or accepted side payments from a third party in exchange for making these misrepresentations. It is therefore clear that Skilling did not commit honest-services fraud.

Skilling had been found guilty of three crimes: honest services fraud, wire fraud, and securities fraud. Although the Supreme Court ruled that Skilling had not violated the honest services statute, they remanded the case to the appeals court to determine if the other two convictions were independent enough to stand on their own without the honest services element. If not, he would have to be retried. The appeals court did uphold Skilling's two other convictions.

Insurance Fraud

Insurance fraud is another common crime. A Ford suddenly swerves in front of a Toyota, causing it to brake hard. A Mercedes, unable to stop, slams into the Toyota, as the Ford races away. Regrettable accident? No: a "swoop and squat" fraud scheme. The Ford and Toyota drivers were working together, hoping to cause an accident with someone else. The "injured" Toyota driver now goes to a third member of the fraud team—a dishonest doctor—who diagnoses serious back and neck injuries and predicts long-term pain and disability. The driver files a claim against the Mercedes's driver, whose insurer may be forced to pay tens or even hundreds of thousands of dollars for an accident that was no accident. Insurance companies investigate countless cases like this each year, trying to distinguish the honest victim from the criminal.

EXAM Strategy

Question: Eric mails glossy brochures to 25,000 people, offering to sell them a one-month time-share in a stylish apartment in Las Vegas. The brochure depicts an imposing building, an opulent apartment, and spectacular pools. To reserve a space, customers need only send in a $2,000 deposit. Three hundred people respond, sending in the money. In fact, there is no such building. Eric, planning to flee with the cash, is arrested and prosecuted. His sentence could be as long as 20 years. (1) With what crime is he charged? (2) Is this a felony or misdemeanor prosecution? (3) Does Eric have a right to a jury trial? (4) What is the government's burden of proof?

Strategy: (1) Eric is deceiving people, and that should tell you the *type* of crime. (2, 3) The potential 20-year sentence determines whether Eric's crime is a misdemeanor or felony, and whether or not he is entitled to a jury trial. (4) We know that the government has the burden of proof in criminal prosecutions—but *how much* evidence must it offer?

Result: Eric has committed fraud. A felony is one in which the sentence could be a year or more. The potential penalty here is 20 years, so the crime is a felony. Eric has a right to a jury, as does any defendant whose sentence could be six months or longer. The prosecution must prove its case beyond a reasonable doubt, a much higher burden than that in a civil case.

Arson

© Patricia Marks/Shutterstock

Tragic accident…or felony?

Robert Dorsey, the Chrysler dealer, committed a second serious crime. **Arson** is the malicious use of fire or explosives to damage or destroy any real estate or personal property. It is both a federal and a state crime. Dorsey used arson to conceal his bank fraud. Most arsonists hope to collect on insurance policies. Every year thousands of buildings burn, particularly in economically depressed neighborhoods, as owners try to make a quick kill or extricate themselves from financial difficulties. Everyone who purchases insurance ends up paying higher premiums because of this immorality.

Embezzlement

This crime also involves illegally obtaining property, but with one big difference: the culprit begins with legal possession. **Embezzlement** is the fraudulent conversion of property already in the defendant's possession.

This is a story without romance: for 15 years, Kristy Watts worked part-time as a bookkeeper for romance writer Danielle Steele, handling payroll and accounting. During that time, Watts stole $768,000 despite earning a salary of $200,000 a year. Watts said that she had been motivated by envy and jealousy. She was sentenced to three years in prison and agreed to pay her former boss almost $1 million.

Arson
The malicious use of fire or explosives to damage or destroy real estate or personal property.

Embezzlement
The fraudulent conversion of property already in the defendant's possession.

Crimes Committed by Business

A corporation can be found guilty of a crime based on the conduct of any of its **agents**, who include anyone undertaking work on behalf of the corporation. An agent can be a corporate officer, an accountant hired to audit a statement, a sales clerk, or almost any other person performing a job at the company's request.

If an agent commits a criminal act within the scope of his employment and with the intent to benefit the corporation, the company is liable.[20] This means that the agent himself must first be guilty. If the agent is guilty, the corporation is, too.

[20]*New York Central & Hudson River R.R. Co. v. United States,* 212 U.S. 481, 29 S. Ct. 304, 1909 U.S. LEXIS 1832 (S. Ct., 1909). Note that what counts is the intention to benefit, not actual benefit. A corporation will not escape liability by showing that the scheme failed.

Critics believe that the criminal law has gone too far. It is unfair, they argue, to impose *criminal* liability on a corporation, and thus penalize the shareholders, unless high-ranking officers were directly involved in the illegal conduct. The following case concerns a corporation's responsibility for a death caused by its employee.

Commonwealth v. Angelo Todesca Corp.

446 Mass. 128, 842 N.E. 2d 930
Supreme Judicial Court of Massachusetts, 2006

Facts: Brian Gauthier, an experienced truck driver, worked for Todesca, a paving company. After about a year driving a particular 10-wheel tri-axle dump truck, Gauthier noticed that the back-up alarm had stopped working. When he reported this, the company mechanic realized that the old alarm needed replacement. The mechanic had none in stock, so the company instructed Gauthier to drive the truck without the alarm.

About a month later, Gauthier and other Todesca drivers were delivering asphalt to the work site on a highway at the entrance to a shopping mall. A police officer directed the construction vehicles and the routine mall traffic. A different driver asked the officer to "watch our backs" as the trucks backed through the intersection. All of the other trucks were equipped with back-up alarms. When it was Gauthier's turn to back up, he struck the police officer, killing him.

The state charged the Todesca corporation with motor vehicle homicide, and the jury found the company guilty. The trial judge imposed a fine—of $2,500. The court of appeals reversed the conviction, and the prosecution appealed to the state's highest court.

Issue: ***Could the company be found guilty of motor vehicle homicide?***

Excerpts from Justice Spina's Decision: Before criminal liability may be imposed on a corporate defendant, the Commonwealth must prove that the individual for whose conduct it seeks to charge the corporation criminally was placed in a position by the corporation where he had enough responsibility to act for the corporation, and that he was acting in behalf of the corporation [when] he committed a criminal act.

The defendant maintains that a corporation never can be criminally liable for motor vehicle homicide because the language of a criminal statute must be construed strictly, and a "corporation" cannot "operate" a vehicle. We agree with the Commonwealth. Because a corporation is not a living person, it can act only through its agents. By the defendant's reasoning, a corporation never could be liable for any crime. A "corporation" can no more serve alcohol to minors, or bribe government officials, or falsify data on loan applications, than operate a vehicle negligently: only human agents, acting for the corporation, are capable of these actions. Nevertheless, we consistently have held that a corporation may be criminally liable for such acts when performed by corporate employees, acting within the scope of their employment and on behalf of the corporation.

It was undisputed that Gauthier's truck was not equipped with a functioning back-up alarm at the time of the collision, and that he knew the alarm was missing. Although a back-up alarm was not required by statute, the defendant had a written safety policy mandating that all its trucks be equipped with such alarms. An employee's violation of his employer's rules, intended to protect the safety of third persons, is evidence of the employee's negligence, for which the employer may be held liable.

Other drivers at the work site had functioning back-up alarms, and although they spoke moments before the collision, Gauthier never informed the victim that his truck did not have an alarm. The jury could have inferred that the victim, a veteran police officer, was aware that the defendant's custom was to equip its trucks with back-up alarms, and that the victim expected to hear a back-up alarm when a driver operated a truck in reverse.

The jury also could have inferred that an alarm on Gauthier's truck would have sounded practically in the victim's ear, alerting him to the truck's movement in time to get out of its way. The back-up alarm makes a distinctive beeping sound, intended to warn people behind the vehicle that it is operating in reverse, and the victim did not realize Gauthier's truck was backing up because he did not hear that sound.

Affirmed.

Selected Crimes Committed by Business

Workplace Crimes

The workplace can be dangerous. Working on an assembly line exposes factory employees to fast-moving machinery. For a roofer, the first slip may be the last. The invisible radiation in a nuclear power plant can be deadlier than a bullet. The most important statute regulating the workplace is the federal **Occupational Safety and Health Act of 1970 (OSHA)**,[21] which sets safety standards for many industries.[22] May a state government go beyond standards set by OSHA and use the criminal law to punish dangerous conditions? In *People v. O'Neill*,[23] the courts of Illinois answered that question with a potent "yes," permitting a *murder prosecution* against corporate executives themselves.

Film Recovery Systems was an Illinois corporation in business to extract silver from used X-ray film and then resell it. Steven O'Neill was president of Film Recovery, Charles Kirschbaum was its plant manager, and Daniel Rodriguez the foreman. To extract the silver, workers at Film Recovery soaked the X-ray film in large, open, bubbling vats that contained sodium cyanide.

A worker named Stefan Golab became faint. He left the production area and walked to the lunchroom, where workers found him trembling and foaming at the mouth. He lost consciousness. Rushed to a hospital, he was pronounced dead on arrival. The Cook County medical examiner determined that Golab died from acute cyanide poisoning caused by inhalation of cyanide fumes in the plant.

Illinois indicted Film Recovery and several of its managers for murder. The indictment charged that O'Neill and Kirschbaum committed murder by failing to disclose to Golab that he was working with cyanide and other potentially lethal substances and by failing to provide him with appropriate and necessary safety equipment.

The case was tried to a judge without a jury. Workers testified that O'Neill, Kirschbaum, and other managers never told them they were using cyanide or that the fumes they inhaled could be harmful; that management made no effort to ventilate the factory; that Film Recovery gave the workers no goggles or protective clothing; that the chemicals they worked with burned their skin; that breathing was difficult in the plant because of strong, foul orders; and that workers suffered frequent dizziness, nausea, and vomiting.

The trial judge found O'Neill, Kirschbaum, and others guilty of murder. Illinois defines murder as performing an act that the defendant *knows will create a strong probability of death* in the victim, and the judge found they had done that. He found Film Recovery guilty of involuntary manslaughter. Involuntary manslaughter is *recklessly* performing an act that causes death. He sentenced O'Neill, Kirschbaum, and Rodriguez to 25 years in prison.

The defendants appealed, contending that the verdicts were inconsistent. They argued, and the Illinois Court of Appeals agreed, that the judge had made contradictory findings. Murder required the specific intent of *knowing there was a strong probability of death*, whereas the manslaughter conviction required *reckless* conduct. The appeals court reversed the convictions and remanded for a new trial.

Moments before the new trial was to start, O'Neill, Kirschbaum, and Rodriguez all pleaded guilty to involuntary manslaughter. They received sentences of three years, two years, and four months, respectively.

[21]29 U.S.C. §§651 et seq. (1982).

[22]See Chapter 29 on employment law.

[23]194 Ill. App. 3d 79, 550 N.E.2d 1090, 1990 Ill. App. LEXIS 65 (Ill. App. Ct. 1990).

Hiring Illegal Workers

Employers are required to verify their workers' eligibility for employment in the United States. It is illegal to knowingly employ unauthorized workers. Within three days of hiring a worker, the employer must complete an I-9 form, which lists the items that can be used as documentation of eligibility. The government has the right to arrest illegal employees, and it can also bring charges against the business that hired them.

RICO

The **Racketeer Influenced and Corrupt Organizations Act** (RICO) is one of the most powerful and controversial statutes ever written.[24] Congress passed the law primarily to prevent gangsters from taking money they earned illegally and investing it in legitimate businesses. But RICO has expanded far beyond the original intentions of Congress and is now used more often against ordinary businesses than against organized criminals. Some regard this wide application as a tremendous advance in law enforcement, but others view it as an oppressive weapon used to club ethical companies into settlements they should never have to make.

Racketeer Influenced and Corrupt Organizations Act (RICO)
A powerful Federal statute, originally aimed at organized crime, now used in many criminal prosecutions and civil lawsuits.

What is a violation of this law? **RICO prohibits using two or more racketeering acts to accomplish any of these goals: (1) investing in or acquiring legitimate businesses with criminal money; (2) maintaining or acquiring businesses through criminal activity; or (3) operating businesses through criminal activity.**

What does that mean in English? It is a two-step process to prove that a person or an organization has violated RICO.

- The prosecutor must show that the defendant committed two or more **racketeering acts**, which are any of a long list of specified crimes: embezzlement, arson, mail fraud, wire fraud, and so forth. Thus, if a gangster ordered a building torched in January and then burned a second building in October, that would be two racketeering acts. If a stockbroker told two customers that Bronx Gold Mines was a promising stock, when she knew that it was worthless, that would be two racketeering acts.

Racketeering acts
Any of a long list of specified crimes, such as embezzlement, arson, mail fraud, wire fraud, and so forth.

- The prosecutor must then show that the defendant used these racketeering acts to accomplish one of the three *purposes* listed above. If the gangster committed two arsons and then used the insurance payments to buy a dry cleaning business, that would violate RICO. If the stockbroker gave fraudulent advice and used the commissions to buy advertising for her firm, that would violate RICO.

The government may prosecute both individuals and organizations for violating RICO. For example, the government prosecuted financier Michael Milken for manipulating stock prices. It also threatened to prosecute his employer, Drexel Burnham Lambert. If the government proves its case, the defendant can be hit with large fines and a prison sentence of up to 20 years. RICO also permits the government to seek forfeiture of the defendant's property. A court may order a convicted defendant to hand over any property or money used in the criminal acts or derived from them. Courts often freeze a defendant's assets once charges are brought to ensure that he will not hide the assets. If all his assets are frozen, he will have a hard time paying his defense lawyer, so a freeze often encourages a defendant to plea bargain on a lesser charge. Both Milken and Drexel entered into plea agreements with the government, rather than face a freeze on their assets, or in Milken's case, a long prison sentence.

---

[24] 18 U.S.C. §§1961–1968.

In addition to criminal penalties, RICO also creates civil law liabilities. The government, organizations, and individuals all have the right to file civil lawsuits, seeking damages and, if necessary, injunctions. For example, a physician sued State Farm Insurance, alleging that the company had hired doctors to produce false medical reports that the company used to cut off claims by injured policy holders. As a result of these fake reports, the company refused to pay the plaintiff for legitimate services he performed on the policy holders. RICO is powerful (and for defendants, frightening) in part because a civil plaintiff can recover **treble damages**, that is, a judgment for three times the harm actually suffered, as well as attorney's fees.

Money Laundering

Money laundering
Using the proceeds of criminal acts either to promote crime or conceal the source of the money.

Money laundering consists of taking the proceeds of certain criminal acts and either (1) using the money to promote crime, or (2) attempting to conceal the source of the money.[25]

Money laundering is an important part of major criminal enterprises. Successful criminals earn enormous sums, which they must filter back into the flow of commerce so that their crimes go undetected. Laundering is an essential part of the corrosive traffic in drugs. Profits, all in cash, may mount so swiftly that dealers struggle to use the money without attracting the government's attention. For example, Colombian drug cartels set up a sophisticated system in which they shipped money to countries such as Dubai that do not keep records on cash transactions. This money was then transferred to the U.S. disguised as offshore loans. Prosecution by the U.S. government led to the demise of some of the banks involved.

But drug money is not the only or even major component of so-called flight capital. Criminals also try to hide the vast sums they earn from arms dealing and tax evasion. Some of this money is used to support terrorist organizations.

EXAM Strategy

Question: Explain the difference between embezzlement and money laundering. Give an example of each.

Strategy: Both crimes involve money illegally obtained, but they are very different. As to embezzlement, how did the criminal obtain the funds? In a laundering case, to what use is the criminal trying to put the cash?

Result: Embezzlement refers to fraudulently taking money that is already in the defendant's possession. For example, if a financial advisor, *lawfully entrusted* with his client's funds for investing, uses some of the cash to buy himself a luxurious yacht, he has embezzled the client's money. Money laundering consists of taking *illegally obtained* money and either using the funds to promote additional crimes or attempting to *conceal* the source of the cash. Thus, an arms dealer might launder money so that he can use it to finance a terrorist organization.

[25] 18 U.S.C. §§1956 et seq.

Other Crimes

Additional crimes that affect business appear elsewhere in the text. An increasing number of federal and state statutes are designed to punish those who harm the environment. (See Chapter 40, on environmental law.) Antitrust violations, in which a corporation fixes prices, can lead to criminal prosecutions. (See Chapter 38, on antitrust law.) Finally, securities fraud is a crime and can lead to severe prison sentences. (See Chapter 36, on securities regulation.)

Punishing a Corporation

Fines

The most common punishment for a corporation is a fine, as demonstrated in the Todesca case. This makes sense in that the purpose of a business is to earn a profit, and a fine, theoretically, hurts. But most fines are modest by the present standards of corporate wealth. In the Todesca prosecution, does a $2,500 fine force corporate leaders to be more cautious, or does it teach them that cutting corners makes economic sense, because the penalties will be a tolerable cost of doing business?

Sometimes the fines are stiffer. British Petroleum was found guilty of two serious environmental violations. In Alaska, the company's failure to inspect and clean pipelines caused 200,000 gallons of crude oil to spill onto the tundra. In Texas, the company's failure to follow standard procedures for ensuring safe refineries caused a catastrophic explosion that killed 15 people and injured 170 more. The total fine for both criminal violations was $62 million.[26] Is that enough to change BP's practices? Evidently not. In the spring of 2010, a BP well called Deepwater Horizon exploded, killing 11 workers and releasing into the Gulf of Mexico the largest marine oil spill ever. The Deepwater rig had violated many safety requirements.

Compliance Programs

The **Federal Sentencing Guidelines** are the detailed rules that judges must follow when sentencing defendants convicted of crimes in federal court. The guidelines instruct judges to determine whether, at the time of the crime, the corporation had in place a serious **compliance program**, that is, a plan to prevent and detect criminal conduct at all levels of the company. A company that can point to a detailed, functioning compliance program may benefit from a dramatic reduction in the fine or other punishment meted out. Indeed, a tough compliance program may even convince federal investigators to curtail an investigation and to limit any prosecution to those directly involved, rather than attempting to get a conviction against high-ranking officers or the company itself.

Federal Sentencing Guidelines
The detailed rules that judges must follow when sentencing defendants convicted of crimes in federal court.

Compliance program
A plan to prevent and detect criminal conduct at all levels of the company.

For a compliance plan to be deemed effective:

- The program must be reasonably capable of reducing the prospect of criminal conduct.
- Specific, high-level officers must be responsible for overseeing the program.
- The company must not place in charge any officers it knows or should have known, from past experience, are likely to engage in illegal conduct.
- The company must effectively communicate the program to all employees and agents.
- The company must ensure compliance by monitoring employees in a position to cheat and by promptly disciplining any who break the law.

---

[26]Source: **http://epa.gov/**.

Chapter Conclusion

Crime has an enormous impact on business. Companies are victims of crimes, and sometimes they also commit criminal actions. Successful business leaders are ever-vigilant to protect their company from those who wish to harm it, whether from the inside or the outside.

Exam Review

1. **BURDEN OF PROOF** In all prosecutions, the government must prove its case beyond a reasonable doubt. (p. 180)

EXAM Strategy

Question: Arnie owns a two-family house in a poor section of the city. A fire breaks out, destroying the building and causing $150,000 damage to an adjacent store. The state charges Arnie with arson. Simultaneously, Vickie, the store owner, sues Arnie for the damage to her property. Both cases are tried to juries, and the two juries hear identical evidence of Arnie's actions. But the criminal jury acquits Arnie, while the civil jury awards Vickie $150,000. How did that happen?

Strategy: The opposite outcomes are probably due to the different burdens of proof in a civil and criminal case. Make sure you know that distinction. (See the "Result" at the end of this section.)

2. **RIGHT TO A JURY.** A criminal defendant has a right to a trial by jury for any charge that could result in a sentence of six months or longer. (p. 180)

3. **DURESS** A defendant is not guilty of a crime if she committed it under duress. However, the defendant bears the burden of proving by a preponderance of the evidence that she acted under duress. (p. 181)

4. **ENTRAPMENT.** When the government induces the defendant to break the law, the prosecution must prove beyond a reasonable doubt that the defendant was predisposed to commit the crime. (p. 181)

5. **FOURTH AMENDMENT.** The Fourth Amendment to the Constitution prohibits the government from making illegal searches and seizures of individuals, corporations, partnerships, and other organizations. (pp. 181–185)

6. **WARRANT.** As a general rule, the police must obtain a warrant before conducting a search but there are seven circumstances under which the police may search without a warrant. (pp. 181–182)

7. **THE EXCLUSIONARY RULE.** Under the exclusionary rule, a prosecutor may not use evidence obtained illegally. (pp. 182–183)

8. **FIFTH AMENDMENT** The Fifth Amendment requires due process in all criminal procedures and prohibits double jeopardy and self-incrimination. (pp. 185–187)

9. **SIXTH AMENDMENT** The Sixth Amendment guarantees criminal defendants the right to a lawyer. (p. 187)

10. **EIGHTH AMENDMENT** The Eighth Amendment prohibits excessive fines and cruel and unusual punishments. (pp. 189–190)

11. **LARCENY** Larceny is the trespassory taking of personal property with the intent to steal. (p. 191)

12. **FRAUD** Fraud refers to a variety of crimes, all of which involve the deception of another person for the purpose of obtaining money or property. (pp. 191–193)

EXAM Strategy

Question: Chuck is a DJ on a radio station. A music company offers to pay him every time he plays one of its songs. Soon enough, Chuck is earning $10,000 a week in these extra payments, and his listeners love the music. In Chuck's view, this is a win-win situation. Is Chuck right?

Strategy: This is not traditional fraud because Chuck is not getting money from the people he is cheating—his listeners. Indeed, they are happy. Is there another type of fraud that applies in this situation? (See the "Result" at the end of this section.)

13. **ARSON** Arson is the malicious use of fire or explosives to damage or destroy real estate or personal property. (p. 193)

14. **EMBEZZLEMENT** Embezzlement is the fraudulent conversion of property already in the defendant's possession. (p. 193)

15. **CORPORATE LIABILITY** If a company's agent commits a criminal act within the scope of her employment and with the intent to benefit the corporation, the company is liable. (pp. 196–197)

16. **RICO** RICO prohibits using two or more racketeering acts to invest in legitimate business or carry on certain other criminal acts. RICO permits civil lawsuits as well as criminal prosecutions. (pp. 197–198)

EXAM Strategy

Question: Cheryl is a bank teller. She figures out a way to steal $99.99 per day in cash without getting caught. She takes the money daily for eight months and invests it in a catering business she is starting with Floyd, another teller. When Floyd learns what she is doing, he tries it, but is caught in his first attempt. He and Cheryl are both prosecuted.

(a) Both are guilty only of larceny.

(b) Both are guilty of larceny and violating RICO.

(c) Both are guilty of embezzlement; Cheryl is also guilty of violating RICO.

(d) Both are guilty of embezzlement and violating RICO.

Strategy: You need to know the difference between larceny and embezzlement. What is it? Once you have that figured out, focus on RICO. The government must prove two things: First, that the defendant committed crimes more than once—how many times? Second, that the defendant used the criminal proceeds for a specific purpose—what? (See the "Result" at the end of this section.)

17. **MONEY LAUNDERING** Money laundering consists of taking profits from a criminal act and either using them to promote crime or attempting to conceal their source. (p. 198)

1. Result: The plaintiff offered enough proof to convince a jury by a preponderance of the evidence that Arnie had damaged her store. However that same evidence, offered in a criminal prosecution, was not enough to persuade the jury beyond a reasonable doubt that Arnie had lit the fire.

12. Result: Chuck has committed a theft of honest services because he has taken a bribe.

16. Result: Cheryl and Floyd both committed embezzlement, which refers to fraudulently taking money that was properly in their possession. Floyd did it once, but a RICO conviction requires two or more racketeering acts—Floyd has not violated RICO. Cheryl embezzled dozens of times and invested the money in a legitimate business. She is guilty of embezzlement and RICO; the correct answer is C.

MULTIPLE-CHOICE QUESTIONS

1. In a criminal case, which statement is true?
   (a) The prosecution must prove the government's case by a preponderance of the evidence.
   (b) The criminal defendant is entitled to a lawyer even if she cannot afford to pay for it herself.
   (c) The police are never allowed to question the accused without a lawyer present.
   (d) All federal crimes are felonies.

2. The police are not required to obtain a warrant before conducting a search if:
   (a) a reliable informant has told them they will find evidence of a crime in a particular location.
   (b) they have a warrant for part of a property and another section of the property is in plain view.
   (c) they see someone on the street who could possibly have committed a criminal act.
   (d) someone living on the property has consented to the search.

3. Under the exclusionary rule, which statement is true?
   (a) Evidence must be excluded from trial if the search warrant is defective, even if the police believed at the time of the search that it was valid.
   (b) The prosecution cannot use any evidence the police found at the site of the illegal search, but it can use any evidence the police discover elsewhere as a result of the illegal search.
   (c) Any statements a defendant makes after arrest are inadmissible if the police do not read him his Miranda rights.
   (d) If a conviction is overturned because of the exclusionary rule, the prosecution is not allowed to retry the defendant.

4. Benry asks his girlfriend, Alina, to drive his car to the repair shop. She drives his car all right—to Las Vegas, where she hits the slots. Alina has committed
   (a) fraud.
   (b) embezzlement.
   (c) larceny.
   (d) a RICO violation.

5. Which of the following elements is required for a RICO conviction?
   (a) Investment in a legitimate business.
   (b) Two or more criminal acts.
   (c) Maintaining or acquiring businesses through criminal activity.
   (d) Operating a business through criminal activity.

Essay Questions

1. **YOU BE THE JUDGE WRITING PROBLEM** An undercover drug informant learned from a mutual friend that Philip Friedman "knew where to get marijuana." The informant asked Friedman three times to get him some marijuana, and Friedman agreed after the third request. Shortly thereafter, Friedman sold the informant a small amount of the drug. The informant later offered to sell Friedman three pounds of marijuana. They negotiated the price and then made the sale. Friedman was tried for trafficking in drugs. He argued entrapment. Was Friedman entrapped? **Argument for Friedman**: The undercover agent had to ask three times before Friedman sold him a small amount of drugs. A real drug dealer, predisposed to commit the crime, leaps at an opportunity to sell. If the government spends time and money luring innocent people into the commission of crimes, all of us are the losers. **Argument for the Government**: Government officials suspected Friedman of being a sophisticated drug dealer, and they were right. When he had a chance to buy three pounds, a quantity only a dealer would purchase, he not only did so, but he bargained with skill, showing a working knowledge of the business. Friedman was not entrapped—he was caught.

2. Conley owned video poker machines. Although they are outlawed in Pennsylvania, he placed them in bars and clubs. He used profits from the machines to buy more machines. Is he guilty of money laundering?

3. Karin made illegal firearm purchases at a gun show. At her trial, she alleged that she had committed this crime because her boyfriend had threatened to harm her and her two daughters if she did not. Her lawyer asked the judge to instruct the jury that the prosecution had an obligation to prove beyond a reasonable doubt that Karin had acted freely. Instead, the judge told the jury that Karin had the burden of proving duress by a preponderance of the evidence. Who is correct?

4. An informant bought drugs from Dorian. The police obtained a search warrant to search Dorian's house. But before they acted on the warrant, they sent the informant back to try again. This time, Dorian said he did not have any drugs. The police then acted on the warrant and searched his house. Did the police have probable cause?

5. Shawn was caught stealing letters from mailboxes. After pleading guilty, he was sentenced to two months in prison and three years supervised release. One of the supervised release conditions required him to stand outside a post office for eight hours wearing a signboard stating, "I stole mail. This is my punishment." He appealed this requirement on the grounds that it constituted cruel and unusual punishment. Do you agree?

Discussion Questions

1. Under British law, a police officer must now say the following to a suspect placed under arrest: "You do not have to say anything. But if you do not mention now something which you later use in your defense, the court may decide that your failure to mention it now strengthens the case against you. A record will be made of anything you say and it may be given in evidence if you are brought to trial." What is the goal of this British law? What does a police officer in the United States have to say, and what difference does it make at the time of an arrest? Which approach is better?

2. **ETHICS** You are a prosecutor who think it is possible that Naonka, in her role as CEO of a brokerage firm, has stolen money from her customers, many of whom are not well off. If you charge her and her company with RICO violations, you know that she is likely to plea bargain because otherwise her assets and those of the company may be frozen by the court. As part of the plea bargain, you might be able to get her to disclose evidence about other people who might have taken part in this criminal activity. But you do not have any hard evidence at this point. Would such an indictment be ethical? Do the ends justify the means? Is it worth it to harm Naonka for the chance of protecting thousands of innocent investors?

3. Van is brought to the police station for questioning about a shooting at a mall. The police read him his Miranda rights. For the rest of the three-hour interrogation, he remains silent except for a few one-word responses. Has he waived his right to remain silent? Can those few words be used against him in court?

4. Police arrested Bennie on a warrant issued in a neighboring county. When they searched him, the police found drugs and a gun. Only later did the police discover that when they had used the warrant, it was not valid because it had been recalled months earlier. The notice of recall had not been entered into the database. Should the evidence of drugs and a gun be suppressed under the exclusionary rule?

5. Andy was arrested for driving under the influence of alcohol (DUI). He had already been convicted of another driving offense. The court in the *first* offense was notified of this later DUI charge and took that information into consideration when determining Andy's sentence. Did the state violate Andy's protection against double jeopardy when it subsequently tried and convicted him for the DUI offense?

CHAPTER 10

Introduction to Contracts

© picsbyst/Shutterstock.com

Austin Electronics had a terrible year. John, the store's owner, decided to get out of the electronics business. Before closing his doors, he hung a sign reading "Everything Must Go!" and held a going-out-of-business sale.

Customer #1—Fran

"Nice TV," Fran commented. "Price says $400. I'll give you $250 for it."

"Sorry, but I need at least $400," John replied.

"Hmm. Nope, that's just too much."

"OK, OK, I'll let it go for $250."

"Well…no. No, I've changed my mind. No deal."

Customer #2—Ricky

"How much for that iPod, mister?" said Ricky, a 10-year-old boy.

"Twenty bucks, kid," John said.

"Wow! I'll take it! Keep it for me while I ride home to get my money."

"Sure thing, kid."

> "Well, how's about you sell them to me for $50 or I'll beat your face in for you."

Customer #3—Carla

"That's a good-looking home theater projector," Carla said. "I don't see a price tag. How much?"

"Well," John replied, "how much are you offering?"

"Hmm … I could give you $700 for it."

John was pleasantly surprised. "You've got yourself a deal." The two shook hands.

"I'll be back with my checkbook later today," Carla said.

Customer #4—Dave

As the sun set and the shadows lengthened, John waited patiently for his last customer to finish looking around. Truth be told, the guy looked kind of creepy.

"I'll give you $50 for these speakers," Dave said in a raspy voice.

"Sorry, man, but I can't let them go for less than $100," John replied.

"Well," Dave said, leaning closer, "how's about you sell them to me for $50 or I'll beat your face in for you."

"O ... kay," John said, startled. "$50 it is, then."

Dave smiled. He slid a fifty-dollar bill across the counter, picked up the speakers, and left without a word.

John has made four agreements, but are they contracts? Can he require Fran to buy the TV for $250? If Ricky and Carla never return to buy the iPod and the projector, can John take them to court and force them to follow through on the deals? Can John undo his transaction with the disreputable Dave?

Throughout this unit on contracts, we will consider issues like these. It is vital for a businessperson to understand the difference between an ordinary promise and a legally enforceable contract.

Most contracts work out precisely as intended because the parties fulfill their obligations. Most—but not all. In this unit, we will study contracts that have gone wrong. We look at these errant deals so that you can learn how to avoid problems.

CONTRACTS

Elements of a Contract

A contract is merely a legally enforceable agreement. People regularly make promises, but only some of them are enforceable. For a contract to be enforceable, seven key characteristics *must* be present. We will study this "checklist" at length in the next several chapters.

- Offer. All contracts begin when a person or a company proposes a deal. It might involve buying something, selling something, doing a job, or anything else. But only proposals made in certain ways amount to a legally recognized offer.
- Acceptance. Once a party receives an offer, he must respond to it in a certain way. We will examine the requirements of both offers and acceptances in the next chapter.
- Consideration. There has to be bargaining that leads to an *exchange* between the parties. Contracts cannot be a one-way street; both sides must receive some measureable benefit.
- Legality. The contract must be for a lawful purpose. Courts will not enforce agreements to sell cocaine, for example.
- Capacity. The parties must be adults of sound mind.
- Consent. Certain kinds of trickery and force can prevent the formation of a contract.
- Writing. While verbal agreements often amount to contracts, some types of contracts must be in writing to be enforceable.

Other Important Issues

Once we have examined the essential parts of contracts, the unit will turn to other important issues:

- Third-Party Interests. If Jerome and Tara have a contract, and if the deal falls apart, can Kevin sue to enforce the agreement? It depends.
- Performance and Discharge. If a party fully accomplishes what the contract requires, his duties are discharged. But what if his obligations are performed poorly, or not at all?
- Remedies. A court will award money or other relief to a party injured by a breach of contract.

Let's apply these principles to the opening scenario.

Fran is not obligated to buy the TV for $250 because John did not accept her offer. Ricky does not have to buy the iPod because he is under 18. If he changes his mind, there is nothing John can do about it. Nor is Carla required to buy the projector. Agreements concerning a sale of goods valued at more than $500 must be in writing. John can successfully sue Dave. He accepted Dave's offer to buy the speakers for $50, but he did so under duress. Agreements made under threats of violence are not enforceable contracts.

All Shapes and Sizes

Some contracts—like those in the opener—are small. But contracts can also be large. Lockheed Martin and Boeing spent years of work and millions of dollars competing for a U.S. Defense Department aircraft contract. Why the fierce effort? The deal was potentially good for 25 years and *$200 billion*. Lockheed won. The company earned the right to build the next generation of fighter jets—3,000 planes, with different varieties of the aircraft to be used by each of the American defense services and some allied forces as well.

Many contracts involve public issues. The Lockheed agreement concerns government agencies deciding how to spend taxpayer money for national defense. Other contracts concern intensely private matters. Mary Beth Whitehead signed a contract with William and Elizabeth Stern, of New Jersey. For a fee of $10,000, Whitehead agreed to act as a surrogate mother, and then deliver the baby to the Sterns for adoption after she carried it to term. But when little Melissa was born, Whitehead changed her mind and fled to Florida with the baby. The Sterns sued for breach of contract. Surrogacy contracts now lead to hundreds of births per year. Are the contracts immoral? Should they be illegal? Are there limits to what one person may pay another to do? The New Jersey Supreme Court, the first to rule on the issue, declared the contract illegal and void. The court nonetheless awarded Melissa to the Sterns, saying that it was in the child's best interest to live with them. Inevitably, legislators disagree about this emotional issue. Some states have passed statutes permitting surrogacy, while others prohibit it.

At times, we even enter contracts without knowing it. Suppose you try to book a flight using your frequent-flyer miles, but the airline tells you the terms of the frequent-flyer program have changed and you must earn more mileage. According to the Supreme Court, you may well have an enforceable agreement based on the terms the airline quoted when you earned the miles.[1]

Contracts Defined

Contract
A legally enforceable agreement.

We have seen that a **contract** is a promise that the law will enforce. As we look more closely at the elements of contract law, we will encounter some intricate issues. This is partly because we live in a complex society, which conducts its business in a wide variety of ways. Remember, though, that we are usually interested in answering three basic questions, all relating to promises:

[1]*American Airlines, Inc. v. Wolens,* 513 U.S. 219, 115 S. Ct. 817, 1995 U.S. LEXIS 690 (1995).

- Is it certain that the defendant promised to do something?
- If she did promise, is it fair to make her honor her word?
- If she did not promise, are there unusual reasons to hold her liable anyway?

Development of Contract Law

Courts have not always assumed that promises are legally significant. In the twelfth and thirteenth centuries, promises were not binding unless a person made them *in writing and affixed a seal* to the document. This was seldom done, and therefore most promises were unenforceable.

The common law changed very slowly, but by the fifteenth century, courts began to allow some suits based on a broken promise. There were still major limitations. Suppose a merchant hired a carpenter to build a new shop, and the carpenter failed to start the job on time. Now courts would permit the suit, but only if the merchant had paid some money to the carpenter. If the merchant made a 10 percent down payment, the contract would be enforceable. But if the merchant merely *promised* to pay when the building was done, and the carpenter never began work, the merchant could recover nothing.

In 1602, English courts began to enforce mutual *promises;* that is, deals in which neither party gave anything to the other but both promised to do something in the future. Thus, if a farmer promised to deliver a certain quantity of wheat to a merchant and the merchant agreed on the price, both parties were now bound by their promise, even though there had been no down payment. This was a huge step forward in the development of contract law, but many issues remained. Consider the following employment case from 1792, which raises issues of public policy that still challenge courts today.

Davis v. Mason

Court of King's Bench
Michaelmas Term, 33d George III, p. 118 (1792)

Facts: Mason was a surgeon/apothecary in the English town of Thetford. Davis wished to apprentice himself to Mason. The two agreed that Davis would work for Mason and learn his profession. They further agreed that if Davis left Mason's practice, he would not set up a competing establishment within 10 miles of Thetford at any time within 14 years. Davis promised to pay £200 if he violated the agreement not to compete.

Davis began working for Mason in July 1789. In August 1791, Mason dismissed Davis, claiming misconduct, though Davis denied it. Davis then established his own practice within 10 miles of Thetford. Mason sued for the £200.

Davis admitted promising to pay the money. But he claimed that the agreement should be declared illegal and unenforceable. He argued that 14 years was unreasonably long to restrict him from the town of Thetford, and that 10 miles was too great a distance. (In those days, 10 miles might take the better part of a day to travel.) He added an additional policy argument, saying that it was harmful to the public health to restrict a doctor from practicing his profession: if the people needed his service, they should have it. Finally, he said that his "consideration" was too great for this deal. In other words, it was unfair that he should pay £200 because he did not receive anything of that value from Mason.

Issue: ***Was the contract too unreasonable to enforce?***

Excerpts from Lord Kenyon's Decision: Here, the plaintiff being established in business as a surgeon at Thetford, the defendant wished to act as his assistant with a view of deriving a degree of credit from that situation; on which the former stipulated that the defendant should not come to live there under his auspices and steal away his patients: this seems to be a fair consideration. Then it was objected that the limits within which the defendant engaged not to practise are unreasonable: but I do not see that they are necessarily unreasonable, nor do I know how to draw the line. Neither are the public likely to be injured by an agreement of this kind, since every other person is at liberty to practise as a surgeon in this town.

Judgment for the Plaintiff.

Noncompetition agreement
A contract in which one party agrees not to compete with another.

The contract between Davis and Mason is called a **noncompetition agreement**. Today they are more common than ever, and frequently litigated. The policy issues that Davis raised have never gone away. You may well be asked to sign a noncompetition agreement sometime in your professional life. We look at the issue in detail in Chapter 12, on consideration. That outcome was typical of contract cases for the next 100 years. Courts took a *laissez-faire* approach, declaring that parties had *freedom to contract* and would have to live with the consequences. Lord Kenyon saw Davis and Mason as equals, entering a bargain that made basic sense, and he had no intention of rewriting it. After 500 years of evolution, courts had come to regard promises as almost sacred. The law had gone from ignoring most promises to enforcing nearly all.

By the early twentieth century, bargaining power in business deals had changed dramatically. Farms and small businesses were yielding place to huge corporations in a trend that accelerated throughout the century. In the twenty-first century, multinational corporations span many continents, wielding larger budgets and more power than many of the nations in which they do business. When such a corporation contracts with a small company or an individual consumer, the latter may have little or no leverage. Courts increasingly looked at the basic fairness of contracts. Noncompetition agreements are no longer automatically enforced. Courts may alter them or ignore them entirely because the parties have such unequal power and because the public may have an interest in letting the employee go on to compete. Davis's argument—that the public is entitled to as many doctors as it needs—is frequently more successful in court today than it was in the days of Lord Kenyon.

Legislatures and the courts limit the effect of promises in other ways. Suppose you purchase a lawn mower with an attached tag, warning you that the manufacturer is not responsible in the event of any malfunction or injury. You are required to sign a form acknowledging that the manufacturer has no liability of any kind. That agreement is clear enough—but a court will not enforce it. The law holds that the manufacturer *has* warranted the product to be good for normal purposes, regardless of any language included in the sales agreement. If the blade flies off and injures a child, the manufacturer is liable. This is socially responsible, even though it interferes with a private agreement.

The law has not come full circle back to the early days of the common law. Courts still enforce the great majority of contracts. But the possibility that a court will ignore an agreement means that any contract is a little less certain than it would have been a century ago.

Types of Contracts

Before undertaking a study of contracts, you need to familiarize yourself with some important vocabulary. This section will present five sets of terms.

Bilateral and Unilateral Contracts

Bilateral contract
A promise made in exchange for another promise.

In a **bilateral contract**, both parties make a promise. A producer says to Gloria, "I'll pay you $2 million to star in my new romantic comedy, which we are shooting three months from now in Santa Fe." Gloria says, "It's a deal." That is a bilateral contract. Each party has made a promise to do something. The producer is now bound to pay Gloria $2 million, and Gloria is obligated to show up on time and act in the movie. The vast majority of contracts are bilateral contracts. They can be for services, such as this acting contract; they can be for the sale of goods, such as 1,000 tons of steel, or for almost any other purpose. When the bargain is a promise for a promise, it is a bilateral agreement.

In a unilateral contract, one party makes a promise that the other party can accept only by *actually doing* something. These contracts are less common. Suppose the movie producer tacks a sign to a community bulletin board. It has a picture of a dog with a phone number, and it reads, "I'll pay $100 to anyone who returns my lost dog." If Leo sees the sign, finds the producer, and merely promises to find the dog, he has not created a contract. Because of the terms on the sign, Leo must actually find and return the dog to stake a claim to the $100.

Executory and Executed Contracts

A contract is **executory** when it has been made, but one or more parties has not yet fulfilled its obligations. Recall Gloria, who agrees to act in the producer's film beginning in three months. The moment Gloria and the producer strike their bargain, they have an executory bilateral express contract.

Executory contract
An agreement in which one or more parties has not yet fulfilled its obligations.

A contract is **executed** when all parties have fulfilled their obligations. When Gloria finishes acting in the movie and the producer pays her final fee, their contract will be fully executed.

Executed contract
An agreement in which all parties have fulfilled their obligations.

EXAM Strategy

Question: Abby has long coveted Nicola's designer handbag because she saw one of them in a movie. Finally, Nicola offers to sell her friend the bag for $350 in cash. "I don't have the money right now," Abby replies, "but I'll have it a week from Friday. Is it a deal?" Nicola agrees to sell the bag. Use two terms to describe the contract.

Strategy: In a bilateral contract, both parties make a promise, but in a unilateral agreement, only one side does so. An executory contract is one with unfulfilled obligations, while an executed agreement is one with nothing left to be done.

Result: Nicola promised to sell the bag for $350 cash, and Abby agreed to pay. Because both parties made a promise, this a bilateral agreement. The deal is not yet completed, meaning that they have an executory contract.

Valid, Unenforceable, Voidable, and Void Agreements

A **valid contract** is one that satisfies all of the law's requirements. It has no problems in any of the seven areas listed at the beginning of this chapter, and a court will enforce it. The contract between Gloria and the producer is a valid contract, and if the producer fails to pay Gloria, she will win a lawsuit to collect the unpaid fee.

An **unenforceable agreement** occurs when the parties intend to form a valid bargain, but a court declares that some rule of law prevents enforcing it. Suppose Gloria and the producer orally agree that she will star in his movie, which he will start filming in 18 months. The law, as we will see in Chapter 15, requires that this contract be in writing because it cannot be completed within one year. If the producer signs up another actress two months later, Gloria has no claim against him.

A **voidable contract** occurs when the law permits one party to terminate the agreement. This happens, for example, when the other party has committed fraud, or when an agreement has been signed under duress. In the opening scenario, Dave threatened John when he would not sell the speakers for $50. The agreement is voidable at John's option. If John later decides that the $50 is acceptable, he may keep it. But if he decides that he wants to cancel the agreement and sue for the return of his speakers, he can do that as well.

Voidable contract
An agreement that may be terminated by one of the parties.

A **void agreement** is one that neither party can enforce, usually because the purpose of the deal is illegal or because one of the parties had no legal authority to make a contract.

Void agreement
A contract that neither party can enforce, because the bargain is illegal or one of the parties had no legal authority to make it.

The following case illustrates the difference between voidable and void agreements.

MR. W FIREWORKS, INC. v. OZUNA

2009 Tex. App. LEXIS 8237
Court of Appeals of Texas, Fourth District, San Antonio, 2009

Facts: Mr. W sells fireworks. Under Texas law, retailers may sell fireworks to the public only during the two weeks immediately before the Fourth of July and during two weeks immediately before New Year's Day. And so, fireworks sellers like Mr. W tend to lease property.

Mr. W leased a portion of Ozuna's land. The lease contract contained two key terms:

> "In the event the sale of fireworks on the aforementioned property is or shall become unlawful during the period of this lease and the term granted, this lease shall become void.
>
> "Lessor(s) agree not to sell or lease any part of said property, including any adjoining, adjacent, or contiguous property, to any person(s) or corporation for the purpose of selling fireworks in competition to the Lessee during the term of this lease, *and for a period of ten years after lease is terminated.*" (Emphasis added.)

A longstanding San Antonio city ordinance bans the sale of fireworks inside city limits, and also within 5,000 feet of city limits. Like all growing cities, San Antonio sometimes annexes new land, and its city limits change. One annexation caused the Ozuna property to fall within 5,000 feet of the new city limits, and it became illegal to sell fireworks from the property. Mr. W stopped selling fireworks and paying rent on Ozuna's land.

Two years later, San Antonio's border shifted again. This time, the city *disannexed* some property and *shrank.* The new city limits placed Ozuna's property just beyond the 5,000-foot no-fireworks zone. Ozuna then leased a part of his land to Alamo Fireworks, a competitor of Mr. W.

Mr. W sued for breach of contract, arguing that Ozuna had no right to lease to a competitor for a period of 10 years. The trial court granted Ozuna's motion for summary judgment. Mr. W appealed.

Issue: ***Did Ozuna breach his contract with Mr. W by leasing his land to a competitor?***

Excerpts from Judge Angelini's Decision: The property owners [argue] that when the city ordinance made the sale of fireworks illegal on the subject properties, the leases became void, resulting in the property owners and Mr. W no longer having an enforceable agreement. Mr. W's argues that the provision restricting the property owners from leasing to competitors survived the agreement. This is inconsistent with the meaning of "voidable" contracts. For example, when a minor enters into a contract, that contract is not void, but is voidable at the election of the minor. This means that the minor may set aside the entire contract at his option, but he *is not entitled to enforce portions that are favorable to him and at the same time disaffirm other provisions that he finds burdensome.* He is not permitted to retain the benefits of a contract while repudiating its obligations.

Could Ozuna declare independence from contractual obligations?

Here, while Mr. W is arguing that the illegalization of the sale of fireworks made the contract "voidable," it is still seeking to enforce the provision of the contract prohibiting the property owners from leasing to competitors. We decline to adopt such an interpretation.

Further, contracts requiring an illegal act are void. We therefore hold that the illegalization of the sale of the fireworks on the respective properties did not trigger the provision in the leases prohibiting the property owners from leasing to competitors of Mr. W.

We affirm the judgment of the trial court.

Express and Implied Contracts

In an **express contract**, the two parties explicitly state all the important terms of their agreement. The vast majority of contracts are express contracts. The contract between the producer and Gloria is an express contract because the parties explicitly state what Gloria will do, where and when she will do it, and how much she will be paid. Some express contracts are oral, as that one was, and some are written. They might be bilateral express contracts, as Gloria's was, or unilateral express contracts, as Leo's was. Obviously, it is wise to make express contracts, and to put them in writing. We emphasize, however, that many oral contracts are fully enforceable.

Express contract
An agreement with all the important terms explicitly stated.

In an implied contract, the words and conduct of the parties indicate that they intended an agreement. Suppose every Friday, for two months, the producer asks Lance to mow his lawn, and loyal Lance does so each weekend. Then, for three more weekends, Lance simply shows up without the producer asking, and the producer continues to pay for the work done. But on the 12th weekend, when Lance rings the doorbell to collect, the producer suddenly says, "I never asked you to mow it. Scram." The producer is correct that there was no express contract because the parties had not spoken for several weeks. But a court will probably rule that the conduct of the parties has *implied* a contract. Not only did Lance mow the lawn every weekend, but the producer even paid on three weekends when they had not spoken. It was reasonable for Lance to assume that he had a weekly deal to mow and be paid.

Today, the hottest disputes about implied contracts continue to arise in the employment setting. Many corporate employees have at-will relationships with their companies. This means that the employees are free to quit at any time and the company has the right to fire them, for virtually any reason. But often a company provides its workers with personnel manuals that lay out certain rights. Does a handbook create a contract guaranteeing those rights? What is your opinion?

You be the Judge

DeMasse v. ITT Corporation

194 Ariz. 500, 984 P.2d 1138
Supreme Court of Arizona, 1999

Facts: Roger DeMasse and five others were employees-at-will at ITT Corporation, where they started working at various times between 1960 and 1979. Each was paid an hourly wage.

ITT issued an employee handbook, which it revised four times over two decades.

The first four editions of the handbook stated that within each job classification, any layoffs would be made in reverse order of seniority. The fifth handbook made two important changes. First, the document stated that "nothing contained herein shall be construed as a guarantee of continued employment. ITT does not guarantee continued employment to employees and retains the right to terminate or lay off employees."

Second, the handbook stated that "ITT reserves the right to amend, modify, or cancel this handbook, as well as any or all of the various policies [or rules] outlined in it." Four years later, ITT notified its hourly employees that layoff guidelines for hourly employees would be based not on seniority, but on ability and performance. About 10 days later, the six employees were laid off, though less-senior employees kept their jobs. The six employees sued.

You Be The Judge: ***Did ITT have the right to unilaterally change the layoff policy?***

Argument for the workers: It is true that all of the plaintiffs were originally employees-at-will, subject to termination at the company's whim. However, things changed when the company issued the first handbook. ITT chose to include a promise that layoffs would be based on seniority. Long-term workers and new employees all understood the promise and relied on it. The company put it there to attract and retain good workers. The policy worked. Responsible employees understood that the longer they remained at ITT, the safer their job was. Company and employees worked together for many years with a common understanding, and that is a textbook definition of an implied contract.

Once a contract is formed, whether express or implied, it is binding on both sides. That is the whole point of a contract. If one side could simply change the terms of an agreement on its own, what value would any contract have? The company's legal argument is a perfect symbol of its arrogance: It believes that because these workers are mere hourly workers, they have no rights, even under contract law. The company is mistaken. Implied contracts are binding, and ITT should not make promises it does not intend to keep.

Argument for ITT: Once an at-will employee, always one. ITT had the right to fire any of its employees at any time—just as the workers had the right to quit whenever they wished. That never changed, and in case any workers forgot it, the company reiterated the point in its most recent handbook. If the plaintiffs thought layoffs would happen in any particular order, that is their error, not ours.

All workers were bound by the terms of whichever handbook was then in place. For many years, the company had made a seniority-layoff promise. Had we fired a senior worker during that period, he or she would have had a legitimate complaint—and that is why we did not do it. Instead, we gave everyone four years' notice that things would change. Any workers unhappy with the new policies should have left to find more congenial work.

Why should an employee be allowed to say, "I prefer to rely on the old, outdated handbooks, not the new one"? The plaintiffs' position would mean that no company is ever free to change its general work policies and rules. Since when does an at-will employee have the right to dictate company policy? That would be disastrous for the whole economy—but fortunately it is not the law.

Promissory Estoppel and Quasi-Contracts

Now we turn away from "true" contracts and consider two unusual circumstances. Sometimes, courts will enforce agreements even if they fail to meet the usual requirement of a contract. We emphasize that these remedies are uncommon exceptions to the general rules. Most of the agreements that courts enforce are the express contracts that we have already studied. Nonetheless, the next two remedies are still pivotal in some lawsuits. In each case, a sympathetic plaintiff can demonstrate an injury but *there is no contract.* The plaintiff cannot claim that the defendant breached a contract, because none ever existed. The plaintiff must hope for more "creative" relief.

The two remedies can be confusingly similar. The best way to distinguish them is this:

- In promissory estoppel cases, the defendant made a promise that the plaintiff relied on.
- In quasi-contract cases, the defendant received a *benefit* from the plaintiff.

Promissory Estoppel

A fierce fire swept through Dana and Derek Andreason's house in Utah, seriously damaging it. The good news was that agents for Aetna Casualty promptly visited the Andreasons and helped them through the crisis. The agents reassured the couple that all of the damage was covered by their insurance, instructed them on which things to throw out and replace, and helped them choose materials for repairing other items. The bad news was that the agents were wrong: the Andreasons' policy had expired six weeks before the fire. When Derek Andreason presented a bill for $41,957 worth of meticulously itemized work that he had done under the agents' supervision, Aetna refused to pay.

Promissory estoppel
A *possible* remedy for an injured plaintiff in a case with no valid contract, where the plaintiff can show a promise, reasonable reliance, and injustice.

The Andreasons sued—but not for breach of contract. There *was* no contract—they allowed their policy to expire. They sued Aetna under the legal theory of promissory estoppel: even when there is no contract, a plaintiff may use **promissory estoppel** to enforce the defendant's promise if he can show that:

- The defendant made a promise knowing that the plaintiff would likely rely on it;
- The plaintiff did rely on the promise; and
- The only way to avoid injustice is to enforce the promise.

Aetna made a promise to the Andreasons—namely, its assurance that all of the damage was covered by insurance. The company knew that the Andreasons would rely on that promise, which they did by ripping up a floor that might have been salvaged, throwing out some furniture, and buying materials to repair the house. Is enforcing the promise the only way to avoid injustice? Yes, ruled the Utah Court of Appeals.[2] The Andreasons' conduct was reasonable and based entirely on what the Aetna agents told them. Under promissory estoppel, the Andreasons received virtually the same amount they would have obtained had the insurance contract been valid.

Is enforcing the promise the only way to avoid injustice?

There was plenty of romance in the following case. Was there an enforceable promise?

Norton v. Hoyt

278 F. Supp. 2d 214
United States District Court for the District of Rhode Island, 2003

Facts: Gail Norton sued Russell Hoyt, and this is what she alleged. The two met when Norton, who was single, worked as an elementary school teacher. Hoyt told her he was also single, and they began an affair. She later learned that he was married, but he assured her he was getting a divorce, and they continued their relationship.

Six years later, Hoyt, who was rich, convinced Norton to quit her job so that they could travel together. The couple lived lavishly, spending time in Newport, Rhode Island, where Hoyt was part of the yachting crowd, in London, the Bahamas, and other agreeable places. Hoyt rented Norton an apartment, bought her cars, and repeated his promises to divorce his wife and marry his lover. He never did either.

After 23 years, Hoyt ended the relationship. Norton became ill, and saw various doctors for anxiety, depression, headaches, stomach maladies, and weight loss. During one joint therapy session, Hoyt told Norton and the psychiatrist that he would continue to support her with $80,000 a year. But he did not.

Norton sued, claiming promissory estoppel. Hoyt moved for summary judgment. In ruling on the motion, the court assumed that Norton's allegations were true.

Issue: ***Was Norton entitled to support, based on promissory estoppel?***

Excerpts from Judge Lageux's Decision: Even viewed most favorably to the Plaintiff, the record fails to reveal a clear, unconditional, and unambiguous promise. Plaintiff's vacillations have not helped her cause. First, she claimed that Hoyt promised to divorce his wife, marry her, and provide lifetime support to her. Then she changed her mind and the promise became one to provide lifetime support to her regardless of whether Hoyt divorced his wife or not. Finally at the hearing on this motion, counsel argued that Hoyt had simply promised to take care of Norton for life. However, there can be many interpretations of the phrase "take care of for life." It could refer to care in a social, emotional, or financial context. As other courts have recognized, this is certainly not a clear and unambiguous promise.

Even assuming, *arguendo,* that there was a clear and unambiguous promise, Norton's reliance upon that promise was unreasonable. Though the couple had discussions about their life together and even discussed potential wedding plans, Plaintiff knew that Hoyt was married, and that he spent time at the marital domicile with his wife and children. Norton and Hoyt never openly associated as husband and wife, their friends and family knew that they were not married, and they did not exclusively cohabitate. Furthermore, Norton knew that Hoyt had lied in the past,

[2] *Andreason v. Aetna Casualty & Surety Co.*, 848 P.2d 171, 1993 Utah App. LEXIS 26 (Utah App. 1993).

was in an adulterous relationship, and apparently had made little effort to fulfill the terms of the promise. Reliance upon an unclear and ambiguous promise made by an apparently unreliable man was imprudent.

In any event, whatever form her reliance took, it is insufficient to overcome the other fatal flaws in her claim. Any promise for support that Hoyt made prior to the breakup is ambiguous at best, and, considering the source, was not a reasonable basis upon which to ground reliance. Sometime between year one and year 23 of the affair, it should have become clear to Norton that her reliance on Hoyt's promise to divorce his wife and marry her was misplaced.

[The defendant's motion for summary judgment is granted.]

Devil's Advocate Why should one person be able to make repeated promises over two decades and escape all responsibility? Even if Hoyt's precise words varied, each of his promises involved long-term emotional and financial security for Norton. Norton was naïve, but Hoyt was dishonest. The law should be a tool for teaching people like him a lesson.

Why have we chosen to illustrate an important point of law—promissory estoppel—with a case that fails? Because that is the typical outcome. Plaintiffs allege promissory estoppel very frequently, but seldom succeed. They do occasionally win, as the Andreasons demonstrated earlier, but courts are skeptical of these claims. The lesson is clear: Before you rely on a promise, negotiate a binding contract.

© Photodisc/Getty Images

Quasi-contract may require compensation even when no contract exists.

Quasi-Contract

Don Easterwood leased over 5,000 acres of farmland in Jackson County, Texas, from PIC Realty for one year. The next year, he obtained a second one-year lease. During each year, Easterwood farmed the land, harvested the crops, and prepared the land for the following year's planting. Toward the end of the second lease, after Easterwood had harvested his crop, he and PIC began discussing the terms of another lease. While they negotiated, Easterwood prepared the land for the following year, cutting and plowing the soil. But the negotiations for a new lease failed, and Easterwood moved off the land. He sued PIC Realty for the value of his work preparing the soil.

Easterwood had neither an express nor an implied contract for the value of his work. How could he make any legal claim? By relying on the legal theory of a quasi-contract: Even when there is no contract, a court may use **quasi-contract** to compensate a plaintiff who can show that:

- The plaintiff gave some benefit to the defendant;
- The plaintiff reasonably expected to be paid for the benefit and the defendant knew this; and
- The defendant would be unjustly enriched if he did not pay.

Quasi-contract
A *possible* remedy for an injured plaintiff in a case with no valid contract, where the plaintiff can show benefit to the defendant, reasonable expectation of payment, and unjust enrichment.

If a court finds all of these elements present, it will generally award the value of the goods or services that the plaintiff has conferred. The damages awarded are called ***quantum meruit***, meaning that the plaintiff gets "as much as he deserves." The court is awarding money that it believes the plaintiff *morally ought to have*, even though there was no valid contract entitling her to it. This again is judicial activism, with the courts inventing a "quasi" contract where no true contract exists. The purpose is justice, the term is contradictory.

Quantum meruit
"As much as he deserves"—the damages awarded in a quasi-contract case.

Don Easterwood testified that in Jackson County, it was quite common for a tenant farmer to prepare the soil for the following year but then be unable to farm the land. In those cases, he claimed, the landowner compensated the farmer for the work done. Other witnesses agreed that this was the local custom. The court ruled that indeed there was no contract, but that all elements of quasi-contract had been satisfied. Easterwood gave a benefit to PIC because the land was ready for planting. Jackson County custom caused Easterwood to assume he would be paid, and PIC Realty knew it. Finally, said the court, it would be unjust to let PIC benefit without paying anything. The court ordered PIC to pay the fair market value of Easterwood's labors.

FOUR THEORIES OF RECOVERY

Theory	Did the Defendant Make a Promise?	Is There a Contract?	Description
Express Contract	Yes	Yes	The parties intend to contract and agree on explicit terms.
Implied Contract	Not explicitly	Yes	The parties do not formally agree, but their words and conduct indicate an intention to create a contract.
Promissory Estoppel	Yes	No	There is no contract, but the defendant makes a promise that she can foresee will induce reliance; the plaintiff relies on it; and it would be unjust not to enforce the promise.
Quasi-Contract	No	No	There is no intention to contract, but the plaintiff gives some benefit to the defendant, who knows that the plaintiff expects compensation; it would be unjust not to award the plaintiff damages.

EXAM Strategy

Question: The table above lists the different theories a plaintiff may use to recover damages in a contract dispute. In the following examples, which one will each plaintiff use in trying to win the case?

1. Company pays all employees 10 percent commission on new business they develop. Company compensates each employee when the new customer pays its first bill. After Leandro obtains three new clients, Company fires him. When

the new customers pay their bill, Company refuses to pay Leandro a commission because he is no longer an employee. Leandro sues.

2. Burt agrees in writing to sell Red 100 lobsters for $15 each, payable by credit card, in exactly 30 days. When the lobsters fail to arrive, Red sues.
3. Company handbook, given to all new hires, states that no employee will be fired without a hearing and an appeal. Company fires Delores without a hearing or appeal. She sues.

Strategy: In (1), the Company never promised to pay a commission to nonemployees, so there is no contract. However, the Company *benefited* from Leandro's work. In (2), the parties have *clearly stated all terms* to a simple sales agreement. In (3), the Company and Delores never negotiated termination, but *the handbook suggests* that all employees have certain rights.

Result: (1) is a case of quasi-contract because the company benefited and should reasonably expect to pay. (2) is an express contract because all terms are clearly stated. (3) is an implied contract, similar to the *DeMasse* case, based on the handbook.

Sources of Contract Law

Common Law

We have seen the evolution of contract law from the twelfth century to the present. Express and implied contracts, promissory estoppel, and quasi-contract were all crafted, over centuries, by courts deciding one contract lawsuit at a time. Many contract lawsuits continue to be decided using common-law principles developed by courts.

Uniform Commercial Code

Business methods changed quickly during the first half of the last century. Transportation speeded up. Corporations routinely conducted business across state borders and around the world. These developments presented a problem. Common-law principles, whether related to contracts, torts, or anything else, sometimes vary from one state to another. New York and California courts often reach similar conclusions when presented with similar cases, but they are under no obligation to do so. Business leaders became frustrated that, to do business across the country, their companies had to deal with many different sets of common-law rules.

Executives, lawyers, and judges wanted a body of law for business transactions that reflected modern commercial methods and provided uniformity throughout the United States. It would be much easier, they thought, if some parts of contract law were the same in every state. That desire gave birth to the Uniform Commercial Code (UCC), created in 1952. The drafters intended the UCC to facilitate the easy formation and enforcement of contracts in a fast-paced world. The Code governs many aspects of commerce, including the sale and leasing of goods, negotiable instruments, bank deposits, letters of credit, investment securities, secured transactions, and other commercial matters. Every state has adopted at least part of the UCC to govern commercial transactions within that state. For our purposes in studying contracts, the most important part of the Code is Article 2, which governs the sale of goods. **"Goods" means anything movable, except for money, securities, and certain legal rights.** Goods include pencils, commercial aircraft, books, and Christmas trees. Goods do not include land or a house because neither is movable, nor do they include a stock certificate. A contract for the sale of 10,000 sneakers is governed by the UCC; a contract for the sale of a condominium in Marina del Rey is governed by the California common law.

When analyzing any contract problem as a student or businessperson, you must note whether the agreement concerns the sale of goods. For many issues, the common law and the UCC are reasonably similar. But sometimes, the law is quite different under the two sets of rules.

And so, the UCC governs contracts for a sale of goods, while common-law principles govern contracts for sales of services and everything else. Most of the time, it will be clear whether the UCC or the common law applies. But what if a contract involves both goods and services? When you get your oil changed, you are paying in part for the new oil and oil filter (goods) and in part for the labor required to do the job (services). In a mixed contract, Article 2 governs only if the *primary purpose* was the sale of goods. In the following case, the court had to decide the primary purpose.

Fallsview Glatt Kosher Caterers, Inc. v. Rosenfeld

2005 WL 53623
Civil Court, City of New York, 2005

Facts: During the Jewish holidays, Fallsview Glatt Kosher Caterers organized programs at Kutcher's Country Club, where it provided all accommodations, food, and entertainment.

Fallsview sued Willie Rosenfeld, alleging that he had requested accommodations for 15 members of his family, agreeing to pay $24,050, and then failed to appear or pay.

Rosenfeld moved to dismiss, claiming that even if there had been an agreement, it was never put in writing. Under UCC §2-201, any contract for the sale of goods worth $500 or more can be enforced only if it is in writing and signed. Fallsview argued that the agreement was not for the sale of goods, but for services. The company claimed that because the contract was not governed by the UCC, it should be enforced even with no writing.

Issue: ***Was the agreement one for the sale of goods, requiring a writing, or for services, enforceable with no writing?***

Excerpts from Judge Battaglia's Decision: Mr. Rosenfeld contends that the "predominant purpose" and "main objective" of the agreement alleged by Fallsview was the "service of Kosher food," while the hotel accommodations and entertainment were merely "incidental or collateral" services.

Defendant's contention that the "predominant purpose" of the alleged agreement is the sale of food is said to be compelled by the very nature of the Passover holiday. [He argues that] "the essential religious obligation during this eight-day period and the principal reason why people attend events similar to the Program sponsored by plaintiff is in order to facilitate their fulfillment of the requirement to eat only food which is prepared in strict accordance with the mandate of Jewish law for Passover, i.e., food which is 'Kosher for Passover.' It is the desire to obtain these 'goods' and not the urge for 'entertainment' or 'accommodations' that motivates customers to subscribe to such 'Programs.' "

[Fallsview submitted] ten sheets, designated "Kutcher's Country Club Daily Activities" for Sunday, April 4, through Tuesday, April 13, 2004. The activities possible include tennis, racquetball, swimming, Swedish massage, "make over face lift show," "trivia time," aerobics, bingo, ice skating, dancing, "showtime," "power walk," arts and crafts, day camp, ping-pong, Yiddish theater, board games, horse racing, horseback riding, wine tasting, and indoor baci and that is only through Wednesday. These activities are provided, together with accommodations and food, for an "all inclusive" price that is apparently determined by the size and location of the room(s) and the numbers and ages of the persons in each party.

A review of the characteristics of the "program," which is the subject matter of the alleged agreement, leads the Court to conclude that the "essence" of the family and communal "experience" is defined primarily by "services" and not by "goods."

The intended scope of UCC section 2-201 is also indicated by its provision that "[a] writing is not insufficient because it omits or incorrectly states a term agreed upon but the contract is not enforceable under this paragraph beyond the quantity of goods shown in the writing." For the Code, quantity is even more important than price. A contract of the type involved here would rarely, if ever, specify the "quantity" of the "goods" to be provided. Nor would, for example, a contract for a week's stay at a weight-loss spa, or a zen-vegetarian retreat, or a cruise of the islands.

Plaintiff argues that "Defendant's proposition that a hotel reservation is a sale of goods would render all reservations made via telephone or the Internet unenforceable and would leave hotels in a precarious economic position." That may or may not be true, but the argument does highlight the importance of ensuring that a Statute of Frauds structured and outfitted by the Legislature for a particular transactional context not be casually applied to a very different commercial segment and model. The structure and terms of section 2-201 tell us that it was not intended to cover the agreement alleged in this Complaint.

Defendant's motion to dismiss is denied.

EXAM Strategy

Question: Leila agrees to pay Kendrick $35,000 to repair windmills. Confident of this cash, Kendrick contracts to buy Derrick's used Porsche for $33,000. Then Leila informs Kendrick she does not need his help and will not pay him. Kendrick tells Derrick that he no longer wants the Porsche. Derrick sues Kendrick, and Kendrick files suit against Leila. What law or laws govern these lawsuits?

Strategy: Always be conscious of whether a contract is for services or the sale of goods. Different laws govern. To make that distinction, you must understand the term "goods." If you are clear about that, the question is answered easily.

Result: *Goods* means anything movable, and a Porsche is movable—one might say "super-movable." The UCC will control Derrick's suit. Repairing windmills is primarily a service. Kendrick's lawsuit is governed by the common law of contracts.

Chapter Conclusion

Contracts govern countless areas of our lives, from intimate family issues to multibillion-dollar corporate deals. Understanding contract principles is essential for a successful business or professional career and is invaluable in private life. This knowledge is especially important because courts no longer rubber-stamp any agreement that two parties have made. If we know the issues that courts scrutinize, the agreement we draft is likelier to be enforced. We thus achieve greater control over our affairs—the very purpose of a contract.

Exam Review

1. **CONTRACTS: DEFINITION AND ELEMENTS** A contract is a legally enforceable promise. Analyzing whether a contract exists involves inquiring into these issues: offer, acceptance, consideration, capacity, legal purpose, consent, and sometimes, whether the deal is in writing. (pp. 232–233)

2. **DEVELOPMENT** The development of contract law stretches into the distant past. Before the fifteenth century, courts rarely enforced promises at all. By the 1600s, courts enforced many mutual promises, and by 1900, most promises containing the seven elements of a contract were strictly enforced. (pp. 233–235)

3. **UNILATERAL AND BILATERAL CONTRACTS** In bilateral contracts, the parties exchange promises. In a unilateral contract, only one party makes a promise, and the other must take some action—his return promise is insufficient to form a contract. (p. 235)

4. **EXECUTORY AND EXECUTED CONTRACTS** In an executory contract, one or both of the parties have not yet have not done everything that they promised to do. In an executed contract, all parties have fully performed. (pp. 235–236)

5. **ENFORCEABILITY**
   - Valid contracts are fully enforceable.
   - An unenforceable agreement is one with a legal defect.
   - A voidable contract occurs when one party has an option to cancel the agreement.
   - A void agreement means that the law will ignore the deal regardless of what the parties want. (pp. 236–237)

EXAM Strategy

Question: Yasmine is negotiating to buy Stewart's house. She asks him what condition the roof is in.

"Excellent," he replies. "It is only 2 years old, and should last 25 more." In fact, Stewart knows that the roof is 26 years old and has had a series of leaks. The parties sign a sales contract for $600,000. A week before Yasmine is to pay for the house and take possession, she discovers the leaks and learns that the mandatory new roof will cost $35,000. At the same time, she learns that the house has increased in value by $60,000 since she signed the agreement. What options does Yasmine have?

Strategy: You know intuitively that Stewart's conduct is as shabby as his roof. What is the legal term for his deception? Fraud. Does fraud make an agreement void or voidable? Does it matter? (See the "Result" at the end of this section.)

6. **EXPRESS AND IMPLIED CONTRACTS** If the parties formally agreed and stated explicit terms, there is probably an express contract. If the parties did not formally agree but their conduct, words, or past dealings indicate they intended a binding agreement, there may be an implied contract. (pp. 237–238)

7. **OTHER REMEDIES** If there is no contract, are there other reasons to give the plaintiff damages?
   - A claim of promissory estoppel requires that the defendant made a promise knowing that the plaintiff would likely *rely,* and the plaintiff did so. It would be wrong to deny recovery.

- A claim of quasi-contract requires that the defendant received a benefit, knowing that the plaintiff would expect compensation, and it would be unjust not to grant it. (pp. 239–242)

EXAM Strategy

Question: The Hoffmans owned and operated a successful small bakery and grocery store. They spoke with Lukowitz, an agent of Red Owl Stores, who told them that for $18,000, Red Owl would build a store and fully stock it for them. The Hoffmans sold their bakery and grocery store and purchased a lot on which Red Owl was to build the store. Lukowitz then told Hoffman that the price had gone up to $26,000. The Hoffmans borrowed the extra money from relatives, but then Lukowitz informed them that the cost would be $34,000. Negotiations broke off, and the Hoffmans sued. The court determined that there was no contract because too many details had not been worked out—the size of the store, its design, and the cost of constructing it. Can the Hoffmans recover any money?

Strategy: Because there is no contract, the Hoffmans must rely on either promissory estoppel or quasi-contract. Promissory estoppel focuses on the defendant's promise and the plaintiff's reliance. Those suing in quasi-contract must show that the defendant received a benefit for which it should reasonably expect to pay. Does either fit here? (See the "Result" at the end of this section.)

8. **SOURCES OF CONTRACT LAW** If a contract is for the sale of goods, the UCC is the relevant body of law. For anything else, the common law governs. If a contract involves both goods and services, a court will determine the agreement's primary purpose. (pp. 243–244)

EXAM Strategy

Question: Honeywell, Inc., and Minolta Camera Co. had a contract providing that Honeywell would give to Minolta various technical information on the design of a specialized camera lens. Minolta would have the right to use the information in its cameras, provided that Minolta also used certain Honeywell parts in its cameras. Honeywell delivered to Minolta numerous technical documents, computer software, and test equipment, and Honeywell engineers met with Minolta engineers at least 20 times to discuss the equipment. Several years later, Honeywell sued, claiming that Minolta had taken the design information but failed to use Honeywell parts in its cameras. Minolta moved to dismiss, claiming that the UCC required lawsuits concerning the sale of goods to be filed within four years of the breach and that this lawsuit was too late. Honeywell answered that the UCC did not apply, and that therefore, Minnesota's six-year statute of limitations governed. Who is right?

Strategy: Like many contracts, this one involves both goods, which are governed by the UCC, and services, controlled by the common law. We decide which of those two laws governs by using the predominant purpose test. Was this contract primarily about selling goods or about providing services? (See the "Result" at the end of this section.)

5. Result: Indeed, it does matter. Stewart's fraud makes the contract voidable by Yasmine. She has the right to terminate the agreement and pay nothing. However, she may go through with the contract if she prefers. The choice is hers—but not Stewart's.

7. Result: Red Owl received no benefit from the Hoffmans' sale of their store or purchase of the lot. However, Red Owl did make a promise and expected the Hoffmans to rely on it, which they did. The Hoffmans won their claim of promissory estoppel.

8. Result: The primary purpose of this agreement was not the sale of goods, but rather the exchange of technical data, ideas, designs, and so forth. The common law governs the contract, and Honeywell's suit may go forward.

Multiple-Choice Questions

1. A sitcom actor, exhausted after his 10-hour workweek, agrees to buy a briefcase full of cocaine from Lewis for $12,000. Lewis and the actor have a ____________ contract.
   (a) valid
   (b) unenforceable
   (c) voidable
   (d) void

2. Carol says, "Pam, you're my best friend in the world. I just inherited a million bucks, and I want you to have some of it. Come with me to the bank tomorrow, and I'll give you $10,000." "Sweet!" Pam replies. Later that day, Carol has a change of heart. She is allowed to do so. Examine the list of the elements of a contract, and cite the correct reason.
   (a) The agreement was not put into writing.
   (b) The agreement lacks a legal purpose.
   (c) Pam did not give consideration.
   (d) Pam does not have the capacity to make a contract.

3. On the first day of the baseball season, Dean orders a new Cardinals hat from Amazon. At the moment he submits his order, Dean and Amazon have an ____________ contract. Two days later, Amazon delivers the hat to Dean's house. At this point, Dean and Amazon have an ____________ contract.
   (a) executory; executory
   (b) executory; executed
   (c) executed; executory
   (d) executed; executed

4. Linda goes to an electronics store and buys a high-definition TV. Lauren hires a company to clean her swimming pool once a week. The ____________ governs Linda's contract with the store, and the ____________ governs Lauren's contract with the cleaning company.

(a) common law; common law
(b) common law; UCC
(c) UCC; common law
(d) UCC; UCC

5. Consider the following scenarios:

I. Madison says to a group of students, "I'll pay $35 to the first one of you who shows up at my house and mows my lawn."

II. Lea posts a flyer around town that reads, "Reward: $500 for information about the person who keyed my truck last Saturday night in the Wag-a-Bag parking lot. Call Lea at 555-5309."

Which of these proposes a *unilateral* contract?

(a) I only
(b) II only
(c) Both I and II
(d) None of the above

Essay Questions

1. Pennsylvania contracted with Envirotest Systems, Inc., an Arizona company, to build 86 automobile emissions inspection stations in 25 counties and operate them for seven years. This contract is worth hundreds of millions of dollars to Envirotest. But Pennsylvania legislators suddenly opposed the entire system, claiming that it would lead to long delays and high expenses for motorists. These lawmakers urged that Pennsylvania simply stop construction of the new system. Was Pennsylvania allowed to get out of the contract because its legislators concluded the whole system is unwise?

2. Central Maine Power Co. made a promotional offer in which it promised to pay a substantial sum to any homeowner or builder who constructed new housing heated with electricity. Motel Services, Inc., which was building a small housing project for the city of Waterville, Maine, decided to install electrical heat in the units in order to qualify for the offer. It built the units and requested payment for the full amount of the promotional offer. Is Central Maine obligated to pay? Why or why not?

3. Interactive Data Corp. hired Daniel Foley as an assistant product manager at a starting salary of $18,500. Over the next six years, Interactive steadily promoted Foley until he became Los Angeles branch manager at a salary of $56,116. Interactive's officers repeatedly told Foley that he would have his job as long as his performance was adequate. In addition, Interactive distributed an employee handbook that specified "termination guidelines," including a mandatory seven-step pre-termination procedure. Two years later, Foley learned that his recently hired supervisor, Robert Kuhne, was under investigation by the FBI for embezzlement at his previous job. Foley reported this to Interactive officers. Shortly thereafter, Interactive fired Foley. He sued, claiming that Interactive could fire him only for good

cause, after the seven-step procedure. What kind of a claim is he making? Should he succeed?

4. ***ETHICS*** You want to lease your automobile to a friend for the summer but do not want to pay a lawyer to draw up the lease. Joanna, a neighbor, is in law school. She is not licensed to practice law. She offers to draft a lease for you for $100, and you unwisely accept. Later, you refuse to pay her fee, and she sues to collect. Who will win the lawsuit, and why? Apart from the law, was it morally right for the law student to try to help you by drafting the lease? Was she acting helpfully, or foolishly, or fraudulently? Is it just for you to agree to her fee and then refuse to pay it? What is society's interest in this dispute? Should a court be more concerned with the ethical issue raised by the conduct of the two parties or with the social consequences of this agreement?

5. ***YOU BE THE JUDGE*** **WRITING PROBLEM** John Stevens owned a dilapidated apartment that he rented to James and Cora Chesney for a low rent. The Chesneys began to remodel and rehabilitate the unit. Over a four-year period, they installed two new bathrooms, carpeted the floors, installed new septic and heating systems, and rewired, replumbed, and painted. Stevens periodically stopped by and saw the work in progress. The Chesneys transformed the unit into a respectable apartment. Three years after their work was done, Stevens served the Chesneys with an eviction notice. The Chesneys counterclaimed, seeking the value of the work they had done. Are they entitled to it? **Argument for Stevens:** Mr. Stevens is willing to pay the Chesneys exactly the amount he agreed to pay: nothing. The parties never contracted for the Chesneys to fix up the apartment. In fact, they never even discussed such an agreement. The Chesneys are making the absurd argument that anyone who chooses to perform certain work, without ever discussing it with another party, can finish the job and then charge it to the other person. If the Chesneys expected to get paid, obviously they should have said so. If the court were to allow this claim, it would be inviting other tenants to make improvements and then bill the landlord. The law has never been so foolish. **Argument for the Chesneys:** The law of quasi-contract was crafted for cases exactly like this. The Chesneys have given an enormous benefit to Stevens by transforming the apartment and enabling him to rent it at greater profit for many years to come. Stevens saw the work being done and understood that the Chesneys expected some compensation for these major renovations. If Stevens never intended to pay the fair value of the work, he should have stopped the couple from doing the work or notified them that there would be no compensation. It would be unjust to allow the landlord to seize the value of the work, evict the tenants who did it, and pay nothing.

Discussion Questions

1. Have you ever made an agreement that mattered to you, only to have the other person refuse to follow through on the deal? Looking at the list of elements in the chapter, did your agreement amount to a contract? If not, which element did it lack?

2. Consider promissory estoppel and quasi-contracts. Do you like the fact that these doctrines exist? Should courts have "wiggle room" to enforce deals that fail to meet

formal contract requirements? Or, should the rule be "If it's not an actual contract, too bad. No deal."

3. Is it sensible to have two different sets of contract rules—one for sales of goods and another for everything else? Would it be better to have a single set of rules for all contracts?

4. In the case *Davis v. Mason*, a court considered an early non-compete agreement. Did the court in that case reach a proper conclusion? What should courts say in similar cases in modern times?

5. Return to the opening scenario. Fran, Ricky, Carla, and Dave each made an agreement with John. None is valid under contract law. For the sake of fairness, *should* any of them be legally enforceable? If so, which?

The Agreement: Offers and Acceptances

> I should talk with my agent. I'd need something in writing about the nude scene ...

Interior. A glitzy café, New York. Evening. Bob, a famous director, and Katrina, a glamorous actress, sit at a table, near a wall of glass looking onto a New York sidewalk that is filled with life and motion. Bob sips a margarita while carefully eyeing Katrina. Katrina stares at her wine glass.

BOB *(smiling confidently)*: *Body Work* is going to be huge—for the right actress. I know a film that's gonna gross a hundred million when I'm holding one. I'm holding one.

KATRINA *(perking up at the mention of money)*: It is quirky. It's fun. And she's very strong, very real.

BOB: She's you. That's why we're sitting here. We start shooting in seven months.

KATRINA *(edging away from the table)*: I have a few questions. That nude scene.

BOB: The one on the toboggan run?

KATRINA: *That* one was O.K. But the one in the poultry factory—very explicit. I don't work nude.

BOB: It's not really nude. Think of all those feathers fluttering around.

KATRINA: It's nude.

BOB: We'll work it out. This is a romantic comedy, not tawdry exploitation. Katrina, we're talking $2.5 million. A little accommodation, please. We'll give you $600,000 up front, and the rest deferred, the usual percentages.

KATRINA: Bob, my fee is $3 million. As you know. That hasn't changed.

Katrina picks up her drink, doesn't sip it, places it on the coaster, using both hands to center it perfectly. He waits, as she stares silently at her glass.

BOB: We're shooting in Santa Fe, the weather will be perfect. You have a suite at the Excelsior, plus a trailer on location.

KATRINA: I should talk with my agent. I'd need something in writing about the nude scene, the fee, percentages—all the business stuff. I never sign without talking to her.

Bob shrugs and sits back.

KATRINA *(made anxious by the silence)*: I love the character, I really do.

BOB: You and several others love her. *(That jolts her.)* Agents can wait. I have to put this together fast. We can get you the details you want in writing. *Body Work* is going to be bigger than *Sex in the City*.

That one hooks her. She looks at Bob. He nods reassuringly. Bob sticks out his hand, smiling. Katrina hesitates, lets go of her drink, and SHAKES HANDS, looking unsure. Bob signals for the check.

Do Bob and Katrina have a deal? *They* seem to think so. But is her fee $2.5 million or $3 million? What if Katrina demands that all nude scenes be taken out, and Bob refuses? Must she still act in the film? Or suppose her agent convinces her that *Body Work* is no good even with changes. Has Katrina committed herself? What if Bob auditions another actress the next day, likes her, and signs her? Does he owe Katrina her fee? Or suppose Bob learns that the funding has fallen apart and there will be no film. Is Katrina entitled to her money?

Bob and Katrina have acted out a classic problem in *agreement*, one of the basic issues in contract law. Their lack of clarity means that disputes are likely and lawsuits possible. Similar bargaining goes on every day around the country and around the world, and the problems created are too frequently resolved in court. Some negotiating is done in person; more is done over the phone, by fax, by email—or all of them combined. This chapter highlights the most common sources of misunderstanding and litigation so that you can avoid making contracts you never intended—or deals that you cannot enforce.

There almost certainly is no contract between Bob and Katrina. Bob's offer was unclear. Even if it was valid, Katrina counteroffered. When they shook hands, it is impossible to know what terms each had in mind.

MEETING OF THE MINDS

Remember from the last chapter that contracts have seven key characteristics. Agreements that have a problem in any of the areas do not amount to valid contracts. In this chapter, we examine the first two items on the checklist.

Offer
An act or statement that proposes definite terms and permits the other party to create a contract by accepting those terms.

Parties form a contract only if they have a meeting of the minds. For this to happen, one side must make an **offer** and the other must make an **acceptance**. An offer proposes definite terms, and an acceptance unconditionally agrees to them.

Throughout the chapter, keep in mind that courts make *objective* assessments when evaluating offers and acceptances. A court will not try to get inside Katrina's head and decide what she was thinking as she shook hands. It will look at the handshake *objectively*, deciding how a reasonable person would interpret her words and conduct. Katrina may honestly have meant to conclude a deal for $3 million with no nude scenes, while Bob might in good faith have believed he was committing himself to $2.5 million and absolute control of the script. Neither belief will control the outcome.

OFFER

Bargaining begins with an offer. The person who makes an offer is the **offeror**. The person to whom he makes that offer is the **offeree**. The terms are annoying but inescapable because, like handcuffs, all courts use them.

Offeror
The person who makes an offer.

Offeree
The person to whom an offer is made.

Two questions determine whether a statement is an offer:

- Do the offeror's words and actions indicate an *intention* to make a bargain?
- Are the terms of the offer reasonably definite?

Zachary says to Sharon, "Come work in my English language center as a teacher. I'll pay you $800 per week for a 35-hour week, for six months starting Monday." This is a valid offer. Zachary's words seem to indicate that he intends to make a bargain and his offer is definite. If Sharon accepts, the parties have a contract that either one can enforce.

In the section below, we present several categories of statements that are generally *not* valid offers.

Statements that Usually do not Amount to Offers

Invitations to Bargain

An invitation to bargain is not an offer. Suppose Martha telephones Joe and leaves a message on his answering machine, asking if Joe would consider selling his vacation condo on Lake Michigan. Joe faxes a signed letter to Martha saying, "There is no way I could sell the condo for less than $150,000." Martha promptly sends Joe a cashier's check for that amount. Does she own the condo? No. Joe's fax was not an offer. It is merely an invitation to negotiate. Joe is indicating that he might well be happy to receive an offer from Martha, but he is not promising to sell the condo for $150,000 or for any amount.

Price Quotes

A price quote is generally not an offer. If Imperial Textile sends a list of fabric prices for the new year to its regular customers, the list is not an offer. Once again, the law regards it merely as a solicitation of offers. Suppose Ralph orders 1,000 yards of fabric, quoted in the list at $40 per yard. *Ralph* is making the offer, and Imperial may decline to sell at $40, or at any price, for that matter.

This can be an expensive point to learn. Leviton Manufacturing makes electrical fixtures and switches. Litton Microwave manufactures ovens. Leviton sent a price list to Litton, stating what it would charge for specially modified switches for use in Litton's microwaves. The price letter included a statement greatly limiting Leviton's liability in the event of any problem with the switches. Litton purchased thousands of the switches and used them in manufacturing its microwaves. But consumers reported fires due to defects in the switches. Leviton claimed that under the contract it had no liability. But the court held that the price letter was not an offer. It was a request to receive an offer. Thus the contract ultimately formed did not include Leviton's liability exclusion. Litton won over $4 million.[1] See Exhibit 11.1

Letters of Intent

In complex business negotiations, the parties may spend months bargaining over dozens of interrelated issues. Because each party wants to protect itself during the discussions, ensuring that the other side is serious without binding itself to premature commitments,

[1] *Litton Microwave Cooking Products v. Leviton Manufacturing Co., Inc.*, 15 F.3d 790, 1994 U.S. App. LEXIS 1876 (8th Cir. 1994).

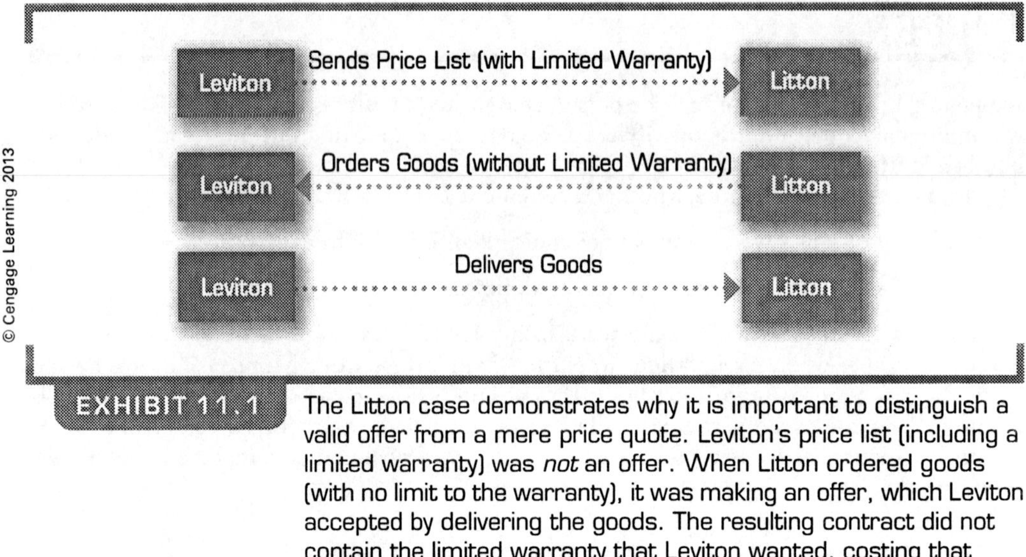

EXHIBIT 11.1 The Litton case demonstrates why it is important to distinguish a valid offer from a mere price quote. Leviton's price list (including a limited warranty) was *not* an offer. When Litton ordered goods (with no limit to the warranty), it was making an offer, which Leviton accepted by delivering the goods. The resulting contract did not contain the limited warranty that Leviton wanted, costing that company a $4 million judgment.

Letter of intent
A letter that summarizes negotiating progress.

it may be tempting during the negotiations to draft a **letter of intent**. The letter *might* help distinguish a serious party from one with a casual interest, summarize the progress made thus far, and assist the parties in securing necessary financing. Usually, letters of intent do not create any legal obligation. They merely state what the parties are considering, not what they have actually agreed to. But note that is possible for a letter of intent to bind the parties if its language indicates that the parties *intended* to be bound.

Advertisements

Mary Mesaros received a notice from the United States Bureau of the Mint, announcing a new $5 gold coin to commemorate the Statue of Liberty. The notice contained an order form stating:

> VERY IMPORTANT—PLEASE READ: YES, Please accept my order for the U.S. Liberty Coins I have indicated. I understand that all sales are final and not subject to refund. Verification of my order will be made by the Department of the Treasury, U.S. Mint. If my order is received by December 31, I will be entitled to purchase the coins at the Pre-Issue Discount price shown.

Mesaros ordered almost $2,000 worth of the coins. But the Mint was inundated with so many requests for the coin that the supply was soon exhausted. Mesaros and thousands of others never got their coins. This was particularly disappointing because the market value of the coins doubled shortly after their issue. Mesaros sued on behalf of the entire class of disappointed purchasers. Like most who sue based on an advertisement, she lost.[2] **An advertisement is generally not an offer.** An advertisement is merely a request for offers. The consumer makes the offer, whether by mail, as above, or by arriving at a merchant's store ready to buy. The seller is free to reject the offer.

Advertisers should be careful, however, not to be too specific in their ads. Some ads do count as offers, as the following case illustrates.

---

[2]*Mesaros v. United States*, 845 F.2d 1576, 1988 U.S. App. LEXIS 6055 (Fed. Cir. 1988).

Landmark Case

Carlill v. Carbolic Smoke Ball Company

1 QB 256
Court of Appeal, 1892

Facts: In the early 1890s, English citizens greatly feared the Russian flu. The Carbolic Smoke Ball Company ran a newspaper ad that contained two key passages:

> "£100 reward will be paid by the Carbolic Smoke Ball Company to any person who contracts the influenza after having used the ball three times daily for two weeks according to the printed directions supplied with each ball.
>
> "£1000 is deposited with the Alliance Bank, shewing our sincerity in the matter."

The product was a ball that contained carbolic acid. Users would inhale vapors from the ball through a long tube.

Carlill purchased a smoke ball and used it as directed for two months. She then caught the flu. She sued, arguing that because her response to the ad had created a contract with the company, she was entitled to £100.

The trial court agreed, awarding Carlill the money. The company appealed.

Issues: ***Did the advertisement amount to an offer? If so, was the offer accepted?***

Excerpts from Lord Justice Lindley's Decision: The first observation I will make is that we are dealing with an express promise to pay £100 in certain events. Read the advertisement how you will, and twist it about as you will, here is a distinct promise expressed in language which is perfectly unmistakable.

We must first consider whether this was intended to be a promise at all. The deposit is called by the advertiser as proof of his sincerity in the matter—that is, the sincerity of his promise to pay this £100 in the event which he has specified. I say there is the promise, as plain as words can make it.

Then it is contended that it is not binding. In the first place, the performance of the conditions is the acceptance of the offer. Unquestionably, as a general proposition, when an offer is made, it is necessary that the acceptance should be notified. But is that so in cases of this kind? I think that in a case of this kind that the person who makes the [offer] shews by his language and from the nature of the transaction that he does not expect and does not require notice of the acceptance apart from notice of the performance.

We, therefore, find here all the elements which are necessary to form a binding contract enforceable in point of law.

It appears to me, therefore, that the defendants must perform their promise, and, if they have been so unwary as to expose themselves to a great many actions, so much the worse for them. Appeal dismissed.

Carlill lived 50 years more, dying at the age of 96—of the flu.

This case serves as a cautionary tale. Running a "normal" ad which describes a product, its features, and its price does not amount to an offer. But, if a company proposes to take an action—like pay $100 to customers who take certain, specific actions—then it may find itself contractually obligated to follow through on its promises. The acceptance of the offer makes a unilateral contract.

Note also that, regardless of whether an ad counts as an offer, consumers have protection from those shopkeepers who are intent upon deceit. Almost every state has some form of **consumer protection statute,** which outlaws false advertising. For example, an automobile dealer who advertises a remarkably low price but then has only one automobile at that price has probably violated a consumer protection statute because the ad was published in bad faith, to trick consumers into coming to the dealership. In the *Mesaros* case, the United States Mint did not violate any consumer protection statute because it acted in good faith and simply ran out of coins.

© AP Photo/Seth Wenig

You have the high bid—but you may not have the property.

Auctions

It is the property you have always dreamed of owning—and it is up for auction! You arrive bright and early, stand in front, bid early, bid often, bid higher, bid highest of all—it's yours! For five seconds. Then, to your horror, the auctioneer announces that none of the bids were juicy enough and he is withdrawing the property. Robbery! Surely he cannot do that? But he can. Auctions are exciting and useful, but you must understand the rules.

Every day, auctions are used to sell exquisite works of art, real estate, and many other things. **Placing an item up for auction is *not* an offer—it is merely a request for an offer.** The *bids* are the offers. If and when the hammer falls, the auctioneer has accepted the offer.

The important thing to know about a particular auction is whether it is conducted with or without reserve. Most auctions are *with reserve,* meaning that the items for sale have a minimum price. The law assumes that an auction is with reserve unless the auctioneer clearly states otherwise. The auctioneer will not sell anything for less than its reserve (minimum price). So when the bidding for your property failed to reach the reserve, the auctioneer was free to withdraw it.

The rules are different in an auction *without reserve.* Here, there is no minimum. Once the first bid is received, the auctioneer *must* sell the merchandise to the highest bidder.

EXAM Strategy

Question: Ahn and Chet are both unhappy. (1) Ahn, an interior designer, is working on a hotel project. In the annual catalog of a furniture wholesaler, she sees that sofa beds cost $3,000. Based on the catalog, she sends an order for 100 sofa beds to the wholesaler. The wholesaler notifies Ahn that the price has gone up to $4,000. (2) At an estate auction, held without reserve, Chet is high bidder on a rare violin. The seller considers Chet's bid too low and refuses to sell. Both Ahn and Chet sue, but only one will win. Which plaintiff will win, and why?

Strategy: (1) A contract requires an offer and an acceptance. When the furniture wholesaler sent out its catalog, did it make an offer that Ahn could accept? (2) Chet was high bidder. At some auctions, the high bidder is merely making an offer, but at others, he wins the item. Which kind of auction was this?

Result: (1) A price quote is generally not an offer. Ahn's order for 100 sofas was the offer, and the company was free to reject it. Ahn loses. (2) Most auctions are with reserve, meaning that the high bidder is merely making an offer. However, this one was without reserve. Chet gets the violin.

Problems with Definiteness

It is not enough that the offeror indicates that she intends to enter into an agreement. **The terms of the offer must also be definite.** If they are vague, then even if the offeree agrees to the deal, a court does not have enough information to enforce it and there is no contract.

You want a friend to work in your store for the holiday season. This is a definite offer: "I offer you a job as a sales clerk in the store from November 1 through December 29, 40 hours per week at $10 per hour." But suppose, by contrast, you say: "I offer you a job as a sales clerk in the store during the holiday season. We will work out a fair wage once we see how busy things get." Your friend replies, "That's fine with me." This offer is indefinite, and there is no contract. What is a fair wage? $15 per hour? Or $20 per hour? What is the "holiday season"? How will the determinations be made? There is no binding agreement.

The following case, which concerns a famous television show, presents a problem with definiteness.

Baer v. Chase

392 F.3d 609
Third Circuit Court of Appeals, 2004

Facts: David Chase was a television writer-producer with many credits, including a detective series called *The Rockford Files*. He became interested in a new program, set in New Jersey, about a "mob boss in therapy," a concept he eventually developed into *The Sopranos*. Robert Baer was a prosecutor in New Jersey who wanted to write for television. He submitted a *Rockford Files* script to Chase, who agreed to meet with Baer.

When they met, Baer pitched a different idea, concerning "a film or television series about the New Jersey Mafia." He did not realize Chase was already working on such an idea. Later that year, Chase visited New Jersey. Baer arranged meetings for Chase with local detectives and prosecutors, who provided the producer with information, material, and personal stories about their experiences with organized crime. Detective Thomas Koczur drove Chase and Baer to various New Jersey locations and introduced Chase to Tony Spirito. Spirito shared stories about loan sharking, power struggles between family members connected with the mob, and two colorful individuals known as Big Pussy and Little Pussy, both of whom later became characters on the show.

Back in Los Angeles, Chase wrote and sent to Baer a draft of the first *Sopranos* teleplay. Baer called Chase and commented on the script. The two spoke at least four times that year, and Baer sent Chase a letter about the script.

When *The Sopranos* became a hit television show, Baer sued Chase. He alleged that on three separate occasions Chase had agreed that if the program succeeded, Chase would "take care of" Baer, and would "remunerate Baer in a manner commensurate to the true value of his services." This happened twice on the phone, Baer claimed, and once during Chase's visit to New Jersey. The understanding was that if the show failed, Chase would owe nothing. Chase never paid Baer anything.

The district court dismissed the case, holding that the alleged promises were too vague to be enforced. Baer appealed.

Issue: ***Was Chase's promise definite enough to be enforced?***

Excerpts from Judge Greenberg's Decision: A contract arises from offer and acceptance, and must be sufficiently definite so that the performance to be rendered by each party can be ascertained with reasonable certainty. Therefore parties create an enforceable contract when they agree on its essential terms and manifest an intent that the terms bind them. If parties to an agreement do not agree on one or more essential terms of the purported agreement courts generally hold it to be unenforceable.

New Jersey law deems the price term, that is, the amount of compensation, an essential term of any contract.

An agreement lacking definiteness of price, however, is not unenforceable if the parties specify a practicable method by which they can determine the amount. However, in the absence of an agreement as to the manner or method of determining compensation the purported agreement is invalid. Additionally, the duration of the contract is deemed an essential term and therefore any agreement must be sufficiently definitive to allow a court to determine the agreed upon length of the contractual relationship.

Baer premises his argument on his view that New Jersey should disregard the well-established requirement of definiteness in its contract law when the subject-matter of the contract is an "idea submission." [However,] New Jersey precedent does not support Baer's attempt to carve out an exception to traditional principles of contract law for submission-of-idea cases. The New Jersey courts have not provided even the slightest indication that they intend to depart from their well-established requirement that enforceability of a contract requires definiteness with respect to the essential terms of that contract.

Nothing in the record indicates that the parties agreed on how, how much, where, or for what period Chase would compensate Baer. The parties did not discuss who would determine the "true value" of Baer's services, when the "true value" would be calculated, or what variables would go into such a calculation. There was no discussion or agreement as to the meaning of "success" of *The Sopranos.* There was no discussion how "profits" were to be defined. There was no contemplation of dates of commencement or termination of the contract. And again, nothing in Baer's or Chase's conduct, or the surrounding circumstances of the relationship, shed light on, or answers, any of these questions.

Affirmed.

Ethics Was it fair for Chase to use Baer's services without compensation? Did Baer really *expect* to get paid, or was he simply hoping that his work would land him a job?

EXAM Strategy

Question: Niels owned three adjoining parcels of land in Arizona ranging from 60 to 120 acres. Hannah wanted to buy one. The two had dinner in Chicago and then sketched this agreement: "Binding Contract: Niels agrees to sell one of his three Arizona lots to Hannah. Within 14 days, the parties will meet on the land, decide which lot Hannah is buying, and settle on a price. If they cannot agree on a price, they will decide a fair method of doing so. Both parties agree to be bound by this contract." Each signed. When they meet in Arizona, Niels refuses to sell any land, and Hannah sues. What will happen?

Strategy: Do not be fooled by wording such as "Binding Contract." Focus on the legal issues: Was there a meeting of the minds? Niels and Hannah *thought* they had a contract—but courts make an objective assessment, not subjective. Did Niels make an offer? Were the terms definite?

Result: Both parties believed they had a binding deal, and both parties were wrong. There are two primary issues—which lot is being sold and how much will it cost—and neither is specified. How are they to select a lot? What is a "fair method" of determining price? Other issues are not touched upon: When will the deal close, how will payment be made, what happens if Hannah cannot finance the purchase? The terms are too vague. The parties never reached a meeting of the minds, and Hannah will lose her suit.

The UCC and Open Terms

In the last chapter, we introduced the Uniform Commercial Code (UCC). Article 2 of the UCC governs contracts when the primary purpose is a sale of goods. Remember that goods are moveable, tangible objects. Usually, UCC provisions are not significantly different from common-law rules. But on occasion, the UCC modifies the common-law rule in some major way. In such cases, we will present a separate description of the key UCC provision. The UCC as a whole is covered in Unit 3. Depending on the class time available, some instructors prefer to discuss the UCC separately, while others like to include it in the general discussion of contracts. This book is designed to work with either approach.

We have just seen that, under the common law, the terms of an offer must be definite. But under the UCC, many indefinite contracts are allowed to stand. Throughout this unit, we witness how the Uniform Commercial Code makes the law of sales more flexible. There are several areas of contract law where imperfect negotiations may still create a binding agreement under the Code, even though the same negotiations under the common law would have yielded no contract. "Open terms" is one such area.

Yuma County Corp. produced natural gas. Yuma wanted a long-term contract to sell its gas so that it could be certain of recouping the expenses of exploration and drilling. Northwest Central Pipeline, which operated an interstate pipeline, also wanted a deal for 10 or more years so it could make its own distribution contracts, knowing it would have a steady supply of natural gas in a competitive market. But neither Yuma nor Northwest wanted to make a long-term *price* commitment, because over a period of years the price of natural gas could double—or crash. Each party wanted a binding agreement without a definitive price. If their negotiations had been governed by the common law, they would have run smack into the requirement of definiteness—no price, no contract. But because this was a sale of goods, it was governed by the UCC.

Under UCC §2-204(3), even though one or more terms are left open, a contract does not fail for indefiniteness if the parties have intended to make a contract and there is a reasonably certain basis for giving an appropriate remedy. Thus, a contract for the sale of goods may be enforced when a key term is missing. Business executives may have many reasons to leave open a delivery date, a price, or some other term. But note that the parties must still have *intended* to create a contract. The UCC will not create a contract where the parties never intended one.

In some cases, the contract will state how the missing term is to be determined. Yuma County and Northwest drafted a contract with alternative methods of determining the price. In the event that the price of natural gas was regulated by the Federal Energy Regulatory Commission (FERC), the price would be the highest allowed by the FERC. If the FERC deregulated the price (as it ultimately did), the contract price would be the average of the two highest prices paid by different gas producers in a specified geographic area.

Gap Filler Provisions

Even if a UCC contract lacks a specific method for determining missing terms, the Code itself contains **gap-filler provisions**, which are rules for *supplying* missing terms. Some of the most important gap-filler provisions of the Code follow.

Gap-filler provisions
UCC rules for supplying missing terms.

Open Price. In general, if the parties do not settle on a price, the Code establishes that the goods will be sold for a reasonable price. This will usually be the market value or a price established by a neutral expert or agency. (UCC §2-305.)

Output and Requirements Provisions. An **output contract** obligates the seller to sell all of his output to the buyer, who agrees to accept it. For example, a cotton grower might agree to sell all of his next crop to a textile firm. A **requirements contract** obligates a buyer to obtain all of his needed goods from the seller. A vineyard might agree to buy all of its wine bottles from one supplier. Output and requirements contracts are by definition

Output contract
Obligates the seller to sell all of his output to the buyer, who agrees to accept it.

Requirements contract
Obligates a buyer to obtain all of his needed goods from the seller.

incomplete, since the exact quantity of the goods is unspecified. The Code requires that in carrying out such contracts, both parties act in good faith. Neither party may suddenly demand a quantity of goods (or offer a quantity of goods) that is disproportionate to their past dealings or their reasonable estimates. (UCC §2-306.)

Termination of Offers

Once an offer has been made, it faces only two possible fates—it can be terminated or accepted. If an offer is terminated, it can never be accepted. If it is accepted, and if there are no problems with any of the five remaining elements on the Contracts Checklist, then a valid contract is created. Offers can be terminated in four ways: revocation, rejection, expiration, and by operation of law.

Termination by Revocation

An offer is **revoked** when the offeror "takes it back" before the offeree accepts. In general, the offeror may revoke the offer any time before it has been accepted. Imagine that I call you and say, "I'm going out of town this weekend. I'll sell you my ticket to this weekend's football game for $75." You tell me that you'll think it over and call me back. An hour later, my plans change. I call you a second time and say, "Sorry, but the deal's off—I'm going to the game after all." I have revoked my offer, and you can no longer accept it.

In the next case, this rule was worth $100,000 to one of the parties.

NADEL V. TOM CAT BAKERY

2009 N.Y. Misc. Lexis 5105
Supreme Court of New York, New York County, 2009

Facts: A Tom Cat Bakery delivery van struck Elizabeth Nadel as she crossed a street. Having suffered significant injuries, Nadel filed suit. Before the trial began, the attorney representing the bakery's owner offered a $100,000 settlement, which Nadel refused.

While the jury was deliberating, the bakery's lawyer again offered Nadel the $100,000 settlement. She decided to think about it during lunch. Later that day, the jury sent a note to the judge. The bakery owner told her lawyer that if the note indicated the jury had reached a verdict, that he should revoke the settlement offer.

Back in the courtroom, the bakery's lawyer said, "My understanding is that there's a note.... I was given an instruction that if the note is a verdict, my client wants to take the verdict."

Nadel's lawyer then said, "My client will take the settlement. My client will take the settlement."

The trial court judge allowed the forewoman to read the verdict, which awarded Nadel—nothing. She appealed, claiming that a $100,000 settlement had been reached.

Issue: ***Did Nadel's lawyer accept the settlement offer in time?***

Excerpts from Judge Figueroa's Decision: Plaintiff's motion to enforce "the settlement" has generated considerable debate between the parties. Plaintiff asserts that the defendant is bound to a settlement. Plaintiff's problem is that there was no "agreement" to speak of. To be sure, there was an offer from defendant. During the above-quoted colloquy, clearly there were also words of acceptance from plaintiff. But when the words, "my client will take the settlement" were uttered, it was too late for them to be effective. By that time, defense counsel had made it clear that if the jury had already come to a verdict, the offer was off the table. That condition could not be ignored, as the verdict that would mean all bets were off had already been reached. For the foregoing reasons, plaintiff's motion is denied.

Making Contracts Temporarily Irrevocable

Some offers cannot be revoked, at least for a time. Often, people and businesses need time to evaluate offers. If a car dealer offers you a green sedan for $25,000, you may want to shop around for a few days to try to find a better price. In the meantime, you may want to make sure that the green sedan is still available if you decide to return. Can you legally prevent the car dealer from selling the car to anyone else while you ponder the offer? In some circumstances, yes.

Option Contract (All types of contracts). With an option contract, an interested purchaser *buys* the right to have the offer held open. **The offeror may not revoke an offer during the option period.** Suppose you pay the car dealer $250 to hold open its offer until February 2. Later that day, the dealership notifies you that it is selling to someone else. Result? You can enforce *your* contract. The car dealer had no power to revoke because you purchased an option.

Firm Offers (UCC contracts only). Once again, the UCC has changed the law on the sale of goods. If a promise made in writing is signed by a *merchant,* and if it agrees to hold open an offer for a stated period, then an offer may not be revoked. The open period may not exceed three months. So, if the car dealer gives you a piece of paper that reads, "The offer on the green sedan is open at $25,000 until Friday at noon," he cannot revoke the offer before Friday at noon, even though you have not paid him anything. (UCC §2-205.)

Termination by Rejection

If an offeree clearly indicates that he does not want to take the offer, then he has **rejected** it. **If an offeree rejects an offer, the rejection immediately terminates the offer.** Suppose a major accounting firm telephones you and offers a job, starting at $80,000. You respond, "Nah. I'm gonna work on my surfing for a year or two." The next day, you come to your senses and write the firm, accepting its offer. No contract. Your rejection terminated the offer and ended your power to accept it.

Counteroffer. A party makes a **counteroffer** when it responds to an offer with a new and different proposal. Frederick faxes Kim, offering to sell a 50 percent interest in the Fab Hotel in New York for only $135 million. Kim faxes back and says, "That's too much, but I'll pay $115 million." Moments later, Kim's business partner convinces her that Frederick's offer was a bargain, and she faxes an acceptance of his $135 million offer. Does Kim have a binding deal? No. **A counteroffer is a rejection.** When Kim offered $115 million, she rejected Frederick's offer. Her original fax created a new offer, for $115 million, which Frederick never accepted. The parties have no contract at any price.

Termination by Expiration

An offeror may set a time limit. Quentin calls you and offers you a job in his next motion picture. He tells you, "I've got to know by tomorrow night." If you call him in three days to accept, you are out of the picture. **When an offer specifies a time limit for acceptance, that period is binding.**

If the offer specifies no time limit, the offeree has a *reasonable* period in which to accept. A reasonable period varies, depending upon the type of offer, previous dealings between the parties, and any normal trade usage or customary practices in a particular industry.

Termination by Operation of Law

In some circumstances, the law itself terminates an offer. **If an offeror dies or becomes mentally incapacitated, the offer terminates automatically and immediately.** Arnie offers you a job as an assistant in his hot-air balloon business. Before you can even accept, Arnie tumbles out of a balloon at 3,000 feet. The offer terminates along with Arnie.

Destruction of the subject matter terminates the offer. A car dealer offers to sell you a rare 1938 Bugatti for $7,500,000 if you bring cash the next day. You arrive, suitcase stuffed with cash, just in time to see Arnie drop 3,000 feet through the air and crush the Bugatti. The dealer's offer is terminated.

Acceptance

As we have seen, when there is a valid offer outstanding, it remains effective until it is terminated or accepted. An offeree accepts by saying or doing something that a reasonable person would understand to mean that he definitely wants to take the offer. Assume that Ellie offers to sell Gene her old iPod for $50. If Gene says, "I accept your offer," then he has indeed accepted, but there is no need to be so formal. He can accept the offer by saying, "It's a deal," or, "I'll take it," or any number of things. He need not even speak. If he hands her a $50 bill, he also accepts the offer.

It is worth noting that **the offeree must say or do *something* to accept.** Marge telephones Vick and leaves a message on his answering machine: "I'll pay $75 for your business law textbook from last semester. I'm desperate to get a copy, so I will assume you agree unless I hear from you by 6:00 tonight." Marge hears nothing by the deadline and assumes she has a deal. She is mistaken. Vick neither said nor did anything to indicate that he accepted.

Mirror Image Rule

If only he had known! A splendid university, an excellent position as department chair—gone. And all because of the mirror image rule.

Was it sensible to deny the professor a job over a mere 14-day difference? Sensible or not, that is the law.

Ohio State University wrote to Philip Foster offering him an appointment as a professor and chair of the art history department. His position was to begin July 1, and he had until June 2 to accept the job. On June 2, Foster telephoned the dean and left a message accepting the position, *effective July 15.* Later, Foster thought better of it and wrote the university, accepting the school's starting date of July 1. Too late! Professor Foster never did occupy that chair at Ohio State. The court held that since his acceptance varied the starting date, it was a counteroffer. And a counteroffer, as we know, is a rejection.[3]

Was it sensible to deny the professor a job over a mere 14-day difference? Sensible or not, that is the law. The common-law **mirror image rule** requires that acceptance be on *precisely* the same terms as the offer. If the acceptance contains terms that add or contradict the offer, even in minor ways, courts generally consider it a counteroffer. The rule worked reasonably well in the 19th century, when parties would write an original contract and exchange it, penciling in any changes. But now that businesses use standardized forms to purchase most goods and services, the rule creates enormous difficulties. Sellers use forms they have prepared, with all conditions stated to their advantage, and buyers employ their own forms, with terms they prefer. The forms are exchanged in the mail or electronically, with neither side clearly agreeing to the other party's terms.

Mirror image rule
Requires that acceptance be on precisely the same terms as the offer.

The problem is known as the "battle of forms." Once again, the UCC has entered the fray, attempting to provide flexibility and common sense for those contracts involving the

[3]*Foster v. Ohio State University*, 41 Ohio App. 3d 86, 534 N.E.2d 1220, 1987 Ohio App. LEXIS 10761 (Ohio Ct. App. 1987).

sale of goods. But for contracts governed by the common law, such as Professor Foster's, the mirror image rule is still the law.

UCC and the Battle of Forms

UCC §2-207 dramatically modifies the mirror image rule for the sale of goods. Under this provision, an acceptance that adds additional or different terms often will create a contract.

Additional or Different Terms

One basic principle of the common law of contracts remains unchanged: the key to creation of a contract is a valid offer that the offeree *intends* to accept. If there is no intent to accept, there is no contract. The big change brought about by UCC §2-207 is this: **an offeree who accepts may include in the acceptance terms that are additional to or different from those in the offer.** Thus, even with additional or different terms, the acceptance may well create a contract.

Example A. Wholesaler writes to Manufacturer, offering to buy "10,000 wheelbarrows at $50 per unit. Payable on delivery, 30 days from today's date." Manufacturer writes back, "We accept your offer of 10,000 wheelbarrows at $50 per unit, payable on delivery. *Interest at normal trade rates for unpaid balances.*" Manufacturer clearly intends to form a contract. The company has added a new term, but there is still a valid contract.

However, if the offeree states that her acceptance is *conditioned on the offeror's assent* to the new terms, there is no contract.

Example B. Same offer as above. Manufacturer adds the interest rate clause and states, "Our acceptance is conditional upon your agreement to this interest rate." Manufacturer has made a counteroffer. There is no contract, yet. If Wholesaler accepts the counteroffer, there is a contract; if Wholesaler does not accept it, there is no contract.

Additional terms are those that bring up *new* issues, such as interest rates, not contained in the original offer. Additional terms in the acceptance are considered proposals to add to the contract. Assuming that both parties are merchants, the additional terms ***will generally become part of the contract.*** Thus, in Example A, the interest rate will become a part of the binding deal. If Wholesaler is late in paying, it must pay whatever interest rate is current.

In three circumstances, the additional terms in the acceptance *do not* become part of the contract:

- If the original offer *insisted on its own terms.* In other words, if Wholesaler wrote, "I offer to buy them on the following terms and *no other terms,*" then the Manufacturer is not free to make additions.
- If the additional terms *materially alter* the original offer. Suppose Manufacturer wrote back, "We accept your offer for 10,000 wheelbarrows. Delivery will be made within 180 days, unless we notify you of late delivery." Manufacturer has changed the time from 30 days to 180 days, with a possible extension beyond that. That is a material alteration, and it will not become part of the contract. By contrast, Manufacturer's new language concerning "interest at normal trade rates" was not a material alteration, and therefore that interest rate becomes part of the contract.
- If the offeror receives the additional terms and *promptly objects* to them.

Different terms are those that contradict terms in the offer. For example, if the seller's form clearly states that no warranty is included, and the buyer's form says the seller warrants all goods for three years, the acceptance contains different terms. An acceptance may contain different terms and still create a contract. But in these cases, courts have struggled to decide what the terms of the contract are. **The majority of states hold that different**

(contradictory) terms cancel each other out. Neither term is included in the contract. Instead, the neutral terms from the Code itself are "read into" the contract. These are the gap-filler terms discussed above. If, for example, the forms had contradictory warranty clauses (as they almost always do), the different terms would cancel each other out, and the warranty clauses from the UCC would be substituted.[4]

EXAM Strategy

Question: Elaine faxes an offer to Raoul. Raoul writes, "I accept. Please note, I will charge 2 percent interest per month for any unpaid money." He signs the document and faxes it back to Elaine. Do the two have a binding contract?

Strategy: Slow down, this is trickier than it seems. Raoul has added a term to Elaine's offer. We must take two steps to decide whether there is a contract. In a contract for services, acceptance must mirror the offer, but not so in an agreement for the sale of goods.

Result: If this is an agreement for services, there is no contract. However, if this agreement is for goods, the additional term *may* become part of an enforceable contract.

Question: Assume that Elaine's offer concerns goods. Is there an agreement?

Strategy: Under UCC §2-207, an additional term will become part of a binding agreement for goods except in three instances. What are the three exceptions?

Result: Raoul's extra term will be incorporated in a binding contract unless (1) Elaine's offer made clear she would accept no other terms; (2) Raoul's interest rate is a material alteration of the offer (almost never the case for interest rates); or (3) Elaine promptly rejects the interest rate.

Clickwraps And Shrinkwraps

You want to purchase Attila brand software and download it to your computer. You type in your credit card number and other information, agreeing to pay $99. Attila also requires that you "read and agree to" all of the company's terms. You click "I agree," without having read one word of the terms. Three frustrating weeks later, tired of trying to operate defective Attilaware, you demand a refund and threaten to sue. The company replies that you are barred from suing because the terms you agreed to included an arbitration clause. To resolve any disputes, you must travel to Attila's hometown, halfway across the nation, use an arbitrator that the company chooses, pay one-half the arbitrator's fee, and also pay Attila's legal bills if you should lose. The agreement makes it financially impossible for you to get your money back. Is that contract enforceable?

You have entered into a "clickwrap" agreement. Similar agreements, called "shrinkwraps," are packaged inside many electronic products. A shrinkwrap notice might require that before inserting a purchased CD into your computer, you must read and agree to all terms in the brochure. Clickwraps and shrinkwraps often include arbitration clauses. They

[4]Not all states follow this rule, however. Some courts have held that when the acceptance contains terms that contradict those in the offer, the language in the offer should be final. A few courts have ruled that the terms in the acceptance should control.

frequently limit the seller's liability if anything goes wrong, saying that the manufacturer's maximum responsibility is to refund the purchase price (even if the software destroys your hard drive).

Many courts that have analyzed these issues have ruled that clickwrap and shrinkwrap agreements are indeed binding, even against consumers. The courts have emphasized that sellers are entitled to offer a product on any terms they wish, and that shrinkwrap and clickwrap are the most efficient methods of including complicated terms in a small space. Think before you click![5]

However, some courts have *refused* to enforce such contracts against a consumer, stating that the buyer never understood or agreed to the shrinkwrapped terms. The court in the following case works hard to balance the competing interests, and in the process demonstrates that this new area of law is very much in flux.

Specht v. Netscape Communications Corporation

306 F.3d 17
Second Circuit Court of Appeals, 2002

Facts: A group of plaintiffs sued Netscape, claiming that two of the company's products illegally captured private information about files that they downloaded from the Internet. The plaintiffs alleged that this was electronic eavesdropping, in violation of two federal statutes.

From Netscape's Web page, the plaintiffs had downloaded SmartDownload, a software plug-in that enabled them to download the company's Communicator software. The Web page advertised the benefits of SmartDownload, and near the bottom of the screen was a tinted button labeled "Download." The plaintiffs clicked to download. If, instead of downloading, they had scrolled further down, they would have seen an invitation to "review and agree to the terms of the Netscape SmartDownload software license agreement." By clicking the appropriate button, they would have been sent to a series of linked pages, and finally arrived at a license agreement. Among the terms was an agreement to arbitrate any dispute. In other words, a consumer downloading SmartDownload was in theory giving up the right to file suit if anything went wrong, and agreeing to settle the dispute by arbitration. However, the plaintiffs never reviewed the license terms.

In the district court, Netscape moved to dismiss the case and compel arbitration. Netscape claimed that the plaintiffs had forfeited any right to sue based on the license agreement. The district court denied the company's motion, ruling that the plaintiffs had not agreed to the terms of the license. Netscape appealed.

Issue: ***Had the plaintiffs agreed to arbitrate their claims?***

Excerpts from Judge Sotomayor's Decision: Defendants argue that plaintiffs must be held to a standard of reasonable prudence and that, because notice of the existence of SmartDownload license terms was on the next scrollable screen, plaintiffs were on "inquiry notice" of those terms. We disagree with the proposition that a reasonably prudent offeree in plaintiffs' position would necessarily have known or learned of the existence of the SmartDownload license agreement prior to acting, so that plaintiffs may be held to have assented to that agreement with constructive notice of its terms.

Receipt of a physical document containing contract terms or notice thereof is frequently deemed, in the world of paper transactions, a sufficient circumstance to place the offeree on inquiry notice of those terms. These principles apply equally to the emergent world of online product delivery, pop-up screens, hyperlinked pages, clickwrap licensing, scrollable documents, and urgent admonitions

[5]*ProCD, Inc. v. Zeidenberg,* 86 F.3d 1447 (7th Cir. 1996), is the leading case to enforce shrinkwrap agreements (and, by extension, clickwraps). *Klocek v. Gateway,* 104 F. Supp. 1332 (D. Kan. 2000), is one of the few cases to reject such contracts. *Klocek,* however, was dismissed for failure to reach the federal court $75,000 jurisdictional level.

to "Download Now!" What plaintiffs saw when they were being invited by defendants to download this fast, free plug-in called SmartDownload was a screen containing praise for the product and, at the very bottom of the screen, a "Download" button. Defendants argue that a fair and prudent person using ordinary care would have been on inquiry notice of SmartDownload's license terms.

We are not persuaded that a reasonably prudent offeree in these circumstances would have known of the existence of license terms. Plaintiffs were responding to an offer that did not carry an immediately visible notice of the existence of license terms or require unambiguous manifestation of assent to those terms. Thus, plaintiffs' apparent manifestation of consent was to terms contained in a document whose contractual nature was not obvious. Moreover, the fact that, given the position of the scroll bar on their computer screens, plaintiffs may have been aware that an unexplored portion of the Netscape Web page remained below the download button does not mean that they reasonably should have concluded that this portion contained a notice of license terms.

We conclude that in circumstances such as these, where consumers are urged to download free software at the immediate click of a button, a reference to the existence of license terms on a submerged screen is not sufficient to place consumers on inquiry or constructive notice of those terms. There is no reason to assume that viewers will scroll down to subsequent screens simply because screens are there.

For the foregoing reasons, we affirm the district court's denial of defendants' motion to compel arbitration and to stay court proceedings.

The plaintiffs in *Specht* won because they knew nothing about the arbitration clause and were unlikely to discover it on the company's website. Notice what happens when a user *does* know about terms posted online. Register.com was a registrar of Internet domain names, meaning that it issued domain names to people and companies establishing a new website. The company was legally obligated to make available to the public, for free, the names and contact information of its customers. Register was also in the business of assisting owners, for a fee, to develop their websites.

Verio, Inc. competed in the site development business. Verio's automated software program (robot) would search Register.com daily, seeking information about new sites. *After* Verio obtained contact information, a notice would appear on the Register site, stating:

> By submitting a query, you agree that under no circumstances will you use this data to support the transmission of mass unsolicited, commercial advertising or solicitation via email.

In fact, though, Verio used the contact information for exactly that purpose, sending mass emailings to owners of new websites, soliciting their development business. Register sued. Verio defended by stating it was not bound by the notice because the notice did not appear until after it had obtained the information. Verio argued that when it sent the queries, it was unaware of any restrictions on use of the data. The court was unpersuaded, and explained its reasoning with a simple but telling metaphor:

> The situation might be compared to one in which plaintiff P maintains a roadside fruit stand displaying bins of apples. A visitor, defendant D, takes an apple and bites into it. As D turns to leave, D sees a sign, visible only as one turns to exit, which says "Apples—50 cents apiece." D does not pay for the apple. D believes he has no obligation to pay because he had no notice when he bit into the apple that 50 cents was expected in return. D's view is that he never agreed to pay for the apple. Thereafter, each day, several times a day, D revisits the stand, takes an apple, and eats it. D never leaves money.
>
> P sues D in contract for the price of the apples taken. D defends on the ground that on no occasion did he see P's price notice until after he had bitten into the apples. D may well prevail as to the first apple taken. D had no reason to understand upon taking it that P was demanding the payment. In our view, however, D cannot continue on a daily basis to take apples for free, knowing full well that P is offering them only in exchange for 50 cents in compensation, merely because the sign demanding payment is so placed that on each occasion D does not see it until he has bitten into the apple.

Register.com won its case. Verio was prohibited from using the contact information for mass emailings because it had actual knowledge of the restrictions placed on its use.[6]

Communication of Acceptance

The offeree must communicate his acceptance for it to be effective. The questions that typically arise concern the method, the manner, and the time of acceptance.

Method and Manner of Acceptance

The term "method" refers to whether acceptance is done in person or by mail, telephone, email, or fax. The term "manner" refers to whether the offeree accepts by promising, by making a down payment, by performing, and so forth. **If an offer demands acceptance in a particular method or manner, the offeree must follow those requirements.** An offer might specify that it be accepted in writing, or in person, or before midnight on June 23. An offeror can set any requirements she wishes. Omri might say to Oliver, "I'll sell you my bike for $200. You must accept my offer by standing on a chair in the lunchroom tomorrow and reciting a poem about a cow." Oliver can only accept the offer in the exact manner specified if he wants to form a contract.

If the offer does not specify a type of acceptance, the offeree may accept in any reasonable manner and method. An offer generally may be accepted by performance or by a promise, unless it specifies a particular method. The same freedom applies to the method. If Masako faxes Eric an offer to sell 1,000 acres in Montana for $800,000, Eric may accept by mail or fax. Both are routinely used in real estate transactions, and either is reasonable.

If the offer does not specify a type of acceptance, the offeree may accept in any reasonable manner and medium.

Time of Acceptance: The Mailbox Rule

An acceptance is generally effective upon dispatch, meaning the moment it is out of the offeree's control. Terminations, on the other hand, are effective when received. When Masako faxes her offer to sell land to Eric, and he mails his acceptance, the contract is binding the moment he puts the letter into the mail. In most cases, this **mailbox rule** is just a detail. But it becomes important when the offeror revokes her offer at about the same time the offeree accepts. Who wins? Suppose Masako's offer has one twist:

Mailbox rule
Acceptance is generally effective upon dispatch. Terminations are effective when received.

- On Monday morning, Masako faxes her offer to Eric.
- On Monday afternoon, Eric writes, "I accept" on the fax, and Masako mails a revocation of her offer.
- On Tuesday morning, Eric mails his acceptance.
- On Thursday morning, Masako's revocation arrives at Eric's office.
- On Friday morning, Eric's acceptance arrives at Masako's office.

[6] *Register.Com v. Verio, Inc.*, 353 F.3d 393 (2d Cir. 2004).

Outcome? Eric has an enforceable contract. Masako's offer was effective when it reached Eric. His acceptance was effective on Tuesday morning, when he mailed it. Nothing that happens later can "undo" the contract.

Soldau v. Organon, Inc.

860 F.2d 355, 1988 U.S. App. LEXIS 14757
United States Court of Appeals for the Ninth Circuit, 1988

Facts: Organon fired John Soldau. Then the company sent to him a letter offering to pay him double the normal severance pay, provided Soldau would sign a full release, that is, a document giving up any and all claims he might have against Organon. The release was included with the letter. Soldau signed it, dated it, and took it to the nearest post office, where he deposited it in the mailbox. When he returned home, Soldau discovered in the mail a check from Organon for the double severance pay. He hustled back to the post office, where he persuaded a postal clerk to open the mailbox and retrieve the release he had posted. He then cashed Organon's check and finally filed a suit against the company, alleging that his firing was age discrimination.

The federal district court gave summary judgment for Organon, ruling that Soldau's acceptance of the proposed release was effective when he mailed it, creating a contract. He appealed.

Issue: ***Did Soldau create a contract by mailing the release?***

Excerpts from the *Per Curiam* Decision: The district court was clearly correct under California law. Soldau does not argue to the contrary. Instead, he contends that the formation and validity of the release are governed by federal law, and would not have been effective unless and until it had been received by Organon. We need not decide which body of law controls. Under federal as well as California law, Soldau's acceptance was effective when it was mailed.

The so-called mailbox or effective when mailed rule was adopted and followed as federal common law by the Supreme Court [at the beginning of the 20th century]. We could not change the rule, and there is no reason to believe the Supreme Court would be inclined to do so. It is almost universally accepted in the common law world. It is enshrined in the Restatement (Second) of Contracts and endorsed by the major contract treatises.

Commentators are also virtually unanimous in [supporting the "effective upon dispatch" rule,] pointing to the long history of the rule; its importance in creating certainty for contracting parties; its essential soundness, on balance, as a means of allocating the risk during the period between the making of the offer and the communication of the acceptance or rejection to the offeror; and the inadequacy of the rationale offered by the Court of Claims for the change.

Since Soldau's contractual obligation to release Organon in return for Organon's obligation to make the enhanced severance payment arose when Soldau deposited his acceptance in the post office mailbox, his subsequent withdrawal of the acceptance was ineffectual.

Affirmed.

Chapter Conclusion

The law of offer and acceptance can be complex. Yet for all its faults, the law is not the principal source of dispute between parties unhappy with negotiations. Most litigation concerning offer and acceptance comes from *lack of clarity* on the part of the people negotiating. The many examples discussed are all understandable given the speed and fluidity of the real world of business. But the executive who insists on clarity is likelier in the long run to spend more time doing business and less time in court.

Exam Review

1. **MEETING OF THE MINDS** The parties can form a contract only if they have a meeting of the minds, which requires that they understand each other and show that they intend to reach an agreement. (p. 252)

EXAM Strategy

Question: Norv owned a Ford dealership and wanted to expand by obtaining a BMW outlet. He spoke with Jackson and other BMW executives on several occasions. Norv now claims that those discussions resulted in an oral contract that requires BMW to grant him a franchise, but the company disagrees. Norv's strongest evidence of a contract is the fact that Jackson gave him forms on which to order BMWs. Jackson answered that it was his standard practice to give such forms to prospective dealers, so that if the franchise were approved, car orders could be processed quickly. Norv states that he was "shocked" when BMW refused to go through with the deal. Is there a contract?

Strategy: A court makes an *objective* assessment of what the parties did and said to determine whether they had a meeting of the minds and intended to form a contract. Norv's "shock" is irrelevant. Do the order forms indicate a meeting of the minds? Was there additional evidence that the parties had reached an agreement? (See the "Result" at the end of this section.)

2. **OFFER** An offer is an act or statement that proposes definite terms and permits the other party to create a contract by accepting those terms. (p. 253)

3. **OTHER STATEMENTS** Invitations to bargain, price quotes, letters of intent, and advertisements are generally not offers. However, an ad in which a company proposes to take a specific action when a customer takes a specific action can amount to an offer. And letters of intent that indicate the parties intended to be bound can also count as offers. (pp. 253–255)

EXAM Strategy

Question: **"Huge** selection of Guernsey sweaters," reads a newspaper ad from Stuffed Shirt, a clothing retailer. "Regularly $135, today only $65." Waldo arrives at Stuffed Shirt at 4:00 that afternoon, but the shop clerk says there are no more sweaters. He shows Waldo a newly arrived Shetland sweater that sells for $145. Waldo sues, claiming breach of contract and violation of a consumer protection statute. Who will prevail?

(a) Waldo will win the breach of contract suit and the consumer protection suit.

(b) Waldo will lose the breach of contract suit but might win the consumer protection suit.

(c) Waldo will lose the consumer protection suit but should win the breach of contract suit.

(d) Waldo will win the consumer protection suit only if he wins the contract case.

(e) Waldo will lose both the breach of contract suit and the consumer protection suit.

Strategy: Waldo assumes that he is accepting the store's offer. But did Stuffed Shirt make an offer? If not, there cannot be a contract. Does the consumer protection statute help him? (See the "Result" at the end of this section.)

4. **DEFINITENESS** The terms of the offer must be definite, although under the UCC the parties may create a contract that has open terms. (pp. 257–258)

5. **TERMINATION** An offer may be terminated by revocation, rejection, expiration, or operation of law. (pp. 260–262)

EXAM Strategy

Question: Rick is selling his Espresso Coffee Maker. He sends Tamara an email, offering to sell the machine for $350. Tamara promptly emails back, offering to buy the item for $300. She hears nothing from Rick, so an hour later Tamara stops by his apartment, where she learns that he just sold the machine to his roommate for $250. She sues Rick. Outcome?

(a) Tamara will win because her offer was higher than the roommate's.

(b) Tamara will win because Rick never responded to her offer.

(c) Tamara will win because both parties made clear offers, in writing.

(d) Tamara will lose because she rejected Rick's offer.

(e) Tamara will lose because her offer was not definite.

Strategy: A valid contract requires a definite offer and acceptance. Rick made a valid offer. When Tamara said she would buy the machine for a lower amount, was that acceptance? If not, what was it? (See the "Result" at the end of this section.)

6. **MIRROR IMAGE RULE AND UCC §2-207** The common-law mirror image rule requires acceptance on precisely the same terms as the offer. Under the UCC, an offeree may often create a contract even when the acceptance includes terms that are additional to or different from those in the offer. (pp. 262–264)

7. **CLICKWRAPS** Clickwrap and shrinkwrap agreements are generally enforceable. (pp. 264–267)

8. **MANNER OF ACCEPTANCE** If an offer demands acceptance in a particular method or manner, the offeree must follow those requirements. If the offer does not specify a type of acceptance, the offeree may accept in any reasonable manner and medium. (p. 267)

9. **MAILBOX RULE** An acceptance is generally effective upon dispatch, meaning from the moment it is out of the offeree's control. Terminations usually are not effective until received. (pp. 267–268)

1. Result: The order forms are neither an offer nor an acceptance. Norv has offered no evidence that the parties agreed on price, date of performance, or any other key terms. There is no contract. Norv allowed eagerness and optimism to replace common sense.[7]

3. Result: An advertisement is usually not an offer, but merely a solicitation of one. It is Waldo who is making the offer, which the store may reject. Waldo loses his contract case, but he may win under the consumer protection statute. The correct answer is B. If Stuffed Shirt proclaimed "Huge selection" when there were only five sweaters, the store was deliberately misleading consumers, and Waldo wins. However, if there was indeed a large selection, and Waldo arrived too late, he is out of luck.

5. Result: Tamara made a counteroffer of $300. A counteroffer is a rejection. Tamara rejected Rick's offer and simultaneously offered to buy the coffee maker at a lower price. Rick was under no obligation to sell to Tamara at any price. He will win Tamara's suit.

Multiple-Choice Questions

1. Rebecca, in Honolulu, faxes a job offer to Spike, in Pittsburgh, saying, "We can pay you $55,000 per year, starting June 1." Spike faxes a reply, saying, "Thank you! I accept your generous offer, though I will also need $3,000 in relocation money. See you June 1. Can't wait!" On June 1, Spike arrives, to find that his position is filled by Gus. He sues Rebecca.

   (a) Spike wins $55,000.
   (b) Spike wins $58,000.
   (c) Spike wins $3,000.
   (d) Spike wins restitution.
   (e) Spike wins nothing.

2. Arturo hires Kate to work in his new sporting goods store. "Look," he explains, "I can only pay you $9.00 an hour. But if business is good a year from now, and you're still here, I'm sure I can pay you a healthy bonus." Four months later, Arturo terminates Kate. She sues.

   (a) Kate will win her job back, plus the year's pay and the bonus.
   (b) Kate will win the year's pay and the bonus.
   (c) Kate will win only the bonus.
   (d) Kate will win only her job back.
   (e) Kate will win nothing.

[7]Based on *Arnold Pontiac-GMC, Inc. v. General Motors Co.*, 786 F.2d 564 (3d Cir. 1986).

3. Manny offers to sell Gina his TV for $100 on January 1. On January 2, Gina writes out a letter of acceptance. On January 3, Gina drops the letter in a mailbox. On January 4, a postal worker gets the letter out of the mailbox and takes it to the post office. On January 5, the letter arrives in Manny's mailbox. When (if ever) was a contract formed?
   (a) January 2
   (b) January 3
   (c) January 4
   (d) January 5
   (e) None of the above—a contract has not been formed.

4. Frank, an accountant, says to Missy, "I'll sell you my laptop for $100." Missy asks, "Will you give me until tomorrow to make up my mind?" "Sure," Frank replies. Which of the following is true?
   (a) Frank cannot revoke his offer, no matter what.
   (b) Frank cannot revoke his offer, but only if Missy pays him to keep the offer open until tomorrow.
   (c) Frank can revoke his offer no matter what, because he is not a merchant.
   (d) Frank can revoke his offer no matter what, because he did not promise Missy anything in writing.

5. Which of the following amounts to an offer?
   (a) Ed says to Carmen, "I offer to sell you my pen for $1."
   (b) Ed says to Carmen, "I'll sell you my pen for $1."
   (c) Ed writes, "I'll sell you my pen for $1," and gives the note to Carmen.
   (d) All of the above.
   (e) A and C only.

Essay Questions

1. The town of Sanford, Maine, decided to auction off a lot it owned. The town advertised that it would accept bids through the mail, up to a specified date. Arthur and Arline Chevalier mailed in a bid that turned out to be the highest. When the town refused to sell them the lot, they sued. Result?

2. The Tufte family leased a 260-acre farm from the Travelers Insurance Co. Toward the end of the lease, Travelers mailed the Tuftes an option to renew the lease. The option arrived at the Tuftes' house on March 30, and gave them until April 14 to accept. On April 13, the Tuftes signed and mailed their acceptance, which Travelers received on April 19. Travelers claimed there was no lease and attempted to evict the Tuftes from the farm. May they stay?

3. Consolidated Edison Co. of New York (Con Ed) sought bids from General Electric Co. (GE) and others to supply it with two huge transformers. Con Ed required that the bids be held open for 90 days. GE submitted a written bid and included a clause

holding the bid open for 90 days. During that period, Con Ed accepted GE's bid, but GE refused to honor it. Is there a contract?

4. The Dukes leased land from Lillian Whatley. Toward the end of their lease, they sent Ms. Whatley a new contract, renewing the lease for three years and giving themselves the option to buy the land at any time during the lease for $50,000. Ms. Whatley crossed out the clause giving them an option to buy. She added a sentence at the bottom, saying, "Should I, Lillian Whatley, decide to sell at end [sic] of three years, I will give the Dukes the first chance to buy." Then she signed the lease, which the Dukes accepted in the changed form. They continued to pay the rent until Ms. Whatley sold the land to another couple for $35,000. The Dukes sued. Are the Dukes entitled to the land at $50,000? At $35,000?

5. ***YOU BE THE JUDGE* WRITING PROBLEM** Academy Chicago Publishers (Academy) approached the widow of author John Cheever about printing some of his unpublished stories. She signed a contract, which stated:

 The Author will deliver to the Publisher on a mutually agreeable date one copy of the manuscript of the Work as finally arranged by the editor and satisfactory to the Publisher in form and content.... Within a reasonable time and a mutually agreeable date after delivery of the final revised manuscript, the Publisher will publish the Work at its own expense, in such style and manner and at such price as it deems best, and will keep the Work in print as long as it deems it expedient.

 Within a year, Academy had located and delivered to Mrs. Cheever more than 60 unpublished stories. But she refused to go ahead with the project. Academy sued for the right to publish the book. The trial court ruled that the agreement was valid; the appeals court affirmed; and the case went to the Illinois Supreme Court. Was Academy's offer valid, and was the contract enforceable? **Argument for Mrs. Cheever:** The agreement is too vague to be enforceable. None of the essential terms are specified: the number of stories, their length, who selects them, the date of publication, the size or cost of the book, or anything else. There is no contract. **Argument for Academy:** Mrs. Cheever wanted to publish this book and agreed in writing to help Academy do so. Both parties understood the essential nature of the book and were willing to permit some flexibility, to ensure a good edition. She has no right to back out now.

Discussion Questions

1. Advertisements usually do not amount to offers. Is this fair? Should businesses have legal obligations to sell items at an advertised price?

2. Most auctions are held "with reserve." If you place the highest bid at such an auction, and if your bid is below the reserve, then you do not get the item. Is this fair? Should the law award you the item at the price you bid?

3. Someone offers to sell you a concert ticket for $50, and you reply, "I'll give you $40," The seller refuses to sell at the lower price, and you say, "OK, OK, I'll pay you $50." Clearly, no contract has been formed, because you made a counteroffer. If the seller has changed her mind and no longer wants to sell for

$50, she doesn't have to. But is this fair? If it is all part of the same conversation, should you be able to accept the $50 offer and get the ticket?

4. If you click an "I agree" box, odds are that its terms are binding on you, even if the box contains dozens or even hundreds of lines of dense text. Is this fair? Should the law change to limit the enforceability of clickwraps?

5. Courts stick to objective (reasonable person) standards when evaluating offers and acceptances. Juries are not asked to "get inside someone's head," they are instructed to determine what a reasonable person would think of offerors' and offereees' statements. Is this practice reasonable? Would it be better if the law directly considered whether people *wanted* to make contracts?

CHAPTER 12

© picsbyst/Shutterstock.com

CONSIDERATION

Have you ever rented a movie that you did not want every one of your friends to know about? Cathryn Harris did. Imagine her shock when she rented a movie online from Blockbuster, only to find out that this news was automatically transmitted to her Facebook page and then broadcast to all her "friends." Just think how bad that could be.

Harris sued Blockbuster for this violation of her privacy, only to find out she had clicked away her right to sue. To rent the movie, she had had to click that little box saying she agreed to all the terms and conditions. And one of those terms and conditions was an agreement to arbitrate, not litigate. Can Blockbuster get away with this?

> To rent the movie, she had to click that little box saying she agreed to all the terms and conditions.

It turns out that this movie has a happy ending. The court ruled that the contract between Harris and Blockbuster was unenforceable because there was no *consideration*.

Consideration is our next step on the road to understanding contracts. In the last chapter, we learned what it takes to create an agreement. But an agreement is not necessarily a legally enforceable contract.

This is the first of four chapters that will examine problems that can prevent an agreement from becoming a contract. A lack of consideration is one of them. Without it, a promise is "just a promise" and nothing more.

What is Consideration?

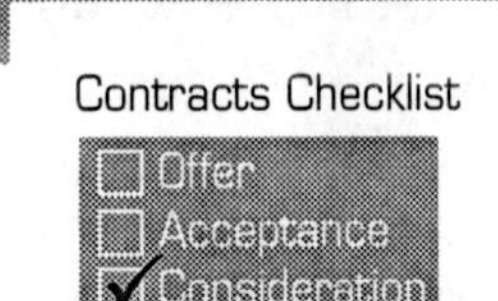

The central idea of consideration is simple: contracts must be a two-way street. If one side gets all the benefit and the other side gets nothing, then an agreement lacks consideration and is not an enforceable contract.

There are three rules of consideration:

1. Both parties must get something of *measureable value* from the contract. That thing can be money, boots, an agreement not to sue, or anything else that has real value.
2. A *promise* to give something of value counts as consideration. A *promise* to mow someone's lawn next week is the equivalent of actually *doing* the yardwork when evaluating whether consideration exists.
3. The two parties must have *bargained for* whatever was exchanged and struck a deal: "If you do this, I'll do that." If you just decide to deliver a cake to your neighbor's house without her knowing, that may be something of value, but since you two did not bargain for it, there is no contract and she does not owe you the price of the cake.

Let's take an example: Sally's Shoe Store and Baker Boots agree that she will pay $20,000 for 100 pairs of boots. They both get something of value—Sally gets the boots, Baker gets the money. A contract is formed when the promises are made because a promise to give something of value counts. The two have bargained for this deal, so there is valid consideration.

Now for an example where there is no consideration. Marvin works at Sally's. At 9 a.m., he is in a good mood and promises to buy his coworker a Starbucks during the lunch hour. The delighted coworker agrees. Later that morning, the coworker is rude to Marvin, who then changes his mind about buying the coffee. He is free to do so. His promise created a one-way street: the coworker stood to receive all the benefit of the agreement, while Marvin got nothing. Because Marvin received no value, there is no contract.

What Is Value?

As we have seen, an essential part of consideration is that both parties must get something of value. That item of value can be either an "act" or a "forbearance."

Act

Act
Any action that a party was not legally required to take in the first place.

A party commits an **act** when she does something she was not legally required to do in the first place. She might do a job, deliver an item, or pay money, for example. An act does not count if the party was simply complying with the law or fulfilling her obligations under an existing contract. Thus, for example, suppose that your professor tells the university that she will not post final grades unless she is paid an extra $5,000. Even if the university agrees to this outrageous demand, that agreement is not a valid contract because the professor is already under an obligation to post final grades.

Forbearance

Forbearance
Refraining from doing something that one has a legal right to do.

A **forbearance** is, in essence, the opposite of an act. A plaintiff forbears if he agrees *not* to do something he had a legal right to do. An entrepreneur might promise a competitor not to open a competing business, or an elderly driver (with a valid driver's license) might promise concerned family members that he will not drive at night.

Let's apply these ideas to the most famous of all consideration lawsuits. Our story begins in 1869, when a well-meaning uncle makes a promise to his nephew. Ever since *Hamer v. Sidway* appeared, generations of American law students have dutifully inhaled the facts and sworn by its wisdom; now you, too, may drink it in.

Landmark Case

Hamer v. Sidway

124 N.Y. 538, 27 N.E. 256, 1891 N.Y. LEXIS 1396
New York Court of Appeals, 1891

Facts: This is a story with two Stories. William Story wanted his nephew to grow up healthy and prosperous. In 1869, he promised the 15-year-old boy (who was also named William Story) $5,000 if the lad would refrain from drinking liquor, using tobacco, swearing, and playing cards or billiards for money until his twenty-first birthday. (In that wild era—can you believe it?—the nephew had a legal right to do all those things.) The nephew agreed and, what is more, he kept his word. When he reached his twenty-first birthday, the nephew notified his uncle that he had honored the agreement. The uncle congratulated the young man and promised to give him the money, but said he would wait a few more years before handing over the cash, until the nephew was mature enough to handle such a large sum. The uncle died in 1887 without having paid, and his estate refused to honor the promise. Because the nephew had transferred his rights in the money, it was a man named Hamer who eventually sought to collect from the uncle's estate. The estate argued that since the nephew had given no consideration for the uncle's promise, there was no enforceable contract. The trial court found for the plaintiff, and the uncle's estate appealed.

Issue: ***Did the nephew give consideration for the uncle's promise?***

Excerpts from Justice Parker's Decision: The defendant contends that the contract was without consideration to support it, and therefore invalid. He asserts that the promisee, by refraining from the use of liquor and tobacco, was not harmed, but benefited; that that which he did was best for him to do, independently of his uncle's promise, and insists that it follows that, unless the promisor was benefited, the contract was without consideration, a contention which, if well founded, would seem to leave open for controversy in many cases whether that which the promisee did or omitted to do was in fact of such benefit to him as to leave no consideration to support the enforcement of the promisor's agreement. Such a rule could not be tolerated, and is without foundation in the law. Courts will not ask whether the thing which forms the consideration does in fact benefit the promisee or a third party, or is of any substantial value to anyone. It is enough that something is promised, done, forborne, or suffered by the party to whom the promise is made as consideration for the promise made to him.

Now applying this rule to the facts before us, the promisee used tobacco, occasionally drank liquor, and he had a legal right to do so. That right he abandoned for a period of years upon the strength of the promise of the testator [that is, the uncle] that for such forbearance he would give him $5,000. We need not speculate on the effort which may have been required to give up the use of those stimulants. It is sufficient that he restricted his lawful freedom of action within certain prescribed limits upon the faith of his uncle's agreement, and now, having fully performed the conditions imposed, it is of no moment whether such performance actually proved a benefit to the promisor, and the court will not inquire into it.

The issue of value in a contract is an important one, so let's look at another case. In the movies, when a character wants to get serious about keeping a promise—*really* serious—he sometimes signs an agreement in blood. As it turns out, this kind of thing actually happens in real life. In the following case, did the promise of forbearance have value? Did a contract signed in blood count? You be the judge.

You be the Judge

Kim v. Son

2009 Cal. App. LEXIS 2011
Court of Appeal of California, 2009

Facts: Stephen Son was a part owner and operator of two corporations. Because the businesses were corporations, Son was not personally liable for the debts of either one.

Jinsoo Kim invested a total of about $170,000 in the companies. Eventually, both of them failed, and Kim lost his investment. Son felt guilty over Kim's losses.

Later, Son and Kim met in a sushi restaurant and drank heroic quantities of alcohol. At one point, Son pricked his finger with a safety pin and wrote the following in his own blood: "Sir, please forgive me. Because of my deeds, you have suffered financially. I will repay you to the best of my ability." In return, Kim agreed not to sue him for the money owed.

Son later refused to honor the bloody document and pay Kim the money. Kim filed suit to enforce their contract.

The judge determined that the promise did not create a contract because there had been no consideration.

You Be The Judge: ***Was there consideration?***

Argument for Kim: As a part of the deal made at the sushi restaurant, Kim agreed not to sue Son. What could be more of a forbearance than that? Kim had a right to sue at any time, and he gave the right up. Even if Kim was unlikely to win, Son would still prefer not to be sued.

Besides, the fact that Son signed the agreement in blood indicates how seriously he took the obligation to repay his loyal investor. At a minimum, Son eased his guilty conscience by making the agreement, and surely that is worth something.

Argument for Son: Who among you has not at one point or another become intoxicated, experienced emotions more powerful than usual, and regretted them the next morning? Whether calling an ex-girlfriend and professing endless love or writing out an agreement in your own blood, it is all the same.

A promise not to file a meritless lawsuit has no value at all. It did not matter to Son whether or not Kim filed suit because Kim could not possibly win. If this promise counts as value, then the concept of consideration is meaningless because anyone can promise not to sue anytime. Son had no obligation to pay Kim. And the bloody napkin does not change that fact because it was made without consideration of any kind. It is an ordinary promise, not a contract that creates any legal obligation.

Adequacy of Consideration

Gold can make people crazy. At the turn of the 20th century, John Tuppela joined the gold rush to Alaska. He bought a mine and worked it hard, a disciplined man in an unforgiving enterprise. Sadly, his prospecting proved futile and mental problems overwhelmed him. In 1914, a court declared him insane and locked him in an institution in Portland, Oregon. Four years later, Tuppela emerged and learned to his ecstasy that gold had been discovered in his mine, now valued at over half a million dollars. Then the bad news hit: a court-appointed guardian had sold the mine for pennies while Tuppela was institutionalized. Destitute and forlorn, Tuppela turned to his lifelong friend, Embola, saying, "If you will give me $50 so I can go to Alaska and get my property back, I will pay you $10,000 when I win my property." Embola accepted the offer, advancing the $50.

After a long and bitter fight, Tuppela won back his mine, though a guardian would still supervise his assets. Tuppela asked the guardian to pay the full $10,000 to Embola, but the guardian refused. Embola sued, and the issue was whether his $50 was *adequate consideration* to support Tuppela's promise of $10,000. A happy ending: Embola won and recovered his money.

Courts seldom inquire into the *adequacy* of consideration. Although the difference between Embola's $50 and Tuppela's $10,000 was huge, it was not for a court to decide whether the parties had made an intelligent bargain. Embola undertook a risk, and his $50 was valid consideration. The question of adequacy is for the parties as they bargain, not for the courts.

Law professors often call this the "peppercorn rule," a reference to a Civil War–era case in which a judge mused, "What is a valuable consideration? A peppercorn."[1] Even the tiniest benefit to a plaintiff counts, so long as it has a measureable value.

REUTERS/Mario Anzuoni

How does the peppercorn rule apply in this situation?

EXAM Strategy

Question: 50 Cent has been rapping all day, and he is very thirsty. He pulls his Ferrari into the parking lot of a convenience store. The store turns out to be closed, but luckily for him, a PepsiCo machine sits outside. While walking over to it, he realizes that he has left his wallet at home. Frustrated, he whistles to a 10-year-old kid who is walking by. "Hey kid!" he shouts. "I need to borrow fifty cents!" "I know you are!" the kid replies. Fiddy tries again. "No, no, I need to *borrow* fifty cents!" The kid walks over. "Well, I'm not going to just give you my last fifty cents. But maybe you can sell me something." 50 Cent cannot believe it, but he really is very thirsty. He takes off a Rolex, which is his least expensive bling. "How about this?" "Deal," the kid says, handing over two quarters. Is the kid entitled to keep the watch?

Strategy: Even in extreme cases, courts rarely take an interest in *how much* consideration is given, or whether everyone got a "good deal." Even though the Rolex is worth thousands of times more than the quarters, the quarters still count under the peppercorn rule.

Result: After this transaction, 50 Cent may have second thoughts, but they will be too late. The kid committed an act by handing over his money—he was under no legal obligation to do so. And 50 Cent received something of small but measureable value. So there is consideration to support this deal, and 50 Cent would not get his watch back.

[1] *Hobbs v. Duff*, 23 Cal. 596 (1863).

Illusory Promises

Annabel calls Jim and says, "I'll sell you my bicycle for 325 bucks. Interested?" Jim says, "I'll look at it tonight in the bike rack. If I like what I see, I'll pay you in the morning." At sunrise, Jim shows up with the $325, but Annabel refuses to sell. Can Jim enforce their deal? No. He said he would buy the bicycle *if he liked it,* keeping for himself the power to get out of the agreement for any reason at all. He is not *committing* himself to do anything, and the law considers his promise illusory—that is, not really a promise at all. **An illusory promise is not consideration.** Because he has given no consideration, there is no contract, and *neither party* can enforce the deal.

Let's revisit the Blockbuster case from the opening scenario. Blockbuster's clickwrap box read, in part:

> "Blockbuster may at any time, and at its sole discretion, modify these Terms and Conditions of Use, including without limitation the Privacy Policy, with or without notice. Such modifications will be effective immediately upon posting."

Because Blockbuster had the ability to change the rules at any time for any reason, the court determined that the contract was illusory and that Harris was not bound by Blockbuster's arbitration clause.[2]

Applications Of Consideration

We will spend the remainder of the chapter looking at specific situations in which consideration plays a central role.

The UCC: Consideration in Requirements and Output Contracts

In a requirements contract, the buyer agrees to purchase 100 percent of her goods from one seller. The seller agrees to sell the buyer whatever quantity she reasonably needs. The quantity is not stated in the contract, though it may be estimated based on previous years or best calculations. The common law regarded requirements contracts as void because the buyer held all the power. She could purchase a vast quantity or none at all. She was making no commitment, and hence was giving no consideration. Common-law courts refused to enforce requirements contracts, as well as their counterpart, output contracts.

In an output contract, the seller guarantees to sell 100 percent of its output to one buyer, and the buyer agrees to accept the entire quantity. For example, a timber company might agree to sell all of its wood products to a lumber wholesaler. The common law frowned on this because now it was the seller who was making no real commitment.

The problem with the common-law rule was that many merchants valued these contracts. Consider the utility of requirements contracts. From the buyer's viewpoint, a requirements contract provides flexibility. The buyer can adjust purchases based on consumer demands. The agreement also guarantees her a source of goods in a competitive market. For a seller, the requirements agreement will ensure him at least this one outlet and will prevent competitors from selling to this buyer. The contract should enable the seller to spend less on marketing and may enable him to predict sales more accurately. Output contracts have similar value.

---

[2]*Harris v. Blockbuster Inc.*, 622 F. Supp. 2d 396 (N.D. Tex. 2009).

The UCC responded in a forthright fashion: **Section 2-306 expressly allows output and requirements contracts in the sale of goods.**[3] However, the Code places one limitation on how much the buyer may demand (or the seller may offer):

> A term which measures the quantity by the output of the seller or the requirements of the buyer means such actual output or requirements as may occur *in good faith*, ...

The "good faith" phrase is critical. In requirements contracts, courts have ruled that it is the "good faith" that a buyer brings to the deal that represents her consideration.[4] In other words, by agreeing to act in good faith, she actually is limiting her options. Because she is obligating herself, the deal becomes binding. Beware that this is not just wordplay. A buyer *must make its requirement demands in good faith,* based on the expectations the parties had when they signed the deal.

Suppose that you operate a T-shirt business. You and a wholesaler agree on a two-year requirements contract with a fixed price of $3 per T-shirt and an estimate of 150 T-shirts per week. If business is slow the first two months, you are permitted to purchase only 25 T-shirts per week if that is all you are selling. Should sales suddenly boom and you need 200 per week, you may also require that many. Both of those demands are made in good faith. But suppose the price of cotton skyrockets and the wholesale cost of T-shirts everywhere suddenly doubles. You have a two-year guaranteed price of $3 per T-shirt. Could you demand 2,000 T-shirts per week, knowing that you will be able to resell the shirts to other retailers for a big profit? No. That is not acting in good faith based on the original expectations of the parties. The wholesaler is free to ignore your exorbitant demand. The legal requirement has come full circle: your good faith is valid consideration and makes the deal enforceable—but it is binding on you, too.

EXAM Strategy

Question: Will bought simple wood furniture and custom-painted it for sale to interior designers. He entered into a written agreement to buy all the furniture he needed, for two years, from Wood Knot, Inc. Wood Knot agreed to supply Will with all the furniture he requested. During the second year, Will's business grew, and he requested 28 percent more furniture than in the first year. Wood Knot would not deliver unless Will would pay a higher price per unit, which Will would not. Will sued. What kind of a contract was this? Will Will win? Why or why not?

Strategy: Because this agreement did not specify the quantity of goods being sold, we know that it was either a requirements contract or an output contract. Review the difference between the two. Which was this agreement? These contracts are now legal, with one major limitation. What is that limitation? Apply it here.

Result: This was a requirements contract because Will agreed to purchase all his furniture from Wood Knot. Under the UCC, requirements contracts are enforceable, provided the buyer makes his demands in good faith. Will's increased order was a result of his booming business. Indeed, he entered into this agreement to protect his ability to grow his company. He made the request in good faith, the contract is enforceable, and yes—Will will win.

---

[3]UCC §2-306(2) permits a related type of contract, the exclusive dealing agreement. Here, either a buyer or a seller of goods agrees to deal exclusively with the other party. The results are similar to an output or requirements agreement. Once again, one party is receiving a guarantee in exchange for a promise that the common law would have considered illusory. Under the Code, such a deal is enforceable.

[4]*Famous Brands, Inc. v. David Sherman Corp.*, 814 F.2d 517, 1987 U.S. App. LEXIS 3634 (8th Cir. 1987).

> Of course, exceptions are the spice of law ...

Preexisting Duty

As we have seen, **a promise to do something that a party is already obligated to do is not consideration.** Of course, exceptions are the spice of law, and the preexisting duty rule provides us with a rackful. Courts have created these exceptions because a rigid application of the rule might interfere with legitimate business goals.

Exception: Additional Work

When a party agrees to do something above and beyond what he is obligated to do, his promise is generally valid consideration. Cecil has promised to build a fabulous swimming pool/cabana for Nathalie for $250,000. When the work is half complete, he offers to build the cabana out of seashells rather than pine wood. If Nathalie agrees to a new price of $300,000 for the pool complex, she is obligated to pay because Cecil's extra work is valid consideration for her promise.

Exception: Modification

If both parties agree that a modification is necessary, the surest way to accomplish that is to rescind the original contract and draft a new one. **To rescind means to cancel.** Thus, if neither party has completed its obligations, the agreement to rescind will terminate each party's rights and obligations under the old contract. This should be done in writing. Then the parties sign the new agreement. Courts will *generally* enforce a rescission and modification provided both parties voluntarily entered into it, in good faith. If one side, determined to earn greater profits, unfairly coerces the other into the changes, the modification is invalid.

Once again, the UCC has changed the common law, making it easier for merchants to modify agreements for the sale of goods. UCC §2-209 provides:

- An agreement modifying a contract within this Article needs no consideration to be binding.
- A signed agreement which excludes modification or rescission except by a signed writing cannot be otherwise modified or rescinded.

Here is how these two provisions work together. Mike's Magic Mania (MMM) agrees to deliver 500 rabbits and 500 top hats to State University for the school's Sleight of Hand 101 course. The goods, including 100 cages and 1,000 pounds of rabbit food, are to arrive no later than September 1, in time for the new semester, with payment on delivery. By September 20, no rabbits have appeared, in or out of hats. The university buys similar products from another supply house at a 25 percent steeper price and sues MMM for the difference. Mike claims that in early September, the dean had orally agreed to permit delivery in October. The dean is on sabbatical in Tahiti and cannot be reached for comment. Is the alleged modification valid?

Under the common law, the modification would have been void because MMM gave no consideration for the extended delivery date. However, this is a sale of goods, and under UCC §2-209, an oral modification may be valid even without consideration. Unfortunately for Mike, though, the original agreement included a clause forbidding oral modification. Any changes had to be in writing, signed by both parties. Mike never obtained such a document. Even if the dean did make the oral agreement, the university wins.

The following case arose in a setting that is traumatic and lamentably common: a homeowner could not make his mortgage payments. Foreclosure loomed. Did the parties agree to save the home?

You be the Judge

CITIZENS TRUST BANK v. WHITE

274 Ga.App.508, 618 S.E.2d 9
Georgia Court of Appeals, 2005

Facts: Herbert White owned a house in Atlanta. He refinanced his home through Citizens Trust Bank, but fell behind on his loan payments. He owed about $43,000. The Bank notified White that it intended to foreclose. After some delays, the Bank sent White a formal notice that it would sell his house at a foreclosure sale on the courthouse steps, on May 7. The finance agreement provided that if the Bank foreclosed, White owed the full amount.

On that date, White arrived and offered the Bank $35,000 to stop the foreclosure. The Bank's collection manager, D.J. Hughlett, accepted the money and drafted a letter, which he and White signed:

> Citizens Trust Bank agrees to postpone the foreclosure [based on] a payment of $33,000.00 in certified funds and a possible $2,000.00 from the account of Cora White Cummings on the above-referenced property. Our Attorney, William A. Broughman, will forward to you a written agreement, for your signature, to consummate this transaction. The payoff balance as of 11:05 AM is $7,986.43. If his sister pays the $2,000.00, the balance will be $5,986.43.

White did pay the extra $2,000. Hughlett decided that the signed letter was a forbearance agreement with White, so he did not bother to send an additional document. Hughlett believed that White would pay the balance within 30 days, but White never did so. The Bank sent a new foreclosure notice and did in fact sell the house.

White sued the Bank, claiming that it had breached its agreement not to foreclose. The jury agreed, awarding White $250,000 in compensatory damages. The Bank appealed, arguing that White gave no consideration for the agreement because he was already obligated to pay the full balance.

You Be The Judge: ***Was the signed letter an enforceable contract?***

Argument for the Bank: Mr. White fell behind on his mortgage payments. As soon as the Bank notified him that it was foreclosing, his full debt became due. When he offered to pay a percentage of that debt, he was fulfilling a preexisting duty. He was *legally obligated* to pay the $35,000 that he "offered," along with the full balance due. A promise to do what a party is required to do is never consideration. Without consideration, there is no contract.

The jury made an emotional decision based on sympathy for the debtor. That leads to bad policy and bad law. The policy is poor because if everyone were allowed to default without suffering a loss, no bank would lend money and most citizens could never buy a house. The law is even worse because the case should not have gone to a jury. The trial judge should have dismissed the suit based on the preexisting duty rule.

Argument for Mr. White: There were two parties to this agreement, and both believed they had a binding agreement. The Bank's officer agreed to postpone foreclosure. He also promised to forward a formal document confirming the understanding but did not do so. And why did he send no other document? Because he believed the Bank had already agreed to halt any foreclosure effort. He was right.

Mr. White paid 80 percent of the balance due. It is wrong for the Bank to take the money and then break its promise. Furthermore, it is absurd to foreclose based on such a modest debt. The legal argument about consideration is nonsense. Mr. White's consideration was a check for $35,000.

The jury award indicates a group of average citizens who were angry about what the Bank did. The verdict should be affirmed.

EXAM Strategy

Question: Star Struck, a Hollywood talent agency, employs Puneet as one of its young agents and Max as a part-time delivery boy. Puneet's contract is for one year. She earns $5,000 per month, payable on the last day of each month. After she has worked at the firm for four months, a Star Struck executive says to her, "We are having cash flow problems. We cannot pay you this month, and will probably fall about two months behind. However, if you will agree to do Max's job for the next few months, we can pay you on time." Puneet cheerfully agrees to the deal. However, after a few weeks of the extra labor, Puneet confesses that she is overwhelmed and can no longer do Max's job. Star Struck fires her. Puneet sues. Was there a binding agreement for Puneet to do Max's work?

Strategy: Star Struck made an offer to Puneet and she accepted it. But a contract needs more than offer and acceptance. Both parties must give consideration. Had they done more than they were required to do under their preexisting duty?

Result: A promise to do what a party is already obligated to do is not consideration. Star Struck was required to pay Puneet every month, so its "offer" included no consideration. Without consideration, there can be no agreement. Puneet was not obligated to do Max's job, and she will win this lawsuit.

Exception: Unforeseen Circumstances

Hugo has a deal to repair major highways. Hugo hires Hal's Hauling to cart soil and debris. Hal's trucks begin work, but after crossing the work site several times, they sink to their axles in sinister, sucking slime. Hal demands an additional 35 percent payment from Hugo to complete the job, pointing out that the surface was dry and cracked and that neither Hal nor Hugo was aware of the subsurface water. Hal howls that he must use different trucks with different tires and work more slowly to permit the soil to dry. Hugo hems and haws and finally agrees. But when the hauling is finished, Hugo refuses to pay the extra money. Is Hugo liable?

Yes. When unforeseen circumstances cause a party to make a promise regarding an unfinished project, that promise is generally valid consideration. Even though Hal is only promising to finish what he was already obligated to do, his promise is valid consideration because neither party knew of the subsoil mud. Hal was facing a situation quite different from what the parties anticipated. It is almost as though he were undertaking a new project. Hal has given consideration, and Hugo is bound by his promise to pay extra money.

SETTLEMENT OF DEBTS

You claim that your friend Felicity owes you $90,000, but she refuses to pay. Finally, when you are desperate, Felicity offers you a cashier's check for $60,000—provided you accept it as full settlement. To get your hands on some money, you agree and cash the check. The next day, you sue Felicity for $30,000. Who wins? It will depend principally upon one major issue: was Felicity's debt liquidated or unliquidated?

Liquidated Debt

A **liquidated debt** is one in which there is no dispute about the amount owed. A loan is a typical example. If a bank lends you $10,000, and the note obligates you to repay that amount on June 1 of the following year, you clearly owe that sum. The debt is liquidated.

Liquidated debt
A debt in which there is no dispute about the amount owed.

In cases of liquidated debt, if the creditor agrees to take less than the full amount as full payment, her agreement is not binding. The debtor has given no consideration to support the creditor's promise to accept a reduced payment, and therefore the creditor is not bound by her word. The reasoning is simply that the debtor is already obligated to pay the full amount, so no bargaining could reasonably cause the creditor to accept less. If Felicity's debt to you is liquidated, your agreement to accept $60,000 is not binding, and you will successfully sue for the balance.

Exception: Different Performance

There is one important exception to this rule. If the debtor offers a *different performance* to settle the liquidated debt, and the creditor agrees to take it as full settlement, the agreement is binding. Suppose that Felicity, instead of paying $60,000, offers you five acres in Alaska, and you accept. When you accept the deed to the land, you have given up your entire claim, regardless of the land's precise value.

Unliquidated Debt: Accord and Satisfaction

A debt is **unliquidated** for either of two reasons: (1) the parties dispute whether any money is owed, or (2) the parties agree that some money is owed but dispute how much. When a debt is unliquidated for either reason, the parties may enter into a binding agreement to settle for less than what the creditor demands.

Unliquidated debt
A debt that is disputed because the parties disagree over its existence or amount.

Such a compromise will be enforced if:

- The debt is unliquidated;
- The parties agree that the creditor will accept as full payment a sum less than she has claimed; and
- The debtor pays the amount agreed upon.

This agreement is called an **accord and satisfaction**. The accord is the agreement to settle for less than the creditor claims. The satisfaction is the actual payment of that compromised sum. An accord and satisfaction is valid consideration to support the creditor's agreement to drop all claims. Each party is giving up something: the creditor gives up her full claim, and the debtor gives up his assertion that he owed little or nothing.

Accord and satisfaction
A completed agreement to settle a debt for less than the sum claimed.

Accord and Satisfaction by Check

Most accord and satisfaction agreements involve payment by check. UCC §3-311 governs these agreements, using the same common-law rules described above.[5] The Code specifies that when the debtor writes "full settlement" on the check, a creditor who cashes the check generally has entered into an accord and satisfaction. If Felicity's debt is unliquidated, and she gives you a check with "full payment of all debts" written on the face in bold letters, the moment you deposit the check, you lose any claim to more money. What happens if the debtor makes such a notation but the creditor changes it? A massage therapist learned the answer and felt sore for days.

[5]A check is legally an instrument, which is why this section comes from Article 3 of the Code. For a full discussion of instruments, see Chapters 23–36.

Henches v. Taylor

138 Wash. App. 1026, 2007 WL 1241525
Washington Court of Appeals, 2007

Facts: Jim Henches, a licensed massage therapist, treated Benjamin Taylor after he was injured in a car accident. When all treatments were finished, Henches billed Taylor for more than $7,000. Taylor's insurance company claimed the bill was exorbitant and paid only $2,625, for 24 massage treatments.

Henches continued to send bills to Taylor, not only for the balance due but for additional time spent consulting with Taylor's other health care providers, preparing to testify in Taylor's personal injury lawsuit, and attempting to collect his debts. In response to a bill for $11,945.86, Taylor's lawyer, James Harris, sent Henches a letter, stating:

> I have reviewed your billing statements and am having a difficult time understanding a number of charges you included. By my calculations, the amount owed to you is approximately $5,243.45. I have enclosed a check for that amount as payment in full to settle Mr. Taylor's account with you.

The letter was accompanied by a check with "final payment" written on the notation line. Henches filed suit, seeking the full balance. Then he wrote "attorney/fee" on the check, over the word "final," and deposited the check.

The trial court gave summary judgment to Taylor, ruling that deposit of the check constituted accord and satisfaction. Henches appealed.

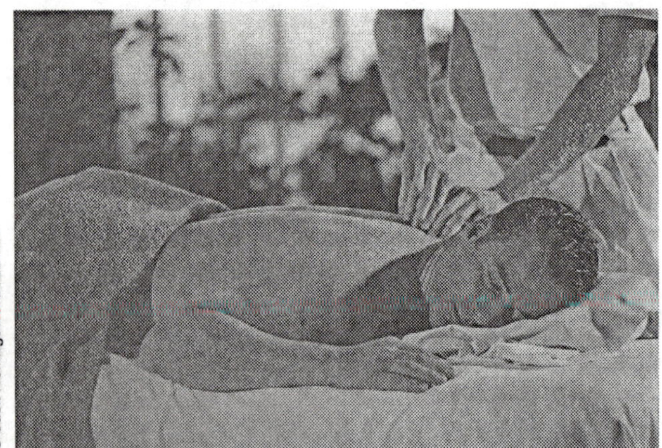

© Jack Hollingsworth/Corbis

The massage feels great, but how much is it really worth?

Issue: ***Was there an accord and satisfaction, discharging the debt?***

Excerpts from Judge Ellington's Decision: A debt is discharged by accord and satisfaction when the debtor and creditor agree to settle a claim by some performance other than that which is claimed due, and the creditor accepts the substituted performance as full satisfaction of the claim. Accord and satisfaction requires a bona fide dispute, an agreement to settle the dispute for a certain sum, and performance of the agreement.

Taylor easily satisfied the first element of accord and satisfaction. The parties' contracts did not establish a liquidated amount for the services provided, and the letter that accompanied Taylor's check to Henches demonstrates a good faith dispute over the amount owed.

As with any contract, an accord and satisfaction cannot be formed without a meeting of the minds. But the required intent is shown when payment is offered in full satisfaction and is accompanied by conduct from which the creditor cannot fail to understand that payment is tendered on condition its acceptance constitutes satisfaction.

Given the undisputed facts here, Henches could not fail to understand that the check was offered on condition of full settlement. Henches' alteration of the "final payment" language is further demonstration that he read and understood the notation. Taylor tendered a check in final payment and Henches deposited the check, thereby accepting that payment.

A creditor can accept payment and avoid formation of an accord only where both parties understand before payment is accepted that the payment will not settle the claim. Henches contends his alteration of the check prevents accord and satisfaction. But a creditor cannot prevent formation of an accord by making a unilateral change to a draft tendered in full payment, even if the creditor endorses the check with the words accepted as partial payment and not as payment in full and not as an accord and satisfaction of the known full amount legally due and owing.

Where the amount due is in dispute, and the debtor sends cash or check for less than the amount claimed, clearly expressing his intention that it is sent as a settlement in full, and not on account or in part payment, the retention and use of the money or the cashing of the check is almost always held to be an acceptance of the offer operating as full satisfaction, even though the creditor may assert or send word to the debtor that the sum is received only in part payment.

Henches' alteration of the check was a unilateral act not communicated to Taylor. Accord and satisfaction discharged Taylor's debts to Henches. We affirm the trial court's summary judgment dismissal of Henches' suit.

UCC Exceptions

The Code creates two exceptions for accord and satisfaction cases involving checks. The first exception concerns "organizations," which typically are businesses. The general rule of §3-311 is potentially calamitous to them because a company that receives thousands of checks every day is unlikely to inspect all notations. A consumer who owes $12,000 on a credit card might write "full settlement" on a $200 check, potentially extinguishing the entire debt through accord and satisfaction. Under the exception, if an organization notifies a debtor that any offers to settle for less than the debt claimed must be made to a particular official, and the check is sent to anyone else in the organization, depositing the check generally does *not* create an accord and satisfaction. Thus a clerk who deposits 900 checks daily for payment of MasterCard debts will not have inadvertently entered into dozens of accord and satisfaction agreements.

The second exception allows a way out to most creditors who have inadvertently created an accord and satisfaction. If, within 90 days of cashing a "full payment" check, the creditor offers repayment of the same amount to the debtor, there is no accord and satisfaction. Homer claims that Virgil owes him $7 million but foolishly cashes Virgil's check for $3 million, without understanding that "paid in full" means just what it says. Homer has created an accord and satisfaction. But if he promptly sends Virgil a check for $3 million, he has undone the agreement and may sue for the full amount.

Consideration: Trends

Employment Agreements

In a noncompete agreement, an employee promises not to work for a competitor for some time after leaving the company. It used to be that these covenants were rare and reserved for top officers, but they have now become commonplace throughout many organizations. We will talk about them more in the next chapter, but often these covenants raise an issue of consideration: what consideration does the employee receive for signing a covenant not to compete? After all, the company is already under an obligation to pay the employee for working. What additional value does the employee receive in return for signing the agreement?

Although this area of law is developing and is a bit murky, the following case reflects the current majority view. Sometimes consideration issues can drive you nuts.

Snider Bolt & Screw v. Quality Screw & Nut

2009 U.S. Dist. LEXIS 50797
United States District Court for the Western District of Kentucky, 2009

Facts: James Scott signed a covenant not to compete when he went to work for Snider Bolt & Screw. The agreement prohibited him from taking a job with a competitor for one year after leaving Snider. Three years later, Scott quit his job at Snider and immediately went to work for Quality Screw & Nut (QSN).

Snider obtained a temporary restraining order that banned Scott from working at his new job. QSN argued that the covenant not to compete was void for lack of consideration. It asked the court to lift the temporary restraining order.

Issue: ***Did the covenant not to compete lack consideration?***

Excerpt from Judge Heyburn's Decision: Snider says that when Scott signed his covenant not to compete, he did so based upon an implied promise that Snider would continue his employment. Indeed, Snider did maintain Scott's employment until Scott himself left his job. Kentucky courts have found quite specifically that "where an employer has fulfilled an implied promise to continue the employee's employment, that promise is sufficient consideration

[to] support enforcement of the employee's promise not to compete." The Kentucky Supreme Court subsequently held that even continued at-will employment would be sufficient consideration. Here, Scott worked for another three years and left on his own accord to join QSN. These circumstances fit within the rule and the Court finds that the Covenant is supported by adequate consideration.

Consequently, the Court has no basis for sustaining QSN's motion.

Promissory Estoppel and "Moral Consideration"

Judges have a tool by which they can enforce agreements even if there is no consideration. Under the doctrine of promissory estoppel, a judge has the discretion to "ignore" the fact that consideration does not exist if a promise causes foreseeable reliance by a plaintiff and a great injustice would be done if the promise were broken. Some courts will use the phrase "moral consideration" to describe this basic idea.

For example, consider a pledge to charity. If Dave promises to give money to charity and then fails to make the donation, there is no consideration because he has received nothing in return. If the charity sues to enforce the promise, it cannot show that it has committed an act or forbearance.[6]

Nevertheless, some courts will force donors to make good on their donations anyway. Especially in the case of large donations, courts will often cite the "grave injustices" that can follow from this kind of promise breaking. "If you don't give the 'Coats for Kids' program the $100,000 you've pledged, then thousands of children will go without a coat this winter," a judge might say. Also, it may be that the charity has relied on the pledge to open another storefront or undertake a new program. Courts are likely to enforce the pledge in these circumstances.

It is unwise to make charitable pledges, especially large pledges, if you might change your mind.

EXAM Strategy

Question: In an Alabama case, Webb saved McGowin's life by preventing a giant block of wood from falling on his head.[7] Webb was permanently disabled in the accident and was never able to work again. Later, McGowin promised to give Webb money every two weeks for the rest of his life. McGowin made the payments for awhile but then stopped. Webb sued.

Strategy: No consideration exists here. McGowin made the promise to pay the money *after* Webb's heroic act. Webb did not give McGowin anything of value *in return for* the promise to pay money. But what about promissory estoppel?

[6] An exception to this, of course, would be if the charity agreed to give Dave something at the time he made the pledge. As a "fix" for consideration problems, many charities send donors something of trivial value when pledges are made—maybe a water bottle or a tote bag. Under the peppercorn rule, even something of small value counts as a legal act, and it converts a mere promise of a donation into an enforceable contract.

[7] *Webb v. McGowin*, 168 So. 196 (Ala.1935).

Result: In the case, the court found that "moral consideration" was present, and that Webb was entitled to the payments to prevent substantial injustice.

It is important to note that applications of promissory estoppel and similar doctrines are rare. Ordinarily, if there is no consideration, then there is no contract. However, in extreme cases, it is possible for a court to enforce a deal even without consideration. But this is not something you can count on.

Chapter Conclusion

This ancient doctrine of consideration is simple to state but subtle to apply. The parties must bargain and enter into an exchange of promises or actions. If they do not, there is no consideration and the courts are unlikely to enforce any promise made. A variety of exceptions modify the law, but a party wishing to render its future more predictable—the purpose of a contract—will rely on a solid bargain and exchange.

Exam Review

1. **CONSIDERATION** There are three rules of consideration:
   - Both parties must get something of *measureable value* from the contract.
   - A *promise* to give something of value counts as consideration.
   - The two parties must have *bargained for* whatever was exchanged. (pp. 276–278)
2. **ACT OR FORBEARANCE** The item of value can be either an act or a forbearance. (pp. 276–277)

EXAM Strategy

Question: An aunt saw her eight-year-old nephew enter the room, remarked what a nice boy he was, and said, "I would like to take care of him now." She promptly wrote a note, promising to pay the boy $3,000 upon her death. Her estate refused to pay. Is it obligated to do so?

Strategy: A contract is enforceable only if the parties have given consideration. The consideration might be an act or a forbearance. Did the nephew give consideration? (See the "Result" at the end of this section.)

3. **ADEQUACY** The courts will seldom inquire into the adequacy of consideration. This is the "peppercorn rule." (pp. 278–279)
4. **ILLUSORY PROMISES** An illusory promise is not consideration. (pp. 278–280)

EXAM Strategy

Question: Eagle ran convenience stores. He entered into an agreement with Commercial Movie in which Commercial would provide Eagle with DVDs for rental. Eagle would pay Commercial 50 percent of the rental revenues. If Eagle stopped using Commercial's service, Eagle could not use a competitor's services for 18 months. The agreement also provided: "Commercial shall not be liable for compensation or damages of any kind, whether on account of the loss by Eagle of profits, sales or expenditures, or on account of any other event or cause whatsoever." Eagle complied with the agreement for two years but then began using a competitor's service, and Commercial sued. Eagle claimed that the agreement was unenforceable for lack of consideration. Please rule.

Strategy: In this case, both parties seem to have given consideration. But there is a flaw in the "promise" that Commercial made. Commercial can never be liable to Eagle—no matter what happens. (See the "Result" at the end of this section.)

5. **REQUIREMENT AND OUTPUT CONTRACTS** Under sales law, requirement and output contracts are valid. Although one side controls the quantity, its agreement to make demands *in good faith* is consideration. (pp. 280–283)

6. **PREEXISTING DUTY** Under the doctrine of preexisting duty, a promise to do something that the party is already legally obligated to perform is generally not consideration. (p. 282)

7. **LIQUIDATED DEBT** A liquidated debt is one in which there is no dispute about the amount owed. For a liquidated debt, a creditor's promise to accept less than the full amount is not binding. (pp. 285–287)

8. **UNLIQUIDATED DEBT** For an unliquidated debt, if the parties agree that the creditor will accept less than the full amount claimed and the debtor performs, there is an accord and satisfaction and the creditor may not claim any balance. (pp. 285–287)

9. **"FULL PAYMENT" NOTATIONS** In most states, payment by a check that has a "full payment" notation will create an accord and satisfaction unless the creditor is an organization that has notified the debtor that full payment offers must go to a certain officer. (pp. 285–287)

EXAM Strategy

Question: When White's wife died, he filed a claim with Boston Mutual for $10,000 death benefits under her insurance policy. The insurer rejected the claim, saying that his wife had misrepresented her medical condition in the application form. The company sent White a check for $478.75, which it said represented "a full refund of all applicable premiums paid" for the coverage. White deposited the check. Had the parties reached an accord and satisfaction?

Strategy: The UCC permits parties to enter into an accord and satisfaction by check. The debtor must make clear that the check is offered in full payment of a disputed debt. Debtors generally do that by writing "Final Settlement," "Accepted as Full Payment of All Debts," or some similar notation on the check. Had the insurance company complied with that requirement? (See the "Result" at the end of this section.)

10. **PROMISSORY ESTOPPEL** Sometimes, to prevent injustice, courts will enforce agreements even if no consideration is present. These deals are still not formal contracts, but the courts will enforce a promise nonetheless. (pp. 288–289)

EXAM Strategy

Question: Phil Philanthropist called PBS during a fund drive and pledged to donate $100,000. PBS then planned and began to produce a Fourth of July *Sesame Street* special, counting on the large donation to fund it. Later, Phil changed his mind and said he had decided not to donate the money after all. PBS sued because without the money, it would not be able to complete the show. Will PBS win the lawsuit?

Strategy: Analyze the promise to donate the $100,000. Does it contain consideration? If not, is there any other legal possibility? (See the "Result" at the end of this section.)

2. Result: The nephew gave no consideration. He did not promise to do anything. He committed no act or forbearance. Without consideration, there is no enforceable contract. The estate wins.

4. Result: Commercial's promise was illusory. The company was free to walk away from the deal at any time. Commercial could never be held liable. Commercial gave no consideration, and there was no binding contract for either party to enforce.

9. Result: The insurer merely stated that its check was a refund of premiums. Nowhere did the company indicate that the check was full payment of its disputed obligation. The company should have made it clear that it would not pay any benefits and that this payment was all that it would offer. There was no accord and satisfaction.

10. Result: There is no "regular" consideration here because Phil received no measureable benefit and PBS did not act or forbear. But PBS can likely make a strong case that a great injustice will be done if the money is not paid. A judge might well decide to apply the doctrine of promissory estoppel and require Phil to make the donation.

Multiple-Choice Questions

1. For consideration to exist, there must be:
   (a) A bargained-for exchange
   (b) A manifestation of mutual assent
   (c) Genuineness of assent
   (d) Substantially equal economic benefits to both parties

2. Which of the following requires consideration in order to be binding on the parties?
   (a) Modification of a contract involving the sale of real estate
   (b) Modification of a sale of goods contract under the UCC
   (c) Both A and B
   (d) None of the above

3. Ted's wallet is as empty as his bank account, and he needs $3,500 immmediately. Fortunately, he has three gold coins that he inherited from his grandfather. Each is worth $2,500, but it is Sunday, and the local rare coins store is closed. When approached, Ted's neighbor Andrea agrees to buy the first coin for $2,300. Another neighbor, Cami, agrees to buy the second for $1,100. A final neighbor, Lorne, offers "all the money I have on me"—$100—for the last coin. Desperate, Ted agrees to the proposal. Which of the deals is supported by consideration?
   (a) Ted's agreement with Andrea only
   (b) Ted's agreements with Andrea and Cami only
   (c) All three of the agreements
   (d) None of the agreements

4. In a(n) ___________ contract, the seller guarantees to sell 100 percent of its output to one buyer, and the buyer agrees to accept the entire quantity. This kind of arrangement ___________ acceptable under the UCC.
   (a) output; is
   (b) output; is not
   (c) requirements; is
   (d) requirements; is not

5. Noncompete agreements are common features of employment contracts. Currently, courts ___________ enforce these clauses.
   (a) always
   (b) usually
   (c) rarely
   (d) never

ESSAY QUESTIONS

1. American Bakeries had a fleet of over 3,000 delivery trucks. Because of the increasing cost of gasoline, the company was interested in converting the trucks to propane fuel. It signed a requirements contract with Empire Gas, in which Empire would convert "approximately 3,000" trucks to propane fuel, as American Bakeries requested, and would then sell all the required propane fuel to run the trucks. But American Bakeries changed its mind and never requested a single conversion. Empire sued for lost profits. Who won?

2. CeCe Hylton and Edward Meztista, partners in a small advertising firm, agreed to terminate the business and split assets evenly. Meztista gave Hylton a two-page document showing assets, liabilities, and a bottom line of $35,235.67, with half due to each partner. Hylton questioned the accounting and asked to see the books. Meztista did not permit Hylton to see any records and refused to answer her phone calls. Instead, he gave her a check in the amount of $17,617.83, on which he wrote "Final payment/payment in full." Hylton cashed the check, but she wrote on it, "Under protest—cashing this check does not constitute my acceptance of this amount as payment in full." Hylton then filed suit, demanding additional monies. Meztista claimed that the parties had made an accord and satisfaction. What is the best argument for each party? Who should win?

3. ***ETHICS*** Melnick built a house for Gintzler, but the foundation was defective. Gintzler agreed to accept the foundation if Melnick guaranteed to make future repairs caused by the defects. Melnick agreed but later refused to make any repairs. Melnick argued that his promise to make future repairs was unsupported by consideration. Who will win the suit? Is either party acting unethically? Which one, and why?

4. Sami walks into a restaurant. She is given a menu, which indicates that lobster is $30. Sami orders the lobster. It arrives, and Sami thinks it is very tasty. When the bill arrives, Sami tries to execute a clever ploy she learned about in her business law class. She writes a check to the restaurant for $20 and writes "full settlement" across the top. The waiter accepts the check without looking at it, and the restaurant manager later deposits it in the restaurant's bank account. Is this a liquidated or an unliquidated debt? Is Sami off the hook for the last $10?

5. In the bleachers…

   "You're a prince, George!" Mike exclaimed. "Who else would give me a ticket to the big game?"

   "No one, Mike, no one."

   "Let me offer my thanks. I'll buy you a beer!"

   "Ah," George said. "A large beer would hit the spot right now."

   "Small. Let me buy you a small beer."

   "Ah, well, good enough."

   Mike stood and took his wallet from his pocket. He was distressed to find a very small number of bills inside. "There's bad news, George!" he said.

   "What's that?"

   "I can't buy you the beer, George."

   George considered that for a moment. "I'll tell you what, Mike," he said. "If you march to the concession stand right this minute and get me my beer, I won't punch you in the face."

   "It's a deal!" Mike said.

   Discuss the consideration issues raised by this exchange.

6. Jack Tallas came to the United States from Greece in 1914. He lived in Salt Lake City for nearly 70 years, achieving great success in insurance and real estate. During the last 14 years of his life, his friend Peter Dementas helped him with numerous personal and business chores. Two months before his death, Tallas dictated a memorandum to Dementas, in Greek, stating:

   > PETER K. DEMENTAS is my best friend I have in this country, and since he came to the United States, he treats me like a father and I think of him as my own son. He takes me in his car grocery shopping. He drives me to the doctor and also takes me every week to Bingham to pick up my mail, collect the rents, and manage my properties. For all the services Peter has given me all these years, I owe to him the amount of $50,000 (Fifty Thousand Dollars). I will shortly change my will to include him as my heir.

   Tallas signed the memorandum, but he did not in fact alter his will to include Dementas. The estate refused to pay, and Dementas sued. Was there consideration? Please rule.

Discussion Questions

Apply the following material to the next three questions.

Some view consideration as a technicality that allows people to make promises and then back out of them. Perhaps all promises should be enforced. In Japan, for example, promises to give gifts are enforceable without consideration.[8]

In the United States, if I promise to give you a gift merely because I feel like being nice, I can freely change my mind as far as contract law is concerned. A court will not make me follow through because there is no consideration.

In Japan, I would be obligated to buy the gift if all other elements of a contract were present—an offer, an acceptance, and so forth.

Some argue that consideration in U.S. law is a doctrine left over from centuries long past, that it lacks any reasonable modern purpose, and that it should be abolished.

1. Do you agree with this statement: "A person should always keep his or her word."

2. When it comes to giving gifts, which is better—the Japanese or American rule?

3. Are there any specific types of agreements (perhaps high-value, long-term, extremely time-consuming ones) that should definitely require consideration?

4. In the gold rush example, Embola gave Tuppela $50 in exchange for a promise of $10,000 later. Under the peppercorn rule, the deal was a contract. Is the peppercorn rule sensible? Should courts require a more *even* exchange of value?

5. In the last two chapters, we have examined clickwrap boxes. Sometimes courts refuse to enforce clickwrap terms because of problems with acceptance or consideration, but usually the terms are enforced. Is there a way to make clickwraps fair to both sides? Would it be better to ban clickwrap boxes altogether?

[8]See Japan's Civil Code, Article 549.

CHAPTER 13

© picsbyst/Shutterstock.com

LEGALITY

Soheil Sadri, a California resident, did some serious gambling at Caesar's Tahoe casino in Nevada. And lost. To keep gambling, he wrote checks to Caesar's and then signed two memoranda pledging to repay all money advanced. After two days, with his losses totaling more than $22,000, he went home. Back in California, Sadri stopped payment on the checks and refused to pay any of the money he owed Caesar's. The casino sued. In defense, Sadri claimed that California law considered his agreements illegal and unenforceable. He was unquestionably correct about one thing: a contract that is illegal is void and unenforceable.

A contract that is illegal is void and unenforceable.

Contracts that Violate a Statute

In this chapter, we examine a variety of contracts that may be void, or unenforceable. Illegal agreements fall into two groups: those that violate a statute, and those that violate public policy.

Wagers

Gambling is big business. Almost all states now permit some form of wagering, from casinos to racetracks to lotteries, and they eagerly collect the billions of dollars in revenue generated. Supporters urge that casinos create jobs and steady income, boost state coffers, and take business away from organized crime. Critics argue that naive citizens inevitably lose money they can ill afford to forfeit, and that addicted gamblers destroy their families and weaken the fabric of communities. With citizens and states divided over the ethics of gambling, it is inevitable that we have conflicts such as the dispute between Sadri and Caesar's. The basic rule, however, is clear: **a gambling contract is illegal unless it is a type of wagering *specifically authorized* by state statute.**

In California, as in many states, gambling on credit is not allowed. In other words, it is illegal to lend money to help someone wager. But in Nevada, gambling on credit is legal, and debt memoranda such as Sadri's are enforceable contracts. Caesar's sued Sadri in California (where he lived). The result? The court admitted that California's attitude toward gambling had changed, and that bingo, poker clubs, and lotteries were common. Nonetheless, the court denied that the new tolerance extended to wagering on credit:

> There is a special reason for treating gambling on credit differently from gambling itself. Having lost his or her cash, the pathological gambler will continue to play on credit, if extended, in an attempt to win back the losses. This is why enforcement of gambling debts has always been against public policy in California and should remain so, regardless of shifting public attitudes about gambling itself. If Californians want to play, so be it. But the law should not invite them to play themselves into debt. The judiciary cannot protect pathological gamblers from themselves, but we can refuse to participate in their financial ruin.[1]

© Elena Ray/Shutterstock

The gambling is legal—but what about a gambling contract?

Caesar's lost and Sadri kept his money. However, do not become too excited at the prospect of risk-free wagering. Casinos responded to cases like *Sadri* by changing their practices. Most now extend credit only to a gambler who agrees that disputes about repayment will be settled in *Nevada* courts. Because such contracts are legal in that state, the casino is able to obtain a judgment against a defaulting debtor and—yes—enforce that judgment in the gambler's home state.

Despite these more restrictive casino practices, Sadri's dispute is a useful starting place from which to examine contract legality because it illustrates two important themes.

First, morality is a significant part of contract legality. In refusing to enforce an obligation that Sadri undeniably had made, the California court relied on the human and social consequences of gambling and on the ethics of judicial enforcement of gambling debts. Second, "void" really means just that: a court will not

[1]*Metropolitan Creditors Service of Sacramento v. Sadri*, 15 Cal. App. 4th 1821, 1993 Cal. App. LEXIS 559, 19 Cal. Rptr. 2d 646 (Cal. Ct. App. 1993).

intercede to assist either party to an illegal agreement, even if its refusal leaves one party shortchanged.

Insurance

Another market in which "wagering" unexpectedly pops up is that of insurance. You may certainly insure your own life for any sum you choose. But may you insure someone else's life? **Anyone taking out a policy on the life of another must have an insurable interest in that person.** The most common insurable interest is family connection, such as spouses or parents. Other valid interests include creditor-debtor status (the creditor wants payment if the debtor dies) and business association (an executive in the company is so valuable that the firm will need compensation if something happens to him). If there is no insurable interest, there is generally no contract.

EXAM Strategy

Question: Jimenez sold Breton a used motorcycle for $5,500, payable in weekly installments. Jimenez then purchased an insurance policy on Breton's life, worth $320,000 if Breton died in an accident. Breton promptly died in a collision with an automobile. The insurance company offered only $5,500, representing the balance due on the motorcycle. Jimenez sued, demanding $320,000. Make an argument that the insurance company should win.

Strategy: The issue is whether Jimenez had an insurable interest in Breton's life. If he had no interest, he cannot collect on an insurance policy. If he had an interest, what was it? For how much money?

Result: Jimenez's had an interest in Breton's life to insure payment of the motorcycle debt—$5,500. Beyond that, this policy represented a wager by Jimenez that Breton was going to die. Contracts for such wagers are unenforceable. Jimenez is entitled only to $5,500.[2]

Licensing Statutes

You sue your next-door neighbor in small claims court, charging that he keeps a kangaroo in his backyard and that the beast has disrupted your family barbecues by leaping over the fence, demanding salad, and even kicking your cousin in the ear. Your friend Foster, a graduate student from Melbourne, offers to help you prepare the case, and you agree to pay him 10 percent of anything you recover. Foster proves surprisingly adept at organizing documents and arguments. You win $1,200, and Foster demands $120. Must you pay? The answer is determined by the law of licensing.

States require licenses for anyone who practices a profession, such as law or medicine, works as a contractor or plumber, and for many other kinds of work. These licenses are required in order to protect the public. States demand that an electrician be licensed because the work is potentially dangerous to a homeowner: the person doing the work must know an amp from a watt. **When a licensing requirement is designed to protect the public, any contract made by an unlicensed worker is unenforceable.** Your friend Foster is

[2] *Jimenez v. Protective Life Insurance Co.*, 8 Cal. App. 4th 528 (Cal. App. 1992).

unlicensed to practice law. Even though Foster did a fine job with your small claims case, he cannot enforce his contract for $120.

States use other licenses simply to raise money. For example, most states require a license to open certain kinds of retail stores. This requirement does not protect the public because the state will not investigate the store owner the way it will examine a prospective lawyer or electrician. The state is simply raising money. **When a licensing requirement is designed merely to raise revenue, a contract made by an unlicensed person is generally enforceable.** Thus, if you open a stationery store and forget to pay the state's licensing fee, you can still enforce a contract to buy 10,000 envelopes from a wholesaler at a bargain price.

Many cases, such as the following one, involve contractors seeking to recover money for work they did without a license.

AUTHENTIC HOME IMPROVEMENTS V. MAYO

2006 WL 2687533
District of Columbia Superior Court, 2006

Facts: Authentic Home Improvements (Authentic) performed work on Diane Mayo's home, but she sued for return of the money she had paid. In court, Authentic's owner acknowledged that he had no contractor's license when it began the work, but he expected to obtain it soon. The court ordered Authentic to refund Mayo the entire sum she had paid, and the company agreed. Later, however, Authentic returned to court, stating that things had changed. The license had in fact been issued soon after work began. Authentic argued that it should not be obligated to return Mayo's money and was in fact entitled to its full fee for the work accomplished.

Issue: ***Did the new license entitle Authentic to its home improvement fee?***

Excerpts from Judge Goodbread's Decision: This is not a matter of a trial judge doggedly cleaving to his original ruling—one that he frankly wishes he could modify under these circumstances. To use the words of Proteus, "My duty pricks me on to utter that which else no worldly good should draw from me." Shakespeare, "The Two Gentlemen of Verona." Not that it makes any difference to anyone, but the undersigned, a carpenter's son dwelling at this end of the Judicial Food Chain, disagrees with the harsh general rule in these cases and [believes that exceptions to the licensing requirement should be made in deserving cases]. Nevertheless, the undersigned is bound by the repeated rulings of the Court of Appeals.

As early as 1974, our Court of Appeals noted the high incidence of complaints emanating from the home improvement industry, noting that, even then, it was estimated that fraudulent practices in the industry cost consumers from 500 million to 1 billion dollars annually (this would amount to over $4.3 billion in today's dollars). A simple search of the Internet for the term "home improvement fraud" brings up over two million sites.

Not only is it immaterial that the parties may be in equal fault in the home improvement contract matter, but it has also been held that the unlicensed contractor may not recover even in instances wherein the homeowner *already knew* at all times relevant that the contractor was not licensed and impliedly or expressly "waived" that requirement in return for the work being done promptly. Moreover—turning the purpose of the rule inside out—even where it was the contractor who was the "victim" and the home owner herself who knew in advance that the contract would be invalid and unenforceable, yet still benefitted unfairly from the contractor's good work, the homeowner was allowed to prevail, despite what might be termed "malice aforethought."

The unique defense of a "retroactive" license presented in this case does not vitiate the rule. [Authentic's owner argues that he] had every reasonable *expectation* of receiving a license and that, in fact, he *did* receive the license within a reasonable time of beginning work. Yet the requirement to have *already* had issued, and in hand, a license or permit to conduct or perform the act at issue is not a difficult concept to grasp and one need go no further than the common driver's permit or license tags to understand it. No one could legally drive a vehicle in *anticipation* of the license and the plates that had already been approved, on the premise that they would eventually arrive in the mail in due course, and that it would be all right to drive until they do.

The Court's original ruling in this case must stand.

Usury

It pays to understand usury.

Henry Paper and Anthony Pugliese were real estate developers. They bought property in Florida, intending to erect an office building. Walter Gross, another developer, agreed to lend them $200,000 at 15 percent interest. Gross knew the partners were desperate for the money, so at the loan closing, he demanded 15 percent equity (ownership) in the partnership, in addition to the interest. Paper and Pugliese had no choice but to sign the agreement. The two partners never repaid the loan, and when Gross sued, the court ruled that they need never pay a cent.

Usury laws prohibit charging excess interest on loans. Some states, such as New York, set very strict limits. Others, like Utah, allow for virtually any rate. A lender who charges a usurious rate of interest may forfeit the illegal interest, all interest, or, in some states, the entire loan.

Florida law requires a lender who exceeds 25 percent interest to forfeit the entire debt. Where was the usury in Gross's case? Just here: when Gross insisted on a 15 percent share of the partnership, he was simply extracting additional interest and disguising it as partnership equity. The Paper-Pugliese partnership had equity assets of $600,000. A 15 percent equity, plus interest payments of 15 percent over 18 months, was the equivalent of a per annum interest rate of 45 percent. Gross probably thought he had made a deal that was too good to be true. And in the state of Florida, it was. He lost the entire debt.[3]

Credit Card Debt

Many consumers are desperate to obtain credit cards on any terms. When First Premier Bank launched a credit card with a 79.9 percent rate of interest, 700,000 people applied for it within the next two years.

How can such a rate exist?

Even if a state's usury statute applies to credit cards, savvy lenders can often avoid limits on interest rates. The Supreme Court has ruled that when national banks issue a credit card, they can use the rate of their own state or of that of the consumer, whichever is higher. Also, many card issuers require borrowers to sign contracts that say the laws of a lender-friendly state will be applied to all future disputes. New York customers might agree to live by Utah laws, for example.

Most courts continue to enforce these contracts that impose high out-of-state rates. But since the financial meltdown of 2008, some courts have started to express distaste for this practice. In the following case, a New York court addressed the issue.

American Express Travel Related Services Company, Inc. v. Assih

893 N.Y.S.2d 438
Civil Court of the City of New York, Richmond County, 2009

Facts: American Express Travel Related Services (American Express) alleged that New York resident Titus Assih missed a credit card payment. His interest rate ballooned from 12.24 percent to 21 percent, and eventually to 27.99 percent. Assih made small payments for a time, but soon he stopped paying altogether.

American Express sued Assih. The company sought to enforce this provision of its agreement: "This Agreement

---

[3] *Jersey Palm-Gross, Inc. v. Paper*, 639 So.2d 664, 1994 Fla. App. LEXIS 6597 (Fla. Ct. App. 1994).

is governed by Utah law and applicable federal law." The agreement's only connection to Utah was that American Express assigned its interest to a one-branch bank in Utah.

Assih argued that New York law, which sets strict limits on maximum rates of credit card interest, should apply instead.

Issues: ***Should New York or Utah law apply? Did the increased rates violate usury statutes?***

Excerpts from Judge Straniere's Opinion: Having dealt with thousands of consumer credit cases over the years, the court is sometimes caused to wonder if the regulations governing this industry originated in the Wonderful Land of Oz. For example, the scene where Dorothy and friends approach the gates of the Emerald City and ring the bell seeking entrance seems to present a number of the issues arising in debt collection litigation.

> Guardian: Well, that's more like it! Now state your business!
> Dorothy and Friends: We want to see the Wizard!
> Guardian: The Wizard? But nobody can see the Great Oz! Nobody's ever seen the Great Oz! Even I've never seen him!
> Dorothy: Well, then how do you know there is one?

Like the Land of Oz, run by a Wizard who no one has ever seen, the Land of Credit Cards permits consumers to be bound by agreements they never sign, agreements they may have never received, subject to change without notice and the laws of a state other than those existing where they reside.

The Utah usury statute provides: The parties to a lawful contract may agree upon any rate of interest for the loan that is the subject of their contract.

Is it any wonder that credit card issuers, such as plaintiff, make their agreements subject to Utah law? An interest rate is not usurious so long as the parties "agree upon any rate of interest." If Nathan Detroit had known he could make loans charging 100% interest a day by reducing them to writing, signed and subject to Utah law, he would not have had to seek a living running the "oldest, established, permanent floating crap game in New York." Incredibly courts are expected to enforce these agreements against unsophisticated, unrepresented consumers who reside in states such as New York which do not have similar statutes and who have no idea that their agreement is subject to Utah law.

Is New York required to apply the Utah usury statute to credit card interest charges which far exceed the legal rate in New York? New York follows the "substantial relationship" approach that provides:

> The law of the state chosen by the parties to govern their contractual rights and duties will be applied.... unless the chosen state has no substantial relationship to the parties.

The corporate plaintiff is incorporated in New York and its principal place of business is in New York. Defendant resides in New York. Most of the transactions charged to the credit card took place in New York. Payments on the credit card are mailed to a New York address. Utah has no substantial relationship to the parties.

Taking all of the above into account, it is clear that New York has the most significant contacts to the parties and New York law will apply to the Agreement.

The legal rate of interest in New York in general obligations [is] sixteen per cent. New York still retains a criminal usury statute for interest rates which exceed twenty-five per cent. Except for the initial interest rate charged on defendant's account by plaintiff of 12.24%, all other interest charges assessed by plaintiff violated the New York civil usury statutes. The last billings on this account in fact exceeded the criminal usury rate of 25% when they reached 27.99%.

Under New York law, all usurious contracts are void and the lender forfeits both principal and interest.

The Wizard in the "Wizard of Oz" warned Dorothy and friends, "Do not arouse the wrath of the great and powerful Oz." I am sure the court will likewise be arousing the wrath of the plaintiff.

Plaintiff's cause of action is dismissed.

Contracts that Violate Public Policy

In the preceding section, we saw that courts refuse to enforce contracts that violate a *statute*. However, a judge may declare a contract illegal even if it does not violate a statute. In this section, we examine cases in which a *public policy* prohibits certain contracts. In other words, we focus primarily on common law rules.

Restraint of Trade: Noncompete Agreements

Free trade is the basis of the U.S. economy, and any bargain that restricts it is suspect. Most restraint of free trade is barred by antitrust law. But it is the common law that still regulates one restriction on trade: agreements to refrain from competition. Some of these agreements are legal, and some are void.

Recall that a noncompete agreement is a contract in which one party agrees not to compete with another in a stated type of business. For example, an anchorwoman for an NBC news affiliate in Miami might agree that she will not anchor any other Miami station's news for one year after she leaves her present employer. Noncompetes are often valid, but the common law places some restrictions on them.

To be valid, an agreement not to compete must be ancillary to a legitimate bargain. "Ancillary" means that the noncompetition agreement must be part of a larger agreement. Suppose Cliff sells his gasoline station to Mina, and the two agree that Cliff will not open a competing gas station within 5 miles anytime during the next two years. Cliff's agreement not to compete is ancillary to the sale of his service station. His noncompetition promise is enforceable. But suppose that Cliff and Mina already had the only two gas stations within 35 miles. They agree between themselves not to hire each other's workers. Their agreement might be profitable to them because each could now keep wages artificially low. But their deal is ancillary to no legitimate bargain, and it is therefore void. Mina is free to hire Cliff's mechanic despite her agreement with Cliff.

The two most common settings for legitimate noncompetition agreements are the sale of a business and an employment relationship.

Sale of a Business

Kory has operated a real estate office, Hearth Attack, in a small city for 35 years, building an excellent reputation and many ties with the community. She offers to sell you the business and its goodwill for $300,000. But you need assurance that Kory will not take your money and promptly open a competing office across the street. With her reputation and connections, she would ruin your chances of success. You insist on a noncompete clause in the sale contract. In this clause, Kory promises that for one year, she will not open a new real estate office or go to work for a competing company within a 10-mile radius of Hearth Attack. Suppose, six months after selling you the business, Kory goes to work for a competing real estate agency two blocks away. You seek an injunction to prevent her from working. Who wins?

> With her reputation and connections, she would ruin your chances of success.

When a noncompete agreement is ancillary to the sale of a business, it is enforceable if reasonable in time, geographic area, and scope of activity. In other words, a court will not enforce a noncompete agreement that lasts an unreasonably long time, covers an unfairly large area, or prohibits the seller of the business from doing a type of work that she never had done before. Measured by this test, Kory is almost certainly bound by her agreement. One year is a reasonable time to allow you to get your new business started. A 10-mile radius is probably about the area that Hearth Attack covers, and realty is obviously a fair business from which to prohibit Kory. A court will probably grant the injunction, barring Kory from her new job.

If, on the other hand, the noncompetition agreement had prevented Kory from working anywhere within 200 miles of Hearth Attack, and she started working 50 miles away, a court would refuse to enforce the contract. That geographic restriction would be unreasonable since Kory never previously did business 50 miles away, and Hearth Attack is unlikely to be affected if she works there now. An overly broad restriction would make for bad public policy, and it would lack a legal purpose.

Employment

When you sign an employment contract, the document may well contain a noncompete clause. Employers have legitimate worries that employees might go to a competitor and take with them trade secrets or other proprietary information. Some employers, though, attempt to place harsh restrictions on their employees, perhaps demanding a blanket agreement that the employee will never go to work for a competitor. Once again, courts look at the reasonableness of restrictions placed on an employee's future work. Because the agreement now involves the very livelihood of the worker, a court scrutinizes the agreement more closely.

A noncompete clause in an employment contract is generally enforceable only if it is essential to the employer, fair to the employee, and harmless to the general public. Judges usually enforce these agreements to protect trade secrets and confidential information. They may protect customer lists that have been expensive to produce. Courts rarely restrain an employee simply because he wants to work for a competitor, and they disfavor agreements that last too long or apply in a very wide area. The following chart summarizes the factors that courts look at in all types of noncompetition agreements.

THE LEGALITY OF NONCOMPETITION CLAUSES (NONCOMPETES)

Type of Noncompetition Agreement	When Enforceable	
Not ancillary to a sale of business or employment	Never	
Ancillary to a sale of business	If reasonable in time, geography, and scope of activity	
Ancillary to employment	Contract is *more* likely to be enforced when it involves:	Contract is *less* likely to be enforced when it involves:
	• Trade secrets or confidential information: these are almost always protected • Customer lists developed over extended period of time and carefully protected • Limited time and geographical scope • Terms essential to protect the employer's business	• Employee who already had the skills when he arrived, or merely developed general skills on the job • Customer lists that can be derived from public sources • Excessive time or geographical scope • Terms that are unduly harsh on the employee or contrary to public interest

Suppose that Gina, an engineer, goes to work for Fission Chips, a silicon chip manufacturer that specializes in defense work. She signs a noncompete agreement promising never to work for a competitor. Over a period of three years, Gina learns some of Fission's proprietary methods of etching information onto the chips. She acquires a great deal of new expertise about chips generally. And she periodically deals with Fission Chip's customers, all of whom are well-known software and hardware manufacturers. Gina accepts an offer from WriteSmall, a competitor. Fission Chips races to court, seeking an injunction that would prevent Gina from (1) working for WriteSmall; (2) working for any other competitor; (3) revealing any of Fission's trade secrets; (4) using any of the general expertise she acquired at Fission Chips; and (5) contacting any of Fission's customers.

This injunction threatens Gina's career. If she cannot work for a competitor, or use her general engineering skills, what *will* she do? And for exactly that reason, no court will grant such a broad order. The court will allow Gina to work for competitors, including WriteSmall. It will order her not to use or reveal any trade secrets belonging to Fission. She will, however, be permitted to use the general expertise she has acquired, and she may contact former customers since anyone could get their names from the yellow pages.

Was the noncompete in the following case styled fairly, or was the employee clipped?

King v. Head Start Family Hair Salons, Inc.

886 So.2d 769
Supreme Court of Alabama, 2004

Facts: Kathy King was a single mother supporting a college-age daughter. For 25 years, she had worked as a hair stylist. For the most recent 16 years, she had worked at Head Start, which provided haircuts, coloring, and styling for men and women. King was primarily a stylist, though she had also managed one of the Head Start facilities.

King quit Head Start and began working as manager of a Sport Clips shop, located in the same mall as the store she just left. Sport Clips offered only haircuts and primarily served men and boys. Head Start filed suit, claiming that King was violating the noncompetition agreement that she had signed. The agreement prohibited King from working at a competing business within a two-mile radius of any Head Start facility for 12 months after leaving the company. The trial court issued an injunction enforcing the noncompete. King appealed.

Issue: ***Was the noncompetition agreement valid?***

Excerpts from Justice Lyons's Decision: King's most persuasive argument is that the geographic restriction contained in the noncompetition agreement imposes an undue hardship on her. King has been in the hair-care industry for 25 years, and it is the only industry in which she is skilled and the only industry in which she can find employment. Head Start has 30 locations throughout the Jefferson County and Shelby County area, making it virtually impossible for her to find employment in the hair-care industry at a facility that does not violate the terms of the noncompetition agreement. According to King, the geographic restriction constitutes a blanket prohibition on practicing her trade.

It cannot reasonably be argued that King, at the age of 40 and having spent more than half of her life as a hair stylist, can learn a new job skill that would allow her to be gainfully employed and meet her needs and the needs of her daughter. Under the circumstances presented here, enforcement of the noncompetition agreement works an undue hardship upon King. The noncompetition agreement cannot so burden King that it would result in her impoverishment.

Head Start is nevertheless entitled to some of the protection it sought in the noncompetition agreement. Head Start has a valid concern that King would be able to attract many of her former Head Start customers if she is allowed to provide hair-care services unencumbered by any limitations. To prevent an undue burden on King and to afford some protection to Head Start, the trial court should enforce a more reasonable geographic restriction—such as one prohibiting King from providing hair-care services within a two-mile radius of the location of the Head Start facility at which she was formerly employed or imposing some other limitation that does not unreasonably interfere with King's right to gainful employment while, at the same time, protecting Head Start's interest in preventing King from unreasonably competing with it during the one-year period following her resignation.

Reversed and remanded.

EXAM Strategy

Question: Caf-Fiend is an expanding chain of coffeehouses. The company offers to buy Bessie's Coffee Shop, in St. Louis, on these terms: Bessie will manage the store, as Caf-Fiend's employee, for one year after the sale. For four years after the sale, Bessie will not open a competing restaurant anywhere within 12 miles. For the same four years, she will not work anywhere in the United States for a competing coffee retailer. Are the last two terms enforceable against Bessie?

Strategy: This contract includes two noncompete clauses. In the first, Bessie agrees not to open a competing business. Courts generally enforce such clauses if they are reasonable in time, geography, and scope of activity. Is this clause reasonable? The second clause involves employment. Courts take a dimmer view of these agreements. Is this clause essential to protect the company's business? Is it unduly harsh for Bessie?

Result: The first restriction is reasonable. Caf-Fiend is entitled to prevent Bessie from opening her own coffeehouse around the corner and drawing her old customers. The second clause is unfair to Bessie. If she wants to move from St. Louis to San Diego and work as a store manager, she is prohibited. It is impossible to see how such employment would harm Caf-Fiend—but it certainly takes away Bessie's career options. The first restriction is valid, the second one unenforceable.

Exculpatory Clauses

You decide to capitalize on your expert ability as a skier and open a ski school in Colorado, "Pike's Pique." But you realize that skiing sometimes causes injuries, so you require anyone signing up for lessons to sign this form:

> I agree to hold Pike's Pique and its employees entirely harmless in the event that I am injured in any way or for any reason or cause, including but not limited to any acts, whether negligent or otherwise, of Pike's Pique or any employee or agent thereof.

The day your school opens, Sara Beth, an instructor, deliberately pushes Toby over a cliff because Toby criticized her clothes. Eddie, a beginning student, "blows out" his knee attempting an advanced racing turn. And Maureen, another student, reaches the bottom of a steep run and slams into a snowmobile that Sara Beth parked there. Maureen, Eddie, and Toby's families all sue Pike's Pique. You defend based on the form you had them sign. Does it save the day?

Exculpatory clause
A contract provision that attempts to release one party from liability in the event the other is injured.

The form on which you are relying is an **exculpatory clause**, that is, one that attempts to release you from liability in the event of injury to another party. Exculpatory clauses are common. Ski schools use them, and so do parking lots, landlords, warehouses, sports franchises, and day-care centers. All manner of businesses hope to avoid large tort judgments by requiring their customers to give up any right to recover. Is such a clause valid? Sometimes. Courts frequently—but do not always—ignore exculpatory clauses, finding that one party was forcing the other party to give up legal rights that no one should be forced to surrender.

An exculpatory clause is generally unenforceable when it attempts to exclude an intentional tort or gross negligence. When Sara Beth pushes Toby over a cliff, that is the intentional tort of battery. A court will not enforce the exculpatory clause. Sara Beth is clearly liable.[4] As to the snowmobile at the bottom of the run, if a court determines that was gross negligence

[4]Note that Pike's Pique is probably not liable under agency law principles that preclude an employer's liability for an employee's intentional tort.

(carelessness far greater than ordinary negligence), then the exculpatory clause will again be ignored. If, however, it was ordinary negligence, then we must continue the analysis.

An exculpatory clause is usually unenforceable when the affected activity is in the public interest, such as medical care, public transportation, or some essential service. Suppose Eddie goes to a doctor for surgery on his damaged knee, and the doctor requires him to sign an exculpatory clause. The doctor negligently performs the surgery, accidentally leaving his cuff links in Eddie's left knee. The exculpatory clause will not protect the doctor. Medical care is an essential service, and the public cannot give up its right to demand reasonable work.

© Photodisc/Getty Images

Exculpatory clauses are important to the operators of businesses that involve some risk, such as ski resorts.

But what about Eddie's suit against Pike's Pique? Eddie claims that he should never have been allowed to attempt an advanced maneuver. His suit is for ordinary negligence, and the exculpatory clause probably *does* bar him from recovery. Skiing is a recreational activity. No one is obligated to do it, and there is no strong public interest in ensuring that we have access to ski slopes.

An exculpatory clause is generally unenforceable when the parties have greatly unequal bargaining power. When Maureen flies to Colorado, suppose that the airline requires her to sign a form contract with an exculpatory clause. Because the airline almost certainly has much greater bargaining power, it can afford to offer a "take it or leave it" contract. The bargaining power is so unequal, though, that the clause is probably unenforceable. Does Pike's Pique have a similar advantage? Probably not. Ski schools are not essential and are much smaller enterprises. A dissatisfied customer might refuse to sign such an agreement and take her business elsewhere. A court probably will not see the parties as *grossly* unequal.

An exculpatory clause is generally unenforceable unless the clause is clearly written and readily visible. If Pike's Pique gave all ski students an eight-page contract, and the exculpatory clause was at the bottom of page seven in small print, the average customer would never notice it. The clause would be void.

In the following case, the court focused on the public policy concerns of exculpatory clauses used in a very common setting. Should the exculpatory clause stop the tenant from suing the landlord? You be the judge.

You be the Judge

Ransburg v. Richards

770 N.E.2d 393
Indiana Court of Appeals, 2002

Facts: Barbara Richards leased an apartment at Twin Lakes, a complex owned by Lenna Ransburg. The written lease declared that:

- Twin Lakes would "gratuitously" maintain the common areas.
- Richards's use of the facilities would be "at her own risk."
- Twin Lakes was not responsible for any harm to the tenant or her guests, anywhere on the property (including the parking lot), even if the damage was caused by Twin Lakes' negligence.

It snowed. As Richards walked across the parking lot to her car, she slipped and fell on snow-covered ice. Richards sued Ransburg, who moved for summary judgment based on the exculpatory clause. The trial court denied Ransburg's motion, and she appealed.

You Be the Judge: ***Was the exculpatory clause valid?***

Argument for Tenant: An exculpatory clause in a contract for an essential service violates public policy. When an ill person seeks medical care, his doctor cannot require him to sign an exculpatory clause. In the same way, a person has to live somewhere. Her landlord cannot force her to sign a waiver.

Landlords tend to be wealthy and powerful. There is generally no equality of bargaining power between them. The tenants are not freely agreeing to the exculpatory language.

Moreover, if a landlord fails to maintain property, not just the tenant is at risk. Visitors, the mail carrier, and the general public could all walk through the Twin Lakes parking lot. The public's interest is served when landlords maintain their properties. They must be held liable when they negligently fail to maintain common areas and injuries result.

Argument for Landlord: Ms. Richards does indeed have to live somewhere, but she does not have to live on the plaintiff's property. Surely there are many dozens of properties nearby. If Richards had been dissatisfied with any part of the proposed lease—excessive rent, strict rules, or an exculpatory clause—she was free to take her business to another landlord.

Landlords may generally be wealthier than their tenants, but that fact alone does not mean that a landlord is so powerful that leases are offered on a "take it or leave it" basis. Here, the landlord stated the exculpatory clause plainly. This is a clear contract between adults, and it should stand in its entirety.

Bailment Cases

Bailment
Giving possession and control of personal property to another person.

Bailor
One who creates a bailment by delivering goods to another.

Bailee
A person who rightfully possesses goods belonging to another.

Exculpatory clauses are very common in bailment cases. **Bailment** means giving possession and control of personal property to another person. The person giving up possession is the **bailor**, and the one accepting possession is the **bailee**. When you leave your laptop computer with a dealer to be repaired, you create a bailment. The same is true when you check your coat at a restaurant or lend your Matisse to a museum. Bailees often try to limit their liability for damage to property by using an exculpatory clause.

Judges are slightly more apt to enforce an exculpatory clause in a bailment case because any harm is to *property* and not persons. But courts will still look at many of the same criteria we have just examined to decide whether a bailment contract is enforceable. In particular, when the bailee is engaged in an important public service, a court is once again likely to ignore the exculpatory clause. The following contrasting cases illustrate this.

In *Weiss v. Freeman,*[5] Weiss stored personal goods in Freeman's self-storage facility. Freeman's contract included an exculpatory clause relieving it of any and all liability. Weiss's goods were damaged by mildew, and she sued. The court held the exculpatory clause valid. The court considered self-storage to be a significant business, but not as vital as medical care or housing. It pointed out that a storage facility would not know what each customer stored and therefore could not anticipate the harm that might occur. Freedom of contract should prevail, the clause was enforceable, and Weiss got no money.

But in *Gardner v. Downtown Porsche Audi,*[6] Gardner left his Porsche 911 at Downtown for repairs. He signed an exculpatory clause saying that Downtown was "Not Responsible for Loss or Damage to Cars or Articles Left in Cars in Case of Fire, Theft, or Any Other Cause Beyond Our Control." Due to Downtown's negligence, Gardner's Porsche was stolen. The court held the exculpatory clause void. It ruled that contemporary society is utterly dependent upon automobile transportation and Downtown was therefore in a business of great

[5]1994 Tenn. App. LEXIS 393 (Tenn. Ct. App. 1993).
[6]180 Cal. App. 3d 713, 225 Cal. Rptr. 757, 1986 Cal. App. LEXIS 1542 (Cal. Ct. App. 1986).

public importance. No repair shop should be able to contract away liability, and Gardner won. (This case also illustrates that using 17 uppercase letters in one sentence does not guarantee legal victory.)

EXAM Strategy

Facts: Shauna flew a World War II fighter aircraft as a member of an exhibition flight team. While the team was performing in a delta formation, another plane collided with Shauna's aircraft, causing her to crash-land and leaving her permanently disabled. Shauna sued the other pilot and the team. The defendants moved to dismiss based on an exculpatory clause that Shauna had signed. The clause was one paragraph long, and it stated that Shauna knew team flying was inherently dangerous and could result in injury or death. She agreed not to hold the team or any members liable in case of an accident. Shauna argued that the clause should not be enforced against her if she could prove the other pilot was negligent. Please rule.

Strategy: The issue is whether the exculpatory clause is valid. Courts are likely to declare such clauses void if they concern vital activities like medical care, exclude an intentional tort or gross negligence, or if the parties had unequal bargaining power.

Result: This is a clear, short clause, between parties with equal bargaining power, and does not exclude an intentional tort or gross negligence. The activity is unimportant to the public welfare. The clause is valid. Even if the other pilot was negligent, Shauna will lose, meaning the court should dismiss her lawsuit.

Unconscionable Contracts

Gail Waters was young, naive, and insecure. A serious injury when she was 12 years old left her with an annuity, that is, a guaranteed annual payment for many years. When Gail was 21, she became involved with Thomas Beauchemin, an ex-convict, who introduced her to drugs. Beauchemin suggested that Gail sell her annuity to some friends of his, and she agreed. Beauchemin arranged for a lawyer to draw up a contract, and Gail signed it. She received $50,000 for her annuity, which at that time had a cash value of $189,000 and was worth, over its remaining 25 years, $694,000. Gail later decided this was not a wise bargain. Was the contract enforceable? That depends on the law of unconscionability.

An unconscionable contract is one that a court refuses to enforce because of fundamental unfairness. Even if a contract does not violate any specific statute or public policy, it may still be void if it "shocks the conscience" of the court.

Historically, a contract was considered unconscionable if it was "such as no man in his senses and not under delusion would make on the one hand, and as no honest and fair man would accept on the other."[7] The two factors that most often led a court to find unconscionability were (1) **oppression**, meaning that one party used its superior power to force a

Oppression
One party uses its superior power to force a contract on the weaker party.

[7] *Hume v. United States,* 132 U.S. 406, 411, 10 S.Ct. 134, 1889 U.S. LEXIS 1888 (1889), quoting *Earl of Chesterfield v. Janssen,* 38 Eng. Rep. 82, 100 (Ch. 1750).

contract on the weaker party, and (2) **surprise**, meaning that the weaker party did not fully understand the consequences of its agreement.

These cases have always been controversial because it is not easy to define oppression and unfair surprise. Further, anytime a court rejects a contract as unconscionable, it diminishes freedom of contract. If one party can escape a deal based on something as hard to define as unconscionability, then no one can rely as confidently on any agreement. As an English jurist said in 1824, "public policy is a very unruly horse, and when once you get astride it, you never know where it will carry you."[8]

Gail Waters won her case. The Massachusetts high court ruled:

> Beauchemin introduced the plaintiff to drugs, exhausted her credit card accounts to the sum of $6,000, unduly influenced her, suggested that the plaintiff sell her annuity contract, initiated the contract negotiations, was the agent of the defendants, and benefited from the contract between the plaintiff and the defendants. The defendants were represented by legal counsel; the plaintiff was not. The cash value of the annuity policy at the time the contract was executed was approximately four times greater than the price to be paid by the defendants. For payment of not more than $50,000 the defendants were to receive an asset that could be immediately exchanged for $189,000, or they could elect to hold it for its guaranteed term and receive $694,000.
>
> The defendants assumed no risk and the plaintiff gained no advantage. We are satisfied that the disparity of interests in this contract is so gross that the court cannot resist the inference that it was improperly obtained and is unconscionable.[9]

Adhesion Contracts

Adhesion contracts
Standard form contracts prepared by one party and presented to the other on a "take it or leave it" basis.

A related issue concerns **adhesion contracts**, which are standard form contracts prepared by one party and given to the other on a "take it or leave it" basis. We have all encountered them many times when purchasing goods or services. When a form contract is vigorously negotiated between equally powerful corporations, the resulting bargain is generally enforced. However, when the contract is simply presented to a consumer who has no ability to bargain, it is an adhesion contract and subject to an unconscionability challenge.

Worldwide Insurance v. Klopp

603 A.2d 788, 1992 Del. LEXIS 13
Supreme Court of Delaware, 1992

Facts: Ruth Klopp had auto insurance with Worldwide. She was injured in a serious accident that left her with permanent neck and back injuries. The other driver was uninsured, so Klopp filed a claim with Worldwide under her "uninsured motorist" coverage. Her policy required arbitration of such a claim, and the arbitrators awarded Klopp $90,000. But the policy also stated that if the arbitrators awarded more than the statutory minimum amount of insurance ($15,000), either side could appeal the award and request a full trial. Worldwide appealed and demanded a trial.

In the trial court, Klopp claimed that the appeal provision was unconscionable and void. The trial court agreed and entered judgment for the full $90,000. Worldwide appealed.

Issue: ***Is the provision that requires arbitration and then permits appeal by either party void as unconscionable?***

---

[8] *Richardson v. Mellish*, 2 Bing. 229, 103 Eng. Rep. 294, 303 (1824).

[9] *Waters v. Min Ltd.*, 412 Mass. 64, 587 N.E.2d 231, 1992 Mass. LEXIS 66 (1992).

Excerpts from Justice Walsh's Decision: The parties' views of the arbitration provision are polar opposites. Worldwide contends that the provision is a clear and unambiguous contractual undertaking granting both the insured and the insurer the right to appeal any award in excess of financial responsibility limits. Klopp argues that this provision is unconscionable and void as against public policy because it affords an advantage to one of the parties under a contract of adhesion.

The public policy of this State favors the resolution of disputes through arbitration. An insurance policy which provides for arbitration as its primary mechanism for dispute resolution is thus enforceable against the wishes of either contractual party. [But] our approval of the arbitration concept does not extend to any feature of a contract of adhesion, which, in whole or in part, is unconscionable.

Under the present policy language, both parties are bound by a low award which an insurance company is unlikely to appeal. While high awards may be appealed by either party, common experience suggests that it is unlikely that an insured would appeal such an award. It is the insurer who, generally, would be dissatisfied with a high award. The policy provision thus presents an "escape hatch" to the insurer for avoidance of high arbitration awards, whether or not the award was fair and reasonable. However, the insured, who would tend to be dissatisfied with a low award, is barred from appealing such an award, i.e., an award under [$15,000].

In our view, the policy provision at issue here promotes litigation, circumvents the arbitration process, and provides an arbitration escape device in favor of an insurance company. So viewed, the provision is contrary to the public policy of this State. Accordingly, we hold that a provision in an insurance policy which allows either party to demand a trial de novo, if the amount of an arbitrators' award exceeds a stated minimum amount but denies review for lesser awards, is void as against public policy and unenforceable. The Chancery Court was correct in striking this unconscionable clause.

The judgment of the Court of Chancery is *affirmed.*

The UCC: Unconscionability and Sales Law

With the creation of the Uniform Commercial Code (UCC), the law of unconscionability got a boost. The Code explicitly adopts unconscionability as a reason to reject a contract.[10] Although the Code directly applies only to the sale of goods, its unconscionability section has proven to be influential in other cases as well, and courts today are more receptive than they were 100 years ago to a contract defense of fundamental unfairness.

The drafters of the UCC reinforced the principle of unconscionability by including it in §2-302:

> If the court as a matter of law finds the contract or any clause of the contract to have been unconscionable at the time it was made the court may refuse to enforce the contract, or it may enforce the remainder of the contract without the unconscionable clause, or it may so limit the application of any unconscionable clause as to avoid any unconscionable result.

In Code cases, the issue of unconscionability often arises when a company attempts to limit the normal contract law remedies. Yet the Code itself allows such limitations, provided they are reasonable.

Section 2-719 provides in part:

> [A contract] may provide for remedies in addition to or in substitution for those provided [by the Code itself] *and may limit or alter the measure of damages recoverable* … as by limiting the buyer's remedies to return of the goods and repayment of the price …

In other words, the Code includes two potentially competing sections: §2-719 permits a seller to insist that the buyer's only remedy for defective goods is return of the purchase

[10]UCC §2-302.

price, but §2-302 says that *any unconscionable* provision is unenforceable. In lawsuits concerning defective goods, the seller often argues that the buyer's only remedies are those stated in the agreement, and the buyer responds that the contract limitation is unconscionable.

Electronic Data Systems (EDS) agreed to create complex software for Chubb Life America at a cost of $21 million. Chubb agreed to make staggered payments over many months as the work proceeded. The contract included a limitation on remedies, stating that if EDS became liable to Chubb, its maximum liability would be equal to two monthly payments.

EDS's work was woefully late and unusable, forcing Chubb to obtain its software elsewhere. Chubb sued, claiming $40 million in damages based on the money paid to EDS and additional funds spent purchasing alternative goods. EDS argued that the contract limited its liability to two monthly payments, a fraction of Chubb's damage. Chubb, of course, responded that the limitation was unconscionable.

The court noted that both parties were large, sophisticated corporations. As they negotiated the agreement, the companies both used experienced attorneys and independent consultants. This was no contract of adhesion presented to a meek consumer, but an allocation of risk resulting from hard bargaining. The court declared that the clause was valid, and EDS owed no more than two monthly payments.[11]

Chapter Conclusion

It is not enough to bargain effectively and obtain a contract that gives you exactly what you want. You must also be sure that the contract is legal. What appears to be an insurance contract might legally be an invalid wager. Unintentionally forgetting to obtain a state license to perform a certain job could mean you will never be paid for it. Bargaining a contract with a noncompete or exculpatory clause that is too one-sided may lead a court to ignore it. Legality is multifaceted, sometimes subtle, and always important.

EXAM REVIEW

Illegal contracts are void and unenforceable. Illegality most often arises in these settings:

1. **WAGERING** A purely speculative contract—whether for gambling or insurance—is likely to be unenforceable. (pp. 296–297)

2. **LICENSING** When the licensing statute is designed to protect the public, a contract by an unlicensed plaintiff is generally unenforceable. When such a statute is designed merely to raise revenue, a contract by an unlicensed plaintiff is generally enforceable. (pp. 297–298)

[11] *Colonial Life Insurance Co. v. Electronic Data Systems Corp.*, 817 F. Supp. 235, 1993 U.S. Dist. LEXIS 4123 (D.N.H. 1993).

EXAM Strategy

Question: James Wagner agreed to build a house for Nancy Graham. Wagner was not licensed as a contractor, and Graham knew it. When the house was finished, Graham refused to pay the final $23,000, and Wagner sued. Who will prevail?

Strategy: A licensing statute designed to protect the public is strictly enforced, but that is not true for one intended only to raise revenue. What was the purpose of this statute? (See the "Result" at the end of this section.)

3. **USURY** Excessive interest is generally unenforceable and may be fatal to the entire debt. Credit card debt is often exempt from usury laws. (pp. 299–300)

EXAM Strategy

Question: McElroy owned 104 acres worth about $230,000. He got into financial difficulties and approached Grisham, asking to borrow $100,000. Grisham refused, but ultimately the two reached this agreement: McElroy would sell Grisham his property for $80,000, and the contract would include a clause allowing McElroy to repurchase the land within two years for $120,000. McElroy later claimed the contract was void. Is he right?

Strategy: Loans involving usury do not always include a clearly visible interest rate. You may have to do some simple math to see the interest being charged. McElroy wanted to borrow $100,000, but instead sold his property, with the right to repurchase. If he did repurchase, how much interest would he have effectively paid? (See the "Result" at the end of this section.)

4. **NONCOMPETE** A noncompete clause in the sale of a business must be limited to a reasonable time, geographic area, and scope of activity. In an employment contract, such a clause is considered reasonable—and enforceable—only to protect trade secrets, confidential information, and customer lists. (pp. 301–304)

EXAM Strategy

Question: The purchaser of a business insisted on putting this clause in the sales contract: The seller would not compete, for five years, "anywhere in the United States, the continent of North America, or anywhere else on earth." What danger does that contract represent *to the purchaser?*

Strategy: This is a noncompete clause based on the sale of a business. Such clauses are valid if reasonable. Is this clause reasonable? If it is unreasonable, what might a court do? (See the "Result" at the end of this section.)

5. **EXCULPATORY CLAUSES** These clauses are generally void if the activity involved is in the public interest, the parties are greatly unequal in bargaining power, or the clause is unclear. In other cases, they are generally enforced. (pp. 304–307)

6. **UNCONSCIONABILITY** Oppression and surprise may create an unconscionable bargain. An adhesion contract is especially suspect when it is imposed by a corporation on a consumer or small company. Under the UCC, a limitation of liability is less likely to be unconscionable when both parties are sophisticated corporations. (pp. 307–310)

2. Result: This statute was designed to protect the public. Wagner was unlicensed and cannot enforce the contract. Graham wins.

3. Result: By selling at $80,000 and repurchasing at $120,000, McElroy would be paying $40,000 in interest on an $80,000 loan. The 50 percent rate is usurious. The court prohibited Graham from collecting the interest.

4. Result: "Anywhere else on earth"? This is almost certainly unreasonable. It is hard to imagine a purchaser who would legitimately need such wide-ranging protection. In some states, a court might rewrite the clause, limiting the effect to the seller's state, or some reasonable area. However, in other states, a court finding a clause unreasonable will declare it void in its entirety—enabling the seller to open a competing business next door.

MULTIPLE-CHOICE QUESTIONS

1. At a fraternity party, George mentions that he is going to learn to hang-glide during spring break. Vicki, a casual friend, overhears him, and the next day she purchases a $100,000 life insurance policy on George's life. George has a happy week of hang-gliding. But on the way home, he is bitten by a parrot and dies of a rare tropical illness. Vicki files a claim for $100,000. The insurance company refuses to pay.
   (a) Vicki will win $100,000, but only if she mentioned animal bites to the insurance agent.
   (b) Vicki will win $100,000 regardless of whether she mentioned animal bites to the insurance agent.
   (c) Vicki will win $50,000.
   (d) Vicki will win nothing.

2. Now assume that Vicky has loaned George $50,000. George again mentions that he is going to learn to hang-glide during spring break, so Vicki purchases the $100,000 life insurance policy on George's life. If George dies and the insurance company refuses to pay...
   (a) Vicki will win $100,000, but only if she mentioned animal bites to the insurance agent.
   (b) Vicki will win $100,000 regardless of whether she mentioned animal bites to the insurance agent.
   (c) Vicki will win $50,000.
   (d) Vicki will win nothing.

3. KwikFix, a Fortune 500 company, contracts with Allied Rocket, another huge company, to provide the software for Allied's new Jupiter Probe rocket for

$14 million. The software is negligently designed, and when the rocket blasts off from Cape Kennedy, it travels only as far as Fort Lauderdale before crashing to Earth. Allied Rocket sues for $200 million and proves that as a result of the disaster, it lost a huge government contract, worth at least that much, which KwikFix was aware of. KwikFix responds that its contract with Allied included a clause limiting its liability to the value of the contract. Is the contract clause valid?

(a) The clause is unenforceable because it is unconscionable.

(b) The clause is unenforceable because it is exculpatory.

(c) The clause is enforceable because both parties are sophisticated corporations.

(d) The clause is enforceable because $200 million is an unconscionable claim.

4. Ricki goes to a baseball game. The back of her ticket clearly reads: "Fan agrees to hold team blameless for all injuries—pay attention to the game at all times for your own safety!" In the first inning, a foul ball hits Ricki in the elbow. She __________ sue the team over the foul ball. Ricki spends the next several innings riding the opposing team's first baseman. The *nicest* thing she says to him is, "You suck, Franklin!" In the eighth inning, Franklin has had enough. He grabs the ballboy's chair and throws it into the stands, injuring Ricki's other elbow. Ricki __________ sue the team over the thrown chair.

(a) can; can

(b) can; cannot

(c) cannot; can

(d) cannot; cannot

5. Jim, about to start a pickup soccer game, asks Desiree if she will hold his wallet while he plays. Desiree, a law student, says, "Sure, if you'll sign this exculpatory clause holding me blameless for negligence." Jim is very surprised, but he signs the paper that Desiree holds out for him. A bailment __________ been created. If Desiree is careless and loses the wallet, she __________ be liable to Jim.

(a) has; will

(b) has; will not

(c) has not; will

(d) has not; will not

Essay Questions

1. For 20 years, Art's Flower Shop relied almost exclusively on advertising in the yellow pages to bring business to its shop in a small West Virginia town. One year, the yellow pages printer accidentally did not print Art's ad, and Art's suffered an enormous drop in business. Art's sued for negligence and won a judgment of $50,000 from the jury, but the printing company appealed, claiming that under an exculpatory clause in the contract, the company could not be liable to Art's for more than the cost of the ad, about $910. Art's claimed that the exculpatory clause was unconscionable. Please rule.

2. Brockwell left his boat to be repaired at Lake Gaston Sales. The boat contained electronic equipment and other personal items. Brockwell signed a form stating that Lake Gaston had no responsibility for any loss to any property in or on the boat. Brockwell's electronic equipment was stolen and other personal items were damaged, and he sued. Is the exculpatory clause enforceable?

3. Guyan Machinery, a West Virginia manufacturing corporation, hired Albert Voorhees as a salesman and required him to sign a contract stating that if he left Guyan, he would not work for a competing corporation anywhere within 250 miles of West Virginia for a two-year period. Later, Voorhees left Guyan and began working at Polydeck Corp., another West Virginia manufacturer. The only product Polydeck made was urethane screens, which comprised half of 1 percent of Guyan's business. Is Guyan entitled to enforce its noncompete clause?

4. 810 Associates owned a 42-story skyscraper in midtown Manhattan. The building had a central station fire alarm system, which was monitored by Holmes Protection. A fire broke out and Holmes received the signal. But Holmes's inexperienced dispatcher misunderstood the signal and failed to summon the fire department for about nine minutes, permitting tremendous damage. 810 sued Holmes, which defended based on an exculpatory clause that relieved Holmes of any liability caused in any way. Holmes's dispatcher was negligent. Does it matter *how* negligent he was?

5. ***YOU BE THE JUDGE* WRITING PROBLEM** Oasis Waterpark, located in Palm Springs, California, sought out Hydrotech Systems, Inc., a New York corporation, to design and construct a surfing pool. Hydrotech replied that it could design the pool and sell all the necessary equipment to Oasis, but it could not build the pool because it was not licensed in California. Oasis insisted that Hydrotech do the construction work because Hydrotech had unique expertise in these pools. Oasis promised to arrange for a licensed California contractor to "work with" Hydrotech on the construction; Oasis also assured Hydrotech that it would pay the full contract price of $850,000, regardless of any licensing issues. Hydrotech designed and installed the pool as ordered. But Oasis failed to make the final payment of $110,000. Hydrotech sued. Can Hydrotech sue for either breach of contract or fraud (trickery)? **Argument for Oasis:** The licensing law protects the public from incompetence and dishonesty. The legislature made the section strict: no license, no payment. If the court were to start picking and choosing which unlicensed contractors could win a suit, it would be inviting incompetent workers to endanger the public and then come into court and try their luck. That is precisely the danger the legislature seeks to avoid. **Argument for Hydrotech:** This is not the kind of case the legislature was worried about. Hydrotech has never solicited work in California. Hydrotech went out of its way to avoid doing any contracting work, informing Oasis that it was unlicensed in the state. Oasis insisted on bringing Hydrotech into the state to do work. If Oasis has its way, word will go out that any owner can get free work done by hiring an *unlicensed* builder. Make any promises you want, get the work done to your satisfaction, and then stiff the contractor—you'll never have to pay.

Discussion Questions

1. ***ETHICS:*** Richard and Michelle Kommit traveled to New Jersey to have fun in the casinos. While in Atlantic City, they used their MasterCard to withdraw cash from an ATM conveniently located in the "pit"—the gambling area of a casino. They ran up debts of $5,500 on the credit card and did not pay. The Connecticut National Bank sued for the money. Law aside, who has the moral high ground? Is it acceptable for the *casino* to offer ATM services in the gambling pit? If a *credit card* company allows customers to withdraw cash in a casino, is it encouraging them to lose money? Do *the Kommits* have any ethical right to use the ATM, attempt to win money by gambling, and then seek to avoid liability?

2. The Justice Department recently shut down three of the most popular online poker websites (Poker Stars, Absolute Poker, and Full Tilt Poker). State agencies take countless actions each year to stop illegal gaming operations. Do you believe that gambling by adults *should* be regulated? If so, which types? Rate the following types of gambling from most acceptable to least acceptable:

- online poker	- state lotteries	- horse racing
- casino gambling	- bets on pro sports	- bets on college sports

3. Van hires Terri to add an electrical outlet to his living room for his new HDTV. Terri does an excellent job, and the new outlet works perfectly. She presents Van with a bill for $200. But Terri is not a licensed electrician. Her state sets licensing standards in the profession to protect the public. And so, Van can refuse to pay Terri's bill. Is this reasonable? *Should* he be able to avoid payment?

4. Should noncompete agreements in employment contracts be illegal altogether? Is there equality of bargaining power between the company and the employee? Should non-competes be limited to top officers of a company? Would you be upset if a prospective employer asked *you* to agree to a one year covenant not to compete?

5. Revisit the Gail Waters example on page **[307]**. Imagine now that Beauchemin was not her boyfriend, and that he had not introduced her to the drugs to which she became addicted. If all other facts in the case remain the same, would the purchase of the annuity for $50,000 still be unconscionable, in your opinion?

CHAPTER 14

VOIDABLE CONTRACTS: CAPACITY AND CONSENT

Katie, age 17, visits her local electronics store to buy a new laptop. At the register, she pays $400 in cash for the machine. No one is with her, and the cashier does not ask her to show her ID.

Out in the parking lot, Katie's cell phone rings. As she fumbles for it, she loses her grip on the new laptop. It falls to the pavement—crack!—bounces once, and comes to rest a few feet away from her.

Just then, an H2 Hummer rounds the corner. It runs over Katie's new laptop. "Ugg …" she says, feeling nauseous. The SUV stops, and the reverse lights come on. It backs slowly over the laptop again. The driver, oblivious, rolls down his window and asks Katie, "Say, is there a gas station around here?"

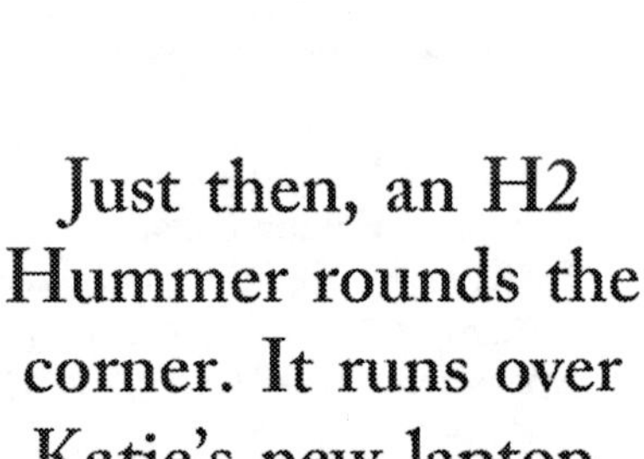
Just then, an H2 Hummer rounds the corner. It runs over Katie's new laptop.

"Ah … that way," a shocked Katie says, pointing to a sign in the distance. "But you just …"

"Oh, I see it! Thanks a million!" The driver puts the Hummer in gear and drives over the laptop a third time. The small jolt loosens the one lug nut securing the spare tire to the back of the SUV. The heavy spare falls directly on top of what remains of Katie's new laptop.

Scooping up wires, bits of plastic, and pieces of metal, she goes back inside the store. Dumping the pieces on the customer service desk, she says, "I've changed my mind about this computer."

The clerk looks at the collection of laptop parts, shakes his head, and points to a sign behind him. "Look, I can't take merchandise back if it's damaged. And this laptop is, ah, damaged."

"Too bad," Katie says. " I want my money back. Now."

Is Katie entitled to a full refund? In most states, *yes*.

This chapter examines **voidable contracts**. When a contract is voidable, one party has the option either to enforce or terminate the agreement. Two specific issues are presented.

Capacity concerns the legal ability of a party to enter a contract in the first place. Someone may lack capacity because of his young age or mental infirmity. **Consent** refers to whether a contracting party truly understood what she was getting into and whether she made the agreement voluntarily. Consent issues arise in cases of fraud, mistake, duress, and undue influence.

Capacity

Capacity is the legal ability to enter into a contract. An adult of sound mind has capacity. Generally, any deal she enters into will be enforced if all elements on the Contracts Checklist—agreement, consideration, and so forth—are present. But two groups of people usually lack legal capacity: minors and those with a mental impairment.

Contracts Checklist

- ☐ Offer
- ☐ Acceptance
- ☐ Consideration
- ☐ Legality
- ☑ Capacity
- ☐ Consent
- ☐ Writing

Minors

In contract law, a minor is someone under the age of 18. Because a minor lacks legal capacity, she normally can create only a voidable contract. **A voidable contract may be canceled by the party who lacks capacity.** Notice that *only the party lacking capacity* may cancel the agreement. So a minor who enters into a contract generally may choose between enforcing the agreement or negating it. The other party—an adult, or perhaps a store—has no such right. Voidable contracts are very different from those that are void, which we examined in Chapter 13, on legality. A *void* contract is illegal from the beginning and may not be enforced by either party. A *voidable* contract is legal but permits one party to escape, if she so wishes.

Disaffirmance

A minor who wishes to escape from a contract generally may **disaffirm** it; that is, he may notify the other party that he refuses to be bound by the agreement. There are several ways a minor may disaffirm a contract. He may simply tell the other party, orally or in writing, that he will not honor the deal. Or he may disaffirm a contract by refusing to perform his obligations under it. A minor may go further—he can undo a contract that has already been completed by filing a suit to **rescind** the contract; that is, to have a court formally cancel it.

Disaffirm
To give notice of refusal to be bound by an agreement.

Rescind
To cancel a contract.

Kevin Green was 16 when he signed a contract with Star Chevrolet to buy a used Camaro. Because he was a minor, the deal was voidable. When the Camaro blew a gasket and Kevin informed Star Chevrolet that he wanted his money back, he was disaffirming the contract. He happened to do it because the car suddenly seemed a poor buy, but he could have disaffirmed for any reason at all, such as deciding that he no longer liked Camaros. When Kevin disaffirmed, he was entitled to his money back.

Restitution

A minor who disaffirms a contract must return the consideration he has received, to the extent he is able. Restoring the other party to its original position is called **restitution**. The consideration that Kevin Green received in the contract was, of course, the Camaro.

Restitution
Restoring an injured party to its original position.

What happens if the minor is not able to return the consideration because he no longer has it or it has been destroyed? Most states hold that the minor is *still* entitled to his money back. A minority of states follow the **status quo rule**, which provides that, if a minor cannot return the consideration, the adult or store is only required to return its *profit margin* to the minor.

In the opening scenario, Katie attempted to return a destroyed laptop for the full purchase price of $400. Assume that the store paid a computer manufacturer $350 for the laptop and then marked it up $50.

In most states, Katie would be entitled to the full $400 purchase price, even though the laptop is now worthless. The sign at the customer service desk would have no effect, and the store would have to absorb the loss. But, if Katie lives in a state with the status quo rule, then the store will have to refund only $50 to Katie. It is permitted to keep the other $350 so that it breaks even on the transaction, or is "returned to the status quo."

Ethics The rule permitting a minor to disaffirm a contract is designed to discourage adults from making deals with innocent children, and it is centuries old. Is this rule still workable in our modern consumer society? There are entire industries devoted to (and dependent upon) minors. Think of children's films, music, sneakers, and toys. Does this rule imperil retailers? Is it *right* to give a 17-year-old high school senior so much power to cancel agreements? In the opening scenario, is it reasonable for Katie to seek a full refund, or is she taking advantage of the system?

Timing of Disaffirmance/Ratification

A minor may disaffirm a contract anytime before she reaches age 18. She also may disaffirm within a reasonable time *after* turning 18. Suppose that 17-year-old Betsy signs a contract to buy a $3,000 stereo. The following week, she picks up the system and pays for it in full. Four months later, she turns 18, and two months after that, she disaffirms the contract. Her disaffirmance is effective. In most states, she gets 100 percent of her money back. In some cases, minors have been entitled to disaffirm a contract several *years* after turning 18. But the minor's right to disaffirm ends if she ratifies the contract. **Ratification** is made by any words or action indicating an intention to be bound by the contract. Suppose Betsy, age 17, buys her stereo on credit, promising to pay $150 per month. She has made only four payments by the time she turns 18, but after reaching her majority, she continues to pay every month for six more months. Then she attempts to disaffirm. Too late. Her actions—payment of the monthly bill for six months as an adult—ratified the contract she entered into as a minor. She is now fully obligated to pay the entire $3,000, on the agreed-upon schedule.

Ratification
Words or actions indicating an intention to be bound by a contract.

Exception: Necessaries

A necessary is something essential to the minor's life and welfare. **On a contract for necessaries, a minor must pay for the value of the benefit received.** In other words, the minor may still disaffirm the contract and return whatever is unused. But he is liable to pay for whatever benefit he obtained from the goods while he had them. Food, clothing, housing, and medical care are necessaries. Thus a 16-year-old who buys and eats a 99-cent cheeseburger cannot later seek his 99 cents from the fast food restaurant.

Exception: Misrepresentation of Age

The rules change somewhat if a minor lies about his age. Sixteen-year-old Dan is delighted to learn from his friend Betsy that a minor can buy a fancy stereo system, use it for a year or so, and then get his money back. Dan drops into SoundBlast and asks to buy a $4,000 surround-sound system. The store clerk says that the store no longer sells expensive systems to underage customers. Dan produces a fake driver's license indicating that he is 18, and the clerk sells him the system. A year later, Dan drives up to SoundBlast and unloads the system, now in shambles. He asks for his $4,000 back. Is he still permitted to disaffirm?

States have been troubled by this problem, and there is no clear rule. A few states will still permit Dan to disaffirm the contract entirely. The theory is that a minor must be saved from his own poor judgment, including his foolish lie. Many states, though, will prohibit Dan from disaffirming the contract. They take the reasonable position that the law was intended to protect childhood innocence, not calculated deceit.

Mentally Impaired Persons

You are a trial court judge. Don wants you to rule that his father, Cedric, is mentally incompetent and, on behalf of Cedric, to terminate a contract he signed. Here is the evidence:

Cedric is a 75-year-old millionaire who keeps $300,000 stuffed in pillow cases in the attic. He lives in a filthy house with a parrot whom he calls the Bishop, an iguana named Orlando, and a tortoise known as Mrs. Sedgely. All of the pets have small beds in Cedric's grungy bedroom, and each one eats at the dining table with its master. Cedric pays college students $50 an hour to read poetry to the animals, but he forbids the reading of sonnets, which he regards as "the devil's handiwork."

Don has been worried about Cedric's bizarre behavior for several years and has urged his father to enter a nursing home. Last week, when Don stopped in to visit, Cedric became angry at him, accusing his son of disrespecting the Bishop and Mrs. Sedgely, who were enjoying a 15th-century Castilian poem that Jane, a college student, was reading. Don then blurted out that Cedric was no longer able to take care of himself. Cedric snapped back, "I'll show you how capable I am." On the back of a 40-year-old menu, he scratched out a contract promising to give Jane "$100,000 today and $200,000 one year from today if she agrees to feed, house, and care for the Bishop, Orlando, and Mrs. Sedgely for the rest of their long lives." Jane *quickly* signed the agreement. Don urges that the court, on Cedric's behalf, declare the contract void. How will you rule? Courts often struggle when deciding cases of mental competence.

A person suffers from a mental impairment if, by reason of mental illness or defect, he is unable to understand the nature and consequences of the transaction.[1] The mental impairment can be due to some mental illness, such as schizophrenia, or to mental retardation, brain injury, senility, or any other cause that renders the person unable to understand the nature and consequences of the contract.

A party suffering a mental impairment usually creates only a voidable contract. The impaired person has the right to disaffirm the contract just as a minor does. But again, the contract is voidable, not void. The mentally impaired party generally has the right to full performance if she wishes.

The law creates an exception: if a person has been adjudicated insane, then all of his future agreements are void. "Adjudicated insane" means that a judge has made a formal finding that a person is mentally incompetent and has assigned the person a guardian.

How will a court evaluate Cedric's mental status? Of course, if there had already been a judicial determination that he was insane, any contract he signed would be void. Since no judge has issued such a ruling about Cedric, the court will listen to doctors or therapists who have evaluated him and to anyone else who can testify about Cedric's recent conduct. The court may also choose to look at the contract itself, to see if it is so lopsided that no competent person would agree to it.

[1]Restatement (Second) of Contracts §15.

How will Don fare in seeking to preserve Cedric's wealth? Poorly. Unless Don has more evidence than we have heard thus far, he is destined to eat canned tuna while Jane and the Bishop dine on caviar. Cedric is decidedly eccentric, and perhaps unwise. But those characteristics do not prove mental impairment. Neither does leaving a fortune to a poetry reader. If Don could produce evidence from a psychiatrist that Cedric, for example, was generally delusional or could not distinguish a parrot from a religious leader, that would persuade a court of mental impairment. But on the evidence presented thus far, Mrs. Sedgely and friends will be living well.[2]

Intoxication

Similar rules apply in cases of drug or alcohol intoxication. When one party is so intoxicated that he cannot understand the nature and consequences of the transaction, the contract is voidable.

We wish to stress that courts are *highly* skeptical of intoxication arguments. If you go out drinking and make a foolish agreement, you are probably stuck with it. Even if you are too drunk to drive, you are probably not nearly too drunk to make a contract. If your blood alcohol level is, say, .08, your coordination and judgment are poor. Driving in such a condition is dangerous. But you probably have a fairly clear awareness of what is going on around you.

Upon the question of his intoxication, he was corroborated abundantly.

To back out of a contract on the grounds of intoxication, you must be able to provide evidence that you did not understand the "nature of the agreement," or the basic deal that you made.

The following landmark case is a rare exception, and the defendant was able to escape the deal. The defendant had lots of witnesses who testified that he had no idea what he was doing.

[2]For a similar case, see *Harwell v. Garrett,* 239 Ark. 551, 393 S.W.2d 256, 1965 Ark. LEXIS 1033 (1965).

Landmark Case

Babcock v. Engel

58 Mont. 597; 194 P. 137
Supreme Court of Montana, 1920

Facts: While Charles Engel's wife was out of town, he sat home alone, drinking mightily. During this period, he made an agreement with G. M. Babcock to trade a 320-acre farm and $2,000 worth of personal property for a hotel. Engel's property was worth approximately twice the value of the hotel. Engel later refused to honor the deal on the grounds that he had been intoxicated when he made the agreement. Babcock sued, but the jury sided with Engel and dismissed the complaint. Babcock appealed.

Issue: ***Was Engel so intoxicated that his agreement with Babcock became voidable?***

Excerpts from Justice Holloway's Decision: If, as a matter of fact, Engel was so far under the influence of intoxicating liquor when he signed the contract that he was incapable of giving his assent, it would be voidable at the election of Engel when he became sober.

[T]he jury answered that on November 22, Engel was "so under the influence of intoxicating liquors as to deprive him of his powers of reasoning and render him unable to comprehend the consequences of his act in executing said agreement."

Engel himself testified to the effect that, availing himself of his wife's absence from home, he had been indulging greatly to excess and had been drunk on November 21; that he drank heavily of whisky which he had at his home on the morning of November 22; that immediately upon his arrival in the town, he had four or five drinks of whisky and blackberry before he entered upon the negotiations with Babcock.

Four other witnesses, each apparently disinterested, testified that at the time in question, Engel was intoxicated, could not comprehend the nature of his acts, in other words, that he was not qualified to transact business. The jury determined upon the credibility of the witnesses.

Intoxication is not made a defense by the Codes, and there was a time in the history of our jurisprudence when courts refused to lend their aid to relieve one from the consequences of his own voluntary intemperance, but the doctrine has long since been abandoned. The courts do not now concern themselves so much with the question of intoxication as with the question of contractual capacity, and if in fact either party is not mentally capable of giving his free consent to the terms disclosed by the writing, it is altogether immaterial by what cause his incapacity was produced. The courts have simply recognized the fact that intoxication, among other things, may render a person incapable of making a binding contract.

The test approved by the great majority of the decisions is the same which is applied in other forms of mental derangement, namely, that the deed or contract will be voidable if the person, at the time of its execution, was so far under the influence of intoxicants as to be unable to understand the nature and consequences of his act, and unable to bring to bear upon the business in hand any degree of intelligent choice and purpose.

Affirmed.

Restitution

A mentally infirm party who seeks to void a contract must make restitution. If a party succeeds with a claim of mental impairment, the court will normally void the contract but will require the impaired party to give back whatever she got. Suppose Danielle buys a Rolls-Royce and promises in writing to pay $4,000 per month for five years. Three weeks later, she seeks to void the contract on the grounds of mental impairment. She must return the Rolls. If the car has depreciated, Danielle normally will have to pay for the decrease in value. What happens if restitution is impossible? Generally, courts require a mentally infirm person to make full restitution if the contract is to be rescinded. If restitution is impossible, the court will not rescind the agreement unless the infirm party can show bad faith by the other. This is because, unlike minority, which is generally easy to establish, mental competence may not be so apparent to the other person negotiating.

REALITY OF CONSENT

Smiley offers to sell you his house for $300,000, and you agree in writing to buy it. After you move in, you discover that the house is sinking into the earth at the rate of six inches per week. In twelve months, your only access to the house may be through the chimney. You sue, seeking to rescind. You argue that when you signed the contract, you did not truly consent because you lacked essential information. In this section we look at four claims that parties make in an effort to rescind a contract based on lack of valid consent: (1) fraud, (2) mistake, (3) duress, and (4) undue influence.

Fraud

Fraud begins when a party to a contract says something that is factually wrong. "This house has no termites," says a homeowner to a prospective buyer. If the house is swarming with the nasty pests, the statement is a misrepresentation. But does it amount to fraud? An injured person must show the following:

1. The defendant knew that his statement was false, or that he made the statement recklessly and without knowledge of whether it was false.
2. The false statement was material.
3. The injured party justifiably relied on the statement.

Element One: Intentional or Reckless Misrepresentation of Fact

The injured party must show a false statement of fact. Notice that this does not mean the statement was a necessarily a "lie." If a homeowner says that the famous architect Stanford White designed her house, but Bozo Loco actually did the work, it is a false statement.

Now, if the owner knows that Loco designed the house, she has committed the first element of fraud. And, if she has no idea who designed the house, her assertion that it was "Stanford White" also meets the first element.

But the owner might have a good reason for the error. Perhaps a local history book identifies the house as a Stanford White. If she makes the statement with a reasonable belief that she is telling the truth, she has made an innocent misrepresentation (discussed in the next section) and not fraud.

Opinions and "puffery" do not amount to fraud. An opinion is not a statement of fact. A seller says, "I think land values around here will be going up 20 or 30 percent for the foreseeable future." That statement is pretty enticing to a buyer, but it is not a false statement of fact. The maker is clearly stating her own opinion, and the buyer who relies on it does so at his peril. A close relative of opinion is something called "puffery."

Get ready for one of the most astonishing experiences you've ever had! This section on puffery is going to be the finest section of any textbook you have ever read! You're going to find the issue intriguing, the writing dazzling, and the legal summary unforgettable!

"But what happens," you might wonder, "if this section fails to astonish? What if I find the issue dull, the writing mediocre, and the legal summary incomprehensible? Can I sue for fraud?" No. The promises we made were mere puffery. A statement is puffery when a reasonable person would realize that it is a sales pitch, representing the exaggerated opinion of the seller. Puffery is not a statement of fact. Because puffery is not factual, it is never a basis for rescission.

Consumers filed a class action against Intel Corporation, claiming fraud. They asserted that Intel advertised its "Pentium 4" computer chip as the "best" in the market when in fact it was no faster than the Pentium III chip. The Illinois Supreme Court dismissed the claims, asserting that no reasonable consumer would make a purchase relying solely on the name "Pentium 4." Even if the consumers could show that Intel plotted to persuade the market that the Pentium 4 was the finest processor, they are demonstrating nothing but puffery.

[Saying that the Pentium 4 is "better" or "best"] could mean that the Pentium 4 is cheaper, smaller, more reliable, of higher quality, better for resale, more durable, creates less heat, uses less electricity, is more compatible with some versions of software, or is simply the latest in a temporal line of processors. Because the term "better" as a mere suggestion in the name "Pentium 4" is not capable of precise measuring, it is mere puffery and therefore not actionable. That is true even if Intel specifically set out to show the market that the Pentium 4 was the best processor to date.[3]

---

[3] *Barbara's Sales, Inc. v. Intel Corp.*, 879 N.E.2d 910 (Ill. 2007).

Courts have found many similar phrases to be puffery, including "high-quality," "expert workmanship," and "you're in good hands with us."

Element Two: Materiality

The injured party must demonstrate that the statement was material, or important. A minor misstatement does not meet this second element of fraud. Was the misstatement likely to influence the decision of the misled party significantly? If so, it was material.

Imagine a farmer selling a piece of his land. He measures the acres himself, and calculates a total of 200. If the actual acreage is 199, he has almost certainly not made a *material* misstatement. But if the actual acreage is 150, he has.

Element Three: Justifiable Reliance

The injured party also must show that she actually did rely on the false statement and that her reliance was reasonable. Suppose the seller of a gas station lies through his teeth about the structural soundness of the building. The buyer believes what he hears but does not much care because he plans to demolish the building and construct a day-care center. There was a material misstatement but no reliance, and the buyer may not rescind.

The reliance must be justifiable—that is, reasonable. If the seller of wilderness land tells Lewis that the area is untouched by pollution, but Lewis can see a large lake on the property covered with six inches of oily red scum, Lewis is not justified in relying on the seller's statements. If he goes forward with the purchase, he may not rescind.

No Duty to Investigate In the previous example, Lewis must act reasonably and keep his eyes open if he walks around the "wilderness" property. But he has no duty to undertake an investigation of what he is told. In other words, if the seller states that the countryside is pure and the lake looks crystal clear, Lewis is not obligated to take water samples and have them tested by a laboratory. A party to a contract has no obligation to investigate the other party's factual statements.

Plaintiff's Remedies for Fraud

In the case of fraud, the injured party generally has a choice of rescinding the contract or suing for damages or, in some cases, doing both. The contract is voidable, which meant that injured party is not *forced* to rescind the deal but may if he wants. Fraud *permits* the injured party to cancel. Alternatively, the injured party can sue for damages—the difference between what the contract promised and what it delivered.

Nancy learns that the building she bought has a terrible heating system. A new one will cost $12,000. If the seller told her the system was "like new," Nancy may rescind the deal. But it may be economically harmful for her to do so. She might have sold her old house, hired a mover, taken a new job, and so forth. What are her other remedies? She could move into the new house and sue for the difference between what she got and what was promised, which is $12,000, the cost of replacing the heating system.

In some states, a party injured by fraud may both rescind *and* sue for damages. In these states, Nancy could rescind her contract, get her deposit back, and then sue the seller for any damages she has suffered. Her damages might be, for example, a lost opportunity to buy another house or wasted moving expenses.

In fact, this last option—rescinding and still suing for damages—is available in all states when a contract is for the sale of goods. **UCC §2-721 permits a party to rescind a contract and then sue for damages when fraud is committed.**

Innocent Misrepresentation

If all elements of fraud are present except the misrepresentation of fact was not made intentionally or recklessly, then **innocent misrepresentation** has occurred. So, if a person misstates a material fact and induces reliance, but he had good reason to believe that his statement was true, then he has not committed fraud. Most states allow recission of a contract, but not damages, in such a case.

Special Problem: Silence

We know that a party negotiating a contract may not misrepresent a material fact. The house seller may not say that "the roof is in great shape" when she sleeps under an umbrella to avoid rain. But what about silence? Suppose the seller knows the roof is in dreadful condition but the buyer never asks. Does the seller have an affirmative obligation to disclose what she knows?

This is perhaps the hottest topic today in the law of misrepresentation. In 1817, the United States Supreme Court laid down the general rule that a party had no duty to disclose, even when he knew that the other person was negotiating under a mistake.[4] In other words, the Court was reinforcing the old rule of *caveat emptor*, "let the buyer beware." But social attitudes about fairness have changed. Today, a seller who knows something that the buyer does not know is often required to divulge it.

Nondisclosure of a fact amounts to misrepresentation in these four cases: (1) where disclosure is necessary to *correct a previous assertion;* (2) where disclosure would correct a *basic mistaken assumption* that the other party is relying on; (3) where disclosure would correct the other party's *mistaken understanding about a writing;* or (4) where there is *a relationship of trust* between the two parties.[5]

To Correct a Previous Assertion. During the course of negotiations, one party's perception of the facts may change. When an earlier statement later appears inaccurate, the change generally must be reported.

W. R. Grace & Co. wanted to buy a natural-gas field in Mississippi. An engineer's report indicated the presence of large gas reserves. On the basis of the engineering report, the Continental Illinois National Bank committed to a $75 million nonrecourse production loan. A "nonrecourse loan" meant that Continental would be repaid only with revenues from the gas field. After Continental committed, but before it had closed on the loan, Grace had an exploratory well drilled and struck it rich—with water. The land would never produce any gas. Without informing Continental of the news, Grace closed the $75 million loan. When Grace failed to repay, Continental sued and won. A party who learns new information indicating that a previous statement is inaccurate must disclose the bad news.[6]

> She also knew that a reasonable buyer might avoid a haunted house, fearing grisly events …

To Correct a Basic Mistaken Assumption. When one party knows that the other is negotiating with a mistaken assumption about an important fact, the party who knows of the error must correct it. Jeffrey Stambovsky agreed to buy Helen Ackley's house in Nyack, New York, for $650,000. Stambovsky signed a contract and made a $32,500 down payment.

---

[4]*Laidlaw v. Organ*, 15 U.S. 178, 1817 U.S. LEXIS 396 (1817).

[5]Restatement (Second) of Contracts §161.

[6]*FDIC v. W.R. Grace & Co.*, 877 F.2d 614, 1989 U.S. App. LEXIS 8905 (7th Cir. 1989).

Before completing the deal, he learned that in several newspaper articles, Ackley had publicized the house as being haunted. Ackley had also permitted the house to be featured in a walking tour of the neighborhood as "a riverfront Victorian (*with ghost*)." Stambovsky refused to go through with the deal and sued to rescind. He won. The court ruled that Ackley sold the house knowing Stambovsky was ignorant of the alleged ghosts. She also knew that a reasonable buyer might avoid a haunted house, fearing grisly events—or diminished resale value. Stambovsky could not have discovered the apparitions himself, and Ackley's failure to warn permitted him to rescind the deal.[7]

What if the defect is…a ghost?

© Galina Barskaya/Shutterstock

A seller generally must report any latent defect he knows about that the buyer should not be expected to discover himself. As social awareness of the environment increases, a buyer potentially worries about more and more problems. We now know that underground toxic waste, carelessly dumped in earlier decades, can be dangerous or even lethal. Accordingly, any property seller who realizes that there is toxic waste underground, or any other hidden hazard, must reveal that fact.

To Correct a Mistaken Understanding about a Writing. Suppose the potential buyer of a vacation property has a town map showing that the land he wants to buy has a legal right of way to a beautiful lake. If the seller of the land knows that the town map is out of date and that there is no such right of way, she must disclose her information.

A Relationship of Trust. Maria is planning to sell her restaurant to her brother Ricardo. Maria has a greater duty to reveal problems in the business because Ricardo assumes she will be honest. **When one party naturally expects openness and honesty, based on a close relationship, the other party must act accordingly.** If the building's owner has told Maria he will not renew her lease, she must pass that information on to Ricardo.

What happens if an owner, rather than disclosing hidden defects, sells the property "as is"? The following case provides insight.

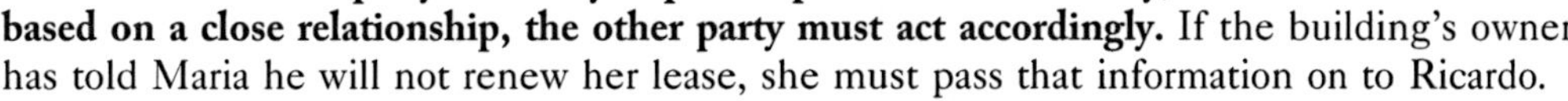

Hess v. Chase Manhattan Bank, USA, N.A.

220 S.W.3d 758
Missouri Supreme Court, 2007

Facts: Billy Stevens owned a paint company. On several occasions, he ordered employees to load a trailer with 55-gallon paint drums and pallets of old paint cans and then dump them on property he owned. This illegal dumping saved Stevens the cost of proper disposal. Later, employees notified the Environmental Protection Agency (EPA) of what Stevens had done, and the EPA began an investigation. (Stevens later served time for environmental crimes.)

Stevens defaulted on his mortgage to the land. While Chase Manhattan Bank was in the process of foreclosing, it learned that the EPA was investigating the property for contamination. Chase foreclosed and put the property up for sale "as is." Several buyers expressed interest. The bank did not inform any of them of the ongoing EPA investigation. Dennis Hess bought the property for $52,000.

[7] *Stambovsky v. Ackley*, 169 A.D.2d 254, 572 N.Y.S.2d 672, 1991 N.Y. App. Div. LEXIS 9873 (N.Y. App. Div. 1991).

After Hess bought the land, he discovered the illegal waste and sued Chase for failing to disclose the EPA's investigation. The jury awarded Hess $52,000 and Chase appealed.

Issue: ***Did Chase have a duty to disclose to Hess the ongoing investigation?***

Excerpts from Judge Stith's Decision: The buyer has a right to rely on the seller to disclose where the undisclosed material information would not be discoverable through ordinary diligence. Chase learned that the EPA was investigating the property before Chase completed its foreclosure of the mortgage. Even with superior knowledge, a duty to disclose will be imposed only if the material facts would not be discovered through the exercise of ordinary diligence. Chase asserts that a reasonable inspection of the property by Hess would have disclosed the presence of the paint cans near the old barn foundation. Chase's argument misapprehends the factual basis of Hess's fraudulent non-disclosure claim. It is the *EPA investigation* into hazardous waste dumping on the property that is the material fact that Hess asserts Chase had a duty to disclose, not the presence (or absence) of paint cans.

Hess presented evidence that two potential buyers who did discover the paint cans each still made an offer to purchase the property. Both testified that the presence of paint cans did not give them notice that the EPA was investigating and that, had they known of its investigation, they would not have made offers for the property. From this evidence, the jury could have found that even had Hess further inspected the property and discovered the paint cans, this would not have put him on notice that the EPA had an ongoing investigation into hazardous waste dumping on the property.

Chase asserts that in spite of the evidence of its knowledge and Hess's inability to discover the EPA investigation, a duty to disclose should not be imposed because the contract specified that Chase was making "no representations, guaranties, or warranties, either written or implied, regarding the property" and that "the property is being sold in AS-IS condition with no express or implied representations or warranties by the seller or its agents." It claims that through these provisions, it bargained for the right to remain silent and no duty to speak ever arose.

What Chase misapprehends is that Hess alleges *fraud in the inducement* to contract, not fraud in the terms of the contract. Missouri law holds that a party may not, by disclaimer or otherwise, contractually exclude liability for fraud in inducing that contract. Each of the individuals who made an offer to purchase this property did so without knowledge that it was under EPA investigation. They all testified that, had they known, they would not have made an offer to purchase this property and would not, therefore, have "bargained for" Chase's silence. Chase's duty to speak arose from its superior knowledge prior to the execution of this contract. The presence of a clause disclaiming warranties in a contract does not negate a pre-contractual duty to speak.

Affirmed.

EXAM Strategy

Question: Mako is selling his country house for $400,000. Guppy, an interested buyer, asks whether there is sufficient water from the property's well. Mako replies, "Are you kidding? Watch this." He turns on the tap, and the water flows bountifully. Mako then shows Guppy the well, which is full. Guppy buys the property, but two weeks later, the well runs dry. In fact, Mako knew the water supply was inadequate, and he had the well filled by a tanker truck while the property was being sold. A hydrologist tells Guppy it will cost $100,000 to dig a better well, with no guarantee of success. Guppy sues Mako. What remedy should Guppy seek? Who will win?

Strategy: Is this a case of innocent misrepresentation or fraud? Fraud. Therefore, Guppy may seek two remedies: damages or rescission. Make sure that you understand the difference. To win, Guppy must show he relied on a fact that was both false and material.

Result: When Mako responded to Guppy's question by demonstrating the apparent abundance of water, he made a false statement. This was fraud (not innocent misrepresentation), because Mako knew the well was inadequate. That was a material fact. Guppy reasonably relied on the demonstration. Guppy will win. He can elect to rescind the contract (return the property to Mako and get his money back) or choose damages (the cost of digging a proper well). Given the uncertain nature of well digging, he would be wise to rescind.

Mistake

Contract law principles come from many sources, and in the area of "legal mistake," a cow significantly influenced the law. The cow was named Rose. She was a gentle animal that lived in Michigan in 1886. Rose's owner, Hiram Walker & Sons, bought her for $850. After a few years, the company concluded that Rose could have no calves. As a barren cow, she was worth much less than $850, so Walker contracted to sell her to T. C. Sherwood for a mere $80. But when Sherwood came to collect Rose, the parties realized that (surprise!) she was pregnant. Walker refused to part with the happy mother, and Sherwood sued. Walker defended, claiming that both parties had made a *mistake* and that the contract was voidable.

A mistake can take many forms. It may be a basic error about an essential characteristic of the thing being sold, as in Rose's case. It could be an erroneous prediction about future prices, such as an expectation that oil prices will rise. It might be a mechanical error, such as a builder offering to build a new home for $300 when he clearly meant to bid $300,000. Some mistakes lead to voidable contracts, others create enforceable deals. The first distinction is between bilateral and unilateral mistakes.

Bilateral Mistake

A **bilateral mistake** occurs when both parties negotiate based on the same factual error. Sherwood and Walker both thought Rose was barren, both negotiated accordingly, and both were wrong. The Michigan Supreme Court gave judgment for Walker, the seller, permitting him to rescind the contract because the parties were *both* wrong about the essence of what they were bargaining for.

Bilateral mistake
Occurs when both parties negotiate based on the same factual error.

If the parties contract based on an important factual error, the contract is voidable by the injured party. Sherwood and Walker were both wrong about Rose's reproductive ability, and the error was basic enough to cause a tenfold difference in price. Walker, the injured party, was entitled to rescind the contract. Note that the error must be *factual.* Suppose Walker sold Rose thinking that the price of beef was going to drop, when in fact the price rose 60 percent in five months. That would be simply a *prediction* that proved wrong, and Walker would have no right to rescind.

Conscious Uncertainty. No rescission is permitted where one of the parties knows he is taking on a risk; that is, he realizes there is uncertainty about the quality of the thing being exchanged. Rufus offers 10 acres of mountainous land to Priscilla. "I can't promise you anything about this land," he says, "but they've found gold on every adjoining parcel." Priscilla, eager for gold, buys the land, digs long and hard, and discovers—mud. She may not rescind the contract. She understood the risk she was assuming, and there was no mutual mistake.

Unilateral Mistake

Sometimes only one party enters a contract under a mistaken assumption, a situation called **unilateral mistake**. In these cases, it is more difficult for the injured party to rescind a contract. This makes sense since in a bilateral error, neither side really knew what it was

Unilateral mistake
Occurs when only one party enters a contract under a mistaken assumption.

getting into, and rescission seems a natural remedy. But with unilateral mistakes, one side may simply have made a better bargain than the other. As we have seen throughout this unit on contracts, courts are unwilling to undo an agreement merely because someone made a foolish deal. Nonetheless, if her proof is strong, the injured party in a case of unilateral mistakes still may sometimes rescind a contract.

To rescind for unilateral mistake, a party must demonstrate that she entered the contract because of a basic factual error and that *either* (1) enforcing the contract would be *unconscionable* or (2) the nonmistaken party *knew* of the error.[8]

A town obtains five bids for construction of a new municipal swimming pool. Four are between $100,000 and $111,000. Fred's bid is for $82,000. His offer includes a figure of $2,000 for excavation work, while the others have allotted about $20,000 for that work. Fred has inadvertently dropped a zero, resulting in a bid that is $18,000 too low. Town officials accept Fred's offer. When he sues to rescind, Fred wins. Town officials knew that the work could not be done that cheaply, and it would be unfair to hold Fred to a mathematical error that the other side perceived.[9]

In contrast, suppose that Rebecca sues Pierce, whose bad driving caused an accident, and Amy, who owned the car that Pierce was driving. While the case is pending, Amy's insurance company, Risknaught, pays Rebecca a $70,000 settlement. Later, the state supreme court rules that Pierce was an unauthorized driver, and an owner's insurer is never liable in such a case. Risknaught seeks to rescind its settlement, claiming unilateral mistake as to its liability. The company loses. Risknaught was aware that an appellate ruling might establish new precedent. The insurer settled based on a decision calculated to minimize its risk.[10]

In the following case an automobile dealer made a mistake—how often does *this* happen?—in the customer's favor.

Donovan v. RRL Corporation

26 Cal.4th 261, 27 P.3d 702, 109 Ca. Rptr.2d 807
Supreme Court of California, 2001

Facts: Brian Donovan was in the market for a used car. As he scanned the Costa Mesa *Daily Pilot,* he came upon a "Pre-Owned Coup-A-Rama Sale!" at Lexus of Westminster. Of the 16 cars listed in the ad (with vehicle identification numbers), one was a sapphire-blue Jaguar XJ6 Vanden Plas, priced at $25,995.

Brian drove to a Jaguar dealership to do some comparison shopping. Jaguars of the same year and mileage cost about $8,000 to $10,000 more than the auto at the Lexus agency. The next day, Brian and his wife hurried over to the Coup-A-Rama event, spotted the Jaguar (which had the correct VIN) and asked a salesperson if they might test-drive it. Pleased with the ride, Brian said to the salesman, "O.K. We will take it at your price, $26,000." This figure startled the sales representative, who glanced at the newspaper ad Brian showed him, and responded, "That's a mistake."

As indeed it was. The Lexus agency had paid $35,000 for the Jaguar and intended to sell it for about $37,000. Brian was adamant. "No, I want to buy it at your advertised price, and I will write you a check right now." The sales manager was called in, and he refused to sell the car for less than $37,000.

It turned out that the *Daily Pilot*'s typographical and proofreading errors had caused the mistake, although the Lexus dealership had failed to review the proof sheet, which would have revealed the error before the ad went to press.

Brian sued. The trial court found that unilateral mistake prevented enforcement of the contract. The appel-

[8]Restatement (Second) of Contracts §153.

[9]See examples provided in Restatement (Second) of Contracts §153.

[10]See, e.g., *AID Hawai'i Ins. Co. v. Bateman,* 82 Haw. 453, 923 P.2d 395 (Haw. 1996).

late court reversed, and Donovan appealed to the state's highest court.

The state supreme court first ruled that there *was* in fact a contract between the parties. (Generally, a newspaper advertisement is merely a solicitation for an offer, but a California statute generally holds *automobile dealers* to the terms of their offers.) The court then went on to examine the mistake.

Issue: ***Did the Lexus dealer's mistake entitle it to rescind the contract?***

Excerpts from Justice George's Decision: A significant error in the price term of a contract constitutes a mistake regarding a basic assumption upon which the contract is made, and such a mistake ordinarily has a material effect adverse to the mistaken party. The defendant must show that the resulting imbalance in the agreed exchange is so severe that it would be unfair to require the defendant to perform.

Measured against this standard, defendant's mistake in the contract for the sale of the Jaguar automobile constitutes a material mistake regarding a basic assumption upon which it made the contract. Enforcing the contract with the mistaken price of $25,995 would require defendant to sell the vehicle to plaintiff for $12,000 less than the intended advertised price of $37,995—an error amounting to 32 percent of the price defendant intended. The exchange of performances would be substantially less desirable for defendant and more desirable for plaintiff.

The mere fact that a mistaken party could have avoided the mistake by the exercise of reasonable care does not preclude avoidance on the ground of mistake. Indeed, since a party can often avoid a mistake by the exercise of such care, the availability of relief would be severely circumscribed if he were to be barred by his negligence. Nevertheless, in *extreme cases,* the mistaken party's fault is a proper ground for denying him relief for a mistake that he otherwise could have avoided.

If we were to accept plaintiff's position that that the dealer always must be held to the strict terms of a contract arising from an advertisement, we would be holding that the dealer intended to assume the risk of all typographical errors in advertisements, no matter how serious the error and regardless of the circumstances in which the error was made. For example, if an automobile dealer proofread an advertisement but, through carelessness, failed to detect a typographical error listing a $75,000 automobile for sale at $75, the defense of mistake would be unavailable to the dealer.

No evidence presented at trial suggested that defendant knew of the mistake before plaintiff attempted to purchase the automobile, that defendant intended to mislead customers, or that it had adopted a practice of deliberate indifference regarding errors in advertisements. The uncontradicted evidence established that the *Daily Pilot* made the proofreading error resulting in defendant's mistake.

We conclude that the municipal court correctly entered judgment in defendant's favor.

EXAM Strategy

Question: Joe buys an Otterhound named Barky, from Purity Dog Shop. He pays $2,500 for the puppy. The high cost is a result of the certificate Purity gives him, indicating that the puppy's parents were both AKC champions (elite dogs). Two months later, Joe sells the hound to Emily for $2,800. Joe and Emily both believe that Barky is descended from champions. Then a state investigation reveals that Purity has been cheating and its certificates are fakes. Barky is just a regular dog, worth about $100. Emily sues Joe. Who wins?

Strategy: Both parties are mistaken about the kind of dog Joe is selling, so this is an instance of bilateral mistake. What is the rule in such cases?

Result: If the two sides agree based on an important factual error, the contract is voidable by the injured party. A mutt is entirely different from a dog that might become a champion. The parties erred about the essence of their deal. Joe's good faith does not save him, and Emily is entitled to rescind.

Duress

Duress
An improper threat made to force another party to enter into a contract.

True consent is also lacking when one party agrees to a contract under **duress**. If kindly Uncle Hugo signs over the deed to the ranch because Niece Nelly is holding a gun to his head, Hugo has not consented in any real sense, and he will have the right to rescind the contract. **If one party makes an improper threat that causes the victim to enter into a contract, and the victim had no reasonable alternative, the contract is voidable.**[11]

On a Sunday morning, Bancroft Hall drove to pick up his daughter Sandra, who had slept at a friend's house. The Halls are black and the neighborhood was white. A suspicious neighbor called the police, who arrived, aggressively prevented the Halls from getting into their own car, and arrested the father. The Halls had not violated any law or done anything wrong whatsoever. Later an officer told Hall that he could leave immediately if he signed a full release (stating that he had no claims of any kind against the police), but that if he refused to sign it, he would be detained for a bail hearing. Hall signed the release but later filed suit. The police defended based on the release.

The court held that the release was voidable because Hall had signed it under duress. The threat to detain Hall for a bail hearing was clearly improper because he had committed no crime. He also had no reasonable alternative to signing. A jury awarded the Halls over half a million dollars.[12]

Can "improper threats" take other forms? Does *economic* intimidation count? Many plaintiffs have posed that question over the last half century, and courts have grudgingly yielded.

Today, in most states, economic duress *can* also be used to void a contract. But economic duress sounds perilously close to hard bargaining—in other words, business. The free market system is expected to produce tough competition. A smart, aggressive executive may bargain fiercely. How do we distinguish economic duress from legal, successful business tactics? Courts have created no single rule to answer the question, but they do focus on certain issues.

In analyzing a claim of economic duress, courts look at these factors:

- Acts that have no legitimate business purpose
- Greatly unequal bargaining power
- An unnaturally large gain for one party
- Financial distress to one party

Is the following case one of duress or hard bargaining?

© Stockbyte/Getty Images

How do we distinguish hard bargaining from economic duress?

---

[11]Restatement (Second) of Contracts §175(1).

[12]*Halls v. Ochs*, 817 F.2d 920, U. S. App. LEXIS 5822 (1st Cir. 1987).

You be the Judge

In Re Rls Legal Solutions, L.L.C.

2005 WL 171381
Texas Court of Appeals, 2005

Facts: Amy Maida sued her employer, RLS Legal Solutions, for various claims relating to her job. RLS asked that the case be dismissed because Maida had signed an arbitration agreement. Maida had in fact signed the contract while already working at RLS. However, she responded that the agreement should not be enforced because she had signed it under economic duress. At trial, she was asked whether she had found the agreement acceptable:

> I did not. The arbitration clause was going to allow me not to be able to be in a position that I needed to be in now, and that is, to have someone represent me to help me where I feel like the company did me wrong.
>
> After I refused to agree to this arbitration clause, I was told that my payroll checks would not be direct deposited into my account until I signed the agreement and that I would not be paid until I signed the agreement. I had received my paychecks by direct deposit for three years. [RLS did in fact stop the direct deposit payment of Maida's salary.]
>
> I needed my paycheck to meet my financial responsibilities since I am a single family income household provider. I had no way to pay my mortgage, vehicle note, car and homeowner's insurance as well as any household bills.

Maida testified that after signing and returning the agreement, she received a manual check. Maida said that when she asked why she had not been paid by direct deposit as usual, she was told her paycheck would be held until she signed the agreement.

RLS argued that Maida had eventually received every paycheck to which she was entitled, had suffered no losses, and was free to leave RLS at any time if she found her employment terms unacceptable.

The trial court refused to dismiss the case or order arbitration, and RLS appealed.

You Be the Judge: ***Did Maida sign the arbitration under economic duress?***

Argument for RLS: Your honors, it is hard to take seriously a claim of economic duress when the plaintiff has not lost one cent and was never forced to sign anything. RLS runs a business, not a community center. To stay competitive, we constantly revise our commercial practices, and this was one such change. We did not ask for a bizarre or inappropriate change: arbitration is a widely favored method of settling disputes, quicker and cheaper *for all parties*. Maida signed. Yes, we stopped direct deposit of her check, but in the end, we paid her all she was due. We were not obligated to pay her in any particular fashion, or even to continue her employment. If she wanted to stay with us, she had to play by our rules.

Argument for Maida: The company could offer an arbitration contract to all workers. But that is distinct from forcing such agreements down employee throats, which is what they did here. RLS knows that its workers depend on prompt payment of payroll checks to avoid falling quickly into debt. The company offered Maida the arbitration agreement, she rejected it, and they responded by stopping direct deposit of her check. Knowing that she was the sole provider for her family, the firm intended to subject her to intolerable economic pressure. It worked. However, the court should have no part of this coercion. The two sides had hugely differing bargaining power, and RLS attempted to use financial distress to obtain what it could not by persuasion.

Undue Influence

She was single and pregnant. A shy young woman in a large city with no family nearby, she needed help and support. She went to the Methodist Mission Home of Texas where she found room and board, support—and a lot of counseling. Her discussions with a minister and a private counselor stressed one point: that she should give up her baby for adoption. She signed the adoption papers, but days later, she decided she wanted the baby after all. Was there any ground to rescind? She claimed *undue influence*, in other words, that the Mission Home so dominated her thinking that she never truly consented. Where one party has used undue influence, the contract is voidable at the option of the injured party. There are two elements to the plaintiff's case. **To prove undue influence, the injured party must demonstrate:**

- A relationship between the two parties either of trust or of domination, and
- Improper persuasion by the stronger party.[13]

In the Methodist Mission case, the court held that the plaintiff had been young and extremely vulnerable during the days following the birth of her child. The mission's counselor, to whom she turned for support, had spent day after day forcefully insisting that the young woman had no moral or legal right to keep her child. This amounted to undue influence. The court voided the adoption agreement.[14] In the following case, the age difference is reversed.

Sepulveda v. Aviles

762 N.Y.S.2d 358, 308 A.D.2d 1
New York Supreme Court, Appellate Division, 2003

Facts: Agnes Seals owned and lived in a 10-unit apartment building on East 119th Street in New York City. When she was 80 years old, a fire damaged much of the building's interior, leaving Seals physically and mentally unable to care for the property. Shortly after the fire, she met David Aviles, a 35-year-old neighbor. Aviles convinced Seals to sell him the building, promising to care for her for the rest of her life. She sold him the building for $50,000, taking a down payment of $10,000, with the rest to be paid over time. At the closing, Seals was represented by an attorney, Martin Freedman, whom she had never met before, and who had been referred to her by Aviles's lawyer (with whom he shared office space).

Three years later, Seals died. Her will left her entire estate to Elba and Victor Sepulveda, but the building had been Seals's principal asset. The Sepulvedas sued Aviles, asking the court to set aside the sale of the building, claiming that Aviles had used undue influence to trick Seals into a sale that was not in her interest. The jury found that Aviles had not used undue influence, and the Sepulvedas appealed.

Issue: ***Did Aviles use undue influence to obtain the apartment building?***

Excerpts from Judge Gonzalez's Decision: The jury's verdict here was completely at odds with any fair interpretation of the evidence. The trial testimony established that at the time of the transfer, Seals was an 80-year-old woman in declining health who had recently suffered a traumatic crisis resulting from [the fire], requiring her to vacate the premises for two months. The testimony of social worker Blair established that only 16 months after the conveyance, Seals was totally homebound and dependent on others, especially Aviles, to do her banking and shopping and to provide her with transportation to medical appointments. She also was suffering from significant memory impairment by that time. This evidence of Seals's mental condition was corroborated by the medical testimony of Dr. Forster, who provided his expert opinion that Seals was suffering from severe Alzheimer's dementia [at the time of the sale]. In our view, the evidence of Seals's severe mental impairment far outweighed the self-serving, lay opinions of Aviles and Freedman that Seals appeared coherent and lucid at the closing.

Seals's dependence on Aviles was further confirmed by the testimony of two disinterested witnesses, Blair and Sister Lachapelle, who testified that Aviles told Seals shortly before the sale that if she transferred the building to him, he would take care of her for the rest of her life. In addition, that Seals was represented at the closing by an attorney she had never met before and who was referred by the buyer, Mr. Aviles, is a circumstance noted in many prior cases as raising a serious question of improper influence.

---

[13]Restatement (Second) of Contracts §177.

[14]*Methodist Mission Home of Texas v. N A B*, 451 S.W.2d 539, 1970 Tex. App. LEXIS 2055 (Tex. Civ. App. 1970).

Additional clear and convincing evidence adduced by plaintiffs reveal a series of transactions permeated by undue influence. Aviles's unfettered use of Seals's funds and credit cards, which Aviles admitted at trial, provides convincing evidence that he was exploiting Seals's impaired condition for his own financial gain. Finally, his brazen conduct in writing out mortgage checks to Seals, having her endorse them, and then depositing them back into his own account raises the strongest inference that the mortgage agreement was a sham, and his intent was to obtain Seals's building through improper means. In light of the trial evidence, we find that the jury's verdict that Aviles did not obtain Seals's property by undue influence could not have been reached on any fair interpretation of the evidence.

[Reversed and remanded for new trial.]

Chapter Conclusion

An agreement between two parties may not be enough to make a contract enforceable. A minor or a mentally impaired person may generally disaffirm contracts. Even if both parties are adults of sound mind, courts will insist that consent be genuine. Misrepresentation, mistake, duress, and undue influence all indicate that at least one party did not truly consent. As the law evolves, it imposes an increasingly greater burden of *good faith negotiating* on the party in the stronger position.

Exam Review

1. **VOIDABLE CONTRACT** Capacity and consent are different contract issues that can lead to the same result: a voidable contract. A voidable agreement is one that can be canceled by a party who lacks legal capacity or who did not give true consent. (p. 317)

2. **MINORS** A minor (someone under the age of 18) generally may disaffirm any contract while she is still a minor or within a reasonable time after reaching age18. (pp. 317–319)

EXAM Strategy

Question: John Marshall and Kirsten Fletcher decided to live together. They leased an apartment, each agreeing to pay one-half of the rent. When he signed the lease, Marshall was 17. Shortly after signing the lease, Marshall turned 18, and two weeks later, he moved into the apartment. He paid his half of the rent for two months and then moved out because he and Fletcher were not getting along. Fletcher sued Marshall for one-half of the monthly rent for the remainder of the lease. Who wins?

Strategy: Marshall was clearly a minor when he signed the lease, and he could have rescinded the agreement at that time. However, after he turned 18, he moved in and began to pay rent. What effect did that have on his contract obligation? (See the "Result" at the end of this section.)

3. **MENTAL IMPAIRMENT** A mentally impaired person may generally disaffirm a contract. In such a case, though, he generally must make restitution. (pp. 319–320)

4. **INTOXICATION** A person who is so intoxicated that he fails to understand the nature of an agreement may disaffirm a contract. (pp. 320–321)

5. **FRAUD** Fraud is grounds for rescinding a contract. The injured party must prove all of the following:

   a. A false statement of fact made intentionally or recklessly

   b. Materiality

   c. Justifiable reliance (pp. 322–324)

6. **INNOCENT MISREPRESENTATION** Innocent misrepresentation also allows an injured party to rescind a contract, but it does not allow a plaintiff to sue for damages. It has the same elements as fraud, but it does not require intent or recklessness. (p. 324)

EXAM Strategy

Question: Ron buys 1,000 "Smudgy Dolls" for his toy store. Karen, the seller, tells him the dolls are in perfect condition, even though she knows their heads are defectively attached. Ron sells all of the products, but then he has to face 1,000 angry customers with headless dolls. Ron sues Karen seeking recission. What is the likely outcome?

a. This is fraud, and Ron will be able to rescind.

b. This is an innocent misrepresentation, and Ron will be able to rescind.

c. This is fraud, but Ron will not be able to rescind.

d. This is an innocent misrepresentation, but Ron will not be able to rescind.

e. This is neither fraud nor an innocent misrepresentation.

Strategy: Karen knew her statement was false, so this is a case of fraud if all elements can be met. Ron must prove a false statement of fact, materiality, and reliance. Can he do so? (See the "Result" at the end of this section.)

7. **SILENCE** Silence amounts to misrepresentation only in four instances:

   - Where disclosure is necessary to *correct a previous assertion*
   - Where disclosure would correct a *basic mistaken assumption* on which the other party is relying
   - Where disclosure would correct the other party's *mistaken understanding about a writing;* or
   - Where there is a *relationship of trust* between the two parties. (pp. 324–327)

8. **MISTAKE** In a case of bilateral mistake, either party may rescind the contract. In a case of unilateral mistake, the injured party may rescind only upon a showing that enforcement would be unconscionable or that the other party knew of her mistake. (pp. 327–330)

9. **DURESS** If one party makes an improper threat that causes the victim to enter into a contract, and the victim had no reasonable alternative, the contract is voidable. (pp. 330–332)

EXAM Strategy

Question: Andreini's nerve problem diminished the use of his hands. Dr. Beck operated, but the problem grew worse. A nurse told the patient that Beck might have committed a serious error that exacerbated the problem. Andreini returned for a second operation, which Beck assured him would correct the problem. But after Andreini had been placed in a surgical gown, shaved, and prepared for surgery, the doctor insisted that he sign a release relieving Beck of liability for the first operation. Andreini did not want to sign it, but Beck refused to operate until he did. Later, Andreini sued Beck for malpractice. A trial court dismissed Andreini's suit based on the release. You are on the appeals court. Will you affirm the dismissal or reverse?

Strategy: Adreini is claiming physical duress. Did Beck act *improperly* in demanding a release? Did Adreini have a *realistic alternative?* (See the "Result" at the end of this section.)

10. **UNDUE INFLUENCE** Once again the injured party may rescind a contract, but only upon a showing of a special relationship and improper persuasion. (pp. 332–333)

2. Result: A minor can disaffirm a contract. However, if he turns 18 and then ratifies the agreement, he is fully liable. When he paid the rent, Marshall ratified the contract, and thus he is fully liable.

5. Result: Karen made a false statement of fact, knowing it was wrong. It was material, and Ron reasonably relied on her. Karen has committed fraud. Ron is entitled to rescind the agreement. The correct answer is "a."

8. Result: The Utah Supreme Court reversed the trial court, so you probably should as well. Beck forced Adreini to sign under duress. The threat to withhold surgery was improper, and Adreini had no reasonable alternative.

MULTIPLE-CHOICE QUESTIONS

1. Kerry finds a big green ring in the street. She shows it to Leroy, who says, "Wow. That could be valuable." Neither Kerry nor Leroy knows what the ring is made of or whether it is valuable. Kerry sells the ring to Leroy for $100, saying, "Don't come

griping if it turns out to be worth two dollars." Leroy takes the ring to a jeweler who tells him it is an unusually perfect emerald, worth at least $75,000. Kerry sues to rescind.

(a) Kerry will win based on fraud.

(b) Kerry will win based on mutual mistake.

(c) Kerry will win based on unilateral mistake.

(d) Kerry will lose.

2. Veronica has a beer and then makes a contract. She continues drinking, and her blood alcohol level eventually rises to .09, which is just above her state's threshold for drunk driving. She makes a second contract while in this condition. Veronica's first contract is ________________, and her second contract is ________________.

(a) valid; valid

(b) valid; voidable

(c) voidable; voidable

(d) voidable; void

3. Jerry is so mentally ill that he is unable to understand the nature and consequences of his transactions, but he has not been adjudicated insane. Penny has been adjudicated insane, and a court has appointed a guardian to handle her affairs. Jerry's contracts are ____________, and Penny's contracts are ____________.

(a) valid; valid

(b) valid; voidable

(c) valid; void

(d) voidable; voidable

(e) voidable; void

4. Angela makes a material misstatement of fact to Lance, which he relies on when he signs Angela's contract. Fraud exists if Angela made the misstatement ...

(a) intentionally

(b) recklessly

(c) carelessly

(d) A and B only

(e) A, B, and C

5. Scarborough's Department Store opens for business on a busy shopping day just before Christmas. A hurried clerk places a sign in the middle of a table piled high with red cashmere sweaters. The sign reads, "SALE—100% Cashmere—$0.99 Each." The sign, of course, was supposed to read "$99 each."

This is a __________ mistake, and customers ____________ be able to demand that Scarborough's sell the sweaters for 99 cents.

(a) unilateral; will

(b) unilateral; will not

(c) bilateral; will

(d) bilateral; will not

Essay Questions

1. Raymond Barrows owned a 17-acre parcel of undeveloped land in Seaford, Delaware. For most of his life, Mr. Barrows had been an astute and successful businessman, but by the time he was 85 years old, he had been diagnosed as "very senile and confused 90 percent of the time." Glenn Bowen offered to buy the land. Barrows had no idea of its value, so Bowen had it appraised by a friend, who said it was worth $50,000. Bowen drew up a contract, which Barrows signed. In the contract, Barrows agreed to sell the land for $45,000, of which Bowen would pay $100 at the time of closing; the remaining $44,900 was due whenever Bowen developed the land and sold it. There was no time limit on Bowen's right to develop the land nor any interest due on the second payment. Comment.

2. On television and in magazines, Maurine and Mamie Mason saw numerous advertisements for Chrysler Fifth Avenue automobiles. The ads described the car as "luxurious," "quality-engineered," and "reliable." When they went to inspect the car, the salesman told them the warranty was "the best ... comparable to Cadillacs and Lincolns." After the Masons bought a Fifth Avenue, they began to have many problems with it. Even after numerous repairs, the car was unsatisfactory and required more work. The Masons sued, seeking to rescind the contract based on the ads and the dealer's statement. Will they win?

3. The McAllisters had several serious problems with their house, including leaks in the ceiling, a buckling wall, and dampness throughout. They repaired the buckling wall by installing I-beams to support it. They never resolved the leaks and the dampness. When they decided to sell the house, they said nothing to prospective buyers about the problems. They stated that the I-beam had been added for reinforcement. The Silvas bought the house for $60,000. Soon afterwards, they began to have problems with leaks, mildew, and dampness. Are the Silvas entitled to any money damages? Why or why not?

4. Roy Newburn borrowed money and bought a $49,000 truck from Treadwell Ford. A few months later, the truck developed transmission problems. Newburn learned that the truck had 170,000 more miles on it than the odometer indicated. The company admitted the mileage error and promised to install a new transmission for free. Treadwell did install the new transmission, but when Newburn came to pick up the truck, Treadwell demanded that he sign a general release absolving the dealership of any claims based on the inaccurate mileage. Treadwell refused to turn over the truck until Newburn finally signed. The truck broke down again, and delays cost Newburn so much income that he fell behind on his loan payments and lost the truck. He sued Treadwell, which defended based on the release. Is the release valid?

5. Morell bought a security guard business from Conley, including the property on which the business was located. Neither party knew that underground storage tanks were leaking and contaminating the property. After the sale, Morell discovered the tanks and sought to rescind the contract. Should he be allowed to do so?

Discussion Questions

1. Sixteen-year-old Travis Mitchell brought his Pontiac GTO into M&M Precision Body and Paint for body work and a paint job. M&M did the work and charged $1,900, which Travis paid. When Travis later complained about the quality of the work, M&M did some touching up, but Travis was still dissatisfied. He demanded his $1,900 back, but M&M refused to refund it because all of the work was "in" the car and Travis could not return it to the shop. The state of Nebraska, where this occurred, follows the majority rule on this issue. Does Travis get his money? Is this a *fair* result?

2. Contract law gives minors substantial legal protection. But does a modern high school student *need* so much protection? Older teens may have been naive in the 1700s, but today, they are quite savvy. Should the law change so that only younger children—perhaps those aged 14 and under—have the ability to undo agreements? Or is the law reasonable the way it currently exists?

3. In the old Michigan case featuring Rose the Cow, the court refused to enforce the agreement. Was this a fair result? Should bilateral mistakes create voidable contracts, or should Walker have been required to sell the cow for $80?

4. Susan drops by Dean's garage sale. She buys a painting for $10. Both she and Dean think that the painting is a copy of a Matisse. Later, Susan is delighted to discover that the painting is actually a Matisse and is worth $50,000,000. Dean hears the news, and wants the painting back. Will he get it? Why or why not?

5. Do you have sympathy for intoxicated people who make agreements? Should the law ever let them back out of deals when they sober up? After all, no one forced them to get drunk. Should the law be more lenient, or is is it reasonable as it currently exists?

CHAPTER 15

© picsbyst/Shutterstock.com

WRITTEN CONTRACTS

Oliver and Perry were college roommates, two sophomores with contrasting personalities. They were sitting in the cafeteria with some friends, Oliver chatting away, Perry slumped on a plastic bench. Oliver suggested that they buy a lottery ticket, as the prize for that week's drawing was $13 million. Perry muttered, "Nah. You never win if you buy just one ticket." Oliver bubbled up, "O.K., we'll buy a ticket every week. We'll keep buying them from now until we graduate. Come on, it'll be fun. This month, I'll buy the tickets. Next month, you will, and so on." Other students urged Perry to do it and, finally, he agreed.

> **Perry moved out of their dorm room into a suite at the Ritz and refused to give Oliver one red cent.**

The two friends carefully reviewed their deal. Each party was providing consideration—namely, the responsibility for purchasing tickets during his month. The amount of each purchase was clearly defined at one dollar. They would start that week and continue until graduation day, two and a half years down the road. Finally, they would share equally any money won. As three witnesses looked on, they shook hands on the bargain. That month, Oliver bought a ticket every week, randomly choosing numbers, and won nothing. The next month, Perry bought a ticket with equally random numbers—and won $52 million. Perry moved out of their dorm room into a suite at the Ritz and refused to give Oliver one red cent. Oliver sued, seeking $26 million, and the return of an Eric Clapton compact disc. If the former friends had understood the Statute of Frauds, they would never have gotten into this mess.[1]

[1]Based loosely on *Lydon v. Beauregard* (Middlesex Sup. Ct., Mass., Dec. 22, 1989), reported in Paul Langher, "Couple Lose Suit to Share $2.8M Prize," *Boston Globe,* December 23, 1989, p. 21.

The rule we examine in this chapter is not exactly news. Originally passed by the British Parliament in 1677, the Statute of Frauds has changed little over the centuries. The purpose was to prevent lying (fraud) in civil lawsuits. Jury trials of that era invited perjury. Neither the plaintiff nor the defendant was permitted to testify, meaning that the jury never heard from the people who really knew what had happened. Instead, the court heard testimony from people who claimed to have witnessed the contract being created. Knowing that he would never be subjected to aggressive cross-examination, a plaintiff might easily allege that a fake contract was real, and then bribe witnesses to support his case. A powerful earl, seeking to acquire 300 acres of valuable land owned by a neighboring commoner, might claim that the neighbor had orally promised to sell his land. Although the claim was utterly false, the earl would win if he could bribe enough "reputable" witnesses to persuade the jury.

To provide juries with more reliable evidence that a contract did or did not exist, Parliament passed the Statute of Frauds. It required that in several types of cases, a contract would be enforced only if it were in writing. Contracts involving interests in land were first on the list.

In the days before the Revolutionary War, when Pennsylvania was still a British possession, the colony's supreme court heard the following case, which centered on the Statute of Frauds. Notice the case citation. This is very nearly the first case reported in United States history. Back then, rulings were expressed quite differently (and everything was capitalized), but you will be able to see Judge Coleman's point.

Landmark Case

The Lessee of Richardson v. Campbell

1 U.S. 10
Supreme Court of Pennsylvania, 1764

Facts: A tenant had rented land from Richardson. However, Campbell claimed the property was really his. Unless the tenant could prove that Richardson owned the land, he would have no right to stay there.

Richardson's tenant offered a deed (which was then called a *patent*) to support his claim; Campbell provided receipts as evidence that he had bought the property.

To prove that the receipts were for the disputed property, Campbell wanted to introduce statements from an important person—Thomas Penn, whose father, William, had founded the Pennsylvania colony. Obviously, the tenant did not want that evidence admitted in court.

Issue: ***Was oral evidence about the ownership of land admissible in court?***

Excerpts from Justice Coleman's Decision: PLAINTIFF supported his Title by a Patent. The Defendant produced Receipts several Years prior to Plaintiff's Patent; but the Plaintiff contend[ed] that the Receipts were only for Money paid on an adjacent Tract; the Defendant produced a Witness to prove a parol Declaration of Mr. Thomas Penn that the Land in dispute was sold to Defendant.

This piece of Evidence was opposed by the Plaintiff, and refused BY THE COURT.

Almost all states of this country have passed their own version of the Statute of Frauds. It is important to remember, as we examine the rules and exceptions, that Parliament and the state legislatures all had a commendable, straightforward purpose in passing their respective statutes of fraud: *to provide a court with the best possible evidence of whether the parties intended to make a contract.* Ironically, the British government has repealed the writing requirement for most contracts. Parliament concluded that the old statute, far from preventing wrongdoing, was *helping* people commit fraud. A wily negotiator could orally agree to terms and then, if the deal turned unprofitable, walk away from the contract, knowing it was unenforceable without written evidence.

Thus far, no state in this country has entirely repealed its Statute of Frauds. Instead, courts have carved exceptions into the original statute to prevent unfairness. Some scholars have urged state legislatures to go further and repeal the law altogether. Other commentators defend the Statute of Frauds as a valuable tool for justice. They argue that, among other benefits, the requirement of a writing cautions people to be careful before making—or relying on—a promise. For now, the Statute of Frauds is a vital part of law. Sadly, Oliver from the opening scenario will learn this the hard way.

The Statute of Frauds: A plaintiff may not enforce any of the following agreements unless the agreement, or some memorandum of it, is in writing and signed by the defendant. The agreements that must be in writing are those:

- For any interest in **land**
- That **cannot be performed within one year**
- To pay the **debt of another**
- Made by an **executor of an estate**
- Made **in consideration of marriage**; and
- For the sale of goods worth $500 or more.

In other words, when two parties make an agreement covered by any one of these six topics, it must be in writing to be enforceable. Oliver and Perry made a definite agreement to purchase lottery tickets during alternate months and share the proceeds of any winning ticket. But their agreement was to last two and a half years. As the second item on the list indicates, a contract must be in writing if it cannot be performed within one year. The good news is that Oliver gets back his Eric Clapton CD. The bad news is he gets none of the lottery money. Even though three witnesses saw the deal made, it is unlikely to be enforced in any state. Perry will walk away with all $52 million.

Note that although the Oliver-Perry agreement is unenforceable, it is not void. Suppose that Perry does the right thing, agreeing to share the winnings with Oliver. Over the next 20 years, as he receives the winnings, Perry gives one-half to his friend. But then, having squandered his own fortune, Perry demands the money back from Oliver, claiming that the original contract violated the Statute of Frauds. Perry loses. **Once a contract is fully executed, it makes no difference that it was unwritten.** The Statute of Frauds prevents the enforcement of an executory contract; that is, one in which the parties have not fulfilled their obligations. But the contract is not *illegal.* Once both parties have fully performed, neither party may demand rescission. The Statute of Frauds allows a party to cancel future obligations but not undo past actions.

Ethics The *law* permits Perry to keep all of the lottery money. But does Perry have a *moral* right to deny Oliver his half-share? Is the Statute of Frauds serving a useful purpose here? Remember that Parliament passed the original Statute of Frauds believing that a written document would be more reliable than the testimony of alleged witnesses. If we permitted Oliver to enforce the oral contract, based on his testimony and that of the witnesses, would we simply be inviting other plaintiffs to invent lottery "contracts" that had never been made?

Common Law Statute of Frauds: Contracts That Must Be in Writing

Agreements for an Interest in Land

A contract for the sale of any interest in land must be in writing to be enforceable. Notice the phrase "interest in land." This means *any legal right* regarding land. A house on a lot is an interest in land. A mortgage, an easement, and a leased apartment are all interests in land. As a general rule, leases must therefore be in writing, although most states have created an exception for short-term leases. A short-term lease is often one for a year or less, although the length varies from state to state.

"Any interest in land" may sound obscure, but those who understand it are better off than those who do not.

Kary Presten and Ken Sailer were roommates in a rental apartment in New Jersey that had a view of the Manhattan skyline. The lease was in Sailer's name, but the two split all expenses. Then the building became a "cooperative," meaning that each tenant would have the option of buying the apartment.[2] Sailer learned he could buy his unit for only $55,800 if he promptly paid a $1,000 fee to maintain his rights. He mentioned to Presten that he planned to buy the unit, and Presten asked if he could become half-owner. Sailer agreed and borrowed the $1,000 from Presten to pay his initial fee. But as the time for closing on the purchase came nearer, Sailer realized that he could sell the apartment for a substantial profit. He placed an ad in a paper and promptly received a firm offer for $125,000. Sailer then told Presten that their deal was off, and that he, Sailer, would be buying the unit alone. He did exactly that, and Presten filed suit. Regrettably, the outcome of Presten's suit was only too easy to predict.

A cooperative apartment is an interest in land, said the court. This agreement could be enforced only if put in writing and signed by Sailer. The parties had put nothing in writing, and therefore Presten was out of luck. He was entitled to his $1,000 back, but nothing more. The apartment belonged to Sailer, who could live in it or sell it for a large, quick profit.[3]

Suppose that you are interested in buying five expensive acres in a fast-growing rural area. There is no water on the property, and the only way to bring public water to it is through land owned by the neighbor, Joanne, who agrees to sell you an easement through her property. An *easement* is a legal right that an owner gives to another person to make some use of the owner's land. In other words, Joanne will permit you to dig a 200-foot trench through her land and lay a water pipe there in exchange for $15,000. May you now safely purchase the five acres? Not until Joanne has signed the written easement. You might ignore this "technicality," since Joanne seems friendly and honest. But

[2]Technically, the residents of a "co-op" do not own their apartments. They own a share of the corporation that owns the building. Along with their ownership shares, residents have a right to lease their unit for a modest fee.

[3]*Presten v. Sailer*, 225 N.J. Super. 178, 542 A.2d 7, 1988 N.J. Super. LEXIS 151 (N.J. Super. Ct. App. Div. 1988).

you could then spend $300,000 buying your property only to learn that Joanne has changed her mind. She might refuse to go through with the deal unless you pay $150,000 for the easement. Without her permission to lay the pipe, your new land is worthless. Avoid such nightmares: get it in writing.

Exception: Full Performance by the Seller

If the seller completely performs her side of a contract for an interest in land, a court is likely to enforce the agreement even if it was oral. Adam orally agrees to sell his condominium to Maggie for $150,000. Adam delivers the deed to Maggie and expects his money a week later, but Maggie fails to pay. Most courts will allow Adam to enforce the oral contract and collect the full purchase price from Maggie.

Exception: Part Performance by the Buyer

The buyer of land may be able to enforce an oral contract if she paid part of the purchase price *and either* entered upon the land *or* made improvements to it. Suppose that Eloise sues Grover to enforce an alleged oral contract to sell a lot in Happydale. She claims they struck a bargain in January. Grover defends based on the Statute of Frauds, saying that even if the two did reach an oral agreement, it is unenforceable. Eloise proves that she paid 10 percent of the purchase price, that she began excavating on the lot in February to build a house, and that Grover knew of the work. Eloise has established part performance and will be allowed to enforce her contract.

This exception makes sense if we recall the purpose of the Statute of Frauds: to provide the best possible evidence of the parties' intentions. The fact that Grover permitted Eloise to enter upon the land and begin building on it is compelling evidence that the two parties had reached an agreement. But be aware that most claims of part performance fail. Merely paying a deposit on a house is not part performance. A plaintiff seeking to rely on part performance must show partial payment *and* either entrance onto the land *or* physical improvements to it.

Exception: Promissory Estoppel

The other exception to the writing requirement is our old friend promissory estoppel. **If a promisor makes an oral promise that should reasonably cause the promisee to rely on it, and the promisee does rely, the promisee may be able to enforce the promise,** despite the Statute of Frauds, if that is the only way to avoid injustice. This exception potentially applies to any contract that must be written, such as those for land, those that cannot be performed within one year, and so forth.

Maureen Sullivan and James Rooney lived together for seven years, although they never married. They decided to buy a house. The two agreed that they would be equal owners, but Rooney told Sullivan that in order to obtain Veterans Administration financing, he would have to be the sole owner on the deed. They each contributed to the purchase and maintenance of the house, and Rooney repeatedly told Sullivan that he would change the deed to joint ownership. He never did. When the couple split up, Sullivan sued, seeking a 50 percent interest in the house. She won. The agreement was for an interest in land and should have been in writing, said the court. But Rooney had clearly promised Sullivan that she would be a half-owner, and she had relied by contributing to the purchase and maintenance. The Statute of Frauds was passed to *prevent* fraud, not to enable one person to mislead another and benefit at her expense.[4]

---

[4]*Sullivan v. Rooney,* 404 Mass. 160, 533 N.E.2d 1372, 1989 Mass. LEXIS 49 (1989).

EXAM Strategy

Question: Aditi and Danielle, MBA students, need an apartment for next September. They find a lovely two-bedroom unit that the owner is rehabbing. The students can see that the owner is honest, his workmanship excellent. The owner agrees to rent them the apartment beginning September 1, for $1,200 per month for one year. "Come back at the end of August. By then, my work will be done and I'll have the papers to sign." Aditi asks, "Should we sign something now, to be sure?" The landlord laughs and replies, "I trust you. You don't trust me?" They both trust him, and they shake hands on the deal. When the students return in August, the landlord has rented it to Danielle's former boyfriend for $1,400 per month. Aditi and Danielle sue. Who wins?

Strategy: Under the statute of frauds, a contract for the sale of any interest in land must be in writing to be enforceable. What does "any interest" mean? Does the Statute of Frauds apply to this case?

Result: An "interest" means any legal right. A lease is an interest in land, meaning that the students cannot enforce this agreement unless it is in writing, signed by the owner—and it is not. The students need to look for a new apartment.

Agreements That Cannot Be Performed within One Year

Contracts that cannot be performed within one year are unenforceable unless they are in writing. This one-year period begins on the date the parties make the agreement. The critical word here is "cannot." If a contract *could possibly* be completed within one year, it need not be in writing. Betty gets a job at Burger Brain, throwing fries in oil. Her boss tells her she can have Fridays off for as long as she works there. That oral contract is enforceable whether Betty stays one week or twenty years. "As long as she works there" *could* last for less than one year. Betty might quit the job after six months. Therefore, it does not need to be in writing.[5]

If an agreement will *necessarily* take longer than one year to finish, it must be in writing to be enforceable. If Betty is hired for a term of three years as manager of Burger Brain, the agreement is unenforceable unless put in writing. She cannot perform three years of work in one year.

Or, if you hire a band to play at your wedding 15 months from today, the agreement must be in writing. The gig may take only a single day, but that day will definitely not fall in the next 12 months.

The following case starts with a notorious diet pill and ends with a paralegal suing her boss. Which argument carries greater weight?

---

[5]This is the majority rule. In most states, for example, if a company hires an employee "for life," the contract need not be in writing because the employee could die within one year. "Contracts of uncertain duration are simply excluded [from the Statute of Frauds]; the provision covers only those contracts whose performance cannot possibly be completed within a year." Restatement (Second) of Contracts §130, Comment a, at 328 (1981). See, e.g., *Mackay v. Four Rivers Packing Co.*, 2008 WL 427789 (Id. 2008). However, a few states disagree. The Illinois Supreme Court ruled that a contract for lifetime employment is enforceable only if written. *McInerney v. Charter Golf, Inc.*, 176 Ill. 2d 482, 680 N.E.2d 1347, 1997 Ill. LEXIS 56 (Ill. 1997).

You be the Judge

Sawyer v. Mills

2007 WL 1113038
Kentucky Court of Appeals, 2007

Facts: Barbara Sawyer, a paralegal, worked for attorney Melbourne Mills, assisting him in a class action lawsuit against the makers of a popular diet drug called Fen-Phen. Mills promised Sawyer a large bonus "when the ship comes in," but he never specified how much he would pay her. Mills successfully settled the Fen-Phen case for millions of dollars, and he later met with Sawyer and her husband to discuss her bonus. The Sawyers secretly recorded the conversation.

The Sawyers asked Mills for a $1 million bonus, to be paid as a lump sum. Mills refused. However, the parties kept talking and Mills eventually agreed to pay Sawyer $1 million, plus $65,000 for a luxury automobile. Payments were to be made in monthly installments of $10,000, for 10 years. Mills also agreed to sign a document confirming his promise. Sawyer's lawyer drafted the writing, but Mills never signed it. He did pay nine monthly installments, along with an extra payment of $100,000.

At trial, jurors heard the tape recording, which confirmed the oral agreement. The jury concluded that the parties had reached a binding agreement and awarded Sawyer $900,000. However, the court granted a judgment notwithstanding the verdict for Mills. He ruled that the agreement was barred by the Statute of Frauds. Sawyer appealed.

You Be the Judge: ***Does the Statute of Frauds prevent enforcement of Mills's promise?***

Argument for Sawyer: The Statute of Frauds exists to make sure that a plaintiff does not come into court and allege an oral promise that never existed. The fear of fraudulent claims is legitimate, but obviously it does not apply in this case. We *know* that Mills agreed to pay a million dollars because we can *hear* him make the promise. We know the exact terms of the agreement, and we know it was a reasonable arrangement based on years of work and a massive settlement. We even hear Mills agree to sign a document confirming his promise.

The Statute of Frauds was designed to prevent fraud—not encourage it. Mills's tiresome, technical arguments did not fool the jurors. After hearing—literally—the evidence, the jury knew there had been a deal and awarded Sawyer her fair share. Let's stop playing legal games, start doing justice, and restore the verdict.

Argument for Mills: This is a simple case. The plaintiffs allege an oral contract for 10 years' worth of installment payments. In other words, *if* there was an agreement, it was for 10 years' duration. Sawyer's own lawyer drafted a contract—never signed—for compensation lasting a full decade. Under the Statute of Frauds, an agreement that cannot be performed within one year is unenforceable unless written and signed. End of case.

If our legislature wanted to encourage secret tape recordings and deception, it could have included an exception to the Statute of Frauds, giving tricky plaintiffs a reward for bad-faith negotiating. However, the legislators wisely have made no such exception. The alleged oral contract is worthless.

Promise to Pay the Debt of Another

When one person agrees to pay the debt of another as a favor to that debtor, it is called a collateral promise, and it must be in writing to be enforceable. D. R. Kemp was a young entrepreneur who wanted to build housing in Tuscaloosa, Alabama. He needed $25,000 to complete a project he was working on, so he went to his old college professor, Jim Hanks, for help. The professor said he would see what he could do about getting Kemp a loan. Professor Hanks spoke with his good friend Travis Chandler, telling him that Kemp was highly responsible and would be certain to repay any money loaned. Chandler trusted Professor Hanks but wanted to be sure of his money. Professor Hanks assured Chandler that if for any reason Kemp did not repay the loan, he, Hanks, would pay Chandler in full.

With that assurance, Chandler wrote out a check for $25,000, payable to Kemp, never having met the young man.

Kemp, of course, never repaid the loan. (Thank goodness he did not; this textbook has no use for people who do what they are supposed to.) Kemp exhausted the cash trying to sustain his business, which failed anyway, so he had nothing to give his creditor. Chandler approached Professor Hanks, who refused to pay, and Chandler sued. The outcome was easy to predict. Professor Hanks had agreed to repay Kemp's debt *as a favor to Kemp,* making it a collateral promise. Chandler had nothing in writing, and that is exactly what he got from his lawsuit—nothing.

Exception: The Leading Object Rule

There is one major exception to the collateral promise rule. When the promisor guarantees to pay the debt of another and *the leading object of the promise is some benefit to the promisor himself,* then the contract will be enforceable even if unwritten. In other words, if the promisor makes the guarantee not as a favor to the debtor, but primarily out of *self-interest,* the Statute of Frauds does not apply.

Robert Perry was a hog farmer in Ohio. He owed $26,000 to Sunrise Cooperative, a supplier of feed. Because Perry was in debt, Sunrise stopped giving him feed on credit and began selling him feed on a cash-only basis. Perry also owed money to Farm Credit Services, a loan agency. Perry promised Farm Credit he would repay his loans as soon as his hogs were big enough to sell. But Perry couldn't raise hogs without feed, which he lacked the money to purchase. Farm Credit was determined to bring home the bacon, so it asked Sunrise Cooperative to give Perry the feed on credit. Farm Credit orally promised to pay any debt that Perry did not take care of. When Perry defaulted on his payments to Sunrise, the feed supplier sued Farm Credit based on its oral guarantee. Farm Credit claimed the promise was unenforceable, based on the Statute of Frauds. But the court found in favor of Sunrise. The *leading object* of Farm Credit's promise to Sunrise was self-interest, and the oral promise was fully enforceable.[6]

Promise Made by an Executor of an Estate

This rule is merely a special application of the previous one, concerning the debt of another person. An executor is the person who is in charge of an estate after someone dies. The executor's job is to pay debts of the deceased, obtain money owed to him, and disburse the assets according to the will. In most cases, the executor will use only the estate's assets to pay those debts. The Statute of Frauds comes into play when an executor promises to pay an estate's debts with her own funds. An executor's promise to use her own funds to pay a debt of the deceased must be in writing to be enforceable.

Suppose Esmeralda dies penniless, owing Tina $35,000. Esmeralda's daughter, Sapphire, is the executor of her estate. Tina comes to Sapphire and demands her $35,000. Sapphire responds, "There is no money in mamma's estate, but don't worry, I'll make it up to you with my own money." Sapphire's oral promise is unenforceable. Tina should get it in writing while Sapphire is feeling generous.

Promise Made in Consideration of Marriage

Barney is a multimillionaire with the integrity of a gangster and the charm of a tax collector. He proposes to Li-Tsing, who promptly rejects him. Barney then pleads that if Li-Tsing will be his bride, he will give her an island he owns off the coast of California. Li-Tsing begins to see his good qualities and accepts. After they are married, Barney refuses to

[6]*Sunrise Cooperative v. Robert Perry*, 1992 Ohio App. LEXIS 3913 (Ohio Ct. App. 1992).

deliver the deed. Li-Tsing will get nothing from a court either, because **a promise made in consideration of marriage must be in writing to be enforceable.**

The Common Law Statute of Frauds: What the Writing Must Contain

Each of the types of contract described above must be in writing in order to be enforceable. What must the writing contain? It may be a carefully typed contract, using precise legal terminology, or an informal memo scrawled on the back of a paper napkin at a business lunch. The writing may consist of more than one document, written at different times, with each document making a piece of the puzzle. But there are some general requirements: the writing

- **Must be signed by the defendant, and**
- **Must state with reasonable certainty the name of each party, the subject matter of the agreement, and all of the essential terms and promises.**[7]

Signature

A state's Statute of Frauds typically requires that the writing be "signed by the party to be charged therewith"; that is, the party who is resisting enforcement of the contract. Throughout this chapter, we refer to that person as the defendant because when these cases go to court, it is the defendant who is disputing the existence of a contract.

Judges define "signature" very broadly. Using a pen to write one's name certainly counts, but it is not required. A secretary who stamps an executive's signature on a letter fulfills this requirement. In fact, any mark or logo placed on a document to indicate acceptance, even an "X," will generally satisfy the Statute of Frauds. And electronic commerce, as we discuss below, creates new methods of signing.

Reasonable Certainty

Suppose Garfield and Hayes are having lunch, discussing the sale of Garfield's vacation condominium. They agree on a price and want to make some notation of the agreement even before their lawyers work out a detailed purchase and sales agreement. A perfectly adequate memorandum might say, "Garfield agrees to sell Hayes his condominium at 234 Baron Boulevard, Apartment 18, for $350,000 cash, payable on June 18, 2015, and Hayes promises to pay the sum on that day." They should make two copies of their agreement and sign both. Notice that although Garfield's memo is short, it is *certain* and *complete*. This is critical because problems of vagueness and incompleteness often doom informal memoranda.

Vagueness

Ella Hayden owned valuable commercial property on a highway called Route 9. She wrote a series of letters to her stepson Mark, promising that several of the children, including Mark, would share the property. One letter said: "We four shall fairly divide on the Route 9 property. [sic]" Other letters said: "When the Route 9 Plaza is sold, you can take a long vacation," and

---

[7]Restatement (Second) of Contracts §131.

"The property will be sold. You and Dennis shall receive the same amount." Ella Hayden died without leaving Mark anything. He sued, but got nothing. The court ruled:

> The above passages written by Ms. Hayden do not recite the essential elements of the alleged contract with reasonable certainty. The writings do not state unequivocally or with sufficient particularity the subject matter to which the writings relate, nor do they provide the terms and conditions of alleged promises made which constitute a contract. The alleged oral contract between Ms. Hayden and Mr. Hayden cannot be identified from the passages from Ms. Hayden's letters quoted above when applied to existing facts. In sum, Mr. Hayden's cause of action seeking an interest in the Route 9 property is foreclosed by the Statute of Frauds.[8]

Incompleteness

During Ronald McCoy's second interview with Spelman Memorial Hospital, the board of directors orally offered him a three-year job as assistant hospital administrator. McCoy accepted. Spelman's CEO, Gene Meyer, sent a letter confirming the offer, which said:

> To reconfirm the offer, it is as follows: 1. We will pay for your moving expenses. 2. I would like you to pursue your Master's Degree at an area program. We will pay 100 percent tuition reimbursement. 3. Effective September 26, you will be eligible for all benefits. 4. A starting salary of $48,000 annually with reviews and eligibility for increases at 6 months, 12 months, and annually thereafter. 5. We will pay for the expenses of 3 trips, if necessary, in order for you to find housing. 6. Vacation will be for 3 weeks a year after one year; however, we do allow for this to be taken earlier. [Signed] Gene Meyer.

Spelman Hospital fired McCoy less than a year after he started work, and McCoy sued. The hospital's letter seems clear, and it is signed by an authorized official. The problem is, it is incomplete. Can you spot the fatal omission? The court did.

McCoy wanted to hold the hospital's board to its spoken promise that he would have a job for a term of three years. To be enforceable, a contract for a term of over one year must be in writing under the Statute of Frauds.

To satisfy the Statute of Frauds, an employment contract—[or] its memorandum or note—must contain *all* essential terms, including *duration of the employment relationship.* Without a statement of duration, an employment-at-will arrangement is created, which is terminable at any time by either party with no liability for breach of contract. McCoy's argument that the letter constituted a memorandum of an oral contract fails because the letter does not state an essential element: duration. The letter did not state that Spelman was granting McCoy employment for any term—only that his salary would be reviewed at 6 months, 12 months, and "annually thereafter."[9]

The lawsuits in this section demonstrate the continuing force of the Statute of Frauds. If the promisor had truly wanted to make a binding commitment, he or she could have written the appropriate contract or memorandum in a matter of minutes. Great formality and expense are unnecessary. But the written document *must be clear and complete,* or it will fail.

EXAM Strategy

Question: Major Retailer and Owner negotiated a lease of a strip mall, the tenancy to begin August 1. Retailer's lawyer then drafted a lease accurately reflecting all terms agreed to, including the parties, exact premises, condition of the store, dates of the

[8] *Hayden v. Hayden,* Mass. Lawyers Weekly No. 12-299-93 (Middlesex Sup. Ct. 1994).

[9] *McCoy v. Spelman Memorial Hospital,* 845 S.W.2d 727, 1993 Mo. App. LEXIS 105 (Mo. Ct. App. 1993).

lease, and monthly rent of $18,000. Retailer signed the lease and delivered it to Owner on July 1. On July 20, Owner leased the same space to a different tenant for $23,000 per month. Retailer sued, claiming that the parties had a binding deal, and the Owner had breached his agreement in order to obtain higher rent. Who will win?

Strategy: To comply with the Statute of Frauds, a writing must state all essential terms. This lease appears to do that. However, the writing must contain one other thing. What is it?

Result: The writing must be *signed* by the party claiming that there is no contract; that is, by the defendant. Owner never signed the lease. This lease does not comply with the Statute of Frauds, and the Retailer will lose his case.

Electronic Contracts and Signatures

E-commerce has grown at a dazzling rate—each year, U.S. enterprises buy and sell tens of billions of dollars worth of goods and services over the Internet. What happens to the writing requirement, though, when there is no paper? The present Statute of Frauds requires some sort of "signature" to ensure that the defendant committed to the deal. Today, an "electronic signature" could mean a name typed (or automatically included) at the bottom of an e-mail message, a retinal or vocal scan, or a name signed by electronic pen on a writing tablet, among others.

E-signatures are valid in all 50 states. Almost all states have adopted the Uniform Electronic Transactions Act[10]. UETA declares that *electronic* contracts and signatures are as enforceable as those on paper. In other words, the normal rules of contract law apply, and neither party can avoid such a deal merely because it originated in cyberspace. A federal statute, the **Electronic Signatures in Global and National Commerce Act (E-SIGN),** also declares that contracts cannot be denied enforcement simply because they are in electronic form, or signed electronically. It applies in states that have not adopted UETA.

Note that, in many states, certain documents still require a traditional (non-electronic) signature. Wills, adoptions, court orders, and notice of foreclosure are common exceptions. If in doubt, get a hard copy, signed in ink.

The UCC's Statute of Frauds

We have reached another section dedicated to the Uniform Commercial Code. Remember that UCC rules govern only contracts involving a sale of goods. Because some merchants make dozens or even hundreds of oral contracts every year, the drafters of the UCC wanted to make the writing requirement less onerous for the sale of goods.

The UCC requires a writing for the sale of goods worth $500 or more. The Code's requirements are easier to meet than those of the common law. **UCC §2-201,** the Statute of Frauds section, has three important elements:

1. The basic rule
2. The merchants' exception
3. Special circumstances

[10]The states that have not adopted the Uniform Electronic Transactions Act, at the time of this writing, are Illinois, New York, and Washington.

The key difference between the common-law rule and the UCC rule is that the Code does *not* require *all* of the terms of the agreement to be in writing.

UCC §2-201(1)—The Basic Rule

A contract for the sale of goods worth $500 or more is not enforceable unless there is some writing, signed by the defendant, indicating that the parties reached an agreement. The key difference between the common-law rule and the UCC rule is that the Code does *not* require *all* of the terms of the agreement to be in writing. The Code looks for something simpler: *an indication that the parties reached an agreement.* Only two things are required: the signature of the defendant and the quantity of goods being sold. Suppose a short memorandum between textile dealers indicates that Seller will sell to Buyer "grade AA 100 percent cotton, white athletic socks." If the writing does not state the price, the parties can testify at court about what the market price was at the time of the deal. If the writing says nothing about the delivery date, the court will assume a reasonable delivery date, say, 60 days. But how many socks were to be delivered? 100 pairs or 100,000? The court will have no objective evidence, and so, the quantity must be written.

Writing	Result
"Confirming phone conversation today, I will send you 1,000 reams of paper for laser printing, usual quality & price. [Signed,] Seller."	This memorandum satisfies UCC §2-201 (1), and the contract may be enforced against the seller. The buyer may testify as to the "usual" quality and price between the two parties, and both sides may rely on normal trade usage.
"Confirming phone conversation today, I will send you best quality paper for laser printing, $3.25 per ream, delivery date next Thursday. [Signed,] Seller."	This memorandum is not enforceable because it states no quantity.

UCC §2-201(2)—The Merchants' Exception

When both parties are "merchants," that is, businesspeople who routinely deal in the goods being sold, the Code will accept an even more informal writing. **Within a reasonable time of making an oral contract, if a merchant sends a written confirmation to another, and if the confirmation is definite enough to bind the *sender herself,* then the merchant who receives the confirmation will *also* be bound by it unless he objects in writing within 10 days.** This exception dramatically changes the rules from the common law, but it applies only between two merchants. The drafters of the Code assumed that experienced merchants are able to take care of themselves in fast-moving negotiations. The critical difference is this: a writing may create a binding contract *even when it is not signed by the defendant.*

Madge manufactures "beanies," that is, silly caps with plastic propellers on top. Rachel, a retailer, telephones her, and they discuss the price of the beanies, shipping time, and other details. Madge then faxes Rachel a memo: "This confirms your order for 2,500 beanies at $12.25 per beanie. Colors: blue, green, black, orange, red. Delivery date: 10 days. [Signed] Madge." Rachel receives the fax, reads it while negotiating with another manufacturer, and throws it in the wastebasket. Rachel buys her beanies elsewhere, and Madge sues. Rachel defends, claiming there is no written contract because she, Rachel, never signed anything. Madge wins under UCC §2-201(2). Both parties were merchants because they routinely dealt in these goods. Madge signed and sent a confirming memo that could have been used to hold her, Madge, to the deal. When Rachel read it, she was not free to disregard it. Obviously, the intelligent business practice would have been to promptly fax a reply saying, "I disagree. We do not have any deal for beanies." Since Rachel failed to respond within 10 days, Madge has an enforceable contract.

For a confirming memo to count, a merchant must send it within a *reasonable* time. But how long is that? A few days certainly qualifies. Could 13 months be quick enough?

Seton Co. v. Lear Corp.

198 Fed. Appx. 496, 2006 WL 2860774
Sixth Circuit Court of Appeals, 2006

Facts: General Motors hired Lear Corporation to supply all of the leather seats for its trucks and SUVs. In October 1998, Lear reached an agreement with Seton Company to provide Lear with the actual cut-to-pattern leather, which Lear would then assemble. Seton agreed to give Lear certain rebates based on the size of the orders. Despite the great value of this contract, the parties initially put nothing in writing. (Note to students: Later in life, if you negotiate a multimillion dollar deal and fail to put it in writing, your grade in this course will be *retroactively lowered!*)

Both parties performed the contract satisfactorily for about a year. Then they agreed to a slight modification in the rebates. All was still well. In the fall of 1999, Lear asked Seton to send a written summary of the agreement, including the modified rebates. In November 1999, Seton sent a one-page memorandum to Lear, summarizing the agreement. It stated: "Lear is to award Seton the entire [truck and SUV program] cut-to-pattern business for the life of the program." The letter ended with a request that Lear "kindly return with acknowledgment signature," but Lear did not do so.

For two more years, the parties worked together amicably. Then Seton became anxious that Lear was planning to take its business elsewhere. In January 2002, Seton sent a letter requesting that Lear affirm its commitment to deal exclusively with Seton for the life of the GMC program. Lear responded that there had never been any such agreement. Seton filed suit.

At trial, Lear claimed that no contract had ever been signed. Seton replied that its memo summarizing the agreement created a valid contract under the "merchant exception" rule. The jury agreed with Seton and awarded the company $34 million. Lear appealed.

Issue: ***Did Seton's memorandum create a contract under the merchant exception?***

Excerpts from the Court's Per Curiam Decision: The attention of the jurors was focused upon two inquiries: first, whether Seton actually produced a "writing in confirmation of the contract"; and second, whether any such writing was sent to Lear "within a reasonable time." The defendant argues that the November 23, 1999, letter from Seton to Lear was not a confirmation of a contract but, rather, an offer to contract. To bolster that argument, Lear now emphasizes language in the letter stating, "We hope that the above meets with your understanding of this agreement." The jury, however, obviously gave more credence to the opening sentence of the letter directing Lear to "please find below the agreement reached by Messrs. M. Duross, Director of Purchasing for Lear Corporation and N. Showich, Vice President of Sales and Marketing for Seton Company."

Similarly, a closer look at the language of the entire November 23 letter reveals the falsity of the defendant's claim that the fact that the correspondence asked for an acknowledgment signature necessarily means that the letter was merely an offer that has not yet been accepted by Lear. As explained by the district judge, "Seton's November 23, 1999 letter did not *require* Lear to take an additional step in order to indicate its acceptance of the letter's terms. Therefore, the Court does not conclude as a matter of law that the letter merely was an offer."

The defendant also contests the timeliness of the letter. Although recognizing that the concept of a "reasonable time" for sending a written confirmation of the agreement depends on the nature, purpose, and circumstances of such action, Lear argues that the 13-month period between the making of the alleged contract and the letter is far too lengthy a period to be considered "reasonable." Again, the jury came to a contrary conclusion, possibly because the parties had engaged in congenial business relations with each other without incident for a lengthy period of time after negotiation of the 1998 agreement. Furthermore, a short time prior to issuance of the letter, Lear and Seton modified the terms of their agreement to extend the rebates that the plaintiff paid to the defendant. Even Lear does not argue that the period of time between that subsequent modification and the November 23 letter should be considered unreasonably long as a matter of law.

Affirmed.

UCC §2-201(3)—Special Circumstances

An oral contract *may* be enforceable, even without a written memorandum, if:

- **The seller is specially manufacturing the goods for the buyer, *or***
- **The defendant admits in court proceedings that there was a contract, *or***
- **The goods have been delivered or they have been paid for.**

Specially Manufactured Goods

If a seller, specially manufacturing goods for the buyer, begins work on them before the buyer cancels, and the goods cannot be sold elsewhere, the oral contract is binding. Bernice manufactures solar heating systems. She phones Jason and orders 75 special electrical converter units designed for her heating system, at $150 per unit. Jason begins manufacturing the units, but then Bernice phones again and says she no longer needs them. Bernice is bound by the contract. The goods are being manufactured for her and cannot be sold elsewhere. Jason had already begun work when she attempted to cancel. If the case goes to court, Jason will win.

Admissions in Court

When the defendant admits in court proceedings that the parties made an oral contract, the agreement is binding. Rex sues Sophie, alleging that she orally agreed to sell him five boa constrictors that have been trained to stand in a line and pass a full wine glass from one snake to the next. Sophie defends the lawsuit, but during a deposition, she says, "OK, we agreed verbally, but nothing was ever put in writing, and I knew I didn't have to go through with it. When I went home, the snakes made me feel really guilty, and I decided not to sell." Sophie's admission under oath dooms her defense.

The UCC gives merchants special leeway—and important responsibilities.

Goods Delivered or Paid For

If the seller has delivered the goods, or the buyer has paid for them, the contract may be enforced even with nothing in writing. Malik orally agrees to sell 500 plastic chairs to a university for use in its cafeteria. Malik delivers 300 of the chairs, but then the university notifies him that it will not honor the deal. Malik is entitled to payment for the 300 chairs, though not for the other 200. Conversely, if the university had sent a check for one-half of the chairs, it would be entitled to 250 chairs.

EXAM Strategy

Question: Beasley is a commercial honey farmer. He orally agrees to sell 500,000 pounds of honey to Grizzly at $1 per pound. Grizzly immediately faxes Beasley a signed confirmation, summarizing the deal. Beasley receives the fax but ignores it, and he never responds to Grizzly. Five days later, Beasley sells his honey to Brown for $1.15 per pound. Grizzly sues Beasley for breach of contract. Beasley claims that he signed nothing and was free to sell his honey anywhere he wanted. Who will win?

Strategy: Honey is a moveable thing, meaning that this contract is governed by the UCC. Under the Code, contracts for the sale of goods worth $500 or more must be in writing. However, the merchant exception changes things when both parties are merchants. Beasley and Grizzly are both merchants. Apply the merchant exception.

Result: Beasley breached the contract. Within a reasonable time after making the agreement, Grizzly sent a memo to Beasley confirming it. Beasley had 10 days either to object in writing or be held to the agreement. Beasley will lose this lawsuit because he ignored the faxed confirmation.

Parol Evidence

Tyrone agrees to buy Martha's house for $800,000. The contract obligates Tyrone to make a 10 percent down payment immediately and pay the remaining $720,000 in 45 days. As the two parties sign the deal, Tyrone discusses his need for financing. Unfortunately, at the end of 45 days, he has been unable to get a mortgage for the full amount. He claims that the parties orally agreed that he would get his deposit back if he could not obtain financing. But the written agreement says no such thing, and Martha disputes the claim. Who will win? Probably Martha, because of the parol evidence rule.

Parol evidence refers to anything (apart from the written contract itself) that was said, done, or written *before* the parties signed the agreement or *as they signed it.* Martha's conversation with Tyrone about financing the house was parol evidence because it occurred as they were signing the contract. Another important term is **integrated contract**, which means a writing that the parties intend as the final, complete expression of their agreement. Now for the rule.

Integrated contract
A writing that the parties intend as the final, complete expression of their agreement.

The parol evidence rule: When two parties make an integrated contract, neither one may use parol evidence to contradict, vary, or add to its terms. Negotiations may last for hours, weeks, or even months. Almost no contract includes everything that the parties said. When parties consider their agreement integrated, any statements they made before or while signing are irrelevant. If a court determines that Martha and Tyrone intended their agreement to be integrated, it will prohibit testimony about Martha's oral promises. One way to avoid parol evidence disputes is to include an *integration clause.* That is a statement clearly proclaiming that this writing is the "full and final expression" of the parties' agreement, and that anything said before signing or while signing is irrelevant. In the following case, learned people learned about parol evidence the hard way.

Mayo v. North Carolina State University

2005 WL 350567
North Carolina Court of Appeals, 2005

Facts: Dr. Robert Mayo was a tenured faculty member of the engineering department at North Carolina State University (NCSU), and director of the school's nuclear engineering program. In July, he informed his department chair, Dr. Paul Turinsky, that he was leaving NCSU effective September 1. Turinsky accepted the resignation.

In October, after Mayo had departed, Phyllis Jennette, the university's payroll coordinator, informed him that he had been overpaid. She explained that for employees who worked 9 months but were paid over 12 months, the salary checks for July and August were in fact prepayments for the period beginning that September. Because Mayo had not worked after September 1, the checks for July and August were overpayment. When he refused to refund the money, NCSU sought to claim it in legal proceedings. The first step was a hearing before an administrative agency.

At the hearing, Turinsky and Brian Simet, the university's payroll director, explained that the "prepayment" rule was a basic part of every employee's contract. However, both acknowledged that the prepayment rule was not included in any of the documents that formed Mayo's contract, including his appointment letter, annual salary letter, and policies adopted by the university's trustees. The university officials used other evidence, outside the written documents, to establish the prepayment policy.

Based on the additional evidence, the agency ruled that NCSU was entitled to its money. However, Mayo appealed to court, and the trial judge declared that he owed nothing, ruling that the university was not permitted to rely on parol evidence to establish its policy. NCSU appealed.

Issue: ***May NCSU rely on parol evidence to establish its prepayment rule?***

Excerpts from Judge Bryant's Decision: Here, the language of the employment agreement is clear and unambiguous—petitioner is to be paid in twelve monthly installments for his service as a nine-month, academic year, tenured faculty member.

The terms relied upon by NCSU were not expressly included in the employment agreement. Dr. Turinsky testified that petitioner's written employment agreement is comprised of terms found in petitioner's appointment letter, annual salary letter, and written policies adopted and amended by the UNC Board of Governors and the NCSU Board of Trustees. However, none of these documents forming the employment agreement set forth the compensation policies upon which NCSU bases its claim. Simet, Director of NCSU's Payroll Department, admitted at the agency hearing that the policies were "not stated anywhere specifically." Further, Dr. Turinsky testified he did not know of the existence of the terms until September, after petitioner left his employment with NCSU. NCSU, however, attempts to offer parol evidence to explain that payments made in July and August were prepayments for the following academic year.

The parol evidence rule prohibits the admission of parol evidence to vary, add to, or contradict a written instrument intended to be the final integration of the transaction. The rule is otherwise where it is shown that the writing is not a full integration of the terms of the contract, or when a contract is ambiguous, parol evidence is admissible to show and make certain the intention behind the contract.

Here Dr. Turinsky testified that petitioner's employment agreement consisted only of petitioner's appointment letter, his annual salary letter, and the policies adopted and amended by the UNC Board of Governors and by the NCSU Board of Trustees. It therefore appears the parties intended the above documents to be the final integration of the employment agreement. Additionally, we have already noted the language contained in the documents are unambiguous; thus, parol evidence may not be introduced to explain the terms of the agreement.

We hold petitioner does not owe a debt to NCSU as result of an alleged overpayment of salary.

[Affirmed.]

Exception: An Incomplete or Ambiguous Contract

If a court determines that a written contract is incomplete or ambiguous, it will permit parol evidence. Suppose that an employment contract states that the company will provide "full health coverage for Robert Watson and his family," but does not define *family*. Three years later, Watson divorces and remarries, acquiring three stepchildren, and a year later, his second wife has a baby. Watson now has two children by his first marriage and four by the second. The company refuses to insure Watson's first wife or his stepchildren. A court will probably find a key clause in his health care contract—"coverage for ... *his family*"—is ambiguous. A judge cannot determine exactly what the clause means from the contract itself, so the parties will be permitted to introduce parol evidence to prove whether or not the company must insure Watson's extended family.[11]

Fraud, Misrepresentation, or Duress

A court will permit parol evidence of fraud, misrepresentation, or duress. To encourage Annette to buy his house, Will assures her that no floodwaters from the nearby river have ever come within two miles of the house. Annette signs a contract that is silent about flooding and includes an integration clause stating that neither party is relying on any oral statements made during negotiations. When Annette moves in, she discovers that the foundation is collapsing due to earlier flooding and that Will knew of the flooding and the damage. Despite the integration clause, a court will probably allow Annette to testify about Will's misrepresentations.[12]

Chapter Conclusion

Some contracts must be in writing to be enforceable, and the writing must be clear and unambiguous. Drafting the contract need not be arduous. The disputes illustrated in this chapter could all have been prevented with a few carefully crafted sentences. It is worth the time and effort to write them.

Exam Review

1. **THE STATUTE OF FRAUDS** Several types of contract are enforceable only if written:
    - **LAND** The sale of any interest in land (pp. 342–344)
    - **ONE YEAR** An agreement that *cannot* be performed within one year (pp. 344–345)

EXAM Strategy

CPA Question: Able hired Carr to restore Able's antique car for $800. The terms of their oral agreement provided that Carr had 18 months to complete the work. Actually, the work could be completed within one year. The agreement is:

(a) Unenforceable because it covers services with a value in excess of $500

(b) Unenforceable because it covers a time period in excess of one year

[11]See, e.g., *Eure v. Norfolk Shipbuilding & Drydock Corp., Inc.*, 561 S.E.2d 663 (Va. 2002).

[12]*Lindberg v. Roseth*, 137 Idaho 222, 46 P.3d 518 (Idaho 2002).

(c) Enforceable because personal service contracts are exempt from the Statute of Frauds

(d) Enforceable because the work could be completed within one year

Strategy: This is a subtle question. Notice that the contract is for a sum greater than $500. But that is a red herring. Why? The contract also might take 18 months to perform. But it *could* be finished in less than a year. (See the "Result" at the end of this section.)

- **DEBT OF ANOTHER** A promise to pay the debt of another, including promises made by executors to pay an estate's debts. (pp. 345–346)

EXAM Strategy

Question: Donald Waide had a contracting business. He bought most of his supplies from Paul Bingham's supply center. Waide fell behind on his bills, and Bingham told Waide that he would extend no more credit to him. That same day, Donald's father, Elmer Waide, came to Bingham's store, and said to Bingham that he would "stand good" for any sales to Donald made on credit. Based on Elmer's statement, Bingham again gave Donald credit, and Donald ran up $10,000 in goods before Bingham sued Donald and Elmer. What defense did Elmer make, and what was the outcome?

Strategy: This was an oral agreement, so the issue is whether the promise had to be in writing to be enforceable. Review the list of six contracts that must be in writing. Is this agreement there? (See the "Result" at the end of this section.)

- **EXECUTORS** A promise made by an executor of an estate (p. 346)
- **MARRIAGE** A promise made in consideration of marriage; and (pp. 346–347)
- **GOODS** The sale of goods worth $500 or more (p. 350)

EXAM Strategy

Question: James River-Norwalk, Inc., was a paper and textile company that needed a constant supply of wood. James River orally contracted with Gary Futch to supply wood for the company, and Futch did so for several years. The deal was worth many thousands of dollars, but nothing was put in writing. Futch actually purchased the wood for his own account and then resold it to James River. After a few years, James River refused to do more business with Futch. Did the parties have a binding contract?

Strategy: If this is a contract for services, it is enforceable without anything in writing. However, if it is one for the sale of goods, it must be in writing. Clearly what James River wanted was the wood, and it did not care where Futch found it. (See the "Result" at the end of this section.)

2. **CONTENTS** The writing must be signed by the defendant and must state the name of all parties, the subject matter of the agreement, and all essential terms and promises. Electronic signatures usually are valid. (pp. 347–349)

3. **UNIFORM COMMERCIAL CODE (UCC)** A contract or memorandum for the sale of goods may be less complete than those required by the common law.

   - The basic UCC rule requires only a memorandum signed by the defendant, indicating that the parties reached an agreement and specifying the quantity of goods.
   - Between merchants, even less is required. If one merchant sends written confirmation of a contract, the merchant who receives the document must object within 10 days or be bound by the writing.
   - In the following special circumstances, no writing may be required: the goods are specially manufactured, one party admits in litigation that there was a contract, or one party pays for part of the goods or delivers some of the goods. (pp. 349–353)

4. **PAROL EVIDENCE** When an integrated contract exists, neither party may generally use parol evidence to contradict, vary, or add to its terms. Parol evidence refers to anything (apart from the written contract itself) that was said, done, or written before the parties signed the agreement or as they signed it. (pp. 353–355)

1. "One Year" Result: (d) A contract for the sale of goods worth $500 or more must be in writing—but this is a contract for *services*, not the sale of goods, so the $800 price is irrelevant. The contract *can* be completed within one year, and thus it falls outside the Statute of Frauds. This is an enforceable agreement.

1. "Debt of Another" Result: Elmer made a promise to pay the debt of another. He did so as a favor to his son. This is a collateral promise. Elmer never signed any such promise, and the agreement cannot be enforced against him.

1. "Goods" Result: James River was buying wood, and this is a contract for the sale of goods. With nothing in writing, signed by James River, Futch has no enforceable agreement.

Multiple-Choice Questions

1. **CPA QUESTION** Two individuals signed a contract that was intended to be their entire agreement. The parol evidence rule will prevent the admission of evidence offered to:
   (a) Explain the meaning of an ambiguity in the written contract
   (b) Establish that fraud had been committed in the formation of the contract
   (c) Prove the existence of a contemporaneous oral agreement modifying the contract
   (d) Prove the existence of a subsequent oral agreement modifying the contract

2. Raul wants to plant a garden, and he agrees to buy a small piece of land for $300. Later, he agrees to buy a table for $300. Neither agreement is put in writing. The

agreement to buy the land ____________ enforceable, and the agreement to buy the table ____________ enforceable.

(a) is; is

(b) is; is not

(c) is not; is

(d) is not; is not

3. The common-law Statute of Frauds requires that to be "in writing," an agreement must be signed by ...

(a) the plaintiff

(b) the defendant

(c) both A and B

(d) none of the above

4. Mandy verbally tells a motorcycle dealer that she will make her son's motorcycle payments if he falls behind on them. Will Mandy be legally required to live up to this agreement?

(a) Yes, absolutely

(b) Yes, if her son is under 18

(c) Yes, if Mandy will be the primary driver of the motorcycle

(d) Yes, if the motorcycle is worth less than $500

(e) No, absolutely not

5. In December 2012, Eric hires a band to play at a huge graduation party he is planning to hold in May, 2014. The deal is never put into writing. In January 2014, if he wanted to cancel the job, Eric ____________ be able to do so. If he does not cancel, and if the band shows up and plays at the party in May 2014, Eric ____________ have to pay them.

(a) will; will

(b) will; will not

(c) will not; will

(d) will not; will not

Essay Questions

1. Richard Griffin and three other men owned a grain company called Bearhouse, Inc., which needed to borrow money. First National Bank was willing to loan $490,000, but it insisted that the four men sign personal guaranties on the loan, committing themselves to repaying up to 25 percent of the loan each if Bearhouse defaulted. Bearhouse went bankrupt. The bank was able to collect some of its money from Bearhouse's assets, but it sued Griffin for the balance. At trial, Griffin wanted to testify that before he signed his guaranty, a bank officer assured him that he would only owe 25 percent of *whatever balance was unpaid*, not 25 percent of the total loan. How will the court decide whether Griffin is entitled to testify about the conversation?

2. When Deana Byers married Steven Byers, she was pregnant with another man's child. Shortly after the marriage, Deana gave birth. The marriage lasted only two months, and the couple separated. In divorce proceedings, Deana sought child support. She claimed that Steven had orally promised to support the child if Deana would marry him. Steven claims he never made the promise. Comment on the outcome.

3. Lonnie Hippen moved to Long Island, Kansas, to work in an insurance company owned by Griffiths. After he moved there, Griffiths offered to sell Hippen a house he owned, and Hippen agreed in writing to buy it. He did buy the house and moved in, but two years later, Hippen left the insurance company. He then claimed that at the time of the sale, Griffiths had orally promised to buy back his house at the selling price if Hippen should happen to leave the company. Griffiths defended based on the Statute of Frauds. Hippen argued that the Statute of Frauds did not apply because the repurchase of the house was essentially part of his employment with Griffiths. Comment.

4. Landlord owned a clothing store and agreed in writing to lease the store's basement to another retailer. The written lease, which both parties signed, (1) described the premises exactly, (2) identified the parties, and (3) stated the monthly rent clearly. But an appeals court held that the lease did not satisfy the Statute of Frauds. Why not?

5. **YOU BE THE JUDGE WRITING PROBLEM** Harrison Epperly operated United Brake Systems in Indianapolis, Indiana, and wanted to open a similar store in Nashville. He offered Kenneth Jarrett a job as manager, promising six months' severance pay if the store was not profitable in six months, and 49 percent ownership if he managed the new store for 10 years. Jarrett agreed, but the two men never put the deal in writing. Under Jarrett's management, the Nashville branch grew dramatically. After four years of renting space, the company purchased the land and buildings it used. Epperly periodically acknowledged his promise to make Jarrett 49 percent owner of the Nashville branch, and from time to time, he mentioned the arrangement to other workers. But after 10 years, Epperly sold United Brake, which had grown to 23 branches, to another company for $11 million. Jarrett sued Epperly for 49 percent of the Nashville branch. The trial court awarded Jarrett $812,000. Epperly appealed. Is Jarrett's contract with Epperly barred by the Statute of Frauds? **Argument for Epperly:** This alleged contract is unenforceable for two reasons. First, the agreement includes real estate; namely, the valuable land and buildings the company uses. A contract for the sale of any interest in land is unenforceable unless written. Second, the contract could not have been performed within 1 year. If there was a deal, then by Jarrett's own words, the parties intended it to last 10 years. And 10 years' work cannot be performed in 1 year. **Argument for Jarrett:** The agreement had nothing to do with land. Jarrett and Epperly agreed that Mr. Jarrett would obtain a 49 percent ownership of the *Nashville branch*. At the time they made that agreement, the Nashville branch had no real estate. There is no rule saying that a valid contract becomes invalid because a corporation acquires some land. The "not in one year" argument also misses the point. The primary obligation was to open the branch and manage it for six months. If it was not profitable, Mr. Jarrett would immediately receive six months' severance pay, and the contract would be fully performed by both parties in less than a year. Finally, Epperly made a binding commitment, and Mr. Jarrett relied. Promissory estoppel prohibits Mr. Epperly from using deceit to profit.

Discussion Questions

1. **ETHICS** Jacob Deutsch owned commercial property. He orally agreed to rent it for six years to Budget Rent-A-Car. Budget took possession, began paying monthly rent, and, over a period of several months, expended about $6,000 in upgrading the property. Deutsch was aware of the repairs. After a year, Deutsch attempted to evict Budget. Budget claimed it had a six-year oral lease, but Deutsch claimed that such a lease was worthless. Please rule. Is it ethical for Deutsch to use the Statute of Frauds in attempting to defeat the lease? Assume that, as landlord, you had orally agreed to rent premises to a tenant, but then for business reasons, you preferred not to carry out the deal. Would you evict a tenant if you thought the Statute of Frauds would enable you to do so? How should you analyze the problem? What values are most important to you?

2. Mast Industries and Bazak International were two textile firms. Mast orally offered to sell certain textiles to Bazak for $103,000. Mast promised to send documents confirming the agreement, but it never did. Finally, Bazak sent a memorandum to Mast confirming the agreement, describing the goods, and specifying their quantity and the price. Bazak's officer signed the memo. Mast received the memo but never agreed to it in writing. When Mast failed to deliver the goods, Bazak sued. Who will win? Why?

3. Is the Statute of Frauds reasonable, or does it unacceptably allow people to escape their obligations on a mere technicality?

4. Does the coverage of the Statute of Frauds make sense as it currently stands? Would it be better to expand the law and require that all contracts be in writing? Or should the law be done away with altogether?

5. Compare the common-law Statute of Frauds to the UCC version. What are the specific differences? Which is more reasonable? Why?

CHAPTER 17

Performance and Discharge

Polly disliked a veal dish and gagged on one of Caesar's soups. She fired her chef.

Polly was elated. It was the grand opening of her new restaurant, Polly's Folly, and everything was bubbling. The wait staff hustled, and Caesar, the chef, churned out succulent dishes. Polly had signed a contract promising him $1,500 per week for one year, "provided Polly is personally satisfied with his cooking." Polly was determined that her restaurant would be glorious. Her three-year lease would cost $6,000 per month, and she had signed an advertising deal with Billboard Bonanza for the same period. Polly had also promised Eddie, a publicity agent, a substantial monthly fee, to begin as soon as the restaurant was 80 percent booked for one month. Tonight, with candles flickering at packed tables, Polly beamed.

After a week, Polly's smiles were a bit forced. Some of Caesar's new dishes had been failures, including a grilled swordfish that was hard to pierce and shrimp jambalaya that was too spicy. The restaurant was only 60 percent full, and the publicity agent yelled at Caesar for costing him money. Later that month, Polly disliked a veal dish and gagged on one of Caesar's soups. She fired her chef.

Then troubles gushed forth—literally. A water main burst in front of Polly's restaurant, flooding the street. The city embarked on a two-month repair job that ultimately took four times that long. The street was closed to traffic, and no one could park within blocks of Polly's restaurant. Patronage dropped steadily as hungry customers refused to deal with the bad parking and construction noise. After several months, behind on the rent and in debt to everyone, Polly closed her doors for good.

Shortly, the court doors swung open, offering a full menu of litigation. Polly's landlord sued for three years' rent, and Billboard Bonanza demanded its money for the same period. Caesar claimed his year's pay. Eddie, the agent, insisted on some money for his hard work. Polly defended vigorously, seeking to be *discharged* from her various contracts.

Discharge
A party is discharged when she has no more duties under the contract.

If a party is **discharged,** she is "finished," and has no more duties under a contract. In each lawsuit, Polly asked a court to declare that her obligations were terminated and that she owed no money.

Most contracts are discharged by full performance. In other words, the parties generally do what they promise. Suppose, before the restaurant opened, Walter had promised to deliver 100 sets of cutlery to Polly and she had promised to pay $20 per set. Walter delivered the goods on time, and Polly paid $2000 on delivery. The parties got what they expected, and that contract was fully discharged.

Rescind
To terminate a contract by mutual agreement.

Sometimes the parties discharge a contract by agreement. For example, the parties may agree to **rescind** their contract, meaning that they terminate it by mutual agreement.[1] If Polly's landlord believed he could get more rent from a new tenant, he might agree to rescind her lease. But he was dubious about the rental market and refused to rescind.

At times, a court may discharge a party who has not performed. When things have gone amiss, a judge must interpret the contract and issues of public policy to determine who in fairness should suffer the loss. In the lawsuits brought by the landlord and Billboard Bonanza, Polly argued a defense called "commercial impracticability," claiming that she should not be forced to rent space that was useless to her or buy advertising for a restaurant that had closed. From Polly's point of view, the claim was understandable. But we can also respect the arguments made by the landlord and the advertiser, that they did not cause the burst water main. Claims of commercial impracticability are difficult to win, and Polly lost against both of these opponents. Though she was making no money at all from the restaurant, the court found her liable in full for the lease and the advertising contract.[2]

Polly's argument against Caesar raised another issue of discharge. Caesar claimed that his cooking was good professional work and that all chefs have occasional disasters, especially in a new restaurant. But Polly responded that they had a "personal satisfaction" contract. Under such contracts, "good" work may not suffice if it fails to please the promisee. Polly won this argument, and Caesar recovered nothing.

As to Eddie's suit, Polly raised a defense called "condition precedent," meaning that some event had to occur before she was obligated to pay. Polly claimed that she owed Eddie money only if and when the restaurant was 80 percent full for a month, and that had never happened. The court agreed and discharged Polly on Eddie's claim.

We will analyze each of these issues, and begin with a look at conditions.

CONDITIONS

Condition
An event that must occur before a party becomes obligated under a contract.

Parties often put conditions in a contract. A **condition** is an event that must occur before a party becomes obligated under a contract. "I'll agree to do something, but only if something else happens first." Polly agreed to pay Eddie, the agent, a percentage of her profits, but with an important condition: 80 percent of the tables had to be booked for a month. Unless and until those tables were occupied, Polly owed Eddie nothing. That never happened, or, in contract language, the *condition failed,* and so Polly was discharged.

Conditions can take many forms. Alex would like to buy Kevin's empty lot and build a movie theater on it, but the city's zoning law will not permit that kind of business in that

[1]The parties could also decide that one party's duties will be performed by someone else, a modification called a **novation**. Alternatively, they could create an **accord and satisfaction,** in which they agree that one party will substitute a new kind of performance in place of his contract obligations. See Chapter 16, on third parties, and Chapter 12, on consideration.

[2]Based on *Luminous Neon v. Parscale,* 17 Kan. App. 2d 241, 836 P.2d 1201, 1992 Kan. App. LEXIS 572 (Kan. Ct. App. 1992).

location. Alex signs a contract to buy Kevin's empty lot in 120 days, *provided that* within 100 days, the city re-zones the area to permit a movie theater. If the city fails to re-zone the area by day 100, Alex is discharged and need not complete the deal.

Another example: Friendly Insurance issues a policy covering Vivian's house, promising to pay for any loss due to fire, but only if Vivian furnishes proof of her losses within 60 days of the damage. If the house burns down, Friendly becomes liable to pay. But if Vivian arrives with her proof 70 days after the fire, she collects nothing. Friendly, though it briefly had a duty to pay, was discharged when Vivian failed to furnish the necessary information on time.

How Conditions Are Created

Express Conditions

The parties may expressly state a condition. Alex's contract with Kevin expressly discharged all obligations if the city failed to re-zone within the stated period. Notice that **no special language is necessary to create the condition**. Phrases such as "provided that" frequently indicate a condition, but neither those nor any other specific words are essential. So long as the contract's language indicates that the parties *intended* to create a condition, a court will enforce it.

Because informal language can create a condition, the parties may dispute whether they intended one or not. Sand Creek Country Club, in Indiana, was eager to expand its clubhouse facilities and awarded the design work to CSO Architects. The club wanted the work done quickly but had not secured financing. The architects sent a letter confirming their agreement:

> It was our intent to allow Mr. Dan Moriarty of our office to start work on your project as early as possible in order to allow you to meet the goals that you have set for next fall. Also, it was the intent of CSO to begin work on your project and delay any billings to you until your financing is in place. As I explained to you earlier, we will continue on this course until we reach a point where we can no longer continue without receiving some payment.

The club gave CSO the go-ahead to begin design work, and the architects did their work and billed Sand Creek for $33,000. But the club, unable to obtain financing, refused to pay. Sand Creek claimed that CSO's letter created a *condition* in their agreement; namely, that the club would have to pay only if and when it obtained financing. The court was unpersuaded and ruled that the parties had never intended to create an express condition. The architects were merely delaying their billing as a convenience to the club. It would be absurd, said the court, to assume that CSO intended to perform $33,000 worth of work for free.[3]

Professional sports contracts are often full of conditions. Assume that the San Francisco Giants want to sign Tony Fleet to play center field. The club considers him a fine defensive player but a dubious offensive performer. The many conditional clauses in his contract reflect hard bargaining over an athlete who may or may not become a star. The Giants guarantee Fleet only $500,000, a very modest salary by Major League Baseball standards. If the speedy outfielder appears in at least 120 games, his pay increases to $1 million. Winning a Gold Glove award is worth an extra $200,000 to him. The Giants insist on a team option to re-sign Fleet for the following season at a salary of $800,000, but if the center-fielder plays in fewer than 100 games, the team loses that right, leaving Fleet free to negotiate for higher pay with other teams.

---

[3] *Sand Creek Country Club, Ltd. v. CSO Architects, Inc.*, 582 N.E.2d 872, 1991 Ind. App. LEXIS 2151 (Ind. Ct. App. 1991).

Implied Conditions

At other times, the parties say nothing about a condition, but it is clear from their agreement that they have implied one. Charlotte orally rents an apartment to Hakan for one year and promises to fix any problems in the unit. It is an implied condition that Hakan will promptly notify Charlotte of anything needing repair. Although the parties have not said anything about notice, it is only common sense that Hakan must inform his landlord of defects since she will have no other way to learn of them.

Types of Conditions

Courts divide conditional clauses into three categories: (1) condition precedent, (2) condition subsequent, and (3) concurrent conditions.[4] But what they have in common is more important than any of their differences. The key to all conditional clauses is this: **if the condition does not occur, one party will probably be discharged without having to perform his obligations under a contract**.

Condition Precedent

In this kind of condition, an event must occur *before* a duty arises. Polly's contract with Eddie concerned a condition precedent. Polly had no obligation to pay Eddie anything *unless and until* the restaurant was 80 percent full for a month. Since that never happened, she was discharged. If the parties agreed to a condition precedent, the *plaintiff* has the burden to prove that the condition happened and that the defendant was obligated to perform.

In the following case, the plaintiff claimed that it had met a condition precedent and was entitled to a payment. Not surprisingly, the defendant had a different point of view.

American Electronic Components, Inc. v. Agere Systems, Inc.

2009 U.S. App. LEXIS 12763
Third Circuit Court of Appeals, 2009

Facts: American Electronic Components, Inc. (AECI), agreed to a three-year contract under which it would sell Agere Systems's equipment. The contract said in part, "AECI shall receive a percentage of the sale price for each item of Equipment sold."

Agere announced that it planned to close a subsidiary in Madrid. AECI found potential buyers for the Madrid equipment, but Agere ultimately sold it to a different buyer.

AECI sued, arguing that it should be paid a commission because of its effort in trying to sell the equipment. It also argued that when Agere sold the equipment, it had interfered with AECI's ability to fulfill the contract's condition precedent.

The trial court dismissed the complaint, and AECI appealed.

Issues: ***Was a* completed sale *a condition precedent in this agreement? Was Agere liable for interfering with AECI's sales efforts?***

Excerpts from Judge Smith's Decision: As the District Court determined, the contract clearly sets forth when AECI is owed a commission: when AECI consummated a sale of equipment.

AECI argues that summary judgment is not appropriate because the parties dispute whether AECI expended substantial effort to find a buyer for the equipment. AECI

[4]The Restatement (Second) of Contracts has officially abandoned the terms *condition precedent* and *condition subsequent.* See Restatement §§224 et seq. But courts routinely use the terms, so it is difficult to avoid the old distinctions.

claims that it acted as Agere's broker and is thus owed a commission for merely finding a buyer for the Madrid equipment. This argument is unavailing, as the contract specifically limits AECI's entitlement to a commission to situations where it actually sold the designated equipment. Thus, whether AECI expended resources to—and did in fact—find a buyer for the Madrid equipment, are not material to whether AECI is owed a commission.

Finally, there is not sufficient evidence for a reasonable jury to conclude that Agere should be required to pay AECI a commission because Agere improperly prevented AECI from fulfilling the contract's condition precedent—consummating the sale. AECI correctly asserts that a party may not escape contractual liability by relying on the failure of a condition precedent where the party wrongfully prevented the performance of that condition. The record does not support this conclusion here. The facts that AECI located potential buyers for the Madrid equipment and that Agere eventually sold the equipment do not lead to the inference that Agere engaged in some sort of subterfuge to prevent AECI from earning a commission. Further, the non-exclusive contract allows Agere to sell its own equipment.

For the reasons stated above, we affirm.

Condition Subsequent

This type of condition must occur *after* a particular duty arises. If the condition does not occur, the duty is discharged. Vivian's policy with Friendly Insurance contains a condition subsequent. As soon as the fire broke out, Friendly became obligated to pay for the damage. But if Vivian failed to produce her proof of loss on time, Friendly's obligation ended – it was discharged. Note that, with a condition subsequent, it is the *defendant* who must prove that the condition occurred, relieving him of any obligation.

CONDITION PRECEDENT AND CONDITION SUBSEQUENT COMPARED

	Condition Created	**Does Condition Occur?**	**Duty Is Determined**	**Result**
Condition Precedent	"Fee to be paid when restaurant is filled to 80% capacity for one month."	Condition DOES occur: restaurant is packed.	Duty arises: Polly owes Eddie his fee.	Polly pays the fee.
		Condition DOES NOT occur: restaurant is empty.	Duty never arises: Polly is discharged.	Polly pays nothing.
	Condition Created	**Duty Is Determined**	**Does Condition Occur?**	**Result**
Condition Subsequent	"Vivian must give proof of loss within 60 days."	Fire damages property, and Friendly Insurance becomes obligated to pay Vivian.	Condition DOES occur: Vivian proves her losses within 60 days.	Friendly pays Vivian for her losses.
			Condition DOES NOT occur: Vivian fails to prove her losses within 60 days.	Friendly is discharged and owes nothing

Concurrent Conditions

Here, both parties have a duty to perform *simultaneously*. Renee agrees to sell her condominium to Tim on July 5. Renee agrees to furnish a valid deed and clear title to the property on that date, and Tim promises to present a cashier's check for $200,000. The parties have agreed to concurrent conditions. Each performance is the condition for the other's performance. If Renee arrives at the Registry of Deeds and can say only, "Don't worry. I'm totally sure I own this property," Tim need not present his check; similarly, if Tim arrives with only an "IOU" scribbled on the back of a candy wrapper, Renee has no duty to hand over a valid deed.

EXAM Strategy

Question: Roberto wants to buy Naomi's house for $350,000 and is willing to make a 20 percent down payment, which satisfies Naomi. However, he needs a $280,000 mortgage in order to complete the purchase, and he is not certain he can obtain one. Naomi is worried that Roberto might change his mind about buying the house and then use alleged financing problems to skip out of the deal. How can the two parties protect themselves?

Strategy: Both parties should use conditional clauses in the sales agreement. Naomi must force Roberto to do his best to obtain a mortgage. How? Roberto's clause should protect him if he cannot obtain a sufficient mortgage. How?

Result: Naomi should demand the 20 percent down payment. Further, her conditional clause should state that Roberto forfeits the down payment unless he demonstrates that, within two weeks, he has applied in good faith for a mortgage to at least three banks. Roberto should insist that if he promptly and fully applies to three banks but fails to obtain a mortgage, his down payment is refunded.

Public Policy

At times, a court will refuse to enforce an express condition on the grounds that it is unfair and harmful to the general public. In other words, a court might agree that the parties created a conditional clause but conclude that permitting its enforcement would hurt society. Did the insurance contract in the following case harm society? You be the judge.

You be the Judge

Anderson v. Country Life Insurance Co.

180 Ariz. 625, 886 P.2d 1381, 1994 Ariz. App. LEXIS 240
Arizona Court of Appeals, 1994

Facts: On November 26, a Country Life Insurance agent went to the house of Donald and Anna Mae Anderson. He persuaded the Andersons to buy a life insurance policy and accepted a check for $1,600. He gave the Andersons a "conditional receipt for medical policy," dated that day. The form stated that the Andersons would have a valid life insurance policy with Country Life, effective November 26, but only when all conditions were met. The most important of these conditions was that the Country Life home office accepts the Andersons as medical risks. The Andersons were pleased with the new policy and glad that it was effective that same day.

It was not. Donald Anderson died of a heart attack a few weeks later. Country Life declined the Andersons as medical risks and refused to issue a policy. Anna Mae Anderson sued. Country Life pointed out that medical approval was a condition precedent. In other words, the company argued that the policy would be effective as of November 26, but only if it later decided to make the policy effective. Based on this argument, the trial court gave summary judgment for Country Life. Ms. Anderson appealed, claiming that the conditional clause was a violation of public policy.

You Be the Judge: ***Did the conditional clause violate public policy?***

Argument for Ms. Anderson: Your honors, this policy is a scam. This so-called "conditional receipt for medical policy" is designed to trick customers and then steal their money. The company leads people to believe they are covered as of the day they write the check. But they aren't covered until *much later*, when the insurer gets around to deciding the applicant's medical status.

The company gets the customer's money right away and gives nothing in exchange. If the company, after taking its time, decides the applicant is not medically fit, it returns the money, having used it for weeks or even months to earn interest. If, on the other hand, the insurance company decides the applicant is a good bet, it then issues the policy effective for weeks or months *in the past, when coverage is of no use.* No one can die retroactively, your honors. The company is being paid for a period during which it had no risk.This is a fraud and a disgrace, and the company should pay the benefits it owes.

Argument for Country Life: Your honors, is Country Life supposed to issue life insurance policies without doing a medical check? That is the road to bankruptcy and would mean that no one could obtain this valuable coverage. Of course we do a medical inquiry, as quickly as possible. It's in our interest to get the policy decided one way or the other.

The policy clearly stated that coverage was effective *only when approved by the home office*, after all inquiries were made. The Andersons knew that as well as the agent. If they were covered immediately, why would the company do a medical check? Country Life resents suggestions that this policy is a scam, when in reality it is Ms. Anderson who is trying to profit from a tragedy that the company had nothing to do with.

The facts of this case are unusual. Obviously, most insureds do not die between application and acceptance. It would be disastrous for society to rewrite every insurance policy in this state based on one very sad fact pattern. The contract was clear and it should be enforced as written.

PERFORMANCE

Caitlin has an architect draw up plans for a monumental new house, and Daniel agrees to build it by September 1. Caitlin promises to pay $900,000 on that date. The house is ready on time, but Caitlin has some complaints. The living room was supposed to be 18 feet high, but it is only 17 feet; the pool was to be azure, yet it is aquamarine; the maid's room was not supposed to be wired for cable television, but it is. Caitlin refuses to pay anything for the house. Is she justified? Of course not, it would be absurd to give her a magnificent house for free when it has only tiny defects. But in this easy answer lurks a danger. Technically, Daniel did breach the contract, and yet the law allows him to recover the full contract price, or virtually all of it. Once that principle is established, how far will a court stretch it? Suppose the living room is only 14 feet high, or 12 feet, or 5 feet? What if the foundation has a small crack? A vast and dangerous split? What if Daniel finishes the house a month late? Six months late? Three years late? At some point, a court will conclude that Daniel has so thoroughly botched the job that he deserves little or no money. But where, exactly, is that point? This is a question that businesses—and judges—face often.

The more complex a contract, the more certain that at least one party will perform imperfectly. Nearly every house ever built has at least some small defects. A delivery of a thousand bushels of apples is sure to include a few rotten ones. A custom-designed computer system for a huge airline is likely to have some glitches. The cases raise several related doctrines, all concerning *how well* a party performed its contractual obligations.

Strict Performance and Substantial Performance

Strict Performance

When Daniel built Caitlin's house with three minor defects, she refused to pay, arguing that he had not *strictly performed* his obligations. Her assertion was correct, yet she lost anyway. Courts dislike strict performance because it enables one party to benefit without paying and sends the other one home empty-handed. A party is generally not required to render

Strict performance
Requires one party to perform its obligations precisely, with no deviation from the contract terms.

strict performance unless the contract expressly demands it *and* such a demand is reasonable. Caitlin's contract never suggested that Daniel would forfeit all payment if there were minor problems. Even if Caitlin had insisted on such a clause, few courts would have enforced it because the requirement would be unreasonable for a project as complicated as the construction of a $900,000 home.

There are some cases where strict performance does make sense. Marshall agrees to deliver 500 sweaters to Leo's store, and Leo promises to pay $20,000 cash on delivery. If Leo has only $19,000 cash and a promissory note for $1,000, he has failed to perform, and Marshall need not give him the sweaters. Leo's payment represents 95 percent of what he promised, but there is a big difference between getting the last $1,000 in cash and receiving a promissory note for that amount.

Substantial Performance

Substantial performance
Occurs when one party fulfills enough of its contract obligations to warrant payment.

Daniel, the house builder, won his case against Caitlin because he fulfilled *most* of his obligations, even though he did an imperfect job. Courts often rely on the substantial performance doctrine, especially in cases involving services as opposed to those concerning the sale of goods or land. In a contract for services, a party that **substantially performs** its obligations will generally receive the full contract price, minus the value of any defects. Daniel receives $900,000, the contract price, minus the value of a ceiling that is 1 foot too low, a pool the wrong color, and so forth. It will be for the trial court to decide how much those defects are worth. If the court decides the low ceiling is a $10,000 defect, the pool color is worth $5,000, and the cable television wiring error is worth $500, then Daniel receives $884,500.

© Wally Stemberger/Shutterstock
Substantial performance is vital, unless you enjoy working for free.

On the other hand, a **party that fails to perform substantially receives nothing on the contract itself and will recover only the value of the work, if any.** If the foundation cracks in Caitlin's house and the walls collapse, Daniel will not receive his $900,000. In such a case, he collects only the market value of the work he has done, which, since the house is a pile of rubble, is probably zero.

When is performance substantial? There is no perfect test, but courts look at these issues:

- How much benefit has the promisee received?
- If it is a construction contract, can the owner use the thing for its intended purpose?
- Can the promisee be compensated with money damages for any defects?
- Did the promisor act in good faith?

EXAM Strategy

Question: Jade owns a straight track used for drag racing. She hires Trevor to resurface it, for $180,000, paying $90,000 down. When the project is completed, Jade refuses to pay the balance and sues Trevor for her down payment. He counterclaims for the $90,000 still due. At trial, Trevor proves that all of the required materials were applied by trained workers in an expert fashion, the dimensions were perfect, and his profit margin very modest. The head of the national drag racing association testifies that his group considers the strip unsafe. He noticed puddles in both asphalt lanes, found the concrete starting pads unsafe, and believed the racing surface needed to be ground off and reapplied. His organization refuses to sanction races at the track until repairs are made. Who wins the suit?

Strategy: When one party has performed imperfectly, we have an issue of substantial performance. To decide whether Trevor is entitled to his money, we apply four factors: (1) How much benefit did Jade receive? (2) Can she use the racing strip for its intended purpose? (3) Can Jade be compensated for defects? (4) Did Trevor act in good faith?

Result: Jade has received no benefit whatsoever. She cannot use her drag strip for racing. Compensation will not help Jade—she needs a new strip. Trevor's work must be ripped up and replaced. Trevor may have acted in good faith, but he failed to deliver what Jade bargained for. Jade wins all of the money she paid. (As we will see in the next chapter, she may also win additional sums for her lost profits.)

Personal Satisfaction Contracts

Sujata, president of a public relations firm, hires Ben to design a huge multimedia project for her company, involving computer software, music, and live actors, all designed to sell frozen bologna sandwiches to supermarkets. His contract guarantees him two years' employment, provided all of his work "is acceptable in the sole judgment of Sujata." Ben's immediate supervisor is delighted with his work and his colleagues are impressed, but Sujata is not. Three months later, she fires him, claiming that his work is "uninspired." Does she have the right to do that?

This is a **personal satisfaction contract**, in which the promisee makes a personal, subjective evaluation of the promisor's performance. Employment contracts may require personal satisfaction of the employer; agreements for the sale of goods may demand that the buyer be personally satisfied with the product; and deals involving a credit analysis of one party may insist that his finances be satisfactory to the other party. In resolving disputes like Ben and Sujata's, judges must decide: when is it *fair* for the promisee to claim that she is not satisfied? May she make that decision for any reason at all, even on a whim?

Personal satisfaction contracts
Permit the promisee to make a subjective evaluations of the promisor's performance.

A court applies a subjective standard only if assessing the work involves personal feelings, taste, or judgment and the contract explicitly demanded personal satisfaction. A "subjective standard" means that the promisee's personal views will greatly influence her judgment, even if her decision is foolish and unfair. Artistic or creative work, or highly specialized tasks designed for a particular employer, may involve subtle issues of quality and personal preference. Ben's work combines several media and revolves around his judgment. Accordingly, the law applies a subjective standard to Sujata's decision. Since she concludes that his work is uninspired, she may legally fire him, even if her decision is irrational.

> Either the system works or it does not.

Note that the promisee, Sujata, has to show two things: that assessing Ben's work involves her personal judgment *and* that their contract explicitly demands personal satisfaction. If the contract were vague on this point, Sujata would lose. Had the agreement merely said, "Ben will at all times make his best efforts," Sujata could not fire him.

In all other cases, a court applies an *objective* standard to the promisee's decision. In other words, the objective standard will be used if assessing the work does not involve personal judgment *or* if the contract failed to explicitly demand personal satisfaction. An objective standard means that the promisee's judgment of the work must be reasonable. Suppose Sujata hires Leila to install an alarm system for her company, and the contract requires that Sujata be "personally satisfied." Leila's system passes all tests, but Sujata claims, "It just doesn't make me feel secure. I know that someday it's going to break down." May Sujata refuse to pay? No. Even though the contract used the phrase "personally satisfied," a mechanical alarm system does not involve personal judgment and taste. Either the system works or it does not. A reasonable person would find that Leila's system is just fine and therefore, under the objective standard, Sujata must pay. The law strongly favors the objective standard because the subjective standard gives unlimited power to the promisee.

Good Faith

The parties to a contract must carry out their obligations in good faith. The difficulty, of course, is applying this general rule to the wide variety of problems that may arise when people or companies do business. How far must one side go to meet its good faith burden? Marvin Shuster was a physician in Florida. Three patients sued him for alleged malpractice. Shuster denied any wrongdoing and asked his insurer to defend the claims. But the insurance company settled all three claims without defending and with a minimum of investigation. Shuster paid nothing out of his own pocket, but he sued the insurance company, claiming that it acted in bad faith. The doctor argued that the company's failure to defend him caused emotional suffering and meant that it would be impossible for him to obtain new malpractice insurance. The Florida Supreme Court found that the insurer acted in good faith. The contract clearly gave all control of malpractice cases to the company. It could settle or defend as it saw fit. Here, the company considered it more economical to settle quickly, and Shuster should have known, from the contract language, that the insurer might choose to do so.[5]

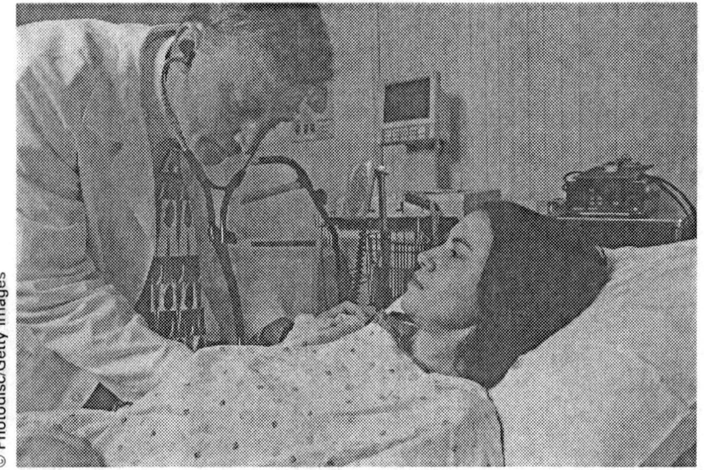

How far must one side go to meet its good faith burden?

In the following case, one party to a contract played its cards very close to its chest. Too close?

Brunswick Hills Racquet Club Inc. v. Route 18 Shopping Center Associates

182 N.J. 210, 864 A.2d 387
Supreme Court of New Jersey, 2005

Facts: Brunswick Hills Racquet Club (Brunswick) owned a tennis club on property that it leased from Route 18 Shopping Center Associates (Route 18). The lease ran for 25 years, and Brunswick had spent about $1 million in capital improvements. The lease expired, and Brunswick had the option of either buying the property

[5]*Shuster v. South Broward Hospital Dist. Physicians' Prof. Liability Ins. Trust*, 591 So. 2d 174, 1992 Fla. LEXIS 20 (Fla. 1992).

or purchasing a 99-year lease, both on very favorable terms. To exercise its option, Brunswick had to notify Route 18 no later than September 30 and had to pay the option price of $150,000. If Brunswick failed to exercise its options, the existing lease automatically renewed as of September 30, for 25 more years, but at more than triple the current rent.

Brunswick's lawyer wrote to Rosen Associates, the company that managed Route 18, nineteen months before the option deadline, stating that Brunswick intended to exercise the option for a 99-year lease. He requested that the lease be sent well in advance so that he could review it. He did not make the required payment of $150,000. Rosen replied that it had forwarded Spector's letter to its attorney, who would be in touch. In April, Spector again wrote, asking for a reply from Rosen or its lawyer.

Over the next six months, the lawyer continually asked for a copy of the lease or further information, but neither Route 18's lawyer nor anyone else provided any data. Eventually, the September deadline passed.

Route 18's lawyer notified Brunswick that it could not exercise its option to lease because it had failed to pay the $150,000 by September 30.

Brunswick sued, claiming that Route 18 had breached its duty of good faith and fair dealing. The trial court found that Route 18 had no duty to notify Brunswick of impending deadlines, and it gave summary judgment for Route 18. The appellate court affirmed, and Brunswick appealed to the state supreme court.

Issue: ***Did Route 18 breach its duty of good faith and fair dealing?***

Excerpts from Justice Albin's Decision: Courts generally should not tinker with a finely drawn and precise contract entered into by experienced business people that regulates their financial affairs. [However,] every party to a contract is bound by a duty of good faith and fair dealing in both the performance and enforcement of the contract. Good faith is a concept that defies precise definition. Good faith conduct is conduct that does not violate community standards of decency, fairness, or reasonableness. The covenant of good faith and fair dealing calls for parties to a contract to refrain from doing anything which will have the effect of destroying or injuring the right of the other party to receive the benefits of the contract.

Our review of the undisputed facts of this case leads us to the inescapable conclusion that defendant breached the covenant of good faith and fair dealing. Nineteen months in advance of the option deadline, plaintiff notified defendant in writing of its intent to exercise the option to purchase the 99-year lease. Plaintiff mistakenly believed that the purchase price was not due until the time of closing.

During a 19-month period, defendant, through its agents, engaged in a pattern of evasion, sidestepping every request by plaintiff to discuss the option and ignoring plaintiff's repeated written and verbal entreaties to move forward on closing the 99-year lease despite the impending option deadline and obvious potential harm to plaintiff.

Defendant never requested the purchase price of the lease. Indeed, as defendant's attorney candidly admitted at oral argument, defendant did not want the purchase price because the successful exercise of the option was not in defendant's economic interest.

Ordinarily, we are content to let experienced commercial parties fend for themselves and do not seek to introduce intolerable uncertainty into a carefully structured contractual relationship by balancing equities. But there are ethical norms that apply even to the harsh and sometimes cutthroat world of commercial transactions. We do not expect a landlord or even an attorney to act as his brother's keeper in a commercial transaction. We do expect, however, that they will act in good faith and deal fairly with an opposing party. Plaintiff's repeated letters and telephone calls to defendant concerning the exercise of the option and the closing of the 99-year lease obliged defendant to respond, and to respond truthfully.

[Plaintiff is entitled to exercise the 99-year lease.]

EXAM Strategy

Question: Sun operates an upscale sandwich shop in New Jersey, in a storefront that she leases from Ricky for $18,000 per month. The lease, which expires soon, allows Sun to renew for five years at $22,000 per month. Ricky knows, but Sun does not, that in a year, Prada will open a store on the same block. The dramatic increase in pedestrian traffic will render Sun's space more valuable. Ricky says nothing about Prada, Sun declines to renew, and Ricky leases the space for $40,000 a month. Sun sues Ricky, claiming he breached his duty of good faith and fair dealing. Based on the *Brunswick Hills* case, how would the New Jersey Supreme Court rule?

Strategy: In the *Brunswick Hills* case, the court, on the one hand, criticized the defendant for cynically evading the plaintiff's efforts to renew. However, the court also said, "We do not expect a landlord or even an attorney to act as his brother's keeper in a commercial transaction." Using those opposing themes as guidelines, examine the court's decision and predict the ruling in Sun's suit.

Result: *Brunswick Hills* begins: "Courts generally should not tinker with a finely drawn and precise contract entered into by experienced business people." Sun's lease imposes no responsibility on Ricky to report on neighborhood changes or forecast profitability. Further, Sun made no requests to Ricky about the area's future. Sun is asking Ricky to be "her brother's keeper," and neither this court nor any other will do that. She loses.

Time of the Essence Clauses

> Go, sir, gallop, and don't forget that the world was made in six days. You can ask me for anything you like, except time.
>
> *Napoleon, to an aide, 1803*

Generals are not the only ones who place a premium on time. Ask Gene LaSalle. The Seabreeze Restaurant agreed to sell him all of its assets. The parties signed a contract stating the price and closing date. Seabreeze insisted on a clause saying, "Seabreeze considers that time is of the essence in consummating the proposed transaction." Such clauses are common in real estate transactions and in any other agreement where a delay would cause serious damage to one party. LaSalle was unable to close on the date specified and asked for an extension. Seabreeze refused and sold its assets elsewhere. A Florida court affirmed that Seabreeze acted legally.

Time of the essence clauses
Generally make contract dates strictly enforceable.

A **time of the essence clause** will generally make contract deadlines strictly enforceable. Seabreeze regarded a timely sale as important, and LaSalle agreed to the provision. There was nothing unreasonable about the clause, and LaSalle suffered the consequences of his delay.[6]

Suppose the contract had named a closing date but included no time of the essence clause. If LaSalle offered to close three days late, could Seabreeze sell elsewhere? No. **Merely including a date for performance does not make time of the essence.** Courts dislike time of the essence arguments because even a short delay may mean that one party forfeits everything it expected to gain from the bargain. If the parties do not *clearly* state that prompt performance is essential, then both are entitled to reasonable delays.

BREACH

When one party breaches a contract, the other party is discharged. The discharged party has no obligation to perform and may sue for damages. Edwin promises that on July 1, he will deliver 20 tuxedos, tailored to fit male chimpanzees, to Bubba's circus for $300 per suit.

[6]*Seabreeze Restaurant, Inc. v. Paumgardhen*, 639 So.2d 69, 1994 Fla. App. LEXIS 4546 (Fla. Dist. Ct. App. 1994).

After weeks of delay, Edwin concedes he hasn't a cummerbund to his name. Bubba is discharged and owes nothing. In addition, he may sue Edwin for damages.

Material Breach

As we know, parties frequently perform their contract duties imperfectly, which is why courts accept substantial performance rather than strict performance, particularly in contracts involving services. In a more general sense, **courts will discharge a contract only if a party committed a *material* breach.** A material breach is one that substantially harms the innocent party and for which it would be hard to compensate without discharging the contract. Suppose Edwin fails to show up with the tuxedos on June 1 but calls to say they will arrive under the big top the next day. He has breached the agreement. Is his breach material? No. This is a trivial breach, and Bubba is not discharged. When the tuxedos arrive, he must pay.

The following case raises the issue in the context of a major college sports program.

O'Brien v. Ohio State University

2007 WL 2729077
Ohio Court of Appeals, 2007

Facts: The Ohio State University (OSU), experiencing a drought in its men's basketball program, brought in Coach Jim O'Brien to turn things around. The plan was successful. In only his second year, he guided the team to its best record ever. The team advanced to the Final Four, and O'Brien was named national coach of the year. OSU's athletic director promptly offered the coach a new, multi-year contract worth about $800,000 per year.

Section 5.1 of the contract included termination provisions. The university could fire O'Brien *for cause* if (a) there was a material breach of the contract by the coach or (b) O'Brien's conduct subjected the school to NCAA sanctions. OSU could also terminate O'Brien *without cause*, but in that case, it had to pay him the full salary owed.

O'Brien began recruiting a talented 21-year-old Serbian player named Alex Radojevic. While getting to know the young man, O'Brien discovered two things. First, it appeared that Radojevic had been paid to play briefly for a Yugoslavian team, meaning that he was ineligible to play college basketball. Second, it was clear that Radojevic's family had suffered terribly during the strife in his homeland.

O'Brien concluded that Radojevic would never play for OSU or any major college. He also decided to loan Radojevic's mother some money. Any such loan would violate an NCAA rule if done to recruit a player, but O'Brien believed the loan was legal since Radojevic could not play in the NCAA anyway. Several years later, the university learned of the loan and realized that O'Brien had never reported it. Hoping to avoid trouble with the NCAA, OSU imposed sanctions on itself. The university also fired the coach, claiming he had lied, destroyed the possibility of postseason play, and harmed the school's reputation.

O'Brien sued, claiming he had not materially breached the contract. The trial court awarded the coach $2.5 million, and the university appealed.

Issue: ***Did O'Brien materially breach the contract?***

Excerpts from Judge Tyack's Decision: OSU argued that it was substantially injured by the self-imposed sanctions, which included a ban from post-season and NCAA tournament play [during the current season], and relinquishing two basketball scholarships from the [next] recruiting class. Contrary to OSU's argument, however, the trial court found these sanctions to be insubstantial. [Athletic Director] Geiger announced the one-year post-season ban in December, and it appears from the timing of that announcement that Geiger made the decision based on the fact that the team was unlikely to be invited to a post-season tournament in the first place.

The second alleged harm was harm to OSU's reputation. The trial court found that any reputational harm was similarly exaggerated, at least as it specifically related to the Radojevic matter. Radojevic never enrolled at OSU, and never played a single second for OSU's basketball team.

NCAA violations happen all the time. It's the nature of the beast. Also relevant to the issue of OSU's allegedly damaged reputation is the fact that almost immediately after firing O'Brien, OSU was able to lure one of the nation's top coaching prospects, [Thad Matta], to assume O'Brien's former position. Shortly thereafter, Matta successfully recruited possibly the best recruiting class ever. Based on this evidence, the trial court could reasonably find the Radojevic loan did not cause serious harm to OSU.

OSU argues that O'Brien acted in bad faith by covering up his misconduct for several years. In the words of OSU's counsel at oral argument: "*If lying to your employer for four years is not a material breach, it's hard to imagine what would be!*" Although the premise for counsel's argument is sound, it is unsound in application because it assumes facts not in evidence. Counsel for OSU assumes for the purposes of the argument that O'Brien systematically either denied allegations about the Radojevic loan, or took affirmative steps to conceal it from OSU. The evidence does not support such a conclusion. After Radojevic was drafted by the NBA, there is not a single inference that can be drawn from the record to suggest that O'Brien even thought about the loan. In O'Brien's own mind, he did not believe he had done anything wrong; thus, he would not have had a motive to conceal what he had done.

[There was no material breach.]

Affirmed.

Anticipatory Breach

Sally will receive her bachelor's degree in May and already has a job lined up for September. She has signed a two-year contract to work as window display designer for Surebet Department Store. The morning of graduation, she reads in the paper that Surebet is going out of business that very day. Surebet has told Sally nothing about her status. Sally need not wait until September to learn her fate. Surebet has committed an **anticipatory breach by making it unmistakably clear that it will not honor the contract.** Sometimes a promisor will actually inform the promisee that it will not perform its duties. At other times, as here, the promisor takes some step that makes the breach evident. Sally is discharged and may immediately seek other work. She is also entitled to file suit for breach of contract. The court will treat Surebet's anticipatory breach just as though the store had actually refused to perform on September 1.

Statute of Limitations

Statute of limitations
A statutory time limit within which an injured party must file suit.

A party injured by a breach of contract should act promptly. A **statute of limitations** begins to run at the time of injury and will limit the time within which the injured party may file suit. These laws set time limits for filing lawsuits. Statutes of limitation vary from state to state and from issue to issue within a state. Failure to file suit within the time limits discharges the party who breached the contract. Always consult a lawyer promptly in the case of a legal injury.

Impossibility

"Your honor, my client wanted to honor the contract. He just couldn't. *Honest.*" This plea often echoes around courtrooms as one party seeks discharge without fulfilling his contract obligations. Does the argument work? It depends. If performing a contract was truly impossible, a court will discharge the agreement. But if honoring the deal merely imposed a financial burden, the law will generally enforce the contract.

True Impossibility

These cases are easy—and rare. **True impossibility means that something has happened making it literally impossible to do what the promisor said he would do.** Francoise owns a vineyard that produces Beaujolais Nouveau wine. She agrees to ship 1,000 cases of her wine to Tyrone, a New York importer, as soon as this year's vintage is ready. Tyrone will pay $50 per case. But a fungus wipes out her entire vineyard. Francoise is discharged. It is theoretically impossible for Francoise to deliver wine from her vineyard, and she owes Tyrone nothing.

Meanwhile, though, Tyrone has a contract with Jackson, a retailer, to sell 1,000 cases of Beaujolais Nouveau wine at $70 per case. Tyrone has no wine from Francoise, and the only other Beaujolais Nouveau available will cost him $85 per case. Instead of earning $20 per case, Tyrone will lose $15. Does this discharge Tyrone's contract with Jackson? No. It is possible for him to perform—it's just more expensive. He must fulfill his agreement.

True impossibility is generally limited to these three causes:

- ***Destruction of the Subject Matter,*** as happened with Francoise's vineyard.
- ***Death of the Promisor in a Personal Services Contract.*** When the promisor agrees personally to render a service that cannot be transferred to someone else, her death discharges the contract. Producer hires Josephine to write the lyrics for a new Broadway musical, but Josephine dies after writing only two words: "Act One." The contract was personal to Josephine and is now discharged. Neither Josephine's estate nor Producer has any obligation to the other. But notice that most contracts are not for personal services. Suppose that Tyrone, the wine importer, dies. His contract to sell wine to Jackson is not discharged because anyone can deliver the required wine. Tyrone's estate remains liable on the deal with Jackson.
- ***Illegality.*** Chet, a Silicon Valley entrepreneur, wants to capitalize on his computer expertise. He contracts with Construction Co. to build a factory in Iran that will manufacture computers for sale in that country. Construction Co. fails to build the factory on time, and Chet sues. Construction Co. defends by pointing out that the President of the United States has issued an executive order barring trade between the United States and Iran. Construction Co. wins; the executive order discharged the contract.

Commercial Impracticability and Frustration of Purpose

It is rare for contract performance to be truly impossible but very common for it to become a financial burden to one party. Suppose Bradshaw Steel in Pittsburgh agrees to deliver 1,000 tons of steel beams to Rice Construction in Saudi Arabia at a given price, but a week later, the cost of raw ore increases 30 percent. A contract once lucrative to the manufacturer is suddenly a major liability. Does that change discharge Bradshaw? Absolutely not. Rice signed the deal *precisely to protect itself against price increases.* As we have seen, the primary purpose of contracts is to enable the parties to control their future.

Yet there may be times when a change in circumstances is so extreme that it would be unfair to enforce a deal. What if a strike made it impossible for Bradshaw to ship the steel to Saudi Arabia, and the only way to deliver would be by air, at *five times* the sea cost? Must Bradshaw fulfill its deal? What if a new war meant that any ships or planes delivering the goods might be fired upon? Other changes could make the contract undesirable for *Rice.* Suppose the builder wanted steel for a major public building in Riyadh, but the Saudi government decided not to go forward with the construction. The steel would then be worthless to Rice. Must the company still accept it?

None of these hypotheticals involves true impossibility. It is physically possible for Bradshaw to deliver the goods and for Rice to receive. But in some cases, it may be so dangerous, costly, or pointless to enforce a bargain that a court will discharge it instead.

Courts use the related doctrines of commercial impracticability and frustration of purpose to decide when a change in circumstances should permit one side to escape its duties.

Commercial impracticability means some event has occurred that neither party anticipated and *fulfilling the contract would now be extraordinarily difficult and unfair to one party.* If a shipping strike forces Bradshaw to ship by air, the company will argue that neither side expected the strike and that Bradshaw should not suffer a fivefold increase in shipping costs. Bradshaw will probably win the argument.

Frustration of purpose means some event has occurred that neither party anticipated and *the contract now has no value for one party.* If Rice's building project is canceled, Rice will argue that the steel now is useless to the company. Frustration cases are hard to predict. Some states would agree with Rice, but others would hold that it was Rice's obligation to protect itself with a government guarantee that the project would be completed. Courts consider the following factors in deciding impracticability and frustration claims:

- *Mere financial difficulties will never suffice to discharge a contract.* Barbara and Michael Luber divorced, and Michael agreed to pay alimony. He stopped making payments and claimed that it was impracticable for him to do so because he had hit hard times and simply did not have the money. The court dismissed his argument, noting that commercial impracticability requires some objective event that neither party anticipated, not merely the financial deterioration of one party.[7]
- *The event must have been truly unexpected.* Wayne Carpenter bought land from the state of Alaska, intending to farm it and agreeing to make monthly payments. The sales contract stated that Alaska did not guarantee the land for agriculture or any other purpose. Carpenter struggled to farm the land but failed; as soon as the ground thawed, the water table rose too high for crops. Carpenter abandoned the land and stopped making payments. Alaska sued and won. The high court rejected Carpenter's claim of impracticability since the "event"—bad soil—was not unexpected. Alaska had warned that the land might prove unworkable, and Carpenter had no claim for commercial impracticability.[8]
- *If the promisor must use a different means to accomplish her task, at a greatly increased cost, she probably does have a valid claim of impracticability.* If a shipping strike forces Bradshaw to use a different means of delivery—say, air—and this multiplies its costs several times, the company is probably discharged. But a mere increase in the cost of raw materials, such as a 30 percent rise in the price of ore, will almost never discharge the promisor.
- *A* force majeure *clause is significant but not necessarily dispositive.* To protect themselves from unexpected events, companies sometimes include a *force majeure* clause, allowing cancellation of the agreement in case of extraordinary and unexpected events. A typical clause might permit the seller of goods to delay or cancel delivery in the event of "acts of God, fire, labor disputes, accidents, or transportation difficulties." A court will always consider a *force majeure* clause, but it may not enforce it if one party is trying to escape from routine financial problems.

---

[7] *Luber v. Luber*, 418 Pa. Super. 542, 614 A.2d 771, 1992 Pa. Super. LEXIS 3338 (Pa. Super. Ct. 1992).
[8] *State v. Carpenter*, 869 P.2d 1181, 1994 Alaska LEXIS 23 (Alaska 1994).

Chapter Conclusion

Negotiate carefully. A casually written letter may imply a condition precedent that the author never intended. The term *personal satisfaction* should be defined so that both parties know whether one party may fire the other on a whim. Never assume that mere inconvenience or financial loss will discharge contractual duties.

Exam Review

1. **CONDITION** A condition is an event that must occur before a party becomes obligated. It may be stated expressly or implied, and no formal language is necessary to create one. (pp. 382–387)

EXAM Strategy

Question: Stephen Krogness, a real estate broker, agreed to act as an agent for Best Buy Co., which wanted to sell several of its stores. The contract provided that Best Buy would pay Krogness a commission of 2 percent for "a sale to any prospect submitted directly to Best Buy by Krogness." Krogness introduced Corporate Realty Capital (CRC) to Best Buy, and the parties negotiated but could not reach agreement. CRC then introduced Best Buy to BB Properties (BB). Best Buy sold several properties to BB for $46 million. CRC acted as the broker. Krogness sought a commission of $528,000. Is he entitled to it?

Strategy: This contract contains a conditional clause. What is it? What must occur before Best Buy is obligated to pay Krogness? Did that event happen? (See the "Result" at the end of this section.)

2. **SUBSTANTIAL PERFORMANCE** Strict performance, which requires one party to fulfill its duties perfectly, is unusual. In construction and service contracts, substantial performance is generally sufficient to entitle the promisor to the contract price, minus the cost of defects in the work. (pp. 388–389)

3. **PERSONAL SATISFACTION** Personal satisfaction contracts are interpreted under an objective standard, requiring reasonable ground for dissatisfaction, unless the work involves personal judgment *and* the parties intended a subjective standard. (pp. 389–390)

4. **GOOD FAITH** Good faith performance is required in all contracts. (pp. 390–392)

5. **TIME OF THE ESSENCE** Time of the essence clauses result in strict enforcement of contract deadlines. (p. 392)

EXAM Strategy

Question: Colony Park Associates signed a contract to buy 44 acres of residential land from John Gall. The contract stated that closing would take place exactly one year later. The delay was to enable Colony Park to obtain building permits to develop condominiums. Colony Park worked diligently to obtain all permits, but delays in sewer permits forced Colony Park to notify Gall it could not close on the agreed date. Colony Park suggested a date exactly one month later. Gall refused the new date and declined to sell. Colony Park sued. Gall argued that since the parties specified a date, time was of the essence and Colony Park's failure to buy on time discharged Gall. Please rule.

Strategy: A time of the essence clause generally makes a contract date strictly enforceable. Was there one in this agreement? (See the "Result" at the end of this section.)

6. **MATERIAL BREACH** A material breach is the only kind that will discharge a contract; a trivial breach will not. (pp. 393–394)

7. **IMPOSSIBILITY** True impossibility means that some event has made it impossible to perform an agreement. It is typically caused by destruction of the subject matter, the death of an essential promisor, or intervening illegality. (pp. 394–396)

EXAM Strategy

Question: Omega Concrete had a gravel pit and factory. Access was difficult, so Omega contracted with Union Pacific Railroad (UP) for the right to use a private road that crossed UP property and tracks. The contract stated that use of the road was solely for Omega employees and that Omega would be responsible for closing a gate that UP planned to build where the private road joined a public highway. In fact, UP never constructed the gate; Omega had no authority to construct the gate. Mathew Rogers, an Omega employee, was killed by a train while using the private road. Rogers's family sued Omega, claiming that Omega failed to keep the gate closed as the contract required. Is Omega liable?

Strategy: True impossibility means that the promisor cannot do what he promised to do. Is this such a case? (See the "Result" at the end of this section.)

8. **COMMERCIAL IMPRACTICABILITY** Commercial impracticability means that some unexpected event has made it extraordinarily difficult and unfair for one party to perform its obligations. (pp. 395–396)

9. **FRUSTRATION OF PURPOSE** Frustration of purpose may occur when an unexpected event renders a contract completely useless to one party. (pp. 395–396)

1. Result: The conditional clause requires Best Buy to pay a commission for "a sale to any prospect submitted directly to Best Buy by Krogness." Krogness did not in fact introduce BB Properties to Best Buy. The condition has not occurred, and Best Buy is under no obligation to pay.

5. Result: Merely including a date for performance does not make time of the essence. A party that considers a date critical must make that clear. This contract did not indicate that the closing date was vital to either party, so a short delay was reasonable. Gail was ordered to convey the land to Colony Park.

7. Result: There was no gate, and Omega had no right to build one. This is a case of true impossibility. Omega was not liable.

Multiple-Choice Questions

1. ***CPA QUESTION*** Nagel and Fields entered into a contract in which Nagel was obligated to deliver certain goods by September 10. On September 3, Nagel told Fields that he had no intention of delivering the goods. Prior to September 10, Fields may successfully sue Nagel under the doctrine of:
   (a) Promissory estoppel
   (b) Accord and satisfaction
   (c) Anticipatory breach
   (d) Substantial performance

2. Most contracts are discharged by …
   (a) Agreement of the parties
   (b) Full performance
   (c) Failure of conditions
   (d) Commercial impracticability
   (e) A material breach

3. If a contract contains a condition precedent, the ____________ has the burden of proving that the condition actually happened. If a condition subsequent exists, the ____________ has the burden of showing that the condition occurred.
   (a) plaintiff; plaintiff
   (b) plaintiff; defendant
   (c) defendant; plaintiff
   (d) defendant; defendant

4. Big Co., a construction company, builds a grocery store. The contract calls for a final price of $5 million. Big Co. incurred $4.5 million in costs and stands to make a profit of $500,000. On a final inspection, the grocery store owner is upset. His blueprints called for 24 skylights, but the finished building has only 12. Installing the additional skylights would cost $100,000. Big Co. made no other errors. How much must the grocery store owner pay Big Co.?
   (a) $5,000,000
   (b) $4,900,000
   (c) $4,500,000
   (d) $0

5. Lenny makes K2, a synthetic form of marijuana, in his basement. He signs an agreement with the Super Smoke Shop to deliver 1,000 cans of K2 for $10,000. After the contract is signed, but before the delivery, Super Smoke Shop's state legislature makes the sale of K2 illegal. Lenny's contract will be discharged because of ____________.
   (a) true impossibility
   (b) commercial impracticability
   (c) frustration of purpose
   (d) None of the above

Essay Questions

1. **ETHICS** Commercial Union Insurance Co. (CU) insured Redux, Ltd. The contract made CU liable for fire damage but stated that the insurer would not pay for harm caused by criminal acts of any Redux employees. Fire destroyed Redux's property. CU claimed that the "criminal acts" clause was a condition precedent, but Redux asserted it was a condition subsequent. What difference does it make, and who is legally right? Does the insurance company's position raise any ethical issues? Who drafted the contract? How clear were its terms?

2. Stephen Muka owned U.S. Robotics. He hired his brother Chris to work in the company. His letter promised Chris $1 million worth of Robotics stock at the end of one year, "provided you work reasonably hard & smart at things in the next year." (We should all have such brothers.) Chris arrived at Robotics and worked the full year, but toward the end of the year, Stephen died. His estate refused to give Chris the stock, claiming their agreement was a personal satisfaction contract and only Stephen could decide whether Chris had earned the reward. Comment.

3. Ken Ward was an Illinois farmer who worked land owned by his father-in-law, Frank Ruda. To finance his operation, he frequently borrowed money from Watseka First National Bank, paying back the loans with farming profits. But Ward fell deeper and deeper into debt, and Watseka became concerned. When Ward sought additional loans, Watseka insisted that Ruda become a guarantor on all of the outstanding debt, and the father-in-law agreed. The new loans had an acceleration clause, permitting the bank to demand payment of the entire debt if it believed itself "insecure"; that is, at risk of a default. Unfortunately, just as Ward's debts reached more than $120,000, Illinois suffered a severe drought, and Ward's crops failed. Watseka asked Ruda to sell some of the land he owned to pay back part of the indebtedness. Ruda reluctantly agreed but never did so. Meanwhile, Ward decreased his payments to the bank because of the terrible crop. Watseka then "accelerated" the loan, demanding that Ruda pay off the entire debt. Ruda defended by claiming that Watseka's acceleration at such a difficult time was bad faith. Who should win?

4. Loehmann's clothing stores, a nationwide chain with headquarters in New York, was the anchor tenant in the Lincoln View Plaza Shopping Center in Phoenix, Arizona, with a 20-year lease from the landlord, Foundation Development, beginning in 1978. Loehmann's was obligated to pay rent the first of every month and to pay common-area charges four times a year. The lease stated that if Loehmann's failed

to pay on time, Foundation could send a notice of default, and that if the store failed to pay all money due within 10 days, Foundation could evict. On February 23, 1987, Foundation sent to Loehmann's the common-area charges for the quarter ending January 31, 1987. The balance due was $3,500. Loehmann's believed the bill was in error and sent an inquiry on March 18, 1987. On April 10, 1987, Foundation insisted on payment of the full amount within 10 days. Foundation sent the letter to the Loehmann's store in Phoenix. On April 13, 1987, the Loehmann's store received the bill and, since it was not responsible for payments, forwarded it to the New York office. Because the company had moved offices in New York, a Loehmann's officer did not see the bill until April 20. Loehmann's issued a check for the full amount on April 24 and mailed it the following day. On April 28, Foundation sued to evict; on April 29, the company received Loehmann's check. Please rule.

5. **YOU BE THE JUDGE WRITING PROBLEM** Kuhn Farm Machinery, a European company, signed an agreement with Scottsdale Plaza Resort, of Arizona, to use the resort for its North American dealers' convention during March 1991. Kuhn agreed to rent 190 guest rooms and spend several thousand dollars on food and beverages. Kuhn invited its top 200 independent dealers from the United States and Canada and about 25 of its own employees from the United States, Europe, and Australia, although it never mentioned those plans to Scottsdale.

   On August 2, 1990, Iraq invaded Kuwait, and on January 16, 1991, the United States and allied forces were at war with Iraq. Saddam Hussein and other Iraqi leaders threatened terrorist acts against the United States and its allies. Kuhn became concerned about the safety of those traveling to Arizona, especially its European employees. By mid-February, 11 of the top 50 dealers with expense-paid trips had either canceled their plans to attend or failed to sign up. Kuhn postponed the convention. The resort sued. The trial court discharged the contract under the doctrines of commercial impracticability and frustration of purpose. The resort appealed. Did commercial impracticability or frustration of purpose discharge the contract? **Argument for Scottsdale Plaza Resort:** The resort had no way of knowing that Kuhn anticipated bringing executives from Europe, and even less reason to expect that if anything interfered with their travel, the entire convention would become pointless. Most of the dealers could have attended the convention, and the resort stood ready to serve them. **Argument for Kuhn:** The parties never anticipated the threat of terrorism. Kuhn wanted this convention so that its European executives, among others, could meet top North American dealers. That is now impossible. No company would risk employee lives for a meeting. As a result, the contract has no value at all to Kuhn, and its obligations should be discharged by law.

Discussion Questions

1. Evans built a house for Sandra Dyer, but the house had some problems. The garage ceiling was too low. Load-bearing beams in the "great room" cracked and appeared to be steadily weakening. The patio did not drain properly. Pipes froze. Evans wanted the money promised for the job, but Dyer refused to pay. Comment.

2. Krug International, an Ohio corporation, had a contract with Iraqi Airways to build aeromedical equipment for training pilots. Krug then contracted for Power Engineering, an Iowa corporation, to build the specialized gearbox to be used in

the training equipment for $150,000. Power did not know that Krug planned to resell the gearbox to Iraqi Airways. When Power had almost completed the gearbox, the Gulf War broke out and the United Nations declared an embargo on all shipments to Iraq. Krug notified Power that it no longer wanted the gearbox. Power sued. Please rule.

3. The death of a promisor in a *personal services* contract discharges an agreement. But if a promisor dies, other kinds of contracts live on. Is this sensible? Would it be better to discharge all kinds of agreements if one of the parties passes away?

4. Is commercial impracticability (such as the shipping strike described earlier in the chapter) a good reason for discharge? What about frustration of purpose (such as the cancellation of the construction project in Saudi Arabia)? Is one more justified than the other? Are parties who back out of contracts on these grounds acting reasonably?

5. Franklin J. Moneypenny hires Angela to paint his portrait. She is to be paid $50,000 if the painting is acceptable "in Franklin's sole judgment." At the big unveiling, 99 of 100 attendees think that Angela has done a masterful job. Franklin disagrees. He thinks the painting makes him look like a toad. (He does in fact look like a toad, but he does not like to contemplate this fact.) Franklin refuses to pay, and, because he signed a personal satisfaction contract, Angela gets nothing. Is this fair? Should the law allow personal satisfaction contracts?

CHAPTER 18

Remedies

© picsbyst/Shutterstock.com

Ben is the general manager of an NFL football team. Driving home in his truck, he is in a sour humor. Spencer, the team's best running back, under contract to play for one more year at $2.5 million, has announced he is leaving the team to act in a new sitcom. Ben wonders whether he can stop Spencer from leaving the team. Even if it is possible, would it be worthwhile to make a disgruntled, out-of-condition athlete carry (and fumble) the ball? If Spencer leaves, it will cost at least $5 million to hire a runner with equal speed and power.

The G.M.'s phone rings. Louise, a dealer in rare autos, has bad news.

"I hate to tell you, Ben, but the deal just fell through."

"What are you talking about? We both signed! That's a binding contract!" A seller in Florida had agreed in writing to sell Ben a 1955 Ferrari for $900,000.

"*I* know it's true, and *you* know it," Louise murmurs soothingly. "But the seller has decided he just can't part with it."

Ben slams his cell phone down, turns into his driveway—and notices that the back door is open. Did he leave it that way? No. The burglar did.

Ben slams his cell phone down, turns into his driveway—and notices that the back door is open. Did he leave it that way? No. The burglar did. Ben has lost about $100,000 worth of jewelry, clothing, and sports memorabilia. Why didn't the alarm sound? When he demands an explanation from Alarmist, his home security provider, the quality assurance representative assures Ben that he will receive the full compensation due under his contract—$600. Later that night, Ben will have a long talk with his lawyer about breached contracts and remedies.

Breaching a Contract

Someone breaches a contract when he fails to perform a duty without a valid excuse. Spencer is legally committed to play for the team for one more year and is clearly breaching his contract when he informs the team that in the future, he will be playing for laughs. But what can the team do about the runner's breach? In other words, what is the team's *remedy?* **A remedy is the method a court uses to compensate an injured party.**

Injunction
A court order that requires someone to do something or refrain from doing something.

Should a court stop Spencer from performing in his new sitcom? Force him to carry the ball instead? An order forcing someone to refrain from doing something is an **injunction.** Courts frequently grant injunctions to an employer, blocking an employee from *leaving* to work elsewhere. However, courts almost never use an order to force an employee to *complete* a contract with his employer because that would force two antagonistic parties to work together. In other words, Ben can probably stop Spencer from working in television, but no court will order the running back to suit up and play.

Expectation damages
The money required to put one party in the position she would have been in had the other side performed the contract.

Courts also award **expectation damages**, meaning the money required to put one party in the position he would have been in had the other side performed the contract. If Spencer's team is forced to hire another running back for double the money they expected to pay Spencer, the team will probably recover the difference between the two players' salaries.

Specific performance
Forces both parties to complete the deal.

The Ferrari seller has breached his deal with Ben. What is Ben's remedy? He does not want money damages; he wants that lovely red car. In cases of property that is rare or difficult to replace, courts often award **specific performance**, forcing both parties to complete the deal. Ben should get his car.

Liquidated damages clause
A provision in the contract that declares in advance what one party will receive if the other side breaches.

Finally, the alarm company is trying to *insist* upon a remedy—a very limited one, which will leave Ben largely uncompensated for the burglary. Alarmist is relying on a **liquidated damages clause,** meaning a provision in the contract that declares in advance what one party will receive if the other side breaches. Courts sometimes enforce these clauses. But as we will see later, Alarmist's liquidated clause may be too harsh, and thus unenforceable.

How to best help an injured party, without unfairly harming the other person, is the focus of remedies. The questions and issues created by Ben's Bad Day are typical remedy problems. Courts have struggled with remedies for centuries, but we will master the subject in one chapter.

Ethics Though a court may have several alternative remedies available, it is important to note that most have one thing in common: the focus is on compensating the injured party rather than punishing the party in breach. A court must decide whether to prevent Spencer from leaving the gridiron for the television studio, but it will not consider fining or jailing him.

Some critics argue that someone who willfully breaches a contract should pay a penalty. The Ferrari seller knows he is obligated to part with his car but tries to keep it anyway. Spencer blithely ignores his obligations to the team. Should a remedy reflect morality? In this chapter, we will see very few instances in which a court *punishes* unethical conduct. Is this right? Should contract law exact a price for bad behavior?

Identifying the "Interest" to Be Protected

Interest
A legal right in something.

The first step that a court takes in choosing a remedy is to decide what interest it is trying to protect. An **interest** is a legal right in something. Someone can have an interest in property, for example, by owning it, or renting it to a tenant, or lending money so someone else may buy it. He can have an interest in a *contract* if the agreement gives him some benefit. There are four principal contract interests that a court may seek to protect:

- ***Expectation interest.*** This refers to what the injured party reasonably thought she would get from the contract. The goal is to put her in the position she would have been in if both parties had fully performed their obligations.
- ***Reliance interest.*** The injured party may be unable to demonstrate expectation damages, perhaps because it is unclear he would have profited. But he may still prove that he *spent money* in reliance on the agreement and that in fairness, he should receive compensation.
- ***Restitution interest.*** The injured party may be unable to show an expectation interest or reliance. But perhaps she has conferred a benefit *on the other party*. Here, the objective is to restore to the injured party the benefit she has provided.
- ***Equitable interest.*** In some cases, money damages will not suffice to help the injured party. Something more is needed, such as an order to transfer property to the injured party (specific performance) or an order forcing one party to stop doing something (an injunction).

In this chapter, we look at all four interests.

Expectation Interest

This is the most common remedy that the law provides for a party injured by a breach of contract. **The expectation interest is designed to put the injured party in the position she would have been in had both sides fully performed their obligations.** A court tries to give the injured party the money she would have made from the contract. If accurately calculated, this should take into account all the gains she reasonably expected and all the expenses and losses she would have incurred. The injured party should not end up better off than she would have been under the agreement, nor should she suffer a loss.

If you ever go to law school, you will almost certainly encounter the following case during your first week of classes. It has been used to introduce the concept of damages in contract lawsuits for generations. Enjoy the famous "case of the hairy hand."

Landmark Case

Hawkins v. McGee

84 N.H. 114, 146 A. 641
Supreme Court of New Hampshire, 1929

Facts: Hawkins suffered a severe electrical burn on the palm of his right hand. After years of living with disfiguring scars, he went to visit Dr. McGee, who was well known for his early attempts at skin-grafting surgery. The doctor told Hawkins "I will guarantee to make the hand a hundred percent perfect." Hawkins hired him to perform the operation.

McGee cut a patch of healthy skin from Hawkins's chest and grafted it over the scar tissue on Hawkins' palm. Unfortunately, the chest hair on the skin graft was very thick, and it continued to grow after the surgery. The operation resulted in a hairy palm for Hawkins. Feeling rather ... embarrassed ... Hawkins sued Dr. McGee.

The trial court judge instructed the jury to calculate damages in this way: "If you find the plaintiff entitled to anything, he is entitled to recover for what pain and suffering he has been made to endure and what injury he has sustained over and above the injury that he had before."

The jury awarded Hawkins $3,000, but the court reduced the award to $500. Dissatisfied, Hawkins appealed.

Issue: ***How should Hawkins' damages be calculated?***

Excerpts from Justice Branch's Decision: The jury was permitted to consider two elements of damage, (1) pain and suffering due to the operation, and (2) positive ill effects of the operation upon the plaintiff's hand. [T]he foregoing instruction was erroneous.

By damages as that term is used in the law of contracts, is intended compensation to put the plaintiff in as good a position as he would have been in had the defendant kept his contract. The measure of recovery is what the defendant should have given the plaintiff, not what the plaintiff has given the defendant or otherwise expended.

We conclude that the true measure of the plaintiff's damage in the present case is the difference between the value to him of a perfect hand and the value of his hand in its present condition, including any incidental consequences fairly within the contemplation of the parties when they made their contract.

The extent of the plaintiff's suffering does not measure this difference in value. The pain necessarily incident to a serious surgical operation was a part of the contribution which the plaintiff was willing to make to his joint undertaking with the defendant to produce a good hand. It furnished no test of the difference between the value of the hand which the defendant promised and the one which resulted from the operation.

[Remanded for a] new trial.

Now let's consider a more modern example.

William Colby was a former director of the CIA. He wanted to write a book about his 15 years in Vietnam. He paid James McCarger $5,000 for help in writing an early draft and promised McCarger another $5,000 if the book was published. Then he hired Alexander Burnham to cowrite the book. Colby's agent secured a contract with Contemporary Books, which included a $100,000 advance. But Burnham was hopelessly late with the manuscript and Colby missed his publication date. Colby fired Burnham and finished the book without him. Contemporary published *Lost Victory* several years late, and the book flopped, earning no significant revenue. Because the book was so late, Contemporary paid Colby a total of only $17,000. Colby sued Burnham for his lost expectation interest. The court awarded him $23,000, calculated as follows:

	$100,000	advance, the only money Colby was promised
	– 10,000	agent's fee
	= 90,000	Fee for the two authors, combined
divided by 2	= 45,000	Colby's fee (the other half went to the coauthor)
	– 5,000	owed to McCarger under the earlier agreement
	= 40,000	Colby's expectation interest
	– 17,000	Fee Colby eventually received from Contemporary
	= 23,000	Colby's expectation damages; that is, the additional amount he would have received had Burnham finished on time

The *Colby* case[1] presented a relatively easy calculation of damages. Other contracts are complex. Courts typically divide the expectation damages into three parts: (1) direct (or "compensatory") damages, which represent harm that flowed directly from the contract's breach; (2) consequential (or "special") damages, which represent harm caused by the injured party's unique situation; and (3) incidental damages, which are minor costs such as

[1] *Colby v. Burnham,* 31 Conn. App. 707, 627 A.2d 457, 1993 Conn. App LEXIS 299 (Conn. App. Ct. 1993).

storing or returning defective goods, advertising for alternative goods, and so forth. The first two, direct and consequential, are the important ones.

Note that punitive damages are absent from our list. The golden rule in contracts cases is to give successful plaintiffs "the benefit of the bargain" and not to punish defendants. Punitive damages are occasionally awarded in lawsuits that involve both a contract *and* either an intentional tort (such as fraud) or a breach of fiduciary duty, but they are not available in "simple" cases involving only a breach of contract.

Direct Damages

Direct damages are those that flow directly from the contract. They are the most common monetary award for the expectation interest. These are the damages that inevitably result from the breach. Suppose Ace Productions hires Reina to star in its new movie, *Inside Straight.* Ace promises Reina $3 million, providing she shows up June 1 and works until the film is finished. But in late May, Joker Entertainment offers Reina $6 million to star in its new feature, and on June 1, Reina informs Ace that she will not appear. Reina has breached her contract, and Ace should recover direct damages.

Direct damages
Are those that flow directly from the contract.

What are the damages that flow directly from the contract? Ace has to replace Reina. If Ace hires Kayla as its star and pays her a fee of $4 million, Ace is entitled to the difference between what it expected to pay ($3 million) and what the breach forced it to pay ($4 million), or $1 million in direct damages.

Consequential Damages

In addition to direct damages, the injured party may seek consequential damages or, as they are also known, "special damages." **Consequential damages** reimburse for harm that results from the *particular* circumstances of the plaintiff. These damages are only available if they are a *foreseeable consequence* of the breach. Suppose, for example, Raould breaches two contracts—he is late picking both Sharon and Paul up for a taxi ride. His breach is the same for both parties, but the consequences are very different. Sharon misses her flight to San Francisco and incurs a substantial fee to rebook the flight. Paul is simply late for the barber, who manages to fit him in anyway. Thus, Raould's damages would be different for these two contracts. The rule concerning this remedy comes from a famous 1854 case, *Hadley v. Baxendale.* This is another case that all American law students read. Now it is your turn.

Consequential damages
Are those resulting from the unique circumstances of *this injured party.*

Landmark Case

Hadley v. Baxendale

9 Ex. 341, 156 Eng. Rep. 145
Court of Exchequer, 1854

Facts: The Hadleys operated a flour mill in Gloucester. The crankshaft broke, causing the mill to grind to a halt. The Hadleys employed Baxendale to cart the damaged part to a foundry in Greenwich, where a new one could be manufactured. Baxendale promised to make the delivery in one day, but he was late transporting the shaft, and as a result, the Hadleys' mill was shut for five extra days. They sued, and the jury awarded damages based in part on their lost profits. Baxendale appealed.

Issue: ***Should the defendant be liable for profits lost because of his delay in delivering the shaft?***

Excerpts from Judge Alderson's Decision: Where two parties have made a contract which one of them has broken, the damages which the other party ought to receive in respect of such breach of contract should be such as may fairly and reasonably be considered either arising naturally, i.e. according to the usual course of things, from such breach of contract itself, or such as may reasonably be supposed to have been in the contemplation of both parties, at the time they made the contract, as the probable result of the breach of it. Now, if the special circumstances under which the contract was actually made were communicated by the plaintiffs to the defendants, and thus known to both parties, the damages resulting from the breach of such a contract, which they would reasonably contemplate, would be the amount of injury which would ordinarily follow from a breach of contract under these special circumstances so known and communicated. But, on the other hand, if these special circumstances were wholly unknown to the party breaking the contract, he, at the most, could only be supposed to have had in his contemplation the amount of injury which would arise generally, and in the great multitude of cases not affected by any special circumstances, from such a breach of contract.

Now, in the present case, if we are to apply the principles above laid down, we find that the only circumstances here communicated by the plaintiffs to the defendants at the time the contract was made, were that the article to be carried was the broken shaft of a mill, and that the plaintiffs were the millers of that mill. But how do these circumstances shew reasonably that the profits of the mill must be stopped by an unreasonable delay in the delivery of the broken shaft by the carrier to the third person? Suppose the plaintiffs had another shaft in their possession put up or putting up at the time, and that they only wished to send back the broken shaft to the engineer who made it; it is clear that this would be quite consistent with the above circumstances, and yet the unreasonable delay in the delivery would have no effect upon the intermediate profits of the mill. It follows, therefore, that the loss of profits here cannot reasonably be considered such a consequence of the breach of contract as could have been fairly and reasonably contemplated by both the parties when they made this contract.

[The court ordered a new trial, in which the jury would *not* be allowed to consider the plaintiffs' lost profits.]

The rule from *Hadley v. Baxendale* has been unchanged ever since: **The injured party may recover consequential damages only if the *breaching party* should have *foreseen* them when the two sides formed the contract.**

Let us return briefly to *Inside Straight.* Suppose that, long before shooting began, Ace had sold the film's soundtrack rights to Spinem Sound for $2 million. Spinem believed it would make a profit only if Reina appeared in the film, so it demanded the right to discharge the agreement if Reina dropped out. When Reina quit, Spinem terminated the contract. Now, when Ace sues Reina, it will also seek $2 million in consequential damages for the lost music revenue.

The $2 million is not a direct damage. The contract between Reina and Act has nothing directly to do with selling soundtrack rights. But the loss is nonetheless a consequence of Reina bailing out on the project. And so, if Reina knew about Ace's contract with Spinem when she signed to do the film, the loss would be foreseeable to her, and she would be liable for $2 million. If she never realized she was an essential part of the music contract, and if a jury determines that she had no reason to expect the $2 million loss, she owes nothing for the lost soundtrack profits.

Injured plaintiffs often try to recover lost profits. Courts will generally award these damages if (1) the lost profits were foreseeable and (2) plaintiff provides enough information so that the fact finder can reasonably estimate a fair amount. The calculation need not be done with mathematical precision. In the following case, the plaintiffs lost not only profits—but their entire business. Can they recover for harm that is so extensive? You decide.

You be the Judge

Bi-Economy Market, Inc. v. Harleysville Ins. Co. of New York

2008 WL 423451
New York Court of Appeals, 2008

Facts: Bi-Economy Market was a family-owned meat market in Rochester, New York. The company was insured by Harleysville Insurance. The "Deluxe Business Owner's" policy provided replacement cost for damage to buildings and inventory. Coverage also included "business interruption insurance" for one year, meaning the loss of pretax profit plus normal operating expenses, including payroll.

The company suffered a disastrous fire, which destroyed its building and all inventory. Bi-Economy immediately filed a claim with Harleysville, but the insurer responded slowly. Harleysville eventually offered a settlement of $163,000. A year later, an arbitrator awarded the Market $407,000. During that year, Harleysville paid for seven months of lost income but declined to pay more. The company never recovered or reopened.

Bi-Economy sued, claiming that Harleysville's slow, inadequate payments destroyed the company. The company also sought consequential damages for the permanent destruction of its business. Harleysville claimed that it was only responsible for damages specified in the contract: the building, inventory, and lost income. The trial court granted summary judgment for Harleysville. The appellate court affirmed, claiming that when they entered into the contract, the parties did not contemplate damages for termination of the business. Bi-Economy appealed to the state's highest court.

You Be the Judge: ***Is Bi-Economy entitled to consequential damages for the destruction of its business?***

Argument for Bi-Economy: Bi-Economy is a small, family business. We paid for business interruption insurance for an obvious reason: in the event of a disaster, we lacked the resources to keep going while buildings were constructed and inventory purchased. We knew that in such a calamity, we would need prompt reimbursement—compensation covering the immediate damage and our ongoing lost income. Why else would we pay the premiums?

At the time we entered into the contract, Harleysville could easily foresee that if it responded slowly, with insufficient payments, we could not survive. They knew that is what we wanted to avoid—and it is just what happened. The insurer's bad faith offer of a low figure, and its payment of only seven months' lost income, ruined a fine family business. When the insurance company agreed to business interruption coverage, it was declaring that it would act fast and fairly to sustain a small firm in crisis. The insurer should now pay for the full harm it has wrought.

Argument for Harleysville: We contracted to insure the Market for three losses: its building, inventory, and lost income. After the fire, we performed a reasonable, careful evaluation and made an offer we considered fair. An arbitrator later awarded Bi-Market additional money, which we paid. However it is absurd to suggest that in addition to that, we are liable for an open-ended commitment for permanent destruction of the business.

Consequential damages are appropriate in cases where a plaintiff suffers a loss that was not covered in the contract. In this case, though, the parties bargained over exactly what Harleysville would pay in the event of a major fire. If the insurer has underpaid for lost income, let the court award a fair sum. However, the parties never contemplated an additional, enormous payment for cessation of the business. There is almost no limit as to what that obligation could be. If Bi-Market was concerned that a fire might put the company permanently out of business, it should have said so at the time of negotiating for insurance. The premium would have been dramatically higher.

Neither Bi-Market nor Harleysville ever imagined such an open-ended insurance obligation, and the insurer should not pay an extra cent.

Incidental Damages

Incidental damages are the relatively minor costs that the injured party suffers when *responding to* the breach. When Reina, the actress, breaches the film contract, the producers may have to leave the set and fly back to Los Angeles to hire a new actress. The travel cost is an incidental damage. In another setting, suppose Maud, a manufacturer, has produced 5,000 pairs of

Incidental damages
Relatively minor costs that the injured party suffers when responding to the breach.

running shoes for Foot The Bill, a retail chain, but Foot The Bill breaches the agreement and refuses to accept the goods. Maud will have to store the shoes and advertise for alternate buyers. The storage and advertising costs are incidental expenses, and Maud will recover them.

The UCC and Damages

Under the Uniform Commercial Code (UCC), remedies for breach of contract in the sale of goods are similar to the general rules discussed throughout this chapter. UCC §§2-703 through 2-715 govern the remedies available to buyers and sellers.[2]

Seller's Remedies

If a buyer breaches a sale of goods contract, the seller generally has at least two remedies. She may resell the goods elsewhere. If she acts in good faith, she will be awarded **the difference between the original contract price and the price she was able to obtain in the open market**. Assume that Maud, the manufacturer, had a contract to sell her shoes to Foot The Bill for $55 per pair and Foot The Bill's breach forces her to sell them on the open market, where she gets only $48 per pair. Maud will win $7 per pair times 5,000 pairs, or $35,000, from Foot The Bill.

Alternatively, the buyer may choose not to resell and settle for the difference between the contract price and the market value of the goods. Maud, in other words, may choose to keep the shoes. If she can prove that their market value is $48 per pair, for example, by showing what other retailers would have paid her for them, she will still get her $7 each, representing the difference between what the contract promised her and what the market would support. In either case, the money represents direct damages. Maud is also entitled to incidental damages, such as the storage and advertising expenses described above. But there is one significant difference under the UCC: **most courts hold that the seller of goods is *not* entitled to consequential damages**. Suppose Maud hired two extra workers to inspect, pack, and ship the shoes for Foot The Bill. Those are consequential damages, but Maud will not recover them because she is the seller and the contract is for the sale of goods.

Buyer's Remedies

Cover
To make a good faith purchase of goods similar to those in the contract.

The buyer's remedies in sale of goods contracts (which are, as always, governed by the Uniform Commercial Code) are similar to those we have already considered. She typically has two options. First, the buyer can "cover" by purchasing substitute goods. To **cover** means to make a good faith purchase of goods similar to those in the contract. The buyer may then obtain **the difference between the original contract price and her cover price**. Alternatively, if the buyer chooses not to cover, she is entitled to the difference between the original contract price and the market value of the goods.

Suppose Mary has contracted to buy 1,000 six-foot Christmas trees at $25 per tree from Elmo. The market suddenly rises, and not feeling the spirit of the season, Elmo breaches his deal and sells the trees elsewhere. If Mary makes a good faith effort to cover but is forced to pay $40 per tree, she may recover the difference from Elmo, meaning $15 per tree times 1,000 trees, or $15,000. Similarly, if she chooses not to cover but can prove that $40 is now the market value of the trees, she is entitled to her $15 per tree.

Under the UCC, **the buyer *is* entitled to consequential damages, provided that the seller could reasonably have foreseen them.** If Mary tells Elmo, when they sign their deal, that she has a dozen contracts to resell the trees for an average price of $50 per tree, she may recover $25 per tree, representing the difference between her contract price with Elmo and the value of the tree *to her*, based on her other contracts.[3] If she failed to inform Elmo of the

[2]We discuss these remedies in greater detail in Unit 3, on commercial transactions.

[3]As we discuss in the section on mitigation later in the chapter, Mary will get only her consequential damages if she attempts to cover.

other contracts, she would not receive any money based on them. The buyer is also entitled to whatever incidental damages may have accrued.

EXAM Strategy

Question: Chloe is a fashion designer. Her recent collection of silk-velvet evening gowns was gobbled up by high-end retailers, who now clamor for more. Chloe needs 300 yards of the same fabric by August 15. Mill House, which has supplied fabric to Chloe for many years, agrees to sell her 300 yards at $100 per yard, delivered on August 15. The market value of the fabric is $125, but Mill House gives Chloe a break because she is a major customer.

Chloe contracts with Barney's and Neiman Marcus to sell a total of 50 dresses, at an *additional* profit to Chloe of $800 per dress. On August 15, Mill House delivers defective fabric. Chloe cannot make her dresses in time, and the retailers cancel their orders. Chloe sues Mill House and wins—but what are her damages?

Strategy: To determine damages, first ask whether the contract is governed by the common law or the UCC. This agreement concerns goods, so the Code applies. The UCC permits a buyer to recover damages for the difference between the contract price and the market value of the goods. The Code also allows consequential damages if the seller could have foreseen them. Apply those standards.

Offscreen/Shutterstock.com

For a fashion designer, defective fabric is a calamity. But how do we calculate the damages?

Result: Because Chloe's contract enabled her to save $25 per yard for 300 yards, she is entitled to $7,500. Chloe has also lost profits of $40,000. Mill House could easily have foreseen those losses because the supplier knew that Chloe was a designer who fabricated and sold dresses. Chloe is entitled to $47,500.

We turn now to cases where the injured party cannot prove expectation damages.

Reliance Interest

To win expectation damages, the injured party must prove the breach of contract caused damages that can be *quantified with reasonable certainty*. This rule sometimes presents plaintiffs with a problem.

George plans to manufacture and sell silk scarves during the holiday season. In the summer, he contracts with Cecily, the owner of a shopping mall, to rent a high-visibility stall for $100 per day. George then buys hundreds of yards of costly silk and gets to work cutting and sewing. But in September, Cecily refuses to honor the contract. George sues and proves Cecily breached a valid contract. But what is his remedy?

George cannot establish an expectation interest in his scarf business. He *hoped* to sell each scarf for a $40 gross profit. He *planned* on making $2,000 per day. But how much would he *actually* have earned? Enough to retire on? Enough to buy a salami sandwich for lunch? He has no way of proving his profits, and a court cannot give him his expectation interest.

Reliance interest
Puts the injured party in the position he would have been in had the parties never entered into a contract.

Instead, George will ask for *reliance damages*. The **reliance interest** is designed to put an injured party in the position he would have been in had the parties never entered into a contract. This remedy focuses on the time and money the injured party spent performing his part of the agreement.

George should be able to recover reliance damages from Cecily. Assuming he is unable to sell the scarves to a retail store, which is probable since retailers will have made purchases long ago, George should be able to recover the cost of the silk fabric he bought and perhaps something for the hours of labor he spent cutting and sewing. But reliance damages can be difficult to win because *they are harder to quantify*. Courts prefer to compute damages using the numbers provided in a contract. If a contract states a price of $25 per Christmas tree and one party breaches, the arithmetic is easy. Judges can become uncomfortable when asked to base damages on vague calculations. How much was George's time worth in making the scarves? How good was his work? How likely were the scarves to sell? If George has a track record in the industry, he will be able to show a market price for his services. Without such a record, his reliance claim becomes a tough battle.

Promissory Estoppel

We have seen in earlier chapters that a plaintiff may sometimes recover damages based on promissory estoppel even when there is no valid contract. The plaintiff must show that the defendant made a promise knowing that the plaintiff would likely rely on it, that the plaintiff did rely, and that the only way to avoid injustice is to enforce the promise. **In promissory estoppel cases, a court will generally award *reliance damages*.** It would be unfair to give expectation damages for the full benefit of the bargain when, legally speaking, there has been no bargain.

In the following case, the victorious plaintiff demonstrates how unreliable reliance damages are and how winning can be hard to distinguish from losing.

Toscano v. Greene Music

124 Ca. App. 4th 685, 21 Ca. Rptr. 3d 732
Court of Appeal of California, 2004

Facts: Joseph Toscano was the general manager of Fields Pianos (Fields) in Santa Ana, California. He was unhappy with his job and decided to seek other employment. Toscano contacted Michael Greene, who owned similar stores. In July, Greene offered Toscano a sales management job starting September 1. Relying on that offer, Toscano resigned from Fields on August 1. However, in mid-August, Greene withdrew his employment offer. Toscano later found lower-paying jobs in other cities.

Toscano sued Greene for breach of contract and promissory estoppel. Greene argued that Toscano was not entitled to any expectation damages because his employment with Greene would have been at will, meaning he could lose the job at any time. Greene also urged that because Toscano was an at-will employee at Fields, he could recover at most one month's lost wage.

The trial court ruled that Toscano was entitled to reliance damages for all lost wages at Fields, starting from the day he resigned, going forward until his anticipated retirement in 2017. Toscano's expert accountant calculated his past losses (until the time of trial) at $119,061, and his future lost earnings at $417,772. The trial court awarded Toscano $536,833, and Greene appealed.

Issue: ***Was Toscano entitled to reliance damages?***

Excerpts from Judge O'Rourke's Decision: Given the equitable underpinnings of the promissory estoppel doctrine, we hold that a plaintiff such as Toscano, who relinquished his job in reliance on an unfulfilled promise of employment, may on an appropriate showing recover the lost wages he would have expected to earn from his former employer but for the defendant's promise. Such a damage measure is in keeping with the equitable nature of promissory estoppel. The object of equity is to do right and justice.

Our holding necessarily rejects the notion that the at-will nature of Toscano's former employment with Fields (undisputed by the parties here) is a strict impediment to recovery of future wages that Toscano would have earned at Fields had he not relied on Greene's promise.

[However,] we conclude that even drawing all inferences in Toscano's favor, the evidence was too speculative to lend support to the trial court's award of Toscano's lost future earnings from September 1 to his retirement.

Roberta Spoon, Toscano's damages expert, testified that in calculating Toscano's lost wages for the remainder of his career, "[a]ll I have done is arithmetic. I have simply analyzed the numbers." She testified she was not aware that Toscano's employment with Fields called for any specific tenure. Indeed, Spoon admitted Toscano could have quit or been fired from that job from the time he resigned to the present. She simply assumed Toscano would have continued employment with Fields or another employer at a comparable salary, observing that he had never in the past changed employers for anything other than a pay increase.

Spoon's testimony does not establish Toscano had a definite expectation of continued employment with Fields for any particular period of time. It is evident her supposition was based only on Toscano's history of remaining with his employers until offered new employment. However, *Toscano's* intentions or practices are not relevant to whether he could expect to remain with Fields until his retirement. Evidence of Toscano's intentions does not establish with any reasonable certainty that Fields, an at-will employer who had the right to terminate Toscano at any time for any reason, had some different understanding of the terms of Toscano's employment, or that it would have continued to employ him until the end of his career. Neither party presented testimony from Jerry Goldman, Toscano's boss at Fields. An expert's opinion must not be based upon speculative or conjectural data.

The award of future earnings calculated from [the day he quit] to the date of Toscano's retirement in 2017 is vacated and the matter remanded for a new trial on the issue of damages only. The judgment is otherwise affirmed.

Notice that the court never even mentions that Toscano acted in good faith, relying on Greene's promise, while the latter offered no excuse for suddenly withdrawing his offer. Is it fair to permit Greene to escape all liability? This court, like most, simply will not award significant damages where there is no contract permitting a clear calculation of losses.

The judges, though, have not entirely closed the door on Toscano. What is the purpose of the remand? What might Toscano demonstrate on remand? What practical difficulties will he encounter?

Restitution Interest

Lillian and Harold Toews signed a contract to sell 1,500 acres of Idaho farmland to Elmer Funk. (No, not him—the Bugs Bunny character you are thinking of is Elmer Fudd.) He was to take possession immediately, but he would not receive the deed until he finished paying for the property, in 10 years. This arrangement enabled him to enroll in a government

He did move onto the land and did receive $76,000 from the government for a year's worth of inactivity. (Nice work if you can get it.)

program that would pay him "set-asides" for *not* farming. Funk kept most aspects of his agreement. He did move onto the land and did receive $76,000 from the government for a year's worth of inactivity. (Nice work if you can get it.) The only part of the bargain Funk did not keep was his promise to pay. Lillian and Harold sued. Funk had clearly breached the deal. But what remedy?

The couple still owned the land, so they did not need it reconveyed. Funk had no money to pay for the farm, so they would never get their expectation interest. And they had expended almost no money based on the deal, so they had no reliance interest. What they had done, though, was to *confer a benefit* on Funk. They had enabled him to obtain $76,000 in government money. Harold and Lillian wanted a return of the benefit they had conferred on Funk, a remedy called *restitution*. The **restitution interest** is designed to return to the injured party a benefit that he has conferred on the other party, which it would be unjust to leave with that person. The couple argued that they had bestowed a $76,000 benefit on Funk and that it made absolutely no sense for him to keep it. The Idaho Court of Appeals agreed. It ruled that the couple had a restitutionary interest in the government set-aside money and ordered Funk to pay them the money.[4]

Restitution interest
Is designed to return to the injured party a benefit he has conferred on the other party.

Restitution is awarded in two types of cases. First, the law allows restitution when the parties have reached a contract and one of them breaches, as Funk did. In such cases, a court may choose restitution because no other remedy is available or because no other remedy would be as fair. Second, courts may award restitution in cases of quasi-contract, which we examined in Chapter 10. In quasi-contract cases, the parties never made a contract, but one side did benefit the other. We consider each kind of restitution interest in turn.

Restitution in Cases of a Voidable Contract

Restitution is a common remedy in contracts involving fraud, misrepresentation, mistake, and duress. In these cases, restitution often goes hand in hand with **rescission**, which means to "undo" a contract and put the parties where they were before they made the agreement. Courtney sells her favorite sculpture to Adam for $95,000, both parties believing the work to be a valuable original by Barbara Hepworth. Two months later, Adam learns that the sculpture is a mere copy, worth very little. A court will permit Adam to rescind the contract on the ground of mutual mistake. At the same time, Adam is entitled to restitution of the purchase price. Courtney gets the worthless carving, and Adam receives his money back.

Rescission
To "undo" a contract and put the parties where they were before they made the agreement.

The following case involved fraud in the sale of a valuable property.

Putnam Construction & Realty Co. v. Byrd

632 So. 2d 961, 1992 Ala. LEXIS 1289
Supreme Court of Alabama, 1992

Facts: Putnam Construction & Realty Co. owned the University Square Business Center (USBC), an office complex with several major tenants. William Byrd and his partners (the "buyers") entered into a contract to buy USBC. They financed the purchase with a $16.2 million loan from Northwestern Mutual Life. Northwestern's loan was secured with a mortgage on the USBC, meaning that if the borrowers failed to repay the loan,

[4] *Toews v. Funk*, 129 Idaho 316, 924 P.2d 217, 1994 Idaho App. LEXIS 75 (Idaho Ct. App. 1994).

Northwestern would own the property. Shortly after the sale closed, Byrd learned that several of the major tenants were leaving. The buyers sued Putnam, seeking rescission of the contract and restitution of their money. The trial court found that Putnam (the "sellers") had committed fraud. It rescinded the sales contract, returning the property to the sellers. It ordered the sellers to assume full liability for the mortgage. The trial court did not, however, order restitution of the buyers' expenses, such as the closing costs. The sellers appealed—which proved to be a big mistake.

Issue: ***Were the buyers entitled to rescission and/or restitution?***

Excerpts from Justice Steagall's Decision: With the departure of its major tenants, the USBC does not have the profit potential the buyers bargained for and is, in fact, a liability to them. While the buyers could receive money damages to approximate the value of the lost leases, such an award would be speculative at best and would not abrogate the fact that the buyers now have a property that operates at an increasing loss. The equitable remedy of rescission, while difficult to execute, would more completely provide the buyers with the compensation they seek. The jury was, therefore, correct in determining that rescission is the proper remedy to be applied in this case.

We agree with the trial court that a reconveyance of USBC to the sellers, subject to the mortgage, "constitutes the most equitable result which can be achieved." Accordingly, we affirm those portions of the court's order relating to the reconveyance of USBC subject to the mortgage. We must also recognize, however, that the buyers incurred other substantial out-of-pocket costs to finance a transaction that was born out of the sellers' fraud. After carefully considering the evidence in this case, we conclude that repayment of the following costs is necessary to more equitably restore the buyers to the position they occupied before the sale: $483,006.75 in closing costs on the purchase of USBC; $121,000 in interest payments they paid to the sellers on the $1.5 million note; and the $500,000 in nonrefundable fees the buyers paid to Northwestern to obtain the loan. We remand this case for the trial court to enter a judgment ordering repayment of these costs.

Ethics Imagine that you are the officer from Putnam in charge of negotiating the sale of USBC to the buyers. You learn that several major tenants are soon to depart and realize that if the buyers learn this, they will lower their offer or reject the deal altogether. Your boss insists you tell the buyers that all tenants will be staying. What will you do? What Life Principles will you apply?

Restitution in Cases of a Quasi-Contract

George Anderson owned a valuable 1936 Plymouth. He took it to Ronald Schwegel's repair shop, and the two orally agreed that Schwegel would restore the car for $6,000. Unfortunately, they never agreed on the meaning of the word *restore*. Anderson thought the term meant complete restoration, including body work and engine repairs, whereas Schwegel intended body work but no engine repairs. After doing some of the work, Schwegel told Anderson that the car needed substantial engine work, and he asked for Anderson's permission to allow an engine shop to do it. Anderson agreed, believing the cost was included in the original estimate. When the car was finished and running smoothly, Schwegel demanded $9,800. Anderson refused to pay more than the $6,000 agreed price, and Schwegel sued.

The court held that there was no valid contract between the parties. A contract requires a meeting of the minds. Here, said the court, there was no meeting of the minds on what *restore* included, and hence Schwegel could not recover either his expectation or his reliance interest since both require an enforceable agreement. Schwegel then argued that a quasi-contract existed. In other words, he claimed that even if there had been no valid agreement, he had performed a service for Anderson and that it would be unjust for Anderson to keep it without paying. **A court may award restitution, even in the absence of a contract, where one party has conferred a benefit on another and it would be unjust for the other party to retain**

the benefit. The court ruled that Schwegel was entitled to the full $3,800 above and beyond the agreed price because that was the fair market value of the additional work. Anderson had asked for the repairs and now had an auto that was substantially improved. It would be unjust, ruled the court, to permit him to keep that benefit for free.[5]

OTHER REMEDIES

In contract lawsuits, plaintiffs are occasionally awarded the remedies of specific performance, injunction, and reformation.

Specific Performance

Leona Claussen owned Iowa farmland. She sold some of it to her sister-in-law, Evelyn Claussen, and, along with the land, granted Evelyn an option to buy additional property at $800 per acre. Evelyn could exercise her option anytime during Leona's lifetime or within six months of Leona's death. When Leona died, Evelyn informed the estate's executor that she was exercising her option. But other relatives wanted the property, and the executor refused to sell. Evelyn sued and asked for *specific performance.* She did not want an award of damages; she wanted *the land itself.* The remedy of specific performance forces the two parties to perform their contract.

A court will award specific performance, ordering the parties to perform the contract, only in cases involving the sale of land or some other asset that is considered "unique." Courts use this remedy when money damages would be inadequate to compensate an injured party. If the subject is unique and irreplaceable, money damages will not put the injured party in the same position she would have been in had the agreement been kept. So a court will order the seller to convey the rare object and the buyer to pay for it.

Historically, every parcel of land has been regarded as unique, and therefore specific performance is always available in real estate contracts. Family heirlooms and works of art are also often considered unique. Evelyn Claussen won specific performance. The Iowa Supreme Court ordered Leona's estate to convey the land to Evelyn for $800 per acre.[6] Generally speaking, either the seller or the buyer may be granted specific performance. One limitation in land sales is that a buyer may obtain specific performance only if she was ready, willing, and able to purchase the property on time. If Evelyn had lacked the money to buy Leona's property for $800 per acre within the six-month time limit, the court would have declined to order the sale.

EXAM Strategy

Question: The Monroes, a retired couple who live in Illinois, want to move to Arizona to escape the northern winter. In May, the Monroes contract in writing to sell their house to the Temples for $450,000. Closing is to take place June 30. The Temples pay a deposit of $90,000. However, in early June, the Monroes travel through Arizona and discover it is too hot for them. They promptly notify the Temples they are no longer willing to sell, and return the $90,000, with interest. The Temples sue, seeking the house. In response, the Monroes offer evidence that

[5]*Anderson v. Schwegel,* 118 Idaho 362, 796 P.2d 1035, 1990 Idaho App. LEXIS 150 (Idaho Ct. App. 1990).
[6]*In re Estate of Claussen,* 482 N.W.2d 381, 1992 Iowa Sup. LEXIS 52 (Iowa 1992).

the value of the house has dropped from about $450,000 to about $400,000. They claim that the Temples have suffered no loss. Who will win?

Strategy: Most contract lawsuits are for money damages, but not this one. The Temples want the house. Because they want the house itself, and not money damages, the drop in value is irrelevant. What legal remedy are the Temples seeking? They are suing for specific performance. When will a court grant specific performance? Should it do so here?

Result: In cases involving the sale of land or some other unique asset, a court will grant specific performance, ordering the parties to perform the agreement,. All houses are regarded as unique. The court will force the Monroes to sell their house, provided the Temples have sufficient money to pay for it.

Other unique items, for which a court will order specific performance, include such things as secret formulas, patents, and shares in a closely held corporation. Money damages would be inadequate for all these things since the injured party, even if she got the cash, could not go out and buy a substitute item. By contrast, a contract for a new Cadillac Escalade is not enforceable by specific performance. If the seller breaches, the buyer is entitled to the difference between the contract price and the market value of the car. The buyer can take his money elsewhere and purchase a virtually identical SUV.

Injunction

In the opening scenario, the NFL team's general manager considered whether to seek an injunction against his running back who wanted to leave the team and act in a TV show. An **injunction** is a court order that requires someone to refrain from doing something.

In the increasingly litigious world of professional sports, injunctions are commonplace. In the following basketball case, the trial court issued a **preliminary injunction;** that is, an order issued early in a lawsuit prohibiting a party from doing something *during the course of the lawsuit.* The court attempts to protect the interests of the plaintiff immediately. If, after trial, it appears that the plaintiff has been injured and is entitled to an injunction, the trial court will make its order a **permanent injunction**. If it appears that the preliminary injunction should never have been issued, the court will terminate the order.

Milicic v. Basketball Marketing Company, Inc.

2004 Pa.A Super. 333, 857 A.2d 689
Superior Court of Pennsylvania, 2004

Facts: The Basketball Marketing Company (BMC) markets, distributes, and sells basketball apparel and related products. BMC signed a long-term endorsement contract with a 16-year-old Serbian player, Darko Milicic, who was virtually unknown in the United States. Two years later, Milicic became the second pick in the National Basketball Association draft, making him an immensely marketable young man.

Four days after his 18th birthday, Milicic made a buyout offer to BMC, seeking release from his contract so that he could arrange a more lucrative one elsewhere. BMC refused to release him. A week later, Milicic notified BMC in writing that he was disaffirming the contract, and he returned all money and goods he had received from the company. BMC again refused to release Milicic.

Believing that Milicic was negotiating an endorsement deal with either Reebok or Adidas, BMC sent both companies letters informing them it had an enforceable endorsement deal with Milicic that was valid for several more years. Because of BMC's letter, Adidas ceased negotiating with Milicic just short of signing a contract. Milicic sued BMC, seeking a preliminary injunction that would prohibit BMC from sending such letters to competitors. The trial court granted the preliminary injunction, and BMC appealed.

Issue: ***Is Milicic entitled to a preliminary injunction?***

Excerpts from Judge McCaffery's Decision:[7] BMC argues that the trial court erred by concluding that Milicic had proven the four essential prerequisites necessary for injunctive relief. However, Milicic did meet these four requirements.

1. Milicic had a strong likelihood of success on the merits.

   Pennsylvania law recognizes, except as to necessities, the contract of a minor is voidable if the minor disaffirms it at any reasonable time after the minor attains majority. Just 11 days after his 18th birthday, Milicic sent BMC a letter withdrawing from the agreement. This letter was sent within a reasonable time after Milicic's reaching the age of majority and stated his unequivocal revocation and voidance of the agreement. There exists more than a reasonable probability that Milicic will succeed in [nullifying the contract with BMC].

2. Injunctive relief was necessary to prevent immediate and irreparable harm that could not be adequately compensated by the awarding of monetary damages.

   Top N.B.A. draft picks generally solicit, negotiate, and secure endorsement contracts within a short time after the draft to take advantage of the publicity, excitement, and attendant marketability associated with the promotion. BMC blocked Milicic's efforts to enter into such an endorsement agreement. After being contacted by BMC, advanced negotiations between Milicic and Adidas were suspended. These business opportunity and market advantage losses may aptly be characterized as irreparable injury for purposes of equitable relief.

3. Greater injury would have occurred from denying the injunction than from granting the injunction.

   BMC's refusal to acknowledge Milicic's ability to disaffirm the contract is at odds with public policy. Because infants are not competent to contract, the ability to disaffirm protects them from their own immaturity and lack of discretion. It is established practice in Pennsylvania to petition the court to appoint a guardian for the child, to protect the interests of both parties. It confounds the Court that BMC, a corporation of great magnitude, whose business may be said to be based in contract law, failed to have a guardian appointed for Milicic. Harm to the public is an additional consideration. The public policy consideration underlying the rule which allows a child to disaffirm a contract within a reasonable time after reaching the age of majority is that minors should not be bound by mistakes resulting from their immaturity or the overbearance of unscrupulous adults.

4. The preliminary injunction restored the parties to the status quo that existed prior to the wrongful conduct:

   Enjoining BMC from further interfering with Milicic's ability to contract will place the parties where they were prior to BMC's wrongful conduct. As all four of the essential prerequisites have been satisfied in this case, the Court properly granted injunctive relief. Order affirmed.

Was Darko Milicic entitled to a preliminary injunction against BMC?

[7] Because we are unwilling to assume, as the court apparently does, that this decision will be read only by robots, the authors have substituted *BMC* for *appellant* and *Milicic* for *appellee*.

Reformation

The final remedy, and perhaps the least common, is **reformation**, a process in which a court will partially rewrite a contract. Courts seldom do this because the whole point of a contract is to enable the parties to control their own futures. But a court may reform a contract if it believes a written agreement includes a simple mistake. Suppose that Roger orally agrees to sell 35 acres to Hannah for $600,000. The parties then draw up a written agreement, accidentally describing the land as including 50 additional acres that neither party considered part of the deal. Roger refuses to sell. Hannah sues for specific performance but asks the court to *reform* the written contract to reflect the true agreement. Most but not all courts would reform the agreement and enforce it.

Reformation
A process in which a court will partially rewrite a contract.

A court may also reform a contract to save it. If Natasha sells her advertising business to Joseph and agrees not to open a competing agency in the same city anytime in the next 10 years, a court may decide that it is unfair to force her to wait a decade. It could reform the agreement and permit Natasha to compete, say, 3 years after the sale. But some courts are reluctant to reform contracts and would throw out the entire noncompetition agreement rather than reform it. Parties should never settle for a contract that is sloppy or overbroad, assuming that a court will later reform errors. They may find themselves stuck with a bargain they dislike, or with no contract at all.

Special Issues

Finally, we consider some special issues of damages, beginning with a party's obligation to minimize its losses.

Mitigation of Damages

A party injured by a breach of contract may not recover for damages that he could have avoided with reasonable efforts. In other words, when one party perceives that the other has breached or will breach the contract, the injured party must try to prevent unnecessary loss. A party is expected to **mitigate** his damages; that is, to keep damages as low as he reasonably can.

Mitigate
To keep damages as low as reasonable.

Malcolm agrees to rent space in his mall to Zena, for a major department store. As part of the lease, Malcolm agrees to redesign the interior to meet her specifications. After Malcolm has spent $20,000 in architect and design fees, Zena informs Malcolm that she is renting other space and will not occupy his mall. Malcolm nonetheless continues the renovation work, spending an additional $50,000 on materials and labor. Malcolm will recover the lost rental payments and the $20,000 expended in reliance on the deal. He will *not* recover the extra $50,000. He should have stopped work when he learned of Zena's breach.

Nominal Damages

Nominal damages are a token sum, such as one dollar, given to a plaintiff who demonstrates that the defendant breached the contract but cannot prove serious injury. A school board unfairly fires Gemma, a teacher. If she obtains a teaching job at a better school for identical pay the very next day, she probably can show no damages at all. Nonetheless, the school wrongfully terminated her, and a court may award nominal damages. Nominal damages provide plaintiff with a "moral victory."

Nominal damages
A token sum, such as one dollar, given to a plaintiff who demonstrates a breach but no serious injury.

Liquidated Damages

It can be difficult or even impossible to prove how much damage the injured party has suffered. So lawyers and executives negotiating a deal may include in the contract a **liquidated damages** clause, a provision stating in advance how much a party must pay if it

Liquidated damages
A clause stating in advance how much a party must pay if it breaches.

breaches. Assume that Laurie has hired Bruce to build a five-unit apartment building for $800,000. Bruce promises to complete construction by May 15. Laurie insists on a liquidated damages clause providing that if Bruce finishes late, Laurie's final price is reduced by $3,000 for each week of delay. Bruce finishes the apartment building June 30, and Laurie reduces her payment by $18,000. Is that fair? The answer depends on two factors: **A court will generally enforce a liquidated damages clause if (1) at the time of creating the contract, it was very difficult to estimate actual damages, and (2) the liquidated amount is reasonable.** In any other case, the liquidated damage will be considered a mere penalty and will prove unenforceable.

We will apply the two factors to Laurie's case. When the parties made their agreement, would it have been difficult to estimate actual damages caused by delay? Yes. Laurie could not prove that all five units would have been occupied or how much rent the tenants would have agreed to pay. Was the $3,000 per week reasonable? Probably. To finance an $800,000 building, Laurie will have to pay at least $6,000 interest per month. She must also pay taxes on the land and may have other expenses. Laurie does not have to prove that every penny of the liquidated damages clause is justified, but only that the figure is reasonable. A court will probably enforce her liquidated damages clause.

On the other hand, suppose Laurie's clause demanded $3,000 per day. There is no basis for such a figure, and a court will declare it a penalty clause and refuse to enforce it. Laurie will be back to square one, forced to prove in court any damages she claims to have suffered from Bruce's delay.

In the chapter's opening scenario, the alarm company tries to invoke a liquidated damages clause that would leave Ben largely uncompensated. Depending on what the parties knew when they made the agreement, a court may well find the clause too harsh and permit Ben to sue for his actual losses.

EXAM Strategy

Question: In March, James was accepted into the September ninth-grade class at the Brookstone Academy, a highly competitive private school. To reserve his spot, James's father, Rex, sent in a deposit of $2,000 and agreed in writing to pay the balance due, $19,000. If James withdrew in writing from the school by August 1, Rex owed nothing more to Brookstone. However, once that date passed, Rex was obliged to pay the full $19,000, whether or not James attended. On August 5, Rex hand-delivered to Brookstone a letter stating that James would not attend. Brookstone demanded the full tuition and, when Rex refused to pay, sued for $19,000. Analyze the case.

Strategy: When one party seeks contract damages that are specified in the agreement, it is relying on a liquidated damages clause. A court will generally enforce a liquidated damages clause provided the plaintiff can prove two things. What are those two things? Can this plaintiff meet that standard?

Result: Brookstone must prove that at the time of creating the contract it was difficult to estimate actual damages and that the liquidated amount is reasonable. Rex will probably argue that the liquidated amount is unreasonable, contending that a competitive school can quickly fill a vacancy with another eager applicant. Brookstone will counter that budgeting, which begins in January, is difficult and imprecise. Tuition money goes toward staff salaries, maintenance, utilities, and many other expenses. If the school cannot not rely in January on a certain income, the calculation becomes impossible. Rex had four months to make up his mind, and by August 1, the school was firmly committed to its class size and budget. In a similar case, the court awarded the full tuition to the school, concluding that the sum was a reasonable estimate of the damages.

Chapter Conclusion

The powers of a court are broad and flexible and may suffice to give an injured party what it deserves. But problems of proof and the uncertainty of remedies demonstrate that the best solution is a carefully drafted contract and socially responsible behavior.

EXAM REVIEW

1. **BREACH** Someone breaches a contract when he fails to perform a duty without a valid excuse. (pp. 404–405)

2. **REMEDY** A remedy is the method a court uses to compensate an injured party. (p. 405)

3. **INTERESTS** An interest is a legal right in something, such as a contract. The first step that a court takes in choosing a remedy is to decide what interest it is protecting. (pp. 404–405)

4. **EXPECTATION** The expectation interest puts the injured party in the position she would have been in had both sides fully performed. It has three components:

   (a) Direct damages, which flow directly from the contract.
   (b) Consequential damages, which result from the unique circumstances of the particular injured party. The injured party may recover consequential damages only if the breaching party should have foreseen them.
   (c) Incidental damages, which are the minor costs an injured party incurs responding to a breach. (pp. 405–411)

EXAM Strategy

Question: Mr. and Ms. Beard contracted for Builder to construct a house on property he owned and sell it to the Beards for $785,000. The house was to be completed by a certain date, and Builder knew that the Beards were selling their own home in reliance on the completion date. Builder was late with construction, forcing the Beards to spend $32,000 in rent. Ultimately, Builder never finished the house, and the Beards moved elsewhere. They sued. At trial, expert testimony indicated the market value of the house as promised would have been $885,000. How much money are the Beards entitled to, and why?

Strategy: Normally, in cases of property, an injured plaintiff may use specific performance to obtain the land or house. However, there *is* no house, so there will be no specific performance. The Beards will seek their expectation interest. Under the contract, what did they reasonably expect? They anticipated a finished house, on a particular date, worth $885,000. They did not expect to pay rent while waiting. Calculate their losses. (See the "Result" at the end of this section.)

5. **RELIANCE** The reliance interest puts the injured party in the position he would have been in had the parties never entered into a contract. It focuses on the time and money that the injured party spent performing his part of the agreement. If there was no valid contract, a court might still award reliance damages under a theory of promissory estoppel. (pp. 412–413)

EXAM Strategy

Question: Bingo is emerging as a rock star. His last five concerts have all sold out. Lucia signs a deal with Bingo to perform two concerts in one evening in Big City for a fee of $50,000 for both shows. Lucia then rents the Auditorium for that evening, guaranteeing to pay $50,000. Bingo promptly breaks the deal before any tickets are sold. Lucia sues, pointing out that the Auditorium seats 3,000 and she anticipated selling all tickets for an average of $40 each, for a total gross of $120,000. How much will Lucia recover, if anything?

Strategy: The parties created a valid contract, and Lucia relied on it. She claims two losses: the payment to rent the hall and her lost profits. A court may award reliance damages if the plaintiff can quantify them, provided the damages are not speculative. Can Lucia quantify either of those losses? Both of them? Were they speculative? (See the "Result" at the end of this section.)

6. **RESTITUTION** The restitution interest returns to the injured party a benefit that she has conferred on the other party which would be unjust to leave with that person. Restitution can be awarded in the case of a contract created, for example, by fraud, or in a case of quasi-contract, where the parties never created a binding agreement. (pp. 413–416)

7. **SPECIFIC PERFORMANCE** Specific performance, ordered only in cases of land or a unique asset, requires both parties to perform the contract. (pp. 416–417)

8. **INJUNCTION** An injunction is a court order that requires someone to do something or refrain from doing something. (pp. 417–418)

9. **REFORMATION** Reformation is the process by which a court will—occasionally—rewrite a contract to ensure that it accurately reflects the parties' agreement and/or to maintain the contract's viability. (p. 419)

10. **MITIGATION** The duty to mitigate means that a party injured by a breach of contract may not recover for damages that he could have avoided with reasonable efforts. (p. 419)

EXAM Strategy

Question: Ambrose hires Bierce for $25,000 to supervise the production of Ambrose's crop, but then breaks the contract by firing Bierce at the beginning of the season. A nearby grower offers Bierce $23,000 for the same growing season, but Bierce refuses to take such a pay cut. He stays home and sues Ambrose. How much money, if any, will Bierce recover from Ambrose, and why?

Strategy: Ambrose has certainly breached the contract. The injured party normally receives the difference between his expectation interest and what he actually received. Bierce expected $25,000 and received nothing. However, Bierce made no effort to minimize his losses. How much would Bierce have lost had he mitigated? (See the "Result" at the end of this section.)

11. **NOMINAL DAMAGES** Nominal damages are a token sum, such as one dollar, given to an injured plaintiff who cannot prove damages. (p. 419)

12. **LIQUIDATED DAMAGES** A liquidated damages clause will be enforced if and only if, at the time of creating the contract, it was very difficult to estimate actual damages and the liquidated amount is reasonable. (pp. 419–420)

4. Result: The Beards' direct damages represent the difference between the market value of the house and the contract price. They expected a house worth $100,000 more than their contract price, and they are entitled to that sum. They also suffered consequential damages. The Builder knew they needed the house as of the contract date, and he could foresee that his breach would force them to pay rent. He is liable for a total of $132,000.
5. Result: Lucia can easily demonstrate that Bingo's breach cost her $50,000—the cost of the hall. However, it is uncertain how many tickets she would have sold. Unless Lucia has a strong track record selling tickets to concerts featuring Bingo, a court is likely to conclude that her anticipated profits were speculative. She will probably receive nothing for that claim.
10. Result: Even if he had mitigated, Bierce would have lost $2,000. He is entitled to that sum. However, he cannot recover the remaining $23,000. After Ambrose breached, Bierce had identical work available to him, but he failed to take it. His failure to mitigate is fatal.

Multiple-Choice Questions

1. *CPA QUESTION* Master Mfg., Inc. contracted with Accur Computer Repair Corp. to maintain Master's computer system. Master's manufacturing process depends on its computer system operating properly at all times. A liquidated damages clause in the contract provided that Accur would pay $1,000 to Master for each day that Accur was

late responding to a service request. On January 12, Accur was notified that Master's computer system had failed. Accur did not respond to Master's service request until January 15. If Master sues Accur under the liquidated damage provision of the contract, Master will:

(a) Win, unless the liquidated damages provision is determined to be a penalty

(b) Win, because under all circumstances liquidated damage provisions are enforceable

(c) Lose, because Accur's breach was not material

(d) Lose, because liquidated damage provisions violate public policy

2. **CPA QUESTION** Kaye contracted to sell Hodges a building for $310,000. The contract required Hodges to pay the entire amount at closing. Kaye refused to close the sale of the building. Hodges sued Kaye. To what relief is Hodges entitled?

(a) Punitive damages and direct damages

(b) Specific performance and direct damages

(c) Consequential damages or punitive damages

(d) Direct damages or specific performance

3. A manufacturer delivers a new tractor to Farmer Ted on the first day of the harvest season. But, the tractor will not start. It takes two weeks for the right parts to be delivered and installed. The repair bill comes to $1,000. During the two weeks, some acres of Farmer Ted's crops die. He argues in court that his lost profit on those acres is $60,000. If a jury awards $1,000 for tractor repairs, it will be in the form of ____________ damages. If it awards $60,000 for the lost crops, it will be in the form of ____________ damages.

(a) direct; direct

(b) direct; consequential

(c) consequential; direct

(d) consequential; consequential

(e) direct; incidental

4. Julie signs a contract to buy Nick's 2002 Mustang GT for $5,000. Later, Nick changes his mind and refuses to sell his car. Julie soon buys a similar 2002 Mustang GT for $5,500. She then sues Nick and wins $500. The $500 represents her ____________.

(a) expectation interest

(b) reliance interest

(c) restitution interest

(d) None of the above

5. Under the Uniform Commercial Code, a seller ____________ generally entitled to recover consequential damages, and a buyer ____________ generally entitled to recover consequential damages.

(a) is; is

(b) is; is not

(c) is not; is

(d) is not; is not

Essay Questions

1. Lewis signed a contract for the rights to all timber located on Nine-Mile Mine. He agreed to pay $70 per thousand board feet ($70/mbf). As he began work, Nine-Mile became convinced that Lewis lacked sufficient equipment to do the job well and forbade him to enter the land. Lewis sued. Nine-Mile moved for summary judgment. The mine offered proof that the market value of the timber was exactly $70/mbf, and Lewis had no evidence to contradict Nine-Mile. The evidence about market value proved decisive. Why? Please rule on the summary judgment motion.

2. Twin Creeks Entertainment signed a deal with U.S. JVC Corp. in which JVC would buy 60,000 feature-film videocassettes from Twin Creeks over a three-year period. JVC intended to distribute the cassettes nationwide. Relying on its deal with JVC, Twin Creeks signed an agreement with Paramount Pictures, agreeing to purchase a minimum of $600,000 worth of Paramount cassettes over a two-year period. JVC breached its deal with Twin Creeks and refused to accept the cassettes it had agreed upon. Twin Creeks sued and claimed, among other damages, the money it owed to Paramount. JVC moved to dismiss the claim based on the Paramount contract, on the ground that Twin Creeks, the seller of goods, was not entitled to such damages. What kind of damages is Twin Creeks seeking? Please rule on the motion to dismiss.

3. Racicky was in the process of buying 320 acres of ranchland. While that sale was being negotiated, Racicky signed a contract to sell the land to Simon. Simon paid $144,000, the full price of the land. But Racicky went bankrupt before he could complete the *purchase* of the land, let alone its sale. Which of these remedies should Simon seek: expectation, restitution, specific performance, or reformation?

4. Parkinson was injured in an auto accident by a driver who had no insurance. Parkinson filed a claim with her insurer, Liberty Mutual, for $2,000 under her "uninsured motorist" coverage. Liberty Mutual told her that if she sought that money, her premiums would go "sky high," so Parkinson dropped the claim. Later, after she had spoken with an attorney, Parkinson sued. What additional claim was her attorney likely to make?

5. **YOU BE THE JUDGE WRITING PROBLEM** John and Susan Verba sold a Vermont lakeshore lot to Shane and Deborah Rancourt for $115,000. The Rancourts intended to build a house on the property, but after preparing the land for construction, they learned that a wetland protection law prevented building near the lake. They sued, seeking rescission of the contract. The trial court concluded that the parties had reached their agreement under a "mutual, but innocent, misunderstanding." The trial judge gave the Verbas a choice: they could rescind the contract and refund the purchase price, or they could give the Rancourts $55,000, the difference between the sales price and the actual market value of the land. The Rancourts appealed. Were the Rancourts entitled to rescission of the contract? **Argument for the Rancourts:** When the parties have made a mutual mistake about an important factual issue, either party is entitled to rescind the contract. The land is of no use to us and we want our money back. **Argument for the Verbas:** Both sides were acting in good faith and both sides made an honest mistake. We are willing to acknowledge that the land is worth somewhat less than we all thought, and we are willing to refund $55,000. The buyers shouldn't complain—they are getting the property at about half the original price, and the error was as much their fault as ours.

Discussion Questions

1. **ETHICS** The National Football League owns the copyright to the broadcasts of its games. It licenses local television stations to telecast certain games and maintains a "blackout rule," which prohibits stations from broadcasting home games that are not sold out 72 hours before the game starts. Certain home games of the Cleveland Browns team were not sold out, and the NFL blocked local broadcast. But several bars in the Cleveland area were able to pick up the game's signal by using special antennas. The NFL wanted the bars to stop showing the games. What did it do? Was it unethical of the bars to broadcast the games that they were able to pick up? Apart from the NFL's legal rights, do you think it had the moral right to stop the bars from broadcasting the games?

2. Consequential damages can be many times higher than direct damages. Consider the "Farmer Ted" scenario raised in multiple-choice question 3, which is based on a real case.[8] Is it fair for consequential damages to be 60 times higher than direct damages? The Supreme Court is skeptical that *punitive* damages should be more than 9 times compensatory damages in a tort case. Should a similar "soft limit" apply to consequential damages in contract cases?

3. Is reformation ever a reasonable remedy? Should courts be in the business of rewriting contracts, or should they stick to determining whether agreements are enforceable?

4. If someone breaks a contract, the other party can generally sue and win some form of damages. But for centuries, the law has considered land to be unique. And so, a lawsuit that involves a broken agreement for a sale of land will usually result in an order of specific performance. Is this ancient rule still reasonable? If someone backs out of an agreement to sell an acre of land, should he be ordered to turn over the land itself? Why not just require him to pay an appropriate number of dollars in damages?

5. Is it reasonable to require the mitigation of damages? If a person is wronged because the other side breached a contract, should she have any obligations at all? For example, suppose that a tenant breaches a lease by leaving early. Should the landlord have an obligation to try to find another tenant before the end of the lease?

---

[8] *Prutch v. Ford*, 574 P.2d 102 (Colo. 1977).

CHAPTER 28

AGENCY LAW

The first time Bella walked into the store, my heart flipped. A lot of hot girls just know you can't keep your eyes off them. But not Bella. She had the shyest, sweetest smile you ever saw. From the beginning, I knew she was out of my league. But it didn't matter. Just to be in the same room with her was awesome. I would have folded shirts forever if I could do it standing next to her. She smelled like flowers, and her skin was beautiful.

Of course, she didn't last long at the store. How could she? All she had to do was walk down the street and good things would happen to her. She got picked to be on one of those reality shows.

Being on TV and all, she had to look good, so a couple of weeks after she left, she texted me: "Need clothes 4 show. Can u help?"

I like to think I wouldn't have murdered someone if Bella had asked me to, but I guess it depends on who the someone was. So I came up with a pretty good idea. I issued merchandise credits made out to fake people, which she used to buy clothes. I also let her use my employee discount. Look, Anthropologie is a big company—it's not like they would miss the clothes or anything. Besides, having Bella wear them on that TV show was great advertising.

I like to think I wouldn't have murdered someone if Bella had asked me to, but I guess it depends on who the someone was.

But you know what those guys at corporate did? Sued me for violating my duty of loyalty! To some big company! Are they kidding?? Like they would ever be loyal to me.

To find out who is in the right here, read the *Otsuka* case later in the chapter. It deals with a similar situation.

Thus far, this book has primarily dealt with issues of individual responsibility: what happens if *you* knock someone down or *you* sign an agreement? Agency law, on the other hand, is concerned with your responsibility for the actions of others. What happens if your agent assaults someone or signs a contract in your name? Agency law presents a significant trade-off: if you do everything yourself, you have control over the result. But the size and scope of your business (and your life) will be severely limited. Once you hire other people, you can accomplish a great deal more, but your risks increase immensely. Your agents may violate your instructions, and still you could be liable for what they have done. Although it might be safer to do everything yourself, that is not a practical decision for most business owners (or most people). The alternative is to hire carefully and to limit the risks as much as possible by understanding the law of agency.

Creating an Agency Relationship

Let us begin with two important definitions:

- **Principal**: A person who has someone else acting for him.
- **Agent:** A person who acts for someone else.

Principals have substantial liability for the actions of their agents.[1] Therefore, disputes about whether an agency relationship exists are not mere legal quibbles but important issues with potentially profound financial consequences.

In an agency relationship, someone (the agent) agrees to perform a task for, and under the control of, someone else (the principal). **To create an agency relationship, there must be:**

- A **principal** and
- An **agent**
- Who mutually **consent** that the agent will act on behalf of the principal and
- Be subject to the principal's **control**
- Thereby creating a **fiduciary** relationship.

Principal
In an agency relationship, the person for whom an agent is acting.

Agent
In an agency relationship, the person who is acting on behalf of a principal.

Consent

To establish consent, the principal must ask the agent to do something, and the agent must agree. In the most straightforward example, you ask a neighbor to walk your dog, and she agrees. Matters were more complicated, however, when Steven James met some friends one evening at a restaurant. During the two hours he was there, he drank four to six beers. (It is probably a bad sign that he cannot remember how many.) From then on, one misfortune piled upon another. After leaving the restaurant at about 7:00 p.m., James sped down a highway and crashed into a car that had stalled on the road, thereby killing the driver. James told the police at the scene that he had not seen the parked car (another bad sign). Evidently, James's lawyer was not as perceptive as the police in recognizing drunkenness. In a misguided attempt to help his client, James's lawyer took him to the local hospital for a blood test. Unfortunately, the test confirmed that James had indeed been drunk at the time of the accident.

[1] The word "principal" is always used when referring to a person. It is not to be confused with the word "principle," which refers to a fundamental idea.

The attorney knew that if this evidence was admitted at trial, his client would soon be receiving free room and board from the Massachusetts Department of Corrections. So at trial, the lawyer argued that the blood test was protected by the client-attorney privilege because the hospital had been his agent and therefore a member of the defense team. The court disagreed, however, holding that the hospital employees were not agents for the lawyer because they had not consented to act in that role.

The court upheld James's conviction of murder in the first degree by reason of extreme atrocity or cruelty.[2]

Control

Principals are liable for the acts of their agents because they exercise control over the agents. If principals direct their agents to commit an act, it seems fair to hold the principal liable when that act causes harm. How would you apply that rule to the following situation?

William Stanford was an employee of the Agency for International Development. While on his way home to Pakistan to spend the holidays with his family, his plane was hijacked and taken to Iran, where he was killed. Stanford had originally purchased a ticket on Northwest Airlines but had traded it for a seat on Kuwait Airways (KA). The airlines had an agreement permitting passengers to exchange tickets from one to the other. Stanford's widow sued Northwest on the theory that KA was Northwest's agent. The court found, however, that no agency relationship existed because Northwest had no control over KA.[3] Northwest did not tell KA how to fly planes or handle terrorists; therefore, it should not be liable when KA made fatal errors. Not only must an agent and principal consent to an agency relationship, but the principal also must have control over the agent.

Fiduciary Relationship

In a **fiduciary relationship**, a trustee acts for the benefit of the beneficiary, always putting the interests of the beneficiary before his own. A fiduciary relationship is a special relationship with high standards. The beneficiary places special confidence in the fiduciary who, in turn, is obligated to act in good faith and candor, putting his own needs second. The purpose of a fiduciary relationship is for one person to benefit another. **Agents have a fiduciary duty to their principals.**

All three elements—consent, control, and a fiduciary duty—are necessary to create an agency relationship. In some relationships, for example, there might be a *fiduciary duty* but no *control*. A trustee of a trust must act for the benefit of the beneficiaries, but the beneficiaries have no right to control the trustee. Therefore, a trustee is not an agent of the beneficiaries. *Consent* is present in every contractual relationship, but that does not necessarily mean that the two parties are agent and principal. If Horace sells his car to Lily, they both expect to benefit under the contract, but neither has a *fiduciary duty* to the other and neither *controls* the other, so there is no agency relationship.

Elements Not Required for an Agency Relationship

Consent, control, and a fiduciary relationship are necessary to establish an agency relationship. The following elements are *not* required:

- *A Written Agreement.* In most cases, an agency agreement does not have to be in writing. An oral understanding is valid, except in one circumstance—the **equal dignities rule**. According to this rule, if an agent is empowered to enter into a contract that must be in writing, then the appointment of the agent must also be written.

Equal dignities rule
If an agent is empowered to enter into a contract that must be in writing, then the appointment of the agent must also be written.

---

[2]*Commonwealth v. James*, 427 Mass. 312, 693 N.E.2nd 148, 1998 Mass. LEXIS 175. (S.J.C. MA, 1998)
[3]*Stanford v. Kuwait Airways Corp.*, 648 F. Supp. 1158, 1986 U.S. Dist. LEXIS 18880 (S.D.N.Y. 1986).

For example, under the statute of frauds, a contract for the sale of land is unenforceable unless in writing, so the agency agreement to sell land must also be in writing.

- *A Formal Agreement.* The principal and agent need not agree formally that they have an agency relationship. They do not even have to think the word "agent." So long as they act like an agent and a principal, the law will treat them as such.
- *Compensation.* An agency relationship need not meet all the standards of contract law. For example, a contract is not valid without consideration, but an agency agreement is valid *even if the agent is not paid.*

Duties of Agents to Principals

Agents owe a fiduciary duty to their principals. There are four elements to this duty.

Duty of Loyalty

An agent has a fiduciary duty to act loyally for the principal's benefit in all matters connected with the agency relationship.[4] The agent has an obligation to put the principal first, to strive to accomplish the principal's goals. As the following case illustrates, this duty applies to all employees, no matter how lowly.

Otsuka v. Polo Ralph Lauren Corporation

2007 U.S. DIST. LEXIS 86523
United States District Court for the Northern District of California, 2007

Facts: Justin Kiser and Germania worked together at a Ralph Lauren Polo store in San Francisco. After she left the job, he let her buy clothing using merchandise credits made out to nonexistent people. He also let her use his employee discount. Not surprisingly, both of these activities were against store policies. Polo sued Kiser, alleging that he had violated his duty of loyalty.

Kiser filed a motion to dismiss on the grounds that he was such a low-level employee that he did not owe a duty of loyalty to Polo.

Issue: ***Do all employees owe a duty of loyalty to their employer?***

Excerpts from Judge Illston's Decision: Kiser moves to dismiss this cause of action, contending that a lower-level employee owes no fiduciary duty to his employer. In response, [Polo] argues that there is a duty of loyalty akin to a fiduciary duty that all employees owe to their employers.

The Court agrees with Kiser that the cases cited by [Polo] address the duty of loyalty with respect to higher-ranking employees than Kiser, who worked as a sales clerk in a retail store. [But t]he Third Restatement provides that all employees are agents, and that "[a]s agents, all employees owe a duty of loyalty to their employers." Restatement (Third) of Agency §1.01. This is true regardless of how ministerial or routinized a work assignment may be.

Accordingly, the Court DENIES Kiser's motion to dismiss the cause of action.

[4]Restatement (Third) of Agency §8.01.

The various components of the duty of loyalty follow.

Outside Benefits

An agent may not receive profits unless the principal knows and approves. Suppose that Hope is an employee of the agency Big Egos and Talents, Inc. (BEAT). She has been representing Will Smith in his latest movie negotiations.[5] Smith often drives her to meetings in his new Maybach. He is so thrilled that she has arranged for him to star in the new movie *Little Men* that he buys her a Maybach. Can Hope keep this generous gift? Only with BEAT's permission. She must tell BEAT about the Maybach; the company may then take the vehicle itself or allow her to keep it.

Confidential Information

The ability to keep secrets is important in any relationship, but especially a fiduciary relationship. Agents can neither disclose nor use for their own benefit any confidential information they acquire during their agency. As the following case shows, this duty continues even after the agency relationship ends.

Abkco Music, Inc. v. Harrisongs Music, Ltd.

722 F.2d 988, 1983 U.S. App. LEXIS 15562
United States Court of Appeals for the Second Circuit, 1983

Facts: Bright Tunes Music Corp. (Bright Tunes) owned the copyright to the song "He's So Fine." The company sued George Harrison, a Beatle, alleging that the Harrison composition "My Sweet Lord" copied "He's So Fine." At the time the suit was filed, Allen B. Klein handled the business affairs of the Beatles.

Klein (representing Harrison) met with the president of Bright Tunes to discuss possible settlement of the copyright lawsuit. Klein suggested that Harrison might be interested in purchasing the copyright to "He's So Fine." Shortly thereafter, Klein's management contract with the Beatles expired. Without telling Harrison, Klein began negotiating with Bright Tunes to purchase the copyright to "He's So Fine" for himself. To advance these negotiations, Klein gave Bright Tunes information about royalty income for "My Sweet Lord"—information that he had gained as Harrison's agent.

The trial judge in the copyright case ultimately found that Harrison had infringed the copyright on "He's So Fine" and assessed damages of $1,599,987. After the trial, Klein purchased the "He's So Fine" copyright from Bright Tunes and with it, the right to recover from Harrison for the breach of copyright.

George Harrison, a few months after writing "My Sweet Lord."

Issue: ***Did Klein violate his fiduciary duty to Harrison by using confidential information after the agency relationship terminated?***

Excerpts from Judge Pierce's Decision: There is no doubt that the relationship between Harrison and [Klein]

[5]Do not be confused by the fact that Hope works as an agent for movie stars. As an employee of BEAT, her duty is to the company. She is an agent of BEAT, and BEAT works for the celebrities.

prior to the termination of the management agreement was that of principal and agent, and that the relationship was fiduciary in nature. [A]n agent has a duty not to use confidential knowledge acquired in his employment in competition with his principal. This duty exists as well after the employment is terminated as during its continuance. On the other hand, use of information based on general business knowledge or gleaned from general business experience is not covered by the rule, and the former agent is permitted to compete with his former principal in reliance on such general publicly available information. The evidence presented herein is not at all convincing that the information imparted to Bright Tunes by Klein was publicly available.

While the initial attempt to purchase [the copyright to "He's So Fine"] was several years removed from the eventual purchase on [Klein]'s own account, we are not of the view that such a fact rendered [Klein] unfettered in the later negotiations. Taking all of these circumstances together, we agree that [Klein's] conduct did not meet the standard required of him as a former fiduciary.

To listen to the two songs involved in this case, google "benedict copyright."

Ethics Klein was angry that the Beatles had failed to renew his management contract. Was it reasonable for him to think that he owed no duty to the principal who had fired him? Why kind of world would it be if everyone acted like Klein? Why would George Harrison prefer to owe money to Bright Tunes rather than to Klein?

Competition with the Principal

Agents are not allowed to compete with their principal in any matter within the scope of the agency business. If Allen Klein had purchased the "He's So Fine" copyright while he was George Harrison's agent, he would have committed an additional sin against the agency relationship. Owning song rights was clearly part of the agency business, so Klein could not make such purchases without Harrison's consent. Once the agency relationship ends, however, so does the rule against competition. Klein was entitled to buy the "He's So Fine" copyright after the agency relationship ended (so long as he did not use confidential information).

Conflict of Interest Between Two Principals

Unless otherwise agreed, an agent may not act for two principals whose interests conflict. Suppose Travis represents both director Steven Spielberg and actor Amy Adams. Spielberg is casting the title role in his new movie, *Nancy Drew: Girl Detective,* a role that Adams covets. Travis cannot represent these two clients when they are negotiating with each other unless they both know about the conflict and agree to ignore it. The following example illustrates the dangers of acting for two principals at once.

EXAM Strategy

Question: The Sisters of Charity was an order of nuns in New Jersey. Faced with growing health care and retirement costs, they decided to sell off a piece of property. The nuns soon found, however, that the world is not always a charitable place. They agreed to sell the land to Linpro for nearly $10 million. But before the deal closed, Linpro signed a contract to resell the property to Sammis for $34 million. So, you say, the sisters made a bad deal. There is no law against that. But it turned out that the nuns' law firm also represented Linpro. Their lawyer at the firm, Peter Berkley, never told the sisters about the deal between Linpro and Sammis. Was that the charitable—or legal—thing to do?

Strategy: Always begin by asking if there is an agency relationship. Was there consent, control, and a fiduciary relationship? *Consent*: Berkley had agreed to work for the nuns. *Control*: they told him what he was to do—sell the land. The purpose of a *fiduciary relationship* is for one person to benefit another. The point of the nuns' relationship with Berkley is for him to help them. Once you know there is an agency relationship, then ask if the agent has violated his duty of loyalty.

Result: You know that an agent is not permitted to act for two principals whose interests conflict. Here, Berkley is working for the nuns, who want the highest possible price for their land, and Linpro, who wants the lowest price. Berkley has violated his duty of loyalty.

Secretly Dealing with the Principal

If a principal hires an agent to arrange a transaction, the agent may not become a party to the transaction without the principal's permission. Matt Damon became an overnight sensation after starring in the movie *Good Will Hunting*. Suppose that he hired Trang to read scripts for him. Unbeknownst to Damon, Trang has written her own script, which she thinks would be ideal for him. She may not sell it to him without revealing that she wrote it herself. Damon may be perfectly happy to buy Trang's script, but he has the right, as her principal, to know that she is the person selling it.

Appropriate Behavior

An agent may not engage in inappropriate behavior that reflects badly on the principal. This rule applies even to *off-duty* conduct. For example, a coed trio of flight attendants went wild at a hotel bar in London. They kissed and caressed each other, showed off their underwear, and poured alcohol down their trousers. The airline fired two of the employees and gave a warning letter to the third.

Other Duties of an Agent

Before Taylor left for a five-week trip to England, he hired Angie to rent his vacation house. Angie never got around to listing his house on the Multiple Listing Service used by all the area brokers, nor did she post it on the Web herself, but when the Fords contacted her looking for rental housing, she did show them Taylor's place. They offered to rent it for $750 per month.

Angie called Taylor in England to tell him. He responded that he would not accept less than $850 a month, which Angie thought the Fords would be willing to pay. He told Angie to call back if there was any problem. The Fords decided that they would go no higher than $800 a month. Although Taylor had told Angie that he could not receive text messages in England, she texted him the Fords' counteroffer. Taylor never received it, so he never responded. When the Fords pressed Angie for an answer, she said she could not get in touch with Taylor. Not until Taylor returned home did he learn that the Fords had rented another house. Did Angie violate any of the duties that agents owe to their principals?

Duty to Obey Instructions

An agent must obey her principal's instructions unless the principal directs her to behave illegally or unethically. Taylor instructed Angie to call him if the Fords rejected the offer. When Angie failed to do so, she violated her duty to obey instructions. If, however, Taylor had asked her to say that the house's basement was dry when in fact it looked like a swamp every spring, Angie would be under no obligation to follow those illegal instructions.

Duty of Care

An agent has a duty to act with reasonable care. In other words, an agent must act as a reasonable person would, under the circumstances. A reasonable person would not have texted Taylor while he was in England.

Under some circumstances, an agent is held to a higher—or lower—standard than usual. **An agent with special skills is held to a higher standard because she is expected to use those skills.** A trained real estate agent should know enough to post all listings on the Web.

But suppose Taylor had asked his neighbor, Jed, to help him sell the house. Jed is not a trained real estate agent, and he is not being paid, which makes him a *gratuitous agent.* A gratuitous agent is held to a lower standard because he is doing his principal a favor and, as the old saying goes, you get what you pay for—up to a point. **Gratuitous agents are liable if they commit *gross* negligence, but not *ordinary* negligence.** If Jed, as a gratuitous agent, texted Taylor an important message because he forgot that Taylor could not receive these messages in England, he would not be liable for that ordinary negligence. But if Taylor had, just that day, sent Jed an email complaining that he could not get any text messages, Jed would be liable for gross negligence and a violation of his duty.

Duty to Provide Information

An agent has a duty to provide the principal with all information in her possession that she has reason to believe the principal wants to know. She also has a duty to provide accurate information. Angie knew that the Fords had counteroffered for $800 a month. She had a duty to pass this information on to Taylor.

EXAM Strategy

Question: Jonah tells his friend Derek that he would like to go parasailing. Derek is very enthusiastic and suggests that they try an outfit called Wind Beneath Your Wings because he has heard good things about them. Derek offers to arrange everything. He makes a reservation, puts the $600 fee on his credit card, and picks Jonah up to drive him to the Wings location. What a friend! But the day does not turn out as Jonah had hoped. While he is soaring up in the air over the Pacific Ocean, his sail springs a leak, he goes plummeting into the sea and breaks both legs. During his recuperation in the hospital, he learns that Wings is unlicensed. He also sees an ad for Wings offering parasailing for only $350. And Derek is listed in the ad as one of the company's owners. Is Derek an agent for Jonah? Has he violated his fiduciary responsibility?

Strategy: There are three issues to consider in answering this question: (1) Was there an agency relationship? This requires consent, control, and a fiduciary relationship. (2) Is anything missing—does it matter if the agent is unpaid or the contract is not in writing? (3) Has the agent fulfilled his duties?

Result: There is an agency relationship: Derek had agreed to help Jonah; it was Jonah who set the goal for the relationship (parasailing); the purpose of this relationship is for one person to benefit another. It does not matter if Derek was not paid or the agreement not written. Derek has violated his duty to exercise due care. He should not have taken Jonah to an unlicensed company. He has also violated his duty to provide information: he should have told Jonah the true cost for the lessons and also revealed that he was a principal of the company. And he violated his duty of loyalty when he worked for two principals whose interests were in conflict.

Principal's Remedies when the Agent Breaches a Duty

A principal has three potential remedies when an agent breaches her duty:

- The principal can recover from the agent any **damages** the breach has caused. Thus, if Taylor can rent his house for only $600 a month instead of the $800 the Fords offered, Angie would be liable for $2,400—$200 a month for one year.
- If an agent breaches the duty of loyalty, he must turn over to the principal any **profits** he has earned as a result of his wrongdoing. Thus, after Klein violated his duty of loyalty to Harrison, he forfeited profits he would have earned from the copyright of "He's So Fine."
- If the agent has violated her duty of loyalty, the principal may **rescind** the transaction. When Trang sold a script to her principal, Matt Damon, without telling him that she was the author, she violated her duty of loyalty. Damon could rescind the contract to buy the script.[6]

Duties of Principals to Agents

In a typical agency relationship, the agent agrees to perform tasks for the principal, and the principal agrees to pay the agent. The range of tasks undertaken by an agent is limited only by the imagination of the principal. Because the agent's job can be so varied, the law needs to define an agent's duties carefully. The role of the principal, on the other hand, is typically less complicated—often little more than paying the agent as required by the agreement. Thus, the law enumerates fewer duties for the principal. Primarily, the principal must reimburse the agent for reasonable expenses and cooperate with the agent in performing agency tasks. The respective duties of agents and principals can be summarized as follows:

Duties of Agents to Principals	Duty of Principals to Agents
Duty of loyalty	Duty to compensate as provided by the agreement
Duty to obey instructions	Duty to reimburse for reasonable expenses
Duty of care	Duty to cooperate
Duty to provide information	

As a general rule, the principal must indemnify (i.e., reimburse) the agent for any expenses she has reasonably incurred. These reimbursable expenses fall into three categories:

- **A principal must indemnify an agent for any expenses or damages reasonably incurred in carrying out his agency responsibilities.** For example, Peace Baptist Church of Birmingham, Alabama, asked its pastor to buy land for a new church. He paid part of the purchase price out of his own pocket, but the church refused to reimburse him. Although the pastor lost in church, he won in court.[7]

---

[6]A principal can rescind his contract with an agent who has violated her duty, but, as we shall see later in the chapter, the principal might not be able to rescind a contract with a third party when the agent misbehaves.

[7]*Lauderdale v. Peace Baptist Church of Birmingham*, 246 Ala. 178, 19 So. 2d 538, 1944 Ala. LEXIS 508 (S. Ct. AL, 1944).

- **A principal must indemnify an agent for tort claims brought by a third party if the principal authorized the agent's behavior and the agent did not realize he was committing a tort.** Marisa owns all the apartment buildings on Elm Street, except one. She hires Rajiv to manage the units and tells him that, under the terms of the leases, she has the right to ask guests to leave if a party becomes too rowdy. But she forgets to tell Rajiv that she does not own one of the buildings, which happens to house a college sorority. One night, when the sorority is having a rambunctious party, Rajiv hustles over and starts ejecting the noisy guests. The sorority is furious and sues Rajiv for trespass. If the sorority wins its suit against Rajiv, Marisa would have to pay the judgment, plus Rajiv's attorney's fees, because she had told him to quell noisy parties and he did not realize he was trespassing.
- **The principal must indemnify the agent for any liability she incurs from third parties as a result of entering into a contract on the principal's behalf, including attorney's fees and reasonable settlements.** An agent signed a contract to buy cucumbers for Vlasic Food Products Co. to use in making pickles. When the first shipment of cucumbers arrived, Vlasic inspectors found them unsuitable and directed the agent to refuse the shipment. The agent found himself in a pickle when the cucumber farmer sued. The agent notified Vlasic, but the company refused to defend him. He settled the claim himself and, in turn, sued Vlasic. The court ordered Vlasic to reimburse the agent because he had notified them of the suit and had acted reasonably and in good faith.[8]

Duty to Cooperate

Principals have a duty to cooperate with their agent:

- **The principal must furnish the agent with the opportunity to work.** If Lewis agrees to serve as Ida's real estate agent in selling her house, Ida must allow Lewis access to the house. It is unlikely that Lewis will be able to sell the house without taking anyone inside.
- **The principal cannot unreasonably interfere with the agent's ability to accomplish his task.** Ida allows Lewis to show the house, but she refuses to clean it and then makes disparaging comments to prospective purchasers. "I really get tired of living in such a dark, dreary house," she says. "And the neighborhood children are vicious thugs." This behavior would constitute unreasonable interference with an agent.
- **The principal must perform her part of the contract.** Once the agent has successfully completed the task, the principal must pay him, even if the principal has changed her mind and no longer wants the agent to perform. Ida is a 78-year-old widow who has lived alone for many years in a house that she loves. Her asking price is outrageously high. But lo and behold, Lewis finds a couple happy to pay Ida's price. There is only one problem. Ida does not really want to sell. She put her house on the market because she enjoys showing it to all the folks who move to town. She rejects the offer. Now there is a second problem. The contract provided that Lewis would find a willing buyer at the asking price. Because he has done so, Ida must pay his real estate commission even if she does not want to sell her house.

Terminating an Agency Relationship

Either the agent or the principal can terminate the agency relationship at any time. In addition, the relationship terminates automatically if the principal or agent no longer can perform their required duties or a change in circumstances renders the agency relationship pointless.

[8]*Long v. Vlasic Food Products Co.*, 439 F.2d 229, 1971 U.S. App. LEXIS 11455 (4th Cir. 1971).

Termination by Agent or Principal

The two parties—principal and agent—have three choices in terminating their relationship:

- *Term Agreement.* If the principal and agent agree in advance how long their relationship will last, they have a term agreement. For example:
  - *Time.* Alexandra hires Boris to help her add to her collection of guitars previously owned by rock stars. If they agree that the relationship will last two years, they have a term agreement.
  - *Achieving a Purpose.* The principal and agent can agree that the agency relationship will terminate when the principal's goals have been achieved. Alexandra and Boris might agree that their relationship will end when Alexandra has purchased 10 guitars.
  - *Mutual Agreement.* No matter what the principal and agent agree at the start, they can always change their minds later on, so long as the change is mutual. If Boris and Alexandra originally agree to a two-year term, but Boris decides he wants to go back to business school and Alexandra runs out of money after only one year, they can decide together to terminate the agency.
- *Agency at Will.* If they make no agreement in advance about the term of the agreement, either principal or agent can terminate at any time.
- *Wrongful Termination.* An agency relationship is a personal relationship. Hiring an agent is not like buying a book. You might not care which copy of the book you buy, but you do care which agent you hire. If an agency relationship is not working out, the courts will not force the agent and principal to stay together. **Either party always has the *power* to walk out. They may not, however, have the *right*.** If one party's departure from the agency relationship violates the agreement and causes harm to the other party, the wrongful party must pay damages. Nonetheless, he will be permitted to leave. If Boris has agreed to work for Alexandra for two years but he wants to leave after one, he can leave, provided he pays Alexandra the cost of hiring and training a replacement.

  If the agent is a **gratuitous** agent (i.e., is not being paid), he has both the power and the right to quit any time he wants, regardless of the agency agreement. If Boris is doing this job for Alexandra as a favor, he will not owe her damages when he stops work.

Principal or Agent Can No Longer Perform Required Duties

If the principal or the agent is unable to perform the duties required under the agency agreement, the agreement terminates.

- **If either the agent or the principal fails to obtain (or keep) a license necessary to perform duties under the agency agreement, the agreement ends.** Caleb hires Allegra to represent him in a lawsuit. If she is disbarred, their agency agreement terminates because the agent is no longer allowed in court. Alternatively, if Emil hires Bess to work in his gun shop, their agency relationship terminates when he loses his license to sell firearms.
- **The bankruptcy of the agent or the principal terminates an agency relationship only if it affects their ability to perform.** Bankruptcy rarely interferes with an agent's responsibilities. After all, there is generally no reason why an agent cannot continue to act for the principal whether the agent is rich or poor. If Lewis, the real estate agent, becomes bankrupt, he can continue to represent Ida or anyone else who wants to sell a house. The bankruptcy of a principal is different, however, because after filing for

bankruptcy, the principal loses control of his assets. A bankrupt principal may be unable to pay the agent or honor contracts that the agent enters into on his behalf. Therefore, the bankruptcy of a principal is more likely to terminate an agency relationship.

- **An agency relationship terminates upon the death or incapacity of either the principal or the agent.** Agency is a personal relationship, and when the principal dies, the agent cannot act on behalf of a nonexistent person.[9] Of course, a nonexistent person cannot act either, so the relationship also terminates when the agent dies. Incapacity has the same legal effect because either the principal or the agent is at least temporarily unable to act.
- **If the agent violates her duty of loyalty, the agency agreement automatically terminates.** Agents are appointed to represent the principal's interest; if they fail to do so, there is no point to the relationship. Louisa is negotiating a military procurement contract on behalf of her employer, Missiles R Us, Inc. In the midst of these negotiations, she becomes very friendly with Sam, the government negotiator. One night over drinks, she tells Sam what Missiles' real costs are on the project and the lowest bid it could possibly make. By passing on this confidential information, Louisa has violated her duty of loyalty, and her agency relationship terminates.

Change in Circumstances

After the agency agreement is negotiated, circumstances may change. If these changes are significant enough to undermine the purpose of the agreement, the relationship ends automatically. Andrew hires Melissa to sell his country farm for $100,000. Shortly thereafter, the largest oil reserve in North America is discovered nearby. The farm is now worth 10 times Andrew's asking price. Melissa's authority terminates automatically.

Other changes in circumstance that affect an agency agreement are:

- *Change of Law.* If the agent's responsibilities become illegal, the agency agreement terminates. Oscar has hired Marta to ship him succulent avocados from California's Imperial Valley. Before she sends the shipment, Mediterranean fruit flies are discovered, and all fruits and vegetables in California are quarantined. The agency agreement terminates because it is now illegal to ship the California avocados.
- *Loss or Destruction of Subject Matter.* Andrew hired Damian to sell his Palm Beach condominium, but before Damian could even measure the living room, Andrew's creditors attached the condo. Damian is no longer authorized to sell the real estate because Andrew has "lost" the subject matter of his agency agreement with Damian.

Effect of Termination

Once an agency relationship ends, the agent no longer has the authority to act for the principal. If she continues to act, she is liable to the principal for any damages he incurs as a result. The Mediterranean fruit fly quarantine ended Marta's agency. If she sends Oscar the avocados anyway and he is fined for possession of a fruit fly, Marta must pay the fine.

The agent loses her authority to act, but some of the duties of both the principal and agent continue even after the relationship ends:

- *Principal's Duty to Indemnify Agent.* Oscar must reimburse Marta for expenses she incurred before the agency ended. If Marta accumulated mileage on her car during her search for the perfect avocado, Oscar must pay her for gasoline and depreciation. But he owes her nothing for her expenses after the agency relationship ends.

[9]Restatement (Third) of Agency §§3.05, 3.06, 3.07, 3.08.

- *Confidential Information.* Remember the "He's So Fine" case earlier in the chapter? George Harrison's agent used confidential information to negotiate on his own behalf the purchase of the "He's So Fine" copyright. An agent is not entitled to use confidential information even after the agency relationship terminates.

LIABILITY

Thus far, this chapter has dealt with the relationship between principals and agents. Although an agent can dramatically increase his principal's ability to accomplish her goals, an agency relationship also dramatically increases the risk of legal liability to third parties. A principal may be liable in tort for any harm the agent causes and also liable in contract for agreements that the agent signs. Indeed, once a principal hires an agent, she may be liable to third parties for his acts, even if he disobeys instructions. Agents may also find themselves liable to third parties.

PRINCIPAL'S LIABILITY FOR CONTRACTS

Many agents are hired for the primary purpose of entering into contracts on behalf of their principals. Salespeople, for example, may do little other than sign on the dotted line. Most of the time, the principal wants to be liable on these contracts. But even if the principal is unhappy (because, say, the agent has disobeyed orders), the principal generally cannot rescind contracts entered into by the agent. After all, if someone is going to be penalized, it should be the principal who hired the disobedient agent, not the innocent third party.

The principal is liable for the acts of an agent if (1) the agent had *authority*, or (2) the principal *ratifies* the acts of the agent.

To say that the principal is "liable for the acts" of the agent means that the principal is as responsible as if he had performed the acts himself. It also means that the principal is liable for statements the agent makes to a third party. Thus, when a lawyer lied on an application for malpractice insurance, the insurance company was allowed to void the policy for the entire law firm. It was as if the firm had lied. In addition, the principal is deemed to know any information that the agent knows or should know.

Authority

A principal is bound by the acts of an agent if the agent has authority. There are three types of authority: express, implied, and apparent. Express and implied authority are categories of actual authority because the agent is truly authorized to act for the principal. In apparent authority, the principal is liable for the agent's actions even though the agent was *not* authorized.

Express Authority

The principal grants **express authority** by words or conduct that, reasonably interpreted, cause the agent to believe the principal desires her to act on the principal's account.[10] In other words, the principal asks the agent to do something and the agent does it. Craig calls his stockbroker, Alice, and asks her to buy 100 shares of Banshee Corp. for his account. She has *express authority* to carry out this transaction.

---

[10]Restatement (Third) of Agency §2.01.

Implied Authority

Unless otherwise agreed, authority to conduct a transaction includes authority to do acts that are reasonably necessary to accomplish it.[11] The principal does not have to micromanage the agent. David has recently inherited a house from his grandmother. He hires Nell to auction off the house and its contents. She hires an auctioneer, advertises the event, rents a tent, and generally does everything necessary to conduct a successful auction. After withholding her expenses, she sends the tidy balance to David. Totally outraged, he calls her on the phone, "How dare you hire an auctioneer and rent a tent? I never gave you permission! I absolutely *refuse* to pay these expenses!"

Did Nell have the authority to hire this auctioneer?

David is wrong. A principal almost never gives an agent absolutely complete instructions. Unless some authority is implied, David would have had to say, "Open the car door, get in, put the key in the ignition, drive to the store, buy stickers, mark an auction number on each sticker ..." and so forth. To solve this problem, the law assumes that the agent has authority to do anything that is reasonably necessary to accomplish her task.

Apparent Authority

A principal can be liable for the acts of an agent who is not, in fact, acting with authority if the *principal's* conduct causes a third party reasonably to believe that the agent is authorized.[12] In the case of *express* and *implied* authority, the principal has authorized the agent to act. Apparent authority is different: the principal has *not* authorized the agent, but has done something to make an innocent third party *believe* the agent is authorized. As a result, the principal is every bit as liable to the third party as if the agent did have authority.

For example, Zbigniew Lambo and Scott Kennedy were brokers at Paulson Investment Co., a stock brokerage firm in Oregon. The two men violated securities laws by selling unregistered stock, which ultimately proved to be worthless. Kennedy and Lambo were liable, but they were unable to repay the money. Either Paulson or its customers would end up bearing the loss. What is the fair result? The law takes the view that the principal is liable, not the third party, because the principal, by word or deed, allowed the third party to believe that the agent was acting on the principal's behalf. The principal could have prevented the third party from losing money.

Although the two brokers did not have *express* or *implied* authority to sell the stock (Paulson had not authorized them to break the law), the company was nonetheless liable on the grounds that the brokers had *apparent* authority. Paulson had sent letters to its customers notifying them when it hired Kennedy. The two brokers made sales presentations at Paulson's offices. The company had never told customers that the two men were not authorized to sell this worthless stock.[13] Thus the agents *appeared* to have authority, even though they did not. Of course, Paulson had the right to recover from Kennedy and Lambo, if it could ever compel them to pay.

Remember that the issue in apparent authority is always what the *principal* has done to make the *third party* believe that the *agent* has authority. Suppose that Kennedy and Lambo never worked for Paulson but, on their own, printed up Paulson stationery. The company would not be liable for the stock the two men sold because it had never done or said anything that would reasonably make a third party believe that the men were its agents.

---

[11]Restatement (Third) of Agency §2.02.

[12]Restatement (Third) of Agency §2.03.

[13]*Badger v. Paulson Investment Co.*, 311 Ore. 14, 803 P.2d 1178, 1991 Ore. LEXIS 7 (S. Ct. OR, 1991).

Ratification

If a person accepts the benefit of an unauthorized transaction or fails to repudiate it, then he is as bound by the act as if he had originally authorized it. He has *ratified* the act.[14] Many of the cases in agency law involve instances in which one person acts *without* authority for another. To avoid liability, the alleged principal shows that he had not authorized the task at issue. But sometimes after the fact, the principal decides that he approves of what the agent has done even though it was not authorized at the time. The law would be perverse if it did not permit the principal, under those circumstances, to agree to the deal the agent has made. The law is not perverse, but it is careful. Even if an agent acts without authority, the principal can decide later to be bound by her actions so long as these requirements are met:

- The "agent" indicates to the third party that she is acting for a principal.
- The "principal" knows all the material facts of the transaction.
- The "principal" accepts the benefit of the whole transaction, not just part.
- The third party does not withdraw from the contract before ratification.

A night clerk at the St. Regis Hotel in Detroit, Michigan, was brutally murdered in the course of a robbery. A few days later, the *Detroit News* reported that the St. Regis management had offered a $1,000 reward for any information leading to the arrest and conviction of the killer. Two days after the article appeared, Robert Jackson turned in the man who was subsequently convicted of the crime. But then it was Jackson's turn to be robbed—the hotel refused to pay the reward on the grounds that the manager who had made the offer had no authority. Jackson still had one weapon left: he convinced the court that the hotel had ratified the offer. One of the hotel's owners admitted he read the *Detroit News*. The court concluded that if someone reads a newspaper, he is sure to read any articles about a business he owns; therefore, the owner must have been aware of the offer. He accepted the benefit of the offer by failing to revoke it publicly by, say, announcing to the press that the reward was invalid. This failure to revoke constituted a ratification, and the hotel was liable.[15]

Subagents

Many of the examples in this chapter involve a single agent acting for a principal. Real life is often more complex. Daniel, the owner of a restaurant, hires Michaela to manage it. She in turn hires chefs, waiters, and dishwashers. Daniel has never even met the restaurant help, yet they are also his agents, albeit a special category called **subagent.** Michaela is called an **intermediary agent**—someone who hires subagents for the principal.

As a general rule, an agent has no authority to delegate her tasks to another unless the principal authorizes her to do so. But when an agent is authorized to hire a subagent, the principal is as liable for the acts of the subagent as he is for the acts of a regular agent. Daniel authorizes Michaela to hire a restaurant staff, so she hires Lydia to serve as produce buyer. When Lydia buys food for the restaurant, Daniel must pay the bill.

Agent's Liability for Contracts

The agent's liability on a contract depends upon how much the third party knows about the principal. Disclosure is the agent's best protection against liability.

[14]Restatement (Third) of Agency §4.01.

[15]*Jackson v. Goodman*, 69 Mich. App. 225, 244 N.W.2d 423, 1976 Mich. App., LEXIS 741 (Mich. Ct. App., 1976).

Fully Disclosed Principal

An agent is not liable for any contracts she makes on behalf of a *fully* disclosed principal. A principal is fully disclosed if the third party knows of his *existence* and his *identity*. Augusta acts as agent for Parker when he buys Tracey's prize-winning show horse. Augusta and Tracey both grew up in posh Grosse Pointe, Michigan, where they attended the same elite schools. Tracey does not know Parker, but she figures any friend of Augusta's must be OK. She figures wrong—Parker is a charming deadbeat. He injures Tracey's horse, fails to pay the full contract price, and promptly disappears. Tracey angrily demands that Augusta make good on Parker's debt. Unfortunately for Tracey, Parker was a fully disclosed principal—Tracey knew of his *existence* and his *identity*. Although Tracey partly relied on Augusta's good character when contracting with Parker, Augusta is not liable because Tracey knew who the principal was and could have (should have) investigated him. Augusta did not promise anything herself, and Tracey's only recourse is against the principal, Parker (wherever he may be).

To avoid liability when signing a contract on behalf of a principal, an agent must clearly state that she is an agent and also must identify the principal. Augusta should sign a contract on behalf of her principal, Parker, as follows: "Augusta, as agent for Parker" or "Parker, by Augusta, Agent."

Unidentified Principal

In the case of an *unidentified* principal, the third party can recover from either the agent or the principal. (An unidentified principal is also sometimes called a "partially disclosed principal.") A principal is unidentified if the third party knew of his *existence* but not his *identity*. Suppose that, when approaching Tracey about the horse, Augusta simply says, "I have a friend who is interested in buying your champion." Any friend of Augusta's is a friend of Tracey's—or so Tracey thinks. Parker is an unidentified principal because Tracey knows only that he exists, not who he is. She cannot investigate his creditworthiness because she does not know his name. Tracey relies solely on what she is able to learn from the agent, Augusta. Both Augusta and Parker are liable to Tracey. (They are jointly and severally liable, which means that Tracey can recover from either or both of them. However, she cannot recover more than the total she is owed: if her damages are $100,000, she can recover that amount from either Augusta or Parker, or partial amounts from both, but in no event more than $100,000.)

Undisclosed Principal

In the case of an *undisclosed* principal, the third party can recover from either the agent or the principal. A principal is undisclosed if the third party did not know of his existence. Suppose that Augusta simply asks to buy the horse herself, without mentioning that she is purchasing it for Parker. In this case, Parker is an undisclosed principal because Tracey does not know that Augusta is acting for someone else. Both Parker and Augusta are jointly and severally liable. As Exhibit 28.1 illustrates, the principal is always liable, but the agent is not unless the principal's identity is a mystery.

In some ways, the concept of an undisclosed principal violates principles of contract law. If Tracey does not even know that Parker exists, how can they have an agreement or a meeting of the minds? Is such an arrangement fair to Tracey? No matter—a contract with an undisclosed principal is binding. The following incident illustrates why.

William Zeckendorf was a man with a plan. For years, he had been eyeing a six-block tract of land along New York's East River. It was a wasteland of slums and slaughterhouses, but he could see its potential. The meat packers had refused to sell to him, however, because they knew they would never be permitted to build slaughterhouses in Manhattan again. Finally, he got the phone call he had been waiting for. The companies were willing to sell—at more than three times the market price of surrounding land. Undeterred, Zeckendorf immediately put down a $1 million deposit. But to make his investment worthwhile, he needed to buy the neighboring property—once the slaughterhouses were gone, the other land would be much more valuable. Zeckendorf was well known as a wealthy developer; he

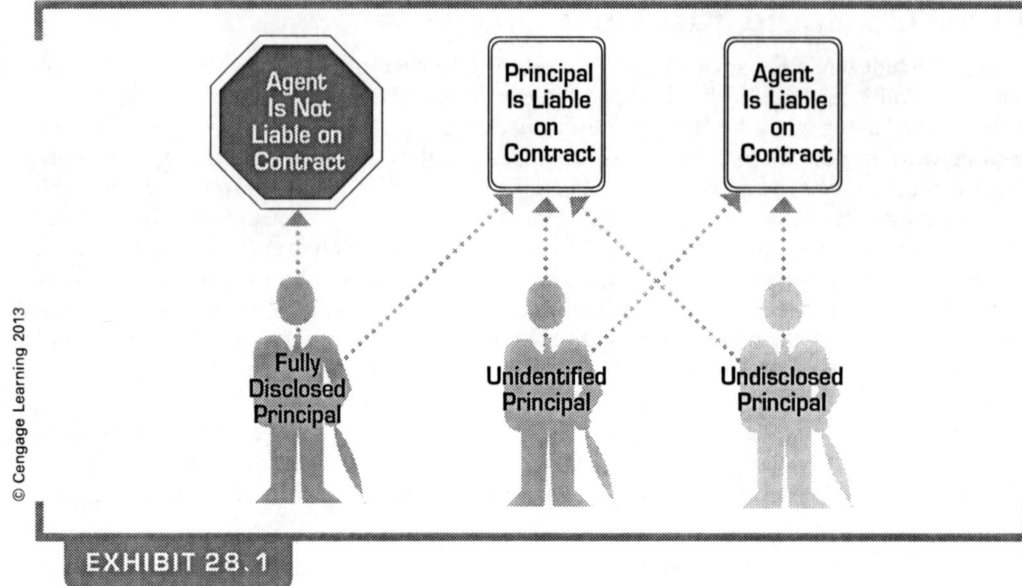

EXHIBIT 28.1

had begun his business career managing the Astor family's real estate holdings. If he personally tried to negotiate the purchase of the surrounding land, word would soon get out that he wanted to put together a large parcel. Prices would skyrocket, and the project would become too costly. So he hired agents to purchase the land for him. To conceal his involvement further, he went to South America for a month. When he returned, his agents had completed 75 different purchases, and he owned 18 acres of land.

Shortly afterwards, the United Nations (UN) began seeking a site for its headquarters. President Truman favored Boston, Philadelphia, or a location in the Midwest. The UN committee suggested Greenwich or Stamford, Connecticut. But John D. Rockefeller settled the question once and for all. He purchased Zeckendorf's land and donated it to the UN (netting Zeckendorf a 25 percent profit). Without the cooperation of agency law, the UN headquarters would not be in New York today.

> Without the cooperation of agency law, the UN headquarters would not be in New York today.

Because of concerns about fair play, there are some exceptions to the rule on undisclosed principals. **A third party is not bound to the contract with an undisclosed principal if (1) the contract specifically provides that the third party is not bound to anyone other than the agent, or (2) the agent lies about the principal because she knows the third party would refuse to contract with him.** Suppose that a large university is buying up land in an impoverished area near its campus. An owner of a house there wants to make sure that if he sells to the university, he gets a higher price than if he sells to an individual with more limited resources. A cagey property owner, when approached by one of the university's agents, could ask for a clause in the contract providing that the agent was not representing someone else. If the agent told the truth, the owner could demand a higher price. If the agent lied, then the owner could rescind the contract when the truth emerged.

Unauthorized Agent

Thus far in this section, we have been discussing an agent's liability to a third party for a transaction that was authorized by the principal. Sometimes, however, agents act without the authority of a principal. **If the agent has no authority (express, implied, or apparent), the**

principal is not liable to the third party, and the agent is. Suppose that Augusta agrees to sell Parker's horse to Tracey. Unfortunately, Parker has never met Augusta and has certainly not authorized this transaction. Augusta is hoping that she can persuade him to sell, but Parker refuses. Augusta, but not Parker, is liable to Tracey for breach of contract.

PRINCIPAL'S LIABILITY FOR TORTS

An employer is liable for a tort committed by its employee acting within the scope of employment or acting with authority.[16] This principle of liability is called ***respondeat superior,*** which is a Latin phrase that means "let the master answer." Under the theory of *respondeat superior,* the employer (that is, the principal) is liable for misbehavior by the employee (that is, the agent) whether or not the employer was at fault. Indeed, the employer is liable even if he *forbade* or tried to *prevent* the employee from misbehaving. Thus a company could be liable for the damage a worker causes while driving and talking on her cell phone, even if she is violating company policy at the time. This sounds like a harsh rule. The logic is that because the principal controls the agent, he should be able to *prevent* misbehavior. If he cannot prevent it, at least he can *insure* against the risks. Furthermore, the principal may have deeper pockets than the agent or the injured third party and thus be better able to *afford* the cost of the agent's misbehavior.

To apply the principle of *respondeat superior,* it is important to understand each part of the rule.

Employee

There are two kinds of agents: (1) *employees* and (2) *independent contractors.* **A principal *may be* liable for the torts of an employee but generally is *not* liable for the torts of an independent contractor.** Because of this rule, the distinction between an employee and an independent contractor is important.

Employee or Independent Contractor?

The more control the principal has over an agent, the more likely that the agent will be considered an employee. Therefore, when determining if agents are employees or independent contractors, courts consider whether:

- The principal supervises details of the work.
- The principal supplies the tools and place of work.
- The agents work full time for the principal.
- The agents receive a salary or hourly wages, not a fixed price for the job.
- The work is part of the regular business of the principal.
- The principal and agents believe they have an employer-employee relationship.
- The principal is in business.[17]

Suppose, for example, that Mutt and Jeff work 40 hours a week at Swansong Media preparing food for the company's onsite dining room. They earn a weekly salary. Swansong provides food, utensils, and kitchen. This year, however, Swansong decides to go all out for its holiday party, so it hires FiFi LaBelle to prepare special food. She buys the food, prepares it in her own kitchen, and delivers it to the company in time for the party. She is an independent contractor, while Mutt and Jeff are employees.

---

[16]Restatement (Third) of Agency §7.07.

[17]Ibid.

Negligent Hiring

Principals prefer agents to be considered independent contractors, not employees, because, as a general rule, principals are not liable for the torts of an independent contractor. There is, however, one exception to this rule: **the principal is liable for the torts of an independent contractor *if* the principal has been negligent in hiring or supervising her.** Remember that, under *respondeat superior*, the principal is liable *without fault* for the torts of employees. The case of independent contractors is different: the principal is liable only if he was *at fault* by being careless in his hiring or supervising.

Exhibit 28.2 illustrates the difference in liability between an employee and an independent contractor.

Scope of Employment

Principals are liable only for torts that an employee commits within the *scope of employment.* If an employee leaves a pool of water on the floor of a store and a customer slips and falls, the employer is liable. But if the same employee leaves water on his own kitchen floor and a friend falls, the employer is not liable because the employee is not acting within the scope of employment. An employee is acting within the scope of employment if the act:

- Is one that employees are generally responsible for
- Takes place during hours that the employee is generally employed
- Is part of the principal's business
- Is similar to the one the principal authorized
- Is one for which the principal supplied the tools; and
- Is not seriously criminal.

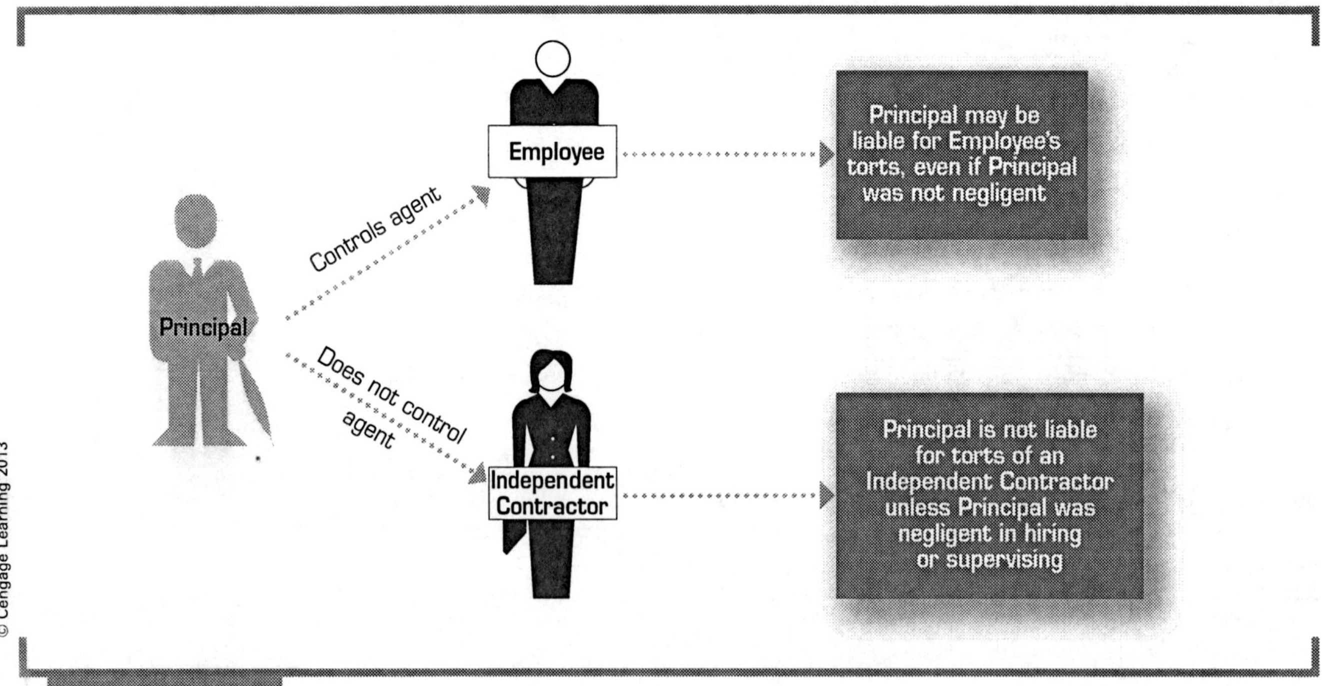

EXHIBIT 28.2

Scope of employment cases raise two major issues: authorization and abandonment.

Authorization

In authorization cases, the agent is clearly working for the principal but commits an act that the principal has not authorized. Although Jane has often told the driver of her delivery van not to speed, Hank ignores her instructions and plows into Bernadette. At the time of the accident, he is working for Jane, delivering flowers for her shop, but his act is not authorized. **An act is within the scope of employment, even if expressly forbidden, if it is of the same general nature as that authorized or if it is incidental to the conduct authorized.** Hank was authorized to drive the van, but not to speed. However, his speeding was of the same general nature as the authorized act, so Jane is liable to Bernadette.

Abandonment

The second major issue in a *scope of employment* case involves abandonment. **The principal is liable for the actions of the employee that occur while the employee is at work, but not for actions that occur after the employee has abandoned the principal's business.** Although the rule sounds straightforward, the difficulty lies in determining whether the employee has in fact abandoned the principal's business. The employer is liable if the employee is simply on a *detour* from company business, but the employer is not liable if the employee is off on a *frolic of his own.* Suppose that Hank, the delivery van driver, speeds during his afternoon commute home. An employee is generally not acting within the scope of his employment when he commutes to and from work, so his principal, Jane, is not liable. Or suppose that, while on the way to a delivery, he stops to view his favorite movie classic, *Dead on Arrival.* Unable to see in the darkened theater, he knocks Anna down, causing grave harm. Jane is not liable because Hank's visit to the movies is outside the scope of his employment. On the other hand, if Hank stops at the Burger Box drive-in window en route to making a delivery, Jane is liable when he crashes into Anna on the way out of the parking lot because this time, he is simply making a detour.

Was the employee in the following case acting within the scope of his employment while driving to work? You be the judge.

You be the Judge

ZANKEL V. UNITED STATES OF AMERICA

2008 U.S. Dist. LEXIS 23655
United States District Court for the Western District of Pennsylvania, 2008

Facts: Staff Sergeant William E. Dreyer was a recruiter for the United States Marine Corps. Driving to work one morning at 6:40 a.m., in a government-owned car, he struck and killed 12-year-old Justin Zankel. The child's parents sued the federal government, claiming that it was liable for Dreyer's actions because he had been acting within the scope of his employment at the time of the accident.

The Marine Corps had provided Dreyer with a car to drive while on government business, but he was not permitted to use this car while commuting to and from home unless he had specific authorization from his boss, Major Michael Sherman. However, Sherman was flexible in giving authorization and even permitted his soldiers simply to leave a message on his voicemail. Indeed, he had denied only about a dozen such requests over a three-year period.

Each month, Dreyer was expected to meet specific quotas for the number of contracts signed and recruits shipped to basic training. However, despite working 16 to 18 hours every day of the week, Dreyer had not met his recruiting quotas for months. Sherman had formally reprimanded him and increased his target for the following month.

On the day before the accident, Dreyer left home at 6:30 a.m., driving his own car. At the office, he switched to a government car and worked until 10:45 p.m. He then discovered that his personal car would not start. He did not want to call Sherman that late, so he drove his government car home without permission. He believed that, had he called, Sherman would have said it was OK.

Dreyer arrived home at midnight. He was under orders to attend an early-morning training session the next day. So he awoke early and left home at 6:35 a.m. At 6:40 a.m., his car hit Justin Zankel.

You Be the Judge: ***Was Dreyer within the scope of employment when he killed Zankel?***

Argument for the Zankels: At the time of the accident, Dreyer was driving a government vehicle. Although he had not requested permission to drive the car, if he had done so, permission certainly would have been granted.

Moreover, even if Dreyer was not authorized to drive the Marine Corps car, the government is still liable because his activity was of the same general nature as that authorized and it was incidental to the conduct authorized. Driving the car was part of Dreyer's work. Indeed, he could not perform his job without it. In addition, Dreyer was on the road early so that he could attend a required training session. He was exhausted from trying to reach impossible goals. The Marine Corps must bear responsibility for this tragic accident.

Argument for United States: The government had a clear policy stating that recruiters were not authorized to drive a government car without first requesting permission. Dreyer had not done so. Therefore, he was not authorized to drive the government car at the time of the accident.

Moreover, it is well established that an employee commuting to and from work is not within the scope of employment. If Dreyer had been driving from one recruiting effort to another, that would be a different story. But in this case, he had not yet started work for the Marine Corps, and therefore the government is not liable.

Intentional Torts

A principal is *not* liable for the *intentional* torts of an employee unless (1) the employee intended to serve some purpose of the employer; or (2) the employer was negligent in hiring or supervising this employee.

During an NBA basketball game, Kobe pushes LeBron into some chairs under the basket to prevent him from scoring a breakaway layup. Kobe's team is liable for his actions because he was motivated, at least in part, by a desire to help his team. But if Kobe hits LeBron in the parking lot after the playoffs are over, Kobe's team is *not* liable because he is no longer motivated by a desire to help the team. His motivation now is personal revenge or frustration.

In the following case, a priest did wrong. Was he serving some purpose of the Church? Was the Church liable for his criminal acts?

Doe v. Liberatore

478 F. Supp. 2d 742; 2007 U.S. Dist. Lexis 19067
United States District Court for the Middle District of Pennsylvania, 2007

Facts: A number of priests wrote to James Timlin, the Bishop of Scranton, warning him that Father Albert Liberatore was engaging in a sexual relationship with one of his male students. Bishop Timlin transferred Liberatore from the school to a parish church.

Fourteen year-old John Doe was a member of Liberatore's parish. Liberatore befriended Doe, taking him on outings and giving him expensive gifts. Doe routinely slept in Liberatore's bed. A number of priests told Bishop Timlin that they feared Liberatore was sexually abusing Doe. One witness reported that she had seen Doe put his hand down Liberatore's pants. Eventually, Doe himself told a priest that he was being sexually abused. The priest instructed Doe to forgive Liberatore and not to tell other people because it would ruin Doe's life and the lives of others.

Only after Liberatore pleaded guilty to multiple counts of sexual abuse did the Church dismiss him from the priesthood. Doe filed suit against the Church and Bishop Timlin, alleging that they were liable for the torts committed by Liberatore. The defendants filed a motion to dismiss.

Issues: ***Was Liberatore acting within the scope of his employment? Was the Church liable for his criminal acts?***

Excerpts from Judge Caputo's Decision: Under Pennsylvania law, an employer is held liable for the negligent acts of his employee which cause injuries to a third party, provided that such acts were committed during the course of and within the scope of the employment.

The conduct of an employee is considered within the scope of employment if: (1) it is of a kind and nature that the employee is employed to perform; (2) it occurs substantially within the authorized time and space limits; (3) it is actuated, at least in part, by a purpose to serve the employer; and (4) if force is intentionally used by the employee against another, the use of force is not unexpected by the employer.

Here, it is clear that Liberatore's sexual molestation of Plaintiff was not within the scope or nature of his employment as a priest. Indeed, the activity of which Plaintiff now complains is wholly inconsistent with the role of one who is received into the Holy Orders as an ordained priest of the Roman Catholic Church. Moreover, the acts of sexual abuse perpetrated by Liberatore were both outrageous and certainly not actuated by any purpose of serving the Diocese, Sacred Heart, or Bishop Timlin. Therefore, the Court will grant summary judgment in favor of the Diocese, Sacred Heart, and Bishop Timlin as to [this issue].

Plaintiff next claims that the Diocese, Sacred Heart, and Bishop Timlin are liable for negligence in their hiring, supervision, and retention of Liberatore as a Diocesan priest. [A]n employer owes a duty to exercise reasonable care in selecting, supervising and controlling employees. The Supreme Court of Pennsylvania has held that, to fasten liability on an employer, it must be shown that the employer knew or, in the exercise of ordinary care, should have known of the necessity for exercising control of his employee.

In the instant case, the Diocese, Sacred Heart, and Bishop Timlin may be liable if they knew or should have known that Liberatore had a propensity for committing sexual abuse and his employment as Pastor at Sacred Heart might create a situation where his propensity would harm a third person, such as Plaintiff. [A] reasonable jury could conclude that the Diocese, Sacred Heart, and Bishop Timlin were negligent or reckless in supervising and retaining Liberatore. However, the Court concludes that a reasonable jury could not find that the Diocese, Sacred Heart, and Bishop Timlin were negligent or reckless in hiring Liberatore because there is no evidence suggesting that Liberatore was or would become a child sex predator when he was hired.

Physical or Non-Physical Harm

In the case of *physical* torts, a principal is liable for the negligent conduct of a employee that occurs within the scope of employment. The rule for *nonphysical* torts (that is, torts that harm only reputation, feelings, or wallet) is different. **Nonphysical torts are treated more like a contract claim, and the principal is liable if the employee acted with express, implied, or apparent authority.**[18] For example, suppose that Dwayne buys a house insurance policy from Andy, who is an agent of the Balls of Fire Insurance Company. Andy throws away Dwayne's policy and pockets his premiums. When Dwayne's house burns down, Balls of Fire is liable because Andy was acting with apparent authority.

EXAM Strategy

Question: Daisy was the founder of an Internet start-up company. Mac was her driver. One day, after he had dropped her at a board meeting, he went to the car wash. There, he told an attractive woman that he worked for a money management firm. She gave him money to invest. On the way out of the car wash, he was so excited that he hit another customer's expensive car. Who is liable for Mac's misdeeds?

Strategy: In determining a principal's liability, begin by figuring out whether the agent has committed a physical or non-physical tort. Remember that the principal is liable for physical torts within the scope of employment, but for nonphysical torts, she is liable only if the employee acted with authority.

Result: In this case, Daisy is liable for the damage to the car because that was a physical tort within the scope of employment. But she is not liable for the investment money because Mac did not have authority (express, implied, or apparent) to take those funds.

Agent's Liability for Torts

The focus of the prior section was on the *principal's* liability for the agent's torts. But it is important to remember that **agents are always liable for their own torts.** Agents who commit torts are personally responsible, whether or not their principal is also liable. Even if the tort was committed to benefit the principal, the agent is still liable. So the sailor who got into a fistfight while rousting a shipmate from bed is liable even though he thought he was acting for the benefit of his principal.

This rule makes obvious sense. If the agent were not liable, he would have little incentive to be careful. Imagine Hank driving his delivery van for Jane. If he were not personally liable for his own torts, he might think, "If I drive fast enough, I can make it through that light even though it just turned red. And if I don't, what the heck, it'll be Jane's problem, not mine." Agents, as a rule, may have fewer assets than their principal, but it is important that their personal assets be at risk in the event of their negligent behavior.

If the agent and principal are *both* liable, which does the injured third party sue? The principal and the agent are *jointly and severally liable,* which means, as we have seen, that the injured third party can sue either one or both, as she chooses. If she recovers from the principal, he can sue the agent.

Chapter Conclusion

When students enroll in a business law course, they fully expect to learn about torts and contracts, corporations and partnerships. They probably do not think much about agency law; many of them have not even heard the term before. Yet it is an area of the law that affects us all because each of us has been and will continue to be both an agent and a principal many times in our lives.

Exam Review

1. **CREATING AN AGENCY RELATIONSHIP** A principal and an agent mutually consent that the agent will act on behalf of the principal and be subject to the principal's control, thereby creating a fiduciary relationship. (pp. 671–672)

2. **ELEMENTS NOT REQUIRED** An agency relationship can exist without either a written agreement, a formal agreement, or compensation. (pp. 672–673)

3. **AN AGENT'S DUTIES TO THE PRINCIPAL** An agent owes these duties to the principal: duty of loyalty, duty to obey instructions, duty of care, and duty to provide information. (pp. 673–677)

4. **THE PRINCIPAL'S REMEDIES IN THE EVENT OF A BREACH** The principal has three potential remedies when the agent breaches her duty: recovery of damages the breach has caused, recovery of any profits earned by the agent from the breach, and rescission of any transaction with the agent. (p. 678)

5. **THE PRINCIPAL'S DUTIES TO THE AGENT** The principal has three duties to the agent: to compensate as provided by the agreement, to reimburse legitimate expenses, and to cooperate with the agent. (pp. 678–679)

6. **POWER AND RIGHT TO TERMINATE** Both the agent and the principal have the power to terminate an agency relationship, but they may not have the right. If the termination violates the agency agreement and causes harm to the other party, the wrongful party must pay damages. (pp. 679–682)

7. **AUTOMATIC TERMINATION** An agency relationship automatically terminates if the principal or agent no longer can perform the required duties or if a change in circumstances renders the agency relationship pointless. (pp. 680–681)

8. **A PRINCIPAL'S LIABILITY FOR CONTRACTS** A principal is liable for the contracts of the agent if the agent has express, implied, or apparent authority. (pp. 682–684)

9. **EXPRESS AUTHORITY** The principal grants express authority by words or conduct that, reasonably interpreted, cause the agent to believe that the principal desires her to act on the principal's account. (p. 682)

10. **IMPLIED AUTHORITY** Implied authority includes authority to do acts that are incidental to a transaction, usually accompany it, or are reasonably necessary to accomplish it. (p. 683)

11. **APPARENT AUTHORITY** Apparent authority means that a principal is liable for the acts of an agent who is not, in fact, acting with authority if the principal's conduct causes a third party reasonably to believe that the agent is authorized. (p. 683)

EXAM Strategy

Question: Dr. James Leonard wrote Dr. Edward Jacobson to offer him the position of chief of audiology at Jefferson Medical College in Philadelphia. In the letter, Leonard stated that this appointment would have to be approved by the promotion and appointment committee. Jacobson believed that the appointment committee acted only as a "rubber stamp," affirming whatever recommendation Leonard made. Jacobson accepted Leonard's offer and proceeded to sell his house and quit his job in Colorado. You can guess what happened next. Two weeks later, Leonard sent Jacobson another letter, rescinding his offer because of opposition from the appointment committee. Did Leonard have apparent authority?

Strategy: In cases of apparent authority, begin by asking what the principal did to make the third party believe that the agent was authorized. What did the Medical College do? (See the "Result" at the end of this section.)

12. **AN AGENT'S LIABILITY FOR A CONTRACT** An agent is not liable for any contract she makes on behalf of a fully disclosed principal. The principal is liable. In the case of a unidentified or undisclosed principal, both the agent and the principal are liable on the contract. (pp. 684–687)

13. **A PRINCIPAL'S LIABILITY FOR TORTS** An employer is liable for a tort committed by its employee acting within the scope of employment or acting with authority. (pp. 687–692)

EXAM Strategy

Question: While drunk, the driver of a subway car plows into the back of the car ahead of him, killing a passenger. It was against the rules for the driver to be drunk. Is the subway authority liable for the negligence of its employee?

Strategy: With a tort case, always determine first if the agents are employees or independent contractors. This worker was an employee. Then ask if the employee was acting within the scope of employment. Yes, he was driving a subway car, which is what he was hired to do. Does it matter than he had violated subway rules? No, his violation of the rules does not eliminate his principal's liability. (See the "Result" at the end of this section.)

14. **INDEPENDENT CONTRACTOR** The principal is liable for the physical torts of an independent contractor only if the principal has been negligent in hiring or supervising him. (p. 687)

15. **INTENTIONAL TORTS** A principal is not liable for the intentional torts of an employee unless (1) the employee intended to serve some purpose of the employer; or (2) the employer was negligent in hiring or supervising the employee. (pp. 690–691)

EXAM Strategy

Question: What if the subway driver mentioned above had stabbed a passenger?

Strategy: In the case of an intentional tort, the principal is liable only if the agent was intending to serve some purpose of the employer or the employer was negligent in hiring or supervising him. (See the "Result" at the end of this section.)

16. **AGENT'S LIABILITY FOR TORTS** Agents are always liable for their own torts. (p. 692)

17. **NONPHYSICAL TORTS** A principal is liable only for the nonphysical torts of an employee who is acting with express, implied or apparent authority. (p. 691)

11. Result: No. Indeed, Leonard had told Jacobson that he did not have authority. If Jacobson chose to believe otherwise, that was his problem.

13. Result: The subway authority is liable.

15. Result: When he stabbed a passenger, the driver was not serving the purpose of the employer, so the subway authority would not be liable. There was no evidence that the subway authority had been negligent in its hiring or supervising of employees.

Multiple-Choice Questions

1. At Business University, semester enrollment begins at midnight on April 1. Jasper asked his roommate, Alonso, to register him for an important required course as a favor. Alonso agreed to do so but then overslept. As a result, Jasper could not enroll in the required course he needed to graduate and had to stay in school for an additional semester. Is Alonso liable to Jasper?
   (a) No, because an agency agreement is invalid unless the agent receives payment.
   (b) No, because Alonso was not grossly negligent.
   (c) No, because the cost of the extra semester is unreasonably high.
   (d) Yes, because Alonso disobeyed his instructions.

2. Finn learns that, despite his stellar record, he is being paid less than other salespeople at Barry Co., so he decides to start his own company. During his last month on the Barry payroll, he tells all of his clients about his new business. He also tells them that Barry is a great company, but his fees will be lower. After he opens the doors of his new business, most of his former clients move with him. Is Finn liable to Barry?
   (a) No, because he has not been disloyal to Barry—he praised the company.
   (b) No, because Barry was underpaying him.
   (c) No, because his clients have the right to hire whichever company they choose.
   (d) Yes, Finn has violated his duty of loyalty to Barry.

3. Kurt asked his car mechanic, Quinn, for help in buying a used car. Quinn recommends a Ford Focus that she has been taking care of its whole life. Quinn was working for the seller. Which of the following statements is true?
   (a) Quinn must pay Kurt the amount of money she received from the Ford's prior owner.
   (b) After buying the car, Kurt finds out that it needs $1,000 in repairs. He can recover that amount from Quinn, but only if Quinn knew about the needed repairs before Kurt bought the car.
   (c) Kurt cannot recover anything because Quinn had no obligation to reveal her relationship with the car's seller.
   (d) Kurt cannot recover anything because he had not paid Quinn for her help.

4. Figgins is the dean of a college. He appointed Sue as acting dean while he was out of the country and posted an announcement on the college website announcing that she was authorized to act in his place. He also told Sue privately that she did not have the right to make admissions decisions. While Figgins was gone, Sue overruled the admissions committee to admit the child of a wealthy alumnus. Does the child have the right to attend this college?
   (a) No, because Sue was not authorized to admit him.
   (b) No, because Figgins did not ratify Sue's decision.
   (c) Yes, because Figgins was a fully disclosed principal.
   (d) Yes, because Sue had apparent authority.

5. ***CPA QUESTION*** A principal will not be liable to a third party for a tort committed by an agent:
   (a) unless the principal instructed the agent to commit the tort.
   (b) unless the tort was committed within the scope of the agency relationship.
   (c) if the agency agreement limits the principal's liability for the agent's tort.
   (d) if the tort is also regarded as a criminal act.

6. ***CPA QUESTION*** Cox engaged Datz as her agent. It was mutually agreed that Datz would not disclose that he was acting as Cox's agent. Instead, he was to deal with prospective customers as if he were a principal acting on his own behalf. This he did and made several contracts for Cox. Assuming Cox, Datz, or the customer seeks to avoid liability on one of the contracts involved, which of the following statements is correct?
   (a) Cox must ratify the Datz contracts to be held liable.
   (b) Datz has no liability once he discloses that Cox was the real principal.
   (c) The third party can avoid liability because he believed he was dealing with Datz as a principal.
   (d) The third party may choose to hold either Datz or Cox liable.

Essay Questions

1. An elementary school custodian hit a child who wrote graffiti on the wall. Is the school district liable for this intentional tort by its employee?

2. What if the custodian hit one of the schoolchildren for calling him a name? Is the school district liable?

3. A soldier was drinking at a training seminar. Although he was told to leave his car at the seminar, he disobeyed orders and drove to a military club. On the way to the club, he was involved in an accident. Is the military liable for the damage he caused?

4. One afternoon while visiting friends, tennis star Vitas Gerulaitis fell asleep in their pool house. A mechanic had improperly installed the swimming pool heater, which leaked carbon monoxide fumes into the house where he slept, killing him.

His mother filed suit against the owners of the estate. On what theory would they be liable?

5. **YOU BE THE JUDGE WRITING PROBLEM** Sarah went to an auction at Christie's to bid on a tapestry for her employer, Fine Arts Gallery. The good news is that she purchased a Dufy tapestry for $77,000. The bad news is that it was not the one her employer had told her to buy. In the excitement of the auction, she forgot her instructions. Fine Art refused to pay, and Christie's filed suit. Is Fine Arts liable for the unauthorized act of its agent? **Argument for Christie's:** Christie's cannot possibly ascertain in each case the exact nature of a bidder's authority. Whether or not Sarah had actual authority, she certainly had apparent authority, and Fine Arts is liable. **Argument for Fine Arts:** Sarah was not authorized to purchase the Dufy tapestry, and therefore Christie's must recover from her, not Fine Arts.

Discussion Questions

1. **ETHICS** Mercedes has just begun work at Photobook.com. What a great place to work! Although the salary is not high, the company has fabulous perks. The dining room provides great food from 7 a.m. to midnight, five days a week. There is also a free laundry and dry-cleaning service. Mercedes's social life has never been better. She invites her friends over for Photobook meals and has their laundry done for free. And because her job requires her to be online all the time, she has plenty of opportunity to stay in touch with her friends by g-chatting, tweeting, and checking Facebook updates. She is, however, shocked that one of her colleagues takes paper home from the office for his children to use at home. Are these employees behaving ethically?

2. Kevin was the manager of a radio station, WABC. A competing station lured him away. In his last month on the job at WABC, he notified two key on-air personalities that if they were to leave the station, he would not hold them to their noncompete agreements. What can WABC do?

3. Jesse worked as a buyer for the Vegetable Co. Rachel offered to sell Jesse 10 tons of tomatoes for the account of Vegetable. Jesse accepted the offer. Later, Jesse discovered that Rachel was an agent for Sylvester Co. Who is liable on this contract?

4. The Pharmaceutical Association holds an annual convention. At the convention, Brittany, who was president of the association, told Luke that Research Corp. had a promising new cancer vaccine. Luke was so excited that he chartered a plane to fly to Research's headquarters. On the way, the plane crashed and Luke was killed. Is the Pharmaceutical Association liable for Luke's death?

5. Betsy has a two-year contract as a producer at Jackson Movie Studios. She produces a remake of the movie *Footloose.* Unfortunately, it bombs, and Jackson is so furious that he fires her on the weekend the movie opens. Does he have the power to do this?

CHAPTER 31

STARTING A BUSINESS: LLCs AND OTHER OPTIONS

© Evan Meyer/Shutterstock.com

Poor Jeffrey Horning. If only he had understood business law. Horning owned a thriving construction company which operated as a corporation—Horning Construction Company, Inc. To lighten his crushing workload, he decided to bring in two partners to handle more day-to-day responsibility. It seemed a good idea at the time.

Horning transferred the business to Horning Construction, LLC and then gave one-third ownership each to two trusted employees, Klimowski and Holdsworth. But Horning did not pay enough attention to the legal formalities—the new LLC had no operating agreement.

> Jeffrey Horning was stuck in purgatory, with two business partners he loathed and no way out.

Nothing worked out as he had planned. The two men did not take on extra work. Horning's relationship with them went from bad to worse, with the parties bickering over every petty detail and each man trying to sabotage the others. It got to the point that Klimowski sent Horning a letter full of foul language. At his wit's end, Horning proposed that the LLC buy out his share of the business. Klimowski and Holdsworth refused. Really frustrated, Horning asked a court to dissolve the business on the grounds that Klimowski despised him, Holdsworth resented him, and neither of them trusted him. In his view, it was their goal "to make my remaining time with Horning, LLC so unbearable that I will relent and give them for a pittance the remainder of the company for which they have paid nothing to date."

Although the court was sympathetic, it refused to help. Because Horning, LLC did not have an operating agreement that provided for a buyout, it had to depend upon the LLC statute, which only permitted dissolution "whenever it is not reasonably practicable to carry on the business." Unfortunately, Horning, LLC was very successful, grossing over $25 million annually. Jeffrey Horning was stuck in purgatory, with two business partners he loathed and no way out.[1]

Every business, no matter how large, was at one point little more than a gleam in an entrepreneur's eye. The goal of the law is to balance the rights, duties, and liabilities of entrepreneurs, managers, investors, and customers. Time and again in these next chapters, we will see that legal issues can have as profound an impact on the success of a company as any business decision. The law affects virtually every aspect of business. Wise (and successful) entrepreneurs know how to use the law to their advantage. Think of the grief Jeffrey Horning could have saved himself if he had understood the implications of the LLC statute.

To begin, entrepreneurs must select a form of organization. The correct choice can reduce taxes, liability, and conflict while facilitating outside investment. If entrepreneurs do not make a choice for themselves, the law will automatically select a (potentially undesirable) default option.

Sole Proprietorships

Sole proprietorships are the most common form of business, so we begin there. A **sole proprietorship** is an unincorporated business owned by one person. For example, Linda runs ExSciTe (which stands for Excellence in Science Teaching), a company that helps teachers prepare hands-on science experiments in the classroom using such basic items as vinegar, lemon juice, and red cabbage.

Sole proprietorship
An unincorporated business owned by one person.

If an individual runs a business without taking any formal steps to create an organization, she automatically has a sole proprietorship. It is, if you will, the default option. She is not required to hire a lawyer or register with the government. The company is not even required to file a separate tax return—because the business is a *flow-through* tax entity. In other words, Linda must pay *personal* income tax on the profits, but the *business* itself does not pay income taxes. A very few states, and some cities and towns, require sole proprietors to obtain a business license. And states generally require sole proprietors to register their business name if it is different from their own. Linda, for example, would file a "d/b/a" or "doing business as" certificate for ExSciTe.

Sole proprietorships also have some serious disadvantages. First, the owner of the business is responsible for all of the business's debts. If ExSciTe cannot pay its suppliers or if a student is injured by an exploding cabbage, Linda is *personally* liable. She may have to sell her house and car to pay the debt. Second, the owner of a sole proprietorship has limited options for financing her business. Debt is generally her only source of working capital because she has no stock or memberships to sell. If someone else brings in capital and helps with the management of the business, then it is a partnership, not a sole proprietorship. For this reason, sole proprietorships work best for small businesses without large capital needs.

[1] *In the Matter of Jeffrey M. Horning*, 816 N.Y.S.2d 877; 2006 N.Y. Misc. LEXIS 555.

CORPORATIONS

Corporations are the dominant form of organization for a simple reason—they have been around for a long time and, as a result, they are numerous and the law that regulates them is well developed.

The concept of a corporation is very old indeed—it began with the Greeks and spread from them through the Romans into English law. At the beginning, however, corporations were viewed with deep suspicion. A British jurist commented that they had "neither bodies to be punished nor souls to be condemned." And what were shareholders doing that they needed limited liability? Why did they have to cower behind a corporate shield? For this reason, shareholders originally had to obtain special permission to form a corporation. In England, corporations could be created only by special charter from the monarch or, later, from Parliament. But with the advent of the Industrial Revolution, large-scale manufacturing enterprises needed huge amounts of capital from investors who were not involved in management and did not want to be personally liable for the debts of an organization that they were not managing. In 1811, New York became the first jurisdiction in the United States to permit routine incorporation.[2]

Despite the initial suspicion with which corporations were viewed, economists now suggest that this form of organization, combined with technological advances such as double-entry bookkeeping and stockmarkets, provided the West with an enormous economic advantage. In particular, corporations permitted the investment of outside capital and were more likely than partnerships to survive the death of their founders. In short, corporations permitted the development of large, enduring businesses.

Corporations in General

As is the case for all forms of organization, corporations have their advantages and disadvantages.

Limited Liability

If a business flops and cannot pay its bills, shareholders lose their investment in the company but not their other assets. Likewise, if an employee is in an accident while driving a company van, the business is liable for any harm to the other driver, but its shareholders are not personally liable. Be aware, however, that limited liability does not protect against all debts. Individuals are always responsible for their *own* acts. Suppose that the careless employee who caused the accident was also a company shareholder. Both he and the company would be liable. If the company did not pay the judgment, the employee would have to, from his personal assets. **A corporation protects managers and investors from personal liability for the debts of the corporation and the actions of others, but not against liability for their *own* negligence (or other torts and crimes).**

Transferability of Interests

Corporations provide flexibility for enterprises small (with one owner) and large (with thousands of shareholders). As we will see, partnership interests are not transferable without the permission of the other partners, whereas corporate stock can be bought and sold easily.

Duration

When a sole proprietor dies, legally so does the business. But corporations have perpetual existence: they can continue without their founders.

---

[2]An Act Relative to Incorporation for Manufacturing Purpose, 1811 N.Y. Laws, ch. 67, §111.

Logistics

Corporations require substantial expense and effort to create and operate. The cost of establishing a corporation includes legal and filing fees, not to mention the cost of the annual filings that states require. Corporations must also hold meetings for both shareholders and directors. Minutes of these meetings must be kept indefinitely in the company minute book.

Taxes

Because corporations are taxable entities, they must pay taxes and file returns. This is a simple sentence that requires a complex explanation. Originally, there were only three ways to do business: as a sole proprietorship, a partnership, or a corporation. The sole proprietor pays taxes on all the business's profits. A partnership is not, as we say, a taxable entity, which means it does not pay taxes itself. All income and losses are passed through to the partners and reported on their personal income tax returns. Corporations, by contrast, are taxable entities and pay income tax on their profits. Shareholders must then pay tax on dividends from the corporation. Thus a dollar is taxed only once before it ends up in a partner's bank account, but twice before it is deposited by a shareholder.

Exhibit 31.1 compares the single taxation of partnerships with the double taxation of corporations. Suppose, as shown in the exhibit, that a corporation and a partnership each receives $10,000 in additional income. The corporation pays tax at a top rate of 35 percent.[3]

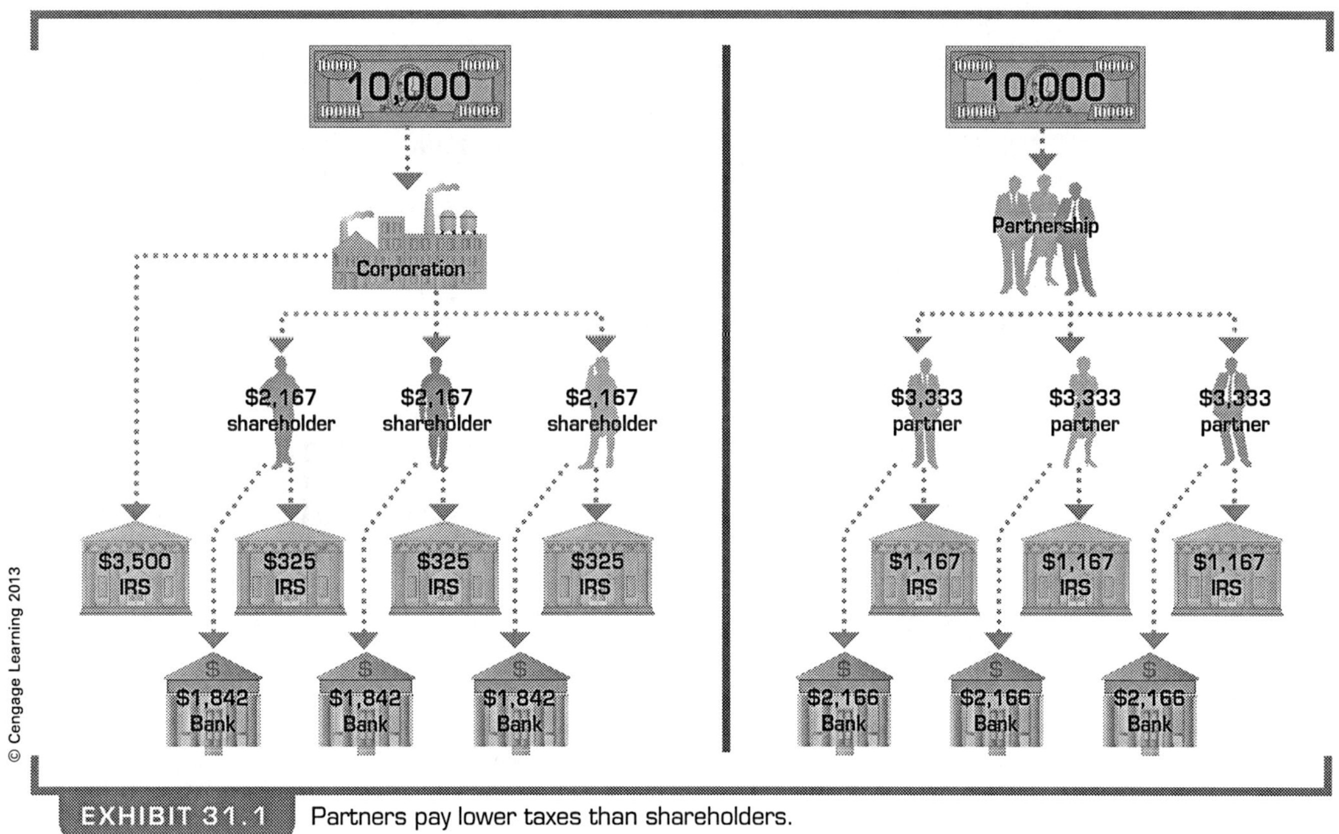

EXHIBIT 31.1 Partners pay lower taxes than shareholders.

[3]This is the federal tax rate; most states also levy a corporate tax.

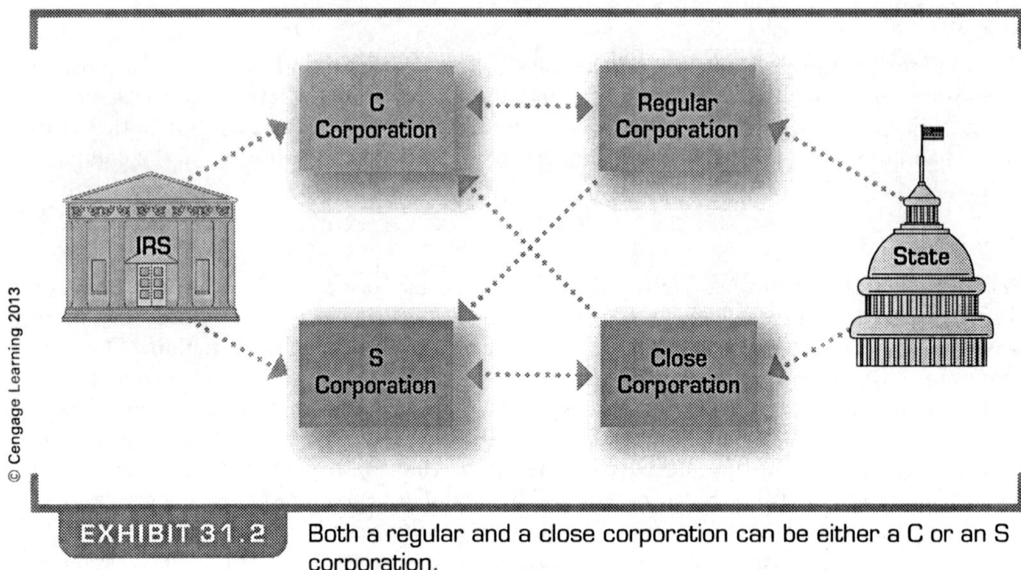

EXHIBIT 31.2 Both a regular and a close corporation can be either a C or an S corporation.

Thus the corporation pays $3,500 of the $10,000 in tax. The corporation pays out the remaining $6,500 as a dividend of $2,167 to each of its three shareholders. Then the shareholders are taxed at the special dividend rate of 15 percent, which means they each pay a tax of $325. They are each left with $1,842. Of the initial $10,000, almost 45 percent ($4,475) has gone to the Internal Revenue Service (IRS).

Compare the corporation to a partnership. The partnership itself pays no taxes, so it can pass on $3,333 to each of its partners. At a 35 percent individual rate, each partner pays an income tax of $1,167. As partners, they pocket $2,166, which is $324 more than they could keep as shareholders. Of the partnership's initial $10,000, 35 percent ($3,501) has gone to the IRS, compared with the corporation's 45 percent.

One further tax issue. Corporations are created and regulated by state law but must pay both federal and state taxes. Federal law gives favorable tax treatment to some small corporations, which it calls "S corporations." Many states also treat small corporations differently but calls them "close corporations." Federal tax law and state corporation statutes are completely independent. Thus, an organization could be a close corporation under state law and not qualify as an S corporation or, conversely, could be an S corporation under federal law but may or may not be a close corporation for state purposes. Exhibit 31.2 illustrates the difference between state corporate law and federal taxation of corporations.

S Corporations

Although entrepreneurs are often optimistic about the likely success of their new enterprise, in truth, the majority of new businesses lose money in their early years. Congress created S corporations (aka "S corps") to encourage entrepreneurship by offering tax breaks. The name "S corporation" comes from the provision of the Internal Revenue Code that created this form of organization.[4] **Shareholders of S corps have both the limited**

[4]26 U.S.C. §1361.

liability of a corporation and the tax status of a partnership. Like a partnership, an S corp is not a taxable entity—all the company's profits and losses pass through to the shareholders, who pay tax at their individual rates. It avoids the double taxation of a regular corporation (called a "C corporation"). If, as is often the case, the startup loses money, investors can deduct these losses against their other income.

S corps do face some major restrictions:

- There can be only one class of stock (although voting rights can vary within the class).
- There can be no more than 100 shareholders.
- Shareholders must be individuals, estates, charities, pension funds, or trusts, not partnerships or corporations.
- Shareholders must be citizens or residents of the United States, not nonresident aliens.
- All shareholders must agree that the company should be an S corporation.

Although *most* states follow the federal lead on S corporations, a small number require these companies to pay state corporate tax.

Close Corporations

Close corporation
A company whose stock is not publicly traded. Also known as a *closely held corporation*.

Originally, the terms ***close corporation*** and ***closely held corporation*** referred simply to a company whose stock was not publicly traded (in other words, a "privately held" company). Most close corporations are small, although some privately held corporations, such as Hallmark Cards, Inc., and Mars, Inc. (maker of Mars candy bars), are huge. Beginning in New York in 1948, some states amended their corporation statutes to make special provisions for entrepreneurs. In some cases, a corporation must affirmatively elect to be treated as a close corporation; in others, any corporation can take advantage of these special provisions. Now when lawyers refer to "close corporations," they usually mean not merely a privately held company, but one that has taken advantage of the close corporation provisions of its state code.

Although the provisions of close corporation statutes vary from state to state, they tend to have certain common themes:

- **Protection of minority shareholders.** As there is no public market for the stock of a close corporation, a minority shareholder who is being mistreated by the majority cannot simply sell his shares and depart. Therefore, close corporation statutes often provide some protection for minority shareholders. For example, the charter of a close corporation could require a unanimous vote of all shareholders to choose officers, set salaries, or pay dividends. It could grant each shareholder veto power over all important corporate decisions.
- **Transfer restrictions.** The shareholders of a close corporation often need to work closely together in the management of the company. Therefore, statutes typically permit the corporation to require that a shareholder first offer shares to the other owners before selling them to an outsider. In that way, the remaining shareholders have some control over who their new co-owners will be.
- **Flexibility.** Close corporations can typically operate without a board of directors, a formal set of bylaws, or annual shareholder meetings.
- **Dispute resolution.** The shareholders are allowed to agree in advance that any one of them can dissolve the corporation if some particular event occurs or, if they choose, for any reason at all. If the shareholders are in a stalemate, the problem

can be solved by dissolving the corporation. Even without such an agreement, a shareholder can ask a court to dissolve a close corporation if the other owners behave "oppressively" or "unfairly."

EXAM Strategy

Question: Consider these two entrepreneurs: Judith formed a corporation to publish a newsletter that will not generate substantial revenues. Drexel operated his construction and remodeling business as a sole proprietorship. Were these forms of organization right for these businesses?

Strategy: Prepare a list of the advantages and disadvantages of each form of organization. Sole proprietorships are best for businesses without substantial capital needs. Corporations can raise capital but are expensive to operate.

Result: Judith would be better off with a sole proprietorship—her revenues will not support the expenses of a corporation. Also, her debts are likely to be small, so she will not need the limited liability of a corporation. And no matter what her form of organization, she would be personally liable for any negligent acts she commits, so a corporation would not provide any additional protection. But for Drexel, a sole proprietorship could be disastrous because his construction company will have substantial expenses and a large number of employees. If an employee causes an injury, Drexel might be personally liable. And if his business fails, the court would liquidate his personal assets. He would be better off with a form of organization that limits his liability, such as a corporation or a limited liability company.

LIMITED LIABILITY COMPANIES

An LLC offers the limited liability of a corporation and the tax status of a partnership.

Limited liability companies (LLCs) are a relatively new form of organization. Wyoming passed the first LLC statute in 1977, but most states did not follow suit until after 1991. An LLC is an extremely useful form of organization increasingly favored by entrepreneurs. It is not, however, as simple as it perhaps should be. Owing to a complex history that involves painful interaction between IRS regulations and state laws (the details of which we will spare you), the specific provisions of state laws vary greatly. An effort to remedy this confusion—the Uniform Limited Liability Company Act—has not at this point been widely accepted. Indeed, it was so heavily criticized that it was revised, but the revised statute has been adopted by only a handful of states. Thus, we can discuss only general trends in state laws. Before forming an LLC, you should review carefully the laws in your particular state.

Limited Liability

Members are not personally liable for the debts of the company. They risk only their investment, as if they were shareholders of a corporation. Are the members of the LLC liable in the following case? You be the judge.

You be the **Judge**

Ridgaway v. Silk

2004 Conn. Super. LEXIS 548
Superior Court of Connecticut, 2004

Facts: Norman Costello and Robert Giordano were members of Silk, LLC, which owned a bar and adult entertainment nightclub in Groton, Connecticut, called Silk Stockings. Anthony Sulls went drinking there one night—and drinking heavily. Although he was obviously drunk, employees at Silk Stockings continued to serve him. Costello and Giordano were working there that night. They both greeted customers (who numbered in the hundreds), supervised employees, and performed "other PR work." When Sulls left the nightclub at 1:45 a.m. with two friends, he drove off the highway at high speed, killing himself and one of his passengers, William Ridgaway, Jr.

Ridgaway's estate sued Costello and Giordano personally. The defendants filed a motion for summary judgment seeking dismissal of the complaint.

You Be the Judge: ***Are Costello and Giordano personally liable to Ridgaway's estate?***

Argument for Costello and Giordano: The defendants did not own Silk Stockings; they were simply members of an LLC that owned the nightclub. The whole point of an LLC is to protect members against personal liability. The assets of Silk, LLC, are at risk, but not the personal assets of Costello and Giordano.

Argument for Ridgaway's Estate: The defendants are not liable for being *members* of Silk, LLC, they are liable for their own misdeeds as *employees* of the LLC. They were both present at Silk Stockings on the night in question, meeting and greeting customers and supervising employees. It is possible that they might actually have served drinks to Sulls, but in any event, they did not adequately supervise and train their employees to prevent them from serving alcohol to someone who was clearly drunk. The world would be an intolerable place to live if employees were free to be as careless as they wished, knowing that they were not liable because they were members of an LLC.

Tax Status

As in a partnership, income flows through the company to the individual members, avoiding the double taxation of a corporation.

Formation

To organize an LLC, you must have a charter and you should have an operating agreement. The charter is short, containing basic information such as name and address. It must be filed with the Secretary of State in the jurisdiction in which it is being formed. An operating agreement sets out the rights and obligations of the owners, who are called "members." If an LLC does not adopt its own operating agreement, LLC statutes provide a default option. However, these standardized provisions may not be what members would choose if they thought about it. Therefore, it is often better for an LLC to prepare its own personalized operating agreement. The Horning case that began this chapter illustrates one of the many things that can go wrong when an LLC does not have an operating agreement.

On this issue, corporations have an advantage over LLCs. Corporations are so familiar that the standard documents (such as a charter, by-laws, and shareholder agreement) are well established and widely available. Lawyers can form a corporation easily, and the Internet offers a host of free forms. This is not the case with LLCs. As yet, the law is so unsettled that standard forms may be dangerous, while customized forms can be expensive. The following case illustrates the importance of a well-drafted operating agreement.

Wyoming.com, LLC v. Lieberman

2005 WY 42; 109 P.3d 883; 2005 Wyo. LEXIS 48
Supreme Court of Wyoming, 2005

Facts: Lieberman was a member of an LLC called Wyoming.com. After he withdrew, he and the other members disagreed about what his membership was worth. Wyoming.com filed a lawsuit asking the court to determine the financial rights and obligations of the parties, if any, upon the withdrawal of a member.

The Supreme Court of Wyoming reached a decision that may have sounded logical but left Lieberman in a sad twilight zone—neither in nor out of the LLC. The court ruled that Lieberman still owned part of the business despite his withdrawal as a member. So far, so good. But neither the LLC statute nor the company's operating agreement required the LLC to pay a member the value of his share. Therefore, neither party had any further rights or obligations. In other words, Lieberman was still an owner, but he was not entitled to any payment. Not quite understanding the implications of this ruling, Lieberman filed a motion seeking financial information about the company. The original trial court denied the request on the theory that since Lieberman had no right to a payout, the company had no obligation to give him financial data.

Issue: ***Does Lieberman have a right to any financial data about Wyoming.com?***

Excerpts from Justice Golden's Decision: [The prior Lieberman case] held that no provision exists either in Wyoming statutes or the operating agreements of Wyoming.com requiring any particular disposition of a member's equity interest upon his withdrawal as a member. Thus, Wyoming.com could not legally force Lieberman to sell his equity interest at any particular value, and Lieberman could not force Wyoming.com to buy his equity interest at any particular value.

This answered the question presented by Wyoming.com in its [lawsuit]. While not explicitly stated in the opinion, with the question answered, nothing remains but to dismiss the [case]. No further proceedings are required to resolve this action. As specifically applied to this case, Lieberman simply retains his equity interest and nothing further is required of either party as a direct result of Lieberman's withdrawal as a member.

Excerpts from Justice Kite's Concurring Decision: I concur with the result reached by the majority in this matter solely because it is mandated by [the prior Lieberman case]. I joined [the] dissenting opinion in that case because I found it more appropriate to allow a minority interest owner in an LLC a mechanism to realize the value of his equity interest. Given the majority's ruling that Mr. Lieberman owns an equity interest, but neither the operating agreement nor the statute provide a method for him to realize the value of that interest, there is nothing left for the district court to order Wyoming.com LLC to do. [The court should consider that] those rights and responsibilities in the context of other forms of business organizations are well developed and may provide guidance in the realm of the LLC.

Flexibility

Unlike S corporations, LLCs can have members that are corporations, partnerships, or nonresident aliens. LLCs can also have different classes of stock. Unlike corporations, LLCs are not required to hold annual meetings or maintain a minute book.

Transferability of Interests

Unless the operating agreement provides otherwise, the members of the LLC must obtain the unanimous permission of the remaining members before transferring their ownership rights. This is yet another reason to have an operating agreement.

LLCs cannot issue stock options, which is potentially a serious problem because options may be an essential lure in attracting and retaining top talent.

Duration

It used to be that LLCs automatically dissolved upon the withdrawal of a member (owing to, for example, death, resignation, or bankruptcy). The current trend in state laws, however, is to permit an LLC to continue in operation even after a member withdraws.

Going Public

Once an LLC goes public, it loses its favorable tax status and is taxed as a corporation, not a partnership.[5] Thus, there is no advantage to using the LLC form of organization for a publicly traded company. And there are some disadvantages: unlike corporations, publicly traded LLCs do not enjoy a well-established set of statutory and case law that is relatively consistent across the many states. For this reason, privately held companies that begin as LLCs usually change to corporations when they go public.

It is worth noting, too, that because of securities laws, it is important for an LLC to have an operating agreement that permits managers the right to convert the LLC into a corporation at the time of a public offering without the consent of the members.[6]

Changing Forms

Some companies that are now corporations might prefer to be LLCs. However, the IRS would consider this change to be a sale of the corporate assets and would levy a tax on the value of these assets. For this reason, few corporations have made the change. However, switching from a partnership to an LLC or from an LLC to a corporation is not considered a sale and does not have the same adverse tax impact.

Piercing the LLC Veil

It has long been the case that, if corporate shareholders do not comply with the technicalities of the law, they may be held personally liable for the debts of the corporation (an issue that will be discussed in more depth in Chapter 33). As the following case illustrates, members of an LLC can also be held liable under the same circumstances.

BLD Products, LTC. v. Technical Plastics of Oregon, LLC

2006 U.S. Dist. LEXIS 89874
United States District Court for the District of Oregon, 2006

Facts: Mark Hardie was the sole member of Technical Plastics of Oregon, LLC (TPO). He operated the business out of an office in his home. Hardie regularly used TPO's accounts to pay such expenses as landscaping and housecleaning. TPO also paid some of Hardie's personal credit card bills, loan payments on his Ford truck, the cost of constructing a deck on his house, his stepson's college bills, and the cost of family vacations to Disneyland, as well as miscellaneous bills from GI Joe's, Wrestler's World, K-Mart, and Mattress World. At the same time, Hardie deposited cash advances from his personal credit cards into the TPO checking account. Hardie did not take a salary from TPO. When TPO filed for bankruptcy, it owed BLD Products approximately $120,000 for goods that it had purchased.

In some cases, a court will "pierce the veil" of a corporation and hold its shareholders personally liable for the debts of the business. BLD argued that the same doctrine should apply to LLCs and the court should hold Hardie personally liable for TPO's debts.

[5]26 U.S.C. §7704.

[6]In this way, under Rule 144 (which is discussed in Chapter 36 on securities regulation), members can include the time during which they owned interests in the LLC when calculating their holding period for stock.

BLD filed for summary judgment.

Issues: ***Does the corporate doctrine of piercing the corporate veil apply to LLCs? Should Hardie be personally liable for TPO's debts?***

Excerpts from Judge King's Decision: I conclude that the piercing doctrine may be applied to LLCs under the same circumstances in which it is applied to corporations. We have characterized that formulation [for piercing a corporate veil] as a three-part test:

1. the defendant controlled the debtor corporation;
2. the defendant engaged in improper conduct; and
3. as a result of that improper conduct plaintiff was unable to collect on a debt against the insolvent corporation.

There is no issue that Hardie, as the sole member and manager of TPO, controlled the company. Turning to the second prong of the test, there is substantial evidence of improper conduct, particularly in the nature of commingling of assets and a general disregard of TPO's LLC form and status as a separate legal entity. Hardie frequently and in significant amounts paid his personal expenses from the TPO business account. The amounts are well beyond small dips into petty cash. There is inadequate documentation about how funds flowed between Hardie, as an individual, and TPO. I realize that Hardie elected to be paid in a manner other than by a regular salary but that does not excuse the lack of documentation. Hardie treated TPO and its assets as his personal funds.

That leaves the third prong of the test, whether Hardie's improper conduct resulted in BLD being unable to collect on its approximately $120,000 debt. I cannot determine as a matter of law that the inability to pay the entire $120,000 debt was due to Hardie's improper conduct over the years. Consequently, I grant partial summary judgment that BLD is entitled to pierce the corporate veil, making Hardie personally liable, but that the amount for which Hardie is personally liable will have to be determined by the jury.

Legal Uncertainty

As we have observed, LLCs are a relatively new form of organization without a consistent and widely developed body of law. As a result, members of an LLC may find themselves in the unhappy position of litigating issues of law which, although well established for corporations, are not yet clear for LLCs. Win or lose, lawsuits are expensive in both time and money.

An important area of legal uncertainty involves managers' duties to the members of the organization. For example, it is not clear in many jurisdictions if managers of an LLC have a legal obligation to act in the best interest of members. Delaware courts have recently ruled that an LLC's managers do have a fiduciary duty to its members unless the operating agreement provides otherwise. (In that state, an operating agreement can limit any duty except the requirement of good faith and fair dealing.) However, this uncertainty means that, before becoming a member of an LLC, it is important to understand both state law and the terms of the operating agreement.

Furthermore, when managers of a corporation violate their duty to the organization by, say, approving a merger without sufficient investigation, shareholders are allowed to bring a so-called **derivative lawsuit** in the name of the corporation against the managers. This right was established by common law. It is unclear, however, if members of an LLC have the same right, especially in a state such as New York where the LLC statute does not explicitly authorize derivative lawsuits. The following case resolves this issue, but only for New York state.

Tzolis v. Wolff

884 N.E.2d 1005; 855 N.Y.S.2d 6; 2008 N.Y. LEXIS 226
Court of Appeals of New York, 2008

Facts: Soterios Tzolis owned 25 percent of Smith Pennington Property Co. LLC, which owned a Manhattan hotel. Herbert Wolff managed the LLC. Tzolis alleged that Wolff first leased and then sold the hotel to family and friends at a price below market value. Tzolis filed a derivative suit against Wolff on the grounds that the man had violated his duties to the LLC.

The trial court ruled that members of an LLC had no right to bring a derivative action because the statute had not explicitly permitted such suits. Tzolis appealed.

Issue: ***Do members of an LLC have the right to bring a derivative suit against managers of the company?***

Excerpts from Justice Smith's Decision: The derivative suit has been part of the general corporate law of this state at least since 1832. It was not created by statute, but by case law. [The judge in a 1832 case said:]

> "no injury the stockholders may sustain by a fraudulent breach of trust, can, upon the general principles of equity, be suffered to pass without a remedy. I will never determine that a court cannot lay hold of every such breach of trust. I will never determine that frauds of this kind are out of the reach of courts of law; for an intolerable grievance would follow from such a determination."

We now consider whether to recognize derivative actions on behalf of the LLC, as to which no statutory provision for such an action exists. In addressing the question, we continue to heed the realization: When fiduciaries are faithless to their trust, the victims must not be left wholly without a remedy. [T]o determine that frauds of this kind are out of the reach of courts of law would lead to "an intolerable grievance."

To hold that there is no remedy when corporate fiduciaries use corporate assets to enrich themselves was unacceptable in 1832, and it is still unacceptable today. Derivative suits are not the only possible remedy, but they are the one that has been recognized for most of two centuries, and to abolish them in the LLC context would be a radical step.

[C]ourts have repeatedly recognized derivative suits in the absence of express statutory authorization. In light of this, it could hardly be argued that the mere absence of authorizing language in the Limited Liability Company Law bars the courts from entertaining derivative suits by LLC members.

We therefore hold that members of LLCs may sue derivatively.

In its reasoning, this court relied on corporate law precedents. However, in a recent case also involving derivative actions, a Delaware court did not follow that approach. The Delaware LLC statute clearly provides that *members* can bring derivative actions. That bit of clarity is helpful. But what about *creditors* of an LLC? We know that creditors of a *corporation* have that right. Does the same rule apply to LLCs?

In the case in question, the board of JetDirect Aviation LLC approved four major acquisitions, all the while knowing that its financials were inaccurate. The company ultimately went bankrupt and, thus, was unable to repay a $34 million loan to CML. The lender filed a derivative action against JetDirect's careless board members. But, much to everyone's surprise, two Delaware courts ruled that CML could *not* bring a derivative action because the Delaware LLC statute had not explicitly authorized such lawsuits. CML was simply out of luck. The lower court observed, "[T]here is nothing absurd about different legal principles applying to corporations and LLCs."

CML would not necessarily agree. And the lower court itself acknowledged that commentators had all assumed that such suits were permitted. It turned out they were wrong. This result may make lenders less willing to finance LLCs and therefore render LLCs a less-desirable form of organization.[7] In short, many issues of law that are well established for corporations still reside in foggy territory when it comes to LLCs.

Choices: LLC v. Corporation

When starting a business, which form makes the most sense—LLC or corporation? The tax status of an LLC is a major advantage over a corporation. Although an S corporation has the same tax status as an LLC, it also has all the annoying rules about classes of stock and number of shareholders. Once an LLC is established, it does not have as many housekeeping rules as corporations—it does not, for example, have to make annual filings or hold annual meetings. However, the LLC is not right for everyone. If done properly, an LLC is more expensive to set up than a corporation because it needs to have a thoughtfully crafted

---

[7] *CML V, LLC v. Bax,* 2011 Del. LEXIS 480 (S. Ct. Del, 2011).

operating agreement. Also, venture capitalists almost always refuse to invest in LLCs, preferring C corporations instead. There are four reasons for this preference: (1) arcane tax issues, (2) C corporations are easier to merge, sell, or take public, (3) corporations can issue stock options, and (4) the general legal uncertainty involving LLCs.

EXAM Strategy

Question: Hortense and Gus are each starting a business. Hortense's business is an Internet startup. Gus will be opening a yarn store. Hortense needs millions of dollars in venture capital and expects to go public soon. Gus has borrowed $10,000 from his girlfriend, which he hopes to pay back soon. Should either of these businesses organize as an LLC?

Strategy: Sole proprietorships may be best for businesses without substantial capital needs and without significant liability issues. Corporations are best for businesses that will need substantial outside capital and expect to go public shortly.

Result: An LLC is not the best choice for either of these businesses. Venture capitalists will insist that Hortense's business be a corporation, especially if it is going public soon. A yarn store has few liability issues, and Gus does not expect to have any outside investors. Hence, a sole proprietorship would be more appropriate for Gus's business.

Benefit Corporations and LLCs

The benefit organization, known as a B corporation or B LLC, is one that has pledged to behave in a socially responsible manner, even as it pursues profits. (Thus, it is *not* a non-profit.) The Benefit company's focus is on the triple bottom line: "people, planet and profits." Currently, a handful of states (such as Maryland, New Jersey, New York, Vermont and Virginia) permit B organizations.

Almost 500 businesses nationwide, including King Arthur Flour Company, Inc. and Seventh Generation, have become Benefit organizations. To obtain B status, shareholders must first give their approval. Then the company has to obtain certification from an independent third party, such as B Lab. Companies with B status must prepare an annual benefit report that includes an assessment of their societal and environmental impact.

General Partnerships

Partnership
An unincorporated association of two or more co-owners who operate a business for profit.

A **partnership** is an unincorporated association of two or more co-owners who carry on a business for profit.[8] Each co-owner is called a *general partner*.

Liability

Each partner is personally liable for the debts of the enterprise whether or not she caused them. Thus, a partner is liable for any injury that another partner or an employee causes while on partnership business as well as for any contract signed on behalf of the partnership.

[8]Uniform Partnership Act §6(1).

This form of organization can be particularly risky if the group of owners is large and the partners do not know each other.

Daniel Matter knows firsthand about the risks of a partnership. A former partner in the accounting firm Pannell Kerr Foster, he thought he had heard the last of the firm when he resigned his partnership. He was wrong. *Seven* years later, he and 260 other former partners of the California firm were served with a 78-page lawsuit seeking $24 million in damages. The lawsuit alleged that Pannell Kerr had been negligent in preparing financial reports for a bankrupt Tennessee savings and loan. Although Daniel Matter had never worked for that particular client, he was potentially liable because he had been a partner when the audit was done. At age 53, Matter feared losing everything he owned.

At age 53, Matter feared losing everything he owned.

Management

As many law, accounting, and consulting firms have grown larger, they have discovered another disadvantage to partnerships: management can be difficult. In theory, all partners in a firm are equal and have an equal right to share in management. When two sisters-in-law form a small accounting firm, they can easily discuss business issues—from hiring a new associate to choosing a photocopy machine. But when the partnership has 1,000 accountants speaking four different languages on three continents, consultation becomes difficult. Although most large firms authorize a management committee to make day-to-day decisions, other partners may still expect to be consulted. One partner in a law firm complained bitterly when all 163 partners were assembled to vote on the style of ceiling tile for the conference room. Yet, to be fair, the managing partner had called for the vote because everyone had complained when he changed the typeface on the firm's stationery without consulting them.

Transfer of Ownership

Financing a partnership may be difficult because the firm cannot sell shares as a corporation does. The capital needs of the partnership must be provided by contributions from partners or by borrowing. Likewise, a partner only has the right to transfer the *value* of her partnership interest, not the interest itself. She cannot, for example, transfer the right to participate in firm management. Take the case of Evan and his mother. She is a partner in the immensely profitable McBain Consulting firm. She dies, leaving him an orphan with no siblings. He overcomes his grief as best he can and goes to her office on the next Monday to take over her job and her partnership. Imagine his surprise when her partners tell him that, as her sole heir, he can inherit the *value* of her partnership but he has no right to be a partner. He is out on the sidewalk within the hour. The partners have promised him a check in the mail.

Dissociation

When a partner quits, that event is called a *dissociation*. A dissociation is a fork in the road: the partnership can either buy out the departing partner(s) and continue in business or wind up the business and terminate the partnership. Most large firms provide in their partnership agreement that, upon dissociation, the business continues.

Formation

Given the disadvantages, why does anyone do business as a partnership? Like sole proprietorships, partnerships are easy to form. Although a partnership should have a written agreement, it is perfectly legal without one. In fact, nothing is required in the way of forms or filings or agreements. If two or more people do business together, sharing management, profits and losses, they have a partnership, whether they know it or not, and are subject to all the rules of partnership law.

A partnership has an important advantage over a sole proprietorship—partners. Sole proprietors are on their own; partners have colleagues to help them and, equally important, to supply capital for the business. Sole proprietorships sometimes turn into partnerships for exactly this reason.

Taxes

As we have seen above, partnerships are not a taxable entity, which means that profits flow through to the owners.

Limited Liability Partnerships

A limited liability partnership (LLP) is a type of general partnership that most states now permit. There is a very important distinction, however, between LLPs and general partnerships: **in an LLP, the partners are not liable for the debts of the partnership.**[9] They are, naturally, liable for their own misdeeds, just as if they were a member of an LLC or a shareholder of a corporation.

To form an LLP, the partners must file a statement of qualification with state officials. LLPs must also file annual reports. The other attributes of a partnership remain the same. Thus, an LLP is not a taxable entity, and it has the right to choose its duration (that is, it can, but does not have to, survive the dissociation of a member).

Although an LLP can be much more advantageous for partners than a general partnership, it is absolutely crucial to comply with all the technicalities of the LLP statute. Otherwise, partners lose protection against personal liability. Note the sad result for Michael Gaus and John West, who formed a Texas LLP. Unfortunately, they did not renew the LLP registration each year, as the statute required. Four years after its initial registration, the partnership entered into a lease. When the partners ultimately stopped paying rent and abandoned the premises, they were both were held personally liable for the rent because the LLP registration had expired. As the court pointed out, the statute did not contain a "substantial compliance" section, nor did it contain a grace period for filing a renewal application. In short, close only counts in horseshoes and hand grenades, not in LLPs.

Limited Partnerships and Limited Liability Limited Partnerships

Although limited partnerships and limited liability limited partnerships sound confusingly similar to limited liability partnerships and general partnerships, like many siblings, they operate very differently. And truth to tell, limited partnerships and limited liability limited partnerships are relatively rare—they are generally used only for estate planning purposes (usually, to reduce estate taxes) and for highly sophisticated investment vehicles. You

[9] UPA §306(c).

should be aware of their existence, but you may not see them very often in your business life. Here are the major features:

Structure

Limited partnerships must have at least one *limited* partner and one *general* partner.

Liability

Limited partners are not *personally* liable, but general partners are. Like corporate shareholders, limited partners risk only their investment in the partnership (which is called their "capital contribution"). In contrast, general partners of the limited partnership are personally liable for the debts of the organization.

However, the revised version of the Uniform Limited Partnership Act permits a limited partnership, in its certificate of formation and partnership agreement, simply to declare itself a *limited liability* limited partnership.[10] **In a limited liability limited partnership, the general partner is not personally liable for the debts of the partnership.** This provision effectively removes the major disadvantage of limited partnerships. Although, at this writing, fewer than half the states have actually passed the revised version of the Uniform Limited Partnership Act, this revision would seem to indicate the trend for the future.

Taxes

Limited partnerships are not taxable entities. Income is taxed only once before landing in a partner's pocket.

Formation

The general partners must file a **certificate of limited partnership** with their Secretary of State. Although most limited partnerships do have a partnership agreement, it is not required.

Management

General partners have the right to manage a limited partnership. Limited partners are essentially passive investors with few management rights beyond the right to be informed about the partnership business. Limited partnership agreements can, however, expand the rights of limited partners.

Transfer of Ownership

Limited partners have the right to transfer the *value* of their partnership interest, but they can sell or give away the interest itself only if the partnership agreement permits.

Duration

Unless the partnership agreement provides otherwise, limited partnerships enjoy perpetual existence—they continue even as partners come and go.

EXAM Strategy

Question: In which one or more of the following forms of organization is it true that none of the partners are liable for the debts of the partnership?

[10]ULPA §102(9).

1. General partnership
2. Limited liability partnership
3. Limited partnership
4. Limited liability limited partnership

Strategy: All these partnerships sound similar, but they are in fact very different, so it is important to keep them straight!

Result: In a general partnership, all the partners are liable. In a limited liability partnership, none are liable. In a limited partnership, the general partners are liable. In a limited liability limited partnership, none of the partners are liable. The correct answers are 2. and 4.

Professional Corporations

Traditionally, most professionals (such as lawyers and doctors) were not permitted to incorporate their businesses, so they organized as partnerships. Now professionals are allowed to incorporate, but in a special way. These organizations are called "professional corporations" or "PCs." **PCs provide more liability protection than a general partnership.** If a member of a PC commits malpractice, the corporation's assets are at risk, but not the personal assets of the innocent members. If Drs. Sharp, Payne, and Graves form a *partnership,* all the partners will be personally liable when Dr. Payne accidentally leaves her scalpel inside a patient. If the three doctors have formed a *PC* instead, Dr. Payne's Aspen condo and the assets of the PC will be at risk, but not the personal assets of the two other doctors.

Generally, the shareholders of a PC are not personally liable for the contract debts of the organization, such as leases or bank loans. Thus, if Sharp, Payne, & Graves, P.C. is unable to pay its rent, the landlord cannot recover from the personal assets of any of the doctors. As partners, the doctors would be personally liable.

PCs have some limitations. First, all shareholders of the corporation must be members of the same profession. For Sharp, Payne, & Graves, P.C., that means all shareholders must be licensed physicians. Other valued employees cannot own stock. Second, like other corporations, the required legal technicalities for forming and maintaining a PC are expensive and time-consuming. Third, tax issues can be complicated. A PC is a separate taxable entity, like any other corporation. It must pay tax on its profits, and then its shareholders pay tax on any dividends they receive. *Salaries,* however, are deductible from firm profits. Thus, the PC can avoid paying taxes on its profits by paying out all the profits as salary. But any profits remaining in firm coffers *at the end of the year* are taxable. To avoid tax, PCs must be careful to calculate their profits accurately and pay them out before year's end. This chore can be time-consuming, and any error may cause unnecessary tax liability.

Joint Ventures

Imax Corp. decided that it would like to partner with cinema operators—it would supply its big screens in return for a share of the box office revenue. The arrangement that Imax is describing is not like the other partnerships we have discussed in this chapter—it is a joint venture. A **joint venture** is a partnership for a limited purpose. Imax and the cinema operators would not merge; they would simply work together. Each organization retains its own identity. Imax would be liable to an electrician whom the cinema operator had hired to install an Imax screen, but not to the cinema's popcorn supplier.

Joint venture
A partnership for a limited purpose.

FRANCHISES

This chapter has presented an overview of the various forms of organization. Franchises are not, strictly speaking, a separate form of organization. They are included here because they represent an important option for entrepreneurs. The United States has nearly half a million franchised businesses, which employ almost 8 million people. Total sales are $1.3 trillion a year. Well-known franchises include Hampton Hotels, McDonald's, and Supercuts. Most franchisors and franchisees are corporations, although they could legally choose to be any of the forms discussed in this chapter.

Buying a franchise is a compromise between starting one's own business as an entrepreneur and working for someone else as an employee. Franchisees are free to choose which franchise to buy, where to locate it, and how to staff it. But they are not completely on their own. They are buying an established business with the kinks worked out. In case the owner has never boiled water before, the McDonald's operations manual explains everything from how to set the temperature controls on the stove, to the number of seconds that fries must cook, to the length of time they can be held in the rack before being discarded. And a well-known name like McDonald's or Subway ought, by itself, to bring customers through the door.

© Andy Z./Shutterstock.com

If you have been to an IMAX movie, you may have benefited from a joint venture between IMAX and cinema operators.

There is, however, a fine line between being helpful and being oppressive. Franchisees sometimes complain that franchisor control is too tight—tips on cooking fries might be appreciated, but rules on how often to sweep the floor are not. Sometimes franchisors, in their zeal to maintain standards, prohibit innovation that appeals to regional tastes. Just because spicy biscuits are not popular in New England does not mean they should be banned in the South.

Franchises can be very costly to acquire, anywhere from several thousand dollars to many millions. That fee is usually payable up front, whether or not a sandwich or burger is ever sold. On top of the up-front fee, franchisees also typically pay an annual fee that is a percentage of *gross sales revenues*, not *profit*. Sometimes the fee seems to eat up all the profits. Franchisees also complain when they are forced to buy supplies from headquarters. In theory, the franchisors can purchase hamburger meat and paper plates more cheaply in bulk and also maintain quality controls. On the other hand, the franchisees are a captive audience, and they sometimes allege that headquarters has little incentive to keep prices low. Indeed, some franchisors make most of their profit from the products they sell to their store owners. Often, the franchise agreement permits the company to change the terms of the agreement by raising fees or expenses. Franchisees also grumble when they are forced to contribute to expensive "co-op advertising" that benefits all the outlets in the region. The sandwich franchise Quiznos recently spent $100 million to settle litigation with potential franchisees, who claimed that the company took their fees without finding a store location for them, and some existing store owners, who complained that the company forced them to buy *everything* (including soap in the bathrooms and the piped-in music) from the company at inflated prices.

All franchisors must comply with the Federal Trade Commission's (FTC) Franchise Rule. In addition, some states also impose their own franchise requirements. Under FTC rules, a franchisor must deliver to a potential purchaser a so-called Franchise Disclosure Document (FDD) at least 14 calendar days before any contract is signed or money is paid. The FDD must provide information on:

- The history of the franchisor and its key executives
- Litigation with franchisees
- Bankruptcy filings by the company and its officers and directors
- Costs to buy and operate a franchise
- Restrictions, if any, on suppliers, products, and customers
- Territory – any limitations (in either the real or virtual worlds) on where the franchisee can sell or any restrictions on other franchisees selling in the same territory
- Business continuity – under what circumstances can the franchisor fire the franchisee and the franchisee's rights to renew or sell the franchise
- Franchisor's training program
- Required advertising expenses
- A list of current franchisees and those that have left in the prior three years (a lot of either may be a bad sign)
- A report on prior owners of stores that the franchisor has reaquired
- Earnings information is not required; but if disclosed, the franchisor must reveal the basis for this information
- Audited financials for the franchisor
- A sample set of the contracts that a franchisee is expected to sign

The purpose of the FDD is to ensure that the franchisor discloses all relevant facts. It is not a guarantee of quality because the FTC does not investigate to make sure that the information is accurate. After the fact, if the FTC discovers the franchisor has violated the rules, it may sue on the franchisee's behalf. (The franchisee does not have the right to bring suit personally against someone who violates

"Be cool, Cat."

FTC franchise rules, but it may be able to sue under state law.)

Suppose you obtain an FDD for "Shrinking Cats," a franchise that offers psychiatric services for neurotic felines. The company has lost money on all the outlets it operates itself; it has sold only three franchises, two of which have gone out of business; and all the required contracts are ridiculously favorable to the franchisor. Nevertheless, the FTC will still permit sales as long as the franchisor discloses all the information required in the FDD.

As the following case illustrates, the franchisor has much of the power in a franchise relationship.

National Franchisee Association v. Burger King Corporation

2010 U.S. Dist. LEXIS 123065
United States District Court for the Southern District of Florida, 2010

Facts: The Burger King Corporation (BKC) would not allow franchisees to have it their way. Instead, BKC forced them to sell the double-cheeseburger (DCB) and, later, the Buck Double (the DCB minus one slice of cheese) for no more than $1.00. Franchisees alleged that, because this price was below their cost, they were losing money on every double cheeseburger they sold. The National Franchisee Association (NFA), to which 75 percent of BKC's individual franchisees belonged, filed suit alleging that (1) BKC did not have the right to set maximum prices; and (2) that even if BKC had such a right, it had violated its obligation under the franchise agreement to act in good faith.

The court dismissed the first claim because the franchise agreement unambiguously permitted BKC to set whatever prices it wanted. But the court allowed the NFA to proceed with the second claim. BKC filed a motion to dismiss.

Issue: ***Was BKC acting in good faith when it forced franchisees to sell items below cost?***

Excerpts from Judge Moore's Decision: The motive of BKC in exercising its discretion to set prices under the contract is key. [B]ad faith involves a subterfuge or evasion of contractual duties. [T]here are at least two ways a plaintiff can go about raising a claim of bad faith. Plaintiffs can allege facts identifying defendant's improper ulterior motive(s). For example, if a franchisee had evidence that a franchisor had a secret agenda to take over the franchise and operate it as a company-owned business, and was deliberately setting prices to weaken the targeted franchisee, such a plaintiff could raise a claim of bad faith by alleging the existence of that plan.

It is more likely, however, that plaintiffs will lack direct evidence of dishonesty. In these cases, plaintiffs must allege some facts tending to show that no reasonable person could have thought that the steps taken by the defendant were a reasonable means of carrying out the contract's defined purposes. If no reasonable person would have exercised discretion as defendant had, the natural inference is that defendant must have had some hidden improper motive.

[T]he magnitude of the injury claimed by plaintiff is of central importance. [A]n inference of bad faith may arise when the defendant exercises discretion in such a manner as to effectively destroy whatever benefits the plaintiff could have reasonably expected under the contract. The logic is that the measure with such severe results could not have been within the contemplation of the parties.

[N]one of the facts alleged by plaintiffs are sufficient to support a claim of bad faith. Plaintiffs rely principally on their allegation that franchisees could not produce and sell DCB or Buck Doubles at a cost less than $1.00, and therefore that franchisees suffer a loss on each of these items sold. There are a variety of legitimate reasons why a firm selling multiple products may choose to set the price of a single product below cost. Among other things, such a strategy might help build goodwill and customer loyalty, hold or shift customer traffic away from competitors, or serve as loss leaders to generate increased sales on other higher margin products.

The issue is not whether such a strategy was wise or ultimately successful or mistaken. In the absence of some other evidence of improper motive, the question is whether it was so irrational and capricious that no reasonable person would have made such a decision. There is nothing about the pricing decision that suggests BKC was doing anything other than seeking to promote the performance of its franchisees. Nothing about this action suggests bad faith.

[T]o the extent plaintiffs seek to raise a claim of bad faith by pointing to the injuries allegedly caused them by

BKC's decision, plaintiffs must allege that the damage to their overall business was so severe as to deprive them of their reasonable expectations under the contract. Plaintiffs come nowhere close to alleging such an impact. Significantly, nowhere do plaintiffs claim that their overall business has been appreciably impaired. Nor do they allege that their overall businesses are no longer profitable or that their competitive positions or economic viability going forward are threatened.

For the foregoing reasons, it is ORDERED AND ADJUDGED that Defendant's Motion to Dismiss is GRANTED.

Chapter Conclusion

The process of starting a business is immensely time-consuming. Eighteen-hour days are the norm. Not surprisingly, entrepreneurs are sometimes reluctant to spend their valuable time on legal issues that, after all, do not contribute directly to the bottom line. No customer buys more fried chicken because the franchise is a limited liability company instead of a corporation. Wise entrepreneurs know, however, that careful attention to legal issues is an essential component of success. The form of organization affects everything from taxes to liability to management control. The idea for the business may come first, but legal considerations occupy a close second place.

Exam Review

	Separate Taxable Entity	**Personal Liability for Owners**	**Ease of Formation**	**Transferable Interests (Easily Bought and Sold)**	**Perpetual Existence**	**Other Features**
Sole Proprietorship	No	Yes	Very easy	No, can only sell entire business	No	
Corporation	Yes	No	Difficult	Yes	Yes	
Close Corporation	Yes, for C corporation No, for S corporation	No	Difficult	Transfer restrictions	Yes	Protection of minority shareholders. No board of directors required
S Corporation	No	No	Difficult	Transfer restrictions	Yes	Only 100 shareholders. Only one class of stock. Shareholders must be individuals, estates, trusts, charities, or pension funds and be citizens or residents of the United States. All shareholders must agree to S status
Limited Liability Company	No	No	Difficult	Yes, if the operating agreement permits	Varies by state, but generally, yes	No limit on the number of shareholders, the number of classes of stock, or the type of shareholder

General Partnership	No	Yes	Easy	No	Depends on the partnership agreement	Management can be difficult
Limited Liability Partnership	No	No	Difficult	No	Depends on the partnership agreement	
Limited Partnership	No	Yes, for general partner No, for limited partners	Difficult	Yes (for limited partners), if partnership agreement permits	Yes	
Limited Liability Limited Partnership	No	No	Difficult	Yes (for limited partners), if partnership agreement permits	Yes	
Professional Corporation	Yes	No	Difficult	Shareholders must all be members of same profession	Yes, as long as it has shareholders	Complex tax issues
Joint Venture	No	Yes	Easy	No	No	Partnership for a limited purpose
Franchise	All these issues depend on the form of organization chosen by participants.					Established business. Name recognition. Management assistance. Loss of control. Fees may be high

Multiple-Choice Questions

1. A sole proprietorship:
   (a) Must file a tax return
   (b) Requires no formal steps for its creation
   (c) Must register with the Secretary of State
   (d) May sell stock
   (e) Provides limited liability to the owner

EXAM Strategy

2. **CPA Question:** Assuming all other requirements are met, a corporation may elect to be treated as an S corporation under the Internal Revenue Code if it has:
(a) Both common and preferred stockholders
(b) A partnership as a stockholder

(c) 100 or fewer stockholders

(d) The consent of a majority of the stockholders

Strategy: Review the list of requirements for an S corporation. (See the "Result" at the end of this section.)

3. A limited liability company:
   (a) Is regulated by a well-established body of law
   (b) Pays taxes on its income
   (c) May issue stock options
   (d) Must register with state authorities
   (e) Protects the owners from personal liability for their own misdeeds

4. **CPA QUESTION** A joint venture is a(n):
   (a) Association limited to no more than two persons in business for profit
   (b) Enterprise of numerous co-owners in a nonprofit undertaking
   (c) Corporate enterprise for a single undertaking of limited duration
   (d) Association of persons engaged as co-owners in a single undertaking for profit

5. A limited liability partnership:
   (a) Has ownership interests that cannot be transferred
   (b) Protects the partners from liability for the debts of the partnership
   (c) Must pay taxes on its income
   (d) Requires no formal steps for its creation
   (e) Permits a limited number of partners

2. Result: An S corporation can have only one class of stock. A partnership cannot be a stockholder, and all the shareholders must consent to S corporation status. C is the correct answer.

ESSAY QUESTIONS

EXAM Strategy

1. Question: Alan Dershowitz, a law professor famous for his wealthy clients (O. J. Simpson, among others), joined with other lawyers to open a kosher delicatessen, Maven's Court. Dershowitz met with greater success at the bar than in the kitchen—the deli failed after barely a year in business. One supplier sued for overdue bills. What form of organization would have been the best choice for Maven's Court?

Strategy: A sole proprietorship would not have worked because there was more than one owner. A partnership would have been a disaster because of unlimited liability. They could have met all the requirements of an S corporation or an LLC. (See the "Result" at the end of this section.)

EXAM Strategy

2. Question: Mrs. Meadows opened a biscuit shop called The Biscuit Bakery. The business was not incorporated. Whenever she ordered supplies, she was careful to sign the contract in the name of the business, not personally: The Biscuit Bakery by Daisy Meadows. Unfortunately, she had no money to pay her flour bill. When the vendor threatened to sue her, Mrs. Meadows told him that he could only sue the business because all the contracts were in the business's name. Will Mrs. Meadows lose her dough?

Strategy: The first step is to figure out what type of organization her business is. Then recall what liability protection that organization offers. (See the "Result" at the end of this section.)

3. **YOU BE THE JUDGE WRITING PROBLEM** Cellwave was a limited partnership that applied to the Federal Communications Commission (FCC) for a license to operate cellular telephone systems. After the FCC awarded the license, it discovered that, although all the limited partners had signed the limited partnership agreement, Cellwave had never filed its limited partnership certificate with the Secretary of State in Delaware. The FCC dismissed Cellwave's application on the grounds that the partnership did not exist when the application was filed. Did the FCC have the right to dismiss Cellwave's application? **Argument for Cellwave:** The limited partnership was effectively in existence as soon as the limited partners signed the agreement. The Secretary of State could not refuse to accept the certificate for filing; that was a mere formality. **Argument for the FCC:** When Cellwave applied for a license, it did not exist legally. Formalities matter.

4. Kristine bought a Rocky Mountain Chocolate Factory franchise. Her franchise agreement required her to purchase a cash register that cost $3,000, with an annual maintenance fee of $773. The agreement also provided that Rocky Mountain could change to a more expensive system. Within a few months after signing the agreement, Kristine learned that she would have to buy a new cash register that cost $20,000, with annual maintenance fees of $2,000. Does Kristine have to buy this new cash register? Did Rocky Mountain act in bad faith?

5. What is the difference between close corporations and S corporations?

1. Result: Maven's Court would have chosen an LLC or an S corporation.

2. Result: The Biscuit Bakery was a sole proprietorship. No matter how Mrs. Meadows signed the contracts, she is still personally liable for the debts of the business.

Discussion Questions

1. **ETHICS** Lee McNeely told Hardee's officials that he was interested in purchasing multiple restaurants in Arkansas. A Hardee's officer assured him that any of the company-owned stores in Arkansas would be available for purchase. However,

the company urged him to open a new store in Maumelle and sent him a letter estimating first-year sales at around $800,000. McNeely built the Maumelle restaurant, but gross sales the first year were only $508,000. When McNeely asked to buy an existing restaurant, a Hardee's officer refused, informing him that Hardee's rarely sold company-owned restaurants. The disclosure document contained no misstatements, but McNeely brought suit alleging fraud in the sale of the Maumelle franchise. Does McNeely have a valid claim against Hardee's? Apart from the legal issues, did Hardee's officers behave ethically? What Life Principles were they applying?

2. Leonard, an attorney, was negligent in his representation of Anthony. In settlement of Anthony's claim against him, Leonard signed a promissory note for $10,400 on behalf of his law firm, an LLC. When the law firm did not pay, Anthony filed suit against Leonard personally for payment of the note. Is a member personally liable for the debt of an LLC that was caused by his own negligence?

3. Think of a business concept that would be appropriate for each of the following: a sole proprietorship, a corporation, and a limited liability company.

4. As you will see in Chapter 33, Facebook began life as a corporation, not an LLC. Why did the founder, Mark Zuckerberg, make that decision?

5. Corporations developed to encourage investors to contribute the capital needed to create large-scale manufacturing enterprises. But LLCs are often start-ups or other small businesses. Why do their members deserve limited liability? And is it fair that LLCs do not have to pay income taxes?

CHAPTER 32

© Evan Meyer/Shutterstock.com

PARTNERSHIPS

Chase stood at the edge of a meadow near the top of the Porcupine Mountains in the Upper Peninsula of Michigan. The sun glistened off apple blossoms, birds called to each other, and the Lake of the Clouds stretched out to the horizon below. Chase had never been happier. As an architect, he believed in designing "green" houses that blended with nature. Sharing his vision, Danielle had hired him to create a house for this perfect location. The large budget would allow Chase to realize many of his architectural and environmental beliefs. But he needed help—a landscape designer and a decorator who could work with the spectacular setting and his splendid design.

Bailey and Chase began to suspect they were in trouble.

Bailey was Chase's choice for the interior design; she could create the sleek, warm look he sought using only natural products. With Zack's landscape plan, the house would appear to be a natural part of the site.

At their first meeting, all three designers committed to the project and rapidly agreed to a deal: Chase would receive 50 percent of the profits, Bailey and Zack 25 percent each. All three would have veto rights over the work of the other two. As the meeting ended, Chase poured glasses of sparkling water. "Here's to our new partnership. We'll build the most beautiful and most environmentally responsible house in America," he said, rising to his feet. The three raised a toast to their success.

The honeymoon lasted only a few weeks. Chase wanted solar panels over the entire roof so that the house could be completely off grid, but Bailey thought the panels were ugly—she insisted on slate instead. When Bailey suggested consulting the owner, Chase blew up. "What do owners know?" he demanded. Zack sided with Bailey on that issue. But then both Chase and Bailey disagreed with Zack, who wanted to relocate the house to save some specimen trees. "Reduce solar efficiency to save a few ratty old trees?" Chase asked incredulously. Outvoted, Zack quit in disgust. Bailey and Chase began to suspect they were in trouble.

Their apprehension proved all too well founded. Outraged that her house was not finished on time, Danielle sued the three designers. When Chase protested that it was not *his* fault Zack quit, Danielle snarled into the phone, "I don't know and I don't care whose fault it is. All I know is that my house isn't ready. I'll see you and your partners in court!" Meanwhile, Zack was last spotted recuperating on Bora Bora, far from the reach of the U.S. legal system.

The plight of this threesome illustrates common partnership problems. Although Chase, Bailey, and Zack never signed an agreement or filed a form, they nonetheless had formed a partnership. Not only did they refer to themselves as partners, but they intended to share profits and co-manage the business. The partnership is liable to Danielle for any damages the delay caused. If the partnership does not have enough assets to pay, each of the partners is personally liable—even if the delay was totally Zack's fault. When Zack left before finishing the project, he wrongfully dissociated from the partnership. Chase and Bailey must pay him the value of his share of the partnership, but they can subtract from that total any damages he caused. If the damages are more than the value of his partnership share, he owes them money. But his former partners must pay Danielle, whether or not they can actually recover from Zack in Bora Bora.

Introduction

Partnerships have two important advantages: they do not pay taxes and they are easy to form.[1] Many professionals, such as accountants and lawyers, traditionally favored this form of organization. Some of the rules can be complex, however, and, like any relationship, a partnership requires careful tending.

Traditionally, partnerships were regulated by common law, but a lack of consistency among the states became troublesome as interstate commerce grew. To solve this problem, the National Conference of Commissioners on Uniform State Laws proposed the Uniform Partnership Act (UPA) in 1914. Since then there have been several revisions, the most recent in 1997. More than two-thirds of the states have now passed the latest revision, so we base our discussion on that version of the law.

Although the UPA has made life easier, common law still plays an important role in regulating partnerships. To some degree, that is always true with statutes. No matter how well written they are, the courts are called upon to interpret some provisions. In addition, the UPA directs courts to apply common law to resolve any issue that it does not cover. Finally, many of the rules in the UPA are so-called **default rules**, meaning that they apply unless the partners reach a different agreement. When partners write their own rules, they must sometimes ask the courts to interpret ambiguous provisions.

Default rules
Rules that govern a partnership unless the partners agree otherwise.

Creating a Partnership

Some legal relationships are carefully delineated. By and large, people know whether or not they are married. Similarly, people usually know if they have formed a corporation. Partnerships are trickier, more like living together than getting married. It can be difficult to tell if a

[1]These issues are discussed at greater length in Chapter 31, on starting a business. Although the partnership itself does not pay taxes, each partner must pay taxes on his share of the partnership's profits.

live-in relationship—or a partnership—really exists. The UPA does not *require* partnerships to prepare a written agreement or make a formal filing. However, the UPA does *permit* a partnership to file a statement with the local Secretary of State that contains basic information about the partnership.[2]

Factors that Matter

How can you tell if you have a partnership? According to the UPA, **the association of two or more persons to carry on as co-owners a business for profit forms a partnership, whether or not the persons intend to form a partnership.**[3]

Note that a partnership is an association of two or more people. If only one person is involved in the business, it is a sole proprietorship, not a partnership.

What factors do the courts consider in determining whether a partnership exists?

- **Sharing profits.** No matter what their arrangement, if two people do not share the profits of their business, they are not partners. Period. However, just because they do share in the profits does not necessarily make them partners. In other words, sharing profits is a necessary but not sufficient condition for being partners.
- **Sharing losses.** Although landlords, employees, and even creditors may share in business profits, usually no one other than a partner is willing to sign on for a share of the losses. Sharing losses is strong evidence of a partnership.
- **Management of the business.** If participants are not involved in management, the courts will generally not consider them to be partners.
- **Oral or written agreement.** The law does not require a formal agreement, either written or oral. Nor is a formal agreement enough on its own to create a partnership. In a partnership, actions speak louder than words. If the people act like partners, then the law will treat them as such. If they do not act like partners, then nothing they say is enough, on its own, to create a partnership. Note, however, that in a close case, referring to yourselves as partners may help sway a court, but it is not enough *by itself* to create a partnership.
- **Charitable businesses.** Because charitable businesses do not technically make profits, they cannot be a partnership. When Aaron and Elijah agree to run the annual jamboree at their children's school, they expect to clear $35,000 after expenses, but they are not partners because their fund-raising has a charitable purpose.

Now let's apply these rules to real examples. Kevin and Brenda formed an electrical contracting business. The business did so well that Kevin's first wife, Cynthia, asked the court to increase his child support payments. Kevin argued that because he and Brenda were partners, he was entitled to only half of the business's profits. Therefore, his child support should not be increased.

Cynthia claimed that Kevin and Brenda were *not* partners because Kevin had reported all the income from the business on his personal tax return, while Brenda had reported none. Kevin had even put "sole proprietorship" in bold letters on the top of his return. No written partnership agreement existed. Kevin and Brenda never informed their accountant that they were a partnership. When Kevin answered interrogatories for Cynthia's lawsuit, he stated that he was sole owner and that Brenda worked for him. Nonetheless, the court held

[2]UPA §105.

[3]UPA §202(a).

that Brenda and Kevin were partners because Brenda helped manage the business and shared in its profits.[4]

In contrast, when Nancy Green borrowed money from Joseph DiFebo to make a down payment on four houses, they agreed that they were partners. Although Green bought the properties in her name alone, the two signed this document:

> Nancy R. Green and Joseph A. DiFebo are equal partners in the following Wilmington, Delaware, properties: 807 Pine Street, 427 East 3rd St., 611 East 7th Street, 613 East 7th Street.
>
> On the death of Nancy R. Green, her half-interest is left to her daughters, Kelly R. Green and Stacy R. Green. On the death of Joseph A. DiFebo, his half-interest is left to his daughters, Amy DiFebo and Beth Durham.
>
> If Nancy R. Green survives Joseph A. DiFebo, she makes all decisions on the above properties.

DiFebo did some repair work on the buildings but never asked Green for a share of the rentals. When the city condemned one of the properties, Green refused to give DiFebo half the proceeds. DiFebo testified that, in his mind, the money he transferred to Green established a partnership between them. Green testified that at no time did she consider their arrangement to be a partnership.

The court was less concerned about what the *agreement said* than how the *parties acted.* Although they had called themselves "equal partners," they did not share profits. DiFebo said he had not taken his share of the profits because he did not want his wife to find out about his arrangements (financial and otherwise) with Green. Ruling that their contract was a will, not a partnership agreement, the court denied DiFebo's claim.[5]

The following case illustrates the adage that a lawyer who represents himself has a fool for a client. Were they partners? You be the judge.

---

[4] *In re Marriage of Cynthia Hassiepen,* 269 Ill. App. 3d 559, 646 N.E.2d 1348, 1995 Ill. App. LEXIS 101 (1995).
[5] *Green v. Schagrin,* 1989 Del. Super. LEXIS 295 (1989).

You be the Judge

NADEL V. STARKMAN

2010 N.J. Super. Unpub. LEXIS 2542
Superior Court of New Jersey, Appellate Division, 2010

Facts: Morris Starkman hired Raymond Nadel just after he graduated from law school. At the beginning, Nadel was clearly an associate, not a partner, but after some years working together, the two men signed an agreement that changed their relationship—although to what is not clear. The agreement clarified many important issues (such as Nadel's vacation time), but it failed to resolve the most crucial question: was Nadel now a partner?

The agreement offered some hints to answering this question, but unfortunately the clues pointed in different directions. It stated that:

- The practice had "heretofore" been owned solely by Starkman;
- Nadel had an "interest in the firm";
- The firm would continue to be owned solely by Starkman, who had the right to make all management decisions;
- Starkman was the sole owner and Nadel was an independent contractor;
- Nadel would receive a percentage of the firm's net income, and he was guaranteed a minimum income each year;
- The firm would pay for Nadel's benefits, but not Starkman's.

Other relevant facts:

- The firm never filed a partnership tax return;

- Its checking accounts remained solely in Starkman's name and were entitled "Morris Starkman, Attorney at Law";
- Nadel never had authority to sign checks, and none of the checks bore his name;
- The firm's signage, letterhead, and advertisements all used the name Starkman & Nadel.

Later, Starkman decided that the firm should become a limited liability company (LLC). The agreement he prepared stated that he would own 99 percent to Nadel's 1 percent. It also stated that Nadel was an employee. Nadel refused to sign the agreement. At trial, Starkman testified that Nadel had refused to sign because he wanted a pension plan and a severance package. Nadel maintained that he had not been willing to give up his partnership interest.

The agreement had referred to the two men's "excellent relationship," but that did not last long. Starkman soon began looking for Nadel's replacement. (He waited to send the termination letter until Nadel was on vacation, which probably did not help their relationship.) Starkman formed a partnership with David Rochman, while Nadel filed suit, asking the court to determine the reasonable value of his ownership interest in the firm.

At trial, Rochman (who had since parted ways with Starkman) and others testified that Starkman had told them that Nadel was his partner and he owed the man a substantial buyout. The trial judge believed Nadel, while finding Starkman evasive and dishonest. She ruled that the two men had intended to form a partnership and had indeed done so. Starkman appealed.

You Be the Judge: ***Were Starkman and Nadel partners?***

Argument for Nadel: There was substantial evidence of a partnership, both in the agreement itself and in the two men's behavior. The agreement provided for the sharing of net profits, which is an important indicator of a partnership. Also, it implied Nadel was a partner when it referred to his "interest in the firm" and stated that the practice was "heretofore" owned solely by Starkman. As for the provision in the agreement that referred to Starkman as the sole owner, that simply meant that he was the managing partner. In any event, if the agreement was unclear, any ambiguity should be interpreted against Starkman because he is the one who drafted it.

As for behavior, the trial judge found that the parties *intended* to create a partnership and that Nadel refused to convert the business to an LLC because he would not give up his partnership interest. Starkman repeatedly referred to the business as a partnership and admitted to other people that he owed Nadel a substantial buyout.

Argument for Starkman: Both the agreement and the two men's behavior provide overwhelming evidence that there was *no* partnership. The agreement does not refer to itself as a partnership agreement. It clearly stated that Nadel was an independent contractor rather than a partner. The agreement did not grant Nadel the right to make management decisions. It did make provisions for his benefits and vacation time, but not Starkman's. These provisions indicated he was an employee, not a partner.

As for behavior, Nadel did not share in the firm's losses and the firm did not file a partnership tax return. (Presumably two lawyers would have known enough to file the appropriate tax return.)

Partnership by Estoppel

Raymond Nadel wanted to be Morris Starkman's partner so that he could share in the profits of the enterprise. *Partnership by estoppel* is concerned with the opposite situation—a person does not want to be considered a partner because he wishes to avoid the *liability* of the partnership. The twist is that partnership by estoppel applies in situations where the participants are *not,* in fact, partners but are held to be liable as if they were.

Partnership by estoppel applies if:

- **Participants tell other people that they are partners (even though they are not), or they allow other people to say, without contradiction, that they are partners;**
- **A third party relies on this assertion; and**
- **The third party suffers harm.**

Dr. William Martin was held liable under a theory of partnership by estoppel because he told a patient that he and Dr. John Maceluch were partners (although they were not); the patient relied on this statement and made appointments to see Dr. Maceluch; and she was harmed by Dr. Maceluch's malpractice. He refused to come to the hospital when she was in labor, and as a result, her child was born with brain damage. Although Dr. Martin was out of the country at the time, he was also liable.[6]

Dr. Martin could have avoided this problem by being very careful *not* to refer to Dr. Maceluch as his partner. Presumably, he used the word "partner" to reassure the patient. Instead of "partner," he could have said "colleague," "associate," or "assistant." Dr. Martin should also have been careful to correct anyone who referred to Dr. Maceluch as his partner.

Note that even if the court determined that Raymond Nadel and Morris Starkman were *not* partners, Nadel could still be liable to a third party who had been harmed by the firm if Starkman had told that person that Nadel was a partner. In short, Nadel could end up with all of the downside but none of the upside of being a partner.

Relationship between Partners and Outsiders

Under the UPA, **the rules governing the liability of partners to outsiders are *mandatory*.** Partners may not change them. **In contrast, most of the rules governing the relationship *among* partners are *default* provisions**, meaning that the partners can change these rules if they desire.[7]

In the relationship between partners and outsiders, two questions arise: When is the partnership liable to outsiders? If the partnership is liable, who must pay the debt?

Liability of the Partnership to Outsiders

Under the UPA, **every partner is an agent of the partnership for the purpose of its business.**[8]

Authority

Partnership liability is based on the rules of agency law, discussed in Chapter 28. As an agent, a partner has three types of authority:

- **Actual authority.** A partnership is liable for any act of a partner that it authorized. Suppose Tamika and Daniel have formed the TD partnership to buy and sell used books. They decide that they would be willing to pay up to $100 for any first-edition *Harry Potter* books. When Daniel agrees to pay $75 to a customer who brings in such a book, the partnership is liable.
- **Implied authority.** A partnership is liable for any act of a partner that is reasonably necessary to carry out an authorized transaction. If Daniel spends $20 to take a taxi to meet a potential customer, the partnership must reimburse him.
- **Apparent authority.** A partnership is liable for an unauthorized act of a partner if the partner *appears* to be carrying on the business of the partnership or even business of the same type. Without Daniel's knowledge, Tamika promises to pay a large sum for Jane's record collection. Jane is a regular customer of the TD partnership and simply assumes that Tamika has authority to act. The TD partnership is liable because buying used records is the same kind of business as buying used books.

---

[6]*Haught v. Maceluch*, 681 F.2d 290, 1982 U.S. App. LEXIS 17123 (5th Cir. 1982).
[7]The exceptions are listed in UPA §103.
[8]UPA §301(1).

This issue frequently arises when a partnership breaks up but fails to notify customers. If Tamika and Daniel terminate their partnership but do not tell Jane, both of the former partners are liable on any deal Tamika enters into with Jane, as long as the transaction reasonably relates to the TD business.

Ratification

As with every agency relationship, partners can ratify unauthorized acts. **If the partnership accepts the benefit of the unauthorized transaction or fails to repudiate it, the partnership has ratified it.** Once ratified, these actions are as valid as if they had been authorized from the beginning. Thus, Daniel exceeds his authority when he offers Matthew $1,000 for any Stephen King first edition. Tamika is outraged, but she never tells Matthew that the deal is no good. After scouring the city, Matthew finds a first edition of *Misery*. The partnership must pay for the book, no matter how miserable it makes Tamika.

Information

As agent, a partner has a duty to pass on all relevant information to the partnership. Whether or not a partner actually fulfills this obligation, the partnership is treated as if it had been notified. Under the UPA, **whatever one partner knows, the partnership is deemed to know**. Under the terms of TD's storefront lease, the landlord must give 90 days' notice if he does not want to renew. He gives notice to Tamika, who forgets to tell Daniel. The notice is nonetheless valid, and the landlord has every right to evict the partnership. If someone is going to suffer harm because of Tamika's mistake, in all fairness, it should be the partnership, which had the bad judgment to take on an unreliable partner.

Tort Liability

A partnership is responsible for the *intentional* and *negligent* torts of a partner that occur *in the ordinary course* of the partnership's business or with the *actual* authority of the partners. When Daniel tells a customer that a book is a valuable, first-edition Tom Clancy when it really is a worthless Book of the Month Club edition, the partnership is liable for this intentional misrepresentation because it occurred in the ordinary course of the partnership's business. But if Daniel gets in a fight at a bar on Saturday night, the partnership is not liable because that had nothing to do with the partnership's business.

Paying the Debts of the Partnership

The basic rule of partnership liability is simply stated: **all partners are personally liable for all debts of the partnership**. All of a partner's assets are at risk. This rule applies whether or not the individual partner was in any way responsible for the debts. Thus, for example, when the accounting firm Laventhol & Horwath went bankrupt, the partners were personally liable, and some had to sell their houses to pay the partnership's debts.

Joint and Several Liability

Partners have *joint and several* liability for partnership obligations. Joint and several liability means that a creditor can sue the partnership and the partners together, or in separate lawsuits, or in any combination. The partnership and the partners are all individually liable for the full amount of the debt, but obviously the creditor cannot keep collecting after he has already received the total amount owed. **Also note that, even if creditors have a judgment against an individual partner, they cannot go after that partner's assets until all the partnership's assets are exhausted.**[9]

[9]UPA §307.

Letitia, one of the world's wealthiest people, enters into a partnership with penniless Harry to drill for oil on her land. While driving on partnership business, Harry crashes into Gus, seriously injuring him. Gus can sue any combination of the partnership, Letitia, and Harry for the full amount, even though Letitia was 2,000 miles away on her Caribbean island when the accident occurred and she had many times cautioned Harry to drive carefully. Even if Gus obtains a judgment against Letitia, however, he cannot recover against her while the partnership still has assets. So, for all practical purposes, he must try to collect first against the partnership. If the partnership is bankrupt and he manages to collect the full amount from Letitia, he cannot then try to recover against Harry. (As we will see in a minute, Letitia may be able to recover from Harry some portion of what she paid Gus.)

Letitia is not wild about Harry's behavior, so she insists that he agree in writing to share all liabilities of the partnership 50/50. Unfortunately for Letitia, the liability rule is *mandatory*, not a default provision, so her agreement with Harry has absolutely no impact on the rights of Gus or any other creditor. He can still recover from Letitia for all debts of the partnership. She can always try to recover from Harry, but he is penniless, so good luck.

Liability of Incoming Partners

A partner is personally liable only for obligations the partnership incurred while he was a partner. His liability for debts incurred before he became partner is limited to his investment in the partnership.[10] Does this rule make sense? Why should an incoming partner be liable in any way for debts the partnership incurred before he became a partner? These issues haunted the investment bank Goldman Sachs when the Englishman Robert Maxwell drowned. Long known as an international wheeler-dealer, Maxwell stole money from his companies' pension plans to pay for the purchase of newspapers and publishing houses around the world. He drowned after falling—or jumping—over the side of his yacht late one evening. After his death, investigators discovered that more than $1 billion was missing from his various enterprises. The looted pension plans sued Goldman, which settled the lawsuits for $250 million. That was the simple part. The more complicated issue was how to divide this liability among the Goldman partners. Current partners argued that the liability should be borne by those who were Goldman partners when the Maxwell transactions occurred. But the ex-partners balked at having to pay as much as $4 million apiece for a settlement they had not agreed to or even had a chance to vote on.

He drowned after falling—or jumping—over the side of his yacht late one evening.

In a sense, the UPA supports both of these positions. Goldman's ex-partners were personally liable for debts incurred while they were members of the firm. However, current partners were also liable, up to the amount of their investment in the partnership, for debts incurred even before they joined.

EXAM Strategy

Question: Mark and Shania are students who also have a business on the side selling baskets of fruit and vegetables that are cut to look like flowers. They advertise that all ingredients are organic. One day, Mark is in a hurry, and instead of driving across town to the organic food co-op, he purchases ingredients from the closest grocery

[10]UPA §306.

store, Unsafeway. Hannibal has a chemical allergy, so when he eats fruit from Mark's basket, he becomes ill. He sues Mark and Shania and is awarded $10,000 in damages. Is Shania personally liable?

Strategy: First decide if Mark and Shania have a partnership. If so, is the partnership liable for Mark's actions? Is Shania liable for the debts of the partnership that were incurred by Mark?

Result: Although Mark and Shania are students, they also run a business for profit and therefore, are partners for purposes of that business. The partnership is liable for Mark's actions because he was authorized to act. Hannibal must first try to recover the judgment from the partnership. Only if the partnership has no assets can he recover from Mark or Shania individually. At that point, Hannibal has the right to recover from Shania, even though she personally did nothing wrong.

Relationship Among Partners

The rules governing the relationship between partners and outsiders are mandatory; the partners cannot change them. In contrast, the rules regulating the relationship among partners are more flexible—the partners can alter many of them by agreement. If these rules can be changed, why are they in the UPA at all? Partnerships are often formed casually. Sometimes the partners themselves do not even realize they have a partnership. In situations such as these, the default rules apply. Also, some partnerships may not want to undertake the effort and expense of preparing their own agreement. For them, the off-the-rack rules work well enough, and they do not need a custom-tailored version.

Financial Rights

Sharing Profits

Partners share profits equally unless they agree otherwise. This basic rule applies no matter how much money, time, or effort an individual partner contributes to the partnership. After graduation, Dawn convinces her friends, Niels and Sonya, to return with her to Jackson, Mississippi, to open a coffee bar. Niels and Sonya each contribute $15,000. Dawn has nothing to contribute financially. But she does know Jackson. When Dawn's Coffee Bar opens for business, she attracts sellout crowds. Meanwhile, Niels and Sonya are working 20-hour days, first renovating the building and then serving customers. Dawn rarely sees the dawn, or even noon. Niels and Sonya have contributed more time and money and may have done more for the bar's success, but they must share profits equally with Dawn unless the three agreed otherwise.

What is Dawn's share of the profits?

Sharing Losses

Partners share losses according to their share of profits unless they agree otherwise. If Dawn's Coffee Bar fizzles after the first few months of success, then Dawn is responsible for one-third of the losses because she received one-third of the profits. It is too late for her to argue that it was not her fault the business failed.

Payment for Work Done

Partners are not entitled to any payment beyond their share of profits unless they agree otherwise. Niels and Sonya have no right to a greater share of the profits in return for their extra work. It is simply too difficult for the courts to evaluate each partner's contributions. ("Sonya didn't get to work until 9:15." "That's not true, I was there at 8:45, but you didn't see me because I was out back washing your dirty dishes....") This rule may seem arbitrary, but at least it is easy to enforce. The only exception, which we will see later, is that partners are entitled to remuneration for services performed in winding up the partnership.

In the following case, the father made a number of mistakes—he died without a will and left his business without a written partnership agreement. The result was the last thing he would ever have wanted: all-out war among his children.

BANKER V. ESTATE OF BANKER

911 N.Y.S.2d 691; 2010 N.Y. Misc. LEXIS 1145
Supreme Court of New York, Delaware County, 2010

Facts: Father Banker owned Peaceful Valley Campground (which more accurately should have been called Angry Family Battleground). Peaceful Valley (PV) operated as both a campground, with cabins and an RV site. When Father Banker died without a will, each of his four sons inherited roughly 10 percent, while his widow got the rest. One son, Arnold, bought out his mother's share, so he owned roughly two-thirds.

Because the four brothers had made no other arrangement, PV operated as a partnership. Arnold was the only brother who worked in the business. He lived year-round in a house on the campground, where he was on call 24 hours a day during the seven-month camping season. He dealt with routine camp business (including reservations and maintenance), as well as emergencies. Off-season, he made repairs and did office work.

The partnership paid Arnold a salary of about $25,000 a year. It also paid his live-in girlfriend, Linda Romeo, about $10,000 a year for office work and cleaning. In addition, PV paid some of Arnold's personal expenses. The other brothers had not agreed to these payments.

The brothers objected to payments from PV to Arnold, alleging that, as a partner, Arnold had no right to payment for the work he performed.

Issue: ***Was Arnold entitled to any payment in addition to his share of partnership profits?***

Excerpts from Justice Peckham's Decision: The personal expenses of Arnold alleged to have been paid from the partnership include meals and lodging, a truck, furniture and fixtures, and sunglasses. The meals and lodging were trips related to campground business. The furniture and fixtures were actually two additional cabins for the campground. The truck was purchased for use at the campground hauling materials and supplies and also canoes the camp rents out. The sunglasses were for Arnold's use working around the camp. [T]he objection to these expenses is denied.

There is no written partnership agreement and no proof was introduced that the partners ever agreed to Arnold's salary. [W]hen there is no written partnership agreement, the New York Partnership Law effectively becomes the partnership agreement. Under the Partnership Law of New York, consent by all the partners was needed [for a partner to receive] compensation for services rendered to the partnership. No such consent was given by the three minority partners in the Peaceful Valley partnership. No consent having been given, the payment of a salary violated the partnership agreement and the law and must be refunded.

The work Ms. Romeo performed is the same type of work done by Arnold and could have been done by him. The other partners did not agree to hire Ms. Romeo, nor to the payments made to her. [Arnold must repay these amounts.]

Partnership Property

All partnership property belongs to the partnership as a whole, not to the individual partners. A partner has no right to use or sell property except for the benefit of the partnership. Suppose that the partnership owns the building that houses their coffee bar. Upstairs, above the bar, are three apartments. "Wow! This is great," says Niels, "I get the front unit." Does Niels have the right to live in one of the three apartments? After all, Dawn and Sonya can have the other two. Although the arrangement sounds fair, in fact, Niels has no right to live there unless the other partners agree.

Right to Transfer a Partnership Interest

A partnership is a personal relationship built on trust. Therefore, a partner can no more sell his partnership share to a stranger than a spouse can come home one night and announce, "I'm leaving the marriage but, don't worry, I've found a substitute." **Without the approval of the other partners, a partner cannot sell her share; she can only transfer her right to receive profits and losses. A new partner can only be admitted to a partnership by unanimous consent of the other partners.**[11] It would be unfair to force partners to work with, or face unlimited liability for, someone they do not consider trustworthy. Sonya gets in serious debt to a fellow gambler, Nathan Detroit. Fearful that Nathan will ruin her manicure if she does not pay her debt, she agrees to give him her share of the partnership, which is her only asset. He knows a lot about coffee, and she is sure he will do fine as a partner. Although Niels and Dawn feel sorry for Sonya's predicament, they refuse to admit Nathan as a partner. Without their permission, Sonya has no right to transfer ownership rights or management authority to Nathan. Niels and Dawn cannot be forced to work with someone they do not want to touch with a 10-foot pole. However, Sonya can transfer to Nathan the right to receive her share of the partnership's profits.

What if Sonya refuses to assign to Nathan her right to receive profits from the partnership? **Creditors can attach partnership profits through a charging order.** A **charging order** is simply a court order granting a third party the right to receive a share of partnership profits.

Similar rules apply when a partner dies. A partner's heirs have no right to specific partnership property; they do not become partners themselves, nor do they have any say in partnership management. They do have a right to receive the value of a partnership share. In large, sophisticated partnerships, the partnership agreement will usually short-circuit arguments by establishing in advance how to calculate the value of a share.

Management Rights

Right to Manage

Each and every partner has equal rights in the management and conduct of the business unless the partners agree otherwise. In a large partnership, with hundreds of partners, too many cooks can definitely spoil the firm's profitability. That is why large partnerships are almost always run by one or a few partners who are designated as managing partners or members of the executive committee. Some firms are run almost dictatorially by the "rainmaker"—the partner who brings in the most business. Nonetheless, even in an autocratic firm, the atmosphere tends to be less hierarchical than in a corporation, where employees are accustomed to the concept of having a boss. Whatever the reality, partners by and large like to think of themselves as being the equal of every other partner.

Right to Bind the Partnership

As we have discussed, partners are agents of the partnership and have the power to bind the partnership through actual, implied, or apparent authority. The partnership is liable to third parties for a partner's actions. **If these actions are not authorized by the partnership, the partner still has the *power* to bind the partnership, but not the *right*.** In this case, the partnership is liable to the third party, and the partner is liable to the partnership. If the

[11]UPA §401(i).

partner has both the *power* and the *right*, he is not personally liable to the partnership no matter how harmful his actions.

A partner is authorized to bind the partnership for any transaction within the ordinary course of its business unless the partner knows that the other partners would disapprove. Dawn decides she would rather buy coffee from Hadley than from the regular supplier in New York. She has the authority to switch suppliers unless she knows that Sonya and Niels would object because Hadley's coffee is not free trade. If Dawn signs a contract with Hadley, knowing that her partners disapprove, the partnership is liable to Hadley, but Dawn is liable to the partnership.

Right to Vote

Unless the partners agree otherwise, all partners have an equal vote, regardless of their contributions to the partnership. For ordinary partnership affairs, the majority has the right to make a decision. To amend the partnership agreement or to make decisions outside the ordinary course of business, the vote must be unanimous. What happens when Dawn wants to introduce organic teas, over Niels's dead body? The partners vote. Since this is an ordinary partnership matter, the majority rules. If Dawn can get Sonya on her side, she will win approval for the healthy teas. It makes no difference that Dawn never contributed any cash to the partnership; she has the right to vote.

This is the default rule, but many partnerships change it by agreement. Accounting and law firms, for instance, often award partners a certain number of points each year based on how much business they bring in or how hard they work. The more points, the higher their compensation and the more their votes count. Some firms, run by a particularly powerful partner, may effectively have only one vote—his. The managing partner of a large law firm once said, "This partnership has a one-man, one-vote rule, and I'm the one man."

Right to Know

It is difficult to manage an enterprise without adequate information. **Therefore, the UPA grants each partner the right to inspect and copy the partnership's books and records.** This right is unconditional and does not depend upon the partner's purpose or motive. However, books and records are not enough, by themselves, to keep a partner fully informed. Therefore, the UPA requires all partners and the partnership to volunteer any information that might reasonably be necessary for other partners to exercise their rights. All partners and the partnership also have a duty to supply any other information that a partner reasonably requests. These rules are mandatory; the partners may not change them by agreement among themselves.

Management Duties

Partners have the right to manage the partnership. In addition, they also have duties to the partnership and the other partners. These duties are mandatory; the partners may not waive them.

Duties of Care

Partners are liable to the partnership for gross negligence, reckless conduct, intentional misconduct, or a knowing violation of the law. Partners are not liable for ordinary negligence.[12] As you remember from earlier in this chapter, a partnership is liable for the intentional and negligent torts of a partner that occur in the ordinary course of business. But, as you have just learned, the partner is not liable to the partnership for ordinary negligence. These two rules intersect in the following case.

---

[12]UPA §404.

Moren v. Jax Restaurant

679 N.W.2d 165, 2004 Minn. App. LEXIS 459
Court of Appeals of Minnesota, 2004

Facts: Jax was a pizza restaurant in Foley, Minnesota, owned by two sisters: Nicole Moren and Amy Benedetti. They operated it as a partnership. One afternoon, Moren ended her regular shift at 4:00 p.m. and left to pick up her two-year-old son, Remington, from day care. When her sister called her to say that one of the cooks had not come to work, Moren returned to the restaurant with Remington. Moren's husband said he would pick the child up in about 20 minutes.

Because Moren did not want Remington running around the restaurant, she brought him into the kitchen with her, set him on top of the counter, and began rolling out pizza dough using the dough-pressing machine. As she was making pizzas, Remington reached his hand into the dough press. His hand was crushed, causing permanent injuries. His father brought suit on Remington's behalf against the partnership for negligence. The partnership, in its turn, sued Moren, arguing that she had to reimburse the partnership for any payments to Remington. The district court granted summary judgment to Moren. The restaurant appealed.

Issue: ***Is Moren liable to the partnership for her own negligence?***

Excerpts from Judge Crippen's Decision: The partnership [argues] that its obligation to compensate Remington is diminished in proportion to the predominating negligence of Moren as a mother, although it is responsible for her conduct as a business owner. Under Minnesota's Uniform Partnership Act of 1994 (UPA), a partnership is liable for loss or injury caused to a person as a result of a wrongful act or omission, or other actionable conduct, of a partner acting in the ordinary course of business of the partnership or with authority of the partnership. [Moreover], a partnership [must] indemnify a partner for liabilities incurred by the partner in the ordinary course of the business of the partnership. Thus, under the plain language of the UPA, a partner has a right to indemnity from the partnership, but the partnership's claim of indemnity from a partner is not authorized or required.

The district court correctly concluded that Nicole Moren's conduct was in the ordinary course of business of the partnership and, as a result, indemnity by the partner to the partnership was inappropriate. It is undisputed that one of the cooks scheduled to work that evening did not come in, and that Moren's partner asked her to help in the kitchen. It also is undisputed that Moren was making pizzas for the partnership when her son was injured. Because her conduct at the time of the injury was in the ordinary course of business of the partnership, under the UPA, her conduct bound the partnership and it owes indemnity to her for her negligence.

[The restaurant] also claims that because Nicole Moren's action of bringing Remington into the kitchen was partly motivated by personal reasons, her conduct was outside the ordinary course of business. Even if the predominant motive of the partner was to benefit himself or third persons, such does not prevent the concurrent business purpose from being within the scope of the partnership. [W]e conclude that the conduct of Nicole Moren was no less in the ordinary course of business because it also served personal purposes. It is undisputed that Moren was acting for the benefit of the partnership by making pizzas when her son was injured, and even though she was simultaneously acting in her role as a mother, her conduct remained in the ordinary course of the partnership business.

Affirmed.

Duty of Loyalty

Partners have a limited fiduciary duty to their partnership.

Competing with the Partnership. **Each partner must turn over to the partnership all earnings from any activity that is related to the partnership's business.** Cara, Max, and Brooke are partners in a Beverly Hills law firm. While Cara is vacationing near Santa Fe, a guest in the next-door hacienda is arrested in the middle of the night for drunk driving. Cara goes down to the police station and persuades the police officer to release the guest. Her new client gratefully insists on paying her $5,000 for her efforts. Cara figures the fee will go a long way toward paying the cost of her vacation. Cara figures wrong. She must turn the fee over to the partnership because she earned it doing the kind of work that the partnership does. It is irrelevant that she was on vacation.

Taking a Business Opportunity. **A partner may not take an opportunity away from the partnership unless the other partners consent.** Suppose that Beverly Hills needs a lawyer to serve as city counsel and offers the post to Max. He cannot take the job himself without the firm's permission. If he violates this duty, the partnership is entitled to the value of the opportunity he has taken.

Using Partnership Property. **A partner must turn over to the partnership any profit he earns from use of partnership property without the consent of the partners.** The partnership's office is in an old, beautifully restored historic building. Max runs a party-planning service on the side—MAXimum Fun. He occasionally holds parties on the weekends in the partnership's elegant foyer without telling Brooke and Cara. When they find out, they are maximum angry, and for good reason—Max has violated his duty to the partnership.

Does Max get to keep the profit from these parties?

Conflict of Interest. **A partner has a conflict of interest whenever the partnership does business with him, a member of his family, or a business partly or fully owned by him. In that case, the partner must turn all profits over to the partnership.** Suppose that Max hires MAXimum Fun to put on the firm's 10th-anniversary celebration. Unless the other partners consent in advance, Max must turn over to the partnership any profits he earns from the party.

In the following case, one partner bought partnership property at a public auction. Is that a conflict of interest?

Marsh v. Gentry

642 S.W.2d 574, 1982 Ky. LEXIS 315
Supreme Court of Kentucky, 1982

Facts: Tom Gentry and John Marsh were partners in a business that bought and sold racehorses. The partnership paid $155,000 for Champagne Woman, who subsequently had a foal named Excitable Lady. The partners decided to sell Champagne Woman at the annual Keeneland auction, the world's premier thoroughbred horse auction. On the day of the auction, Gentry decided to bid on the horse personally, without telling Marsh. Gentry bought Champagne Woman for $135,000. Later, he told Marsh that someone from California had approached him about buying Excitable Lady. Marsh agreed to the sale. Although he repeatedly asked Gentry the name of the purchaser, Gentry refused to tell him. Not until 11 months later, when Excitable Lady won a race at Churchill Downs, did Marsh learn that Gentry had been the purchaser. Marsh became the Excitable Man.

Issue: ***Did Gentry violate his fiduciary duty when he bought partnership property without telling his partner?***

Excerpts from Justice O'Hara's Decision: Admittedly, at an auction sale, the specific identity of a purchaser cannot be ascertained before the sale, but [Kentucky partnership law] required a full disclosure by Gentry to Marsh that he would be a prospective purchaser.

As to the private sale of Excitable Lady, Marsh consented to a sale from the partnership, at a specified price, to the prospective purchaser in California. Even though Marsh obtained the stipulated purchase price, a partner has an absolute right to know when his partner is the purchaser. Partners scrutinize buyouts by their partners in an entirely different light than an ordinary third party sale. This distinction is vividly made without contradiction when Marsh later indicated that he would not have consented to either sale had he known that Gentry was the purchaser. Under these facts, it is obvious that Gentry failed to disclose all that he knew concerning the sales, including his desire to purchase partnership property.

[P]artners, in their relations with other partners, [must] maintain a higher degree of good faith due to the partnership agreement. The requirement of full disclosure among partners as to partnership business cannot be escaped.

Finally, Gentry maintains that it is an accepted practice at auction sales of thoroughbreds for one partner to secretly bid on partnership stock to accomplish a buyout. We would emphatically state, however, for the benefit of those engaged in such practices, that where an "accepted business practice" conflicts with existing law, the law, whether statutory or court ordered, is controlling. To hold otherwise would be chaotic.

Good Faith and Fair Dealing

Partners have an obligation of good faith and fair dealing to each other and to the partnership. They must deal with each other *fairly* and *without coercion.* Behavior that would be acceptable in an arm's-length transaction may be unacceptable between partners. Hartz Mountain Industries, Inc., was the managing partner of a real estate business in northern New Jersey. Eugene Heller was Hartz's partner. According to the partnership agreement, when Heller left the partnership, Hartz would have the properties appraised and buy Heller's share. Hartz had the right to choose the appraiser. Over Heller's objection, Hartz chose Robert DiFalco. Hartz's own internal appraisals valued the properties at more than $214 million, but DiFalco produced an appraisal of $133 million—a slight discrepancy of more than $80 million.

The court found that, while Hartz had technically complied with the partnership agreement, it had breached its obligation of good faith and fair dealing. Courts generally pay a great deal of respect to appraisals, especially when both parties have agreed in advance to the appraisal process. But the court did not accept the appraisal in this case because Hartz had violated its duty to Heller by choosing such an unreliable appraiser.[13]

EXAM Strategy

Question: Tom is a bully. He and Penelope start a test prep business. The partnership agreement specifies that Penelope is entitled to 30 percent of the profits, but that Tom is the managing partner with the right to run the day-to-day affairs of the business. Because students love Penelope's gentle demeanor, the business flourishes. A large university offers the partnership a contract to provide test prep services to all of its students. Tom decides to take that business himself without telling Penelope. He also reduces her income from the partnership. She asks for data on the partnership's profitability, but Tom refuses to give it to her. He also moves the business into a shabbier, cheaper building that Penelope hates. What rights does Penelope have?

[13]*Heller v. Hartz Mountain Industries, Inc.*, 270 N.J. Super. 143, 636 A.2d 599, 1993 N.J. Super. LEXIS 903 (N.J. Super. Ct. Law Div. 1993).

Strategy: The partnership agreement determines most of the rights between partners, but some rights are mandatory and cannot be changed by the partners.

Result: Tom does have the right to move the partnership into a different building, but he cannot take the opportunity to provide services to the university without telling Penelope. She is entitled to see the books and records of the partnership.

Terminating a Partnership

Partnership at will
A partnership with no fixed duration. Any of the partners may leave at any time, for any reason.

Term partnership
A partnership in which the partners agree in advance how long it will last.

The rules on termination depend, in part, on the type of partnership. If the partners have not agreed how long their partnership will last, they have a **partnership at will**, and any of them may leave at any time, for any reason. Taylor, Jay, and Gabriela are partners in the Donut Partnership, which owns a racehorse by the name of Speedy Donut. They see their business as a lark, to last as long as they are having fun, so they make no decision about its duration. When Taylor decamps after only two months, leaving Jay and Gabriela holding the feedbag, they have no legal right to complain.

With a **term partnership**, the partners have agreed in advance how long it will last. At the end of the specified term, the partnership automatically ends. If Taylor, Jay, and Gabriela agree to sell Speedy Donut and end their business relationship in five years, or if they agree the partnership will end when Speedy Donut runs in the Kentucky Derby, they have a term partnership.

Dissociation

Dissociation
When a partner leaves the partnership.

A partnership begins with an association of two or more people. Appropriately, the end of a partnership begins with a *dissociation*. A **dissociation** occurs when a partner quits. However, a dissociation does not inevitably lead to the termination of the partnership business. A dissociation is a fork in the road: **when one or more partners dissociate, the partnership can either buy out the departing partner(s) and continue in business or wind up the business and terminate the partnership**. Exhibit 32.1 illustrates the dissociation process under the UPA.

Rightful versus Wrongful Dissociation

A partnership is a personal relationship built on trust. As we have seen, all partners are agents for the partnership, and each partner is personally liable for its debts. The actions of one partner can profoundly affect the financial health of every other partner. Under these circumstances, courts will not force someone to remain in a partnership, no matter what the partnership agreement says, any more than they will force a couple to stay married because of their vows at the altar. Partners can always dissociate, but like any divorcing spouse, they may have to pay damages for the harm that their departure causes. As courts are wont to say: **a partner always has the power to leave a partnership but may not have the right**.

Rightful Dissociation. A rightful dissociation occurs if:

- *A partner in a partnership at will serves notice that he intends to withdraw.*
- *The partners agree in advance on an event that causes dissociation.* Jay plans to attend business school in three years, so the partnership agreement provides that he will be automatically dissociated from the partnership at that point.

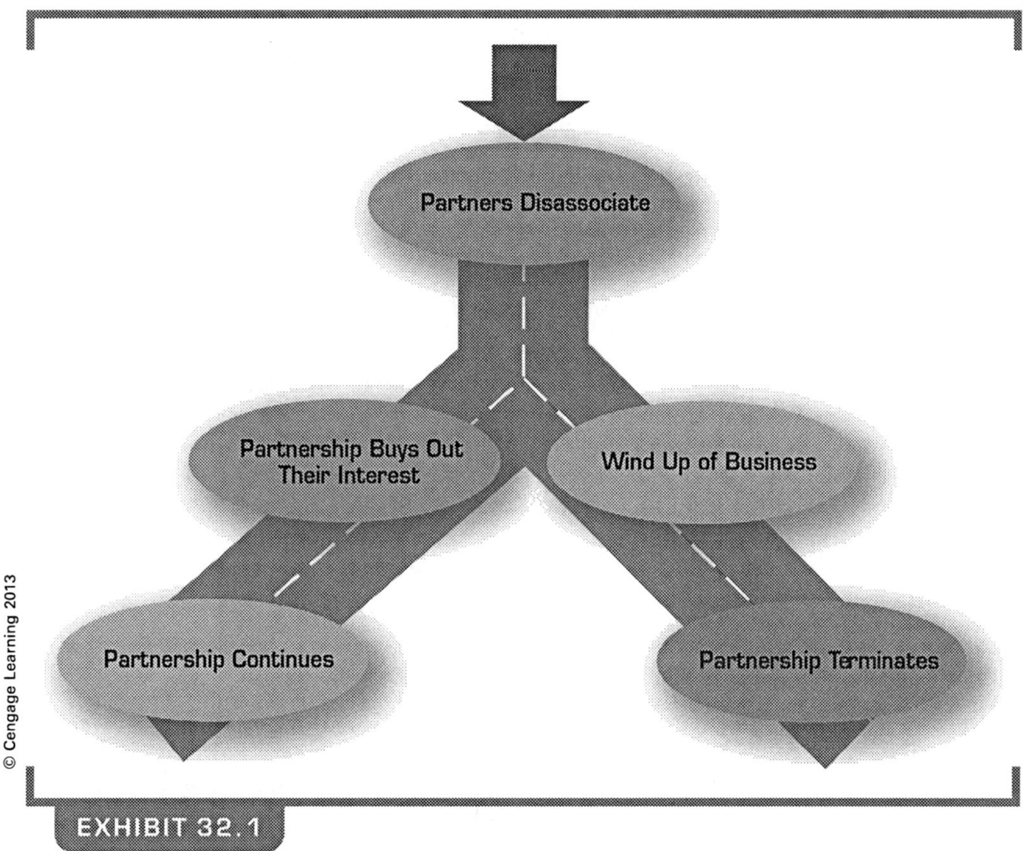

EXHIBIT 32.1

- *A partner dies or becomes incompetent.*
- *A partner is expelled by the other partners.* Partnership agreements can establish a process for expelling a partner. Often, under such agreements, the partnership does not even have to give a reason for expulsion. If a certain percentage of the partners (say, 75 percent) vote against someone, she is out. However, in the absence of such a provision in the partnership agreement, the UPA permits the expulsion of a partner only if (1) it is illegal to carry on the business with her or (2) she has transferred her partnership interest.

Even lawyers sometimes forget the law. The prestigious law firm of Cadwalader, Wickersham, & Taft fired a partner in its New York office. However, the partnership agreement said nothing about expulsion. A court upheld the firing but awarded the former partner $3 million in damages. In short, the law firm had the power, but not the right, to expel a partner. Unlike employees of a corporation, partners cannot be fired unless their partnership agreement specifically allows for it.

Wrongful Dissociation. A wrongful dissociation occurs if:

- *A partner violates the partnership agreement.* The Donut Partnership agreement prohibits racetrack betting. When Taylor wins the Pick Six, he is automatically dissociated.
- *A partner in a term partnership withdraws before the end of the term.* The Donut Partnership is supposed to last five years, but Jay withdraws after five months.
- *A court expels a partner in a term partnership because her behavior is harmful.* A court has the right to expel a partner who engages in wrongful conduct that harms the

partnership or violates the partnership agreement in a serious way. Gabriela drugs the favored Speedy Donut so that she can win a bet on a long shot in the race. A court could expel her, and that would constitute a wrongful dissociation.

- *A partner in a term partnership becomes bankrupt.*

Once a partner is dissociated, the remaining partners must decide how to proceed; they can either continue the partnership as an ongoing business or terminate it.

EXAM Strategy

Question: In their spare time, Maisy and Roland like to build widgets for Facebook.com. (Widgets are software applications that permit Facebook users to do cool things like post bumper stickers on their pages.) Under Facebook rules, Maisy and Roland are paid a small fee each time someone uses one of their applications. After this sideline becomes quite profitable, Maisy tells Roland that she is going to start building widgets on her own without him—she thinks she is more creative than Roland. Does Maisy have the right to exclude Roland?

Strategy: There are three questions to answer: Is there a partnership? If so, what kind of partnership? Does Maisy have the right to withdraw from it?

Result: Maisy and Roland do have a partnership—they are carrying on as co-owners of a business for profit. It does not matter that the word "partnership" has never passed their lips. Because there is no partnership agreement, they have a partnership at will. With this form of partnership, Maisy can withdraw at any time for any reason.

Continuation of the Partnership Business

If a partner is dissociated from the partnership, the other partners can continue the business, but they must buy out the ex-partner.[14] Most large firms provide in their partnership agreement that, upon dissociation, the business continues.

Financial Settlement

If the partnership decides to continue, it must pay the ex-partner the value of her share of the business. This value is equal to her share of the proceeds if (1) the partnership were sold as an ongoing business or (2) the partnership's assets were liquidated, whichever calculation is greater. For example, if Gabriela is adjudged incompetent by a court, she is automatically dissociated from the Donut Partnership. At that point, Speedy Donut is worth $500,000 and the partnership has debts of $50,000, for a total value of $450,000. Gabriela is entitled to at least a one-third share—$150,000. If, however, the partnership is worth $600,000 as an ongoing business, Gabriela is entitled to $200,000.

Now the plot thickens. If Gabriela's dissociation was *wrongful,* the partnership can subtract any damages she caused from the amount it owes her. A court expels Gabriela

[14]If the ex-partner's dissociation was rightful, she can vote in this decision. If her dissociation was wrongful, she has no right to vote.

from the partnership because she drugged Speedy Donut. His recovery is slow and he is unable to race for months, costing the partnership $100,000. Taylor and Jay could subtract that $100,000 from the $200,000 they owe her, so she ultimately receives a check for only $100,000. If her bad acts caused more than $200,000 in damage, she owes them money.

Liability of the Dissociated Partner to Outsiders for Debts Incurred *before* Dissociation

A dissociated partner is liable to outsiders for debts incurred during her term as a partner, but the partnership must indemnify her for these debts. After Gabriela departs, a bank sues the partnership for failure to repay its loan. Although Gabriela is no longer a partner, she was one when the partnership borrowed the money. As we have seen, the bank may be able to recover from her. If it does, however, the partnership must indemnify her, that is, the partnership must reimburse her for any amounts she pays the bank. This outcome is only fair because, when the partnership purchased her share, it reduced the payment to reflect liabilities such as this.

Liability of the Dissociated Partner to Outsiders for Debts Incurred *after* Dissociation

A dissociated partner is liable to outsiders for the debts of the partnership incurred within two years after she leaves, but only if the creditor reasonably believes she is still a partner. The partnership must indemnify her for these debts. If Taylor and Jay buy an expensive saddle on credit from their regular supplier, Gabriela is also liable unless the saddler knows she is dissociated. The partnership would have to reimburse her (if it has enough funds). To protect herself, however, Gabriela can file a statement of dissociation with the Secretary of State. Although the saddler rarely spends his free afternoons perusing the public records, he is deemed to have notice of this filing 90 days after Gabriela makes it.

Liability of the Dissociated Partner to the Partnership

If the ex-partner harms the partnership after she leaves, she is liable for the damage she causes. If Gabriela lets a feed supplier believe that she is still a partner and then buys feed on credit, the partnership may be liable for her charges. If so, she must reimburse the partnership.

Termination of the Partnership Business

When a partner is dissociated, the partnership may choose to terminate the business rather than continue it. **Ending a partnership business involves three steps: dissolution, winding up, and termination.**

Dissolution

Unless the partners agree otherwise, a partnership dissolves under the following circumstances:

- *In a partnership at will, when a partner notifies the partnership that he intends to withdraw and the remaining partners cannot agree unanimously to continue the business.*
- *In a term partnership, when:*
  - *A partner is dissociated before the end of the term and half of the remaining partners vote to wind up the partnership business.* When Jay dies, he is dissociated from the partnership. If Gabriela votes to wind up the business, the partnership is dissolved.
  - *All the partners agree to dissolve.* Although the Donut Partnership is supposed to last five years, Taylor, Jay, and Gabriela can agree among themselves to wind up the

business whenever they want. If Speedy Donut is a cream puff on the racetrack, they can decide to dissolve their partnership and sell the pastry.

- *The term expires or the partnership achieves its goal.* If Speedy Donut runs in the Derby, the Donut Partnership automatically dissolves.

- *In any partnership, when:*
  - *An event occurs which the partners had agreed would cause dissolution.* The Donut Partnership agreement provided that the partnership would dissolve if Speedy Donut failed to win a race in any 12-month period. When Speedy Donut goes winless, the partnership dissolves.
  - *The partnership business becomes illegal.* If horse racing is banned, the Donut Partnership automatically dissolves.
  - *A court determines that the partnership is unlikely to succeed.* If the partners simply cannot get along or they cannot make a profit, any partner has the right to ask a court to dissolve the partnership. If Taylor and Jay quarrel over everything and are unable to reach agreement on anything, a court is likely to agree to dissolve the partnership.

Note that even if one of these events occurs, partners can always decide (by unanimous vote) to continue a partnership. Indeed, even after the winding-up process begins, the partners can change their minds and continue the business.

Winding Up

During the winding-up process, all debts of the partnership are paid, and the remaining proceeds are distributed to the partners.

Who Does It? Unless the partnership agreement provides otherwise, any partner who has not wrongfully dissociated has the right to oversee the winding up.

Are They Paid? Partners are entitled to reasonable compensation for their work in winding up the partnership.

What Do They Do? The winding-up process can be complex and take as long as several years to complete. The partners in charge can either sell the entire business as a whole, sell the individual assets of the business, distribute specific assets to the partners, or some combination of these options. They have the right to complete unfinished transactions and do whatever is necessary to wind up the business, but they do not have the right to take on new business.

If Taylor is winding up the Donut Partnership, he can sell Speedy Donut outright, buy feed for him until the sale, sue to recover any winnings that have not been paid, and settle partnership debts. But can he enter the horse in additional races? In a similar case, a court permitted the partner in charge of winding up a racing business to pay entrance fees for races even though the horses would, in all likelihood, be sold before the races. The court assumed that buyers would pay more for horses that were eligible to race in upcoming events.[15]

The partnership is bound by the acts of the partners in charge of winding up. As the following case illustrates, this rule can sometimes lead to unhappy results.

---

[15]*Central Trust & S. Deposit Co. v. Respass*, 112 Ky. 606, 66 S.W. 421 (1902).

Jefferson Insurance Co. v. Curle

771 S.W.2d 424, 1989 Tenn. App. LEXIS 30
Tennessee Court of Appeals, 1989

Facts: Michael Curle and Steven Shelley were partners doing business under the name C & S Roofing. When the partnership dissolved, Curle agreed to complete one unfinished project (the Bishop house) and left Shelley to wind up the other partnership business. Shelley canceled the partnership's general liability insurance policy without telling Curle. While painting the Bishop house, Dennis Whitsett fell through a hole in the roof that the partnership had left covered only with tar paper. When Whitsett sought to recover from the partnership for his serious injuries, Curle and Shelley asked the insurance company to pay the claim.

The trial court found the policy canceled as to Steven Shelley, individually, but in full force and effect as to the partnership and Michael Curle, individually. The insurance company appealed.

Issue: ***Was the partnership bound by Shelley's decision during the winding-up process to cancel the policy, even though he had not told Curle?***

Excerpts from Judge McLemore's Decision: [The Tennessee Partnership Act] clearly states: "After dissolution a partner can bind the partnership ... by any act appropriate for winding up partnership affairs or completing transactions unfinished at dissolution." The liquidating partner owes a continuing fiduciary duty to the other partners and has an obligation to act equitably toward them. However, these obligations run between partners and do not absolve any partner from being bound by the liquidating partner's actions in winding up partnership affairs. In the present case, we hold Shelley's cancellation of the partnership insurance policy and collection of unused premiums to be within his authority in winding up the partnership's affairs.

For the foregoing reasons, the judgment of the trial court holding the policy canceled as to Steven Shelley, individually, is affirmed, but that portion of the judgment holding that the policy is in full force and effect as to C & S Roofing, a partnership, and Michael Curle, individually, is reversed; and we hold that the policy is canceled as to all insureds and, thus, provides no coverage to any of the defendants for the accident alleged by Dennis Whitsett.

Who Is Liable If a Partner Takes on New Business? During the winding-up process, the partners continue to be liable for the debts of the partnership that were incurred before dissolution. But what if a partner oversteps her bounds during the winding-up process and takes on new business? All of the other partners are liable unless they have filed a statement of dissolution with the Secretary of State. This statement is effective 90 days after it is filed.

How Are Partnership Proceeds Distributed? During the winding-up process, the assets of the partnership are paid out in the following order:

- First, to creditors of the partnership, including creditors who are partners. Suppose that the Donut Partnership has assets of $30,000. It owes $20,000 each to the feed supplier, the stabler, and Jay, for a total of $60,000. It will pay $10,000 to each of the three creditors—Jay is treated exactly like the outsiders.
- Second, any leftover funds (or obligations) are distributed to the partners. Unless the partnership agreement provides otherwise, partners share equally in profits—and losses. In this example, the Donut Partnership had only enough assets to pay half its $60,000 debt. Each partner would then contribute $10,000 to pay the amount still owing. Jay's payment would be a wash—he owes $10,000, but he is also entitled to be paid $10,000.

Termination

After the sometimes lengthy and complex winding up, the actual termination of a partnership is anticlimactic. Termination happens automatically once the winding up is finished. The partnership is not required to do anything official; it can go out of the world even more quietly and simply than it came in.

Chapter Conclusion

In some ways, a partnership is an old-fashioned form of organization. From the late 1770s until the mid-19th century, virtually all businesses were partnerships. Then corporations gained in popularity, and now new forms have arisen such as limited liability companies and limited liability partnerships (both discussed in Chapter 31). These new forms of organization have many of the advantages of a partnership without the disadvantage of unlimited liability.

It is no surprise that to protect their partners from personal liability, many accounting firms, law firms, brokerage houses, advertising agencies, and investment banks that were originally partnerships have changed their form of organization to one of the newer options. But many organizations continue to act like partnerships even though they have changed their official form of organization. And, before the partnership baby gets thrown out with the liability bathwater, it is worth noting that many organizations—law, accounting, and investment banking firms, to name a few—have been highly successful as partnerships. The lack of hierarchy in partnerships encourages collaboration while the lure of ownership motivates employees.

Partnership law is important for another reason. As we have seen in this chapter, partnerships are often formed inadvertently by people who do not realize they are in such a relationship until a dispute arises. It is useful to know in advance the kind of behavior that will create a partnership and understand the consequences.

Exam Review

1. **FORMING A PARTNERSHIP** In determining whether a partnership exists, a court will consider whether the parties:
   - Share the profits of the business,
   - Share the losses of the business,
   - Share management of the business, and
   - Have an oral or written partnership agreement (pp. 788–792)

EXAM Strategy

Question: Suppose that in the chapter's opening vignette, Chase, Bailey, and Zack signed a document stating, "The undersigned expressly agree that they are not partners." If they continued to work together on the house, sharing the profits and the management, would they have been partners?

Strategy: Remember that in the case of partnerships, actions speak louder than words. (See the "Result" at the end of this section.)

2. **PARTNERSHIP BY ESTOPPEL** If someone is not a member of a partnership, she will nonetheless be considered a partner by estoppel if (1) she tells other people she is a partner or allows other people to say, without contradiction, that she is a partner; (2) a third party relies on this assertion; and (3) the third party suffers harm. (pp. 791–792)

EXAM Strategy

Question: Helen parked her new Chevrolet in the parking lot at the airport in Springfield, Ohio. Bryan was giving flying lessons to Edward. Bryan told Edward to taxi a plane off the runway. Edward, standing on the ground next to the plane, cranked up the engine. The throttle was set too far open, so the plane began to move. Edward chased the plane on foot, grabbed its left wing, and swung the airplane in a semicircle, crashing it into Helen's car. Bryan operated his flying business under the name Bryan-Carl Air Service. Bryan and Carl were not partners, but Helen sued them both on a theory of partnership by estoppel. She argued that they had used a name for their business that sounded like a partnership. She had never heard of their business until the collision. Is Carl liable to Helen as a partner by estoppel?

Strategy: These elements are required for partnership by estoppel: the participants must have held themselves out as partners even though they are not; a third party must have relied on that representation and suffered harm. (See the "Result" at the end of this section.)

3. **PARTNERS AS AGENTS** Every partner is an agent of the partnership for the purpose of its business. A partnership is responsible for the intentional and negligent torts of a partner that occur in the ordinary course of the partnership's business or with the actual, implied or apparent authority of the other partners. (pp. 792–793)

EXAM Strategy

Question: While Warren Lyon was representing Betty Cook in divorce proceedings, she inherited $60,000. Lyon suggested Cook invest her money in a corporation of which he was president. Although he promised her a substantial return, the company went bankrupt shortly thereafter. Lyon was a partner in a law firm. The firm was not in the business of giving investment advice, it did not know that Lyon was giving such advice, nor did it receive any fee from Cook for the "investment service." Is the law firm liable for Cook's loss?

Strategy: Was Lyon acting within the ordinary course of the partnership's business? Was he acting with actual, implied or apparent authority? (See the "Result" at the end of this section.)

4. **A PARTNER'S LIABILITY FOR THE DEBTS OF THE PARTNERSHIP** All partners are personally liable for all debts of the partnership incurred while they were members of the partnership. Partners have joint and several liability for partnership obligations. A partner's liability for debts incurred before she became a partner is limited to her investment in the partnership. (pp. 793–795)

5. **DEFAULT RULES AMONG PARTNERS** Unless they agree otherwise, partners:
    - Share profits equally,
    - Share losses according to their share of profits,
    - Are not entitled to any payment beyond their share of profits, even if they perform work for the partnership,
    - Have no right to use or sell specific partnership property except for the benefit of the partnership,
    - Each have an equal vote, regardless of their contributions to the partnership, and
    - Each have an equal right in the management of the business. (pp. 795–798)
6. **TRANSFERRING A PARTNERSHIP SHARE** Without the approval of the other partners, a partner cannot sell her share. She can only transfer the right to receive profits and losses. A new partner can be admitted to a partnership only by unanimous consent of the other partners. (p. 797)
7. **CREDITORS' RIGHTS** Creditors can attach partnership profits through a charging order. (p. 797)
8. **A PARTNER'S LIABILITY TO THE PARTNERSHIP** Partners are liable to the partnership for any damages resulting from their gross negligence, reckless conduct, intentional misconduct, or a knowing violation of the law. Partners are not liable to the partnership for ordinary negligence. (pp. 793–795)
9. **OUTSIDE EARNINGS** Each partner must turn over to the partnership all earnings from any activity that is related to the partnership's business. (pp. 799–800)
10. **PARTNERSHIP OPPORTUNITY** A partner may not take an opportunity away from the partnership unless the other partners consent. (p. 800)
11. **CONFLICT OF INTEREST** A partner has a conflict of interest whenever the partnership does business with him, a member of his family, or a business partly or fully owned by him. The partner must turn all profits over to the partnership. (p. 800)
12. **A PARTNER'S OBLIGATION TO THE PARTNERSHIP** Partners have an obligation of good faith and fair dealing to each other and to the partnership. (pp. 798–802)
13. **DISSOCIATION** A dissociation occurs when a partner leaves the partnership. (pp. 802–805)
14. **AFTER DISSOCIATION** When one or more partners dissociate, the partnership can either buy out the departing partner(s) and continue in business or wind up the business and terminate the partnership. (pp. 804–805)
15. **THE RIGHT TO WITHDRAW** A partner always has the power to leave a partnership but may not have the right. (p. 805)
16. **PARTNERSHIP AT WILL** If partners do not have an agreement about the duration of their partnership, it is called a partnership at will, and any of them can leave at any time for any reason. (p. 805)

17. **TERM PARTNERSHIP** With a term partnership, the partners have agreed in advance how long the partnership will last. (p. 806)

18. **DISSOCIATED PARTNER** A dissociated partner is liable to outsiders for debts incurred during her term as a partner, but the partnership must indemnify her for these debts. A dissociated partner is liable for the debts of the partnership incurred within two years after she leaves, but only if the creditor reasonably believes she is still a partner. The partnership must indemnify her for these debts. (pp. 805–806)

19. **ENDING A PARTNERSHIP** If the partners decide to end the partnership business, they must take three steps: dissolution, winding up, and termination. (pp. 805–806)

20. **THE WINDING-UP PROCESS** During the winding-up process, the partners have the right to complete unfinished transactions and do whatever is necessary to terminate the business. They do not have the right to take on new business. The assets of the partnership are paid out:
    - First, to creditors of the partnership, including creditors who are partners.
    - Second, to partners. (pp. 806–807)

1. Result: The document would have had no impact. So long as they act like partners, they are partners.

2. Result: Two of the three elements are there—Brian and Carl held themselves out as partners and Helen suffered harm. But Carl was not a partner by estoppel because, before the accident, Helen did not know that Carl had held himself out as Bryan's partner. She had not *relied on* their representation.

3. Result: The firm was not in the investment advisory business, so Lyon was not acting within the ordinary course of business. He did not have actual authority, but he might have had apparent authority, in which case the firm would be liable.

MULTIPLE-CHOICE QUESTIONS

1. **CPA QUESTION** Which of the following is not necessary to create a partnership?
   (a) Execution of a written partnership agreement
   (b) Agreement to share ownership of the partnership
   (c) Intention of conducting a business for profit
   (d) Intention of creating a relationship recognized as a partnership

2. If a partner dissociates, he is entitled to:
   (a) Force the termination of the partnership
   (b) Receive indemnification from liability for present partnership debt
   (c) Receive indemnification from damages he caused the partnership
   (d) Receive only his share of the value of the partnership assets when it ultimately liquidates

3. **CPA QUESTION** Cobb, Inc., a partner in TLC Partnership, assigns its partnership interest to Bean, who is not made a partner. After the assignment, Bean asserts the right to (1) participate in the management of TLC and (2) Cobb's share of TLC's partnership profits. Bean is correct as to which of these rights?
   (a) 1 only
   (b) 2 only
   (c) 1 and 2
   (d) Neither 1 nor 2

4. **CPA QUESTION** Ted Fein, a partner in the ABC Partnership, wishes to withdraw from the partnership and sell his interest to Gold. All of the other partners in ABC have agreed to admit Gold as a partner and to hold Fein harmless for the past, present, and future liabilities of ABC. A provision in the original partnership agreement states that the partnership will continue upon the death or withdrawal of one or more of the partners. As a result of Fein's withdrawal and Gold's admission to the partnership, Gold:
   (a) Is personally liable for partnership liabilities arising before and after his admission as a partner
   (b) Has the right to participate in the management of ABC
   (c) Acquired only the right to receive Fein's share of the profits of ABC
   (d) Must contribute cash or property to ABC in order to be admitted with the same rights as the other partners

5. Blackriver Partnership is in the process of winding up. It has three partners: Jason, Keira, and Lancelot. The partnership has assets of $90,000, but debts of $60,000, including $30,000 it owes to Jason. Who gets what?
   (a) Each partner receives $10,000.
   (b) Each partner receives $30,000.
   (c) Jason receives $30,000 and the other two get $10,000 each.
   (d) Jason receives $40,000 and the other two get $10,000 each.

Essay Questions

1. **ETHICS** Arthur, John, and George formed a partnership to drill and maintain cesspools for two years. After less than two months, John and George sent a letter to Arthur, informing him that they were dissolving the partnership. Arthur sued the two other men, asking the court to declare that the partnership still existed and he had the right to continue in the business. Do John and George have the power to dissolve a term partnership before the end of the term? Aside from the legal issue, is it fair to Arthur for the court to allow his two partners to walk away from their partnership? He had counted on a two-year commitment; they gave only two months.

2. **YOU BE THE JUDGE WRITING PROBLEM** Herbert, an artist, entered into an agreement with Randy for the reproduction and distribution of his paintings. Herbert was to receive 50 percent of the gross sales revenues. Randy was responsible for all losses and for management of the business. Before leaving on a trip to Israel,

where he feared he might be in some danger, Randy signed a partnership agreement with Herbert stating that they jointly owned the business. Shortly after Randy returned from the trip, the two men terminated their business relationship, and Herbert revoked his authorization for the sale of prints. When Randy continued selling the prints, Herbert filed suit. Randy argued that the two had formed a partnership and that he was authorized to sell assets of the partnership. Were Herbert and Randy partners? **Argument for Herbert:** A partnership agreement does not create a partnership. Randy alone managed the business. Herbert shared only revenues, not profits or losses. **Argument for Randy:** Herbert and Randy both provided services to the business: Randy paid for the printing, and Herbert did the artwork. These two men signed a partnership agreement, and they obviously intended to be partners.

3. Seventy-Three Land, Inc., sued Maxlar Partners for the balance due on a note made by the partnership. Max, a partner, asked the court to dismiss the claim against him personally because the plaintiff had not first tried to collect against the partnership. Does Max have a valid claim?

4. Pedro and Juan have a business selling ties with fraternity insignia. Pedro finds out that an online shirt business is for sale. It sounds like a great idea—customers send in their measurements and get back a custom-made shirt at a price no higher than an off-the-rack shirt at the local department store. Does Pedro have to let Juan in on the great opportunity?

5. Brothers Sydney and Ashley were partners in a real estate partnership in Pennsylvania. They received identical salaries. Sydney moved to Florida to establish residency so that he could obtain a divorce there. His lawyer told him not to return to Pennsylvania until he had resolved his marital problems. After Sydney had been gone almost a year, Ashley decided to increase his own salary to compensate for the additional work he was doing. Does Ashley have the right to pay himself more if he is doing more work?

Discussion Questions

1. Mike Love and Brian Wilson were members of the Beach Boys. In the 1960s, they wrote songs together. The copyrights for these songs were later sold to Rondor, which paid the two men royalties when the songs were played. In 2004, Wilson re-recorded some of these songs on a CD called *Good Vibrations*. This CD was distributed in the United Kingdom by the newspaper *The Mail on Sunday*. Love sued Wilson, arguing that the two men had a partnership and Wilson had violated the partnership agreement by re-recording the songs without Love's permission. Did Mike Love and Brian Wilson have a partnership?

2. Dutch, Bill, and Heidi were equal partners in a lawn care business. Bill and Heidi wanted to borrow money from the bank to buy more trucks and expand the business. Dutch was dead set against the idea. When the matter came to a vote, Bill and Heidi voted in favor, Dutch against. Dutch was so annoyed that he told the bank not to lend the money and, further, that he would not be responsible for repaying the loan. The bank loaned the money, the business failed, and the bank sued all three partners. Is Dutch liable on the loan?

3. Carrie and Laura started a business together to sell bridesmaid dresses online. Carrie spent months preparing the financials and meeting with potential investors while Laura designed dresses and found suppliers. Once Carrie was finished with the financials and had identified some potential investors, Laura announced that she preferred to work with Scott and Carrie was out of the business. What rights does Carrie have?

4. Is it fair that partners are not entitled to be paid for work they do for the partnership? What about poor Arnold in the Peaceful Valley case—he was on call 24/7 and his girlfriend was cleaning the latrines, but they were not entitled to be paid.

5. Is there any good reason to be in a partnership? If so, for what sort of business would it make sense?

CHAPTER 33

© Evan Meyer/Shutterstock.com

Life and Death of a Corporation

On July 26, 2004, Mark Zuckerberg signed a certificate of incorporation for his company, which he called TheFacebook, Inc. At 11:34 a.m. on July 29, 2004, that certificate was filed with the Secretary of State for Delaware, and TheFacebook began its life as a corporation. Zuckerberg had started this social networking Internet site the previous February in his dorm room at Harvard. By December 2004, TheFacebook had almost 1 million users. By the beginning of 2006, the company was estimated to be worth between $750 million and $2 billion. Today, TheFacebook is valued at more than $50 billion. As Zuckerberg built his company, what did he need to know about the law?

Zuckerberg started TheFacebook in his dorm room at Harvard. Within 10 months, it had almost 1 million users.

Most of the country's largest businesses, and many of its small ones, are corporations. In this chapter, you will learn how to form a corporation and also how to avoid traps that await the unwary entrepreneur before and after a business is formed. Finally, you will learn how to dissolve a corporation.

BEFORE THE CORPORATION IS FORMED

TheFacebook operated for five months before it was incorporated. During this period, Zuckerberg needed to be careful to avoid liability as a promoter.

Promoter's Liability

The promoter is the person who creates the corporation. It is his idea; he raises the capital, hires the lawyers, calls the shots. Mark Zuckerberg was TheFacebook's promoter. Sometimes, promoters are so eager to get their business going that they sign contracts on behalf of the corporation before it is legally formed. Zuckerberg had moved company headquarters to Palo Alto, California before the certificate of incorporation was filed. Suppose that he finds the perfect location for his headquarters. He is eager to sign the lease before someone else snatches the opportunity away, but TheFacebook does not yet legally exist—it is not incorporated. What would happen if he signed the lease anyway?

© AP Photo/Paul Sakuma

Within a few years, Mark Zuckerberg went from college student to Silicon Valley billionaire.

- **The promoter is personally liable on any contract signed before the corporation is formed.** If Zuckerberg signs the lease before TheFacebook, Inc., legally exists, he is personally liable for the rent due.
- **The corporation is not liable on any contracts signed *before* incorporation unless it *adopts* the contract *after* incorporation.** What does **adoption** mean? Either the board of directors takes a formal vote saying, "We hereby adopt this contract," or they act as if they had adopted it. If TheFacebook uses the space Zuckerberg rented, it has adopted the contract. But Zuckerberg is still on the hook.

Novation
A new contract.

- **Even if the corporation adopts the contract, the promoter is still liable until the third party (in this case, the landlord) agrees to a *novation*.** A **novation** creates a *new* contract. Even if TheFacebook adopts the contract, Zuckerberg is still personally liable to the landlord until the landlord signs a new contract with him and TheFacebook explicitly stating that only the corporation is liable, not Zuckerberg.

Like many sets of rules, this one has an exception:

- **If it is clear that the parties did not intend the promoter to be liable, then he is released from liability once the corporation adopts the contract.** To protect himself, Zuckerberg would want the lease to state that TheFacebook is not yet formed but will be liable when it is formed, and that he is not personally liable for rental payments once TheFacebook adopts the contract.

EXAM Strategy

Question: Dr. Warfield hired Wolfe, a young carpenter, to build his house. A week or so after they signed the contract, Wolfe filed Articles of Incorporation for Wolfe Construction, Inc. Warfield made payments to the corporation. Unfortunately, the work on the house was shoddy—the architect said he did not know whether to blow up the house or try to salvage what was there. Warfield sued Wolfe and Wolfe Construction, Inc. for damages. Wolfe argued that if he was liable as a promoter, then the corporation must be absolved and that, conversely, if the corporation was held liable he, as an individual, must not be. Who is liable to Warfield? Does it matter if Wolfe signed the contract in his own name or in the name of the corporation?

Strategy: Wolfe's argument is wrong—Warfield does not have to choose between suing him individually or suing the corporation. He can certainly sue both.

Result: Wolfe is personally liable on any contract signed before the corporation is filed, no matter whose name is on the contract. The corporation is liable only if it adopts the contract. Did it do so here? The fact that the corporation cashed checks that were made out to it means that the corporation is also liable. So Warfield can sue both Wolfe and the corporation.

Defective Incorporation

A promoter is liable on contracts signed before the corporation exists. What happens, though, if the promoter makes some reasonable effort to incorporate but does not succeed? In these situations, the law can be reasonably tolerant. (Remember, however, that litigation is extremely painful and it is far, far better simply to comply with all the rules from the start.)

De Jure Corporation

"De jure" is Latin for "by law." **A *de jure* corporation means that the promoter has substantially complied with the requirements for incorporation but has made some minor error.** He has perhaps misspelled the name of the corporation's registered agent (more about the registered agent later). In this case, no one, not even the state, can challenge the validity of the corporation.

De Facto Corporation

"De facto" is Latin for "in fact." **A *de facto* corporation means that the promoter has made a good faith effort to incorporate and has actually used the corporation to conduct business.** In this case, the state can challenge the validity of the corporation, but a third party cannot. Suppose that Mark Zuckerberg fills out the incorporation form and files it, but the Secretary of State does not stamp it for weeks. In the meantime, Zuckerberg signs a lease for TheFacebook. In many states, no stamp means no corporation. Nonetheless, Zuckerberg has a *de facto* corporation because he made a reasonable effort to incorporate and has used the corporation to conduct business. The landlord cannot challenge the validity of the corporation and claim that Zuckerberg is personally liable on the lease. Only the corporation is liable.

Corporation by Estoppel

A corporation by estoppel means that, if a party enters into a contract *believing* in good faith that the corporation exists, he cannot later take advantage of the fact that it does not. Suppose that Zuckerberg's attorney tells him that TheFacebook, Inc., has been formed, but in fact he never even attempted to incorporate it. In the meantime, Zuckerberg buys many Apple computers in TheFacebook's name. Under the theory of corporation by estoppel, Zuckerberg is *not* personally liable even though the corporation does not exist. Both he and Apple thought he was buying on behalf of the corporation. Why should Apple receive a windfall, and why should Zuckerberg be penalized, simply because his lawyer made a mistake? This rule works both ways: If a bank loans money to TheFacebook, Inc., Zuckerberg cannot refuse to pay it back simply because TheFacebook does not yet exist. At the time Zuckerberg received the loan, he believed the corporation had been formed.

In the following case, a contract is so unclear, the courts have to step in. What is the proper legal result? Is that the most reasonable outcome?

You be the Judge

GS Petroleum, Inc. v. R and S Fuel, Inc.

2009 Del. Super. LEXIS 200
Superior Court of Delaware, 2009

Facts: On March 13, GS Petroleum (GS) signed an agreement to sell a Shell gas station to R and S Fuel, Inc. (Fuel). On April 2, Fuel opened a corporate bank account and began writing checks on it. On April 15, Fuel took possession of the Shell station. Later, it took out insurance in the company's name. Unfortunately, what Fuel did not do was pay the money it owed under the contract.

So far, this looks like just a breach of contract case. But there is one more fact that greatly complicates this simple picture: Fuel did not actually come into existence until March 27, two weeks after the contract was signed. The introduction to the contract stated that it was "entered by and between R and S Fuel, Inc., and GS Petroleum, Inc." The signature lines at the end looked like this:

Richard Simpson
R And S Fuel Inc.
Buyer
Susan Stamm and Richard Simpson

GS filed suit for $124,000 against the corporation but also personally against Richard Simpson and Susan Stamm. The two individuals filed a motion for summary judgment.

You Be the Judge: ***Were Simpson and Stamm personally liable for the debts of Fuel?***

Argument for GS: The corporation did not exist when the contract was signed, so someone else has to be liable. Simpson and Stamm were the promoters, their names appear on the contract, and Simpson actually signed it. No corporate title is attached to his name on the signature line, which indicates he was signing as an individual, not a corporate officer. And when Simpson signed the contract, he was acting as Stamm's agent. So she is liable, too.

The defendants argue that the business was a *de facto* corporation, but they need to read this textbook more carefully. To qualify, they must have made a good faith effort to comply with corporate law, but here they had not bothered to file the forms with the Secretary of State. That is not a good faith effort.

While they are reviewing the text, Simpson and Stamm should also note that even if Fuel adopted the contract, they are still liable until the parties sign a novation. That did not happen here. And no provision of the contract explicitly or impliedly released the two defendants.

To find Simpson and Stamm liable is the only fair result. Someone is going to be out a lot of money. It should be the people responsible for losing that money, not the innocent party who sold them a perfectly good business.

Argument for Simpson and Stamm: It is true that Simpson's signature line did not list a corporate title, but that was simply an oversight. He was clearly signing for the corporation. As for Stamm, she cannot be liable for an agreement she did not sign.

Promoters who sign an agreement on behalf of a corporation are only liable if the parties *intended* that result. GS entered into this agreement with a corporation. Note that the document states it is an agreement with just Fuel; not Fuel, Simpson, and Stamm. Everyone understood that to be the case. GS has not alleged that Fuel was a sham corporation. Even before the corporate documents were filed, Simpson and Stamm ran the business as a corporation. They opened a bank account in the company's name, they used only business checks, and they bought insurance in the corporate name. If GS wanted the two individuals to be liable, the document should have said so.

Also, R and S Fuel was a *de facto* corporation at the time the agreement was signed. Simpson and Stamm were in the process of organizing it, they were making a good faith effort, and they were using the corporation to conduct business. In the case of a *de facto* corporation, third parties such as GS have no right to challenge its validity.

Incorporation Process

The mechanics of incorporation are easy: simply download the form and mail or fax it to the Secretary of State for your state. But do not let this easy process fool you; the incorporation document needs to be completed with some care. The corporate charter defines the corporation, including everything from the company's name to the number of shares it will issue and the liability of its directors. States use different terms to refer to a charter; some call it the "articles of incorporation," others use "articles of organization," and still others say "certificate" instead of "articles." All of these terms mean the same thing. Similarly, some states use the term "shareholders," and others use "stockholders;" they are both the same.

There is no federal corporation code, which means that a company can incorporate only under state law, not federal law. No matter where a company actually does business, it may incorporate in any state. This decision is important because the organization must live by the laws of whichever state it chooses for incorporation. To encourage similarity among state corporation statutes, the American Bar Association drafted the Model Business Corporation Act as a guide. Many states do use the Act as a model, although Delaware does not. In discussing corporate law in this and the following chapters, we will give examples from both the Model Act and specific states, especially Delaware. Why Delaware? Despite its small size, it has a disproportionate influence on corporate law. More than half of all public companies are incorporated there, including 60 percent of Fortune 500 companies.

Where to Incorporate?

Traditionally, companies incorporated either in their home state or in Delaware. They typically must pay filing fees and franchise taxes in their state of incorporation, as well as in any state in which they do business. To avoid this double set of fees, a business that will be operating primarily in one state would probably select that state for incorporation rather than Delaware. But if a company is going to do business in several states, it might consider choosing Delaware.

Delaware has not always been a popular choice for corporations. In the early 1900s, New Jersey held the position that Delaware does today. When Woodrow Wilson became governor (on his way to the White House), he toughened New Jersey's laws. Looking for a state with a more hospitable environment, companies found one across the Delaware River. What is good for business is good for Delaware, too. Each year, it collects substantial filing fees and taxes from companies that, for the most part, conduct little business in the state.

Delaware offers corporations several advantages:

- *Laws that favor management.* Delaware laws offer flexibility. For example, if the shareholders want to take a vote in writing instead of holding a meeting, many other states require the vote to be unanimous; Delaware requires only a majority to agree. The Delaware legislature also tries to keep up to date by changing its code to reflect new developments in corporate law. For example, it was one of the first states to eliminate a rigid format for corporate charters.
- *An efficient court system.* Delaware has a special court (called "Chancery Court") that hears nothing but business cases and has judges who are experts in corporate law. In other states, judges who practiced in fields such as criminal law or divorce also hear corporate cases.[1] In an emergency involving, say, a hostile takeover, Delaware judges will hear cases and reach decisions on short notice. This preferential treatment is typically not available in other states.

[1]When Pennzoil sued Texaco in Texas over a breach of contract, the judge who tried the case was experienced in hearing divorce cases. Many lawyers felt that his ignorance of corporate matters contributed to the jury's Texas-sized verdict—$11 *billion*.

- *An established body of precedent.* Because so many businesses incorporate in the state, its courts hear a vast number of corporate cases, creating a large body of precedent. Thus lawyers feel they can more easily predict the outcome of a case in Delaware than in a state where few corporate disputes are tried.

The financial bonanza that Delaware realizes from its incorporation business has not gone unnoticed by other states. New York, Ohio, Pennsylvania, and, ironically, New Jersey have all modified their corporate laws to attract incorporation business. Large companies in the western part of the country often choose Nevada as their home state because of its attractive laws. Of course, management—not shareholders—chooses the state of incorporation and pays the state fees. Some commentators argue that states are so eager to attract corporate revenue that their laws unfairly favor management over shareholders. They refer to this competition as the "race to the bottom."[2] However, some recent studies indicate that, when a company reincorporates in Delaware, its stock price does not go down. Evidently, financial markets do not perceive shareholders to be at a disadvantage in Delaware.

Once a company has decided *where* to incorporate, the next step is to prepare and file the charter. The charter must always be filed with the Secretary of State; some jurisdictions also require that it be filed in a county office. Some states supply a form to be completed. Delaware and the Model Act require that certain information be included, but the incorporators can list it any way they want. The incorporators may also include some optional provisions.

Charter's Required Provisions

Name

The Model Act imposes two requirements in selecting a name. First, all corporations must use one of the following words in their name: "corporation," "incorporated," "company," or "limited." Delaware also accepts some additional terms, such as "association" or "institute." Both the Model Act and Delaware permit abbreviations (such as "inc." or "corp.") or equivalent terms in another language (such as "S.A.," which is the French abbreviation for corporation).

Second, under both the Model Act and Delaware law, a new corporate name must be different from that of any corporation that already exists in that state. If your name is Freddy du Pont, you cannot name your corporation "Freddy du Pont, Inc.," because Delaware already has a company named E. I. du Pont de Nemours and Company. It does not matter that Freddy du Pont is your real name or that the existing company is a large chemical business while you want to open a video arcade. The names are too similar. In addition, some states ban improper names. For example, Pennsylvania refused to accept "I Choose Hell Productions" because its statute prohibits names that "constitute blasphemy, profane cursing or swearing, or that profane the Lord's name." The state did accept ICH Productions. Zuckerberg chose "TheFacebook" because that was what Harvard students called their freshman directory.

What if you wake from a deep sleep late one night with the perfect corporate name in your head, but the charter is not quite ready for filling? In Delaware, you can reserve a name for 120 days for a fee of $75. That takes care of Delaware, but you know your corporation will soon be going national. How can you protect your name in other states? The Model Act also permits the advance registration of a corporate name. Alternatively, you can form a "nameholder" organization: a corporation that incurs minimum annual fees because it is inactive but does reserve its name.

[2]When Delaware passed its corporation law in 1899, the *American Law Review* attacked its pro-management bias as an effort by a "little community of truck-farmers and clam diggers ... determined to get her little, tiny, sweet, round, baby hand into the grab bag." Quoted in the *Economist* October 25, 2003, p. 55.

All this bother and expense discourage most start-ups from reserving their names nationwide. If they later expand into another state where someone else is already using their name, they either buy the name back or use a different name in that jurisdiction. The problem multiplies if they want to register their name overseas as well. When Steven Spielberg, Jeffrey Katzenberg, and David Geffen launched their Hollywood studio, DreamWorks SKG, they spent nearly $500,000 to clear rights to the name in 108 countries around the world. (Of course, that was a small drop in the $2 billion bucket they raised from investors.)

Address and Registered Agent

A company must have an official address in the state in which it is incorporated so that the Secretary of State knows where to contact it—and so that anyone who wants to sue the corporation can serve the complaint in the state. Since most companies incorporated in Delaware do not actually have an office there, they hire a registered agent to serve as their official presence in the state.

Incorporators

The incorporator signs the charter and delivers it to the Secretary of State for filing. The incorporator is not required to buy stock, nor does he necessarily have any future relationship with the company. Often, the lawyer who prepares the charter serves as incorporator. If no lawyer is involved, typically the promoter is also the incorporator. That is what happened with TheFacebook—Mark Zuckerberg served as the incorporator. The incorporator incurs liability only if he knows that something in the charter is not true when he signs it.

Purpose

The corporation is required to give its purpose for existence. In the 19th century, when corporations were a new concept, states thought it important to keep tight control over them. Under the ***ultra vires* doctrine**, a corporation cannot undertake any transaction unless its charter permits it. Corporate officers understandably chafed at this restriction. To avoid problems of *ultra vires,* most companies now use a very broad purpose clause such as TheFacebook's:

Ultra vires doctrine
A corporation cannot undertake a transaction unless permitted to do so by its charter.

> The purpose of the Corporation is to engage in any lawful act or activity for which corporations may be organized under the General Corporation Law of Delaware.

Essentially, the only way to violate this purpose clause is to commit an illegal act.

Stock

The charter must provide three items of information about the company's stock.

Par Value. The concept of par value was designed to protect investors. Originally, par value was supposed to be close to market price. A company could not issue stock at a price less than par, which meant that it could not sell to insiders at a sweetheart price well below market value. (Once the stock was *issued,* it could be *traded* at any price.) In modern times, par value does not relate to market value; it is usually some nominal figure such as 1¢ or $1 per share. Companies can dispense with the concept altogether and issue stock that has no par value. When making this decision, the company should check the state's filing fees because they may be based on the par value of the company's stock. TheFacebook stock has a par value of $0.0001 (one-hundredth of one cent) per share.

Number of Shares. Before stock can be sold, it must first be authorized in the charter. The corporation can authorize as many shares as the incorporators choose, but the more shares, the higher the filing fee. After incorporation, a company can add authorized shares by simply amending its charter and paying the additional fee. TheFacebook charter authorizes the creation of 10,000,000 shares.

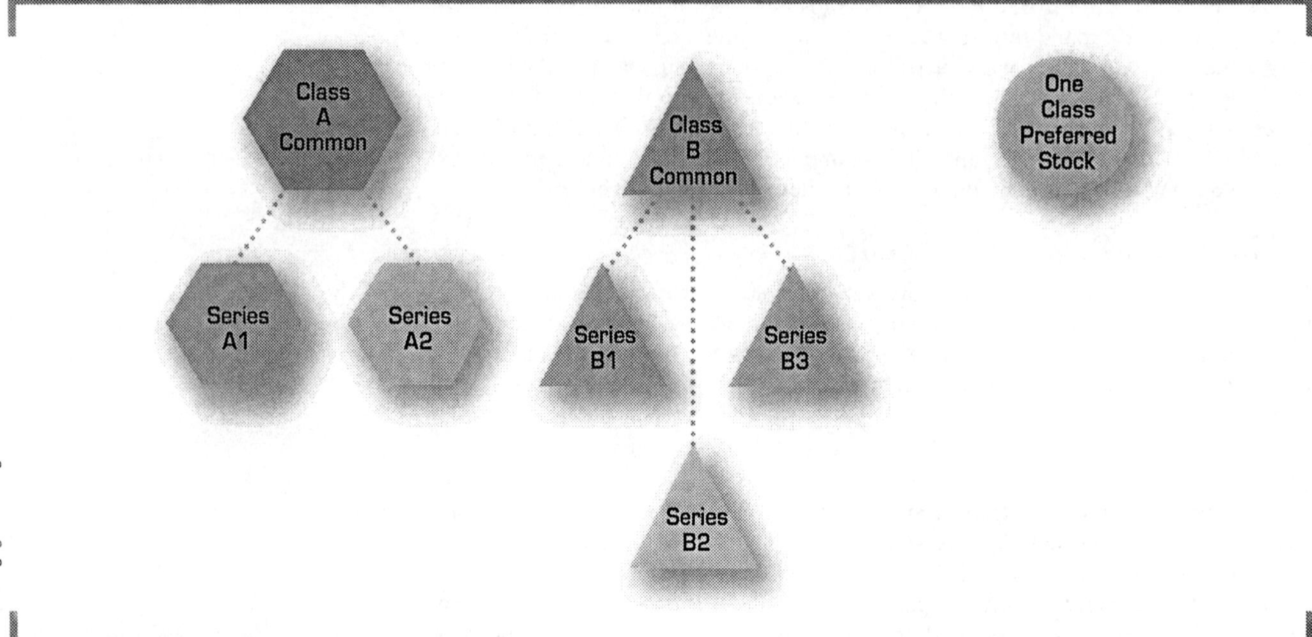

EXHIBIT 33.1

Authorized and unissued
Stock that has been authorized, but not yet sold.

Authorized and issued
Stock has been authorized and sold; another word for it is outstanding.

Treasury stock
Stock that a company has sold, but later bought back.

Stock that has been authorized but not yet sold is called **authorized and unissued**. Stock that has been sold is termed **authorized and issued** or **outstanding**. Stock that the company has sold but later bought back is **treasury stock**.

Classes and Series. Different shareholders often make different contributions to a company. Some may be involved in management, while others may simply contribute financially. Early investors may feel that they are entitled to more control than those who come along later (and who perhaps take less risk). Corporate structure can be infinitely flexible in defining the rights of these various shareholders. Stock can be divided into categories called **classes**, and these classes can be further divided into subcategories called **series**. All stock in a series has the same rights, and all series in a class are fundamentally the same, except for minor distinctions. For example, in a class of preferred stock, all shareholders may be entitled to a dividend, but the amount of the dividend may vary by series. Different classes of stock, however, may have very different rights—a class of preferred stock is different from a class of common stock. Exhibit 33.1 illustrates the concept of class and series. Defining the rights of a class or series of stock is like baking a cake—the stock can contain virtually any combination of the following ingredients (although the result may not be to everyone's taste):

- *Dividend rights.* The charter establishes whether the shareholder is entitled to dividends and, if so, in what amount. No matter what the charter says, the corporation may not pay dividends unless it is solvent, that is, unless it has enough assets to pay its debts.
- *Voting rights.* Shareholders are usually entitled to elect directors and vote on charter amendments, among other issues, but these rights can vary among different series and classes of stock. When Ford Motor Co. went public in 1956, it issued Class B common stock to members of the Ford family. This class of stock holds about 40 percent of the voting power and, thereby, effectively controls the company. Not surprisingly, the chairman of the company has often been named "Ford." TheFacebook recently amended its charter to create two classes of stock with different voting rights, presumably so that Zuckerberg can maintain control after the company goes public.

- *Liquidation rights.* The charter specifies the order in which classes of stockholders will be paid upon dissolution of the company. This provision is important if there are not enough assets to pay everyone.
- *Preemptive rights.* If a corporation later issues additional shares of its stock, the original shareholders will own a smaller percentage of the company. For example, if a company has 10 shareholders, each owning 1 share, and it later issues another 10 shares to others, each of the old shareholders will then own 5 percent of the company instead of 10 percent. To prevent this **dilution**, some companies grant preemptive rights: the old shareholders have the right to acquire enough new stock to prevent their share of the company from being diminished. In our example, each old shareholder would be entitled to buy enough new shares to keep their ownership at 10 percent. Of course, they are not required to buy this stock.
- *Conversion rights.* Some classes of stock may have the right to convert into shares of a different class. For example, if a company does not meet its financial projections, nonvoting stock may have the right to convert into voting stock.
- *Redemption rights.* Similarly, the shareholders of some classes of stock may have the right to force a company to buy their stock back if, for example, the company does not meet its financial goals.

These are the ingredients for any class or series of stock. Some stock comes prepackaged like a cake mix. "Preferred" and "common" stock are two classic types.

Preferred stock
The owners of preferred stock have preference on dividends and also, typically, in liquidation.

Owners of **preferred stock** have preference on dividends and also, typically, in liquidation. If a class of preferred stock is entitled to dividends, then it must receive its dividends before common stockholders are paid theirs. If holders of **cumulative preferred** stock miss their dividend one year, common shareholders cannot receive a dividend until the cumulative preferred shareholders have been paid all that they are owed, no matter how long that takes. Alternatively, holders of **non-cumulative preferred** stock lose an annual dividend for good if the company cannot afford it in the year it is due. When a company dissolves, preferred stockholders typically have the right to receive their share of corporate assets before common shareholders. Exhibit 33.2 illustrates the order of payment for dividends. Preferred stock can have any combination of other ingredients, such

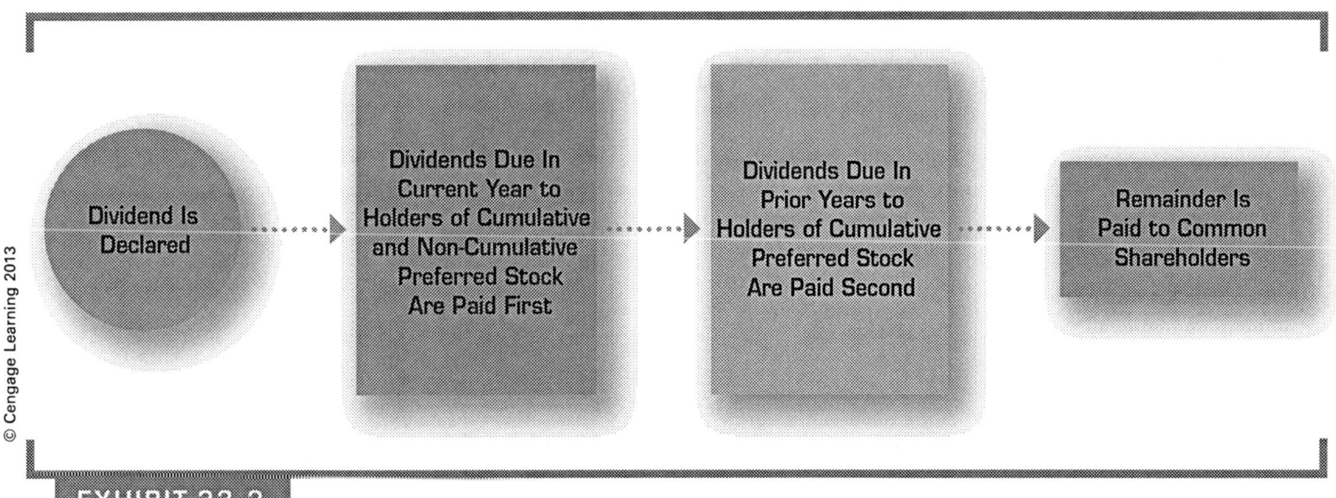

EXHIBIT 33.2

as preemptive rights or conversion rights. Sometimes preferred shareholders have voting rights, but usually they do not.

***Common stock* is last in line for any corporate payouts, including dividends and liquidation payments.** If the company is liquidated, creditors of the company and preferred shareholders are typically paid before common shareholders. But being a common shareholder is not all bad news—common shareholders often have most of the voting rights. They also have greater profit potential; preferred stock typically has a limit on the size of dividends, common does not. If the business does well, common stock will often increase in value faster than preferred stock.

Venture capitalists (professional investors who are in the business of financing companies) often choose a type of stock called **participating preferred stock**, which permits them to have their cake and eat it, too. Upon liquidation of the company, these shareholders are paid first, receiving whatever they paid for the stock plus accrued dividends. Then they are treated as if they had converted their preferred shares into common stock, so they get to share the rest of the proceeds with common shareholders.

Charter's Optional Provisions

Many corporations add optional provisions to their charters. Bear in mind, however, that once a provision is in the charter, it can be changed only by a vote of the shareholders and the filing of an amendment with the Secretary of State. This process can be cumbersome and expensive. Therefore, when in doubt, it is usually a good idea not to include extra provisions in the charter. Nonetheless, some provisions are so important that they belong there, despite the effort and expense required to change them.

Director Liability

Although incorporation protects shareholders against personal liability for the debts of the company, anyone involved in the management of the business can be personally liable for his own wrongdoing. For example, shareholders may sue directors for making an unprofitable decision. The potential liability in such a lawsuit is enormous. Even if the director is found not liable, the legal fees can be devastating.

Under most state statutes, a corporation may include in its charter a provision that protects directors from personal liability to the corporation or its shareholders for anything other than egregious misbehavior involving, for example, bad faith or intentional misconduct.[3] These provisions are called **exculpatory clauses**. TheFacebook charter has an exculpatory clause stating:

Exculpatory clause
A provision that protects directors from personal liability to the corporation and its shareholders for anything other than egregious misbehavior.

> To the fullest extent permitted by the Delaware General Corporation Law...a director of the Corporation shall not be personally liable to the Corporation or its stockholders for monetary damages for breach of fiduciary duty as a director.

Corporations also typically add an **indemnification** provision to their charter that requires the company to pay the legal fees of directors who are sued for any actions taken on behalf of the company. Without these protective provisions, companies would be unable to hire directors.

Indemnification
Requires a company to pay the legal fees of directors who are sued for actions taken on behalf of the company.

The following case illustrates the power of an exculpatory clause. Note that the directors are not liable even for acts of gross negligence.

[3]See, for example, 8 Del. C. §102(7).

Rodriguez v. Loudeye Corporation

2008 Wash. App. LEXIS 767
Court of Appeals of Washington, 2008

Facts: Loudeye Corporation provided digital music for cell phones and other consumer electronics. It was headquartered in Seattle, Washington, but incorporated in Delaware (where it did not have any offices). As permitted under Delaware law, Loudeye's charter had an exculpatory clause protecting directors from liability. Such provisions were unenforceable under Washington law.

Loudeye's directors decided to sell the company because it was not generating enough revenue to compete effectively. Nokia offered a price that was three times market value. After extensive negotiations with Nokia and an unsuccessful search for other buyers, Loudeye's board accepted Nokia's bid.

A Loudeye shareholder named Eli Rodriguez filed suit against five members of the board of directors, alleging that the directors had breached their fiduciary duties by failing to obtain the best price. He thought the board should have conducted a formal auction. He also alleged that the board had conflicts of interest and had approved the sale because they would receive special financial benefits (such as severance payments and stock options).

The Loudeye directors filed a motion to dismiss, alleging that the exculpatory clause in the company's charter protected them from liability. Rodriguez argued that Washington law should apply and, therefore, the clause was invalid. He also argued that, even if the exculpatory clause was valid, it did not apply in this case. The trial court granted the motion to dismiss and Rodriguez appealed.

Issues: ***Which state law applies to a company that is headquartered in Washington but incorporated in Delaware? Does the exculpatory clause in the Loudeye charter protect its directors from liability?***

Excerpts from Judge Agid's Decision: Shareholder claims involving a corporation's internal affairs are governed by the law of the state in which the corporation was incorporated. Thus, because Loudeye is a Delaware corporation, Delaware law applies here.

[T]o the extent these allegations describe gross negligence in the sale of the corporation, their conduct is not actionable. [O]nly if there are allegations establishing that the director's conduct is motivated by an actual intent to do harm, or occurs when directors consciously and intentionally disregard their responsibilities, and is conduct so far beyond the bounds of reasonable judgment that it seems essentially inexplicable on any ground other than bad faith [are the directors liable].

[A]s the directors point out, [that] situation typically is when the directors in the acquired corporation also have interests in the acquiring corporation or when directors seek to entrench themselves in their positions of control. But neither situation is present here. The complaint therefore fails to state a claim.

We affirm the trial court's dismissal of the complaint.

Cumulative Voting

For sheer drama, few corporate battles have exceeded the fight between the elephant, Gulf Oil, and the flea, Mesa Petroleum. When T. Boone Pickens, the CEO of Mesa, announced that Gulf Oil was badly managed, he was picking on the sixth-largest oil company in America. Pickens nominated himself to be Gulf's savior. His plan was to buy enough of the company's shares so that he could elect himself to the board of directors. Pickens's goal was possible only because Gulf was incorporated in Pennsylvania, a state that then had cumulative voting.

For sheer drama, few corporate battles have exceeded the fight between the elephant, Gulf Oil, and the flea, Mesa Petroleum.

At the time, Gulf Oil had 15 directors, all elected annually. Under a *regular* voting system, the 15 people who receive the most votes are awarded the seats. If Pickens owned one share, he could vote for as many as 15 *different* candidates, but he could not pool his votes; that is, he could not cast multiple votes for any one candidate. Thus, he could only vote for himself to be director once. To be sure of getting elected to the board, he would have to buy half of Gulf's shares, plus one. Gulf had 165 million shares outstanding, so Pickens would have to buy 82,500,001 shares. Once he had bought that many shares, he could elect *all* the directors because he would own a majority of the company's stock. As Gulf's stock was trading at around $40 per share, Pickens would have had to invest more than $3 billion ($3,300,000,040) to achieve his goal.

Under a cumulative voting system, however, Pickens is allowed to pool his shares and vote them all for the same person (in this case, himself). How many shares would Pickens have to own to elect himself to the board? This is the formula:

$$\text{Number of shares needed to elect one director} = \frac{\text{Number of shares outstanding}}{\text{Number of directors being elected} + 1} + 1$$

This is how the formula worked in Pickens's case, where x stands for the number of shares he needed to elect one director:

$$x = \frac{165,000,000}{15+1} + 1$$

$$x = 10,312,501$$

This 10 million shares is a lot less than the 82 million he needed under a regular voting system. At a price per share of $40, Pickens would have to invest roughly $400 million ($412,500,040) under a cumulative voting system, compared with $3 billion under a regular system.

In a desperate effort to prevent Pickens from being elected to its board of directors, Gulf called a special meeting of shareholders to change its state of incorporation from Pennsylvania to Delaware and eliminate cumulative voting. (Delaware and the Model Act both permit, but do not require, it.) For months, both sides ran full-page advertisements in newspapers across the country to persuade shareholders. Gulf spent $9 million and Mesa $8 million on the fight alone, not counting money spent buying Gulf shares. In the end, Gulf won the battle but lost the war. It won the shareholder vote by a small margin, but the company was so weakened by this fight that it sold out to Chevron Oil shortly thereafter. The fight so frightened other companies that many changed their state of organization to Delaware. Pennsylvania then changed its statue to be like Delaware's.

After Incorporation

Once the charter has been filed (and the filing fee paid), the corporation legally exists, but work is not done yet. The shareholders must still complete a few additional tasks.

Directors and Officers

Once the corporation is organized, the incorporators elect the first set of directors. Thereafter, shareholders elect directors. Under the Model Act, a corporation is required to have at least one director unless (1) *all* the shareholders sign an agreement that eliminates the board, or (2) the corporation has 50 or fewer shareholders. To elect directors, the shareholders may hold a meeting, or, in the more typical case for a small company, they elect directors by **written consent**. (In most states and under the Model Act, all the shareholders must sign, but in Delaware, a majority is sufficient.) A typical written consent looks like this:

Classic American Novels, Inc.
Written Consent

The undersigned shareholders of Classic American Novels, Inc., a corporation organized and existing under the General Corporation Law of the State of Wherever, hereby agree that the following action shall be taken with full force and effect as if voted at a validly called and held meeting of the shareholders of the corporation:

Agreed: That the following people are elected to serve as directors for one year, or until their successors have been duly elected and qualified:

Herman Melville
Louisa May Alcott
Mark Twain

Dated: ____________________ Signed: ________________________
Willa Cather

Dated: ____________________ Signed: ________________________
Nathaniel Hawthorne

Dated: ____________________ Signed: ________________________
Harriet Beecher Stowe

Once the incorporators or shareholders have chosen the directors, the directors must elect the officers of the corporation. They can use a consent form, if they wish. The Model Act is flexible. It simply requires a corporation to have whatever officers are described in the bylaws. The same person can hold more than one office. Exhibit 33.3 illustrates the election process in corporations.

The written consents and any records of actual meetings are kept in a **minute book**, which is the official record of the corporation. Entrepreneurs sometimes feel they are too busy to bother with all these details, but if a corporation is ever sold, the lawyers for the buyers will *insist* on a well-organized and complete minute book. In one case, a company that was seeking a $100,000 bank loan could not find all of its minutes. Many of its early shareholders and directors were not available to reauthorize prior deeds. In the end, the company had to merge itself into a newly created corporation so it could start fresh with a new set of corporate records. The company spent $10,000 on this task, a large chunk out of the $100,000 loan.

Minute book
A book that contains a summary of a company's official actions.

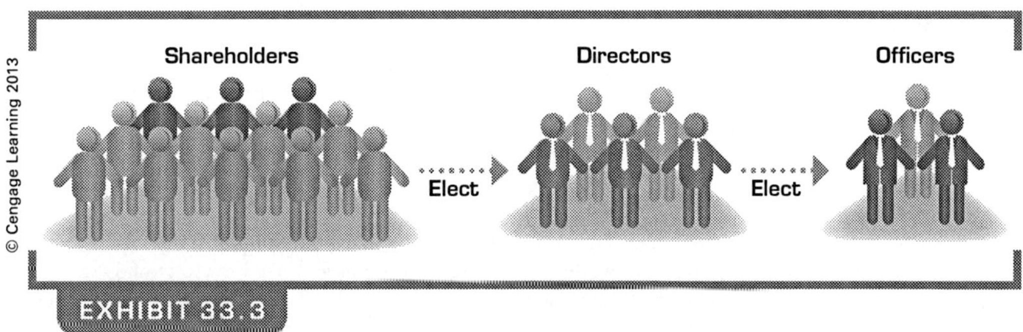

EXHIBIT 33.3

Bylaws

Bylaws
A document that specifies the organizational rules of a corporation or other organization, such as the date of the annual meeting and the required number of directors.

Quorum
The percentage of stock that must be represented for a meeting to count.

The **bylaws** list all the "housekeeping" details for the corporation. For example, bylaws set the date of the annual shareholders' meeting, define what a **quorum** is (i.e., what percentage of stock must be represented for a meeting to count), indicate how many directors there will be, give titles to officers, fix the procedure for calling a special meeting of the shareholders or directors, and establish the fiscal (i.e., tax) year of the corporation. When there is a choice, it is usually better to place provisions in the bylaws rather than the charter, because the bylaws are easier to change. Under the Model Act, directors can amend the bylaws without calling a meeting of the shareholders or paying a filing fee. TheFacebook charter provides that "....the Board of Directors of the Corporation is expressly authorized to make, amend, or repeal Bylaws of the Corporation."

The shareholders can always override the directors if they want, but they rarely do. In the following case, the directors' ignorance of company bylaws led to disaster.

In Re Bigmar

2002 Del. Ch. LEXIS 45
Court of Chancery, Delaware, 2002

Facts: Bigmar was a Delaware corporation that manufactured and marketed pharmaceuticals in Europe. While trying to raise additional capital, the company's founder, John Tramontana, met Cynthia May. She lied to him about her education, wealth, and connections in the investment community. Unfortunately, he believed her. The upshot was that May became Bigmar's president and a director of the company. She soon took control of the company's financial records and refused to give Tramontana any information (always a bad sign).[4] When Bigmar ran out of money, Tramontana sent May an email asking for her resignation. She did not respond. (Also a bad sign.)

The company was in desperate financial shape, but Tramontana managed to find a bank willing to buy $1 million of Bigmar stock. He called a special meeting of the board of directors to approve the sale of shares and to fire May. The meeting was to take place by telephone. To establish a quorum necessary for the meeting to be valid, at least five of the nine directors had to take part. May and her three allies on the board refused to participate.

Tramontana testified that, at the appointed time, he met with two directors in his office. They used a speaker feature on a cell phone that Tramontana borrowed from Danilo Graticola to call two other directors, one of whom was in Heathrow Airport in London. The five directors unanimously resolved to issue the stock to the bank. The meeting then adjourned so that they could consult counsel. It was reconvened the next day, at which time they voted to fire May.

The following day, the bank transferred $1 million to Bigmar. Tramontana instructed the company's transfer agent to send stock certificates to the bank, but May contradicted his order. Tramontana and May went to court to determine if the director's meeting was valid and the bank entitled to the shares.

Issue: ***Was the meeting of the Bigmar board of directors valid?***

Excerpts from Judge Jacobs's Decision: Ms. May attacks the validity of the meeting(s) [claiming that] no meeting at which a quorum of directors was present ever took place.

There is evidence that the meeting(s) did occur. Minutes of the meetings were prepared, and all but one of the Tramontana directors gave sworn testimony that the meeting(s) took place exactly as the minutes recite. Ordinarily that would be sufficient, but this is not an ordinary case, for several reasons.

First, the minutes were prepared by counsel, who was not present at the meetings and who simply reduced to writing what Mr. Tramontana told him had occurred. Second, there is no independent documentation or testimony of any third party witness that corroborates the directors'

[4]She did, however, send him this email: I wish for GOd's sake that you would GROW [UP] just a little...you've F the banking up here in Sweden so I can't get the money that I made [arrangements] for...damn idiot...take a shower and clean your ears out...you can't follow a straight line without having your ego and little hissy fits...Get off the playground...before the big boys beat you up...

testimony. Moreover, any notes taken at the meeting(s) were destroyed. Further, many of the telephone records whose production was requested were not produced, and the records that were produced either fail to corroborate the Tramontana directors' testimony,[5] or those documents are inconsistent with that testimony.[6]

Third, for the directors' testimony to be accepted, the Court would have to "buy into" a scenario that (to put it charitably) is most improbable. Although Mr. Tramontana had a speaker phone in his office, he testified that he decided to conduct the board meeting on Mr. Graticola's borrowed cell phone. His explanation for that unusual decision was that Mr. Graticola had described his new cell phone's technology in glowing terms and Mr. Tramontana elected to use the telephone to ingratiate his company with Graticola. [T]he story does have some plausibility, however slight. But even that minimal plausibility vanishes when one is told that the same identical scenario occurred a second time, at the adjourned meeting. I find this scenario too implausible for even a gullible factfinder to swallow. Accordingly, the Court is unable to determine that those directors' meetings were validly convened and conducted.

Although the analysis could stop here, that would leave the Court (and perhaps a reader of this Opinion) with a sense of dissatisfaction because Mr. Tramontana's testimony leaves unanswered questions. In purely human terms, this issue was most difficult and perplexing for the Court.

It is plausible, and the available evidence does indicate, that Mr. Tramontana attempted to assemble all of his colleagues for a telephonic meeting. [But one director] was unavailable, as he was en route from London to Ireland at that time. Because a quorum required the attendance of five directors, [this director's] unavailability meant that the telephonic meeting failed for lack of a quorum. Mr. Tramontana believed, nonetheless, that the problem could be solved by obtaining from himself and his colleagues' individual written consent resolutions taking the actions recited in the minutes. Unfortunately (and unbeknownst to Mr. Tramontana), Bigmar's by-laws required that any director action by written consent must be unanimous. [When] Mr. Tramontana learned of that unanimity requirement, [he] decided to [say] that a quorum of five directors was present and that a board meeting was held.

I am persuaded that [Mr. Tramontana and his colleagues acted] in the good-faith belief that unless the issuance of the shares to the Bank was upheld, the Company would fall into the hands of Ms. May, who was incapable of saving the Company. I think it plausible that they believed that at worst, they failed to observe a highly technical legal requirement that, on balance, was too insignificant to justify the ruination of the Company.

The principles of corporate governance, such as those violated here, exist precisely because those procedures enable courts and parties to distinguish between acts that lawfully bind the corporation and its constituents, from those that do not. The directors may have believed in good faith that they had no alternative but to testify as they did, but good faith is not sufficient to validate a procedurally invalid proceeding.

Shareholder Agreements

The shareholders of a start-up company often work together intensively. If a shareholder sells her stock to someone who does not share the same vision, conflict is inevitable. To avoid this situation, shareholders of start-ups often sign a shareholder agreement granting a right of first refusal on the company's stock. In a typical agreement, if a shareholder wants to sell, she must first offer the stock to the company at the same price that the outsider has offered. If, after 30 days, the company has not agreed to buy the stock, she must then offer it to the other shareholders. Only if they also refuse to buy it within 30 days can she then sell it to an outsider at the same price that she offered to the company and shareholders.

[5][The] cell phone bills for the [director who is supposed to have received a call in the London airport] do not show any incoming calls to him at Heathrow Airport at 3:00 p.m., London time, which is when the meeting is said to have started. Since [his] cell phone provider was located in Ireland where he lived, [this director] would have incurred a roaming charge for any calls received outside of Ireland, and the roaming charge would have been reflected on his cell phone bill.

[6]For example, Mr. Tramontana's telephone records show that he made an 11-minute telephone call to Mr. Graticola's cell phone number at 7:12 p.m.—a time that Mr. Tramontana claimed to have had Mr. Graticola's cell phone in his possession.

Similarly, if a shareholder dies, his estate may be required to offer the stock to the company or other shareholders. In the case of death, it is more difficult to determine the market value of the stock, so the shareholder agreement often provides a formula for making this determination.

Sometimes shareholder agreements focus not on who owns the company but how their stock is voted. For example, Craig O. McCaw was willing to sell a majority interest in Cellular One to Affiliated Publications, but he was not willing to give up control of the company. After all, he had single-handedly built it into the largest cell phone company in the United States. His solution? McCaw and Affiliated entered into a shareholder agreement requiring Affiliated to vote its stock in Cellular One as McCaw directed. Affiliated trusted McCaw's business acumen enough to want him to continue running the company even though he was only a minority shareholder. This same goal can be achieved by means of a so-called voting trust.

Issuing Debt

Most start-up companies begin with some combination of equity and debt. Equity (i.e., stock) is described in the charter; debt is not. Authorizing debt is often one of the first steps a new company takes. There are several types of debt:

Bonds
Long-term secured debt.

- **Bonds** are long-term debt secured by some of the company's assets. If the company is unable to pay the debt, creditors have a right to specific assets, such as accounts receivable or inventory.

Debentures
Long-term unsecured debt.

- **Debentures** are long-term *unsecured* debt. If the company cannot meet its obligations, the debenture holders are paid after bondholders, but before stockholders.

Notes
When issued by a company, short-term debt, typically payable within five years.

- **Notes** are short-term debt, typically payable within five years. They may be either secured or unsecured.

Foreign Corporations

A company is called a *domestic* corporation in the state where it incorporates and a *foreign* corporation everywhere else.

Ned has sworn that he will never again suffer through a bitter Chicago winter. No, he is not relocating; he has invented a new fabric that looks like fur. It is better than real fur, though, because it breathes, repels water, and is washable. He knows that his business will soon be a national success.

Ned, like many entrepreneurs before him, incorporates Fabulous Fake Furs, Inc. (FFF), in Delaware. He is still, however, living in Chicago (where he now *adores* the winter). Company headquarters are down the street from his condominium. The main manufacturing facility is in Texas, with warehouses in Minnesota and New York. A sales staff calls on all the major department stores and online merchants across the country.

Ned has obligations to the state of Delaware because he incorporated there—he must pay taxes and annual fees. But what about the other states where he is doing business? Someone had to pay to build the roads and educate the workforce in these states. Must he contribute, too? The states certainly think so. They require a foreign corporation that is doing business within their borders to register with them and obtain a "certificate of authority." This registration process is called **qualifying to do business**.

Qualifying to do business
Registering a corporation in a state in which it is not organized but in which it has an ongoing presence.

What constitutes "doing business"? **Opening an office or establishing any other ongoing presence counts as doing business.** Clearly, FFF must register in Illinois, Texas, Minnesota, and New York because it has a permanent presence in these states. Typically, the following activities do *not* count as doing business: holding meetings, opening a bank account, soliciting sales orders, or any isolated transaction. If FFF's directors hold a meeting in Alaska, Ned attends a trade show in Wisconsin, or a sales rep takes an order at a store in California, these activities do not constitute doing business, and FFF does not have to register in these states.

To qualify, a company must file corporate documents with the state, list a registered agent, and pay annual fees and taxes on income generated in that jurisdiction. As a general rule, of course, companies would prefer not to register. Some states fine any companies they catch doing business without registering. Under the Model Act, a company that is doing business without qualifying cannot bring a lawsuit in that state until it registers (and pays back fees, taxes, and penalties). But note that, if the company is not actually doing business, then it may file suit without qualifying first. And whether or not it has qualified, a company can always *defend* against a lawsuit.

EXAM Strategy

Question: You are about to form a corporation. What do you have to do before filling out the form? Which provisions are boilerplate and, therefore, do not require special effort on your part?

Strategy: Review the description of required and optional charter provisions.

Result: Before filling out the form, you need to choose a name and check to make sure it is available. If you are incorporating someplace where you do not have an office, you will also have to hire a registered agent. You do not have to decide the purpose of the corporation; standard boilerplate works here. Unless you will have outside investors from the beginning, you do not have to think a lot about your capital structure—that is, the number and par value of your shares. Just authorize as many shares as you can for the base filing fee, and choose a nominal par value. It makes sense to add an exculpatory clause to protect your directors from liability, especially if you are going to be one. There is no need for cumulative voting at this stage.

DEATH OF THE CORPORATION

Sometimes, business ideas are not successful and the corporation fails. This death can be voluntary (the shareholders elect to terminate the corporation) or forced (by court order). Sometimes, a court takes a step that is much more damaging to shareholders than simply dissolving the corporation—it removes the shareholders' limited liability.

Piercing the Corporate Veil

One of the major purposes of a corporation is to protect its owners—the shareholders—from personal liability for the debts of the organization. Sometimes, however, a court will **pierce the corporate veil**; that is, the court will hold shareholders personally liable for the debts of the corporation. Courts generally pierce a corporate veil in four circumstances:

Pierce the corporate veil
A court holds shareholders personally liable for the debts of the corporation.

- *Failure to observe formalities.* If an organization does not act like a corporation, it will not be treated like one. It must, for example, hold required shareholders' and directors' meetings (or sign consents), keep a minute book as a record of these meetings, and make all the required state filings. Even a corporation with only one shareholder must comply with these formalities. Sole shareholders usually just sign a written consent in lieu of a meeting. In addition, as we saw in the *GS Petroleum* case, officers must be careful to sign all corporate documents with a corporate title, not as an individual. Otherwise, creditors may well be in doubt about whether they were dealing with an individual or a corporation. An officer should sign like this:

Classic American Novels, Inc.
By: Stephen Crane
Stephen Crane, President
If he signs simply "Stephen Crane," creditors may successfully claim that he is personally liable.

- *Commingling of assets*. Nothing makes a court more willing to pierce a corporate veil than evidence that shareholders have mixed their assets with those of the corporation. Sometimes, for example, shareholders use corporate assets to pay their personal debts or even mix corporate and personal funds in one bank account. If shareholders commingle assets, it is genuinely difficult for creditors to determine which assets belong to whom. This confusion is generally resolved in favor of the creditors—*all* assets are deemed to belong to the corporation.
- *Inadequate capitalization*. If the founders of a corporation do not raise enough capital (either through debt or equity) to give the business a fighting chance of paying its debts, courts may require shareholders to pay corporate obligations. Therefore, if the corporation does not have sufficient capital, it needs to buy insurance, particularly to protect against tort liability. Judges are likelier to hold shareholders liable if the alternative is to send an injured tort victim away empty-handed. For example, Oriental Fireworks Co. had hundreds of thousands of dollars in annual sales but only $13,000 in assets. The company did not bother to obtain any liability insurance, keep a minute book, or defend lawsuits. There was no need because the company had no money. But then a court pierced the corporate veil and found the owner of the company personally liable.[7]
- *Fraud*. Corporations cannot be used to shelter fraud. Imagine that a con artist forms a corporation entitled Brooklyn Bridge, Inc. He then sells shares in the organization by convincing "investors," aka "victims," that the company really does own the famous New York landmark. If he is caught, the victims can go after his personal assets, even though the fraud was committed in the name of a corporation.

The following case is a good example of when a court should pierce the corporate veil.

If the owner of this amusement park fails to purchase adequate insurance, its shareholders may be personally liable.

[7] *Rice v. Oriental Fireworks Co.*, 75 Or. App. 627, 707 P.2d 1250, 1985 Ore. App. LEXIS 3928.

Brooks v. Becker

2005 Va. Cir. LEXIS 13
Circuit Court of Fairfax County, Virginia, 2005

Facts: Ronald Becker was the sole shareholder, officer, and director of Becker Interiors. Becker and his partner, Robert LaPointe, used approximately $300,000 of Becker Interiors' funds to renovate their residence, pay their personal credit card bills, and invest in another company of which Becker was president. Becker sold a corporate car for $73,700 and deposited those funds into his personal account, along with the corporation's income tax refund check of $12,850.

Becker Interiors supervised the major renovation of a house in McLean, Virginia. The company hired Stephen Brooks as a subcontractor on the project. When the company refused to pay Brooks, he filed suit, winning a judgment against the company for $54,597.09. But it turned out that Becker Interiors had no assets.

Brooks then sued Ronald Becker in an attempt to pierce the corporate veil and hold Becker personally liable for the debts of the corporation.

Issues: ***Can Brooks pierce the corporate veil? Is Becker personally liable for the debts of the corporation?***

Excerpts from Judge Roush's Decision: The decision to ignore the separate existence of a corporate entity and impose personal liability upon shareholders for debts of the corporation is an extraordinary act to be taken only when necessary to promote justice. Disregarding the corporate entity is usually warranted only under the extraordinary circumstances where: the shareholder sought to be held personally liable has controlled or used the corporation to evade a personal obligation, to perpetrate fraud or a crime, to commit an injustice, or to gain an unfair advantage. Piercing the corporate veil is justified when the unity of interest and ownership is such that the separate personalities of the corporation and the individual no longer exist and to adhere to that separateness would work an injustice.

In this case, the evidence convinces the court that the extraordinary remedy of piercing the corporate veil should be granted. Becker knowingly violated his duties as an officer, director, and shareholder of Becker Interiors and treated the corporation's funds as his personal piggy bank. His testimony that the corporate expenditures on his personal residence were a legitimate business expense because he wanted to use the residence as a showcase of his work was simply not credible. Nor did the court believe Becker's testimony that he commingled his personal funds with the corporation's funds on the advice of his accountant. The court found more credible Becker's later testimony that his accountant was "mystified" by his comingling of funds between his personal and corporate accounts.

Accordingly, the court will enter judgment against Becker in the amount of $54,597.09.

EXAM Strategy

Question: Jose is an employee and shareholder of Birdsong, a company that sells farm equipment. Jose shows Marta how to use the hay baler she has just bought from the company. He also gives her an instructional pamphlet that Birdsong had prepared. Unfortunately, Jose's advice is wrong, and so is the pamphlet's. Marta is injured while using the baler. It turns out that Birdsong's charter was revoked for failure to make the required annual filings with the Arkansas Secretary of State. In all other ways, Birdsong operated as a corporation. Is Birdsong liable to Marta? Is Jose personally liable to her?

Strategy: In theory, Jose could be liable as a shareholder because the charter of the corporation had been revoked or if the corporate veil was pierced. In addition, he could be personally liable for his own wrongdoing.

Result: Birdsong is liable for its carelessness in preparing the pamphlet. Although Birdsong was not technically a corporation, it has operated as one. Therefore, under the theory of corporation by estoppel, Jose is not liable. Nor has Birdsong done anything to warrant its veil being pierced. Jose is, however, liable for his own negligence. Therefore, he is liable for the bad advice he gave Marta.

Termination

Terminating a corporation is a three-step process:

- *Vote.* The directors recommend to the shareholders that the corporation be dissolved, and a majority of the shareholders agree.
- *Filing.* The corporation files "Articles of Dissolution" with the Secretary of State.
- *Winding up.* The officers of the corporation pay its debts and distribute the remaining property to shareholders. When the winding up is completed, the corporation ceases to exist.

The Secretary of State may dissolve a corporation that violates state law by, for example, failing to pay the required annual fees. Indeed, many corporations, particularly small ones, do not bother with the formal dissolution process. They simply cease paying their annual fees and let the Secretary of State act. A court may dissolve a corporation if it is insolvent or if its directors and shareholders cannot resolve conflict over how the corporation should be managed. The court will then appoint a receiver to oversee the winding up.

Chapter Conclusion

Virtually every businessperson will, at some point, work for a corporation or own shares in one. Indeed, corporations are so important that we devote three chapters to them. Although they are an exceedingly useful form of organization, they are also exceedingly formal. State corporation codes contain precise rules that must be followed to the letter. To do otherwise is to court disaster.

Exam Review

1. **PROMOTERS** Promoters are personally liable for contracts they sign before the corporation is formed unless the corporation and the third party agree to a novation. (p. 816)

EXAM Strategy

Question: Ajouelo signed an employment contract with Wilkerson. The contract stated: "Whatever company, partnership, or corporation that Wilkerson may form for the purpose of manufacturing shall succeed Wilkerson and exercise the rights and assume all of Wilkerson's obligations as fixed by this contract." Two months later, Wilkerson formed Auto-Soler Co. Ajouelo entered into a new contract with Auto-Soler that provided that the company was liable for Wilkerson's obligations under the old contract. Neither Wilkerson nor the company ever paid Ajouelo. He sued Wilkerson personally. Does Wilkerson have any obligations to Ajouelo?

Strategy: A promoter is not liable for a contract he signed on behalf of a yet-to-be-formed corporation if the third party (in this case, Wilkinson) agrees to a novation. (See the "Result" at the end of this section.)

2. **STATE OF INCORPORATION** Companies generally incorporate in the state in which they will be doing business. However, if they intend to operate in several states, they may choose to incorporate in a jurisdiction known for its favorable corporate laws, such as Delaware or Nevada. (pp. 816–817)

3. **THE CHARTER**

Required Provisions A corporate charter must generally include the company's name, address, registered agent, purpose, and a description of its stock. The charter must be signed by at least one incorporator. (pp. 820–824)
Optional Provisions A company's charter may include a number of optional provisions, such as cumulative voting and indemnification for officers and directors. (pp. 824–826)

EXAM Strategy

Question: Does par value matter? Did it ever?

Strategy: There are a lot of terms in this chapter, but it is a good idea to remember what they mean because you are likely to hear them again in your life as a businessperson. (See the "Result" at the end of this section.)

Question: At this writing, TheFacebook, Inc. is estimated to have 2.2 billion shares outstanding and four directors. Without cumulative voting, how many shares would you have to purchase to be sure of electing yourself to the board? If the company's charter required cumulative voting, how many shares would you have to buy to achieve this goal? What if there were 15 directors?

Strategy: The formula is

$$\text{Number of shares needed to elect one director} = \frac{\text{Number of shares outstanding}}{\text{Number of directors being elected}+1} + 1$$

(See the "Result" at the end of this section.)

4. **FOREIGN CORPORATION** A corporation must register in every state in which it is doing business. (pp. 830–831)

5. **PIERCING THE CORPORATE VEIL** A court may, under certain circumstances, pierce the corporate veil and hold shareholders personally liable for the debts of the corporation. (pp. 831–834)

6. **TERMINATION** Termination of a corporation is a three-step process requiring a shareholder vote, the filing of "Articles of Dissolution," and the winding up of the enterprise's business. (p. 834)

1. Result: Wilkerson may have had an ethical obligation to Ajouelo but not a legal one. The court held that the second contract was a novation, which ended Wilkerson's obligations under the first contract.

3. Result: *First question:* The original purpose of par value was to protect shareholders from unscrupulous managers who wanted to issue stock at below market value. Now, it has no purpose other than as the basis for state filing fees. The only issue is that you want to set it low enough that it does not trigger a higher-than-necessary fee.
Second question: Without cumulative voting, you would have to buy 1 share more than 1.1 billion shares. With four directors, you would have to buy 1 share more than 440 million. With 15 directors, you would have to buy 1 share more than 137.5 million.

MULTIPLE-CHOICE QUESTIONS

1. **CPA QUESTION** Generally, a corporation's articles of incorporation must include all of the following **except** the:
   (a) Name of the corporation's registered agent
   (b) Name of each incorporator
   (c) Number of authorized shares
   (d) Quorum requirements

2. **CPA QUESTION** Destiny Manufacturing, Inc., is incorporated under the laws of Nevada. Its principal place of business is in California, and it has permanent sales offices in several other states. Under the circumstances, which of the following is correct?
   (a) California may validly demand that Destiny incorporate under the laws of the state of California.
   (b) Destiny must obtain a certificate of authority to transact business in California and the other states in which it does business.
   (c) Destiny is a foreign corporation in California, but *not* in the other states.
   (d) California may prevent Destiny from operating as a corporation if the laws of California differ regarding organization and conduct of the corporation's internal affairs.

3. **CPA QUESTION** A corporate stockholder is entitled to which of the following rights?
   (a) Elect officers
   (b) Receive annual dividends
   (c) Approve dissolution
   (d) Prevent corporate borrowing

4. Participating preferred stockholders:
   (a) only receive payment after other preferred shareholders have been paid
   (b) only receive payment after common shareholders have been paid
   (c) are treated like both a preferred shareholder and a common shareholder
   (d) receive all their payments before all other shareholders

5. Debentures are:
   (a) long-term secured debt
   (b) short-term secured debt
   (c) long-term unsecured debt
   (d) short-term unsecured debt

6. If the terms of a company's charter and bylaws conflict, which governs?
   (a) The charter governs.
   (b) The bylaw governs.
   (c) They are both invalid.
   (d) Shareholders must vote to determine which is valid.

Essay Questions

1. In the *GS Petroleum* case earlier in this chapter, what should the signature line have looked like?

2. Michael incorporated Erin Homes, Inc., to manufacture mobile homes. He issued himself a stock certificate for 100 shares for which he made no payment. He and his wife served as officers and directors of the organization, but, during the eight years of its existence, the corporation held only one meeting. Erin always had its own checking account, and all proceeds from the sales of mobile homes were deposited there. It filed federal income tax returns each year using its own federal identification number. John and Thelma paid $17,500 to purchase a mobile home from Erin, but the company never delivered it to them. John and Thelma sued Erin Homes and Michael, individually. Should the court "pierce the corporate veil" and hold Michael personally liable?

3. The Resolution Trust Corp. (RTC) sued the directors of the Commonwealth Savings Association seeking to recover from them personally $200 million that the bank lost in bad real estate loans. The directors approved the loans after state and federal regulatory agencies had issued reports criticizing the bank's loan practices. The directors failed to implement policies and procedures to prevent problems with the loan portfolio and failed to monitor loan officers adequately. There was no evidence that the directors knowingly committed illegal acts or acts outside their authority. Under Texas law, the RTC could recover for the directors' negligence only if their acts were *ultra vires.* Were these acts *ultra vires?*

4. Waste Management, Inc., the country's largest waste hauler, changed its name to WMX Technologies, Inc. Similarly, U.S. Steel changed its moniker to USX Corp. and

American Airlines became AMR Corp. What legal steps would be necessary for these companies to protect their new corporate names?

5. Dickens, Inc. is a bookstore incorporated in Nevada. From its warehouse in Montana, it ships books to all 50 states. The company's owner lives in New York, and its web designer lives in California. Where is Dickens a domestic corporation? Where must it qualify to do business?

Discussion Questions

1. In the *Loudeye* case, the court ruled that if the charter has an exculpatory clause, directors are not liable unless they are grossly negligent, motivated by an actual intent to do harm, or intentionally disregard their responsibilities. Is that a reasonable standard?

2. **ETHICS** In the *Bigmar* case, the court clearly believed that the directors had lied on the witness stand. Should the directors have been charged with perjury? Did they do the right thing when they lied on the stand to protect their company from the evil Ms. May?

3. Angelica is planning to start a home security business in McGehee, Arkansas. She plans to start modestly but hopes to expand her business within 5 years to neighboring towns and, perhaps, within 10 years to neighboring states. Her inclination is to incorporate her business in Delaware. Is her inclination correct?

4. States compete for lucrative filing fees by passing corporate statutes that favor management. One proposed solution to this problem would be a federal system of corporate registration. Is this a good idea? What are the impediments to such as system?

5. Ford Motor Co. and TheFacebook, Inc. have both created dual classes of stock so that the founders can continue to control their company even after it goes public. Should corporate laws permit this? Should some shareholders be more equal than others? If the founders want to control a company, why shouldn't they buy enough regular stock to do so?

CHAPTER 34

© Evan Meyer/Shutterstock.com

Corporate Management

Rick says: Bob and I own a bar and restaurant in Nevada. It's a pretty good business, but what really brings in the bucks is the keno game in the lounge. Keno is like bingo, only you get to choose the numbers you play. Here is the weird thing—there is absolutely *no* skill involved, but people just *love* to play the game. It is a license to print money. It's as if the folks just want to hand us their cash. We have each pulled in 4 *million* big ones since we bought this business.

You'd think that amount of money would be enough to get Bob's attention, but he acts like the business just runs itself. He can barely be bothered to show up. So I've set up a meeting with city officials, hoping to convince them to put the keno contract up for bid. I'll get the contract in my own name and cut Bob out. He's nothing but dead weight.

Bob says: Whine, whine, whine. Something must be going right with our business; we've made four million bucks, for Pete's sake. It's true that I don't spend as much time at the restaurant as Rick does, but then again, my girlfriend isn't the "manager" there. What Rick's doing there doesn't really count as work. Also, any time he asks me to do something, I'm all over it. I don't know what he's so hot and bothered about.

It's true that I don't spend as much time at the restaurant as Rick does, but then again, my girlfriend isn't the "manager" there.

What obligations does Rick have to the business he owns with Bob? In a similar case later in the chapter—*Anderson v. Bellino*—the court ruled that Rick could not take the keno contract away from their jointly owned corporation. Read on to see why.

Stakeholder
Anyone who is affected by the activities of a corporation, such as employees, customers, creditors, suppliers, shareholders, and neighbors.

Corporations are complicated creatures with many different interest groups: shareholders, officers, directors, and **stakeholders**, such as the community, employees, suppliers, creditors, and customers. Business life was not always so complicated. Before the Industrial Revolution in the 18th and 19th centuries, a business owner typically supplied both capital and management. However, the cash needs of the great manufacturing enterprises spawned by the Industrial Revolution were larger than any small group of individuals could supply. To find capital, firms sought outside investors, who often had neither the knowledge nor the desire to manage the enterprise. Investors without management skills complemented managers without capital. (Throughout these corporation chapters, the term "manager" includes both directors and officers.)

Modern businesses still have the same vast need for capital and the same division between managers and investors. Because shareholders are too numerous and too uninformed to manage the enterprises they own, they elect directors to manage for them. The directors set policy and then appoint officers to implement corporate goals. The Model Business Corporation Act describes the directors' role thus: "All corporate powers shall be exercised by or under the authority of, and the business and affairs of the corporation managed by or under the direction of, its board of directors…."[1]

Directors have the authority to manage the corporate business, but they also have important responsibilities to shareholders and stakeholders. However, the interests of these various groups often conflict. In the 2000s, the world faced two financial crises which were caused, in part, by corporate executives who engaged in highly risky activities that left them wealthy and their shareholders broke. Because of abuses by managers that in some cases included outright fraud, Congress and other regulators have tried to rebalance the power among managers, shareholders, and stakeholders. Part of their goal has been to enhance shareholder oversight of the companies they own. These two chapters are about this balance of rights and responsibilities.

Managers Versus Shareholders: The Fundamental Conflict

The following newspaper excerpt illustrates the natural conflict between managers and shareholders:

> The mood here in reaction to the sale of *The Los Angeles Times* to the Tribune Company may have been best summed up by Mark H. Willes, the company's chairman, when he left the board meeting that approved the transaction late Sunday evening. Mr. Willes burst into tears and wept openly, according to several people who saw him. The sale of the paper and its parent, the Times Mirror Company, would make Mr. Willes an immensely wealthy man. And it would earn tens of thousands of dollars, in some instances more, for each of the reporters, editors and many other employees of the Times Mirror Company who hold stock and stock options.
>
> But for many people in this city, both in *The Los Angeles Times* newsroom and outside, the deal felt humiliating, they said, as if something precious had been stolen away. "There is a feeling that yesterday, a part of this city's soul was *The Los Angeles Times*," said Geoffrey Cowan, dean of the Annenberg School of Communications at the University of Southern California. "I'm not sure how much that is true tomorrow." He added, "There is a loss of identity."

---

[1]A committee of the American Bar Association drafted the Model Business Corporation Act to serve as a guideline for states to use when enacting a corporate code. More than half the states have now adopted some version of it. The corporate statutes of Delaware also serve as a model for other states.

Within the newsroom, many people expressed anger that the Chandler family, which has controlled the company for decades, had sold the company to an outsider, in spite of assurances in recent years that it never would. "The Chandler family long ago lost interest in running a newspaper and they're just interested in the profits," said Ken Reich, a columnist who has worked at *The Los Angeles Times* for 35 years.[2]

This episode illustrates the ongoing debate over corporate governance in America. Managers serve at least three masters: themselves, shareholders, and other stakeholders. These masters have conflicting goals:

- **Managers** want two things: first, to keep their jobs, and second, to build an institution that will survive them. Mark Willes, chairman of *The Los Angeles Times,* wept when his company was sold despite the immense wealth he received from the sale. To him, the job was what mattered.
- **Shareholders** want a high stock price, *right now,* not five years from now. As owners, the members of the Chandler family cared more about their own profits than they did about the newspaper and its important role in the life of the city.
- **Stakeholders**, those who work for the *Los Angeles Times,* read it, sell it ink, or own the food shop across the street from its plant want the newspaper to stay in business. The speaker of the California State Assembly lamented the sale because the paper had been a booster for the whole city of Los Angeles. (Generally, managers are not included in the stakeholder category because their interests may be different from those of lower-level employees.)

Did the Chandler family have a legal or ethical obligation to consider the impact of this sale on the managers and stakeholders? Or should everyone simply accept that shareholders—and their profits—come first? Would it have been fair to shareholders if the managers had vetoed the sale? These are the difficult issues of corporate governance that companies face. Only one thing is clear: managers cannot please all the stakeholders all the time.

The courts have generally held that **managers have a fiduciary duty to act in the best interests of the corporation's shareholders**. Since shareholders are primarily concerned about their return on investment, managers must *maximize shareholder value,* which means providing shareholders with the highest possible financial return from dividends and stock price. However, reality is more complicated than this simple rule indicates. It is often difficult to determine which strategy will best maximize shareholder value. And what about *stakeholders*? Must managers totally ignore their interests? In the following landmark case, the court explicitly permits the board to consider the interests of stakeholders over those of some shareholders. Commentators have described this case as "the most innovative and promising case in our corporation law."

[2]James Sterngold, "In Los Angeles, Tears and a Feeling of Loss," p. C16. From *The New York Times,* March 14, 2000.

Landmark Case

Unocal Corp. v. Mesa Petroleum Co.

493 A.2d 946, 1985 Del. LEXIS 482
Supreme Court of Delaware, 1985

Facts: Mesa Petroleum Co. offered to purchase 64 million shares of Unocal's stock at a cash price of $54 per share. Upon merger of the two companies, Mesa planned to exchange the remaining Unocal shares for "junk bonds" that Mesa (but no one else, including the court) valued at $54 per share. Unocal's investment bankers advised the board of directors that the Mesa proposal was wholly inadequate and that an offer of over $60 per share would have been reasonable. The board rejected the Mesa offer and then made its own competing offer of $72 per share to all shareholders except Mesa. (This type of offer is called a "selective exchange offer.") The board's offer effectively preempted Mesa because no shareholder would accept the $54 Mesa offer when the $72 Unocal offer was also available. The Delaware court issued a preliminary injunction against Unocal's offer unless it included Mesa.

Issues: ***Could Unocal make an offer to buy stock from all shareholders except Mesa? In making this offer, did Unocal have the right to consider the interests of other stakeholders?***

Excerpts from Justice Moore's Decision: In the board's exercise of corporate power to forestall a takeover bid, our analysis begins with the basic principle that corporate directors have a fiduciary duty to act in the best interests of the corporation's stockholders. The restriction placed upon a selective stock repurchase is that the directors may not have acted solely or primarily out of a desire to perpetuate themselves in office. This entails an analysis by the directors of the nature of the takeover bid and its effect on the corporate enterprise. Examples of such concerns may include inadequacy of the price offered, nature and timing of the offer, questions of illegality, the impact on "constituencies" other than shareholders (i.e., creditors, customers, employees, and perhaps even the community generally), the risk of nonconsummation, and the quality of securities being offered in the exchange. While not a controlling factor, it also seems to us that a board may reasonably consider the basic stockholder interests at stake, including those of short term speculators, whose actions may have fueled the coercive aspect of the offer at the expense of the long-term investor.

In adopting the selective exchange offer, the board stated that its objective was either to defeat the inadequate Mesa offer or, should the offer still succeed, provide its stockholders with $72 a share. We find that both purposes are valid. However, such efforts would have been thwarted by Mesa's participation in the exchange offer. First, if Mesa could tender its shares, Unocal would effectively be subsidizing the former's continuing effort to buy Unocal stock at $54 per share. Second, Mesa could not, by definition, fit within the class of shareholders being protected from its own coercive and inadequate tender offer. Thus, we are satisfied that the selective exchange offer is reasonably related to the threats posed.

The decision of the Court of Chancery is therefore *reversed*, and the preliminary injunction is *vacated*.

Devil's Advocate In this case, the court says that the board cannot act with the primary goal of keeping itself in office. One could argue, however, that that is precisely what the board did. It *said* that it was concerned about stakeholders but, conveniently, stakeholder interests coincided precisely with its own. When forced to choose between shareholders, who in fact *own the company*, and stakeholders, why should the board be allowed to choose stakeholders? This choice seems particularly tainted given the board's conflict of interest.

A number of states have adopted statutes that codify the *Unocal* decision. These statutes permit directors, when making a decision, to consider, for example, "both the short-term and long-term best interests of the corporation, taking into account, and weighing as the directors deem appropriate, the effects thereof on the corporation's shareholders and the other corporate constituent groups...."[3] The next section looks more closely at directors' responsibilities to their various constituencies.

Resolving the Conflict: The Business Judgment Rule

Officers and directors have a fiduciary duty to act in the best interests of their stockholders, but under the **business judgment rule,** the courts allow managers great leeway in carrying out this responsibility. The business judgment rule is a common law concept that has achieved national acceptance. It is a fundamental principle of corporate law. To be protected by the business judgment rule, managers must act in good faith:

Duty of Loyalty	1. Without a conflict of interest
Duty of Care	2. With the care that an ordinarily prudent person would take in a similar situation, and 3. In a manner they reasonably believe to be in the best interests of the corporation.

The business judgment rule is two shields in one: it protects both the manager and her decision. **If a manager has complied with the rule, a court will not hold her personally liable for any harm her decision has caused the company, nor will the court rescind her decision.** If the manager violates the business judgment rule, then she has the burden of proving that her decision was entirely fair to the shareholders. If it was not entirely fair, she may be held personally liable and the decision can be rescinded.

The business judgment rule accomplishes three goals:

- *It permits directors to do their job.* Business is risky. No one can guarantee perfect decision making all the time. If directors were afraid they would be liable for every decision that led to a loss, they would never make a decision, or at least not a risky one.
- *It keeps judges out of corporate management.* Shareholders would generally prefer that their investments be overseen by experienced corporate managers, not judges. Without the business judgment rule, judges would be tempted, if not required, to second-guess managers' decisions.
- *It encourages directors to serve.* No one in his right mind would serve as a director if he knew that every decision was open to attack in the courtroom. Even if the company pays the legal bills, who wants to spend years in litigation?

Analysis of the business judgment rule is typically divided into two parts. The obligation of a manager to act without a conflict of interest is called the **duty of loyalty**. The requirements that a manager act with care and in the best interests of the corporation are referred to as the **duty of care**.

Duty of loyalty
The obligation of a manager to act without a conflict of interest.

Duty of care
The requirement that a manager act with care and in the best interests of the corporation.

Duty of Loyalty

The duty of loyalty prohibits managers from making a decision that benefits them at the expense of the corporation.

[3] Indiana Code §23-1-35-1.

Self-Dealing

Self-dealing means that a manager makes a decision benefiting either himself or another company with which he has a relationship. While working at the Blue Moon restaurant, Zeke signs a contract on behalf of the restaurant to purchase bread from Rising Sun Bakery. Unbeknownst to anyone at Blue Moon, he is a part owner of Rising Sun. Zeke has engaged in self-dealing, which is a violation of the duty of loyalty.

Once a manager engages in self-dealing, the business judgment rule no longer applies. This does not mean the manager is automatically liable to the corporation or that his decision is automatically void. All it means is that the court will no longer presume that the transaction was acceptable. Instead, the court will scrutinize the deal more carefully. A self-dealing transaction is valid in any one of the following situations:

- **The disinterested members of the board of directors approve the transaction.** Disinterested directors are those who do not themselves benefit from the transaction.
- **The disinterested shareholders approve it.** The transaction is valid if the shareholders who do not benefit from it are willing to approve it.
- **The transaction was entirely fair to the corporation.** In determining fairness, the courts will consider whether the price was reasonable and the impact of the transaction on the corporation.

Exhibit 34.1 illustrates the rules on self-dealing.

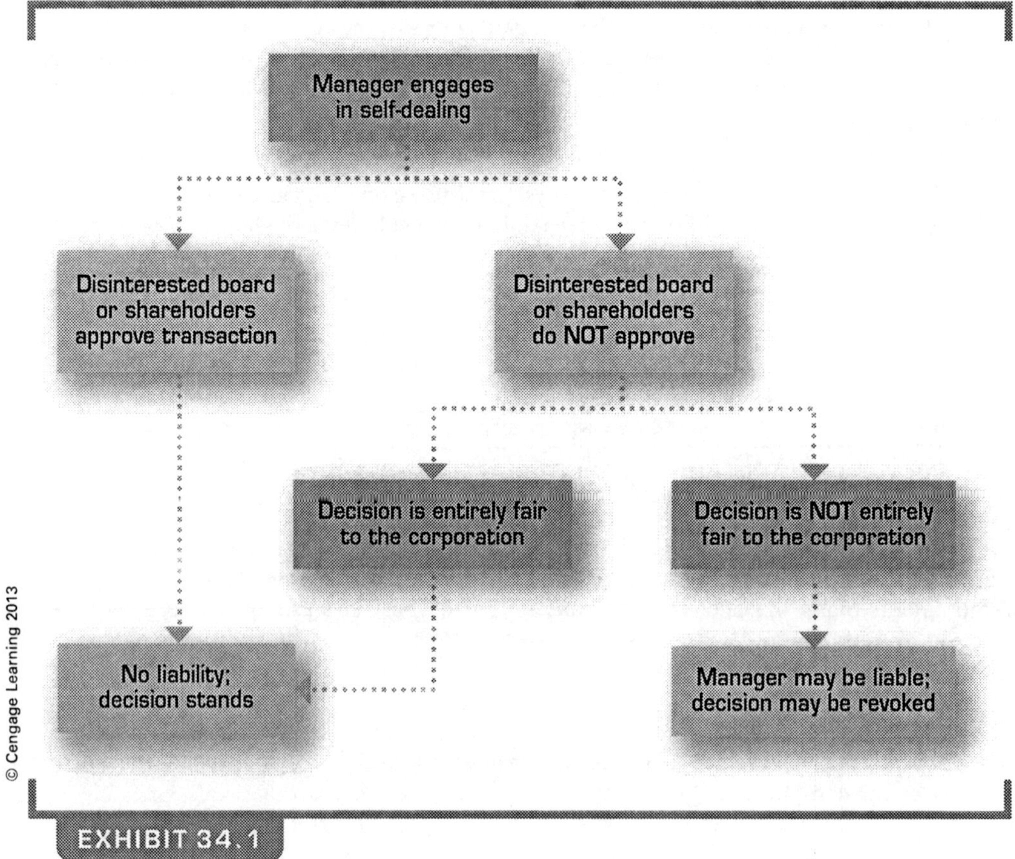

EXHIBIT 34.1

Corporate officers, especially in family businesses, sometimes forget that they do not have the right to do whatever they want. The following case illustrates the business judgment rule and also the enduring principle that litigation is a very sad method for resolving family disputes.

Lippman v. Shaffer

15 Misc. 3d 705; 836 N.Y.S.2d 766; 2006 N.Y. Misc. LEXIS 4212
Supreme Court of New York, 2006

Facts: Years ago, Harry Lippman purchased Despatch Industries, Inc., which manufactured hardware for cabinets. His son, James, worked for the company. Later, James's son, Wade, and son-in-law, Alan Shaffer, also went on the company payroll. Both young men signed identical employment contracts. After Wade and James had a falling out, Wade resigned from the company. The Despatch board agreed to pay $1.3 million to both Wade and Alan. Company tax returns referred to these as "severance" payments, although Alan continued to work for the company and receive a salary.

Wade filed suit against Alan and Despatch, alleging that the payments to Alan were improper and should be returned. The defendants argued that the payments were protected by the business judgment rule. Wade filed a motion for summary judgment.

Issue: ***Were the payments to Alan protected by the business judgment rule?***

Excerpts from Judge Fisher's Decision: Generally, the actions of directors are protected by the business judgment rule, which bars judicial inquiry into actions of corporate directors taken in good faith and in the exercise of honest judgment in the lawful and legitimate furtherance of corporate purposes. As such, the business judgment rule prevents a court from second-guessing corporate decision making.

[T]he business judgment rule is not applicable when the directors have an interest in the challenged transaction. Directors are self-interested in a challenged transaction where they will receive a direct financial benefit from the transaction which is different from the benefit to shareholders generally.

The court's first inquiry is whether the business judgment rule applies. Here, it does not. Plaintiffs have established that there was no contractual or other legitimate reason to give [Alan] the equivalent of the so-called severance payments made to Wade because the severance terms of [Alan's] employment contract covering such payments were not then triggered. To avoid liability, the board will have to demonstrate entire fairness by presenting evidence of the manner by which it otherwise discharged all of its fiduciary duties.

The difficulty in defendants' position lies in the undisputed fact that no events had transpired to trigger any severance payments to [Alan] under the agreements. [Alan] states the following rationale for the payments: "Whatever Wade got, I would get. Whatever I got, Wade would get." Inasmuch as severance payments were contractually due to Wade, but not to [Alan, his] payments may only be described as a gift of corporate assets and therefore he got more than Wade got, to the tune of $ 1.3 million.

[Wade's motion for summary judgment is granted.]

Corporate Opportunity

The self-dealing rules prevent managers from *forcing* their companies into unfair deals. The corporate opportunity doctrine is the reverse—it prohibits managers from *excluding* their company from favorable deals. **Managers are in violation of the corporate opportunity doctrine if they compete against the corporation without its consent.**

Long ago, Charles Guth was president of Loft, Inc., which operated a chain of candy stores. These stores sold Coca-Cola. Guth purchased the Pepsi-Cola Company personally, without offering the opportunity to Loft. The Delaware court found that Guth had violated the corporate opportunity doctrine and ordered him to transfer all his shares in PepsiCo to Loft.[4] That was in 1939 and Pepsi-Cola was bankrupt; today, PepsiCo, Inc., is worth more than $100 billion.

[4]*Guth v. Loft,* 5 A.2d 503, 23 Del. Ch. 255, 1939 Del. LEXIS 13 (Del. 1939).

> **If a manager suspects that company officers would be displeased to learn about his new sideline, that is an indication he is skating on thin ice.**

If a manager first offers an opportunity to disinterested directors or shareholders, and they turn it down, the manager then has the right to take advantage of the opportunity himself. (Remember that "disinterested directors or shareholders" are those who do not personally benefit from the transaction.) Sometimes, however, either through oversight or ignorance, managers do not seek permission in advance. To avoid violating the corporate opportunity doctrine, the manager must show after the fact that the company would have been unable to benefit from the opportunity. For example, Cellular Information Systems, Inc., had just emerged from bankruptcy proceedings when one of its directors learned that a cell-phone license covering part of Michigan was for sale. The director purchased the license himself, and the company sued. The court found the director not liable because the company could not have afforded to purchase the license itself.[5]

A manager will often find it difficult to prove that the company could not have used an opportunity itself. However, these disputes are easy to avoid—the manager must simply ask permission first. Certainly, if a manager suspects that company officers would be displeased to learn about his new sideline, that is an indication that he is skating on thin ice.

In the following case, the manager felt that he had a good reason for taking a corporate opportunity. Unfortunately, the court disagreed.

Anderson v. Bellino

265 Neb. 577, 658 N.W.2d 645, 2003 Neb. LEXIS 49
Supreme Court of Nebraska, 2003

Facts: Richard Bellino and Robert Anderson formed LaVista Lottery, Inc. (Lottery) to operate a restaurant, lounge, and keno game in LaVista, Nevada. They each owned 50 percent of the stock of Lottery, and both were officers and directors.

During the next nine years, Lottery grossed more than $100 million. Bellino and Anderson each received over $4 million in salary and dividends. Although Bellino and Anderson were both involved in Lottery, Bellino spent more time, in part because of his personal relationship with Lottery's lounge manager. During this period, Bellino did not complain to Anderson about his lack of involvement in Lottery, and Anderson never refused to do anything that Bellino asked him to do.

Resentful of Anderson's work ethic, Bellino set up a meeting with LaVista's city administrator. Until that meeting, the city had been satisfied with Lottery's performance. But after the meeting, the administrator recommended to the city council that the keno contract be put up for competitive bid. Bellino incorporated LaVista Keno, Inc. (Keno) to bid on the contract.

Bellino wrote to Anderson complaining that he (Bellino) was doing too much work for Lottery at too little pay. (Evidently, $4 million is not as much as it used to be.) Therefore, Bellino intended to resign from Lottery and bid on the city contract himself. Anderson offered to do more work or whatever Bellino wanted, but Bellino refused any effort at reconciliation. He then submitted a bid on behalf of Keno. At the time he submitted the bid, Bellino was still an officer of Lottery, as well as a director and a 50 percent shareholder. Anderson also bid on the contract on behalf of Lottery. The city awarded the new contract to Keno.

Anderson and Lottery filed suit against Bellino and Keno, alleging that they had usurped a corporate opportunity. The lower court found for Anderson and Lottery. It ordered Bellino to pay $644,992.63 but provided that Bellino could receive a credit of $172,514.63 against the judgment if Bellino transferred the stock of Keno to Lottery and persuaded the city to relicense the keno contract from Keno to Lottery.

---

[5] *Broz v. Cellular Information Systems, Inc.*, 673 A.2d 148, 1996 Del. LEXIS 105.

Issues: ***Did Bellino usurp a corporate opportunity? Is he liable to Lottery?***

Excerpts from Justice Miller-Lerman's Decision: Bellino and Keno claim that if a corporate opportunity existed, it was limited to the opportunity to bid for the keno contract, that Bellino did nothing to impede Lottery from bidding for the keno contract by merely submitting a competing bid, and that, therefore, Bellino did not usurp a corporate opportunity.

Contrary to the arguments asserted by Bellino and Keno, the corporate opportunity was not the right to bid; the bidding process was merely the "preliminary step" by which Lottery sought to acquire the opportunity embodied in the award of the keno contract. The facts thus establish that the keno contract was a corporate opportunity for Lottery.

When discussing a corporate officer or director's fiduciary duty to the corporation, we have stated:

> Although an officer or a director of a corporation is not necessarily precluded from entering into a separate business because it is in competition with the corporation, his fiduciary relationship to the corporation and its stockholders is such that if he does so he must prove that he did so in good faith and did not act in such a manner as to cause or contribute to the injury or damage of the corporation, or deprive it of business; if he fails in this proof, there has been a breach of that fiduciary trust or relationship.

The evidence is uncontroverted that Bellino's successful bid for the LaVista keno contract deprived Lottery of its only source of business. Bellino, through Keno, should not have competed with Lottery for the LaVista keno contract.

We affirm the district court's order.

EXAM Strategy

Question: Otto signed a lease with Landlord on a storefront in Georgetown, in Washington, D.C. He convinced his nephew Nick to start a furniture store in the space. Otto and Nick formed a corporation to operate the store. Otto owned 51 percent and Nick 49 percent of the company's stock. Otto signed a lease between himself and the store at a price that was 20 percent higher than the rent Otto was paying Landlord. Otto purchased a warehouse and then rented it to the corporation at a fair market rent. Nick sued, alleging that the two leases were not valid. Were they?

Strategy: Under the business judgment rule, the courts will not second-guess a corporate action. However, if a manager engages in self-dealing, the business judgment rule does not apply.

Result: Otto violated the duty of loyalty twice. The lease for the storefront was self-dealing—it directly benefited him. When he purchased the warehouse, he took a corporate opportunity that he should have offered first to the company. He is personally liable for any damages to the corporation. The company also has the right to cancel both leases and to purchase the warehouse from him.

Duty of Care

In addition to the *duty of loyalty*, managers also owe a *duty of care.* **The duty of care requires officers and directors to act in the best interests of the corporation and to use the same care that an ordinarily prudent person would in a similar situation.** An ordinarily prudent person would have a rational business purpose, avoid illegal behavior, and make informed decisions. Officers and directors of corporations must do no less.

Rational Business Purpose

Courts generally agree in principle that directors and officers are liable to shareholders for decisions that have no rational business purpose. In practice, however, these same courts have been extremely supportive of managerial decisions, looking hard to find some justification. For years, the Chicago Cubs baseball team was the only major American professional sports team whose home field did not have lights. Cubs fans could only take themselves out to the ball game during the day. A shareholder sued on the grounds that the Cubs' revenues were peanuts and Cracker Jack compared with those generated by other teams that played at night. The Cubs defended their decision on the grounds that a large night crowd would cause the neighborhood to deteriorate, depressing the value of Wrigley Field (which was not owned by the Cubs). The court rooted for the home team and found that the Cubs' excuse was a "rational purpose" and a legitimate exercise of the business judgment rule.[6]

If a decision does not have a rational business purpose, the managers are liable and the decision can be rescinded. If a court decides that there is a rational business purpose, both the manager and the decision are protected.

Legality

Courts are generally unsympathetic to managers who engage in illegal behavior, even if their goal is to help the company. For example, the managing director of an amusement park in New York used corporate funds to purchase the silence of people who threatened to complain that the park was illegally operating on Sunday. The court ordered the director to repay the money he had spent on bribes, even though the company had earned large profits on Sundays.[7]

Informed Decision

Generally, courts will protect managers who make an *informed* decision, even if the decision ultimately harms the company. Making an informed decision means carefully investigating the facts. However, even if the decision is uninformed, the directors will not be held liable if the decision was entirely fair to the shareholders. The board of Technicolor, Inc., agreed to sell the film processing company, knowing little about the terms of the deal and without seeking other bidders. The directors simply knew that the sales price was higher than the appraised value of the company. Five years later, the buyer sold the company for a $750 million profit. The former shareholders sued, alleging that the directors had made an uninformed decision. The state supreme court held that, because the directors had been so careless, they had to prove that the price and the process by which it had been determined were both fair.[8]

Exhibit 34.2 provides an overview of the duty of care.

---

[6] *Shlensky v. Wrigley*, 95 Ill. App. 2d 173, 237 N.E.2d 776, 1968 Ill. App. LEXIS 1107 (Ill. App. Ct. 1968).

[7] *Roth v. Robertson*, 64 Misc. 343, 118 N.Y.S. 351, 1909 N.Y. Misc. LEXIS 279 (N.Y. 1909).

[8] The state supreme court sent the case back to the lower court to determine whether the deal had been fair to the shareholders. *Cede & Co., Inc. v. Technicolor, Inc.*, 634 A.2d 345, 1993 Del. LEXIS 398 (Del. 1993). The lower court ultimately decided that the transaction had indeed been fair. *Cinerama, Inc. v. Technicolor, Inc.*, 663 A.2d 1134, 1994 Del. Ch. LEXIS 178 (Del. Ch. 1994). The state supreme court, however, disagreeing with the valuation method used by the trial court, reversed that decision and remanded it once again to the trial court for further proceedings. *Cede & Co. v. Technicolor*, 684A.2d 289, 1996 Del. LEXIS 386 (Del. 1996). Yet again, in 2000, the Delaware Supreme Court (somewhat apologetically) overruled the trial court and returned the case for another trial. *Cede & Co. v. Technicolor, Inc.*, 758 A.2d 485, 2000 Del. LEXIS 283 (Del. 2000). The results from this trial were again appealed. Finally, in 2005, the Supreme Court of Delaware upheld most of the trial court rulings and remanded with simple instructions to change the interest rate it used to calculate damages. *Cede & Co. v. Technicolor, Inc.*, 2005 Del. LEXIS 177 (Del. 2005). The original sale of stock took place in 1983. This has been the longest case in the 200-year history of the Delaware Court of Chancery.

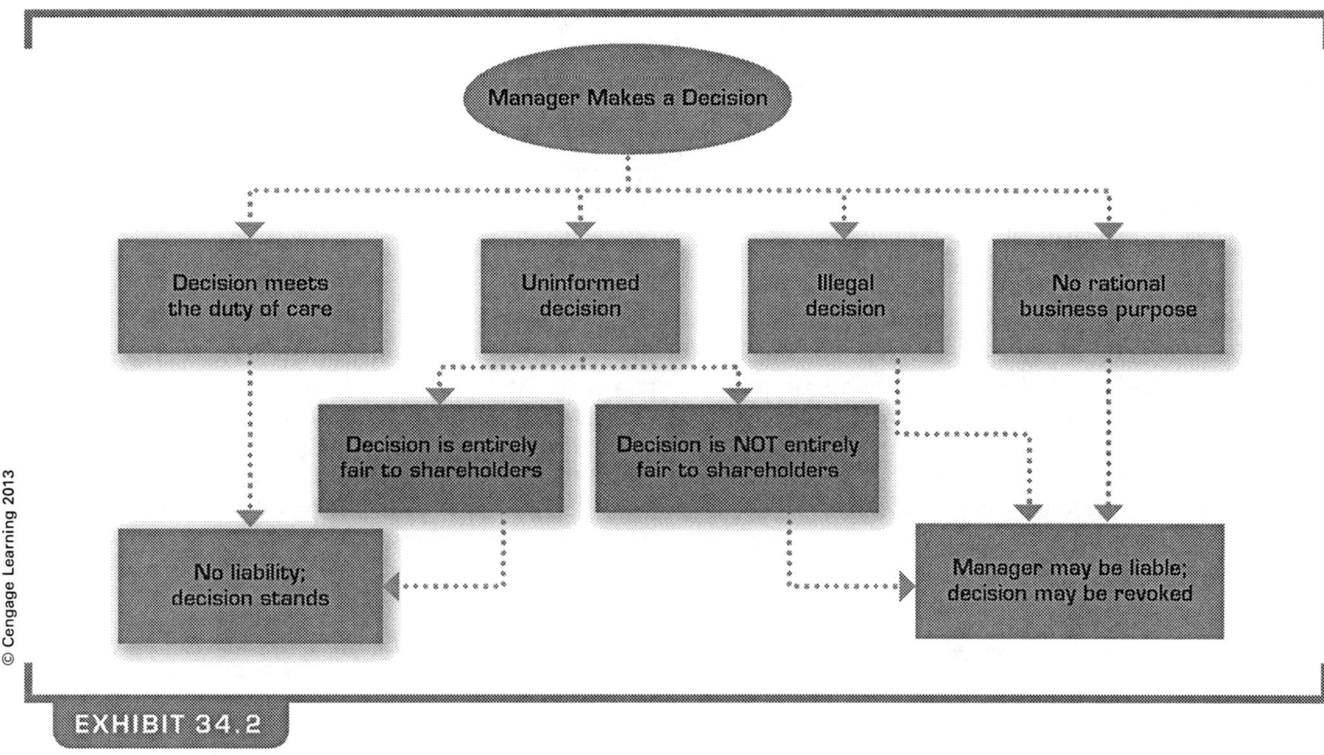

EXHIBIT 34.2

In the following case, the board of directors failed to hold meetings. Were their decisions informed?

RSL Communications v. Bildirici

2006 U.S. Dist. LEXIS 67548
United States District Court for the Southern District of New York, 2006

Facts: Ronald S. Lauder founded RSL Ltd., a multinational telecommunications corporation. RSL Plc was a subsidiary of RSL Ltd. The subsidiary began by issuing $1.4 billion of bonds. A few years later, in July, Lauder provided it with a $100 million line of credit. The company's board of directors did not hold a meeting to approve the Lauder loan. In August, RSL Plc drew down $25 million from that loan. The following March, the company's directors held their first board meeting in a year. Five days later, RSL Plc filed for bankruptcy.

The issue before the court is whether the members of the board of directors of RSL Plc breached their duty of care to the company when they failed to hold a board meeting for a year at a time when the company was in a precarious financial position.

Issue: ***Did the directors of RCL Plc violate their duty of care to the corporation?***

Excerpts from Judge Karas's Decision: Under New York law, a director shall perform his duties as a director, in good faith and with that degree of care which an ordinarily prudent person in a like position would use under similar circumstances. It is well settled that the duty of due care requires that a director's decision be made on the basis of reasonable diligence in gathering and considering material information.

When faced with allegations of misconduct, a defendant director may raise the business judgment rule as an absolute defense. [U]nder Delaware law the business judgment rule applies even where conclusions were stupid or irrational, as long as the process employed was either rational or employed in a *good faith* effort to advance corporate interests.

Although the standard of review for business judgments is deferential, to receive the protection of the business judgment rule, a director must show an exercise of judgment, not simply the existence of a business decision. Directors' fiduciary duties require them to do more than passively rubber-stamp the decisions of the active managers. Thus, where the directors' methodologies and procedures are so restricted in scope, so shallow in execution, or otherwise so *pro forma* or halfhearted as to constitute a pretext or a sham, inquiry into their acts is not shielded by the business judgment rule. The Directors may not seek the protection of the business judgment rule on the ground that they made no decisions and took no actions.

It is undisputed that the Defendants did not hold board meetings on behalf of RSL Plc during the time period relevant to this action. Despite this, RSL Plc still operated and took actions such as drawing down $25 million from the Lauder loan, apparently at the direction of RSL Ltd. However, no independent board discussions regarding the propriety of this and other business decisions were held on behalf of RSL Plc by its board of directors.

Indeed, the law does not tolerate inaction of the sort Defendants are alleged to have engaged in, as Defendants allegedly failed to consider any information they had regarding the company's financial health and allegedly failed to make a business judgment as a board regarding any financial decision on behalf of RSL Plc.

Defendants point to cases which hold that small, closely held corporations with directors frequently in close contact with one another may dispense with formalities such as board meetings when making business decisions. However, RSL Plc is not a small corporation, as it accrued more than $1.4 billion in debt. Further, while it is clear that some of RSL Plc's board members had some contact during the period in question, [there were no] behind-the-scenes meetings where the business of RSL Plc was discussed by these members, let alone an agreement not to have a board meeting.

Defendants argue that they were fully informed regarding RSL Plc's financial matters because some Defendants were also board members of RSL Ltd., and that in that capacity, they exercised judgment on behalf of RSL Ltd, the parent of RSL Plc. This argument is unpersuasive. [I]ndividuals who act in a dual capacity as directors of two corporations, one of whom is parent and the other subsidiary, owe the same duty of good management to both corporations.

EXAM Strategy

Question: You are the CEO of a software company. You will only allow your engineers to create software for Apple computers, not for PCs, because you think Apple is cooler. Some of your shareholders disagree with this policy. Is your decision protected by the business judgment rule?

Strategy: Remember that you owe a duty of care to the corporation. This means that you must have a rational business purpose for your decision.

Result: The courts are very generous in defining a rational business purpose. They would probably uphold your decision as long as it was not in some way personally benefitting you, e.g., as long as you are not a major shareholder of Apple.

MORE CONFLICT: TAKEOVERS

The business judgment rule is an important guideline for officers and directors in the routine management of corporations. The business judgment rule also plays a crucial role in corporate takeover battles. But the business judgment rule is not, by itself, sufficient for resolving all the issues that arise in these battles. Therefore, both Congress and many state legislatures have passed statutes that define the roles of the various combatants in hostile takeovers. Thus, the law of takeovers is rooted in both common and statutory law.

There are three ways to acquire control of a company:

- **Buy the company's assets.** Such a sale must be approved by both the shareholders and the board of directors of the acquired company.

- **Merge with the company.** In a merger, one company absorbs another. The acquired company ceases to exist. A merger must be approved by the shareholders and the board of directors of the target.
- **Buy stock from the shareholders.** This method is called a **tender offer** because the acquirer asks shareholders to "tender," or offer their stock for sale. As long as shareholders tender enough stock, the acquirer gains control. Typically, the bidder makes an offer (at a price above market value). This offer is usually contingent—that is, if a certain percentage of the shareholders do not tender, the offer terminates automatically. Although an acquisition can proceed without the approval of the board of the target company, resistance from the board can hinder the deal and even torpedo it. We will discuss shortly some of the weapons available to the target board. A tender offer is called a **hostile takeover** if the board of the target resists.

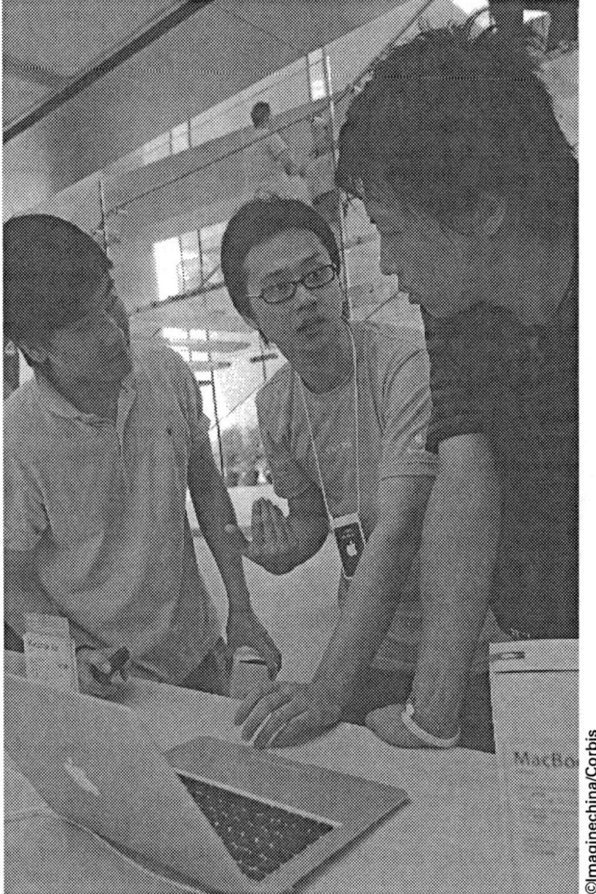
©Imaginechina/Corbis

Apple may be cooler but is that reason enough to refuse to write software for PCs?

Two scenarios are common in hostile takeovers:

- The target has assets that the bidder genuinely wants.
- A speculator plans to acquire control and then resell all or part of the company at a profit. Speculators, sometimes called **corporate raiders**, often say that they are acquiring stock in a company because it is undervalued; their ostensible goal is to improve management and raise stock prices. In practice, however, oftentimes another bidder comes along who buys their stock at a higher price; the raiders dismember the company and sell its parts; or the target company buys its own stock back at a higher-than-market price. (Management is willing to pay a premium price to keep the company intact and their jobs safe.)

In the beginning, state and federal governments barely regulated tender offers at all. Over time, targets began to ask Congress and their state legislatures to umpire these increasingly rancorous battles. Both states and the federal government have stepped into the ring as referees, generally more on the side of the target than of the bidder.[9]

Tender offer
A public offer to buy a block of stock directly from shareholders.

Hostile takeover
An outsider buys a company in the face of opposition from the target company's board of directors.

Federal Regulation of Tender Offers: The Williams Act

The Williams Act applies only if the target company's stock is publicly traded. **Under the Williams Act:**

- Any individual or group who together acquire more than 5 percent of a company's stock must file a public disclosure document (called a "Schedule 13D") with the Securities and Exchange Commission (SEC).

[9]R. Morck, A. Schleifer, and R.W. Vishny, "Management Ownership and Market Valuation: An Empirical Analysis," Working Paper No. 23, Institute for Financial Research, Faculty of Business, University of Alberta, quoted in P.-O. Bjuggren, "Ownership and Efficiency in Companies Listed on Stockholm Stock Exchange 1985," in M. Faure and R. Van den Bergh, *Essays in Law and Economics* (MAKLU, Antwerp, 1985).

- On the day a tender offer begins, a bidder must file a disclosure statement with the SEC;
- A bidder must keep a tender offer open for at least 20 business days initially, and for at least 10 business days after any substantial change in the terms of the offer;
- Any shareholder may withdraw acceptance of the tender offer at any time while the offer is still open;
- If the bidder raises the price offered, all selling shareholders must be paid the higher price, regardless of when they tendered; and
- If the stockholders tender more shares than the bidder wants to buy, it must purchase shares *pro rata* (in other words, it must buy the same proportion from everyone, *not* first come, first served).

Observe that the Williams Act regulates only the behavior of the *bidder*, not that of the *target company*. After Congress passed the Act, the number of tender offers declined and the average premium over market price increased. But target companies did not rely merely on the Williams Act to protect against the threat of takeovers. They were busy formulating other defenses.

State Regulation of Takeovers

A company's response to a takeover attempt is largely governed by state law, both common and statutory.

Common Law of Takeovers

To protect themselves from hostile takeovers, companies adopt defensive measures known as **antitakeover devices** or **shark repellents**. (The acquiring shareholder in a hostile takeover is sometimes referred to as a "shark.") Common shark repellents include the following:

- **Asset lockup.** The target sells off the assets that the shark most wants. Suppose that Ingrid is the CEO of Casablanca, Inc., a successful film production company that owns a vast and valuable library of old films. Turner has indicated that he may want to acquire Casablanca because he covets its library. Ingrid tries to pass the bait to someone else, either by selling the film library or by giving someone else the option to buy it.
- **Greenmail.** The target buys back the shark's stock at a premium price. Ingrid suspects that Turner is not really interested in owning Casablanca stock; he simply wants to turn a quick profit. Ingrid offers to buy back Turner's stock at a price 30 percent higher than he paid for it.
- **Shareholder rights plan ("poison pill").** When an outside shareholder acquires more than a certain percentage of company stock, a rights plan dilutes the value of these shares.[10] Now Ingrid becomes truly creative. She gets Casablanca to issue a special share of preferred stock to each current shareholder.[11] If a shark purchases more than

[10]In a recent case, a Delaware court explicitly permitted a poison pill that applied to outside shareholders but not the chairman of the company. *Yucaipa Am. Alliance Fund II, L.P. v. Riggio*, 1 A.3d 310; 2010 Del. Ch. LEXIS 172.

[11]Although in theory, the shareholders must approve the issuance of a new class of stock, some companies have so-called *blank check preferred stock* in their charters. When this stock is authorized, its rights and other characteristics are left blank, to be filled in by the board of directors upon issuance. It is like an unloaded gun that can be armed by the board whenever a shark threatens.

20 percent of Casablanca's stock and subsequently merges with Casablanca, this preferred stock can be converted into 10 shares of the acquiring company. Thus, for each share of Casablanca that Turner buys, he also has to give away 10 of his own shares, making the takeover much more expensive for him. No wonder these, and other similar tactics, are called "poison pills;" they could certainly prove fatal to a shark.

Jupiterimages

Target companies are often afraid of sharks.

- **Chewable poison pills.** These pills are exactly like a poison pill except that they expire automatically if a cash tender offer is made for 100 percent of the company's stock, at a price at least, say, 25 percent above market value. Chewable poison pills were adopted in response to complaints by institutional shareholders that regular pills are nothing more than protection for incompetent managers. A chewable pill would give Ingrid plenty of clout when negotiating with outsiders but limit her ability to turn down an offer that is clearly in the shareholders' best interest.
- **Dead-hand poison pills.** A dead-hand poison pill can be removed only by vote of the directors who installed the pill or by their handpicked successors. In this way, the decision is in the "dead hands" of the prior board. Without a dead-hand poison pill, Turner could dismantle Casablanca's shark repellents by electing some of his supporters to the board. Dead-hand poison pills are invalid in some states, but if Casablanca is incorporated in a state that does permit this defense, Turner's nominees to the board would not be able to remove the company's poison pill.
- **Staggered board of directors.** With a typical board of directors, all directors run for election each year, with the result that the entire board can be voted out at the same time. With a staggered board, only a portion of the directors are elected each year. Therefore, replacing the entire board takes some years to accomplish. Casablanca has a staggered board, in which each director serves a three-year term and only 4 of the 12 directors are elected each year. If Turner takes over the company, he will not gain control of the board for two years, and it will be three before he can replace all the directors.
- **Supermajority voting.** Ordinarily, shareholders can approve charter amendments by a majority vote, but some companies require a higher percentage to approve important changes. If Ingrid wants to make a takeover more difficult, she can ask shareholders to amend Casablanca's charter to require a *supermajority* vote of, say, 80 percent to approve a merger. Thus, Turner will not be able to merge his company with Casablanca unless he buys 80 percent of Casablanca.
- **White knight.** A white knight is another company that rescues the target from a hostile takeover. Because Turner has publicly criticized Ingrid's management of Casablanca, she despises him and would prefer to sell to *anyone* else. She locates another buyer who she hopes will retain her management team.

Management typically cannot use poison pills, staggered boards of directors, supermajority voting, and white knights without shareholder approval. (Although management could issue stock under a poison pill plan, the stock would first have to be authorized by the shareholders.) Shareholder approval is not required to implement the other shark repellents.

As a general rule, Delaware courts defer to boards of directors, allowing them great latitude in fighting off takeovers. (Not all states are as protective.) Like so much in corporate law, a balancing act is involved: the courts need to allow the board of a target company enough time to communicate with shareholders, search for alternatives, and force a higher price from the bidder, while at the same time allowing shareholders enough power to sell the company if they desire. Perhaps for this reason, legal rules on antitakeover devices are complex and sometimes seem to depend on the specific details of a particular case. But these are the general guidelines:

- **When establishing takeover defenses, shareholder welfare must be the board's primary concern.** The directors may institute shark repellents, but they must do so to ensure that bids are high, not to protect their own jobs. A poison pill is acceptable if it gives management enough bargaining power to negotiate a high price for shareholders, but not if it makes a takeover impossible.
- **If it is clear that the company will ultimately be sold, the board must auction the company to the highest bidder; it cannot give preferential treatment to a lower bidder.** The board cannot sell the company to a white knight at a lower price than someone else has offered, no matter how much management might personally dislike the shark.

In the following case, a bidder tried a new approach to winning a hostile takeover. Should the court permit this action? You be the judge.

You be the Judge

Airgas, Inc. v. Air Products and Chemicals, Inc.

8 A.3d 1182; 2010 Del. LEXIS 585
Supreme Court of Delaware, 2010

Facts: Air Products and Chemicals, Inc. (Air Products) launched a tender offer to acquire 100 percent of the shares of Airgas, Inc. (Airgas). The Airgas board of directors rejected these bids because they were lower than the market price. Airgas's charter provided for a staggered board of nine directors—at each annual meeting, three would run for election.

At Airgas's annual meeting in September, shareholders elected three of Air Products's nominees to the board. Air Products also proposed a bylaw (the January Bylaw) that switched Airgas's annual meeting to January rather than September. This change would mean that the next annual meeting would be in only four months. Air Products's plan was to vote out three more directors in January, which would have the effect of reducing their terms by eight months. Shareholders approved this amendment with a 51 percent vote in favor. Because not all shareholders voted, the favorable vote actually constituted only 45.8 percent of the outstanding shares. To amend the Airgas charter and eliminate the staggered board would have taken a 67 percent vote of the shareholders who cast ballots.

Airgas filed suit, alleging that the January Bylaw was invalid because it was a back-door method of eliminating the staggered board without a 67 percent vote of the shareholders. (A bylaw is invalid if it conflicts with the charter.) The lower court upheld the January Bylaw, and Airgas appealed.

You Be the Judge: ***Was the January Bylaw valid?***

Argument for Air Products: Airgas's charter provides that directors serve terms that expire at "the annual meeting of stockholders held in the third year following the year of their election." The January Bylaw complies with this charter provision as written because the January meeting will take place "in the third year after the directors' election." Nowhere does the charter say that directors have to serve three full years. If Airgas wins this case, corporations in Delaware will have to calculate the dates of their annual meetings with mathematical precision.

Moreover, 51 percent of the shares at the annual meeting voted in favor of the January Bylaw. If it was unfair or against the best interests of shareholders, they could have voted against it. Why should the court thwart the shareholders' intent?

Argument for Airgas: In 25 years, Airgas has never held its annual meeting earlier than July 28. We are not arguing that Airgas has to wait exactly 365 days to schedule its next annual meeting, but it should delay at least 11 months. Moreover, the company's fiscal year ends on March 31, so if the meeting were to be held in January, Airgas would not have new financial results to report to its shareholders.

The charter term is ambiguous—does it mean that directors have to serve into the start of the third year, or do they have to serve three full years? Regardless of what the actual language says, the *intent* is clear—directors are meant to serve three years. Air Products has found a loophole that violates the spirit of the charter provision and frustrates the purpose of staggered boards, which is to provide stability. The court should not allow Air Products to avoid the clear intent of the charter so that it can acquire a company at less than market value.

It is true that that 51 percent of the shares *at the meeting* voted in favor of the January Bylaw, but this was only 45.8 percent of the shares outstanding. That is not even a majority, never mind the 67 percent vote required to amend the charter. Moreover, if the January Bylaw is upheld, effectively three of the board members will be removed without cause. Under the charter, removal without cause also requires a 67 percent vote.

EXAM Strategy

Question: You are the CEO of Bubble Gum, Inc., a publicly traded company. Pink Co. has just made an offer to buy Bubble. Pink is particularly interested in Bubble's farmland, on which grows the corn for the sweetener used in the gum. You despise the CEO of Pink and know if Pink takes over the company, you will be fired. Your friend at ChewCo says his company would be interested in buying Bubble, but at a lower price than Pink is willing to pay. You are convinced that the company is better off long-term with ChewCo. What can you do immediately to protect Bubble from Pink?

Strategy: Shark repellents that require shareholder approval will not work because you do not have time to call a shareholders' meeting. Remember that your primary duty is to your shareholders.

Result: You cannot simply agree to a sale to ChewCo—once it is clear that the company will be sold, you must auction it to the highest bidder. You could try an asset lockup—selling off the company's farmland. Perhaps that would discourage Pink from making the purchase.

State Antitakeover Statutes

In fighting takeover battles, companies have also found support in state governments because legislators fear the impact on the local economy if a major employer leaves. When the Belzberg family threatened a hostile takeover of auto parts manufacturer Arvin Industries, the Indiana legislature quickly passed a tough antitakeover bill that had been drafted by Arvin's own lawyers. Shortly thereafter, Arvin and the Belzbergs settled. Arvin was not only the second-largest employer in Columbus, Indiana, it was an all-purpose fairy godmother. Among its charitable activities, it built two new schools, subsidized the salary of the school superintendent, and opened a summer camp. Columbus residents were delighted that Arvin survived the takeover attempt, but company shareholders might have preferred a bidding war for their stock. After all, shareholders do not necessarily care if the children of

Columbus spend their summers at leafy Camp Grenada or sleazy Mall City. Once again, the interests of these two corporate constituencies clash.

Most states have now passed laws to deter hostile takeovers. Among the common varieties are the following:

- **Statutes that automatically impede hostile takeovers.** These statutes, for instance, might ban hostile mergers for five years after the acquirer buys 10 percent of a company. Or investors who acquire as much as 20 percent of a company lose their voting rights unless the other shareholders move to reinstate the rights (not likely!). These provisions do not apply to bids that have been approved by the board of directors of the target company. In many states, such as Delaware, the board can opt out of the statute altogether and refuse to accept its protection.
- **Statutes that authorize companies to fight off hostile takeovers.** These statutes typically permit management, when responding to a hostile takeover, to consider the welfare of company stakeholders, such as the community, customers, suppliers, and employees. Some even go so far as to allow management to consider the regional or national economy. Since takeovers are almost always harmful to these other constituencies, company management has a ready excuse for fighting the takeover.

Most of these statutes do not totally eliminate hostile takeovers. A determined, well-financed bidder can still be successful. But these state statutes do tip the playing field in favor of management. Research indicates that takeover battles are much more profitable to the shareholders of targets than to bidders.

Ethics Supporters of these state statutes argue that large, publicly traded corporations owe a duty to all of their constituencies. The loss of a large corporate presence can be immensely disruptive to a community. Perhaps a state should have the right to prevent economic upheaval within its borders.

Opponents contend that shareholders own the company and their interests ought to be paramount. Antitakeover legislation entrenches management and prevents shareholders from obtaining the premium that accompanies a takeover. Opponents also argue that, if other *stake*holders are so concerned with the well-being of the company, let them put their money where their mouths are and buy stock. And if current managers cannot offer shareholders as high a stock price as an outside raider, they ought to be replaced.

Delaware companies can choose not to accept the protection of the antitakeover statute. What is the ethical choice for directors?

Chapter Conclusion

Managers of corporations have a fiduciary duty to shareholders and are charged with running the organization for their benefit. The law, whether federal or state, common or statutory, grants managers great freedom in deciding how to promote the shareholders' interest. In the takeover arena, lawmakers have given managers considerable leeway in defending their organizations from outside attack.

Exam Review

1. **FIDUCIARY DUTY** Officers and directors have a fiduciary duty to act in the best interests of the shareholders of the corporation. (p. 841)

2. **BUSINESS JUDGMENT RULE** If managers comply with the business judgment rule, a court will not hold them personally liable for any harm their decisions cause the company, nor will the court rescind the decision. (pp. 843–850)

EXAM Strategy

Question: Employees of Exxon Corp. paid some $59 million in corporate funds as bribes to Italian political parties to secure special favors and other illegal commitments. The board of directors decided not to sue the employees who had committed the illegal acts. Were these decisions protected by the business judgment rule?

Strategy: Two decisions are at issue here: illegal payments and the decision not to sue. (See the "Result" at the end of this section.)

3. **DUTY OF LOYALTY** Managers may not enter into an agreement on behalf of their corporation that benefits them personally unless the disinterested directors or shareholders have first approved it. If the manager does not seek the necessary approval, the business judgment rule no longer applies, and the manager will be liable unless the transaction was entirely fair to the corporation. (pp. 843–847)

4. **CORPORATE OPPORTUNITY** Under the duty of loyalty, managers may not take advantage of an opportunity that rightfully belongs to the corporation. (pp. 845–846)

EXAM Strategy

Question: Vern owned 32 percent of Coast Oyster Co. and served as president and director. Coast was struggling to pay its debts, so Vern suggested that the company sell some of its oyster beds to Keypoint Co. After the sale, officers at Coast discovered that Vern owned 50 percent of Keypoint. They demanded that he give the Keypoint stock to Coast. Did Vern violate his duty to Coast?

Strategy: Here, Vern has violated the duty of loyalty not once, but twice. (See the "Result" at the end of this section.)

5. **DUTY OF CARE** Under the duty of care, managers must make legal, informed decisions that have a rational business purpose. (pp. 847–850)

6. **WILLIAMS ACT** The Williams Act regulates the activities of a bidder in a tender offer for stock in a publicly traded corporation. (pp. 851–852)

7. **TAKEOVER DEFENSES** Under common law, shareholder welfare must be the board's primary concern when establishing takeover defenses. If it is clear that the company will ultimately be sold, the board must auction the company to the highest bidder; it cannot give preferential treatment to a lower bidder. (pp. 852–855)

EXAM Strategy

Question: The board of Harmony, Inc., is concerned that the company may be the target of a hostile takeover. It has decided to adopt antitakeover devices. Which one of the following statements is *false*?

a. Harmony may divest one of its divisions, as long as it does so at fair market value.

b. Harmony may adopt a poison pill, as long as the purpose is to give management enough bargaining power to negotiate a high price for shareholders.

c. If it becomes clear that Harmony is going to be sold, the directors have an obligation to auction the company off to the highest bidder, no matter how loathsome the directors find the bidder to be.

d. If Harmony offers to buy back any of its stock, it must treat its shareholders equally.

Strategy: Apply the principle established in the *Unocal* case earlier in the chapter. (See the "Result" at the end of this section.)

8. **STATE STATUTES** Many states have passed antitakeover statutes that render hostile takeovers more difficult for the bidder. (pp. 855–856)

2. Result: The business judgment rule would not protect the underlying illegal payments, but it did protect the decision not to sue. In other words, anyone who *made* an illegal payment had violated the business judgment rule, but the people who had decided not to pursue the violators had not themselves breached the business judgment rule because they had not violated the duty of care or the duty of loyalty.

4. Result: If the shareholders and directors did not know of Vern's interest in Keypoint, they could not evaluate the contract properly. Vern should have told them. Also, by purchasing stock in Keypoint, Vern took a corporate opportunity. He had to turn over any profits he had earned on the transaction, as well as his stock in Keypoint.

7. Result: In the *Unocal* case, the court permitted the company to exclude one shareholder from its buyback offer. D is the correct answer.

MULTIPLE-CHOICE QUESTIONS

1. If a manager engages in self-dealing, which of the following answers will *NOT* protect him from a finding that he violated the business judgment rule:
   (a) The disinterested members of the board approved the transaction.
   (b) The transaction was of minor importance to the company.
   (c) The disinterested shareholders approved the transaction.
   (d) The transaction was entirely fair to the corporation.

2. In the *Lippman* case involving a payout to the son and son-in-law:
   (a) The son-in-law was entitled to the payment because he represented the daughter's interest in the company.
   (b) The son-in-law was entitled to the payment because he had the same employment contract as the son.
   (c) The son-in-law was entitled to the payment because the business judgment rule protects decisions by corporate directors.
   (d) The son-in-law was not entitled to the payment.

3. The duty of care:
   (a) Is not a requirement of the business judgment rule
   (b) Protects directors who make an uninformed decision if it was entirely fair to the company
   (c) Protects a decision that has a rational business purpose, even if the activity was illegal
   (d) Will not protect directors who make a decision that harms the company

4. Under the Williams Act:
   (a) If shareholders offer more stock than the bidder wants, it must purchase shares *pro rata*.
   (b) Target companies must reveal the names of any shareholders who acquire more than 5 percent of its stock.
   (c) A bidder must file a disclosure statement at least 24 hours before the tender offer begins.
   (d) Once a shareholder has accepted a tender offer, she cannot withdraw it.

5. Takeovers are *NOT* regulated by:
   (a) Federal statute
   (b) Federal common law
   (c) State statutes
   (d) State common law

ESSAY QUESTIONS

1. **YOU BE THE JUDGE WRITING PROBLEM** Asher and Stephen formed a corporation named "Ampersand" to produce plays. Both men were employed by the corporation. Stephen decided to write *Philly's Beat,* focusing on the history of rock and roll in Philadelphia. As the play went into production, however, the two men quarreled over Asher's repeated absences from work and the company's serious financial difficulties. Stephen resigned from Ampersand and formed another corporation to produce the play. Did the opportunity to produce *Philly's Beat* belong to Ampersand? **Argument for Stephen:** Ampersand was formed for the purpose of producing plays, not writing them. When Stephen wrote *Philly's Beat,* he was not competing against Ampersand. Furthermore, Ampersand could not afford to produce the play even if it had had the opportunity. **Argument for**

Asher: Ampersand was in the business of producing plays, and it wanted *Philly's Beat.* Ampersand was perfectly able to afford the cost of production—until Stephen resigned.

2. Both Viacom and Paramount owned a diverse group of entertainment businesses. QVC was a televised shopping channel. The Paramount board of directors accepted a merger offer from Viacom at a price of $69 per share. QVC and Viacom then entered a bidding war for Paramount. QVC ultimately made the highest offer, at $90 per share. The Paramount board rejected QVC's bid on the grounds that a Viacom merger would be more in keeping with Paramount's business strategy. Does a board of directors have the right to reject a high bidder on the belief that the low bidder would be better for the company?

3. Eve bought defective ball bearings from Saginaw Corp. Alfred was the sole shareholder of the company and also its landlord. After Alfred sold all of Saginaw's assets, he withheld enough money to cover the rent that Saginaw owed him. As a result, Saginaw had no money to pay Eve. Does Eve have a claim against Alfred?

4. Ulrick and Birger started an air taxi service in Berlin, Germany, under the name Berlinair, Inc. Birger was approached by a group of travel agents who were interested in hiring an air charter business to take German tourists on vacation. Birger formed Air Berlin Charter Co. (ABC) and was its sole owner. On behalf of ABC, he entered into a contract with the Berlin travel agents. Birger concealed his negotiations from Ulrick, even though he used Berlinair working time, staff, money, and facilities. Birger defended his behavior on the grounds that Berlinair could not afford to enter into a contract with the travel agents. Has Birger violated the corporate opportunity doctrine?

5. Wallace, Inc. adopted a poison pill. Five years later, Moore Corp. offered to buy all Wallace's stock for $56 a share, which was 27 percent over the existing market price. However, the offer was contingent upon the Wallace board eliminating the poison pill. Wallace consulted with its investment banker, which advised the company that the offer was inadequate but did not indicate what the shares were really worth. Moore then raised its offer price to $60 per share, and again the bankers opined that the offer was inadequate. Both the board and its banker believed that Wallace's recently adopted corporate strategy would lead to an increased stock price. Indeed, the company's recent financial results had been better than expected. Despite these improved results, more than 73 percent of Wallace shareholders offered their shares to Moore. When Wallace refused to remove the poison pill, Moore filed suit. Was the board's refusal to remove the poison pill a violation of the business judgment rule?

Discussion Questions

1. Some companies adopt a staggered board of directors as an antitakeover defense. How does a staggered board affect cumulative voting?

2. Congressional Airlines was highly profitable operating flights between Washington, D.C., and New York City. The directors approved a plan to offer flights from Washington to Boston. This decision turned out to be a major mistake, and the

airline ultimately went bankrupt. Under what circumstances would shareholders be successful in bringing suit against the directors?

3. **ETHICS** Ronald O. Perelman, chairman of the board and CEO of Pantry Pride, met with his counterpart at Revlon, Michel C. Bergerac, to discuss a friendly acquisition of Revlon by Pantry Pride. Revlon rebuffed Pantry Pride's overtures, perhaps in part because Bergerac did not like Perelman. The Revlon board of directors agreed to sell the company to Forstmann Little & Co. at a price of $56 per share. Pantry Pride announced that it would engage in fractional bidding to top any Forstmann offer by a slightly higher one. To discourage Pantry Pride, the Revlon board granted Forstmann the right to purchase Revlon's Vision Care and National Health Laboratories divisions at a price some $100–$175 million below their value. Was the board within its rights in selling off these two divisions? Do the shareholders of Revlon have the right to prevent a sale of the company to Forstmann at a price lower than Pantry Pride offered? Is it ethical for a board to base a takeover decision on personal animosity? What are a board's ethical obligations to shareholders?

4. An appraiser valued a subsidiary of Signal Co. at between $230 million and $260 million. Six months later, Burmah Oil offered to buy the subsidiary at $480 million, giving Signal only three days to respond. The board of directors accepted the offer without obtaining an updated valuation of the subsidiary or determining if other companies would offer a higher price. Members of the board were sophisticated, with a great deal of experience in the oil industry. A Signal Co. shareholder sued to prevent the sale. Is the Signal board protected by the business judgment rule?

5. Courts have tended to be protective of managers who fight against hostile takeovers, even if the bidder is offering a price much higher than the market value of the shares. Why? Do the courts have the balance right when resolving disputes between these two groups?

CHAPTER 35

SHAREHOLDERS

© Evan Meyer/Shutterstock.com

In little more than a decade, Enron Corp. transformed itself from a modest pipeline company into a $65 billion global energy business. Enron's officers earned fabulous wealth and became major celebrities. But no sooner had the ink dried on newspaper and magazine articles lauding the Enron business model when suddenly, shockingly, the company collapsed into bankruptcy court. What happened to Enron?

Enron had become, in essence, an energy trading enterprise that required a lot of cash. To obtain the cash, it created subsidiaries that held substantial sums in safe investments. Enron borrowed money that was secured by these subsidiaries, but—and here is the catch—it excluded this debt from its financial statements. The income from energy sales appeared as revenue for Enron, but the debt to support this income was off the books. None of these "special" arrangements was disclosed clearly to shareholders.

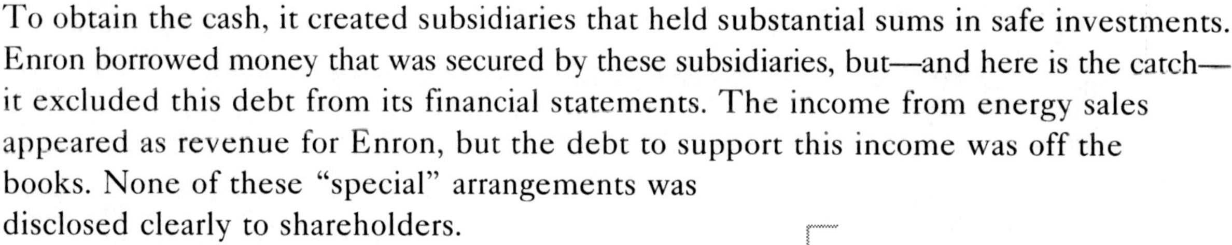

Moreover, compensation for top executives was tied directly to the company's stock price. So managers had a powerful incentive to raise the stock price in any way possible, legal or not. Stock manipulation and questionable accounting practices became standard operating procedure at the firm. The company would, for example, book as current revenues its (optimistic) assessment of what future revenues might be for new deals.

Managers had a powerful incentive to raise the stock price in any way possible, legal or not.

After a few stock analysts began to ask tough questions, Enron restated its earnings by nearly $600 million, which caused investors to lose confidence. Enron stock entered a death spiral into bankruptcy, destroying the net worth (and the dreams) of many employees and shareholders. It turned out, however, that not all employees suffered dramatic financial losses—the top executives had sold hundreds of millions of dollars in stock before the collapse, even as they were exhorting other employees and shareholders to continue buying.

Outrage and uproar ensued. Inquiring minds wanted to know: Why did the law fail to protect Enron shareholders? Why did the impressive board of directors miss—or ignore—obvious signs of trouble? At the same time, other prominent companies confessed to shady accounting practices: Xerox Corp., Merrill Lynch, and Lucent, among others. The CEO of investment bank Goldman Sachs said, "I cannot think of a time when business overall has been held in less repute."

What is the solution to this raft of corporate wrongdoing? Some commentators claim that there are simply a few bad apples in the executive orchard. More pessimistic commentators argue that wholesale changes are needed in the regulation of public companies. After reading this chapter, you decide.

INTRODUCTION

Shareholders technically own the companies in which they invest, but their power over these enterprises is very limited. As Chapter 34 revealed, **directors, not shareholders, have the right to manage the corporate business**. In this chapter, we look at shareholder rights—what control do they exercise over the enterprises they own?

The topic of shareholder rights is a contentious, controversial topic. In this century, we have already experienced two financial meltdowns—one at the beginning of the 2000s and one at the end—that starkly revealed the different incentives faced by shareholders and managers. Too often, managers earned exorbitant compensation from highly risky, short-term decisions that in the longer run left shareholders holding an empty bag. If CEOs made a risky decision that paid off, they profited enormously. If the decision failed, they might be fired, but even then they were likely to have received generous compensation all along. On the way out the door, many also got severance payments that left them wealthy beyond most people's dreams. For example, in the two years before investment banks Bear Stearns Companies, Inc. and Lehman Brothers Holdings, Inc. failed, their top five executives took home $1.4 billion and $1 billion respectively, even as their shareholders were left with nothing.

Even worse, investigations after the fact revealed that too many managers had gamed compensation plans, stacked the boards of their companies with their friends, and ignored shareholder interests. Compliant boards had been little more than rubber stamps, approving whatever the officers wanted. In anger and frustration, shareholders, Congress, the Securities and Exchange Commission (SEC), and stock exchanges undertook an unprecedented effort to rebalance corporate power. Yet these changes are little more than a shot in the dark, without compelling evidence that they will enhance financial stability or improve shareholder results.

A note before we begin: at one time, corporate stock was primarily owned by individuals. But now, institutional investors—pension plans, mutual funds, insurance companies, banks, foundations, and university endowments—own more than 50 percent of all shares publicly traded in the United States.[1] Institutional investors, with enormous sums to invest,

---

[1]Shareholders play a very different role in privately held companies than in publicly traded corporations. Not only do privately held corporations have fewer shareholders, but these owners take a more active role in management, often serving as a director, officer, or employee. A public corporation is one that (1) has completed a public offering under the Securities Act of 1933, or (2) has securities traded on a national exchange, or (3) has at least 500 shareholders and total assets that exceed $10 million. For a discussion of public corporations, see Chapter 36, on securities law.

have little choice but to buy the stocks of large companies. If they are unhappy with management, it is difficult for them to do the "Wall Street walk"—that is, sell their shares—because a sale of their large stock holdings would depress the market price. And where would they invest the proceeds? Institutional investors cannot all profit simply by trading shares among themselves. For better or worse, the fate of fund managers hangs on the success of these large companies.

Rights of Shareholders

If you own a car, you expect to be able to drive it whenever you want. If you own it with four of your friends, you may not be able to use it every Saturday night, but you will get to drive it *sometimes*, even if only on Sunday mornings. Of course, you will also be responsible for changing the oil sometimes, too. Owning stock in a corporation is different. As an owner, you have no right to use any *specific* asset of the corporation. If you own stock in Starbucks Corp., your share of stock plus $6.25 entitles you to a triple grande soy vanilla latte, the same as everyone else. By the same token, if the pipes freeze and the local Starbucks store floods, the manager has no right to call you, as a shareholder, to help clean up the mess. **As a shareholder, you have neither the *right* nor the *obligation* to manage the day-to-day business of the enterprise.** So what rights do you have?

Right to Information

A company's obligation to provide shareholders with information depends on whether it is publicly or privately held. Privately held companies are regulated by state law, while publicly traded enterprises must also meet SEC standards. More than half the states have adopted as state law some version of the Model Business Corporation Act (Model Act), which requires only limited disclosure.[2] In contrast, the SEC requires companies to provide shareholders with extensive information.

Even if a corporation is not required to volunteer information, shareholders have the right to obtain certain data upon request. **Under the Model Act, shareholders acting in good faith and with a proper purpose have the right to inspect and copy the corporation's minute book, accounting records, and shareholder lists.** A **proper purpose** is one that aids the shareholder in managing and protecting her investment. If Celeste receives an offer to sell her shares in a bakery called Devil Desserts, Inc., she may want to look carefully at the company's accounting records to determine the value of her stock. Or, if she is convinced the directors are mismanaging the company, she might demand a list of shareholders so that she can ask them to join her in a lawsuit. This purpose is proper—though the company may not like it—and the company is required to give her the list. If, however, Celeste wants to use the shareholder list as a potential source for her new business selling exercise equipment, the company could legitimately turn her down. The following case is typical: the court must decide if the shareholder is acting in his role as owner or competitor.

[2]A committee of the American Bar Association drafted the Model Business Corporation Act to serve as a guideline for states to use when enacting a corporate code. The corporate statutes of Delaware also serve as a model for some states.

You be the Judge

Chopra v. Helio Solutions, Inc.

2007 Cal. App. Unpub. LEXIS 5909
Court of Appeal of California, 2007

Facts: Paul Chopra was a minority shareholder and former director of Helio Solutions, Inc. Both he and Helio were in the business of reselling Sun Microsystems hardware and software. Chopra suspected that (1) some of Helio's majority shareholders had purchased a building and leased it to Helio at an excessive rent; (2) the company had broken a lease so that it could rent this building; (3) some shareholders had used assets of the corporation to secure a personal loan; (4) Helio had permitted ex-employees to take away substantial business; and (5) the company had not collected a $1 million debt it was owed. In addition, he wanted to know if Helio was planning to issue stock and thereby dilute his ownership. Finally, he felt that his dividend of $1,952.55 was unreasonably low, given that Helio had $88 million in revenue.

Chopra hired a forensic accountant to help him investigate Helio's finances. At the accountant's request, Chopra asked Helio for these documents:

1. Articles of incorporation;
2. Minutes for meetings of the board of directors and shareholders;
3. All financial statements;
4. All tax returns;
5. The general ledger with accompanying journals;
6. Income and balance sheets;
7. Schedule of accounts payable and received and inventory;
8. Depreciation schedule for fixed assets;
9. Supporting documents, including bank loans, lines of credit, accrued payroll liabilities, sales tax liabilities, other receivables, loans to officers and owners, significant prepayments or deposits, and equipment lease agreements;
10. Monthly bank statements;
11. Company credit card statements;
12. Compensation records;
13. The following contracts: life insurance policies for officers and/or stockholders, pension plan and profit sharing plans, stock purchase plans, equipment and building leases, employment and bonus agreements for owners or key employees, covenants not to compete, loan agreements and credit information, documents connected with the company's real property, option grants, and each owner's curriculum vitae;
14. A list of patents held by the company;
15. Budget projections for the current year;
16. Company brochures and/or marketing information;
17. A list of key management personnel with job titles;
18. An overview of company positions and objectives for each department manager; and
19. Information regarding contingencies and lawsuits.

Helio Solutions gave Chopra items 1–6 but refused to turn over the other material. He filed suit.

You Be the Judge: ***Which of these documents must a company provide to its shareholders?***

Argument for Chopra: All these documents are necessary for assessing the value of Chopra's investment in the company and determining whether his interests as a minority shareholder are being protected. For example, without employee agreements and compensation information, he cannot assess the current corporate financial situation, value the business, determine if the business is being properly managed, or discover whether the majority shareholders or directors are improperly diverting corporate funds for their own benefit. He needs the contracts and agreements related to equipment and building leases to determine whether the majority shareholders had purchased a building and leased it to Helio at an excessive rate.

Argument for Helio: Chopra is simply on a fishing expedition to find information that would help him compete against Helio. It seems as if he wants to use Helio's budget projections and managerial objectives so that he can beat them to the punch on some of their new initiatives. Many of the requests relate to specific shareholders rather than to the company. Complying with these requests would be unreasonably burdensome to Helio. It would take weeks of work to pull these documents together and photocopy them. Shareholders have some rights to corporate information, but they are not entitled to unlimited access to corporate confidences and secrets.

Right to Vote

A corporation must have at least one class of stock with voting rights. Typically, common shareholders have the right to vote and preferred shareholders do not, but there are many exceptions to this rule.

Shareholder Meetings

Annual shareholder meetings are the norm for publicly traded companies. Although technically not all states require public companies to hold an annual meeting of shareholders, the New York Stock Exchange (NYSE) requires companies listed with it to do so. Companies whose stock is not publicly traded can either hold an annual meeting or use written consents from their shareholders. (Written consents are discussed in Chapter 33.) Under the Model Act, the board of directors and shareholders owning at least 10 percent of the company's stock each have the right to call a *special* meeting to vote on an emergency issue that cannot wait until the next annual meeting—for example, to conclude a merger or sell off substantial assets.

Everyone who owns stock on the **record date** must be sent notice of a meeting, whether it is an annual or a special meeting. The record date can be any day that is no more than 70 days before the meeting. The votes taken at a shareholder meeting are not valid unless a **quorum** is present, meaning that shareholders owning a certain percentage of the shares are represented, either in person or by proxy.

Quorum
The percentage of voters who must be present for a meeting to count.

Companies are permitted to hold shareholder meetings online rather than in person. Many companies do both, conducting a live meeting with virtual access. In 2010, Symantec Corporation became the first Fortune 500 company to eliminate the in-person meeting and hold a virtual-only version. Unfortunately, the company used this opportunity to limit rather than expand access. It broadcast only in audio, not video, which meant that participants had no opportunity to read body language or even know that three directors were absent. In the question-and-answer period, management read and answered only two questions from shareholders, without providing an opportunity for follow-up questions. Nor did they reveal who had asked the questions or even what questions they had chosen not to answer.

Proxy
The person whom a shareholder appoints to vote for her at a meeting of the corporation. Also, the document a shareholder signs appointing this substitute voter.

Ethics Symantec's actions in holding a virtual shareholder meeting were legal. If you had been a shareholder and had attended the meeting in cyberspace, would you have been satisfied with the company's virtual format?

© REUTERS/Tim Shaffer

A traditional shareholder meeting looks like this. Is a virtual meeting a reasonable substitute?

Proxies

Under common law, shareholders could cast a vote only by attending the shareholders' meeting. Such a rule in a publicly traded corporation would effectively disfranchise many shareholders who have neither the time nor the interest to travel around the country attending meetings. Modern statutory law permits shareholders to appoint someone else to vote for them. Confusingly, both this person and the card the shareholder signs to appoint the substitute voter are called a **proxy**.

Under the Model Act, a proxy is valid for only 11 months unless the form provides for a longer period. For public corporations, however, SEC rules specify that a proxy is valid only for the next meeting. After that, it automatically expires. Under both state and federal law, the shareholder can generally revoke a proxy at any time.

Under SEC rules, companies are not required to solicit proxies, but virtually all of them do because that is the only practical way to obtain a quorum. Along with the proxy, the company must also give shareholders a **proxy statement** and an **annual report**. The proxy statement provides information on everything from management compensation to a list of directors who miss too many meetings. The annual report contains detailed financial data. Under SEC rules, companies are required to post all of this information on their website. They must then mail to shareholders either hard copies of all the information, including ballots, or a card telling shareholders how to view the materials and vote online. But shareholders always have the right to request hard-copy versions.

Annual report
A document that the SEC requires public companies to provide to their shareholders each year.

Even if a company decides not to solicit proxies for a shareholder meeting, it cannot avoid its obligation to communicate with its shareholders. The SEC requires public companies, whether or not they solicit proxies, to give shareholders all the information required in a proxy statement and an annual report.

Shareholder Proposals

Shareholders who oppose a company policy may use the proxy process to challenge that policy. **Under SEC rules, any shareholder who has continuously owned for one year at least 1 percent of the company or $2,000 of stock can require that one proposal be placed in the company's proxy statement to be voted on at the shareholder meeting.**

If a company refuses to include a shareholder proposal in its proxy material, shareholders can appeal to the SEC. These are the major SEC regulations on shareholder resolutions:[3]

- *The proposal cannot relate to the ordinary business operations of the corporation.* For example, the SEC used to routinely exclude all proposals that asked a board of directors to develop a succession plan for the CEO, on the theory that this request related to the management of the workforce, which is part of the ordinary business operations of a company. But the SEC recently overruled itself and decided that succession planning is an important board function that raises significant policy issues. Now these proposals are permitted in proxy statements.
- *The proposal must relate to operations accounting for at least 5 percent of total assets, gross sales, or net earnings.* AT&T refused to include in its proxy statement an anti-Israel proposal from a white supremacy group on the grounds that the company's business with Israel accounted for less than 1 percent of sales.
- *The proposal cannot interfere with the company's proxy solicitation.* Management can exclude more than one proposal on the same topic and proposals that were voted down decisively in the past.
- *The proposal cannot require the company to violate a federal or state law.* Bell & Howell excluded a shareholder proposal that called for the company to hire qualified women because the proposal might require the company to violate federal and state antidiscrimination laws.
- *The shareholder cannot use a proposal to seek satisfaction of a personal grievance against the company.* Lee Data Corp. excluded a proposal requested by an employee/shareholder who had been fired for sexual harassment. The goal of his proposal was to embarrass the company and provide fodder for his lawsuit.

Traditionally, many shareholder proposals had a social policy agenda: cut greenhouse gases, withdraw from Myanmar, or ban genetically modified ingredients, for example. Now, many relate to corporate-governance issues: permit secret ballots, adopt cumulative voting,

[3]Rule 14a-8.

or repeal takeover defenses. Prior to 1985, only *two* proposals had been approved—*ever*. In recent years, shareholders of the 100 largest American companies have approved 20 percent of the corporate governance resolutions, but none of the social policy proposals.

Note, however, that even if a proposal meets SEC standards *and* is approved by a majority of shareholders, the company may not necessarily implement it. Resolutions are binding on a company only if they are within the narrow realm of shareholder power. For example, because shareholders have the right to amend company bylaws, such proposals are binding. But a shareholder vote that requires the board to take action is not binding because the board that has the right to manage the company, not the shareholders. Thus, even though the SEC requires companies to allow a vote on proposals about succession planning, the board still does not *have* to develop a succession plan, even if a majority of shareholders vote in favor. Most proposals are *non-binding*, and companies implement fewer than half of those that their shareholders approve.

Frustrated at this unresponsive behavior by boards, shareholders have begun to withhold their vote from any director who fails to support a successful shareholder proposal. Even this threat has not yet had a significant impact on board response to shareholder proposals.

Ironically, companies sometimes implement shareholder proposals that have not received support from a majority of the shareholders. The pressure of shareholder proposals is credited with inducing many American companies to withdraw from South Africa when its government had apartheid laws. Other companies implement shareholder proposals without even putting them up for a vote. Indeed, a substantial number of shareholder proposals are now withdrawn before a vote because the company is willing to negotiate and accommodate. For instance, Colgate-Palmolive Co. agreed to a proposal by institutional investors to permit secret ballots at shareholder meetings.

EXAM Strategy

Question: Shareholders of Beazer Homes USA asked for a proposal requiring disclosure about the construction company's risks in the mortgage market. This was a time when many companies were struggling with bad loans to home buyers. Beazer asked the SEC for permission to exclude this proposal from its proxy statement. What did the SEC rule?

Strategy: The SEC allows companies to exclude proposals that relate to the ordinary business operations of the company.

Result: The SEC ruled that Beazer Homes was required to include the mortgage proposal because these risks directly affected the value of the company in a time of extraordinary challenges in this industry. Shortly thereafter, Beazer announced that it would stop originating mortgages.

Election and Removal of Directors

The process of electing directors to the board of a publicly traded company is different from what most people think. At this writing, shareholders do *not* have the right to use the company's proxy statement to propose nominees for director. Instead, the nominating committee of the board of directors produces a slate of directors, with one name per opening. Typically, the names are approved by the CEO. This slate is then placed in the proxy statement and sent to shareholders, whose only choice is to vote in favor of a nominee or to withhold their vote (i.e., not vote at all). If shareholders want to vote for someone who was not selected by the company, they have to nominate their own slate, prepare and distribute a proxy statement to other shareholders, and then communicate why their slate is superior, all the while fighting against the company's almost unlimited financial resources. This process is complex, expensive, and disruptive to the company. Not surprisingly, only a few shareholder groups undertake this effort each year. Recent research does indicate, however, that companies with a director elected through proxy contests outperform their peers in both the short and long run.[4]

This traditional corporate voting method is called **plurality voting**. A successful candidate does not need to receive a majority vote; he must simply receive more than any competitor. Since there are no competitors, one vote is sufficient (and that vote could be his own). Even if a large number of shareholders withhold their votes, the nominee may be embarrassed, but as long as he receives that one vote, he is elected. Thus, for example, in the waning years of Michael Eisner's rule at Disney Enterprises Inc., shareholders withheld 43 percent of their votes from him. But that vote of no confidence did not cause the board to fire him, nor did he immediately resign.

Plurality voting
To be elected, a candidate only needs to receive more votes than her opponent, not a majority of the votes cast.

Congress, other regulators, and major shareholders are now reforming corporate democracy in an effort to rebalance the relationship between managers and shareholders.

Independent Directors. Congress began its reform effort by passing the Sarbanes-Oxley Act (SOX), which applies to all publicly traded corporations in the United States, as well as to all foreign companies listed on a U.S. stock exchange. Among other provisions, SOX stipulates that **all members of a board's audit committee must be independent, and at least one of these members must be a financial expert. Independent directors** are those who are not employees of the company and, therefore, presumably not in the pocket of the CEO.

Independent directors
Members of the board of directors who are not employees of the company. Also known as outside directors.

Likewise, the NYSE and NASDAQ require that, for companies listed on these exchanges:

- Independent directors must comprise a majority of the board;
- They must meet regularly on their own without **inside directors**, that is, members of the board who are also employees of the corporation;
- Only independent directors can serve on audit, compensation, or nominating committees; and
- Audit committees must have at least three directors who are financially literate.

Inside directors
Members of the board of directors who are also employees of the corporation.

The effectiveness of these reforms, however, is uncertain. One study found that 45 percent of directors who are technically "independent" have friendship ties to the CEO. And, as the second eBay case in this chapter illustrates, even independent directors are often financially beholden to the CEO. At a minimum, the CEO is more likely to fire them from their lucrative directorships than shareholders are, so their incentives are often more aligned with the CEO. Also, some commentators argue that because independent directors do not work full time for the company, they know *less* about what is really going on and have to rely *more* on company executives.

What happens to independent directors who fail to carry out their watchdog responsibilities? Unless they personally commit fraud, the answer is: not much. After all, if the SEC were aggressive about going after independent directors, few people would be willing to serve in that role. Even if they are sued, the corporation or its insurance company usually pays the damages. For the first time, however, the SEC has brought suit against three independent directors. As friends and neighbors of the CEO at DHB Industries, Inc. they actively assisted him in a cover-up of wrong-doing.

[4]The Investor Responsibility Research Center Institute. See *http://www.irrcinstitute.org/pdf/PR_5_25_09.pdf*.

Shareholder Activists. Proxy advisors, such as Institutional Shareholder Services, Inc. (ISS), are a new development in corporate democracy. They advise institutional investors on how to vote their shares. Proxy advisors and hedge funds (which often own substantial stockholdings) wield significant power. ISS alone can affect up to 20 to 40 percent of the vote at a company. Corporate managers argue that this is too much power—that activists may well have an agenda that is contrary to that of other shareholders, and that they support corporate governance initiatives without proof of effectiveness. In any event, boards have become more responsive to the demands of shareholder activists and, as a result, are more likely to replace executives who perform badly, either in their corporate or personal lives. For example, the board of Hewlett-Packard fired CEO Mark Hurd for a combination of reasons that included his fudging of expense reports to hide his relationship with someone who accused him of sexual harassment, and, perhaps worst of all, bad press.

Majority voting systems. Because of pressure from shareholder activists, two-thirds of the S&P 500 (large companies) now refuse to seat a director if fewer than half of the shares that vote tick off her name on the ballot. However, among smaller companies—those in the Russell 3000 Index—three-quarters still permit plurality voting, where one vote is often sufficient to insure election.[5]

Proxy access. By a 3-2 vote of the commissioners, the SEC approved proxy access rules that required companies to include in their proxy material the names of board nominees selected by large shareholders (that is, those who had owned 3 percent of the company for three years). But when business groups sued the SEC to prevent implementation, a federal appeals court invalidated the proxy access rule on the grounds that the SEC had not followed required procedures in adopting it. The SEC elected not to appeal this decision.[6] However, proxy access survives in a weakened form because the SEC amended Rule 14a-8 so that shareholders can now make proposals which would change company bylaws to permit proxy access. This two-step process is more complicated, and less likely to succeed, than the one-step version the SEC originally proposed. Also, such proposals are binding on the company only if state law permits. Such a proposal could be binding in Delaware.

The effectiveness of this rule change is uncertain. At this stage, it has not changed the reality that for most companies, shareholders have little say on board nominations.

Compensation for Officers and Directors—The Problem

Given the control that the CEO has over the selection process for the board of directors, it is not surprising that when the board sets the CEO's compensation, the results can sometimes appear to unfairly favor the CEO over the shareholders whose money is being used to pay him. After all, the CEO can easily replace stingy directors. Between 2001 and 2003, public companies spent 9.8 percent of their net income on compensation for top executives. In 1975, the top 100 CEOs earned 39 times as much as the average worker. By 2005, that ratio was over 400. See Exhibit 35.1 for an illustration of this trend.

The ratio in Japan is 11 to 1; in Britain, it is 22 to 1. Or, to look at it another way, the average salary of the CEO of a Fortune 500 company in 1960 was twice that of the president of the United States. In 2006, the ratio was 30 to 1.

Here are some examples of executive compensation that particularly agitated shareholders:

- Michael Eisner was the head of Walt Disney Corporation for 20 years. At the beginning of his tenure, the company did very well, and few complained when he was exceedingly well paid. But for the final *13* years, he earned $800 million

---

[5]The S&P 500 is composed of 500 leading companies in the most important U.S. industries, while the Russell 3000 is made up of the largest 3000 companies in the United States, representing 98 percent of the investable U.S. equity market.

[6]*Business Roundtable v. SEC*, 2011 U.S. App. LEXIS 14988 (D.C. Cir, 2011).

EXHIBIT 35.1 CEOs' pay as a multiple of the average worker's pay, 1960-2007
Source: *Executive Excess 2008*, the 15th Annual CEO Compensation Survey from the Institute for Policy Studies and United for a Fair Economy.[7]

while the stock performed worse than government bonds (a much less risky investment).

- The CEO of Fannie Mae earned $90 million during a time when the company's accounting system was so flawed that it overstated its earnings by $11 billion.
- Executives whose companies survived the 2008 financial crisis only because of taxpayer bailouts still received enormous bonuses. For example, taxpayers spent $180 billion to save American International Group, Inc., even as the company awarded bonuses of $165 million.

To many investors, sky-high executive salaries have become the symbol of all that is wrong with corporate governance. In many companies, salaries are the least of the compensation. Executives also received:

Stock options. Concerned about escalating executive salaries, shareholder activists began advocating "pay-for-performance" plans. The theory was that if executives received stock options instead of cash salaries, their incentives would be more closely aligned with those of shareholders. It was a good theory, but in practice, it did not work as intended.

[7]Prepared by Professor G. William Miller, University of California at Santa Cruz, ***http://sociology.ucsc.edu/whorulesamerica/power/wealth.html.***

Stock options became a "heads, I win; tails, you lose" game. When stock prices soared in a bull market, options became unexpectedly valuable. In some cases, managers were richly rewarded even when their company had underperformed the (rising) market. However, when stock prices fell, boards lowered the price of the options.

Also, companies played games with options. After the 9/11 terrorist attack, the stock market was closed for four days. When it reopened, stocks took a bigger plunge than they had in any week since Nazi Germany invaded France at the beginning of World War II. In what appeared to be an unseemly exploitation of a national tragedy, 186 companies granted stock options to 511 executives during those few weeks. That is more than twice the number of companies that usually issued stock options in September.[8] These grants, if questionable, were at least legal; not so the backdated options that more than 2,000 companies appear to have issued their executives. In granting options, companies claimed that they had been issued on an earlier date, when the stock price was lower. This practice is fraud.

Termination, retirement plans, and death benefits. Most public companies provide their top executives with generous termination payments, no matter whether the person dies or is fired. Indeed, many CEO employment contracts provide that employees are entitled to severance pay unless fired for committing a particular type of felony. Dying also pays. For example, Nabor Industries Ltd. agreed to pay its 78-year-old CEO $263 million when he dies. The CEO of the Shaw Group was entitled to $17 million if he did not compete with the company after he dies. Yes, you read that right—he was to be paid for not competing after death.

Lavish perks. Executives had long received perks such as country club memberships and cars, but the roster of options expanded. One of the most popular perks was use of the corporate jet. One study found a high correlation between the use of the company plane and membership in far-flung golf clubs. Unfortunately, the correlation is inverse: the more companies spent on private jets, the worse their stock performed.

No wonder that executive compensation became a hot topic for shareholder proposals. Why did executive pay become so lavish?

Directors, not Shareholders, Set Executive Compensation. Directors set the CEO's compensation, but shareholders are the ones who pay the money. People tend to spend someone else's money more generously than their own. Also, directors and the CEO are often friends. Imagine if you got to decide how much your friend could spend dining out, knowing that someone else, whom you had never met, would have to pay the bill. It would be easy to be generous.

Shareholders Bear the Risk. Once again, executive compensation is a "heads I win; tails you lose" game. As we discussed at the beginning of the chapter, if CEOs make a risky decision that pays off, they typically profit enormously. Even if the decision turns out badly, they are often well paid anyway.

Benchmarking Games. Compensation is rarely linked closely to individual performance but instead to overall industry or stock market performance, which is defined in a way to favor executives. Two-thirds of the largest 1,000 U.S. companies report that they performed better than their peers.[9] That is, in part, because benchmarks can be manipulated.

---

[8]Charles Forelle, James Bandler, and Mark Maremont, "Executive Pay: The 9/11 Factor," *The Wall Street Journal*, July 15, 2006, p. A1.

[9]Kevin J. Murphy, "Politics, Economics and Executive Compensation," reported in Lucian Bebchuk and Jesse Fried, *Pay without Performance*, Harvard University Press, 2004, p. 71.

For example, Tootsie Roll Industries Inc., with $500 million in sales, benchmarked against Kraft Foods Inc., with $42.2 billion in earnings. Indeed, every company Tootsie Roll benchmarked against had higher revenues.

Campbell Soup used one set of benchmark companies to determine executive compensation but another set to evaluate its total shareholder return. In all fairness, it seems that Campbell ought to be consistent—presumably only one set of companies is the right comparison group.

The CEO Gets All the Credit. Compensation committees sometimes act as if the CEO and (maybe) a few other top executives are solely responsible for a company's success. Although there is much talk about "pay for performance," the reality is that luck can be as important a determinant of executive compensation as good performance.[10] After James Kilts became CEO of Gillette Co., the stock price went up 61 percent. He had added $20 billion in shareholder value, and therefore, to many, it seemed only fair when he was rewarded with a $153 million payout. But was it? About half the increase in Gillette revenues during the time that Kilts was running the show were attributable to currency fluctuations. A cheaper dollar increased revenue overseas. If the dollar had moved in the opposite direction, there might not have been any increase in revenue.

The Busier the Directors, the Higher the Executive Pay. Generally, executives are more likely to be overpaid if directors serve on many boards. These directors may be too busy to pay attention to such details. Also, trophy directors may be afraid that if they offend a chief executive at one company, word will get around, jeopardizing their position on other boards.

Most Executives Are Above Average. Of course, not everyone can be above average, but most directors believe that their executives are. No one wants to admit to hiring incompetents. Suppose that you are on a company's compensation committee and have data about industry averages. If your executives are above average in performance, you should pay them above-average salaries. If they are not above average, you should fire them, which few boards want to do, except in the face of disaster. If *you* raise salaries, the industry average also rises. Thus, the next company that sets compensation has an even higher bar to jump. For example, Colgate-Palmolive awarded 2 million stock options to its CEO on the understanding that he would receive no further grants for five years. Three years later, however, when consultants found that the CEO's compensation had fallen below the median, the company immediately awarded him an additional 2.6 million options.

Compensation Consultants Often Have Conflicts of Interest. Many companies hire compensation consultants to offer advice on executive pay. These same consultants may also provide other services to the company—such as human resource management—for which the fees can be substantial. The consultants have every incentive to suggest generous packages. In any event, it is not their money.

To make matters even worse for shareholders, lavish compensation does not appear to improve a business's success. A study of the 58 companies that were most generous to their CEOs found that, on average, these companies significantly underperformed both the market generally and their industry in particular.[11]

---

[10]See, for example, Marianne Bertrand and Sendhil Mullainathan, "Are CEOs Rewarded for Luck? The Ones Without Principals Are," *The Quarterly Journal of Economics*, August 2001.

[11]Reed Abelson, "Who Profits If the Boss Is Overfed?" *New York Times*, June 20, 1999, Business Section, p. 9.

Corporate executives are not the only people to earn fabulous salaries. Some athletes earn even more than CEOs. What is the difference between athletes and executives (besides a hook shot)? Athletes' salaries are indeed negotiated at arm's length with the team owner who will actually be paying the bill. This negotiation process means that (1) athletes' pay is not camouflaged; (2) they do not receive enormous severance packages on their way out the door; and (3) their retirement pay ranges from modest to nonexistent.[12] Also, an athlete's performance is transparent and easy to measure.

Compensation for Officers and Directors—A Solution?

The federal government has begun to respond to these perceived abuses.

Proxy Rules. The SEC began this process by amending its proxy rules to require more information about executive compensation. A proxy statement must now include a summary table setting out the full amount of compensation for the five highest-earning executives. The company must explain, for example, why option grants were approved and how much retirement benefits are worth. Companies must also disclose if the pay package increases the risk of large losses. The goal of this provision is to discourage companies from offering pay plans that reward executives for taking excessive risks.

SOX. Under SOX:

- A company cannot make personal loans to its directors or officers.
- If a company has to restate its earnings, the SEC has the right to demand that the CEO and CFO reimburse the company for any bonus or profits they received from selling company stock within a year of the release of the flawed financials. This is a so-called clawback provision. (See bizlawupdate.com for an article about how this clawback provision is working.)

Dodd-Frank. In 2010, Congress passed the Dodd-Frank Wall Street Reform and Consumer Protection Act. Dodd-Frank:

- Requires that compensation committees for all companies listed on a stock exchange must be composed solely of independent directors.
- Strengthens the clawback provisions of SOX and extends it to three years.
- Requires so-called "say-on-pay." At least once every three years, companies must take a *non-binding* shareholder vote on executive compensation (that is, for executive officers, but not for directors). In 2010, for the first time ever, shareholders voted against an executive pay plan—54 percent of Motorola's shareholders opposed CEO Sanjay Jha's compensation. The board had promised him 3 percent of the company if the plan to split Motorola in two succeeded, or a guaranteed payment if it did not. This vote was non-binding, and the company made no promise to respond.
- At least once every six years, companies must take a *non-binding* shareholder vote on how often to hold the say-on-pay vote—once a year, every two years, or every three years.
- In the event of a merger or sale of all company assets, shareholders have the right to a *non-binding* vote on so-called golden parachutes—special payments to executives because of the transaction.

---

[12]Some of the material in this section on executive compensation is drawn from Lucian Bebchuk and Jesse Fried, *Pay without Performance,* Harvard University Press, 2004.

- Companies must disclose the relationship between financial performance and the executive compensation they actually paid.
- Companies must disclose the CEO's compensation and the median compensation of all other company employees, as well as the ratio of these two numbers.

Even with these new protections in place, shareholder influence over executive compensation is far from guaranteed. Note that the shareholder resolutions are non-binding. And there is little shareholders can do to challenge executive compensation in the courts. To be successful, shareholders must prove that the board violated the business judgment rule, either by making a decision that was *grossly uninformed* or by setting an amount so high that it had *no relation* to the value of the services performed and was really a gift.[13] As the following case indicates, courts tend to be unsympathetic to this line of argument.

Brehm v. Eisner

2006 Del. LEXIS 307
Supreme Court of Delaware, 2006

Facts: Michael Ovitz founded Creative Artists Agency (CAA), the premier talent agency in Hollywood. As a partner at this agency, he earned between $20 and $25 million per year. He was also a longtime friend of Michael Eisner, chairman and CEO of the Walt Disney Company. Ovitz lacked experience managing a diversified public company, but Disney hired him to be its president with the hope that he could improve the company's talent relationships and increase foreign revenues. Upon the advice of Graef Crystal, a compensation consultant, the board approved Ovitz's contract.

After 14 months, all parties agreed that the experiment had failed, so Ovitz left Disney—but not empty-handed. Under his contract, he was entitled to $130 million in severance pay.[14]

Shareholders of Disney sued the board, alleging that it had violated the business judgment rule and that such a large payout was a waste of corporate assets. The trial court held for Disney, and the shareholders appealed.

Issues: ***Did Disney directors have the right to pay $130 million to an employee who had worked unsuccessfully at the company for only 14 months?***

Excerpts from Justice Jacobs's Decision: [T]he compensation committee [of the Board of Directors] was informed of the material facts relating to the payout. If measured in terms of the documentation that would have been generated if "best practices" had been followed, that record leaves much to be desired. [But, the] committee reasonably believed that the analysis of the terms of the [contract] was within Crystal's professional or expert competence, and the committee relied on the information, opinions, reports, and statements made by Crystal. Furthermore, Crystal appears to have been selected with reasonable care, especially in light of his previous engagements with the company.

[The purpose of the business judgment rule] is to protect directors who rely in good faith upon information presented to them from various sources, including any other person as to matters the member reasonably believes are within such person's professional or expert competence and who has been selected with reasonable care by and on behalf of the corporation. For these reasons, we uphold the Chancellor's [that is, the trial court's] determination that the compensation committee members did not breach their fiduciary duty of care.

The shareholders claim the payment of the severance amount to Ovitz constituted waste. A claim of waste will arise only in the rare, unconscionable case where directors irrationally squander or give away corporate assets.

[The shareholders] claim that provisions of the [contract] were wasteful because they incentivized Ovitz to perform poorly in order to obtain payment. The approval

[13]The business judgment rule is discussed at length in Chapter 34.

[14]As Ira Gershwin put it, "Nice work if you can get it, and if you get it—won't you tell me how?"

of the [contract] had a rational business purpose: to induce Ovitz to leave CAA, at what would otherwise be a considerable cost to him, in order to join Disney. To suggest that at the time he entered into the [contract,] Ovitz would engineer an early departure at the cost of his extraordinary reputation in the entertainment industry and his historical friendship with Eisner is not only fanciful but also without proof in the record.

For the reasons stated above, the judgment of the Chancellor is affirmed.

Fundamental Corporate Changes

A corporation must seek shareholder approval before undergoing any of the following fundamental changes:

- **Mergers.** As a general rule, one corporation cannot merge with another unless a majority of both sets of shareholders approve. This rule is always true for shareholders of the *acquired* company because they are always affected by the merger. But when an elephant acquires a peanut, it makes little sense for the elephant to vote. So, shareholders of the *acquiring* company vote only if the merger will have a major impact on their company.
- **Sale of assets.** Generally, shareholders are not asked to approve the sale of corporate assets. After all, one could hardly ask shareholders of the Coca-Cola Company to approve the sale of every bottle of Coke at every grocery store in the country. But shareholders must approve any sale that involves "all or substantially all" of the company's assets.
- **Dissolution.** A corporation cannot *voluntarily* dissolve without shareholder approval. However, as discussed in Chapter 33, the state or a court can *involuntarily* dissolve a corporation regardless of shareholder views.
- **Amendments to the charter.** Directors propose amendments to the charter, but these amendments are not valid unless approved by shareholders.
- **Amendments to the bylaws.** Both directors and shareholders have the right to amend the bylaws.

Right to Dissent

If a private corporation (i.e., one whose stock is not publicly traded) decides to undertake a fundamental change, the Model Act and many state laws require the company to buy back the stock of any shareholders who object to this decision. This process is referred to as **dissenters' rights**, and the company must pay "fair value" for the stock. Fundamental changes include a merger or a sale of most of the company's assets. Devil Desserts, Inc., manufactures sinfully rich chocolate delights. The board of directors is now considering a merger with Angel Treats Ltd., a company that sells low-fat, low-calorie (and in shareholder Celeste's opinion, low-taste) desserts. Celeste fully expects the value of the company to plummet after the merger, but her fellow shareholders support the board's decision. In a public company, Celeste could simply sell her stock, but Devil is a private corporation, and there is no market for its stock. She has the right to dissent because a merger is a fundamental change.

Right to Protection from Other Shareholders

Anyone who owns enough stock to control a corporation has a fiduciary duty to minority shareholders (those with less than a controlling interest). The courts have long recognized that minority shareholders are entitled to extra protection because it is easy (perhaps even natural) for controlling shareholders to take advantage of them. In the following case, craigslist adopted a rights plan (which, as you may remember from the prior chapter, is also called a poison pill). But the pill was too bitter for eBay to swallow.

EBAY DOMESTIC HOLDINGS, INC. V. NEWMARK

2010 Del. Ch. LEXIS 187
Court of Chancery of Delaware, 2010

Facts: The company craigslist, Inc., owned the most popular website in the country for classified ads. It had just two shareholders—Craig Newmark and Jim Buckmaster—and only 34 employees. eBay, Inc. was a publicly traded company that operated online auction sites worldwide. It employed over 16,000 people. eBay bought a minority interest in craigslist, with the goal of ultimately acquiring the company or, failing that, learning the "secret sauce" of craigslist's success. It turned out, though, that craigslist and eBay were not a good match because they had entirely different cultures and approaches to business. While craigslist focused on enhancing its user community rather than maximizing its profits or expanding its business model, eBay's primary focus was to increase profitability and market share.

Without undergoing any premarital discussions in which these divergent goals might have been revealed, eBay purchased 28.4 percent of craigslist's shares. Under the explicit terms of the deal, it had the right to compete with craigslist. Craig and Jim said that if eBay was able to offer customers a better experience, then it should be allowed to do so.

As eBay gradually realized that Craig and Jim would never sell out to them, at least in this lifetime, it launched a competing classifieds website at **www.Kijiji.com**. In this process, it used nonpublic information about craigslist that it garnered, without Craig and Jim's knowledge, from its relationship with the company. That "betrayal" further inflamed the situation. As other people have discovered, agreeing in theory to an open marriage is very different from experiencing it in practice. Jim and Craig were furious about eBay's foray into online classifieds. They asked for a divorce, but eBay refused to sell its stock.

Craig and Jim, in their role as directors, responded by adopting a rights plan that restricted eBay's ability to buy more shares of craigslist or sell its existing shares to third parties. They also eliminated its right to choose one board member. In response, eBay filed suit, alleging that this rights plan violated craigslist's fidcuciary rights to eBay as a minority shareholder.

Issue: ***Did Craig, Jim, and craiglist violate their fiduciary duty to the minority shareholder?***

Excerpts from Chancellor Chandler's Decision: All directors of Delaware corporations are fiduciaries of the corporations' stockholders. Similarly, controlling stockholders are fiduciaries of their corporations' minority stockholders.

[In a situation such as this,] directors must (1) identify the proper corporate objectives served by their actions; and (2) justify their actions as reasonable in relationship to those objectives. Thus, the two main issues I confront are: First, did Jim and Craig properly and reasonably perceive a threat to craigslist's corporate policy and effectiveness? Second, if they did, is the Rights Plan a proportional response to that threat?

Jim and Craig contend that they identified a threat to craigslist and its corporate policies that will materialize after they both die and their craigslist shares are distributed to their heirs. To prevent this unwanted potential future reality, Jim and Craig have adopted the Rights Plan *now* so that their vision of craigslist's culture can bind *future* fiduciaries and stockholders from beyond the grave. Having given new meaning to the concept of a "dead-hand pill," Jim and Craig ask this Court to validate their attempt to use a pill to shape the future of the space-time continuum.

Ultimately, defendants failed to prove that craigslist possesses a palpable, distinctive, and advantageous culture that sufficiently promotes stockholder value to support the indefinite implementation of a poison pill. Jim and Craig did not make any serious attempt to prove that the craigslist culture, which rejects any attempt to further monetize its services, translates into increased profitability for stockholders.

I am sure that part of the reason craigslist is so popular is because it offers a free service that is also extremely useful. It may be that offering free classifieds is an essential component of a successful online classifieds venture. After all, by offering free classifieds, craigslist is able to attract such a large community of users that real estate brokers in New York City gladly pay fees to list apartment rentals in order to access the vast community of craigslist users. Giving away services to attract business is a sales tactic, however, not a corporate culture. To the extent business measures like loss-leading products, money-back coupons, or putting products on sale are cultural artifacts, they reflect the American capitalist culture, not something unique to craigslist.

The defendants also failed to prove at trial that when adopting the Rights Plan, they concluded in good faith that there was a sufficient connection between the craigslist "culture" (however amorphous and intangible it might be) and the promotion of stockholder value. Jim and Craig simply disliked the possibility that the Grim Reaper someday will catch up with them and that a company like eBay might, in the future, purchase a controlling interest in craigslist. They considered this possible future state unpalatable, not because of how it affects the value of the entity for its stockholders, but rather because of their own personal preferences. Jim and Craig therefore failed to prove at trial that they acted in the good faith pursuit of a proper *corporate* purpose when they deployed the Rights Plan.

I personally appreciate and admire Jim's and Craig's desire to be of service to communities. The corporate form in which craigslist operates, however, is not an appropriate vehicle for purely philanthropic ends, at least not when there are other stockholders interested in realizing a return on their investment. If Jim and Craig were the only stockholders affected by their decisions, then there would be no one to object. eBay, however, holds a significant stake in craigslist, and Jim and Craig's actions affect others besides themselves.

As long as Jim and Craig have control, they can maintain the craigslist "culture" regardless of whether eBay sells some or all of its shares. The Rights Plan therefore does not have a reasonable connection to Jim and Craig's professed goal. It therefore falls outside the range of reasonableness.

I rescind the Rights Plan in its entirety.

Ordinary Business Transactions

Minority shareholders have the right to overturn an ordinary business transaction between the corporation and a controlling shareholder unless the corporation can show that the transaction is fair to the minority shareholders. The Sinclair Oil Co. owned 97 percent of Sinclair Venezuelan Oil Co. (Sinven). Sinven's minority shareholders complained that Sinclair

- Forced Sinven to pay dividends so large that the subsidiary faced bankruptcy
- Hired other, wholly owned, subsidiaries but not Sinven, and
- Refused to force its other subsidiaries to abide by their contracts with Sinven; for instance, a Sinclair subsidiary signed a contract with Sinven to buy crude oil but failed to purchase the required amount.[15]

The court ruled that the dividend policy was fair to the minority shareholders because they received the dividends, too. Sinclair was not under any obligation to hire Sinven. But Sinclair did have to ensure that other subsidiaries complied with their Sinven contracts.

Excluding Minority Shareholders

Controlling shareholders must include minority shareholders in any favorable arrangements that they make for their own stock. A successful savings and loan (S&L) had stock that, in theory, was worth $2,400 a share but, in reality, it rarely traded because of the high price. The controlling shareholder could have split the stock so that shareholders received 100 shares worth $24 each. Instead, he concocted a shrewd plan whereby he and his friends (who together owned 85 percent of the stock) exchanged their S&L stock for shares in a new corporation. Stock of the new company sold well, but there was still

[15] *Sinclair Oil Corp. v. Levien*, 280 A.2d 717, 1971 Del. LEXIS 225 (Del. 1971).

virtually no market for the remaining S&L shares. The court held that the controlling shareholders could not exclude the minority without a compelling business purpose, which did not exist in this case.[16]

Expelling Shareholders

There is an old saying that you can choose your friends, but not your family. Can you choose your fellow shareholders? Sometimes, relations between shareholders become so bitter that the majority attempts to expel a minority owner. **Many states prohibit a company from expelling shareholders unless the firm pays a fair price for the minority stock and the expulsion has a legitimate business purpose.** Delaware has an even higher standard—the transaction must be "entirely fair." This standard requires that both the price and the process of approval be fair. Theodore Lerner owned 70 shares in the family real estate company, Lawrence Lerner only 25. When Lawrence sued Theodore for mismanagement, Theodore amended the charter to reclassify each share of stock into 1/35th of a share and to buy out any fractional shares. Lawrence ended up with 5/7ths of a share, which the company purchased. The court, however, halted the squeeze-out because it had no legitimate business purpose.[17]

> Sometimes, relations between shareholders become so bitter that the majority attempts to expel a minority owner.

Right to Monitor

As owners of an enterprise, shareholders play a relatively passive role. Primarily, they have the right to *monitor*, meaning the right to receive information and the right to vote on proposals put to them by the board. Shareholders do not, by and large, have the right to *initiate* corporate changes.

EXAM Strategy

Question: The five Brown children were all owners of the Roundup Ranch, Inc., in Montana. Peter owned 51 percent of the corporation; the rest was evenly divided among his four siblings. Because coal companies were encroaching on Roundup, Peter traded the Montana ranch for equivalent land in New Mexico. His siblings were not happy—their only interest in owning the ranch had been to maintain a connection with their family homestead. What could they do?

Strategy: Because Peter owned a majority of the shares, he had the right to sell the ranch. But because he is undertaking a fundamental change, his siblings do have some rights.

Result: The siblings have the right to dissent—that is, to require the company to buy back their stock, which is what the unhappy siblings required the unhappier Peter to do.

---

[16] *Jones v. H. F. Ahmanson & Co.*, 1 Cal. 3d 93, 460 P.2d 464, 1969 Cal. LEXIS 195 (1969).
[17] *Lerner v. Lerner*, 306 Md. 771, 511 A.2d 501 (Md. App. 1986).

Enforcing Shareholder Rights

Shareholders in serious conflict with management have two different mechanisms for enforcing their rights: a derivative lawsuit or a direct lawsuit.

Derivative Lawsuits

A derivative lawsuit is brought by *shareholders* to remedy a wrong to the *corporation*. The suit is brought in the name of the corporation, and all proceeds of the litigation go to the corporation. For example, as you saw in the earlier case, shareholders of Disney were upset when the board of directors approved a $130 million severance package for Michael Ovitz, who had served as Disney's president for a rocky 14 months. Shareholders wanted to sue the directors for having approved this compensation plan. But they had no right to sue on their *own* behalf because it was the *company* that had been harmed. Any injury to the shareholders was indirect. Thus, only the corporation could sue. And who would authorize a suit against the directors on behalf of the corporation? The directors, of course. Because the directors are unlikely to sue themselves, the law permits derivative actions, by which shareholders can sue managers who have violated their duty to the corporation. Because damages go to the *corporation,* the individual shareholders benefit only to the extent that the settlement causes their stock to rise in value.

The same rule applies if an outsider harms the corporation. If Disney decided not to sue a customer that refused to pay its bill, the shareholders could do so, but only in a derivative action, that is, only in the name of the corporation. Once again, any recovery goes to the corporation.

Litigation is tremendously expensive. How can shareholders afford to sue if they are not entitled to damages? A corporation that loses a derivative suit must pay the legal fees of the victorious shareholders. Most derivative lawsuits are litigated by lawyers eager to earn these fees. (Losing shareholders are not required to pay the corporation's legal fees.[18]) Most derivative lawsuits are initiated by lawyers who seek out shareholders and persuade them to sue. Without this incentive, few shareholders would bring derivative suits and much corporate wrongdoing would go unpunished. As we have seen, shareholders have limited power; derivative lawsuits are a means of protecting their rights.

Most derivative suits are brought in Delaware, so this discussion is based on Delaware law. Most other corporate statutes are similar to those of Delaware.

Making Demand

Before bringing suit, shareholders must first "make demand" on the board of directors. In other words, they must notify the board that the corporation has been wronged and ask the board to bring suit in the name of the corporation directly. There is one crucial exception to this rule: shareholders are not required to make demand if it would *clearly be futile* because a majority of the directors either have a conflict of interest or were careless when making the decision. In the following case, the court ruled that making demand on eBay would be futile.

[18]Under the Private Securities Litigation Reform Act, class action plaintiffs in suits brought under the securities laws must pay the corporation's legal expenses if the court determines that the suit was frivolous or abusive. 104 Pub. L. No. 67, 109 Stat. 737.

In Re eBay, Inc. Shareholders Litigation

2004 Del. Ch. LEXIS 4
Court of Chancery of Delaware, 2004

Facts: Pierre M. Omidyar and Jeffrey Skoll founded eBay, Inc., a company that hosts an online auction site. Later, Robert C. Kagle and Margaret C. Whitman joined the eBay board. Whitman also became president and CEO. Goldman Sachs Group Inc. twice served as lead underwriter when eBay sold shares to the public. Then Whitman became a director of Goldman. Afterwards, Goldman served as eBay's financial advisor when it acquired PayPal, Inc.

During this period in which Goldman engaged in three major transactions with eBay, the investment bank also served as underwriter for a substantial number of technology companies that went public. Many investors wanted to buy stock in these initial public offerings (IPOs) because an immediate and large profit was virtually guaranteed. Often stock prices doubled or tripled on the day of the offering. Goldman allowed Omidyar, Skoll, Kagle, and Whitman, all directors of eBay, to buy shares in hundreds of its IPOs, effectively giving them millions of dollars in profits. The following chart reveals the percentage of eBay shares that each director owned and the number of Goldman IPOs in which he or she was allowed to invest:

Director	Percentage of eBay shares owned	Number of IPOs in which director took part
Omidyar	>23%	40
Skoll	13%	75
Whitman	3.3%	>100
Kagle	Not disclosed in case	25

In each case, the eBay directors sold the stock immediately, and did earn millions of dollars in total profit.

eBay shareholders sued, alleging that Goldman had effectively bribed the defendants to continue giving business to the bank. The lawsuit was brought as a derivative action in the name of eBay. The plaintiffs alleged that demand was futile because the directors had a conflict of interest.

The board of directors of eBay had seven members: Omidyar, Kagle, Whitman, Philippe Bourguignon, Scott D. Cook, Dawn G. Lepore, and Howard D. Schultz. (At the time of the lawsuit, Skoll was no longer a director.) The court determined that the three defendants had a conflict of interest because they were the targets of the lawsuit. It was obvious they would not vote for eBay to pursue the litigation. If one of the remaining four directors also had a conflict, then that would constitute a majority and demand would be excused. The shareholders could then proceed with the lawsuit.

Issues: ***Did a majority of the board of directors have a conflict of interest? Was demand on the board futile?***

Excerpts from Chancellor Chandler's Decision: Plaintiffs allege that Cook, Lepore, Schultz, and Bourguignon have received huge financial benefits as a result of their positions as eBay directors and, furthermore, that they owe their positions on the board to Omidyar, Whitman, Kagle, and Skoll.

[I]n 1998, when Cook joined eBay's board, it awarded him 900,000 [stock] options. In 1998, eBay adopted a director's stock option plan pursuant to which each non-employee director was to be awarded 30,000 options each year. [T]he stock options are worth potentially millions of dollars.

© AP Photo/Paul Sakuma

Was it right for Meg Whitman to buy stock in Goldman IPOs?

I need not address each of the four outside directors, as I agree with plaintiffs that the allegations of the complaint are sufficient to raise a reasonable doubt as to Cook's independence from the eBay insider directors who accepted Goldman Sachs' IPO allocations.

First, Whitman, Omidyar, Kagle, and Skoll (and their affiliates) own about one-half of eBay's outstanding common stock. As a result, these eBay officers and directors effectively have the ability to control eBay and to direct its affairs and business, including the election of directors and the approval of significant corporate transactions.

Second, a significant number of options have not yet vested and will never vest unless the outside directors remain directors of eBay. ["Vested" means that the owner is allowed to keep the options, even if he leaves the company.] Given that the value of the options for Cook (and allegedly for the other outside directors) potentially run into the millions of dollars, one cannot conclude realistically that Cook would be able to objectively and impartially consider a demand to bring litigation against those to whom he is beholden for his current position and future position on eBay's board. With the specific allegations of the complaint in mind, I conclude that plaintiffs have adequately demonstrated that demand on eBay's board should be excused as futile.

Ethics The activities described in this case were standard operating procedure at the time. Yet, these defendants were *billionaires*. Why would they engage in behavior that was potentially damaging to their reputation and to their company? Would you have done the same? Why or why not?

If Demand Is Required

If shareholders are required to make demand, the board has three choices:

1. It can agree with the shareholders and file suit on behalf of the corporation. In this case, the shareholders cannot bring their own derivative action. Although technically, the board is required to put the interests of the corporation first, it is, shall we say, very unlikely that a board will decide to file suit.
2. The board can reject the demand (or fail to respond). To proceed with their suit in this case, the plaintiffs must convince the court that the board has violated the business judgment rule because it had a conflict of interest or was careless in rejecting the demand. Again, this is a low-probability event.
3. The board can appoint a Special Litigation Committee (SLC). The SLC is typically comprised of at least two independent directors (usually those elected after the disputed activity occurred). If the SLC determines that the lawsuit is without merit, then the court must generally dismiss the case unless the shareholders can show the rejection was uninformed or not in good faith. There does not appear to be a single case in which an SLC recommended that litigation continue or a court overturned the decision of an SLC.

Exhibit 35.2 illustrates the course of derivative litigation. The most important issue is whether a court will require demand. Shareholders know that if they make demand, the directors will appoint an SLC, which will then kill the suit. Therefore, shareholders typically file suit without making demand and wait for the company to go to court to ask that the suit be dismissed unless demand is made. If the court indeed requires demand, the shareholders know they have lost and typically withdraw the case. If, however, the shareholders can convince the court that demand is not required, the shareholders have won and the parties settle.

More Fortune 500 companies are incorporated in Delaware than in any other state, making its corporate law the most influential in the nation. The Model Act has, however, deviated from Delaware law by proposing that demand be required in *all* derivative cases. This approach essentially ignores the possibility that demand might be futile.

Must shareholders make demand?
Board had conflict of interest or was careless in making decision
Demand is futile
Proceed to litigation or settlement
Board was independent and careful in making decision
Demand is required—board has three choices
Board can take over shareholder case and proceed to litigation (not likely)
Board rejects demand
Board appoints SLC
Did board have conflict of interest or was it careless in rejecting demand?
SLC votes "No"
SLC votes "Yes"
Yes
No
Proceed to litigation or settlement
Suit terminates

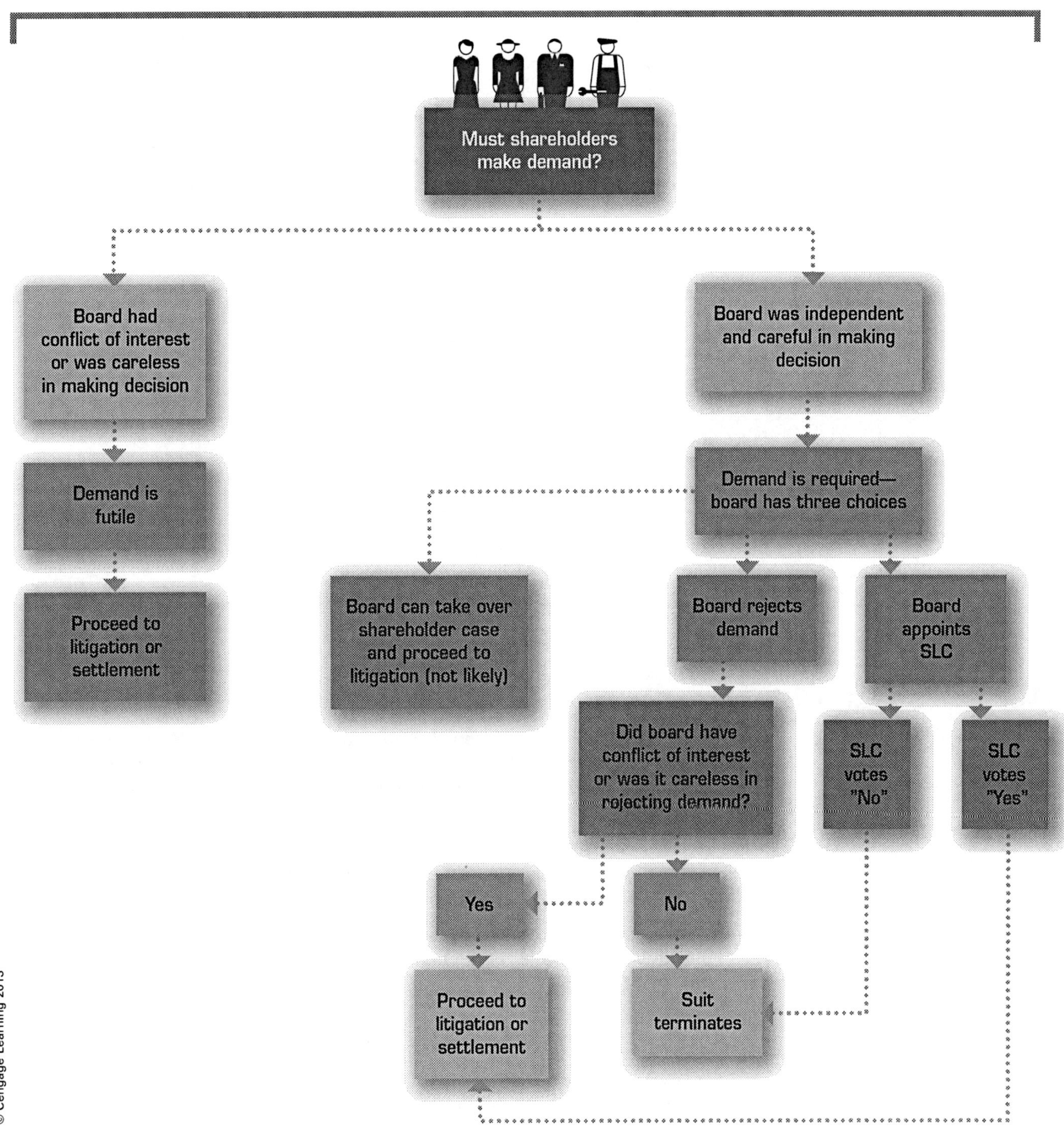

EXHIBIT 35.2

Direct Lawsuits

Shareholders are permitted to sue the corporation directly only if their own rights have been harmed. If, for example, the corporation denies shareholders the right to inspect its books and records or to hold a shareholder meeting, they may sue in their own name and keep any damages awarded. The corporation is not required to pay the shareholders' legal fees; winning shareholders can use part of any damage award for this purpose. With a direct action, shareholders are more likely to get their day in court because they are not required to make demand first.

The following table displays some of the important distinguishing features of derivative suits and direct actions:

Features	Derivative Action	Direct Action
Enforces the Rights of:	The corporation	The shareholder(s)
Damages Are Paid to:	The corporation	The shareholder(s)
Procedural Requirements	• Plaintiffs make demand on the board unless clearly futile. • If demand is futile, plaintiffs proceed with the case. • If demand is made, either the board or the SLC can terminate the case.	The same as regular litigation

EXAM Strategy

Question: Shareholders of Hewlett-Packard Co. were outraged that the board of directors paid CEO Carleton Fiorina $40 million after it fired her. The shareholders filed suit directly. Do the shareholders have the right to bring this suit on their own behalf against the board of directors?

Strategy: Shareholders can bring suit directly only if they have been personally harmed. If the harm is to the corporation, then shareholders must bring a derivative action in the name of the company.

Result: In this case, the harm was to the corporation. The shareholders were harmed only indirectly, when the price of their stock went down. A derivative action was their only option.

Chapter Conclusion

Two major financial collapses in the first decade of this century led to harsher scrutiny of corporate governance. The sight of huge payouts to top executives, even as their companies fell in heaps around them, spurred shareholder—and governmental—anger. We are now engaged in a great experiment—what can shareholders do, with and without government aid, to improve corporate accountability and performance? What is the right balance of power between shareholders and managers?

Regulatory changes and shareholder power have led to some concrete results. At the beginning of this century, about half of publicly traded companies combined the position of CEO and chairman of the board of directors. For most companies, those two jobs are now separate. CEOs now serve an average of 6.3 years, down from 8.1 years a decade ago. More independent directors, who take their independence more seriously, populate boards.

But corporate governance is not an end in itself—its goal is to improve performance. It is early days yet, but so far there is no compelling evidence of a significant relationship between good corporate governance and improved financial results.

In the end, it may be that the answer lies, at least in part, in the character of corporate leaders. In analyzing Enron and its aftermath, a *Wall Street Journal* article concluded: "[N]ot one of the instances of egregious abuse of shareholder interest could have occurred if the CEO had simply said, 'No!' It takes a person of character to know what lines you don't cross."[19]

Exam Review

1. **DIRECTORS** Directors, not shareholders, have the right to manage the corporate business. (p. 863)

2. **THE SEC** The Securities and Exchange Commission regulates the relationship between publicly held corporations and their shareholders. The SEC plays a less active role in privately held corporations. (p. 863)

3. **SHAREHOLDER RIGHTS** Shareholders have the right to:
   - Receive annual financial statements (if their company is publicly traded),
   - Inspect and copy the corporation's records (for a proper purpose),
   - Elect and remove directors, and
   - Approve fundamental corporate changes, such as a merger or a major sale of assets. (pp. 864–879)

EXAM Strategy

Question: The board of directors of Finalco Group, Inc., decided to sell most of the company's assets to Western Savings. Shortly after the proposed sale was announced, Finalco's largest shareholder said he opposed the transaction. Does Finalco need his approval for the sale?

Strategy: Shareholders have the right to approve fundamental corporate changes. Was this a fundamental change? (See the "Result" at the end of this section.)

[19]David Wessel, "Why the Bad Guys of the Boardroom Emerged en Masse," *Wall Street Journal*, June 20, 2002, p. A1.

4. **PROXIES** Virtually all publicly held companies solicit proxies from their shareholders. A proxy authorizes someone else to vote in place of the shareholder. (pp. 866–867)

5. **SHAREHOLDER PROPOSALS** Under certain circumstances, public companies must include shareholder proposals in the proxy statement. (pp. 867–868)

EXAM Strategy

Question: An institutional investor wanted A&P, the grocery store chain, to permit large shareholders to place comments about the company's financial performance in its proxy statement. Which would be a better strategy for achieving this goal: a shareholder proposal or an amendment to the company's bylaws?

Strategy: Shareholder proposals are treated differently from bylaw amendments. Which one is more likely to affect the behavior of the company? (See the "Result" at the end of this section.)

6. **INDEPENDENT DIRECTORS** Under SOX, all members of a board's audit committee must be independent. For companies listed on the NYSE or NASDAQ, independent directors must comprise a majority of the board and only independent directors can serve on audit, compensation, or nominating committees. (p. 869)

7. **EXECUTIVE COMPENSATION**

   - Under SOX, a company cannot make personal loans to its directors or officers. If a company has to restate its earnings, its CEO and CFO must reimburse the company for any bonus or profits they received from selling company stock within a year of the release of the flawed financials.
   - Dodd-Frank requires shareholder "say-on-pay." In addition, companies must disclose the CEO's compensation and the median compensation of all other company employees, as well as the ratio of these two numbers. (pp. 870–876)

8. **DISSENTERS' RIGHTS** A shareholder who objects to a fundamental change in the corporation can insist that her shares be bought out at fair value. (p. 876)

9. **RIGHTS AND OBLIGATIONS OF CONTROLLING SHAREHOLDERS** Controlling shareholders:

   - May not enter into unfair business transactions with the corporation,
   - Have a fiduciary duty to minority shareholders,
   - May not exclude minority shareholders from beneficial arrangements involving stock, and
   - Are prohibited from expelling minority shareholders unless the expulsion is done for a legitimate business purpose. (pp. 876–879)

10. **DERIVATIVE LAWSUITS** A derivative lawsuit is brought by shareholders to remedy a wrong to the corporation. The suit is brought in the name of the corporation, and all proceeds of the litigation go to the corporation. (pp. 880–883)

EXAM Strategy

Question: Daniel Cowin was a minority shareholder of Bresler & Reiner, Inc., a public company that developed real estate in Washington, D.C. He alleged numerous instances of corporate mismanagement, fraud, self-dealing, and breach of fiduciary duty by the board of directors. He sought damages for the diminished value of his stock. Could Cowin bring this suit as a direct action, or must it be a derivative suit?

Strategy: If the wrong was to the corporation, then Cowin must bring a derivative lawsuit. He can bring a direct action only if the harm was to him personally. (See the "Result" at the end of this section.)

3. Result: Yes, it was a sale of most of the company's assets. The board could not proceed without the approval of the owners of a majority of shares.

5. Result: A shareholder proposal is not binding on the company. Even if the shareholders approved a proposal, A&P would be under no obligation to carry it out. A bylaw amendment, on the other hand, would be binding on the company.

10. Result: The court ruled that the injury had fallen equally on all the shareholders, and therefore, a derivative suit was appropriate.

MULTIPLE-CHOICE QUESTIONS

1. The president of R. Hoe & Co., Inc., refused to call a special meeting of the shareholders although 55 percent of them requested it. One purpose of the meeting was to demand that the former president be reinstated. Do shareholders have the right to make these two requests?
   (a) Yes to both.
   (b) No to both.
   (c) The shareholders have the right to call a meeting, but not to reinstate the president.
   (d) The shareholders have the right to reinstate the president, but not to call a meeting.

2. Under SOX and Dodd-Frank:
   (a) Companies are prohibited from making personal loans to directors and officers.
   (b) If a company restates its earnings, the five top executives must reimburse the company for any income they have received during that period.

(c) All directors must be independent.
(d) Shareholders have the right to strike down golden parachutes.

3. A company is allowed to hold its annual meeting online:
   (a) If a majority of its shareholders approve
   (b) If it also hold a live meeting for shareholders who want to attend in person
   (c) If it simulcasts a video of the meeting
   (d) Any way it wants, as long as shareholders are notified

4. To be elected to a board of a publicly traded company, a candidate must:
   (a) Receive a majority of the votes cast
   (b) Receive a majority vote of the shares outstanding
   (c) Receive a plurality of the votes cast
   (d) Receive a plurality of the shares outstanding

5. If directors and officers cause harm to their company:
   (a) Shareholders have the right to file suit against them and recover damages.
   (b) Shareholders have the right to file suit against them and recover damages only if the board permits the suit.
   (c) Shareholders have the right to file suit against them and recover damages only if the board permits the suit or a court deems the demand futile.
   (d) Shareholders do not have the right to file suit against them.

Essay Questions

1. William H. Sullivan, Jr., purchased all the voting shares of the New England Patriots Football Club, Inc. (the Old Patriots). He organized a new corporation called the New Patriots Football Club, Inc. The boards of directors of the two companies agreed to merge. After the merger, the nonvoting stock in the Old Patriots was to be exchanged for cash. Do minority shareholders of the Old Patriots have the right to prevent the merger? If so, under what theory?

2. **ETHICS** Edgar Bronfman, Jr., dropped out of high school to go to Hollywood and write songs and produce movies. Eventually, he left Hollywood to work in the family business—the Bronfmans owned 36 percent of Seagram Co., a liquor and beverage conglomerate. Promoted to president of the company at the age of 32, Bronfman seized a second chance to live his dream. Seagram received 70 percent of its earnings from its 24 percent ownership of DuPont Co. Bronfman sold this stock *at less than market value* to purchase (at an inflated price) 80 percent of MCA, a movie and music company that had been a financial disaster for its prior owners. Some observers thought Bronfman had gone Hollywood, others that he had gone crazy. After the deal was announced, the price of Seagram shares fell 18 percent. Was there anything Seagram shareholders could do to prevent what to them was not a dream but a nightmare? Apart from legal issues, was Bronfman's decision ethical? What ethical obligations does he owe Seagram's shareholders?

3. **YOU BE THE JUDGE WRITING PROBLEM** Two shareholders of Bruce Co., Harry and Yolan Gilbert, were fighting management for control of the company. They asked for permission to inspect Bruce's stockholder list so that they could either solicit support for their slate of directors at the upcoming stockholder meeting, attempt to buy additional stock from other stockholders, or both. Bruce's board refused to allow the Gilberts to see the shareholder list on the grounds that the Gilberts owned another corporation that competed with Bruce. Do the Gilberts have the right to see Bruce's shareholder list? **Argument for the Gilberts:** If shareholders of a company have a proper purpose, they are entitled to inspect shareholder lists. Soliciting votes and buying stock are both proper purposes. **Argument for Bruce:** The Gilberts are simply offering a pretext. They could use this information to compete against the company. No shareholder has the right to cause harm.

4. When Classic Corp. went public at $12 a share, its waterbed business was floating along nicely—the company had annual sales of $23 million and turned a hefty profit. The company then sprang a leak and suffered through many years of losses. Isaac, who owned 64 percent of the stock, decided to take the company private again (by buying shareholders' stock) at a price of 20 *cents* a share. Classic hired two financial advisers who opined that the buyout price was fair. The board of directors voted in favor of the sale and then scheduled a special shareholder meeting to vote on the buyout. Do the minority shareholders have any rights?

5. Shareholders lost their gamble when they bought stock of Jackpot Enterprises, Inc. Fed up with management, a shareholder asked the company to include a proposal in the proxy statement that would require the board of directors to sell or merge the company. Must Jackpot include this proposal in its proxy statement?

Discussion Questions

1. Pfizer Inc. paid $2.3 billion to settle civil and criminal charges alleging that it had illegally marketed 13 of its most important drugs. This settlement made history, but not in a good way. It was both the largest criminal fine and the largest settlement of civil health care fraud charges *ever* paid. Shareholders filed a derivative suit against the Pfizer board and top executives. Defendants responded with a motion to dismiss on the grounds that shareholders had not made demand on the board. Is demand necessary?

2. **ETHICS** After a recent annual meeting, Cisco Systems reported the results of the votes on both management and shareholder proposals. The company reported the results of its own proposals as a simple ratio of those in favor divided by the total number of votes cast. But for shareholder proposals, it reported the percentage as a ratio of those in favor divided by all outstanding shares. As a result, it reported the favorable vote for one shareholder proposal as 19 percent when, in fact, 34 percent of the votes cast supported this proposal. Is Cisco behaving ethically?

3. For several years, CSK Auto, Inc., fraudulently reported inflated earnings. During this period, Maynard Jenkins was CEO. He was not involved in the fraud, however, and was never charged with a crime. Nonetheless, using a SOX provision, the SEC sought

to claw back some of his earnings during this period. Should Jenkins be financially responsible for fraud that occurred on his watch, even though he did not participate?

4. Prior to the DuPont Co.'s annual shareholder meeting, Friends of the Earth Oceanic Society submitted a proposal requiring the company to (1) accelerate its phaseout of the production of chlorofluorocarbons and halons, (2) present to shareholders a report detailing research and development efforts to find environmentally sound substitutes, and (3) report to shareholders on marketing plans to sell those substitutes. Must DuPont include this proposal in its proxy material for the annual meeting?

5. Would the following initiatives improve corporate governance? Can you think of others that would?

   a. Shareholder proposals: require the board of directors to implement shareholder proposals that receive a majority vote,

   b. Proxy access: as proposed by the SEC,

   c. Majority vote: prohibit boards of directors from seating directors who fail to receive a majority vote of shares cast,

   d. Compensation: base compensation on the company's growth in earnings compared with those of its competitors, not just increases in earnings (that might be caused by a general market rise).